Handbook of Communication in Organisations and Professions
HAL 3

Handbooks of Applied Linguistics

Communication Competence
Language and Communication Problems
Practical Solutions

Editors
Karlfried Knapp and Gerd Antos

Volume 3

De Gruyter Mouton

Handbook of Communication in Organisations and Professions

Edited by
Christopher N. Candlin and Srikant Sarangi

De Gruyter Mouton

ISBN 978-3-11-018831-8
e-ISBN 978-3-11-021422-2

Library of Congress Cataloging-in-Publication Data

Handbook of communication in organisations and professions / edited
by Christopher N. Candlin, Srikant Sarangi.
    p. cm. − (Handbooks of applied linguistics; 3)
    Includes bibliographical references and index.
    ISBN 978-3-11-018831-8 (alk. paper)
    1. Communication.   2. Oral communication − Research.   3. Busi-
ness communication.   4. Discourse analysis.   I. Candlin, Christopher.   II. Sarangi, Srikant, 1956−
    P91.H3626   2011
    302.2−dc22
                                                          2011014961

Bibliographic information published by the Deutsche Nationalbibliothek

The Deutsche Nationalbibliothek lists this publication in the Deutsche Nationalbibliografie;
detailed bibliographic data are available in the Internet at http://dnb.d-nb.de.

© 2011 Walter de Gruyter GmbH & Co. KG, Berlin/Boston

Cover design: Martin Zech, Bremen
Typesetting: Dörlemann Satz GmbH & Co. KG, Lemförde
Printing: Hubert & Co. GmbH & Co. KG, Göttingen
∞ Printed on acid-free paper

Printed in Germany

www.degruyter.com

Introduction to the handbook series
Linguistics for problem solving

Karlfried Knapp and Gerd Antos

1. Science and application at the turn of the millennium

The distinction between "pure" and "applied" sciences is an old one. According to Meinel (2000), it was introduced by the Swedish chemist Wallerius in 1751, as part of the dispute of that time between the scholastic disciplines and the then emerging epistemic sciences. However, although the concept of "Applied Science" gained currency rapidly since that time, it has remained problematic.

Until recently, the distinction between "pure" and "applied" mirrored the distinction between "theory and "practice". The latter ran all the way through Western history of science since its beginnings in antique times. At first, it was only philosophy that was regarded as a scholarly and, hence, theoretical discipline. Later it was followed by other leading disciplines, as e.g., the sciences. However, as academic disciplines, all of them remained theoretical. In fact, the process of achieving independence of theory was essential for the academic disciplines to become independent from political, religious or other contingencies and to establish themselves at universities and academies. This also implied a process of emancipation from practical concerns – an at times painful development which manifested (and occasionally still manifests) itself in the discrediting of and disdain for practice and practitioners. To some, already the very meaning of the notion "applied" carries a negative connotation, as is suggested by the contrast between the widely used synonym for "theoretical", i.e. "pure" (as used, e.g. in the distinction between "Pure" and "Applied Mathematics") and its natural antonym "impure". On a different level, a lower academic status sometimes is attributed to applied disciplines because of their alleged lack of originality – they are perceived as simply and one-directionally applying insights gained in basic research and watering them down by neglecting the limiting conditions under which these insights were achieved.

Today, however, the academic system is confronted with a new understanding of science. In politics, in society and, above all, in economy a new concept of science has gained acceptance which questions traditional views. In recent philosophy of science, this is labelled as "science under the pressure to succeed" – i.e. as science whose theoretical structure and criteria of evaluation are increasingly conditioned by the pressure of application (Carrier, Stöltzner, and Wette 2004):

Whenever the public is interested in a particular subject, e.g. when a new disease develops that cannot be cured by conventional medication, the public requests science
to provide new insights in this area as quickly as possible. In doing so, the public is
less interested in whether these new insights fit seamlessly into an existing theoretical
framework, but rather whether they make new methods of treatment and curing possible. (Institut für Wirtschafts- und Technikforschung 2004, our translation).

With most of the practical problems like these, sciences cannot rely on knowledge that is already available, simply because such knowledge does not yet
exist. Very often, the problems at hand do not fit neatly into the theoretical
framework of one particular "pure science", and there is competition among disciplines with respect to which one provides the best theoretical and methodological resources for potential solutions. And more often than not the problems
can be tackled only by adopting an interdisciplinary approach.

As a result, the traditional "Cascade Model", where insights were applied
top-down from basic research to practice, no longer works in many cases. Instead, a kind of "application oriented basic research" is needed, where disciplines – conditioned by the pressure of application – take up a certain still dif-
fuse practical issue, define it as a problem against the background of their
respective theoretical and methodological paradigms, study this problem and
finally develop various application oriented suggestions for solutions. In this
sense, applied science, on the one hand, has to be conceived of as a scientific
strategy for problem solving – a strategy that starts from mundane practical
problems and ultimately aims at solving them. On the other hand, despite the
dominance of application that applied sciences are subjected to, as sciences they
can do nothing but develop such solutions in a theoretically reflected and methodologically well founded manner. The latter, of course, may lead to the well-
known fact that even applied sciences often tend to concentrate on "application
oriented basic research" only and thus appear to lose sight of the original practical problem. But despite such shifts in focus: Both the boundaries between
disciplines and between pure and applied research are getting more and more
blurred.

Today, after the turn of the millennium, it is obvious that sciences are requested to provide more and something different than just theory, basic research
or pure knowledge. Rather, sciences are increasingly being regarded as partners
in a more comprehensive social and economic context of problem solving and
are evaluated against expectations to be practically relevant. This also implies
that sciences are expected to be critical, reflecting their impact on society. This
new "applied" type of science is confronted with the question: Which role can
the sciences play in solving individual, interpersonal, social, intercultural,
political or technical problems? This question is typical of a conception of
science that was especially developed and propagated by the influential philos-
opher Sir Karl Popper – a conception that also this handbook series is based on.

2.   "Applied Linguistics": Concepts and controversies

The concept of "Applied Linguistics" is not as old as the notion of "Applied Science", but it has also been problematical in its relation to theoretical linguistics since its beginning. There seems to be a widespread consensus that the notion "Applied Linguistics" emerged in 1948 with the first issue of the journal *Language Learning* which used this compound in its subtitle *A Quarterly Journal of Applied Linguistics*. This history of its origin certainly explains why even today "Applied Linguistics" still tends to be predominantly associated with foreign language teaching and learning in the Anglophone literature in particular, as can bee seen e.g. from Johnson and Johnson (1998), whose *Encyclopedic Dictionary of Applied Linguistics* is explicitly subtitled *A Handbook for Language Teaching*. However, this theory of origin is historically wrong. As is pointed out by Back (1970), the concept of applying linguistics can be traced back to the early 19th century in Europe, and the very notion "Applied Linguistics" was used in the early 20th already.

2.1.   Theoretically Applied vs. Practically Applied Linguistics

As with the relation between "Pure" and "Applied" sciences pointed out above, also with "Applied Linguistics" the first question to be asked is what makes it different from "Pure" or "Theoretical Linguistics". It is not surprising, then, that the terminologist Back takes this difference as the point of departure for his discussion of what constitutes "Applied Linguistics". In the light of recent controversies about this concept it is no doubt useful to remind us of his terminological distinctions.

Back (1970) distinguishes between "Theoretical Linguistics" – which aims at achieving knowledge for its own sake, without considering any other value –, "Practice" – i.e. any kind of activity that serves to achieve any purpose in life in the widest sense, apart from the striving for knowledge for its own sake – and "Applied Linguistics", as a being based on "Theoretical Linguistics" on the one hand and as aiming at usability in "Practice" on the other. In addition, he makes a difference between "Theoretical Applied Linguistics" and "Practical Applied Linguistics", which is of particular interest here. The former is defined as the use of insights and methods of "Theoretical Linguistics" for gaining knowledge in another, non-linguistic discipline, such as ethnology, sociology, law or literary studies, the latter as the application of insights from linguistics in a practical field related to language, such as language teaching, translation, and the like. For Back, the contribution of applied linguistics is to be seen in the planning of practical action. Language teaching, for example, is practical action done by practitioners, and what applied linguistics can contribute to this is, e.g., to provide contrastive descriptions of the languages involved as a foundation for teaching methods. These contrastive descriptions in turn have to be based on the descriptive methods developed in theoretical linguistics.

However, in the light of the recent epistemological developments outlined above, it may be useful to reinterpret Back's notion of "Theoretically Applied Linguistics". As he himself points out, dealing with practical problems can have repercussions on the development of the theoretical field. Often new approaches, new theoretical concepts and new methods are a prerequisite for dealing with a particular type of practical problems, which may lead to an – at least in the beginning – "application oriented basic research" in applied linguistics itself, which with some justification could also be labelled "theoretically applied", as many such problems require the transgression of disciplinary boundaries. It is not rare that a domain of "Theoretically Applied Linguistics" or "application oriented basic research" takes on a life of its own, and that also something which is labelled as "Applied Linguistics" might in fact be rather remote from the mundane practical problems that originally initiated the respective subject area. But as long as a relation to the original practical problem can be established, it may be justified to count a particular field or discussion as belonging to applied linguistics, even if only "theoretically applied".

2.2.   Applied linguistics as a response to structuralism and generativism

As mentioned before, in the Anglophone world in particular the view still appears to be widespread that the primary concerns of the subject area of applied linguistics should be restricted to second language acquisition and language instruction in the first place (see, e.g., Davies 1999 or Schmitt and Celce-Murcia 2002). However, in other parts of the world, and above all in Europe, there has been a development away from aspects of language learning to a wider focus on more general issues of language and communication.

This broadening of scope was in part a reaction to the narrowing down the focus in linguistics that resulted from self-imposed methodological constraints which, as Ehlich (1999) points out, began with Saussurean structuralism and culminated in generative linguistics. For almost three decades since the late 1950s, these developments made "language" in a comprehensive sense, as related to the everyday experience of its users, vanish in favour of an idealised and basically artificial entity. This led in "Core" or theoretical linguistics to a neglect of almost all everyday problems with language and communication encountered by individuals and societies and made it necessary for those interested in socially accountable research into language and communication to draw on a wider range of disciplines, thus giving rise to a flourishing of interdisciplinary areas that have come to be referred to as hyphenated variants of linguistics, such as sociolinguistics, ethnolinguistics, psycholinguistics, conversation analysis, pragmatics, and so on (Davies and Elder 2004).

That these hyphenated variants of linguistics can be said to have originated from dealing with problems may lead to the impression that they fall completely into the scope of applied linguistics. This the more so as their original thematic focus is in line with a frequently quoted definition of applied linguistics as "the theoretical and empirical investigation of real world problems in which language is a central issue" (Brumfit 1997: 93). However, in the recent past much of the work done in these fields has itself been rather "theoretically applied" in the sense introduced above and ultimately even become mainstream in linguistics. Also, in view of the current epistemological developments that see all sciences under the pressure of application, one might even wonder if there is anything distinctive about applied linguistics at all.

Indeed it would be difficult if not impossible to delimit applied linguistics with respect to the practical problems studied and the disciplinary approaches used: Real-world problems with language (to which, for greater clarity, should be added: "with communication") are unlimited in principle. Also, many problems of this kind are unique and require quite different approaches. Some might be tackled successfully by applying already available linguistic theories and methods. Others might require for their solution the development of new methods and even new theories. Following a frequently used distinction first proposed by Widdowson (1980), one might label these approaches as "Linguistics Applied" or "Applied Linguistics". In addition, language is a trans-disciplinary subject par excellence, with the result that problems do not come labelled and may require for their solution the cooperation of various disciplines.

2.3.   Conceptualisations and communities

The questions of what should be its reference discipline and which themes, areas of research and sub-disciplines it should deal with, have been discussed constantly and were also the subject of an intensive debate (e.g. Seidlhofer 2003). In the recent past, a number of edited volumes on applied linguistics have appeared which in their respective introductory chapters attempt at giving a definition of "Applied Linguistics". As can be seen from the existence of the Association Internationale de Linguistique Appliquée (AILA) and its numerous national affiliates, from the number of congresses held or books and journals published with the label "Applied Linguistics", applied linguistics appears to be a well-established and flourishing enterprise. Therefore, the collective need felt by authors and editors to introduce their publication with a definition of the subject area it is supposed to be about is astonishing at first sight. Quite obviously, what Ehlich (2006) has termed "the struggle for the object of inquiry" appears to be characteristic of linguistics – both of linguistics at large and applied linguistics. Its seems then, that the meaning and scope of "Applied Linguistics" cannot be taken for granted, and this is why a wide variety of controversial conceptualisations exist.

For example, in addition to the dichotomy mentioned above with respect to whether approaches to applied linguistics should in their theoretical foundations and methods be autonomous from theoretical linguistics or not, and apart from other controversies, there are diverging views on whether applied linguistics is an independent academic discipline (e.g. Kaplan and Grabe 2000) or not (e.g. Davies and Elder 2004), whether its scope should be mainly restricted to language teaching related topics (e.g. Schmitt and Celce-Murcia 2002) or not (e.g. Knapp 2006), or whether applied linguistics is a field of interdisciplinary synthesis where theories with their own integrity develop in close interaction with language users and professionals (e.g. Rampton 1997/2003) or whether this view should be rejected, as a true interdisciplinary approach is ultimately impossible (e.g. Widdowson 2005).

In contrast to such controversies Candlin and Sarangi (2004) point out that applied linguistics should be defined in the first place by the actions of those who practically *do* applied linguistics:

> [...] we see no especial purpose in reopening what has become a somewhat sterile debate on what applied linguistics is, or whether it is a distinctive and coherent discipline. [...] we see applied linguistics as a many centered and interdisciplinary endeavour whose coherence is achieved in purposeful, mediated action by its practitioners. [...]
> What we want to ask of applied linguistics is less what it is and more what it does, or rather what its practitioners do. (Candlin/Sarangi 2004:1–2)

Against this background, they see applied linguistics as less characterised by its thematic scope – which indeed is hard to delimit – but rather by the two aspects of "relevance" and "reflexivity". Relevance refers to the purpose applied linguistic activities have for the targeted audience and to the degree that these activities in their collaborative practices meet the background and needs of those addressed – which, as matter of comprehensibility, also includes taking their conceptual and language level into account. Reflexivity means the contextualisation of the intellectual principles and practices, which is at the core of what characterises a professional community, and which is achieved by asking leading questions like "What kinds of purposes underlie what is done?", "Who is involved in their determination?", "By whom, and in what ways, is their achievement appraised?", "Who owns the outcomes?".

We agree with these authors that applied linguistics in dealing with real world problems is determined by disciplinary givens – such as e.g. theories, methods or standards of linguistics or any other discipline – but that it is determined at least as much by the social and situational givens of the practices of life. These do not only include the concrete practical problems themselves but also the theoretical and methodological standards of cooperating experts from other disciplines, as well as the conceptual and practical standards of the practitioners who are confronted with the practical problems in the first place. Thus, as Sarangi and van Leeuwen (2003) point out, applied linguists have to become part of the respective "community of practice".

If, however, applied linguists have to regard themselves as part of a community of practice, it is obvious that it is the entire community which determines what the respective subject matter is that the applied linguist deals with and how. In particular, it is the respective community of practice which determines which problems of the practitioners have to be considered. The consequence of this is that applied linguistics can be understood from very comprehensive to very specific, depending on what kind of problems are considered relevant by the respective community. Of course, following this participative understanding of applied linguistics also has consequences for the Handbooks of Applied Linguistics both with respect to the subjects covered and the way they are theoretically and practically treated.

3.   Applied linguistics for problem solving

Against this background, it seems reasonable not to define applied linguistics as an autonomous discipline or even only to delimit it by specifying a set of subjects it is supposed to study and typical disciplinary approaches it should use. Rather, in line with the collaborative and participatory perspective of the communities of practice applied linguists are involved in, this handbook series is based on the assumption that applied linguistics is a specific, problem-oriented way of "doing linguistics" related to the real-life world. In other words: applied linguistics is conceived of here as "linguistics for problem solving".

To outline what we think is distinctive about this area of inquiry: Entirely in line with Popper's conception of science, we take it that applied linguistics starts from the assumption of an imperfect world in the areas of language and communication. This means, firstly, that linguistic and communicative competence in individuals, like other forms of human knowledge, is fragmentary and defective – if it exists at all. To express it more pointedly: Human linguistic and communicative behaviour is not "perfect". And on a different level, this imperfection also applies to the use and status of language and communication in and among groups or societies.

Secondly, we take it that applied linguists are convinced that the imperfection both of individual linguistic and communicative behaviour and language based relations between groups and societies can be clarified, understood and to some extent resolved by their intervention, e.g. by means of education, training or consultancy.

Thirdly, we take it that applied linguistics proceeds by a specific mode of inquiry in that it mediates between the way language and communication is expertly studied in the linguistic disciplines and the way it is directly experienced in different domains of use. This implies that applied linguists are able to demonstrate that their findings – be they of a "Linguistics Applied" or "Applied Linguistics" nature – are not just "application oriented basic research" but can be made relevant to the real-life world.

Fourthly, we take it that applied linguistics is socially accountable. To the extent that the imperfections initiating applied linguistic activity involve both social actors and social structures, we take it that applied linguistics has to be critical and reflexive with respect to the results of its suggestions and solutions.

These assumptions yield the following questions which at the same time define objectives for applied linguistics:

1. Which linguistic problems are typical of which areas of language competence and language use?
2. How can linguistics define and describe these problems?
3. How can linguistics suggest, develop, or achieve solutions of these problems?
4. Which solutions result in which improvements in speakers' linguistic and communicative abilities or in the use and status of languages in and between groups?
5. What are additional effects of the linguistic intervention?

4.   Objectives of this handbook series

These questions also determine the objectives of this book series. However, in view of the present boom in handbooks of linguistics and applied linguistics, one should ask what is specific about this series of nine thematically different volumes.

To begin with, it is important to emphasise what it is not aiming at:

– The handbook series does not want to take a snapshot view or even a "hit list" of fashionable topics, theories, debates or fields of study.
– Nor does it aim at a comprehensive coverage of linguistics because some selectivity with regard to the subject areas is both inevitable in a book series of this kind and part of its specific profile.

Instead, the book series will try

– to show that applied linguistics can offer a comprehensive, trustworthy and scientifically well-founded understanding of a wide range of problems,
– to show that applied linguistics can provide or develop instruments for solving new, still unpredictable problems,

− to show that applied linguistics is not confined to a restricted number of topics such as, e.g. foreign language learning, but that it successfully deals with a wide range of both everyday problems and areas of linguistics,
− to provide a state-of-the-art description of applied linguistics against the background of the ability of this area of academic inquiry to provide descriptions, analyses, explanations and, if possible, solutions of everyday problems. On the one hand, this criterion is the link to trans-disciplinary cooperation. On the other, it is crucial in assessing to what extent linguistics can in fact be made relevant.

In short, it is by no means the intention of this series to duplicate the present state of knowledge about linguistics as represented in other publications with the supposed aim of providing a comprehensive survey. Rather, the intention is to present the knowledge available in applied linguistics today firstly from an explicitly problem solving perspective and secondly, in a non-technical, easily comprehensible way. Also it is intended with this publication to build bridges to neighbouring disciplines and to critically discuss which impact the solutions discussed do in fact have on practice. This is particularly necessary in areas like language teaching and learning − where for years there has been a tendency to fashionable solutions without sufficient consideration of their actual impact on the reality in schools.

5.   Criteria for the selection of topics

Based on the arguments outlined above, the handbook series has the following structure: Findings and applications of linguistics will be presented in concentric circles, as it were, starting out from the communication competence of the individual, proceeding via aspects of interpersonal and inter-group communication to technical communication and, ultimately, to the more general level of society. Thus, the topics of the nine volumes are as follows:

1. Handbook of Individual Communication Competence
2. Handbook of Interpersonal Communication
3. Handbook of Communication in Organisations and Professions
4. Handbook of Communication in the Public Sphere
5. Handbook of Multilingualism and Multilingual Communication
6. Handbook of Foreign Language Communication and Learning
7. Handbook of Intercultural Communication
8. Handbook of Technical Communication
9. Handbook of Language and Communication: Diversity and Change

This thematic structure can be said to follow the sequence of experience with problems related to language and communication a human passes through in the course of his or her personal biographical development. This is why the topic areas of applied linguistics are structured here in ever-increasing concentric circles: in line with biographical development, the first circle starts with the communicative competence of the individual and also includes interpersonal communication as belonging to a person's private sphere. The second circle proceeds to the everyday environment and includes the professional and public sphere. The third circle extends to the experience of foreign languages and cultures, which at least in officially monolingual societies, is not made by everybody and if so, only later in life. Technical communication as the fourth circle is even more exclusive and restricted to a more special professional clientele. The final volume extends this process to focus on more general, supra-individual national and international issues.

For almost all of these topics, there already exist introductions, handbooks or other types of survey literature. However, what makes the present volumes unique is their explicit claim to focus on topics in language and communication as areas of everyday problems and their emphasis on pointing out the relevance of applied linguistics in dealing with them.

Bibliography

Back, Otto
  1970   Was bedeutet und was bezeichnet der Begriff 'angewandte Sprachwissenschaft'? *Die Sprache* 16: 21–53.
Brumfit, Christopher
  1997   How applied linguistics is the same as any other science. *International Journal of Applied Linguistics* 7(1): 86–94.
Candlin, Chris N. and Srikant Sarangi
  2004   Making applied linguistics matter. *Journal of Applied Linguistics* 1(1): 1–8.
Carrier, Michael, Martin Stöltzner, and Jeanette Wette
  2004   *Theorienstruktur und Beurteilungsmaßstäbe unter den Bedingungen der Anwendungsdominanz.* Universität Bielefeld: Institut für Wissenschafts- und Technikforschung [http://www.uni-bielefeld.de/iwt/projekte/wissen/anwendungsdominanz.html, accessed Jan 5, 2007].
Davies, Alan
  1999   *Introduction to Applied Linguistics. From Practice to Theory.* Edinburgh: Edinburgh University Press.
Davies, Alan and Catherine Elder
  2004   General introduction – Applied linguistics: Subject to discipline? In: Alan Davies and Catherine Elder (eds.), *The Handbook of Applied Linguistics*, 1–16. Malden etc.: Blackwell.
Ehlich, Konrad
  1999   Vom Nutzen der „Funktionalen Pragmatik" für die angewandte Linguistik. In: Michael Becker-Mrotzek und Christine Doppler (eds.), *Medium Sprache im Beruf. Eine Aufgabe für* die *Linguistik*, 23–36. Tübingen: Narr.

Ehlich, Konrad
  2006   Mehrsprachigkeit für Europa – öffentliches Schweigen, linguistische Distanzen. In: Sergio Cigada, Jean-Francois de Pietro, Daniel Elmiger, and Markus Nussbaumer (eds.), *Öffentliche Sprachdebatten – linguistische Positionen. Bulletin Suisse de Linguistique Appliquée/VALS-ASLA-Bulletin* 83/1: 11–28.
Grabe, William
  2002   Applied linguistics: An emerging discipline for the twenty-first century. In: Robert B. Kaplan (ed.), *The Oxford Handbook of Applied Linguistics*, 3–12. Oxford: Oxford University Press.
Johnson, Keith and Helen Johnson (eds.)
  1998   *Encyclopedic Dictionary of Applied Linguistics. A Handbook for Language Teaching.* Oxford: Blackwell.
Kaplan, Robert B. and William Grabe
  2000   Applied linguistics and the Annual Review of Applied Linguistics. In: W. Grabe (ed.), *Applied Linguistics as an Emerging Discipline. Annual Review of Applied Linguistics* 20: 3–17.
Knapp, Karlfried
  2006   Vorwort. In: Karlfried Knapp, Gerd Antos, Michael Becker-Mrotzek, Arnulf Deppermann, Susanne Göpferich, Joachim Gabowski, Michael Klemm und Claudia Villiger (eds.), *Angewandte Linguistik. Ein Lehrbuch.* 2nd ed., xix–xxiii. Tübingen: Francke – UTB.
Meinel, Christoph
  2000   Reine und angewandte Wissenschaft. In: *Das Magazin.* Ed. Wissenschaftszentrum Nordrhein-Westfalen 11(1): 10–11.
Rampton, Ben
  1997 [2003]   Retuning in applied linguistics. *International Journal of Applied Linguistics* 7 (1): 3–25, quoted from Seidlhofer (2003), 273–295.
Sarangi, Srikant and Theo van Leeuwen
  2003   Applied linguistics and communities of practice: Gaining communality or losing disciplinary autonomy? In: Srikant Sarangi and Theo van Leeuwen (eds.), *Applied Linguistics and Communities of Practice*, 1–8. London: Continuum.
Schmitt, Norbert and Marianne Celce-Murcia
  2002   An overview of applied linguistics. In: Norbert Schmitt (ed.), *An Introduction to Applied Linguistics.* London: Arnold.
Seidlhofer, Barbara (ed.)
  2003   *Controversies in Applied Linguistics.* Oxford: Oxford University Press.
Widdowson, Henry
  1984 [1980]   Model and fictions. In: Henry Widdowson (1984) *Explorations in Applied Linguistics 2*, 21–27. Oxford: Oxford University Press.
Widdowson, Henry
  2005   Applied linguistics, interdisciplinarity, and disparate realities. In: Paul Bruthiaux, Dwight Atkinson, William G. Egginton, William Grabe, and Vaidehi Ramanathan (eds.), *Directions in Applied Linguistics. Essays in Honor of Robert B. Kaplan*, 12–25. Clevedon: Multilingual Matters.

Contents

Part I

Professional and organisational practice: A discourse/communication perspective

Srikant Sarangi and Christopher N. Candlin

1. Preamble

This volume is conceived as a contribution to the field of Applied Linguistics and Communication Studies. More precisely, it straddles two domains of study: applied linguistics and studies in professional and organisational communication. It is possible, historically, to draw a dividing line between these two domains. While studies in professional and organisational communication in areas such as health and social care, law, bureaucracy, management and business have engaged in micro-level analysis of text and talk to discover style- and setting-specific features of language use related to particular institutional practices and organisational structures, mainstream applied linguistic studies have focused principally on language education and language acquisition/learning, also with a micro-level orientation, but clearly oriented towards influencing pedagogic practice and policy.

Recently, however, we have seen many studies in Applied Linguistics going well beyond such a narrow construction of its field to include the broader domains of professional practice. It is on these broader domains, seen from the viewpoint of more traditionally focused Applied Linguistics, that this volume places its emphasis on real world issues, principally on fields such as healthcare, law, social work, business organisations. Such an extension of the domains of Applied Linguistics is a conscious attempt on our part in this volume to move towards what Sarangi (2005) calls an "Applied Linguistics of Professions" along the lines of cognate social scientific approaches to professions, for example the Sociology of Professions, Anthropology of Professions *inter alia*, aiming thus to "expand the boundaries of applied linguistic themes and sites as a way of recognising the emerging interest in language-focused activities in professions" (Sarangi 2005: 380). One needs, however, to acknowledge that not all professions, or sub-categories within a profession, rely on language use to the same degree. For instance, within the healthcare profession, surgeons, dentists, radiologists and psychotherapists are bound to differ considerably in the significance they attach to language in dealing with patients/clients, and within the legal profession such differences in significance vary as between advocates in court, solicitors in the community, arbitrators in tribunals, and those involved in Alternative Dispute Resolution (ADR). In a similar vein, it will be an overstatement to claim that language is the only modality in which professional practice is manifest. In reality, professional practice is essentially multimodal, although in this volume we primarily focus on the language/interaction dimensions.

The study of professions and organizations – healthcare, law, social welfare, bureaucracy, education, business and management – from the perspective of language and communication (in the broad sense of discourse) has a long-standing history, beginning with the mid 1970s and the early 1980s (book-length studies include Labov and Fanshel 1977; Atkinson and Drew 1979; Erickson and Shultz 1982; Di Pietro 1982; O'Barr 1982, 1983; Fisher and Todd 1983, 1986; Coleman 1984, 1985, 1989; Drew and Heritage 1992; Gee, Hull, and Lankshear 1996; Sarangi and Slembrouck 1996; Gunnarsson, Linell, and Nordberg 1997; Sarangi and Roberts 1999; Candlin 2002; Thornborrow 2002; Iedema 2003; Hall, Slembrouck, and Sarangi 2006; Gunnarsson 2009; Freed and Ehrlich 2010; Candlin and Crichton 2010; Sarangi and Linell [forthcoming]). This body of literature can be generally grouped under three categories. The first category relates to those descriptive, genre-based studies focusing on specialised registers, mainly involving written texts, drawn chiefly from the world of the academy (e.g. Bazerman 1989; Swales 1990; Myers 1990; Bhatia 1993; Christie and Martin 1997; Hyland 2000). The focus on linguistic and metalinguistic features characterises this tradition. The second category includes interpretive studies of talk and interaction in workplace settings (e.g. Drew and Heritage 1992; Boden 1994; Firth 1994; Sarangi and Roberts 1999; Holmes and Stubbe 2003; Koester 2006) sometimes involving critical sites such as team meetings, cross-examination in the courtroom, symptoms presentation and delivery of diagnosis in clinics, information and advice giving in counselling, conflict resolution in mediation etc. A key difference between these two strands could be seen in terms of their respective emphases on lexico-grammatical and discursive aspects of language use. In more recent years, a third category of studies is emerging which constitutes a problem-centred, interventionist agenda in the spirit of what many have identified as the central focus and commitment of Applied Linguistics, often involving close collaboration between discourse analysts and members of various professions. Accounts of research involving such collaborations have mainly appeared in the form of applied linguistic journal articles and book chapters, or as journal Special Issues, as for example in *Applied Linguistics* (Sarangi and Candlin 2003a), in *Journal of Applied Linguistics* (Iedema 2005), in *Text* (Freeman and Heller 1987) and in *Health, Risk & Society* (Sarangi and Candlin 2003b). New journals such as *Communication & Medicine*, *International Journal of Speech, Language and the Law* (formerly, *Forensic Linguistics*) and the newly relaunched *Journal of Applied Linguistics and Professional Practice* are testimony to this growing field of interdisciplinary and inter-professional interest.

The present volume is organised into four Parts. The first Part constitutes the Editorial Introduction which offers a broad overview of the cross-cutting domains and analytical/methodological themes as well as synopses of individual chapters. The second Part consisting of three contributions offers an historical perspective, selectively, on the interface of language and communication studies and three emblematic professional, organisational domains, viz. healthcare, law and organisational studies. The third Part comprises more detailed accounts of specific professional and organisational sites, focusing on a set of "focal themes" (Roberts and Sarangi 2005) which cut across a diversity of such sites. The contributions in the fourth Part of the volume address issues of *praxis*, exemplifying a range of reflexively methodological and epistemological contributions from canonical domains, while also emphasising issues of researcher-participant collaboration, interdisciplinarity, interprofessionality and uptake of discourse analytic findings.

Before elaborating further the scope of each individual part of the volume (parts 2–4), our Introduction first draws attention to a distinction between what may be called the discourse of the institutional order and that of the professional order, and their interface (Sarangi and Roberts 1999).

2.   Discourse across institutional and professional orders

Professional practices are institutionally and organisationally embedded. Although there is a ritual dimension to professional conduct, which gives rise to distinctive "communities of practice" (Lave and Wenger 1991) and the possibility of socialisation through apprenticeship and experience, a given communicative practice is situationally accomplished. So, before we examine professional practice (text and talk) in specific communicative contexts we need a broader understanding of the institutional order which underpins it.

2.1.   Institutional order/discourse

Berger and Luckmann (1967), in their classic treatise *The Social Construction of Reality*, characterise the institutional order in terms of *habitualisation, typification or routinisation*. As they suggest, "the institution posits that actions of type X will be performed by actors of type X" (1967: 72). In other words, when some practices become typified, they become emblematic of institutions (e.g., family, club, social groups). Ritual activities such as administering a marriage, a funeral, an oath of office, executions etc. become institutional practices, thus assuming a form of "objective reality". Typification, according to Berger and Luckmann (1967), equals "just whatness", marked by economy of effort, anticipation, depersonalisation, legitimation as well as rules and procedures which afford institutions a stable, habitual disposition: "The priority of the institutional definitions of situations must be consistently maintained over individual temptations at redefinition" (1967: 80).

The institutional order is enacted through professionals performing specific roles, which we elaborate further below in our discussion of professional order. Berger and Luckmann characterise the interdependence between professional roles and the institutional order as follows:

> [O]n the one hand, the institutional order is real only in so far as it is *realized* in performed roles and that, on the other hand, roles are representative of an institutional order that defines their character (including their appendages of knowledge) and from which they derive their objective sense.
> (Berger and Luckmann 1967: 96; emphasis in original)

Goffman's (1961) distinction between the *regular performance of a role* and a *regular performer of a role* is useful. The institutional representative (a doctor, a priest, a lawyer) regularly performs a professional role, whereas their clients may be less familiar in such role performance. We can, however, identify contexts where patients with chronic illnesses, clients with access to institutional rules and procedures, and other associated support persons, for example expert witnesses, draw on specific knowledge and expertise to assume ritualised role performance.

In *How Institutions Think*, Mary Douglas (1986) identifies the following features of an institutional order:

– Institutions as "legitimised grouping"
– Institutions as organisers of information
– Institutions confer identity/sameness: "Sameness is not a quality that can be recognised in things themselves; it is conferred upon elements within a coherent scheme" (Douglas 1986: 59).

Interpreting Douglas' features of the institutional order in discourse terms, there is a sense in which institutions are quintessentially *categorisation/classification systems* realised by particular linguistic and discursive choices. For instance, when it comes to rationing access to restricted healthcare resources, the institution may devise ways of categorising risk as "low", "medium" and "high" against set criteria. Such rationing practices may seem rational from an institutional perspective but one which could be contested both by healthcare professionals and clients.

With regard to categorisation, Douglas provides the following Biblical example:

> So the unlikely threesome, the camel, the hare, and rock badger, get classed together in Leviticus 11 as animals that chew the cud, and so they would seem to belong to the class of cud-chewing ungulates; but since their hooves do not part like the rest of the class, they are excluded from it. In the same chapter, the pig is put in a class of one member; it is the only creature whose hoof does part that does not chew the cud.
> (Douglas 1986: 58–59)

This example of Douglas' resonates with Rosch's (1978) prototype theory where she moves away from a simple *either/or* categorization towards a *more/less* categorization, arguing that members of a given category do not always share properties (actions, beliefs, discourses) to the same degree. Such a model of *prototypicality* is central to institutional engagements with accommodating uncertainties in determining risk and probability, but also how, for example, actors and actions may be categorised (see here in particular Sacks' [1992] work on "membership categorization").

Categorisation is primarily accomplished through language. As Lee (1992: 16) observes: "Language [is] a classificatory instrument ... categories are not objective, ready-made, inherent properties of the external world but are subject to processes of perception and interpretation". Grint (1991) provides an example of one such categorisation in terms of his account of the "unemployed":

> For example, to be categorized as "unemployed" today not only signifies the histori-
> cally atypical creation of a formal division between the economy and the polity, em-
> ployment and work, but also embodies the significance attached to one particular
> facet of contemporary Western social life. Unemployment is not a category that
> would be recognised outside a very limited slice of space and time; that it is today,
> and that the label is crucial to the status of the individual, tells us as much about the
> kind of society we inhabit as about the kind of individual stigmatized.
> (Grint 1991: 7)

Categorisations are routinely drawn upon by institutional members to classify particular cases, actions, policies in the context of providing of written or spoken accounts. In healthcare encounters, the doctor offering a diagnostic label is a form of categorisation which is based on identification of specific symptoms and signs and which in turn anticipates the treatment regime to be followed. Categorisation thus involves a set of discursive processes ("formulations", to use Heritage and Watson's [1979] terminology, and reformulations) which result in facts, opinions, or circumstances being established as one type of category rather than another. In sum, categorisation processes are constitutive of the institution which gives rise to them.

It is important to acknowledge that lay people also categorise events and experiences which may not align with the institutional viewpoint. Within a given institutional order, categorisation can be linked to what is often referred to as *recontextualisation*. According to Linell:

> Recontextualisation may be defined as the dynamic transfer-and-transformation of
> something from one discourse/text-in-context (the context being in reality a matrix
> or field of contexts) to another. Recontextualisation involves the extrication of some
> part or aspect from a text or discourse, or from a genre of texts or discourses, and
> the fitting of this part or aspect into another context, i.e., another text or discourse
> (or discourse genre) and its use and environment.
> (Linell 1998: 144–145)

It is in recontextualisation practices that the institutional order and the professional order overlap, with underlying assumptions about power relations and knowledge asymmetries that characterise expert-lay communication (Linell and Luckmann 1991; Linell and Sarangi 1998; Hak 1994).

At the most general level, institutional recontextualisation practices involve transformation of spoken interaction into written language. In this transformation process the institutional form/style overrides everyday language use, and what becomes institutionally recorded (e.g., meeting minutes, patient records, case reports) constitutes the institutional reality for future action (Mehan 1993). With regard to medical patient records, Cicourel (1983) observes:

> The language they [physician and patient] use reflects the two forms of literacy alluded to earlier: the physician recodes the patient's often ambiguous, rambling, and somewhat emotional language into fairly abstract categories; the patients' unclear or particular or concrete terms are converted into crisp and explicit medical terminology, interpretations, and factual statements. The two forms of literacy imply modes of thinking that are different.
> (Cicourel 1983: 227–228)

Similar practices can be seen in the legal setting. Jönsson and Linell (1991) compare police reports and police interviews along the written/spoken continuum and find how the medium contributes to the construction of two different versions of the same story. According to them:

> [T]he monological text has a more clearly elaborated narrative structure and a legally relevant perspective. In addition, the transformation from spoken dialogue to written text involves changes from vagueness to precision, from relative incoherence to coherence and a clear chronology, from emotionality to an objectively identified sequence of events and actions etc.
> (Jönsson and Linell 1991: 419)

At another level, institutional recontextualisation practices are more context-specific. Institutional representatives and professionals reformulate clients' utterances in strategic ways (see below the discussion of professional vision). Sarangi and Slembrouck (1996) in their analysis of discourse in bureaucratic settings illustrate how categorisation of a missing item as "lost" vs "stolen" can lead to very different police actions. They refer to this process as *bureaupretation*.

Dorothy Smith (1990) draws attention to the power of the institutional text vis-à-vis the lay perspective. She provides an example of two texts concerning a confrontation between the police and street people in Berkeley, California in 1968 (the eye witness account published as a letter in the underground newspaper and the mayor's account):

> Between the two accounts, there is little disagreement on the particulars of the story. But the official version reconstructs the witnessed events as moments in extended sequences of institutional action, locating them in textual time, dependent on textual realities already institutionally accomplished. What the witness saw and thought was going on is shown to be only a partial and imperfect knowledge of proper police work. (Smith 1990: 65)

This claim underpins our earlier observation that professional practices are institutionally embedded. The "textual realities" professionals and lay persons create are constitutive of specific stakes and interests rather than being representations of "objective reality" (Smith 1978). The concept of language and discourse as both a mode of representation and as a tool for the construction of reality takes on a different meaning in institutional settings, in particular in determining whose construction of events and how such events are to be categorised, prevails.

As can be seen from the above discussion, such recontextualisation practices reveal an inherent mismatch between what Agar (1985) calls "institutional frames" and "client frames". According to Agar, institutional discourse must accomplish three things.

> First, the institutional representative must *diagnose* the client ... The institution provides a limited number of ways to describe people, their problems and the possible solutions. These ways are called Institutional Frames. Clients, on the other hand, come to the encounter with a variety of ways of thinking about themselves, their problems, and the institution's relationship to them. They have their own Client Frames. Diagnosis is that part of the discourse where the institutional representative fits the client's ways of talking about the encounter to ways that fit the institution's.

> Another part of institutional discourse is the *directives*. They are one of the goals of the diagnosis; the institutional representative directs the client to do certain things or directs an organization to do certain things to or for the client.

> A third part of the institutional discourse is the *report*. A report is the summary of the institutional discourse that the institutional representative produces ... the report, in written or oral form, may be directed only to other institutional representatives. The institutional frames prescribe how a report should look and what it should contain. (Agar 1985: 149; emphasis in original)

While the diagnostic element refers to the problem-definition aspect, the directive dimension refers to problem-solution as characteristic of institutional intervention. However, what constitutes a diagnosis and a directive can be contested within and across institutional orders. The reports function in part as "accounts" (Garfinkel 1967) of the practices of institutional members in terms of which such members may be held "accountable" by clients and professional colleagues, say for advice (not) given, decisions (not) made, and actions (not) taken. "Accountable" here is not to suggest that descriptive accounts in themselves provide unproblematic access to the nature of the activities they describe. On the contrary,

Garfinkel emphasises that accounts have a "loose fit" with the circumstances they depict, and the nature of the fit between accounts and their circumstance is to be established through sense-making.

The realisation of these "accounts" and their "sense-making" draws chiefly on the notion of *indexicality* (Garfinkel 1967). Garfinkel argues that the importance of institutional texts (e.g., clinic records, coroner reports) lies not in the text itself, but in the ties between texts and social systems that service, and are serviced by, these textual records – what he refers to as the "indexical nature" of accounts. This view is reflected in his key assertion that "accounts are not independent of the socially organised occasions of their use" (Garfinkel 1967: 3), which also foregrounds the premise surrounding the "documentary method of interpretation". Hence, in his two classic studies where he uses institutional documents as primary data, Garfinkel identifies how coroner reports and clinic records are both situated *sense-making devices* through which institutional members, in this case the coroner and the doctor, keep account of their daily work and make it visible to a range of ratified participants. Case notes, clinic records and reports of various forms are important sites of professional work where decision-making is displayed as Hall, Slembrouck and Sarangi (2006: 18) point out (see also Barrett 1996; Hak 1989, 1992; Pettinari 1988; Firkins and Candlin 2006).

It is apparent therefore that institutional discourse, at the micro-level, is task-driven and goal-oriented, with constraints on participation and language use (in text as well as talk format). Following Levinson's (1992) seminal work on "activity types and language", Drew and Heritage suggest that:

> 1. Institutional interaction involves an orientation by at least one of the participants to some core goal, task or identity (or set of them) conventionally associated with the institution in question. In short, institutional talk is normally informed by *goal orientations* of a relatively restricted conventional form.
>
> 2. Institutional interaction may often involve *special and particular constraints* on what one or both of the participants will treat as allowable contributions to the business in hand.
>
> 3. Institutional talk may be associated with *inferential frameworks* and procedures that are particular to specific institutional contexts.
> (Drew and Heritage 1992: 22; emphasis in original)

This task/goal-orientation of institutional discourse is manifest at the levels of interactional and linguistic structures and styles (Sarangi 1998). In terms of structure, a clinic visit in primary care settings is organised along certain sequential phases, e.g., symptoms presentation, history taking, physical examination, treatment (Byrne and Long 1976). With regard to style, a clinic encounter, like courtroom encounters or encounters between clients and accountants or clients and social workers, is an activity mediated by questions and answers.

The task-orientation of institutional encounters is indeed manifest in the prevalence of question-answer sequences (Freed and Ehrlich 2010) where the questions have institution-specific purposes, e.g., categorising a disease condition, guilt status, welfare entitlement.

Notions such as categorisation and recontextualisation as discussed above are traditionally linked to the concept of systemic rationality which governs the institutional order. According to Weber (1964), institutional/bureaucratic rationality is manifest in the following of rules and procedures. Habermas (1987) draws a distinction between the systems world and the lifeworld and suggests that there is increasing colonisation of the lifeworld by the systems world, which can be noticed at the levels of linguistic structures and styles. Fairclough (1992) uses the notion of "conversationalisation" to refer to how institutions increasingly use conversational, informal style to give an impression of debureaucratisation (Sarangi and Slembrouck 1996), although at a deeper level the rules and procedures may remain unchanged. In contemporary societies, we even notice the lifeworld and the private sphere adopting bureaucratic structures and styles in their attempt to colonise the systems world (see for instance Bauman's [2000] thesis of "liquid modernity" which stresses "the colonization of the public sphere by issues previously classified as private and unsuitable for public venting").

2.2.   Professional order/discourse

In the previous section we have suggested that professional practices are institutionally embedded. But this statement should not blind us to the tensions between institutions and professions which exist within a given socio-political context, historically and in contemporary terms. At times of conflict the institutional order dominates and constricts the other. As a means of emphasising this point, we can briefly outline the key role that the state plays in mediating institutions and professions. Bureaucratisation and professional control have long emerged as a focus of sociological studies of professions and organisations (e.g., Etzioni 1961; Elliott 1972; Johnson 1972; Larson 1977; Abbott and Wallace 1990; Torstendahl and Burrage 1990; Hugman 1991; Macdonald 1995). For Weber (1964), bureaucratisation and professionalisation are products of the increasing rationalisation of Western civilisation. In more general terms, Johnson (1972) refers to the mediated role of the state:

> State mediation has, then, the effect of creating divergent interests and orientations within an occupational community as a result of the creation of varied specialist and hierarchical organisational forms. These divisions threaten the maintenance or inhibit the emergence of the "complete community" of professionalism and even the belief in occupation-wide colleagueship ...
> (Johnson 1972: 80)

Freidson (1994: 137) makes a similar point when he claims that "bureaucratic organisation is assumed to be antithetical to the freedom of activity traditionally imputed to the professional". Elsewhere he characterises "professionalism" as the third logic (the first and second being "consumerism" and "managerialism"): "a set of interconnected institutions providing the economic support and social organisation that sustains the occupational control of work" (Freidson 2001: 2).

As Johnson (1993) sees it:

> From a Foucauldian perspective, both state and professions are, in part, the emergent effects of an interplay between changing government policies and occupational strategies. This is a view that undermines the dominant conception of the state-profession relationship in sociology, wedded, as it is, to a notion of the state … whose interventions are inimicable to the development of autonomous professionalism.
> (Johnson 1993: 144–146)

Professionalism can be understood by referring to the polarisation between specialisation and localisation tendencies in the professions. Hugman (1991) observes:

> Where specialisation is based on concepts of counselling and advising, localisation is grounded in concepts of liaising and networking, in which knowledge of a small geographical area and the resources within it takes priority over individualised knowledge about causes and solutions to social problems.
> (Hugman 1991: 205)

The discussion so far points to the crucial dimensions of specialised knowledge in the working of professions. There is a strong association between professions and the development of scientific knowledge systems – or what Murphy (1988: 245) calls "formally rational abstract utilitarian knowledge". According to Larson (1977), "professionalisation is thus an attempt to translate one order of scarce resources – special knowledge and skills – into another – social and economic rewards". Focusing mainly on the post-industrial Anglo-American society, Freidson (1994) draws attention to a shift in work control: from bureaucratic, administrative forms of work control to professional forms – knowledge-based occupations of experts. At the same time, Freidson is keen to draw a distinction between what he terms "scholarly, learned, or scientific professions" and what he labels as "practising or consulting professions", and again between "professions" and "para professions" which suggests that there exist tensions not only between professions and the institutions of the state, but also within and among "professions" themselves.

The managerial revolution of the pre-war period has been followed by the revolution of the knowledge-workers in the post-war period. Against this backdrop, occupations such as social work and nursing have been regarded as "semi-professions" since they seem to be based on skills rather than knowledge (Abbott and Wallace 1990; Etzioni 1969; Torstendahl and Burrage 1990; Wilding 1982). Such pigeonholing of professions is constantly contested, however, because the line of demarcation between skill and knowledge is not always so clear-cut, and because neither is systematically linked to the overarching construct of expertise. Kanes' collection of articles (Kanes 2010), for example, emphasises how the concept of "professionalism" is increasingly under challenge in terms of its boundaries, the demands for accountability placed upon it, and the increasingly limiting constraints on professional action imposed by external regulation and ethical considerations.

Linked with skill/knowledge is the notion of power (for structures of power and control in the profession, see Freidson 1970; Johnson 1972). In this context, Freidson (1970) refers to the ideological character of professional claims: how professional institutions create and sustain authority over clients and associated occupations, and the ways they think about deviant behaviour. The display of knowledge through discursive practice offers a key to understanding how professions sustain their power and expertise. As Foucault (1980) would see it, knowledge and power strategies are inextricably intertwined:

> Knowledge is inextricably entwined in relations of power and advances of knowledge are associated with advances and developments in the exercise of power ... knowledge and power are mutually and inextricably interdependent. A site where power is exercised is also a place where knowledge is produced ... knowledge and power are inextricably and necessarily linked.
> (Smart 1985: 64)

In Foucauldian terms, this is "interiorisation of (disciplinary) power" working through the "invisible" and "capillary" ways in which it is exercised. Power is thus not tied to specific locations or individuals: the rational discourses of professions operate through constructing versions of truths and clienthoods that align with institutional priorities. This suggests that professions would first try to intervene through a reinstatement of a "normal situation" before they go for coercive intervention. In that respect, it is true that coercion (the older form of power) is very much a last resort in modern society and it is often cloaked in rationalising discourse which supports Gramsci's (1971) construct of *collusive power*.

Before we move to a discourse/communication based approach to professional practice, it may be useful to consider briefly, from the sociological viewpoint, the *traits theory* of professions and occupations. At base, the trait model is concerned with identifying lists of attributes which are said to represent the common core of professional occupations, i.e. ideal-types (Etzioni 1969). As Becker (1962) points out:

> "[P]rofession" is not a neutral and scientific concept but, rather ... a folk concept, a part of the apparatus of the society we study, to be studied by knowing how it is used and what role it plays in the operations of that society. (Becker 1962: 32)

For Parsons (1951), it is about elite status and economic self-interest. Parsons traces the primacy of cognitive rationality as it is expressed through "functional specificity" and "affective neutrality" of the professional role. He goes on to suggest an inherent contradiction: on the one hand, professions manifest altruistic rather than self-interested behaviour; but, on the other hand, in terms of economic utilitarianism, all behaviour is self-interested. This is echoed by Illich (1977):

> Neither income, long training, delicate tasks nor social standing is the mark of the professional. Rather, it is his authority to define a person as client, to determine that person's need and to find the person a prescription. This professional authority comprises three roles: the sapiential authority to advise, instruct and direct, the moral authority that makes its acceptance not just useful but obligatory; and charismatic authority that allows the professional to appeal to some supreme interest of his client that not only outranks conscience but sometimes even the *raison d'état*.
> (Illich 1977: 17–18)

Among other things, Johnson (1972: 25) maintains, "'trait' theory, because of its atheoretical character, too easily falls into the error of accepting the professionals' own definitions of themselves". There is also the contentious issue of what separates a profession from an occupational group and how certain occupations have over time managed to climb up and assume professional status. Greenwood's (1962: 207) designation of professional work offers some useful criteria:

– A system of theoretical knowledge which serves as the basis for the professional skill.
– Professional authority: the power to prescribe a course of action for a client because of superior knowledge, for example, doctor's orders.
– Approval of authority claims by the community.
– A code of ethics designed to protect the client, provide service to the community, and provide a basis for elimination of unethical practitioners.
– Professional culture patterns consisting of values (for example, the conviction that the professional service is valuable to the community), norms which provide guides for behaviour in professional practice, symbols of professional status such as the title "Doctor" and the concept of a professional career.

In summary, then, the construct and term "profession" may be characterised *inter alia* by the following attributes:

– Specialised knowledge, functional specificity
– Specialised language, jargons
– Corporate organisation
– Monopoly, power, authority

- Autonomy/Independence
- Code of ethics
- Ethic of public service; altruism
- Affective neutrality

Professionals can be seen as belonging to *communities of practice* (Lave and Wenger 1991). The construct of community of practice has been since its invention centrally linked to three sets of defining concepts: the domain of interest and domain-related competence; membership, relationship and community; and, activity, practice, and shared repertoires of experience. Members are said to be "mutually engaged", their engagement is located in a "joint enterprise", and the pursuance of this enterprise over extensive periods of time and within recognizable routines in established space is seen to develop among them a "shared repertoire" of recognized and mutually intelligible performances and interpretations, including, we may assume – although Lave and Wenger do not single this out especially – common discourses. These discourses are constitutive of professional practice: involving acknowledging and claiming identities in interactions; representing in appropriate genres what is accepted and conventional knowledge; signalling membership by a range of semiotic and sociolinguistic performances; managing inter- and intra-community relationships by acknowledgement of rights, duties and roles; and enabling and achieving outcomes for agreed and determined tasks in which processes of resourceful and appropriate deployment of communication competency are clearly at a premium.

From a discourse/communication perspective, Goodwin (1994) argues that

> [P]rofessional settings provide a perspicuous site for the investigation of how objects of knowledge, controlled by and relevant to the defining work of a specific community, are socially constructed from within the settings that make up the lifeworld of that community – that is, endogeneously, through systematic discursive procedures.
> (Goodwin 1994: 630)

Heath (1979) offers a useful historical overview of the characteristics of professionalism (in the USA context, between 1840s and 1960s) drawing particular attention to the development of a specialised professional vocabulary and ways of presenting knowledge in the healthcare setting:

> First, the language of the professional set him (sic) apart from the client or patient. His language was a mark of the special province of knowledge which was the basis of what it was the patient was told, though the knowledge itself could not be transmitted to the patient … A second feature of the language of the professional was his (sic) articulated knowledge of ways to obtain information from patients while restricting the amount and types of information transmitted to the patient … Professionals have, therefore, been socialised to have certain perceptions of their role in communicative tasks, and they have been trained to use language as an instrument to maintain that role and to accomplish ends often known only to them in interchanges.
> (Heath 1979: 108)

This characterisation of professional socialisation is echoed in Goodwin's (1994) conceptualisation at a micro-level of professional practice as ways of seeing and articulating specific knowledge systems, i.e., discursive procedures. Goodwin (1994) proposes the notion of *professional vision*, constituted in three discursive procedures:

(1) coding (i.e., ways in which one transforms what they see/hear/read into objects which can be studied)

(2) *highlighting* (i.e., ways of marking specific phenomena as salient)

(3) *producing and articulating representations* (i.e., documenting how one interprets these phenomena and these objects as a socially situated activity and not just as a cognitive process).

The discursive manifestation of professional vision is informed by different types of (tacit) knowledge: scientific/disciplinary; experiential (practice-based); institutional/organisational and interactional/communicative (with clients, fellow-professionals, inter-professional and inter-institutional; both spoken and written) (Sarangi 2010b). In a sense, "professional vision" is a form of categorisation and recontextualisation as discussed earlier. In the domain of law, Maley et al. (1995) elaborate how the professional vision of lawyers in conferences with clients regularly transforms and recontextualises clients' relational accounts into tractable understandings from a legal perspective, which then need to be re-transformed into appropriately lay-directed spoken language for the non-expert client. The work on police-suspect interviews (Rock 2007) and studies of courtroom interaction between prosecutors and witnesses and accused (Cotterill 2002, 2003) provide parallel examples where such recontextualisations have a strategic adversarial purpose, i.e., to obtain confirmation of actions, to imply guilt etc.

With regard to the discourse of professional-client encounters more generally, at the interpersonal pragmatic level, Thomas (1985) suggests that certain features (as is recontextualisation) are characteristic of the speech of dominant participants, which are systematically absent from that of the subordinate participants. She calls these strategies "metapragmatic acts" – where "dominant participants make explicit reference to the intended pragmatic force of their own or their subordinate's utterances" (Thomas 1985: 767). Specific mechanisms such as illocutionary force indicating devices (IFIDs), metapragmatic comments, upshots and reformulations, appeals to felicity conditions, count as recontextualisation practices within a given institutional order.

Many studies dealing with institutional discourse settings (both theoretical and empirical) draw our attention to the expert-lay communication systems. There is an assumption that the lay and expert systems in themselves are homogeneous entities and the tensions or problems only occur across the boundaries. However, it is quite possible to argue that individual professionals and clients occupy different positions in a continuum (see Sarangi and Slembrouck [1996] on professional clients). The notion of role-set, rather than binary roles, is a better way to characterise situated professional-client encounters (Sarangi 2010a).

Against this backdrop, it is useful to revisit Roberts and Sarangi's (1999) corresponding differentiation between institutional, professional and personal experience modes of talk in the context of healthcare. The "what" and "how" of clinical practice is distinctive both from the "why" of medicine, health and illness and the lifeworld voices inhabited by the clients (as well as professionals). However, the situated talk and text in professional and institutional settings is increasingly characterised by *hybridity*. It is difficult to maintain an orderly discreteness and integrity in terms of which we have come to identify ideal text and interaction types.

The intimate connection between workplaces and their discourses is now well established in the research literature. It has become something of a commonplace to assert that workplaces are in some sense held together by the communicative practices to which they give rise, or even, more boldly, that such communicative practices constitute the work of the workplaces themselves. As Sarangi and Roberts (1999: 1) observe: "workplaces are social institutions where resources are produced and regulated, problems are solved, identities are played out and professional knowledge is constituted". That such workplaces are not unitary in their discourse but frequently complex, overlapping and with unclear and often confusing boundaries, manifesting what Sarangi and Roberts (1999) refer to as discursive *hybridity*, is similarly both recognised and well attested. As Fairclough (1992) observes:

> As producers and interpreters combine discursive conventions, codes and elements in new ways in innovatory discursive events, they are of course cumulatively producing structural changes in the orders of discourse, and rearticulating new orders of discourse, new discursive hegemonies. Such structural changes may affect only the "local" order of discourse of an institution, or they may transcend institutions and affect the societal order of discourse.
> (Fairclough 1992: 97)

As one example of such a shift and change both socio-culturally and discursively, Candlin and Maley (1997) in their study of alternative dispute resolution (ADR) identify what they refer to as *interdiscursivity*. By interdiscursivity, they mean that elements from one discourse, with their institutional and social meanings, may be interpellated in another (Fairclough 1992), and may come to create what is in effect a "new" professional discourse associated with correspondingly new institutional practices. According to them, ADR discourse combines aspects of adjudication and counselling (see also Sarangi [2000] on how genetic counselling as a hybrid activity type variously draws upon clinical, gatekeeping and service encounter discourses). These are active and dynamic processes of "recontextualisation" as discussed earlier.

3.   The historical turn: Professional discourse studies

The three chapters in Part 2 – Aaron Cicourel, Roger Shuy and James Taylor – provide a historically oriented account of the overall field of professional and organisational communication. Each chapter is written not only from the perspective of a different domain (i.e., healthcare, law and organisation studies), but also orients itself to the world of discourse and language in an individual way. At the same time, each chapter identifies issues which cross and transcend domain boundaries: Cicourel, in relation to the interplay between qualitative and quantitative methodologies in applied linguistic research and the accommodation of research outcomes deriving from different data sets and different emphases in research; Shuy, in relation to the issues of practical relevance of domain-specific applied linguistic research, emphasising applications to professional practice; and Taylor, in addressing theoretical issues of where applied linguistics should direct its key research attention: whether on the performance of individuals within organisations or rather on the key interactional relationships between and among individuals vis-à-vis their discursive practices.

From his focus on the biomedical and healthcare domain, Aaron Cicourel, in his chapter titled "Evidence and inference in macro-level and micro-level healthcare studies", identifies two parallel but potentially contested perspectives on research. The first perspective addresses the professional practices of clinicians and researchers in the micro contexts of the delivery of healthcare, emphasising how evidence for clinical decision-making arises from a complex of tacit knowledge, professional communication skills and knowledge of research findings. The second perspective, more policy and programme directed, derives from the outcomes of large scale epidemiological surveys and clinical trials.

The historical angle here is a methodological one. How there is a struggle between quantitative code-driven studies and more context-sensitive qualitative analysis of medical communication in specific encounters. Waitzkin (1991), among others, summarises the drawbacks of both quantitative and qualitative paradigms. Quantification studies, while being costly and tedious to carry out, cannot deal with the complex, deep structure of interaction as they systematically disregard underlying themes in context-sensitive ways. In qualitative studies, by contrast, data selection procedures and text analysis presentations run the risk of arbitrariness and bias, and whose interpretation is neither straightforward nor easy to warrant and evaluate.

In his chapter, Cicourel seeks a common ground between these paradigms whereby, he argues, micro-level analysis of language in interaction together with an associated ethnographically informed exploration of the reasoning behind professional behaviour, could be made to inform the quality of information gathering in quantitatively focused macro-level policy research and in clinical trials. Such a triangulation thus aims to authenticate and ground more narrowly policy outcomes in the healthcare arena, which is a precondition for accomplishing "ecological validity" (Cicourel 1992, 2007).

The importance of the chapter for applied linguistics research more widely is two-fold. Firstly, it indicates how the discursive analysis of the interactive engagements at the micro-level may produce evidence and questions which can affect the direction and organisation of more institutionally macro-oriented policy related research. Secondly, and now quite generally, the emphasis on collaborative and mutually informed research, as here between clinicians and health policy makers, can point the way for the development of an applied linguistics research programme committed to reflexivity and relevance, where such partnerships also involve applied linguists in attempts, as he says, to view organisational structure through the lens of the analysis of process. It is this programme to which the chapters in Part 4 of this volume direct themselves.

Roger Shuy's chapter titled "Applied Linguistics in the legal arena" signals its intent directly: what contribution can applied linguistics make to the world, or in his terms, the "arena", of legal practice? His approach is historical in the sense of tracing the development of such an interdisciplinary engagement, focusing in particular on the applied linguistic specialism of forensic linguistics. Shuy's approach is also developmental in terms of identifying a gradual shift from text-based genre analytical studies towards research which engages more with interactional behaviour in legal contexts. Further, the focus on forensic linguistics signals a movement in applied linguistics towards a more engaged and interventionist position in collaborative research with other professions. This issue of collaboration is quite central both for Shuy and, as we argue, for applied linguists more generally (Candlin and Sarangi 2004).

Shuy takes the view that the starting point for research has to come from the professional arena – in his work that of the law; it is that arena that engages with applied linguistics (see Roberts and Sarangi [1999] on "joint problematisation"). Once engaged, however, an issue arises which is perhaps hidden in Shuy's chapter: what is the role of the applied linguist? Is it to marshal the array of applied linguistic tools (which he outlines fully in the chapter) and in some sense "bring" them to the lawyer as a way of documenting the linguistic aspects of evidential data – what he refers to as "preparing the lawyers"? Or, is it rather to engage in a process of joint problematisation which evolves a "common discourse" for identifying and characterising such evidence (Sarangi 2007)? In our view attaining the latter would be a hoped-for goal for applied linguistics, emphasising the strengths of inter-professionality, but to be in a position to arrive at that will need not only a considerable record of valuable provision of forensic evidence, say, drawing on our applied linguistic toolbox, but will have to address ways of circumventing deep and ingrained disciplinary boundaries.

Perhaps the first step is indeed Shuy's "cross-pollination" metaphor and the accumulation in applied linguistics research of a body of "cases" which is recognised and accepted as evidence. Such evidence can then be channelled towards domain-relevant presentation of such outcomes in professional as well as academic outlets, and schemes of lawyer induction and training in the values of applied linguistic research to legal practice. Shuy's chapter offers from his considerable experience ways in which this may be achieved. And as a counter-point, Coulthard's contribution in Part 4 of this volume gives detailed accounts of how a forensic applied linguist can engage successfully, but also at times with considerable difficulty, in the role of expert witness in the legal arena.

The third of these scoping chapters for the development of applied linguistics in the context of professional and organizational communication is that of James Taylor, entitled "Communication is *not* neutral: 'Worldview' and the science of organizational communication". Taylor presents an historical and conceptual account of two opposing positions in the study of organizational communication: in brief, studies that focus on organizational structures (the discourses of the firm); and studies that focus on the interactional relationships of individuals as they go about the discursive interactions characteristic of their positions, roles and functions *within* the organization.

If, as he claims, "the communicative interaction is the constitutive basis of the organization", then a close data-driven analysis of such interactional relationships, emphasising characteristic behaviours of participants, has to be a primary commitment. It is also, of course, a warrant for applied linguistic research premised on that engagement of the macro- and the micro-levels that Cicourel advocates. Of special importance here is the advocacy of Taylor for applied linguistic research which is *revelatory* and explanatory, as well as descriptive and interpretive.

It is no surprise then that the intellectual sources he names – Luckmann, Bourdieu, Goffman, Gumperz, Giddens, Cicourel *inter alia* – are ones that are key to any appraisal of current work in applied linguistics. Note also how this shift from Functionalism to Interpretivism in the study of organisational structures entails a shift in methodology (not distant from that already suggested in Cicourel's and Shuy's chapters) viz a discursive turn towards a more data-driven qualitative methodology focusing on the structure of exchanges in a range of organisational sites. At the same time, text is not ignored; it could not be since exchanges are frequently not directly interactional but mediated by textualisations (including recontextualisations) of various forms and kinds. Thus, in emphasising a shift from text to interaction in applied linguistic research, we should not ignore the mediating function of textualisation.

Mediation does not imply agreement; indeed there is a clear sense from Taylor's focus on the "worldview" of organisations that such worldviews may be contested, subject to critical account, where the organisation as a kind of living *organism* seeks moments of complementarity and stability in what is always a dynamic system of processual and functional change. In short, we may say, the organisation embodies the dynamics of discourse and is a meaning-making and meaning-interpreting system, requiring for its analysis, perhaps, the kind of analytical procedures suggested in Checkland's (2001) concept of Soft Systems Methodology.

4.   The discursive turn: Specific studies in professional/organisational settings

Part 3 of the volume covers a range of studies in specific professional/organisational settings. Given the close association between applied linguistic research and sociolinguistic mapping of domains, especially in the tradition of languages for special purposes, we introduce them in relation to specific settings, in keeping with the three broad overarching domains of health and social care, law, and management and organisational studies. Accordingly, we have clustered the chapters as follows: in the domains of health and social care, the seven chapters of Aronsson and Rindstedt; Hamilton and Bartell; Måseide; Kovarsky and Walsh; Barton; Sarangi, Brookes-Howell, Bennert and Clarke; and White and Wastell. The second domain specific cluster highlights the legal domain and consists of three chapters, those of Harris; Hobbs; and Garzone. Finally, the third cluster comprises a broader range of sites, focusing on the interactional and relational dimensions of organisations: Heath and Luff; Smart; do Carmo Leite de Oliveira; Roberts; and Erickson.

Notwithstanding this domain-focused organisational structuring of the chapters in Part 3, such a structuring runs a certain risk. What it does, in a rather traditional way, is to reinforce the blackboxing of different professions and their sites as if they each belonged to completely different communities of practice. Languages for Specific Purposes has had this, as we indicate above, as a long-standing and enshrined operating principle. It highlights and further embeds the sociolinguistic basis of much applied linguistic research. What it disguises, however, is how, when looked at from the point of view of the professional practices relevant to such domains, we can discern a number of what we may call *crucial discursive sites of engagement* (Scollon and Scollon 2004; Candlin 1997) which parallel themselves across domains, and indeed which may reveal cross-cutting and inter-professional *critical moments within* and *across* the sites of these domains. Examples of such boundary crossing, focusing on cross-cutting themes, are Candlin and Crichton (2010) on the theme of "deficit" and Sarangi and Linell (forthcoming) on the theme of "team decision making".

On this argument, the exemplary sites of engagement for each domain in question, say, for example, in the domain of healthcare and social work as in our Part 3 (paediatric visits, responses to drug-induced effects on patients, hospital-based medical examinations, speech therapy consultations, genetic counselling for predictive testing, child welfare narratives), or, for example, in the field of law and legal practice (courtroom encounters and police interviews, both monolingual and interpreter-mediated) may evince some discursive parallels with other sites. This would be one such discovery and one way of *reading* such discourse-based studies.

Nor should we necessarily stop here: if we were to lift our eyes above the actual goings-on in these sites we would discover that there are what we may call *critical themes* which regularly emerge, or, better, are seen as salient and relevant, and which are distanced some way from the traditional accounts of applied linguistic research. These critical themes are manifest through a range of discursive realisations – they are what is talked about, written about, drawn on in professional development, and featured in schemata of professional appraisal. Such critical themes (what Roberts and Sarangi [2005] call *"focal themes"*) would typically include the following:

– The communicative aspects of professional *action & practice*
– The nature of professional *expertise* and the role of communication repertoire in such expertise
– The nature and importance of *evidence,* and its potentially contested nature
– The extent of *relevant knowledge – knowing what & knowing how*
– The quality of, and differences in, professional and lay *reasoning & argument – the evidencing of rationality*
– The difficulty of achieving and the importance of maintaining professional *neutrality*
– The role of communication in *assessing* and *appraising* the quality of professional practice, including *professional socialization*

Nor do we need necessarily to stop there in our focus on themes rather than exclusively on domains. We can bring into our research programme focus those critical *macro-themes* that engage debate in many, if not all, professional and organisational communities. As examples, we might list that almost canonical post-modern sextet of *Risk, Trust, Autonomy, Consensus, Quality of Life* and *Professional Values*, each of which is characteristically plinthed, conceptualised, categorised and metaphorised across a range of domains and sites, but which have been characteristically *not* linked to occasions of discursive construction in anything but a highly domain- and site-restricted way, if evidenced at all. Here, as we indicate in our synopses of the chapters in Part 3 of the volume, there is something of a *terra incognita* for applied linguistics, waiting as it were for our collaborative exploration.

For the purposes of realising an applied linguistic research programme, these critical focal themes must be aligned with particular discursive practices. Indeed, the manner in which they are accomplished and aligned in and through discourse (what Roberts and Sarangi (2005) refer to as *analytic themes*, which can be paraphrased as discourse devices) renders them key objects of our collaborative professional and applied linguistic/discourse analytical study. The task for discovery, then, becomes one of exploring inter-professional synergies, of knowing what and knowing how, which cut across domains. Such a programme of discovery calls for the application of a range of methodological tools from our applied linguistic toolbox, tools which range over ethnographic research, for example, a focus on narrative accounts, categorisation; discourse analytical studies; over interaction analysis, for example, a focus on alignment, face work, topic management, repairs, questioning patterns, modes of reported speech, frame shifts; and more social psychologically informed studies of participant reaction and response, including management of rapport and empathy. Taken together, the instruments and foci of such a multi-perspectived research programme directed at a range of potential ways and modes of describing, interpreting and explaining discourse data reflects just that interdiscursivity and hybridity we have indentified earlier.

In what follows we offer brief individual synopses of the chapters in Part 3, structured in the domain-related manner as described above. At the same time we seek to guide the reader and to evidence what we argue for above in terms of cross-cutting focal themes and associated possible analytic themes which serve to align disparate discourses in what for us is a more encompassing applied linguistic approach to professional and organisational communication research. Each domain is prefaced by a brief contextualisation of relevant previous studies.

4.1.   Health and social care domains

The discourse analytic studies in the healthcare domain fall into two broad strands (for an overview, see Candlin and Candlin [2003]; Sarangi [2004]). One strand is informed by conversation analysis with its focus on sequential organisation of talk (e.g., Heath 1986; Drew and Heritage 1992; Heritage and Maynard 2006; Stivers 2007); the other strand is informed by discourse analysis which draws insights from a number of analytical frameworks such as pragmatics, sociolinguistics, and microsociology (e.g., Wadsworth and Robinson 1976; Cicourel 1981, 1985, 1992; Fisher and Todd 1983; West 1984; Mishler 1984; Silverman 1987; Waitzkin 1991; Atkinson 1995; Ainsworth-Vaughn 1998; Sarangi and Roberts 1999; Gwyn 2002; Gotti and Salagar-Meyer 2006; Iedema 2007).

Some of the book-length publications that have had significant impact include the following. Mishler (1984) characterises clinical encounters as a tension between the voice of medicine and the voice of the lifeworld. This tension is manifested at the interactional level and can influence health outcomes. Silverman (1987) and Atkinson (1995), working in settings such as paediatric cardiology and haematology respectively, have shown that the tension between the two voices is quite nuanced and the different voices are strategically drawn upon by healthcare professionals and patients for specific purposes. Adopting a broader societal perspective, Waitzkin (1991) demonstrates that the medical and the social are inextricably linked, requiring a more social contextual approach to interpreting medical encounters both by healthcare practitioners and analysts. From a traditional sociolinguistic angle, West (1984) examines the uneven distribution of questions across doctors and patients, which is suggestive of a power imbalance, especially surrounding gender relations, with important consequences for the clinical encounter.

There are also studies that go beyond mainstream doctor-patient consultation (see Morris and Chenail 1995). Fisher (1995) examines the different communicative styles of doctors and nurses and the extent to which their different styles may foreground or background psychosocial dimensions of patients' lives and thus influence the consultation process and outcome. Ribeiro (1994) investigates the psychiatric setting by focusing on frames and topic coherence vis-à-vis joint construction of meaning. Studies in psychotherapy, especially those by Labov and Fanshel (1977) and Ferrara (1994), are very rich in interactional detail, exploring, respectively, the role of specific interactional features such as cuing of shared knowledge and patterns of repetition following interpretive summaries. Another domain is counselling where information giving and advice giving are delicately managed (Peräkylä 1995; Silverman 1997). Discourse analytic studies in nursing include Fisher (1988, 1995), Crawford, Brown and Nolan (1998) and S. Candlin (2008).

We now offer brief synopses of the chapters dealing with health and social care in Part 3 of the volume.

In their chapter, "Alignments and facework in paediatric visits: Toward a social choreography of multiparty talk", Karin Aronsson and Camilla Rindstedt examine paediatric consultations in the site of a child oncology unit and highlight a number of focal themes with associated analytic themes which arise from the study of multi-party talk. We may identify among these focal themes those of the discursive management of participation and consensus through double ambiguities – ambiguity concerning *what* is said, and ambiguity concerning *who* is addressed (child and/or parent). They show how in the context of agreements and disagreements doctors achieve alignments with the child patient through style shifting and how parents seek to align themselves with the doctor through playful respectfulness in their use of address forms. In terms of Goffman's (1981) participation framework, parents are positioned either as third parties, or as spokespersons, rather than just bystanders as they upgrade or downgrade the doctor's recommendations, or by signalling their alignment with the doctor by means of sentence completions, partial repeats and emphatic acknowledgement tokens – at times positioning themselves as allies of the doctor, perhaps to display responsible parenthood in the interaction.

Heidi Hamilton and Ashley Bartell, in their chapter titled "Peering inside the black box: Lay and professional reasoning surrounding patient claims of adverse drug effects", focus on the interplay between lay and professional reasoning and its consequences arising from patients' claims of adverse drug effects. Such a theme invokes the salience of evidentiality, and how this may be alternatively constructed by professional and lay participants. They demonstrate how doctors' obligation to announce risks associated with treatment options, for example in relation to the negative consequences of medication, can be matched against patients' reports of adverse reactions to drugs and how doctors respond to such claims. Such a focal theme of the acceptance and rejection of validity of expert evidence involves a corresponding analytic theme of facework, where the discourse work involved in disagreeing may influence some physicians to avoid patients' negative responses entirely, perhaps by topic shifting. Tensions may possibly arise, leading to non-compliance, between the voice of medicine articulated by the doctor with reference to published evidence, and the patient's voice of the lifeworld drawing on underlying health beliefs, physical experiences and hearsay. Methodologically, Hamilton and Bartell combine quantitative and qualitative approaches, including interactional sociolinguistics, linguistics of evidentiality (modes of knowing and sources of knowledge) and systemic functional linguistics (process types, material clauses, mental clauses, doing-and-happening) and outline how their findings can have relevance for healthcare practice.

Per Måseide, in his chapter titled "Institutional bodies and social selves: The discourse of medical examinations in hospital settings", explores the distinctive medical examination phase involving bronchoscopy (pre- and post-examination phases) in thoracic wards. While the examination is instrumental and routine, involving collaborative teamwork (surgeons, nurses, radiographer, anaesthetist), he highlights the analytic themes of frame and footing shifts as moral tensions arise when the patient has to be attended to as both a physical and as a social (lived) body, which is the focal theme. During the examination, boundaries are generated between the patient and his body as physical object and between the professionals and the patient as social subject. The communicative management of the frontstage and backstage of the examination becomes salient as the principles of deference and demeanour are enacted in relation to the patient and his body. Complex discursive hybridity characterises the encounter as the patient's body is "objectivised" in the act of medical "invasion" and as the doctor shifts between a focus on the object of examination and on the means of examining. Within the examination, the doctor may talk like a strict empiricist, referring exactly to what is seen, and not to how it might be interpreted from the patient's perspective, combining to render such information situationally adequate and to reduce the patient's discursive rights. Methodologically, Måseide uses a case study approach, based on ethnographic fieldnotes.

Dana Kovarsky and Irene Walsh, in their chapter titled "Uncomfortable moments in speech-language therapy discourse", deal with uncomfortable critical moments where positive rapport is threatened in encounters between speech-language therapists and clients (adults with aphasia and traumatic brain injury). Competing interpretations of communicative events where the therapeutic agenda is strictly followed even in the face of the client's apparent communicative deficiency mirror medical encounters where the voice of medicine juxtaposes with the lifeworld of the patient. Therapy encounters with their typical initiation-response-feedback (IRF) structures, introduced by specific contextualisation cues, bear similarities to classroom encounters where conduit models of communication predominate, ignoring issues of identity. Central to the argument is how clients' genuine concerns are transformed into symptoms of intrinsic underlying pathologies and how the "impairment focus of intervention" manifests interactional asymmetry, leading to the construction of miscommunication as incompetent performance occasions the need for explicit repair work. Methodologically, Kovarsky and Walsh draw on a case study approach, linked to the use of feedback sessions for triangulation of interpretation. The chapter follows an interventionist approach in inter-professional applied linguistics work in its outlining of alternative models of therapeutic intervention aimed at achieving greater communicative parity between professionals and clients.

Ellen Barton's focus, in "Speaking for another: Ethics-in-interaction in medical encounters", is on the theme of decision-making in end-of-life and clinical trial recruitments. Such a focus is essentially a matter of ethics where, in the argument of the chapter, abstract principles need to be examined interactionally – e.g., how autonomy is managed – and, like the chapter by Sarangi et al. below, are linked to moral issues. Such ethical issues are both biomedical, for example concerning medical futility or pain management, and psychosocial, given the other-orientation since in end-of-life settings family members speak on behalf of the patient. Typically, the voice of medicine prevails over others in reaching a decision. There are thus continuing tensions between the medical and ethical bases of decision making: how doctors and family members negotiate medical futility, how reaching a consensus amounts to shared decision making between professionals and family members. Objectivity and persuasion become intertwined in relation to decision-making rights on the part of patients in clinical trials, leading to the lack of true equipoise in such encounters. Methodologically, Barton draws on extensive transcribed records of such encounters, approached in close interactional sociolinguistic and discourse analytic modes.

Srikant Sarangi, Lucy Brookes-Howell, Kristina Bennert and Angus Clarke, in their chapter titled "Psychological and sociomoral frames in genetic counselling for predictive testing", examine genetic counselling as a hybrid activity type in which characterisation of distinctive frames of reference between counsellors and clients is a key object of focus. The chapter displays how psychosocial aspects of illness may be deconstructed into self-focused psychological and other-focused sociomoral frames surrounding the genetic testing process and the disclosure of test results. In strategically shifting between these frames, counsellors strive to maintain their professional ethos of non-directiveness in the light of clients' foregrounding of their lifeworld concerns, including misaligned family relations, character work etc. Such sociomoral dimensions, Sarangi et al. argue, are characteristic of most healthcare encounters. Here, as in Barton's chapter, general ethical principles need to be examined at the interactional level focusing in particular on role-relations and alignment between counsellors and clients, and with significant others. Methodologically, Sarangi et al. combine coding of transcribed data with fine-grained discourse analysis.

Sue White and David Wastell, in "Theoretical vocabularies and moral negotiation in child welfare: The saga of Evie and Seb", focus on moral issues in the context of child welfare. They argue that the making of moral judgements and an engagement in professional reasoning are essential characteristics of professional work in institutional settings, in particular how clients and cases are categorised intra- and inter-professionally, and how such categorisations can give rise to specific consequences for clients. Integral to such client categorisation are processes of evaluation and assessment involving interfaces of institutional and professional framing. Understanding such processes and such framing involves characterising how such professional sense-making is interactionally and rhetorically achieved, for example, in the context of child welfare and specifically in relation to responsible parenting and culpability more generally. When clients present themselves as moral selves, professional decision-making becomes itself morally contestable. Methodologically, White and Wastell combine case conference data and case notes, explore recontextualisation practices as they display how professionals document their work, and exploit insider ethnographic insights in seeking to understand tacit relevances in a single case study.

4.2.   The legal domain

Key discourse analytic studies in the legal domain broadly fall into different strands. The first strand focuses on descriptions of legal genres with an emphasis on text analysis (see Danet [1985, 1990] for overviews), or more generally on relationships between language and the law and the legal system (see Gibbons 1994, 2003), within which strand we can identify a range of foci, for example, studies of judgements (Maley 1985); barristers' opinions (Hafner 2006); and legislative writing (Bhatia 1987; Gunnarsson 1984). The second strand is oriented towards studies of distinct interaction orders in the domain of law, for example, Cotterill (2002); Komter (1993); and Heffer (2005) on courtroom trials; Heydon (2005) and Rock (2007) on police-witness interviewing, within which strand we also note a focus on issues of power and dominance, for example Eades' (2008) work on indigenous Australians in courtroom confrontation, and Cotterill's (2003) and Matoesian's (1993, 2001) work on identity, especially in the context of rape trials.

The following are book length studies that have had a significant impact. Atkinson and Drew's (1979) pioneering study first highlighted the interactional processes of courts of law, focusing on the verbal expression of the different roles, status, and purposes of key participants, the nature of key legal exchanges as typical of such encounters. O'Barr (1982) is an early analysis of how linguistic evidence is presented in courtroom proceedings, innovative for its focus on issues of power in relation to adversarial strategies employed by prosecuting counsel. Conley and O'Barr (1990) follow this tradition by drawing on ethnographic analysis of courtroom proceedings to highlight key differences between the relational presentation of narratives by clients and non-legal participants in the legal process as opposed to the more transactional and law-focused accounts of lawyers. The book shows how such relational accounts are transformed into tractable legal matters with consequent disparities in the display of power. Solan (1993), Tiersma (2000) and Solan and Tiersma (2005) provide a comprehensive account of the role of language and discourse in criminal justice, particularly in the USA, emphasising both the participants in the process and the interaction order of the courtroom.

Coulthard and Johnson's (2007) book draws together their and others' research into the burgeoning field of forensic linguistics, examining not only how careful analysis of linguistic data could make a significant, and at times, contested, contribution to elucidating legal evidence, but also how expert witnesses engage with legal practitioners in a range of crucial sites. Their more recent handbook collection of key papers (Coulthard and Johnson 2010) not only extends the domain of forensic linguistics but serves to mark it out as a defined and specialised field of study in legal discourse (see also Gibbons 2003). Shuy (2006) draws on his very considerable experience in the analysis of legal discourse (see Shuy 1998) and in forensic linguistics in particular, to provide what he refers to as a "Practical Guide" to the analysis of courtroom language, the discursive contributions of its protagonists, and to the role of linguists as expert witnesses and analysts.

Here we turn to brief synopses of the chapters dealing with the legal domain in Part 3 of the volume.

In her chapter titled "Interrogation and evidence: Questioning sequences in courtroom discourse and police interviews", Sandra Harris is interested in the validity of evidence seen through a focus on questioning in relation to the participant structure of knower and teller in the distinctive sites of courtroom trials and police interviews. She argues that evidence underlies the whole of the legal system where the language of evidence assumes significance: specifically, the processes of eliciting, establishing, negotiating, presenting, disputing and, ultimately, assessing of such evidence. Characteristic of such processes is an asymmetry of power and knowledge in the institutional participant roles where conflicting goals generate different interactional strategies on the part of participants. As exemplification, Harris identifies the tensions which result from attempts to present evidence in both factual and narrative modes of discourse; how modes of questioning, especially in their coercive nature and intent, differ as between defendants and suspects in these different sites. The analysis covers the following trajectories: how the putting forward of a hostile proposition accompanied by a coercive "tag form" occurs only in cross-examination; how defendants in courts are allowed more interactional space to develop a narrative account; how the prosecuting lawyer's concluding questions contain built-in accusations of guilt in a coercive form which tend to prohibit a simple "yes/no" denial and are intended to provoke a defensive response, while police interviews allow for more flexibility in such suspects' responses. Methodologically, Harris adopts a case study approach, drawing on transcript data from both sites and offers a comparative perspective at different levels.

Pamela Hobbs' chapter, "Judging by what you're saying: Judges' questioning of lawyers as interactive interpretation", complements that of Harris in focusing on a neglected area of discourse analytic study of legal processes, that of judges' questioning of lawyers and their subsequent interpretive practices. She argues that such questions are consequential for the courtroom process, as it is through their use that judges seek lawyers' input, not only in the framing of the issues and in the display of judges' authority, but also in formulating the interpretations by which they apply the law to the specific facts. As evidence she identifies and elaborates four questioning strategies that judges use to engage lawyers: taking candidate positions on the facts or law; displaying confidence or doubt in their own interpretations; posing "examination-type" questions that engage lawyers in Socratic dialogue; and using humour or displays of rhetorical virtuosity to challenge lawyers' interpretations. Methodologically, the chapter draws on case studies and Hobbs' long-standing experience as personal injury litigator. The discussion raises a number of key implications for legal education.

Giuliana Garzone's focus, in "Professional discourses in contact: Interpreters in the legal and medical settings", is on the interpreting profession as she compares site-specific interpreting practices in medical and legal settings. Such a comparative perspective offers interesting insights into differences where professional discourses connect through the medium of a related practice, as here in interpreting. In the police setting the succession of turns is more systematic and there is closer textual rendering, while the overall organisation of the healthcare interaction is much less orderly, as can be seen in patterns of turn-taking. These elements suggest that interpreters' roles vary in different settings and situations, thus instigating distinctive discursive dynamics. In the police interrogation, a word-by-word translating technique avoids interpreting meaning or making discretionary choices while summarised renditions by interpreters common in healthcare setting can engender different participant structures and agency with interpreters sometimes acting as "patient-substitutes", answering the doctor directly. In this sense, interpreters' professional discourse is typically a form of metadiscourse. Methodologically, the chapter contrasts two sets of transcripts from these settings, employing interactional sociolinguistic and conversational analytical modes of description.

4.3.   Organisational domains

In the organisational domain, we can discern two principal strands; the first theory-led and principally from the field of Organisational and Management Studies (see Bittner 1965; Silverman 1970; Pugh 1971; Handy 1976) and the second more discourse analytically and interactionally-focused. Major textbooks and overarching accounts such as Miller (2008); Modaff, DeWine, and Butler (2007); Shockley-Zalabak (2008); Eisenberg, Goodall, and Trethway (2009) present analyses of communication in organisations from a theory-rich perspective, drawing chiefly on organisational science, while the central role of communication in understanding organisational structures is captured by Putnam and Pacanowsky (1983); Weick (1995, 2001); and Taylor and van Every (2000); and more recently by Putnam and Nicotera (2008). A key theme linking organisational analysis with social psychologically influenced studies of interpersonal relations is that of impression management, especially in the field of management consultancy (Clark 1995). One can trace a growing focus in Organisational Studies for the evidencing of theoretical constructs by close reference to discourse data, coupled often with socio-political engagement with issues of power and informed by pragmatics. Examples here would be Vine (2004) and Clegg, Courpasson, and Phillips (2006), and for a case study approach to understanding communication processes in organisations, Keyton (2002, 2005) and Keyton and Shockley-Zalabak (2009). For more specifically targeted works in terms of theme and domain, drawing closely on discourse and interaction analysis, examples of relevance include Mullany's (2010) work on gendered discourse in the workplace, Mautner's (2010) study of discourse and dominance in the market society and Iedema's (2003) study of the consequences for the interactional and discursive order occasioned by post-bureaucratic and post-Taylorist structural reorganisation in the workplace (see here the impact of the pervasive redefining of the nature of "work" and working roles associated with what Gee, Hull, and Lankshear [1996] identify as the New Work Order).

Turning to monographs in organisational studies which explicitly signal their connection to discourse analysis, the following works form a key locus.

Boden's (1994) study evidences organisational processes in considerable discursive detail, including a special focus on particular activity types, such as business meetings. Sarangi and Slembrouck (1996), adopting a social pragmatics perspective, analyse everyday institutional interactions (talk and text) as they connect micro-level discourse practices to broader processes of bureaucratisation and debureaucratisation (see Eisenstadt 1959). Cameron (2000) provides a detailed account of the "communication culture" in everyday work lives where "talk" is elevated to a therapeutic status, while drawing attention to how "communication" is generally misconstrued as a checklist of skills. Grant et al. (2004) is a key reference work setting out both principles of application of discourse analysis to organisational processes, and is rich in its examples. Fox and Fox (2004) explicitly draw on linguistic and discourse analytical methodologies to underpin a critical analysis of workplace processes.

Increasingly, there are discourse analysts and applied linguists who have focused on the workplace as a site for domain- and site-specific studies, as in the study by Holmes and Stubbe (2003) from the Wellington (New Zealand) Language in the Workplace project. More generally, Koester (2006) draws on different pragmatic and discourse analytic frameworks to investigate notions of power, politeness, conflict and consensus in talk and text across workplace settings. In the field of business discourse, Bargiela-Chiappini, Nickerson, and Planken (2007) provide a comprehensive account of both business discourse genres and interactionally focused case studies of research and practice, with a valuable emphasis on intercultural encounters. From a corpus analytical perspective, Handford's (2010) recent book draws on an extensive corpus of business meeting discourse (CANBEC) (The Cambridge and Nottingham Business English Corpus). For discourse analytical studies employing specific methodologies, Smart's (2006) work on the analysis of written genres in the world of banking is seminal.

In sum, there is an increasing engagement of applied linguists and discourse analysts with the discourses of work and organisations across a range of domains and sites, making use of multiple research methodologies but quite markedly seeking to marry close textual and discourse analytical research with institutionally sited ethnographic accounts.

We now offer brief synopses of the chapters dealing with the organisational domain in Part 3 of the volume.

Christian Heath and Paul Luff's chapter titled "Enabling bids: Occupational practice and 'multi-modal' interaction in auctions of fine art and antiques" examines the distinctive discursive practices of Fine Art auctioneering highlighting in particular the semiotically multi-modal – through body positioning, gesture etc – orchestration of bids in such auctions. They demonstrate how bids are not accomplished through talk but rather through the strategically managed nonverbal or visible conduct of auctioneers. The focal theme is participation and their analytic focus is on the systematic escalation of the price of goods through an ascending sequence of bids by encouraging competition among bidders. Here a central strategy of the auctioneer is to establish particular orders of action conducive to this goal: an economy of behaviour where the serial escalation of price depends not on involving numerous bidders but rather the successive contributions of two participants, thus ensuring direct competition; the postponing of participation by further bidders until one bidder withdraws; the use of "absentee bidders", and from a discursive perspective, the rapid repetition of particular phrases (chants) to maintain rhythm and pace in the face of temporary absence of bids – to engender further bids. Pervasive to such auctions and to such auctioneer behaviour are issues of trust and fairness: it is these which underpin the auctioneers' ability to establish price and value and guarantee the legitimate exchange of goods. Methodologically, the chapter draws on a multimodal set of records of auctioneers' behaviour *in situ*, complemented by explanatory ethnographic data collected from practising auctioneers.

Graham Smart, in "Argumentation across Web-based organisational discourses: The case of climate-change debate", begins with an historical analysis of the science and politics associated with the phenomena of global warming and climate change. This necessary background allows him then to direct his main focus on argumentation as a central activity in characterising opposing positions in debates surrounding such phenomena. His thesis is that by means of a range of representations, opposing parties discursively construct a coalition of forces in support of their central arguments. They do so, Smart argues, by adopting specific lines of what he refers to as "collective argument" in respect of their opposing positions, whether, for example to see these phenomena as signals of crisis, or as objects of sceptical debate. The chapter has, however, wider and more general relevance: how opposing camps each selectively draw on science and scientific experimentation to advance their particular and partisan cause. Methodologically, the chapter is innovative in suggesting that we need to expand our current categorisations of discursive phenomena, say in terms of orders of discourse or discursive formations, or genre systems, in order to do justice to what he refers to as "the discursive phenomenon of time-spanning, multi-participant public debates featuring arguments produced by different professional organizations", making necessary, as he demonstrates in the chapter, just that longitudinal, ecological interpenetratedness of hybrid discourses.

In her chapter titled "E-mail messaging in the corporate sector: Tensions between technological affordances and rapport management", Maria do Carmo Leite de Oliveira examines the use of email in organisational settings but with a particular critical focus on the technological affordances provided by such computer-mediated messaging in organisational communication. Her focal theme is collegial rapport management, in particular the development of a sense of community and the building and maintenance of trust. She identifies tensions that occur in such a context between efficiency in information management and the enhancing (or not) of interpersonal relationships. She argues that the asynchronicity and high visibility of such communication leads to outcomes where in the recording and storage of information the risk of adversative recontextualisation is higher. Rather than encouraging greater integration and collegiality, her study suggests greater isolation, less collaboration and less productive outcomes in a communicative environment where issues of potential accusation and unfolding incompetency accompany mere information sharing. The research needs to be seen in the wider sociocultural context where social contact is highly valued and is threatened by new communicative technologies. Methodologically, the chapter draws on a case study of a Brazilian firm using a range of data sources including close analysis of email data and an ethnographic exploration of the workplace site. Again the orientation is towards interventionist research aimed at modifying organisational communicative practices.

Celia Roberts, in "Gatekeeping discourse in employment interviews", characterises employment interviews as janus-faced – looking both outward and inward in a hybrid manner – exploring how such interviews are becoming an institutional norm for screening candidates even for low paid jobs. Her research identifies how the conduct of such interviews has become an additional hurdle for minority ethnic groups who are already socially disadvantaged. This group has to play the game and pass the gatekeeping barrier by following certain, chiefly implicit, interactional and discursive norms, for example, how questions seeking elaboration may be misinterpreted as requiring confirmation. Such gatekeeping interviews, Roberts argues, are meant to be objective and fair, guaranteeing equality of opportunity, but in reality this is far from the case, bordering on penalty. Drawing on a corpus of authentic video-recorded data, she contrasts successful and unsuccessful candidates and shows how the former call up a shared set of assumptions and combine institutional and personal modes of narration in order to display competency and accountability. Such strategies are examined at the most subtle levels of the utilisation of appropriately placed contextualisation cues such as pause, pitch, falling tone. More generally, the findings suggest that in order to be successful, candidates have to display a balance between "selling oneself" and expressing reticence, so as to foster trust. Methodologically, Roberts combines interactional sociolinguistic analysis with ethnographic insights and identifies specific avenues for practically relevant intervention through staff training.

Staying with the gatekeeping site, in his chapter titled "The gatekeeping encounter as a social form and as a site for face work", Frederick Erickson selects academic advising and clinic encounters and, as with earlier chapters, for example that of Aronsson and Ringstedt, focuses on face work. Erickson argues that most institutional encounters can be seen as involving gatekeeping with particular, and usually negative or inhibiting, consequences for the gate-kept.

Such encounters are never value-neutral and are further complicated in intercultural, inter-racial settings involving social mobility, or access to valued goods, and where obtaining professional judgement is key. He identifies the rhetorical complexity involved in self-presentation and display of co-membership even in the context of gatekeeping barriers. Role distancing and face-threats are central to gatekeeping where the mutual avoidance of face threat, including indirectness and hedging, are characteristic strategies. His illustrative sites evidence how role ambivalence of the gatekeeper both represents the best interests of the institution *and* the best interests of the applicant. The analysis draws attention to the misalignments between institutional goal and the student's career; and in the clinical encounter, the mother presents herself as faultless, as a good and responsible mother despite being a working mother, but not the child care provider. Methodologically, Erickson makes a reference to data feedback sessions as part of triangulated interpretation.

5.   The reflexive turn: Towards a problematisation of professional discourse studies

Central to the integrity of any discipline, or research space, has to be the articulation of a set of principles of inquiry which underpin its practices and underwrite the expertise of its practitioners. We set out below what we see as the core principles in terms of which, from our perspective, applied linguists could develop a research agenda focused on professional and organisational communication. We associate with these principles some key constructs and some emergent themes. These derive in part from, and are evidenced in, the chapters in Part Four of this volume which are summarised later in this Section, and will serve as a grounding for those chapters taken together, with their focus on practices and attendant discourses and their elaboration of researcher and participant identities and roles.

Elsewhere (Sarangi and Candlin 2001) we have introduced the concept of *motivational relevancies* which would be our *first principle* of inquiry into professional and organisational discourse. This concerns the ways in which social scientists study phenomena in line with their own preferred motivations, and how this orientation may condition, in turn, the way in which discourse analysts in collaboration with professional practitioners may approach discourse data. We have suggested two broad orientations:

> First we could say that participants and analysts bring different perspectives to data, very much in the objectivist, scientific mode of inquiry. Such an assumption of difference leads to the analyst imposing or transforming the "observed" into a form of order. A second position would maintain that participants and analysts view the world in the same way, through the same lens, using the same coding devices – very

much in the hermeneutic, ethnomethodological mode of inquiry. Here the assumption is one of similarity demanding that both perspectives need to be aligned in any study of social events.
(Sarangi and Candlin 2001: 379)

Determining which of these positions to adopt as an analyst of professional and organisational discourse is for us probably the key principled choice. It is so because it goes to the heart of what constitutes relevant data, how we approach data, what methodologies and theories of language and discourse we ground our analytical practice in, and, most of all, what our relationships are with those co-participants with whom we collaboratively research, or for whom our findings may have practical relevance. We argue that given the case for acknowledging *motivational relevancies* and recognising the demands imposed on analysts' knowledge by the need to interpret and explain discourse data, these would be grounds enough for preferring the *second position* outlined in the quotation above. The freedom that that position then accords allows us to make apposite selections from a range of exploratory methodologies, in a form of triangulation, rather than fitting the data into some predetermined theoretical or analytical model. It also encourages participative and collaborative inquiry, likely in itself to meet an overarching applied linguistic requirement of relevance and potential uptake of discourse analytic findings. At the same time, it sets researchers a challenge, as outsiders, of finding ways of accessing the tacit knowledge of professionals with whom they work, by means of reflexive inquiry. Relevant here is what Sarangi (2007) refers to as "thick participation", including long-term informal ethnography. As we point out, "the issue of shared perspectives of analyst and participant is, quite clearly and routinely, an issue of access to mutuality" (Sarangi and Candlin 2001: 383).

Such "differential viewing" of the research process is not, however, just a matter of whether a researcher imposes a pre-existing model of analysis into which he or she "fits" the data, or, alternatively, whether researchers and participants seek to achieve hermeneutic alignment in some joint endeavour. What is key is that any accounts we provide are always *indexical* of practice; they cannot, following Garfinkel (1967: 3), be independent of what he terms "the socially organised occasions of their use".

This focus on "occasions of use" evokes our *second principle*, namely, how we may interpret the key construct of *context*. We may interpret this construct in three ways: firstly as an engagement with what Duranti and Goodwin (1992) refer to as relations of figure and ground; secondly, as a layering of context to take account of social and ideological dimensions underpinning language use, as in critical discourse analysis (Fairclough 1992, 1995), and thirdly, as a means of taking account of Cicourel's concern for "ecological validity" in research into macro and micro contexts of language use (Cicourel 1992, 2007).

Our *third principle* has to do with *modality*, in particular how modality is closely linked to field and topic. Because of our central concern with discourse, it may be that we are influenced towards the privileging of talk over silence, or over gesture, for example, or within a particular interaction to focus on some specific discursive feature and associate it with a particular mode of speaking. As one example, if "our interest lies in gendered ways of speaking, it is plausible that our focus of analysis will fall on patterns of interruption in doctor-patient interaction" (Sarangi and Candlin 2001: 370).

Such constraints on being open to a range of modalities and to an array of features of potential relevance, raise broader research issues of "discovery" and "search"; whether we are able and prepared to notice and identify not only features we are seeking to find instances of, but also whether we remain open to noticing those that are not *a priori* in our research agenda (Sacks 1984).

These three principles may be subsumed under a more general guideline for practice in professional/organisational discourse studies, that of elevating our research gaze beyond the immediacy of the text or the transcript. In other words, the researcher should embody "motivational relevancies" with regard to data analysis and findings – the latter constituting potential uptake. We reiterate this point further:

> So far, then discourse analysis, whether primarily descriptive or seeking also interpretation, confines itself to the classification of pattern. The question remains, is pattern-seeking enough? … [What is needed is] not just a matter of some internally generated warrant, from the data and the participants, but an external warrant in terms of what the analysis can offer to our understandings of (as here) professional or personal practice. In most cases the warrant lies outside the data, but it is also likely to be delayed. Here we are talking about consequent validity – the extent to which the study of any particular interaction has an effect, on the ensuing actions of the individuals concerned, on the practices of their, or of related professional communities, on public policy.
> (Sarangi and Candlin 2003b: 122)

Addressing this challenge is very much the substance of Part 4 of this volume. The chapters collectively point the way in which analyses of discourse can achieve such an explanatory effect on the practices and systems of those from whom the data derive. Their legitimation of such practices lies in great measure in the procedure- and system-changing effects they support on professional and personal practice. Such a challenge is not addressed to applied linguists alone; meeting it is incumbent both upon them and on the professional practitioners with whom they collaborate. However, such mutuality raises in turn profound questions surrounding researcher identity and researcher stance, and which are directed as well at the practical relevance of the evidential data drawn upon by such collaborative accounts.

One way in which this key issue of mutuality, and in particular questions surrounding researcher identity and stance, can be highlighted is by identifying a number of constructs and key questions, together with a set of associated conditioning factors. These can serve as criteria underpinning any research agenda against which to characterise and to evaluate reflexivity and relevance in applied linguistic research (Sarangi and Candlin 2003c).

Constructs

Identity (who is engaged in the research and which roles do they occupy in its design and execution?)

Agency (who is responsible for which actions in relation to the research and to what degree are they responsible for its progress?)

Participation (who is involved in these research-related actions and in what ways is their participation determined and managed?)

Conditioning Factors

Transparency (to what extent are the objectives and processes of the research project open to scrutiny and subject to ethical conditions on research practice?)

Reasoning (in what terms, from a researcher or participant perspective, are the arguments in the analysis being formulated?)

Expertise (to what extent and how patently does the research draw on researcher and participant expertise?)

Reflexivity (to what extent and in what ways is the research directed at engaging with system- and practice change?

The chapters in Part 4, to different degrees, engage with these criteria and these issues. They evidence how in the process of designing and conducting research in the field of professional and organisational discourse, researchers may occupy a range of roles extending from outsider to insider, to befriender, to consultant and agent of change (Sarangi and Candlin 2003c). Such researcher roles are not fixed and static: they may interchange and vary according to domain, site and occasions of use. In a similar way, researchers are not identical in terms of their engagement, membership and expertise. Inevitably, as we again see in the chapters in Part 4 of this volume, they will display themselves as less specifically knowledgeable in domain terms than those professional participants with whom they collaborate. At the same time, we should not forget that such collaborating professionals are frequently in their public and professional lives analysts of their own professional discourses, albeit not necessarily in our terms. The challenge faced in the chapters that follow, and indeed in applied linguistics research quite generally, becomes not only one of construing and adopting appropriate roles qua researchers, but of collaboratively devising and making mutually meaningful and relevant a shared and novel discourse.

If we now turn to appraising the expertise in language and interaction of participants in professional/organisational settings with whom we work, we can draw on what Peräkylä and Vehviläinen (2003) call professional "stocks of interactional knowledge" (SIK) as set out in the normative models and theories found in communication textbooks and manuals. As we see from the chapters in Part 4, and Slembrouck and Hall's chapter is a case in point, we need to focus our attention more on how professional practitioners conceptualise and operationalise interaction and communication in their everyday practice rather than on such textbook characterisations. It is only when we interview professional practitioners, especially against a backdrop of long-term ethnographic fieldwork, that we come to realise the complex nature of tacit interactional knowledge which is shared among such professionals (Sarangi 2002, 2010b) and which cannot be captured in such textbooks and manuals, however detailed. Moreover, such knowledge extends beyond a reflective awareness of, say, trajectories of professional-client or inter-professional interaction. It is more a matter of accessing an *expert system* (Sarangi, 2010b) imbuing both knowledge and action. In the words of Lynch and Sharrock (2003):

> Although the sequential procedures that make up what conversation analysts call "talk in interaction" are evident in, and important for, the organisation of practices in a variety of social institutions, it is not enough to say that, for example, a jury deliberation or a medical diagnosis is merely an "organisation of talk".
> (Lynch and Sharrock 2003: xxxix)

Such interactions and their management go to the heart of what the respective professions regard as "being a lawyer", or "being a doctor". Content, process, and interactional structure converge in such characterisations of identity, as Cicourel (1992: 307–308) emphasised when he argued that we need to focus on both the "processual" as well as the "structural" in any framework for research into interaction.

Such processual and structural interactional knowledge is never static: it always intimately reflects other professional, organisational and societal changes taking place within the particular professional sector under review. Accordingly, applied linguists who focus on such processes and structures need close awareness of the professional histories and tensions within contemporary practice which serve as a "backstage" to the "frontstage" of discourse. As one example among very many, in the domain of nursing practice, Candlin and Candlin (2007) suggest that professional changes brought about by the emergence of multi-disciplinary teams have evidenced new and distinctive interactional patterns of discourse, as has the advent and provision of telemedicine with its utilisation of nurses in new roles and relationships with clients via a new modality. Further, changes in nurse education and the development of an expanded role for nurses as nurse consultants and nurse specialists have greatly diversified how this particular profession can be characterised.

In what follows, we offer brief synopses of the chapters in Part 4 of the volume, focusing on *reflective practice* (Schon 1983) involving collaborative work between discourse analysts and professional practitioners (e.g., Taylor, Karnieli-Miller, Inui, Ivy and Frankel; Slembrouck and Hall; Jones and McCracken) as well as professional practitioners themselves when challenged by discourse researchers (e.g., S. Candlin, Clarke). Here, the chapters are not arranged, as earlier in Part 3, into domains and associated focal themes. This is deliberate since we wish to make the point that cutting across such traditional domains and inherent in the construct of focal themes are those significant practices in which both researchers and participants engage, in collaborative, or at least, cooperative research, trading between reflexivity and relevance (Sarangi and Candlin 2003c). As a consequence, we draw readers' attention in particular to the *methodologies* involved in such jointly inspired reflexive research.

In their chapter titled "Appreciating the power of narratives in healthcare: A tool for understanding organisational complexity and values", Amanda Taylor, Orit Karnieli-Miller, Tom Inui, Stephen Ivy and Richard Frankel explore through the medium of narratives of experience the "human dimensions of organizational life". Methodologically, the chapter elaborates a very extensive case study of employees in a large-scale healthcare organisation, focusing on issues surrounding alignments or misalignments between the personal actions and values of such employees on the one hand, and those values espoused and promulgated by the organisation of which they are a part, on the other. The chapter outlines a process the authors refer to as Appreciative Inquiry where the personal "lived" stories of participants are sampled and systematically calibrated against each other through systematic grounded analysis of qualitative semi-structured interview data, and, in turn, "tested" against the core values of the organisation. Issues surrounding the non-resolution or partial resolution of value-conflicts are explored. Of greatest interest is, firstly, the way that researchers worked closely with professional participants in the research, not only in data gathering but in appraising the ongoing interpretation of that data; and secondly, the premium placed by the researchers (and the participants) in disseminating the outcomes of the research through the medium of structured presentation sessions to organisational management, some of which confronted directly the challenges and mismatches, and the alignments, exposed by the research project. Above all, the chapter serves to highlight the different roles of the researcher and the way that targeted applied linguistic research can become engaged with organisational intervention and change.

Professional-client communication and assumptions concerning what constitutes "good practice" is the focus of Stef Slembrouck and Christopher Hall's chapter, "Family support and home visiting: Understanding communication, 'good practice' and interactional skills". Central to the chapter is its voicing of professional social workers' experiences, and those of their clients, in the domain of home visiting. The chapter is directed at a discourse-based process of examining professional practices in action. The close exploration of professional interaction is an innovation in social worker training (including here the provision of human services more widely), requiring considerable attention by professionals to client and encounter diversity. Where such exploration involves discourse-based research, it requires, the authors argue, a parallel informativeness on the part of the discourse analysts of the histories, concerns and challenges of the professional work with which they engage. Methodologically, knowledge of the relevant institutional and professional orders is thus a *sine qua non* for an interventionist-oriented applied linguistics in professional contexts. More than that, making connections between analysis and professional understandings impels a collaborative positioning and affiliation of researchers and participants, just as it does between professionals and their clients, sensitive to each others' "motivational relevancies" (Sarangi and Candlin 2001) and where, over time, the accommodating of roles, although always challenging, becomes both possible and desirable.

Alan Jones and Sheelagh McCracken's chapter, "Crossing the boundary between finance and law: The collaborative problematisation of professional learning in a postgraduate classroom", foregrounds the benefits to be gained from collaborative interdisciplinary, inter-professional research. In the chapter, the authors – an applied linguist and an academic lawyer – draw on a mutuality of interest in issues of language and meaning to problematise and conceptualise learning materials for finance professionals. Grounded in Goodwin's (1994) construct of "professional vision", Jones and McCracken negotiate alternate meanings of profession-specific concepts and practices from finance professional's and discourse analyst's perspectives, seeking to devise professional development materials at tertiary level which will engage learners themselves in such a collaborative enterprise. This curriculum design process is emblematic of the pedagogically directed collaboration. What is quite novel here, however, is how the "backstage" of the inter-professional collaboration of discourse analyst and academic lawyer as they negotiate their understandings of each others' approach to a distinctive domain, involving yet another discipline, that of Finance, is related to the "frontstage" of cooperatively developed classroom-based curriculum. As the authors point out, at issue are discourse and meaning-focused processes of acculturation and socialisation of their learners; more than that, however, the chapter evidences how such processes are also those invested in applied linguists engaged in the understanding of the complexities of cross-boundary professional partnerships in the fields of processional and organisational communication.

In their chapter titled "Making the difference in interagency working: Professional learning in communicating what matters", David Middleton, in association with colleagues, takes up the theme of research-informed intervention, focusing on professional learning across a range of multi-agency sites in the domain of children's services, and in particular focusing on social exclusion of children and young people. What is of particular relevance is, firstly, the array of professional backgrounds of the participants in the research in addition to the researchers themselves: educational psychologists, teachers, children and family workers, education welfare officers, health professionals, speech and language therapists and voluntary sector workers; and, secondly, how the research itself was focused on a discourse analytically-based exploration of challenges and contradictions in situated professional practice. Methodologically, informed by work on Activity Theory (Engeström 1987), the research draws on conversation analytical data in an attempt to provide a "bottom up" protocol for the analysis of communicative action within and across the multi-agency sites. From an applied linguistic perspective, the chapter introduces a future-focused dimension: rather than dwelling on accounts of past actions, the research explores how members *distinctively* categorise their work, their memberships and collectively accomplished knowledge, their professional purposes, and how such categorisation is dynamically and discursively accomplished, and "learned". Exploring by means of an analytical protocol what the authors refer to as "what-it-is-to-be-in-the-know" lies at the heart of accounting for such inter-professional learning, and provides a translatable methodology for collaborative research in other complex sites.

Janet Holmes, Angela Joe, Meredith Marra, Jonathan Newton, Nicky Riddiford and Bernadette Vine, in their chapter "Applying linguistic research to real world problems: The social meaning of talk in workplace interaction", address issues of practical relevance in applied linguistic research. Set in the context of a long-standing project on workplace language and associated language training in New Zealand, the chapter is notable for the way it explores and documents a long-standing relationship between discourse analysts and workplace participants. The chapter focuses on the analysis of communication associated with grounded training in communication skills but with the particular purpose of empowering migrant participants to communicate to advantage in their new workplaces. Becoming analysts of the socio-pragmatics of their own discourse is now a classic formula for engaging language learners in issues of personal communicative relevance; it is also a classic example of how the methodology of training can become translated into a methodology for language acquisition, thus connecting researcher-trainers with language learners in a collaborative and partnered enterprise. Working "for and with" participants (see Cameron et al. 1992), and addressing the challenges of "applied linguistics applied" (Roberts 2003) is, however, still more the exception than the rule in applied linguistic research in the profession and its application. Partly, this is due to lack of experience on the part of researcher-trainers, partly because of problems of access to authentic sites, partly because of a lack of ability in managing consultative research (Sarangi 2005), but also because of the limited availability of clear curriculum designs for ensuing training, a key theme of the chapter.

The theme of inter-professional understanding and engagement between applied linguists and professional partners is a central focus of Sally Candlin's chapter, "Changes in identities: Nursing roles, nurses' practices". For her, a key underpinning for such cooperative engagement is the development of mutual understanding of each other's roles, both vis-à-vis each other and within each other's interpretive worlds. Such roles, she argues, emerge from, and are only construable through, a deep awareness of professional and institutional structures, much in the manner proposed by Cicourel's chapter in Part 2 of this volume. It is these structures which offer insights into the processes of categorisation which, as we have argued earlier, are definitive of particular professional communities of practice. Understanding membership, its conventional behaviours, its discourses and its interpretive repertoires lies at the heart of her chapter, the mutual explanation of which among professionals and discourse analysts is the core challenge to achieving the collaborative goals of an explanatory applied linguistics of the professions. However, as Layder (1993) argues, an awareness of history is a prerequisite of any such explanatory endeavour focused on understanding actions in the settings and sites of particular institutions. Such awareness has clear implications for a reflexive research methodology. It implies, as S. Candlin shows, that any interactional data analysis, however fine, is doomed to remain at the level of pattern-seeking if it fails to incorporate, before, during, and post analysis, understandings of the professionally and institutionally bounded identities of the participants and their discursive affordances and constraints as they engage with their patients and their clients. This echoes Sarangi's (2007) insistence that "thick participation" on the part of the discourse researcher is a condition for making sense of professional practice, thus minimising the "analyst's paradox". Striving for mutuality and cooperation between discourse researchers and professionals, as it were in a multi-professional team – as here with nurses – is for S. Candlin not just a matter of desirability; it is an imperative in aspiring to research relevance.

Reflexivity, inherent in S. Candlin's chapter, and in that of others in this Part of the volume, is a core theme in Angus Clarke's chapter, "Crossing the practitioner-researcher boundary: Working with another discipline to examine one's practice". "Crossing the practitioner-researcher boundary" in his title is to be read, however, not as some occupying of another space, rather as the creation of a new environment for collaborative research in which, it is hoped, both "crossing" parties discern reflexively from the joint experience matters of value for interpreting their own stance and orientation in their professional practice. Not that the "crossings" are without problem and challenge; indeed, Clarke's chapter can be read as something of a cautionary tale for those professionals willing to open their practice – in his case that of clinical inquiry – to outside scrutiny. Joint working entails considerable demands on inter-professional and interpersonal tact and empathy, as here between social science researchers and a geneticist, as it does axiomatically between such professionals and their patients. These demands go beyond the individual and the volitional; they are mandated by external constraints, in particular those governing ethical behaviour. Where, as in this chapter, the roles of social science researcher and professional may merge into a single person, "crossings" take on another intrapersonal dimension, one becoming more visible as discourse-based training is incorporated into professional curricula. Inter- and intra-professionality has its rewards, as Clarke emphasises in his accounts of the affordances provided through access to distinctive bodies of knowledge and professional practice, among which is that of the *discourse practitioner* (Sarangi 2002). Perhaps the time has come for a more sensitively calibrated code of practice for such discourse practitioners as they engage with professional practice (see Sarangi 2007). A reading of Clarke would suggest that both reflexivity and boundary crossing by discourse practitioners would find that valuable.

Earlier (see Part 2), Roger Shuy outlined some of the ways by which applied linguists could make a contribution to professional forensic practice. That such a contribution goes beyond the straightforward description of relatively standardised linguistic features of a range of legal genres into a matter of judgement over questions of evidential value is the focus of Malcolm Coulthard's final chapter titled "The linguist in the witness box". Such judgement goes to the heart of inter-professional engagement since, like all evidence, it needs to be appraised not just against linguistic criteria but in action, by lawyers, in the professional arena of the court. Appraisals in such sites will not at all necessarily be grounded in the evaluations of analyses characteristic of the professional world of linguists or discourse analysts. Nor would the latter expect, or be familiar *a priori* with their evidence, say as expert witnesses, being subject to vigorous cross examination by professional barristers. Becoming an expert witness, then, for linguists and discourse analysts is as much a matter of how convincingly they can display their expertise in a novel arena, governed by its own professional and institutional rules, as it is a matter of any linguistic analytical competence. Coulthard's chapter, then, addresses uncomfortable issues where inter-professional engagement is frequently subject to sharp contestation, not just where the presentation of well grounded linguistic evidence will carry the day. Such a contestation is not just about issues of evidential validity, central though that is, it extends to debates about the appropriateness of analytical methodologies, how the data was gained, and to challenges to the expertise and soundness of expert witnesses. It is in the crucial site of the court, where much hangs in the balance, that issues of professional credibility, achievable degrees of inter-professional understanding, the determination of relevance, are placed in focus, indicating that notwithstanding the advantages to be gained by mutuality among professionals, the discriminatory power of "motivational relevancies" can never be underestimated.

6.   Conclusion

We believe that applied linguistics can make a significant contribution to our understanding of communication processes, participants and their roles, their objectives and goals, and the communication contexts within which knowledge-based professional/organisational practice takes place. This is inherently an interdisciplinary and collaborative undertaking, as the contributions in Part 4 of this volume reflect. It privileges a broad view of language and communication including both formal studies of text and discourse in a range of modes, grounded ethnographic studies of contexts of use, and more social psychological studies of participants' orientations, identities and interpretive processes.

Accordingly, in conducting the analysis of discourse in such sites, we as researchers are always taking a position on the relationship between micro- and macro-phenomena; we are always making assumptions about social organisation and social processes. Any analysis of text and talk which aspires to some explanatory rather than merely descriptive adequacy presupposes an engagement with social action within the context of the institution in question, and needs to take account of the distinctive perspectives of the involved participants (including the researcher). This inevitably means a "thick engagement" with an institutional/professional research site, rather than being constrained by a particular analytical/methodological mentality. At the same time, our awareness of institutional dynamism in a changing and unstable world makes hybridity and interdiscursivity not some aberrant phenomenon, some momentary disorder, but what actually is the discursive case. The task remains, then, as Harvey Sacks noted some time ago, the discovery of orderliness in a disorderly world – "that there is order at all points" (1984: 22).

In exploring this "orderliness" it makes sense to extend Goodwin's (1994) concept of "professional vision" (see earlier discussion) to our own analytical endeavour as applied linguists and discourse analysts. Central to Goodwin's concept is how actors in engaging in an action regard that action, and how we as researchers and analysts may come to discover what that particular professional vision of the participants (including the lay members) might be in performing that action, and how, in doing so, what our professional vision as analysts might be in relation to these actions.

There are thus two professional visions involved – that of the *participant* (*professional actor*) and that of the *researcher (professional analyst)*. The three discursive procedures Goodwin identifies (i.e. *coding*, *highlighting* and *articu-*

lating representations) offer us guidance towards the way in which we "accomplish" this interpretation of "a meaningful event" (i.e., an object plus action) against a background of our (and their) histories (the *interpretive potential*). In this sense, "professional vision" can be linked to "motivational relevancies": how analysts in professional and institutional domains need to engage with critical moments, and through "thick participation" minimise the "analyst's paradox" (Sarangi 2007) and maximise "ecological validity" (Cicourel 2007). An interventionist, real-world preoccupation of applied linguistics necessitates a change in our professional analytical mentality – a mentality which combines discursive and ethnographic endeavours.

An applied linguistic perspective, then, as evidenced in this volume, not only builds on the cumulative insights gained from discourse based studies and the vast body of literature in the sociology of professions and the sociology of work, but also foregrounds a problem-orientation, deeply embedded in methodological and analytical challenges, so that research outcomes are made practically relevant. We refer to this as "Making applied linguistics matter" in an inaugural Editorial in the Journal of Applied Linguistics:

> What we would want to ask of Applied Linguistics is less what it is and more what it does, or rather what its practitioners do. This stance is, of course, not new; many early writers on Applied Linguistics have seen this question as one among several of its characteristics, and it has consistently featured in programmatic statements about the field. What may be more novel is to take doing a step further and address the question of with whom one does the doing, for what purposes, and with what anticipated outcomes and impacts. So, while acknowledging the goal of cumulative coherence, the need to establish principle and not just catalogue practices, the need to address the issue of whether Applied Linguistics is more like a research space than it is a tightly defined discipline, we return to relevance, and ask what it is that we do, how, and why. How this relevance may be characterised, how it can be appraised, how it can be disseminated.
> (Candlin and Sarangi 2004: 2)

Such a perspective opens up fresh avenues for application of linguistic research beyond the mainstream focus on the education sites, while remedying the established paradigm of *Language for Specific Purposes*. A particular challenge for applied linguists, in their chosen sites of engagement, is to access the tacit knowledge base that underlies professional and organisational practice, but not clearly indexed (Cicourel 1992; Sarangi 2007), making indispensable a reflexive approach both for themselves and for members of their target and collaborating groups.

References

Abbott, Pamela and Claire Wallace
   1990   *The Sociology of the Caring Professions.* London: Falmer.
Agar, Michael
   1985   Institutional discourse. *Text* 5(3): 147–168.
Ainsworth-Vaughn, Nancy
   1998   *Claiming Power in Doctor-Patient Talk.* Oxford: Oxford University Press.
Atkinson, J. Maxwell and Paul Drew
   1979   *Order in Court: The Organisation of Verbal Interaction in Judicial Set-*
           tings. London: Macmillan.
Atkinson, Paul
   1995   *Medical Talk and Medical Work.* London: Sage.
Bargiela-Chiappini, Francesca, Catherine Nickerson and Brigitte Planken
   2007   *Business Discourse.* Basingstoke: Palgrave Macmillan.
Barrett, Robert J.
   1996   *The Psychiatric Team and the Social Definition of Schizophrenia: An An-*
           thropological Study of Person and Illness. Cambridge: Cambridge Univer-
           sity Press.
Bauman, Zygmunt
   2000   *Liquid Modernity.* Cambridge: Polity Press.
Bazerman, Charles
   1989   *Shaping Written Knowledge: The Form and Activity of the Experimental*
           Report in Science. Madison: University of Wisconsin Press.
Becker, Howard S.
   1962   The nature of a profession. In: *Education for the Professions,* (1962) *Year-*
           book of the National Society for the Study of Education, 27–46. Chicago:
           University of Chicago Press.
Berger, Peter L. and Thomas Luckmann
   1967   *The Social Construction of Reality: A Treatise in the Sociology of Knowl-*
           edge. Harmondsworth: Penguin.
Bhatia, Vijay K.
   1987   Textual-mapping in British legislative writing. *World Englishes* 6(1): 1–10.
Bhatia, Vijay K.
   1993   *Analysing Genre: Language Use in Professional Settings.* London: Longman.
Bhatia, Vijay K.
   2004   *Worlds of Written Discourse.* London: Continuum.
Bittner, Egon
   1965   The concept of organisation. *Social Research* 32(3): 239–255.
Boden, Deirdre
   1994   *The Business of Talk: Organizations in Action.* Cambridge: Polity Press.
Byrne, Patrick S. and B. Long
   1976   *Doctors Talking to Patients.* London: HMSO.
Cameron, Deborah
   2000   *Good to Talk? Living and Working in a Communication Culture.* London: Sage.
Cameron, Deborah, Elizabeth Fraser, Penelope Harvey, Ben Rampton and Kay Richardson
   1992   *Researching Language: Issues of Power and Method.* London: Routledge.

Candlin, Christopher N.
  1997   General editor's preface. In: Britt-Louise Gunnarsson, Per Linell and Bengt
            Nordberg (eds.), *The Construction of Professional Discourse*, viii-xiv. Har-
            low: Longman.
Candlin, Christopher N. (ed.)
  2002   *Research and Practice in Professional Discourse*. Hong Kong: City Uni-
            versity of Hong Kong Press.
Candlin, Christopher N. and Sally Candlin
  2003   Healthcare communication: A problematic site for applied linguistics re-
            search. *Annual Review of Applied Linguistics* 23: 134–154.
Candlin, Christopher N. and Jonathan Crichton (eds.)
  2010   *Discourses of Deficit*. Basingstoke: Palgrave Macmillan.
Candlin Christopher N. and Yon Maley
  1997   Intertextuality and interdiscursivity in the discourse of alternative dispute
            resolution. In: B-L. Gunnarsson et al. (eds.), *The Construction of Profes-
            sional Discourse*, 201–222. Harlow: Longman.
Candlin Christopher N. and Srikant Sarangi
  2004   Making applied linguistics matter. *Journal of Applied Linguistics* 1(1): 1–8.
Candlin, Sally
  2008   *Therapeutic Communication: A Lifespan Approach*. Sydney: Pearson Edu-
            cation.
Candlin, Sally and Christopher N. Candlin
  2007   Nursing over time and space: Some issues for the construct "community of
            practice". In: R. Iedema (ed.), *The Discourses of Hospital Communication:
            Tracing Complexities in Contemporary Health Organisations*, 244–267.
            Basingstoke: Palgrave Macmillan.
Checkland, Peter
  2001   *Systems Thinking, Systems Practice*. Chichester: John Wiley.
Christie, Frances and James R. Martin (eds.)
  1997   *Genres and Institutions: Social Processes in the Workplace and School*.
            London: Pinter.
Cicourel, Aaron V.
  1981   Language and medicine. In: C. A. Ferguson and S. B. Heath (eds.), *Lan-
            guage in the USA*, 347–367. Cambridge: Cambridge University Press.
Cicourel, Aaron V.
  1983   Hearing is not believing: Language and the structure of belief in medical
            communication. In: S. Fisher and A. Todd (eds.) *The Social Organisation
            of Doctor-Patient Communication*, 138–155. Washington DC: Centre for
            Applied Linguistics.
Cicourel, Aaron V.
  1985   Doctor-patient discourse. In: T. van Dijk (ed.), *Handbook of Discourse
            Analysis*, Volume 4, 193–202. New York: Academic Press.
Cicourel, Aaron V.
  1992   The interpretation of communicative contexts: Examples from medical
            encounters. In: A. Duranti and C. Goodwin (eds.), *Rethinking Context:
            Language as an Interactive Phenomenon*, 291–310. Cambridge: Cam-
            bridge University Press.

Cicourel, Aaron V.
    2007   A personal, retrospective view of ecological validity. *Text & Talk* 27(5):
            734–752.
Clark, Timothy
    1995   *Managing Consultants: Consultancy as the Management of Impressions.*
            Buckingham: Open University Press.
Clegg, Stewart, David Courpasson and Nelson Phillips
    2006   *Power and Organizations.* London: Sage.
Coleman, Hywel (ed.)
    1984   Language and work 1: Law, industry, education. [Special Issue] *Inter-
            national Journal of the Sociology of Language* 49.
Coleman, Hywel (ed.)
    1985   Language and work 2: The health professions. [Special Issue] *International
            Journal of the Sociology of Language* 51.
Coleman, Hywel (ed.)
    1989   *Working with Language: A Multidisciplinary Consideration of Language
            Use in Work Contexts.* Berlin/New York: Mouton de Gruyter.
Conley, John M. and William M. O'Barr
    1990   *Rules versus Relationships: The Ethnography of Legal Discourse.* Chicago:
            The University of Chicago Press.
Cotterill, Janet
    2002   *Language in the Legal Process.* Basingstoke: Palgrave Macmillan.
Cotterill, Janet
    2003   *Language and Power in Court: A Linguistic Analysis of the O. J. Simpson
            Trial.* Basingstoke: Palgrave Macmillan.
Coulthard, Malcolm and Alison Johnson
    2007   *An Introduction to Forensic Linguistics: Language in Evidence.* Abingdon,
            Oxon: Routledge.
Coulthard, Malcolm and Alison Johnson
    2010   *Handbook of Forensic Linguistics.* Abingdon, Oxon: Routledge.
Crawford, Paul, Brian Brown and Peter Nolan
    1998   C*ommunicating Care: The Language of Nursing.* Cheltenham, Gloucester:
            Stanley Thornes.
Danet, Brenda
    1985   Legal discourse. In: T. van Dijk (ed.), *Handbook of Discourse Analysis,*
            Volume 1, 273–291. London: Academic Press.
Danet, Brenda
    1990   Language and law: An overview of 15 years of research. In: H. Giles and
            W. P. Robinson (eds.), *Handbook of Language and Social Psychology,*
            537–559. Chichester: Wiley.
Di Pietro, Robert J. (ed.)
    1982   *Linguistics and the Professions.* Norwood, NJ: Ablex.
Douglas, Mary
    1986   *How Institutions Think.* New York: Syracuse University Press.
Drew, Paul and John Heritage (eds.)
    1992   *Talk at Work: Interaction in Institutional Settings.* Cambridge: Cambridge
            University Press.

Duranti, Alessandro and Charles Goodwin (eds.)
  1992   *Rethinking Context: Language as an Interactive Phenomenon*. Cambridge: Cambridge University Press.
Eades, Diana
  2008   *Courtroom Talk and Neocolonial Control*. Berlin/New York: Mouton de Gruyter.
Eisenberg, Eric M., H. L. Goodall and Angela Trethwey
  2009   *Organisational Communication: Balancing Creativity and Constraint*. New York: Bedford/St Martins.
Eisenstadt, S. N.
  1959   Bureaucracy, bureaucratisation, and debureaucratisation. *Administrative Science Quarterly* 4: 302–320.
Elliott, Philip
  1972   *The Sociology of the Professions*. London: Macmillan.
Engeström, Yrjo
  1987   *Learning by Expanding: An Activity-Theoretical Approach to Developmental Research*. Helsinki: Orienta-Konsultit.
Erickson, Frederick and Jeffrey Shultz
  1982   *The Counsellor as Gatekeeper: Social Interaction in Interviews*. New York: Academic Press.
Etzioni, Amitai (ed.)
  1961   *A Sociological Reader on Complex Organisations*. New York: Holt, Rinehart and Winston.
Etzioni, Amitai (ed.)
  1969   *The Semi-Professions and their Organisation*. New York: Free Press.
Fairclough, Norman
  1992   *Discourse and Social Change*. Cambridge: Polity Press.
Fairclough, Norman
  1995   *Critical Discourse Analysis*. Harlow: Longman
Ferrara, Kathleen W.
  1994   *Therapeutic Ways with Words*. New York: Oxford University Press.
Firkins, Arthur and Christopher N. Candlin
  2006   Framing the child at risk. *Health, Risk & Society* 8(3): 273–291.
Firth, Alan (ed.)
  1994   *The Discourse of Negotiation: Studies of Language in the Workplace*. Oxford. Pergamon.
Fisher, Sue
  1988   *In the Patient's Best Interest: Women and the Politics of Medical Decisions*. New Brunswick, NJ: Rutgers University Press.
Fisher, Sue
  1995   *Nursing Wounds: Nurse Practitioners/Doctors/Women Patients/ and the Negotiation of Meaning*. New Brunswick, NJ: Rutgers University Press.
Fisher, Sue and Alexandra Dundas Todd (eds.)
  1983   *The Social Organisation of Doctor-Patient Communication*. Washington DC: Centre for Applied Linguistics.
Fisher, Sue and Alexandra Dundas Todd (eds.)
  1986   *Discourse and Institutional Authority: Medicine, Education and Law*. Norwood, NJ: Ablex.

Foucault, Michel
  1980   *Power/Knowledge: Selected Interviews and Other Writings.* Edited and
          translated by C. Gordon. Harlow: Prentice Hall.
Fox, Renata and John Fox
  2004   *Organisational Discourse: A Language-Ideology-Power Perspective.*
          Westport, CT: Praeger.
Freed, Alice F. and Susan Ehrlich (eds.)
  2010   *"Why Do You Ask?": The Function of Questions in Institutional Discourse.*
          Oxford: Oxford University Press.
Freeman, Sarah and Monica Heller (eds.)
  1987   Medical Discourse. [Special issue] *Text* 7(1).
Freidson, Eliot
  1970   *Profession of Medicine: A Study of the Sociology of Applied Knowledge.*
          New York: Dodd Mead.
Freidson, Eliot
  1994   *Professionalism Reborn: Theory, Prophecy and Policy.* Cambridge: Polity
          Press.
Freidson, Eliot
  2001   *Professionalism: The Third Logic.* Cambridge: Polity Press.
Garfinkel, Harold
  1967   *Studies in Ethnomethodology.* Englewood Cliffs, NJ: Prentice Hall.
Gee, James P., Glynda Hull and Colin Lankshear
  1996   *The New Work Order.* London: Allen and Unwin.
Gibbons, John
  2003   *Forensic Linguistics: An Introduction to Language in the Justice System.*
          Oxford: Blackwell.
Gibbons, John (ed.)
  1994   *Language and the Law.* Harlow: Longman.
Goffman, Erving
  1961   *Encounters: Two Studies in the Sociology of Interaction.* Indianapolis:
          Bobbs-Merrill.
Goffman, Erving
  1981   *Forms of Talk.* Oxford: Blackwell.
Goodwin, Charles
  1994   Professional vision. *American Anthropologist* 96: 606–633.
Gotti, Maurizio and Francoise Salagar-Meyer (eds.)
  2006   *Advances in Medical Discourse Analysis: Oral and Written Contexts.* Bern:
          Peter Lang.
Gramsci, Antonio
  1971   *Selections from the Prison Notebooks.* Edited and translated by Q. Hoare
          and G. Nowell-Smith. London: Lawrence Wishart.
Grant, David, Cynthia Hardy, Cliff Oswick and Linda Putnam (eds.)
  2004   *The SAGE Handbook of Organizational Discourse.* Thousand Oaks: Sage.
Greenwood, Ernest
  1962   Attributes of a profession. In: S. Nosow and W. F. Form (eds.), *Man, Work
          and Society*, 137–158. New York: Basic Books.

Grimshaw, Allen D.
1989   *Collegial Discourse: Professional Conversation Among Peers*. Norwood, NJ: Ablex.
Grint, Keith
1991   *The Sociology of Work: An Introduction*. Cambridge: Polity Press.
Gunnarsson, Britt-Louise
1984   Functional comprehensibility of legislative texts: Experiments with a Swedish act of parliament. *Text* 4(1/3): 71–106.
Gunnarsson, Britt-Louise
2009   *Professional Discourse*. London: Continuum.
Gunnarsson, Britt-Louise, Per Linell and Bengt Nordberg (eds.)
1997   *The Construction of Professional Discourse*. Harlow: Longman.
Gwyn, Richard
2002   *Communicating Health and Illness*. London: Sage.
Habermas, Jürgen
1987   *Theory of Communicative Action,* Volume 2: *Lifeworld and System: A Critique of Functionalist Reason*. Cambridge: Polity Press.
Hafner, Christoph A.
2006   Understanding barristers' opinions: A discourse analytical study. *Clarity 56*: 37–39.
Hak, Tony
1989   Constructing a psychiatric case. In: B. Torode (ed.), *Text and Talk as Social Practice*, 72–92. Dordrecht: Foris.
Hak, Tony
1992   Psychiatric records as transformations of other Texts. In: G. Watson and R. M. Seiler eds., *Text in Context: Contributions to Ethnomethodology*, 138–155. Newbury Park, CA: Sage.
Hak, Tony
1994   The interactional form of professional dominance. *Sociology of Health and Illness* 16(4): 469–488.
Hall, Christopher J., Stefaan Slembrouck and Srikant Sarangi
2006   *Language Practices in Social Work: Categorisation and Accountability in Child Welfare*. London: Routledge.
Handford, Michael
2010   *The Language of Business Meetings*. Cambridge: Cambridge University Press.
Handy, Charles B.
1976   *Understanding Organisations*. Harmondsworth: Penguin Books.
Heath, Christian
1986   *Body Movement and Speech in Medical Interaction*. Cambridge: Cambridge University Press.
Heath, Shirley Brice
1979   The context of professional languages: An historical overview. In: J. E. Alatis and R. G. Tucker (eds.), *Language in Public Life*, 101–118. Washington, DC: Georgetown University Press.
Heffer, Chris
2005   *The Language of Jury Trial: A Corpus-aided Analysis of Legal-Lay Discourse*. Basingstoke: Palgrave Macmillan.

Heritage, J. C. and Watson, D. R.
  1979   Formulations as conversational objects. In: G. Psathas (ed.), *Everyday Language: Studies in Ethnomethodology*, 123–162. New York: Irvington Publishers.
Heritage, John and Douglas Maynard (eds.)
  2006   *Communication in Medical Care: Interaction between Primary Care Physicians and Patients.* Cambridge: Cambridge University Press.
Heydon, Georgina
  2005   *The Language of Police Interviewing.* Basingstoke: Palgrave Macmillan.
Holmes, Janet and Maria Stubbe
  2003   *Power and Politeness in the Workplace: A Sociolinguistic Analysis of Talk at Work.* London: Longman.
Hugman, Richard
  1991   *Power in the Caring Professions.* London: Macmillan.
Hyland, Ken
  2000   *Disciplinary Discourses: Social Interaction in Academic Writing.* London: Pearson Education.
Iedema, Rick
  2003   *Discourses of Post-Bureaucratic Organisations.* Amsterdam: John Benjamins.
Iedema, Rick (ed.)
  2005   Professional and Organisational Practices in the Hospital Setting. [Special Issue] *Journal of Applied Linguistics* 2(3).
Iedema, Rick (ed.)
  2007   *The Discourses of Hospital Communication: Tracing Complexities in Contemporary Health Organisations.* Basingstoke: Palgrave Macmillan.
Illich, Ivan
  1977   Disabling professions. In: I. Illich, I. K. Zola, J. McNight, J. Caplan, and H. Shaiken (eds.), *Disabling Professions*, 11–39. London: Marion Boyars.
Johnson, Terrence
  1972   *Professions and Power.* London: Macmillan.
Johnson, Terrence
  1993   Expertise and the state. In: Mike Gane and T. Johnson (eds.), *Foucault's New Domains.* London: Routledge.
Jönsson, Linda and Per Linell
  1991   Story generations: From dialogical Interviews to written reports in police interrogations. *Text* 11(3): 419–440.
Kanes, Clive (ed.)
  2010   *Elaborating Professionalism: Studies in Practice and Theory.* London: Springer.
Keyton, Joann
  2002   *Communication in Groups: Developing Relationships for Effective Decision-Making.* Boston: McGraw Hill.
Keyton, Joann
  2005   *Communication and Organisational Culture: A key to Understanding Work Experiences.* Thousand Oaks: Sage.

Keyton, Joann and Pamela Shockley-Zalabak
    2009   *Case Studies for Organisational Communication: Understanding Communication Processes*. Oxford: Oxford University Press.
Koester, Almut
    2006   *Investigating Workplace Discourse*. London: Routledge.
Komter, Martha J.
    1993   *Dilemmas in the Courtroom: A Study of Trials of Violent Crime in the Netherlands*. Mahwah, NJ: Lawrence Erlbaum
Labov, William and David Fanshel
    1977   *Therapeutic Discourse: Psychotherapy as Conversation*. New York: Academic Press.
Larson, Magali Sarfatti
    1977   *The Rise of Professionalism: A Sociological Analysis*. Berkeley: University of California Press.
Lave, Jean and Etienne Wenger
    1991   *Situated Learning: Legitimate Peripheral Participation*. Cambridge: Cambridge University Press.
Layder, Derek
    1993   *New Strategies for Social Research*. Cambridge: Polity Press.
Lee, David
    1992   *Competing Discourses*. London: Longman.
Levinson, Stephen
    1992   Activity types and language. In: P. Drew and J. Heritage (eds.), *Talk at Work: Interaction in Institutional Settings*, 66–100. Cambridge: Cambridge University Press. Originally published in *Linguistics* 17(5/6): 364–399 [1979].
Linell, Per
    1998   Discourse across boundaries: On recontextualisations and blending of voices in professional discourse. *Text* 18(2): 143–157.
Linell, Per and Thomas Luckmann
    1991   Asymmetries in dialogue: Some conceptual preliminaries. In: I. Markova and K. Foppa (eds.), *Asymmetries in Dialogue*, 1–20. Hemel Hempstead: Harvester Wheatsheaf.
Linell, Per and Srikant Sarangi
    1998   Discourse across professional boundaries. [Special Issue] *Text* 18(2).
Lynch, Michael and Wes Sharrock
    2003   Editors' introduction. In: M. Lynch and W. Sharrock (eds.), *Harold Garfinkel*, vii–xlvi. London: Sage.
Macdonald, Keith M.
    1995   *The Sociology of the Professions*. London: Sage.
Maley, Yon
    1985   Judicial discourse: The case of the legal judgment. *Beitraege zur Phonetik und Linguistik* 48: 159–173.
Maley, Yon, Christopher N. Candlin, Jonathan Crichton and Pieter Koster
    1995   Orientations in lawyer-client interviews. *Forensic Linguistics* 2(1): 42–55.
Mather, Lynn, M. McEwen, A. Craig and Richard J. Maiman
    2001   *Divorce Lawyers at Work*. New York: Oxford University Press.

Matoesian, Greg
    1993   *Reproducing Rape: Domination through Talk in the Courtroom.* Cambridge: Polity Press.
Matoesian, Greg
    2001   *Law and the Language of Identity: Discourse in the Kennedy Smith Rape Trial.* Oxford: Oxford University Press.
Mautner, Gerlinde
    2010   *Language and the Market Society: Critical Reflections on Discourse and Dominance.* London: Routledge.
Mehan, Hugh
    1993   Beneath the skin and between the ears: A case study in the politics of representation. In: S. Chaiklin and J. Lave (eds.), *Understanding Practice: Perspectives on Activity and Context*, 241–268. Cambridge: Cambridge University Press.
Miller, Katherine
    2008   *Organizational Communication: Approaches and Processes.* Belmont. CA: Wadsworth Publishing.
Mishler, Elliot G.
    1984   *The Discourse of Medicine: Dialectics of Medical Interviews.* Norwood, N.J.: Ablex.
Modaff, Daniel, Sue DeWine and Jennifer Butler
    2007   *Organisational Communication: Foundations, Challenges and Misunderstandings.* New York: Allyn and Bacon.
Morris, G. H. and Ronald J. Chenail (eds.)
    1995   *The Talk of the Clinic: Explorations in the Analysis of Medical and Therapeutic Discourse.* Hillsdale, NJ: Lawrence Erlbaum.
Mullany, Louise
    2010   *Gendered Discourse in the Professional Workplace.* Basingstoke: Palgrave Macmillan.
Murphy, Raymond
    1988   *Social Closure.* Oxford: The Clarendon Press.
Myers, Greg
    1990   *Writing Biology: Texts in the Social Construction of Scientific Knowledge.* Madison: University of Wisconsin Press.
O'Barr, William
    1982   *Linguistic Evidence: Language, Power and Strategy in the Courtroom.* New York: Academic Press.
O'Barr, William
    1983   The study of language in institutional context. *Journal of Language and Social Psychology* 2: 241–251.
Parsons, Talcott
    1951   *The Social System.* London: Tavistock.
Peräkylä, Anssi
    1995   *AIDS Counselling: Institutional Interaction and Clinical Practice.* Cambridge: Cambridge University Press.
Peräkylä, Anssi and Sanna Vehviläinen
    2003   Conversation analysis and the professional stocks of interactional knowledge. *Discourse & Society* 14(6): 727–750.

Pettinari, Catherine J.
    1988   *Task, Talk, and Text in the Operating Room: A Study in Medical Discourse.*
            Norwood, NJ: Ablex.
Pugh, D. S. (ed.)
    1971   *Organisation Theory: Selected Readings.* Harmondsworth: Penguin Books.
Putnam, Linda L. and Anne M. Nicotera (eds.)
    2008   *Building Theories of Organisation: The Constitutive Role of Communi-
            cation.* Mahwah, NJ: Erlbaum.
Putnam, Linda L. and M. E. Pacanowsky
    1983   *Organisational Communication: An Interpretive Approach.* Newbury Park,
            CA: Sage.
Ribeiro, Branca T.
    1994   *Coherence in Psychotic Discourse.* Oxford: Oxford University Press.
Roberts, Celia
    2003   Applied linguistics applied. In: S. Sarangi and T. van Leeuwen (eds.),
            Applied Linguistics and Communities of Practice, 132–149. London: Con-
            tinuum.
Roberts, Celia and Srikant Sarangi
    1999   Hybridity in gatekeeping discourse: Issues of practical relevance for the
            researcher. In: S. Sarangi and C. Roberts (cds.), *Talk, Work and Institutional
            Order: Discourse in Medical, Mediation and Management Settings*,
            473–503. Berlin/New York: Mouton de Gruyter.
Roberts, Celia and Srikant Sarangi
    2003   Uptake of discourse research in interprofessional settings: Reporting from
            medical consultancy. *Applied Linguistics* 24(3): 338–359.
Roberts, Celia and Srikant Sarangi
    2005   Theme-oriented Discourse Analysis of medical encounters. *Medical Edu-
            cation* 39: 632–640.
Rock, Frances
    2007   *Communicating Rights: The Language of Arrest and Detention.* Basing-
            toke: Palgrave Macmillan.
Rosch, Eleanor
    1978   Principles of categorisation. In: E. Rosch and L. Lloyd (eds.), *Cognition
            and Categorisation*, 27–48. Hillsdale, NJ: Lawrence Erlbaum.
Sacks, Harvey
    1984   Notes on methodology. In: J. M. Atkinson and J. Heritage (eds.), *Structures
            of Social Action: Studies in Conversation Analysis*, 21–27. Cambridge:
            Cambridge University Press.
Sacks, Harvey
    1992   *Lectures on Conversation,* Volumes I and II. Oxford: Blackwell.
Sarangi, Srikant
    1998   Institutional language. In: J. Mey (ed.), *Concise Encyclopedia of Prag-
            matics*, 382–386. Oxford: Elsevier.
Sarangi, Srikant
    2000   Activity types, discourse types and interactional hybridity: The case of
            genetic counselling. In: S. Sarangi and M. Coulthard (eds.), *Discourse and
            Social Life*, 1–27. London: Pearson.

Sarangi, Srikant
    2002   Discourse practitioners as a community of interprofessional practice:
            Some insights from health communication research. In: C. N. Candlin (ed.),
            Research and Practice in Professional Discourse, 94–135. Hong Kong:
            City University of Hong Kong Press.
Sarangi, Srikant
    2004   Towards a communicative mentality in medical and healthcare practice.
            Communication & Medicine 1(1): 1–11.
Sarangi, Srikant
    2005   The conditions and consequences of professional discourse studies. *Journal
            of Applied Linguistics* 2(3): 371–394. Also published in R. Kiely, P. Rea-
            Dickins, H. Woodfield and G. Clibbon (eds.), *Language, Culture and Iden-
            tity in Applied Linguistics*, 199–220. London: Equinox [2006].
Sarangi, Srikant
    2007   The anatomy of interpretation: Coming to terms with the analyst's paradox
            in professional discourse studies. *Text & Talk* 27(5): 567–584.
Sarangi, Srikant
    2010a   Reconfiguring self/identity/status/role: The case of professional role per-
            formance in healthcare encounters. *Journal of Applied Linguistics and Pro-
            fessional Practice* 7(1). Also published in J. Archibald and G. Garzone
            (eds.), *Discourse, Identities and Roles in Specialised Communication*,
            33–57. Bern: Peter Lang [2010].
Sarangi, Srikant
    2010b   Healthcare interaction as an expert communicative system: An activity
            analysis perspective. In: J. Streeck (ed.), *New Adventures in Language and
            Interaction*, 167–197. Amsterdam: John Benjamins.
Sarangi, Srikant and Christopher N. Candlin
    2001   Motivational relevancies: Some methodological reflections on socioling-
            uistic practice. In: N. Coupland, S. Sarangi and C. N. Candlin (eds.), *So-
            ciolinguistics and Social Theory*, 350–388. London: Pearson.
Sarangi, Srikant and Christopher N. Candlin (eds.)
    2003a   Researching the discourses of workplace practice. [Special Issue] *Applied
            Linguistics* 24(3).
Sarangi, Srikant and Christopher N. Candlin (eds.)
    2003b   Categorisation and explanation of risk: A Discourse Analytical perspective.
            [Special Issue] *Health, Risk & Society* 5(2).
Sarangi, Srikant and Christopher N. Candlin
    2003c   Trading between reflexivity and relevance: New challenges for applied lin-
            guistics. *Applied Linguistics* 24(3): 271–285.
Sarangi, Srikant and Per Linell (eds.)
    Forth- *Team Talk: Decision-Making across the Boundaries in Health and Social
    coming Care Professions*. London: Equinox.
Sarangi, Srikant and Celia Roberts
    1999   The dynamics of interactional and institutional orders in work-related
            settings. In: S. Sarangi and C. Roberts (eds.), *Talk, Work and Institutional
            Order: Discourse in Medical, Mediation and Management Settings*, 1–57.
            Berlin/New York: Mouton de Gruyter.

Sarangi, Srikant and Celia Roberts (eds.)
  1999   *Talk, Work and Institutional Order: Discourse in Medical, Mediation and Management Settings*. Berlin/New York: Mouton de Gruyter.
Sarangi, Srikant and Stefaan Slembrouck
  1996   *Language, Bureaucracy and Social Control*. London: Longman.
Schon, Donald
  1983   *The Reflective Practitioner: How Professionals Think in Action*. New York: Basic Books.
Scollon, Ron and Suzie W. Scollon
  2004   *Nexus Analysis: Discourse and the Emerging Internet*. London: Routledge.
Shockley-Zalabak, Pamela
  2008   *Fundamentals of Organizational Communication Knowledge*. New York: Allyn and Bacon.
Shuy, Roger W.
  1998   *The Language of Confession, Interrogation, and Deception*. Thousand Oaks, CA: Sage.
Shuy, Roger W.
  2005   *Creating Language Crimes: How Law Enforcement Uses (and Misuses) Language*. New York: Oxford University Press.
Shuy, Roger W.
  2006   *Linguistics in the Courtroom: A Practical Guide*. New York: Oxford University Press.
Silverman, David
  1970   *The Theory of Organisations: A Sociological Framework*. London: Heinmann Educational Books.
Silverman, David
  1987   *Communication and Medical Practice: Social Relations in the Clinic*. London: Sage.
Silverman, David
  1997   *Discourses of Counselling: HIV Counselling as Social Interaction*. London: Sage.
Smart, Barry
  1985   *Michel Foucault*. London: Tavistock.
Smart, Graham
  2006   *Writing the Economy: Activity, Genre and Technology in the World of Banking*. London: Equinox.
Smith, Dorothy E.
  1978   K is mentally ill: The anatomy of a factual account. *Sociology* 12: 23–53.
Smith, Dorothy E.
  1990   *The Conceptual Practices of Power: A Feminist Sociology of Knowledge*. Boston: Northeastern University Press.
Solan, Larry
  1993   *The Language of Judges*. Chicago: The University of Chicago Press.
Solan, Larry and Peter Tiersma
  2005   *Speaking of Crime: The Language of Criminal Justice*. Chicago: The University of Chicago Press.

Stivers, Tanya
    2007   *Prescribing under Pressure: Patient-Physician Conversations and Antibiotics*. Oxford: Oxford University Press.
Swales, John
    1990   *Genre Analysis: English in Academic and Research Settings*. Cambridge: Cambridge University Press.
Taylor, Jim R. and Elizabeth J. van Every
    2000   *The Emergent Organization: Communication as its Site and Surface*. Mahway, NJ: Lawrence Erlbaum.
Thomas, Jenny A.
    1985   The language of power: Towards a dynamic pragmatics. *Journal of Pragmatics* 9: 764–783.
Thornborrow, Joanna
    2002   *Power Talk: Language and Interaction in Institutional Discourse*. London: Longman.
Tiersma, Peter
    2000   *Legal Language*. Chicago: The University of Chicago Press.
Torstendahl, Rolf and Michael Burrage
    1990   *The Formation of Professions: Knowledge, State and Strategy*. London: Sage.
Vine, Bernadette
    2004   *Getting Things Done at Work: The Discourse of Power in Workplace Interaction*. Amsterdam: John Benjamins.
Wadsworth, Michael and David Robinson (eds.)
    1976   *Studies in Everyday Medical Life*. London: Martin Robertson.
Waitzkin, Howard
    1991   *The Politics of Medical Encounters: How Doctors and Patients Deal with Social Problems*. New Haven, Conn.: Yale University Press.
Weber, Max
    1964   *The Theory of Social and Economic Organization*. Translated by A. M. Henderson and T. Parsons, with an introduction by T. Parsons. New York: Free Press.
Weick, Karl E.
    1995   *Sense Making in Organisations*. Thousand Oaks: Sage.
Weick, Karl E.
    2001   *Making Sense of the Organisation*. Oxford: Blackwell.
West, Candice
    1984   *Routine Complications: Troubles in Talk between Doctors and Patients*. Bloomington: Indiana University Press.
Wilding, Paul
    1982   *Professional Power and Social Welfare*. London: Routledge and Kegan Paul.

Part II

1. Evidence and inference in macro-level and micro-level healthcare studies

Aaron V. Cicourel

Abstract

This chapter addresses two parallel medical issues; clinical healthcare delivery and research motivated by the distribution of disease and health policies. The two medical issues, however, are preoccupied with clinical trial outcomes. Healthcare delivery can be viewed as the interaction of rule-based and intuitive clinical decision-making (tacit, embodied, somatic) anchored in clinical practices and evidence-based medicine. Healthcare delivery, however, is buttressed by bureaucratic and economic constraints. Healthcare professionals rely on animal and human models or bench (wet-lab) controlled experiments and labor-intensive clinical trial studies. A daunting challenge is to understand the clinician's use of implicit clinical knowledge, communicative skills, and research findings in reaching a differential diagnosis that must re-represent clinical and laboratory findings in an official record. Healthcare policies and programs, on the other hand, have an indirect impact on day-to-day clinical practice, but can have a direct effect on bureaucratic cost and management practices by healthcare facilities and third party payers. Such policies and programs emerge from large-scale epidemiological and demographic studies of patients or respondents, clinical trials, and macro-level social science research that may be historical, organizational or survey-based.

1. Introduction

Significant differences exist between the gathering and use of evidence and inference during clinical practice and clinical trial studies and the data gathered and used for population research on healthcare issues and policies (epidemiology, management issues, demographic and actuarial data).

Consider the conceptual notion of "blending" (Turner 2006: 5–7), which allows us to achieve mental activations that produce differential human-scale time frames of reference. We can think of macro and micro accounts of healthcare delivery as two attempts to create different human-scale time blends that will convince people to take immediate action vis-à-vis their health, in contrast to a level in which human-scale time is likely to be less actionable as when information is packaged in such forms as reading media reports, and hearing about healthcare problems from family members, colleagues at work, and friends. At the micro level, healthcare personnel with patients must address the immediate kinds of concrete action that are possible and feasible, information about what needs to be done, including the possibility of repeated consultations and treatments.

Public health studies based on demographic and survey data have a sweeping range of human-scale time, and have the advantage of suggestive (and perhaps "seductive" or deceptive) generalizations despite the benefit of large samples. The research can be constrained by the amount of implicit and explicit knowledge or information that is compressed in the construction of reported outcomes. Readers often have little knowledge of the way the research is designed, how questions come to be framed and asked by research personnel, and answered and interpreted by respondents.

Real-time differential diagnoses are seldom longitudinal but are usually based on the physician's implicit and explicit clinical knowledge and contingent on years of local clinical experiences with patients, ward rounds and grand rounds, continuing medical education, selective reading of medical literature, and interaction with colleagues. A contrasting macro level strategy is to look at the natural history of a disease and correlational studies of its pathogenesis. The study of the physician's (and nurse's) knowledge by cognitive and social scientists is constrained by temporal demands of field research, and the normal intrusion of information processing obstacles like an observer's, physician's, nurse's, and patient's selective attention and memory, and hectic (hence often stressful) procedures and bureaucratic obligations. I do not address professional motivation for money and socio-cultural respect, power and honors.

2.   Macro-level of analysis

Public health research, including much epidemiological research, targets a wide range of medical outcomes and the use of sample survey methods and access to large populations. A given population may be studied prospectively as part of an ongoing study such as the New Haven cohort called the Established Populations for the Epidemiologic Studies of the Elderly (Avendano et al. 2006) or retrospectively by making use of existing data from the well-known Framingham Study (Kannel and Tavia 1968). Such populations enable public health professionals to conduct many longitudinal research studies with the same respondents or patients. Large-sample macro research requires a fairly extensive team of assistants and a few specialists.

The historically proven value of public health research can be found in accounts of cholera epidemics in Britain during the middle of the nineteenth century (Hempel 2007; Johnson 2007; Wohl 1983). The city of London, notes

Johnson, was subject to a "rising tide of excrement" building up inside and outside of homes in London and other cities. The cholera epidemics of 1831–1832, 1848–1849, and 1854 were devastating. The pioneering work of a physician, John Snow, identified water sources as the cause. He visited the homes affected and the source of their water. Those obtaining water from a company in the worst part of the Thames in central London became ill while those getting their water from a company that used a source upstream were likely to be spared the illness. Snow's diligent field work was enhanced by statistics gathered by the General Registry Office that recorded the number of cholera cases and the location of those who fell ill (Cohen 2005). The combination of micro-level, on-site observations and a nascent demography proved to be invaluable for promoting modern public health and epidemiology research.

Creating quantitative measures of macro-level data to achieve generalizations based on sample surveys depend on theoretical assumptions that are in correspondence with a metric and a commitment to a given level of error. Measurement problems in the behavioral and social sciences were succinctly summarized by Coombs:

> Almost anyone is willing to say that any given set of data contains some error, but just what is to be classified as error depends a good deal on the level of measurement assumed to hold in the data.
>
> The social scientist is faced by his dilemma when he chooses between mapping his data into a simple order and *asking* his data whether they satisfy a simple order. By selecting a strong enough system, the social scientist can always succeed in constructing a unidimensional scale of measurement, commonly an interval scale, thus requiring a portion of the data to be classified as error. By not *requiring* a strong system, the social scientist permits the data to determine whether a simple unidimensional solution is adequate. Unidimensionality, obtained by a method of analysis which guarantees it, obviously cannot thereby be shown to be a characteristic of the behavior in question. This is merely a special case of a more general principle that no property of data can be said to hold unless the methods of collecting and of analyzing the data permit alternative properties to exhibit themselves. The problem of the social scientist, in blunt terms, is whether he knows what he wants or whether he wants to know.
>
> (Coombs 1953: 486–487)

If we follow Coombs' useful cautions, an important question is: What do we claim as evidence in epidemiological studies? Data from public health and epidemiological studies often assume an interval scale. The numerical properties of such data often risk classifying a high proportion of data as "error". Survey data are derived from questions that are usually ordinal in nature, despite such interval-appearing distributions as socioeconomic status and age.

3.   Micro-level clinical medicine

The micro-level study of individual and distributed knowledge systems requires labor-intensive, direct observation of actual interaction, eliciting blended or compressed information from physicians as they perform their activities, and then asking them to listen to the tape and reconstruct their experiences. The documentation is always selective because of information processing limitations on both research personnel and physician. Ethnographic studies and the use of recorded discourse of actual clinical practice have the advantage of direct observation of the everyday activities of healthcare delivery that can augment the validity of the research. Using a few case studies or small samples constrains the generalizations that are possible, but the examination of many small samples can be useful for identifying possible invariant elements of clinical practices.

I suggest we characterize the complexities of medical diagnostic reasoning by reference to what Charles Sanders Peirce (1960) called "abductive" reasoning, or real time reasoning; the role of induction, deduction and abduction. Can we distinguish deductive from inductive and abductive inferences when we conduct and analyze epidemiological and public health data on healthcare outcomes? Can we apply Peirce's ideas to the evolving, ongoing, compressed inferential hypotheses attributed to the practice of real-time clinical medicine suggested earlier?

Peirce (1960: 160) notes that "An apodictic or deductive syllogism is one whose validity depends unconditionally upon the relation of the fact inferred to the facts posited in the premises." If additional explicit or implicit knowledge is used, states Peirce, then the inference would be "incomplete". According to Peirce (1960: 162), "All valid reasoning is either deductive, inductive, or hypothetic; or else it combines two or more of these characteristics."

Does clinical practice, including the appearance and mannerisms of the professionals, their nonverbal behavior, the language used, and the use of different instruments or tests, resemble a fusion of elements from deduction and induction, namely what Peirce called "abduction?" The gist of "abduction" is the fact that several contingencies can exist simultaneously from which we must make inferences that may be partially deductive as well as inductive. In other words, in deduction we follow a rule, and in induction we create a generalization about, say, a collection of characteristics. Thus, we create transient hypotheses whose outcomes can be coded with a classificatory label or a numeral.

Can accounts by clinicians such as Groopman's (2007) informative narratives about medical practice be linked to the structural generality of the way evidence is gathered in public health and epidemiological studies? Such measures as blood pressure, cholesterol, sedimentation rate, and temperature are presented quantitatively, and are useful, but their interval scale relevance is

not self-evident and contingent on a physician's clinical judgments and other aspects of the patient's condition. The different levels of analysis are not commensurate despite their common reference to healthcare delivery.

4.   Cognitive aspects of medical decision making

Within academic medicine, there is interest in the general idea of the physician's
possession and use of a "'causal model' of the patient: a description of the
mechanisms of the human body and how they influence each other" (Kuipers
and Kassirer 1984: 363). Kuipers and Kassirer (1984) follow the advice of Newell and Simon (1972) by seeking a verbatim transcript of a "talking out loud"
interview with a physician about a nephrotic syndrome case in order to access
the limits of physicians' knowledge representations. The study by Kuipers and
Kassirer, however, does not examine the physician's real-time reasoning while
interviewing the patient (e.g., recording what the physician and patient say to
each other), but instead creates a "causal" frame by inviting the physician to use
her or his explicit knowledge about a syndrome independently of how the syndrome would be inductively or abductively hypothesized during (or after) an
audio- or video-taped interview. The analysis presented by Kuipers and Kassirer, however, does not show how they redacted their activities into a clinical
history. What aspects were addressed, altered, and ignored? As Joshua Fierer
(personal communication) notes, physicians filter out "'the irrelevant' material
that patients offer and the redundant material". What remains is "reshaped ...
condensed into a standard format. A lot is lost". Neither Kuipers and Kassirer
nor Groupman (see below) address these issues empirically.

Expert systems utilize the physician's standard medical history terminology
and propositions about a patient. Writing algorithms using such compressed
summary information is feasible, but cognitive/emotional and interpersonal
sources of information are thereby masked. The reasoning attributed to the patient, and the physician's reasoning represented in the written clinical record or
history are not readily inferable from the question-answer discourse that motivated the official medical history, but are a necessary point of departure for an
expert system.

I have called attention to cognitive aspects of decision making that attribute
a conceptual frame to diagnostic reasoning (Boshuizen and Schmidt 1992;
Kuipers and Kassirer 1984). The cognitive perspective is an essential part of
healthcare delivery, but research in this area neglects the important roles played
by structural/organizational constraints and the ever-present discourse practices
that sustain and modify the dynamic aspects of healthcare delivery. Epidemiological, structural/organizational, cognitive and discourse approaches to the
study of healthcare professionals and healthcare delivery systems are semi-in-

dependent, loosely connected systems. A particular study may focus on one aspect of these loosely linked substantive areas, but its impact on the other areas remains ambiguous.

5.   Institutional aspects of healthcare

Western medical activities reflect cultural beliefs in the value of scientific medicine. For example, a competitive educational system exists that makes use of special testing procedures and includes admission interviews with students, residents, fellows, and faculty.

The process whereby physicians are accorded special professional status in the U.S. resides in loosely-coupled state and private organizations. These organizations possess the authority and/or power to attribute, exercise, assign, or confer higher professional status to individuals. Scholars such as Fox (1977), Freidson (1970, 1975), Mechanic (1978), and Starr (1982), among others, have focused on structural aspects of the authority and power possessed by healthcare delivery systems and practitioners. A different and more recent focus has been on case studies at the level of doctor-patient social interaction. These micro-level studies have sought to identify the practical activities and local decision making associated with diagnostic inferences, the assessment of medical competence, and the power physicians enjoy within healthcare organizations (Atkinson 1981, 1995; Bosk 1979; Groopman, 2007; Mishler 1984; Silverman 1987; Styles 1982; Waitzkin 1991).

Structural views of healthcare and the profession of medicine provide theoretical frameworks for understanding healthcare delivery as a societal or nation-state phenomenon. Closely linked to such structural studies is the extensive impact of public health research, and epidemiological studies in particular, on how healthcare professionals, the media, and some patients obtain information about trends and symptoms associated with health and illness from colleagues, family members and friends, and neighbors.

One early structural view of health was Talcott Parsons' use of a more abstract terminology that characterizes medical knowledge and practice as "affectively neutral", "universalistic", "functionally specific" and "collectively oriented". Practicing physicians are presumed to be "applied scientists" who "treat an objective problem in objective, scientifically justifiable terms" (Parsons 1951: 435). This view (suggests Joshua Fierer, personal communication) might have been relevant when physicians had relatively little to offer patients except for surgery and pain relief. It is also difficult to sustain Parson's view in light of the recent movement towards patient-centered healthcare.

The economic and political intrigues associated with healthcare costs and policies cast serious doubts on Parsons' (1951) notion of moral neutrality in the generation and use of medical knowledge. Healthcare is a highly profitable commodity in which differentially available diagnostic judgments and technology are related to patient resources, physicians' interests, power, and prestige, both monetary and social. Parsons viewed "neutrality" as part of the bio-physiological state of disease, but did not recognize social class aspects of medical care. Parsons' description of the "sick role" suggests the idea of illness as a part of a system, a socially institutionalized set of expectations or behavior by those designated as "ill".

An empirical issue is the extent to which observing and analyzing actual discourse material generated in physician-patient exchanges supports Parsons' position when the economic constraints of healthcare delivery are not always evident in a routine encounter between doctor and patient. Physicians, however, can tailor their use of a diagnostic armamentarium and treatment programs according to what they think or know a health plan and/or patient will or can pay for, allow, or accept, especially in the context of managed healthcare systems in the USA. But this latter statement needs to be tempered by what is known about the patient's life outside the examination room. For example, what is known about their "lifestyle", diet and related issues such as the likelihood of treatment compliance? Such decisions and information are not available in social science structural studies, health policy studies and much of epidemiological research on healthcare, nor are they self-evident when observing routine healthcare delivery. "Crossing" the "neutrality" line is more likely to occur when a patient lacks (or possesses) viable health insurance, and especially if faced with a life-threatening illness requiring expensive specialists, medications, laboratory and related diagnostic procedures.

Max Weber's (1968) structural view of authority and power refers to the notion of "official" authority or "functional" authority (Schluchter, 1986) or "scientific" authority (Bourdieu, 1981). Weber's cogent but abstract theory viewed domination in modern societies as a special case of power that is linked closely to the possession and use of knowledge. Status systems and the acquisition and use of authority and power, therefore, are for the most part contingent on the possession and control of knowledge resources. The physician-patient relationship, and especially their exchanges, can be viewed as reflecting Weber's broad structural view of power because the physician is viewed as possessing the authority to heal and prevent death, but what is missing is how the physician assigns meaning or significance to his observations, classifies them, and allocates resources. Provisions that allow those with more resources to receive "excessive" or prolonged care can be viewed as "crossing" Parsons' "neutrality line" and as "bad" medical policy.

According to another earlier view but no longer the case, hospitals are like "advisory bureaucracies" that create organizational conditions for distributing resources to the occupants of different decision making positions (Goss 1961).

Such positions assumed the existence of credentialing specifications described by Randall Collins (1980), and the types of authority and autonomous environments noted by Freidson (1970, 1975) as the medical division of labor.

6.   Macro-level research on healthcare

The hallmark of public health research and most of the social sciences is to seek data from large samples of patients or respondents that would lead to generalizations about the relationship between socio-cultural, environmental, personal hygiene, including diet and exercise, "lifestyle", and pressure for research on adequate healthcare. Surveys usually follow a data-driven, bottom-up methodology in which the larger the sample, the more likely that significant correlations will emerge. The correlations are useful for generating hypotheses, but not testing them with similar data. For over one hundred years, sampling theory has become a reliable staple of macro-level research for many aspects of social science and policy research.

An epidemiological component often has become a mandated requirement for funding many long-term governmental and foundation-sponsored medical research projects. In epidemiological research, sample surveys have become a gold standard for eliciting information on relationships between particular diseases like cancer, diabetes, and cardiovascular problems and patients' age of onset, race or ethnicity, socioeconomic levels, membership in social networks, participation in religious organizations, rural/urban differences, familial incidence of illness, and the like. Epidemiologists seek to summarize and explain the consequences of the use of vitamins, exercise, proximity to toxic sites, and so on.

A key component of survey research questions is the creation and processing of semantic content by the investigator, interviewer, and respondent. But not all epidemiological research is necessarily survey-oriented if they recognize the non-independence of many of the factors associated with semantic processing. Survey questions must propagate coherent conceptual representational states across communication activities. Ethnicity, social class, gender, formal and practical education, religious beliefs and/or church attendance, cultural life styles, cognitive skills or deficits are viewed as independent, quantitative variables to explain health outcomes. As independent variables, the categories utilized necessarily compress information but sometimes enable the emergence of a useful, succinct, general normative depiction of a large community or society or nation-state. The questions they design and choose frame and reflect the normative content of the research findings. As noted earlier, Coomb's (1953) cautions cannot be avoided.

A kind of logic of questions and answers (Harrah 1973) is presumed to exist in the use of sample surveys in which the investigator expects the respondent

(a) knows what the problem is about, (b) finds the topic expressed in an effective manner, (c) understands the possible alternatives, and (d) is assumed to know which alternative is relevant. Respondents, therefore, (i) are expected to cooperate with survey goals for eliciting information, and (ii) expect investigators will create brief, unambiguous questions about issues or topics presumed to be known to respondents. Differential understanding or misunderstanding of survey questions can seriously compromise the way responses are coded, aggregated, and analyzed. Pre-tests of questionnaire items have become essential and their syntactic, semantic, and pragmatic vulnerability have sometimes become a focus of attention.

7.   Epidemiological studies of social factors and coronary heart disease

Considerable attention has been directed to the role of social factors associated with the incidence of, say, stroke among the elderly. One study (Avendano et al. 2006) used the "New Haven cohort of the Established Populations of the Elderly" to examine the demographic make-up of 2812 men and women over 65 years of age, the incidence of cardiovascular disease, and psychological risk factors associated with stroke. The sample was followed for 12 years. Findings suggested that 270 "subjects developed incident stroke" and that lower SES (socio-economic status in terms of education and income) "was associated with higher stroke [rates]". On the other hand, after age 75 the rates of stroke were higher for respondents with higher education and income. Josh Fierer (personal communication) noted that the results suggest that lower SES accelerated the onset of "strokes" developing, but may not have changed the incidence.

A study entitled "Social ties and change in social ties in relation to subsequent total and cause-specific mortality and coronary heart disease incidence in men" (Eng et al. 2002) used data from a sample of " ... 28,369 US male health professionals aged 41–77 in 1988". The study " ... reexamined the relations between social ties, as measured by the Berkman-Syme social network index (1), and cause-specific mortality and coronary heart disease in the Health Professionals Follow-up Study (2)".

The validity of the relationship between social interaction and health outcomes suggests that we explore the kinds of informal exchanges and lack thereof that are assumed to influence and are linked to "smoking, heavy alcohol consumption, poor dietary habits, sedentary lifestyle, and suboptimal health service utilization" and the local, everyday dynamics of social exchanges. There is, however, little discussion of how to study the everyday dynamics of social exchanges associated with smoking, heavy alcohol consumption, and the like. Nor is there any mention of the role of the patient's material status and economic knowledge. The authors continue with additional useful observations: marital transition, recent widowhood, grief and bereavement, social isolation, and general mortality across an extended family appear to have credible effects on health outcomes, and the authors provide important details about how they seek to document the relevance of the index.

The Berkman-Syme index addresses plausible issues and generates meaningful hypotheses about the possible relationship between measures of social integration and illness. Is there research on the discourse processes employed during interviews that seek information about how social networks are elicited and coded? For example, obtaining information on what respondents say and do in the context of their residences, and under what circumstances? Also, obtaining details about how they pursue activities at home and in the community, in order to follow who they have contacted and who have contacted them vis-à-vis planned and actual social relations over the course of a week, a month, and up to a year?

The pioneering work of Granovetter (1973) and one of its applications (Burt 1992) is based primarily on retrospective elicitation of information from respondents that conveniently coincides with research in epidemiology and related public health studies. Can we document how often, and under what circumstances, social network participants engage in face-to-face or telephone or electronic social interaction in which different forms of activities are initiated or suggested, settled, modified, and culminated in subsequent social action?

The notion of "social integration" was coined in sociology to address the idea of a breakdown in traditional social relationships. For example, the breakdown and change of traditional family structure, values, and social relations associated with rural ways of life in contrast to the labor and social conditions that forced or attracted people to more "urban-like" settings. Most studies of social integration have used surveys rather than the labor-intensive observation of persons who have been forced to change communities or who have lost a spouse, in order to see what the consequences were.

One way to extend the social network index would be to follow the activities of a cohort of recent widows and widowers to observe directly the extent to which their families, religious and other social or community organizations, close friends and weak social ties converge to fill the "vacuum". How many subjects left their communities and their strong and weak ties? Were efforts made or not pursued to help those affected establish new relationships?

The measurement of social networks necessarily relies on reconstructed memory and the impressions respondents would like to convey to themselves and others. The evidence constructed from respondents, while lacking independent observable evidence, has created hypotheses that have become the focus of many contemporary social science and public health studies. The quality of the evidence and its validity requires more detailed study.

8.   Viewing structure through process

The study of structural conditions is useful for developing healthcare policies. The extent to which such studies are commensurate with, or orthogonal to, the actual delivery of healthcare practices remains an empirical issue. A paradox emerges. We must learn to speak the "language" of medical science and everyday speech, but also claim to analyze these speech events as if we are detached from the particular cultural tradition being studied. In what follows, I briefly address cognitive and interaction processes of healthcare delivery that are not routinely examined in public health and social science research on medical professional practices.

Studies of real-time, moment-to-moment healthcare delivery practices usually include small samples of patient visits to clinics and hospitals that address clinical diagnoses and treatment plans and interpreting subsequent laboratory results and procedures. Healthcare settings include the way physical space is organized and furnished with particular kinds of artifacts; for example, wearing particular clothing, the presence of an examining table, and having access to specific instruments (e. g., thermometer, blood pressure device, rubber gloves) used in physical examinations. Appearances, therefore, convey legitimacy and always complement the local use of verbal and nonverbal behavior. The local medical ecology is more than sets of resources and practices that are ubiquitous in healthcare delivery; they can also constrain and facilitate the quality of medical care.

Documenting how the local medical ecology affects the quality of healthcare delivery requires labor-intensive research. Micro-level research, therefore, seeks the assessments of healthcare delivery in clinic and hospital settings using systematic ethnographic methods, and must contend with the criticism that the samples are often viewed as too small to generalize to larger populations.

We are left, therefore, with a complicated impasse: a modicum of validity may be possible by detailed studies of healthcare practices with methods that include ethnographic, behavioral sampling (Altmann 1974) and sociolinguistic data or discourse methods. It is difficult, however, to link ethnographic findings to correlation measures based on sample surveys, that is, to generate comparable evidence and generalizations. Generalizing from small samples or a few case studies is contingent on a strong theory and seeking aspects of invariance in one's data despite elements of variation.

9.   Professional medical aspirations and the assessment of clinical practice

The medical profession represents the cultural belief in scientific medicine and the ability to train individuals who will be competent experts to assess patients' medical problems while recognizing the necessity of providing humane, personalized treatment to all who need care. The assessment of quality medical care (quality assurance) is a delicate matter and poses many challenges. Recently, Groopman (2007) has addressed the problem of quality medical care with insight based on years of professional experience at well-known medical centers. He provides the reader with a convincing "insider's" perspective as both a practicing physician who is steeped in scientific medicine, and publications that can be readily understood by educated lay-persons.

A key and unusual aspect of Groopman's book is its concern with reasoning processes used by physicians to reach medical decisions. It is rare to find medical practitioners explicitly advocating that physicians must monitor their own decision making activities, including paying close attention to the occasions when they mis-diagnose their patients' problems. The open way in which Groopman addresses delicate issues associated with physicians' decision-making activities may make many medical doctors uneasy. One reason for this unease is the obvious one of inviting possible litigation.

It is easy to admire Groopman's willingness to address what he calls the "cognitive trap" that afflicts medical diagnostic reasoning, but difficult to clarify such reasoning by examining clinical practices using controlled research methods in actual medical settings. We must first convince a human subjects review committee and various physicians that a recorded study of their everyday medical practices in real time should be done routinely to identify misdiagnoses. Groopman carefully points out various reasons for misdiagnoses, especially those linked to training. In the U.S., for example, people are more likely to think first about legal consequences. Yet we must also ask: what is it about medical education and practice in different bureaucratic settings, under the variable resources available to physicians and patients, that make misdiagnoses inevitable yet reducible with better training environments?

The brief reference to cognition in Groopman's book is useful but he does not elaborate on his reference to work by Amos Tversky and Daniel Kahneman (1981) on risk taking and risk-aversion. Some physicians may find Groopman's reference to the role of cognition during decision-making under conditions of uncertainty and limited capacity information processing intriguing, but wonder how to examine such notions as part of their daily medical practices. There is a fairly large cognitive science literature on, for example, the development of expert systems for medical diagnosis (Cicourel 2000; Kuipers and Kassier 1984; Boshuizen and Schmidt 1992).

We will return to this issue because the convincing and carefully designed experiments conducted by Tversky and Kahneman (and favored by Groopman for improving the way medical doctors think) make the experimental subjects' reasoning appear conclusive and at the heart of human cognition. Within the narrowly circumscribed contexts in which experiments are conducted by cognitive psychologists, Tversky and Kahneman's results are sophisticated and convincing vis-à-vis how people make decisions about risk taking and risk aversion under controlled stimulus conditions. Such results, however, do not reveal how such conditions come into existence and unfold across everyday life settings. What remains unclear is how to create experiments in human cognition that can be applied to the complex settings in which physicians assess elicited information from patients, and their use of other sources of evidence to create a differential diagnosis.

Groopman's useful examples of problems associated with medical diagnostic reasoning, and his (July 7, 2007) article in the New York Times on how he and his wife (also a physician) introduced cognitive psychology into their continuing education courses and to fourth year medical students, reminded me of my teaching experiences, e. g., lecturing to medical students, and helping to train first year pediatric residents using videotapes of their interviews of parents and children in a clinic. For each group, I introduced concepts from cognitive science and how to use elicitation procedures with patients.

Groopman's illuminating cases always reveal an expertise that is informative and convincing. His readily understood how descriptions underscore the image of a physician with a strong knowledge of basic science research and clinical practice that lend a distinctive aura of validity to his credentials and expertise. In science and healthcare delivery, doubting one's hypotheses or diagnoses may be an explicit goal, but an element of denial is often present; we tend to favor our pet hypothesis or diagnosis.

The following excerpts from the initial pages of Groopman's (2007) book illustrate his ability to convey a clear understanding of clinical medicine.

> Anne Dodge had lost count of all the doctors she had seen over the past fifteen years. She guessed it was close to thirty. Now, two days after Christmas 2004, on a surprisingly mild morning, she was driving again into Boston to see yet another physician. Her primary care doctor has opposed the trip, arguing that Anne's problems were so long-standing and so well defined that his consultation would be useless. But her boyfriend had stubbornly insisted. Anne told herself the visit would mollify her boyfriend and she would be back home by midday.
> Anne is in her thirties, with sandy brown hair and soft blue eyes. She grew up in a small town in Massachusetts, one of four sisters. No one had had an illness like hers. After a meal, she would feel as if a hand were griping her stomach and twisting it. The nausea and pain were so intense that occasionally she vomited. Her family doctor examined her and found nothing wrong. He gave her antacids. But the symptoms continued. (Groopman 2007: 1)

The description of Anne Dodge's medical symptoms are presented skillfully and may appear to be self-evident to some readers. We learn that the diagnosis was based on inadequate reasoning.

The examples presented throughout the book are equally clear and always convincing. Given Groopman's concern with how medical doctors think, it would be helpful to know what kinds of questions were asked by her initial physician and a psychiatrist she also visited, and how did Anne Dodge respond to these questions?

Groopman provides some indication of how Anne Dodge's subsequent consultation with a gastroenterologist in Boston followed a different strategy. Different questions were asked, and presumably different answers were received, that were revealing, such that the second physician came up with a different diagnosis that probably saved Anne Dodge's life.

For another page and one-half, Groopman continues to tell the reader about Anne Dodge and then returns to her visit to Boston at the end of December 2004 and her visit with Dr. Falchuk, a gastroenterologist. A key issue is why Dr. Falchuk did not follow Anne Dodge's internist's expectations, and instead, "began to question, and listen, and observe, and then to think differently about Anne's case". What details about the case led Dr. Falchuk to a different strategy, what questions did he ask, what did he hear from the patient, and what did he observe? How did he arrive at the diagnosis of Celiac disease (a reaction to gluten)? A verbatim transcript would have been helpful in following Groopman's readable but selective reconstruction of details not available to the reader. What was it about the patient reported by the internist and elicited from the patient by Dr. Falchuk that brought into existence a frame of reference (Kahneman and Miller 1986) that resulted in a path to a different conclusion?

Attending (experienced) physicians present technical details and specific information about clinical medicine, but seldom explain the tacit, real time, often taken-for-granted thinking that led to their decisions.

Groopman (2007: 5) then notes how current changes have emphasized " … preset algorithms and practice guidelines in the form of decision trees" rather than what he believes is a core issue for understanding healthcare delivery:

> Clinical algorithms can be useful for run-of-the-mill diagnosis and treatment – distinguishing strep throat from viral pharyngitis, for example. But they quickly fall apart when a doctor needs to think outside their boxes, when symptoms are vague, or multiple and confusing, or when test results are inexact. In such cases – the kinds of cases where we most need a discerning doctor – algorithms discourage physicians from thinking independently and creatively. Instead of expanding a doctor's thinking, they can constrain it.
> (Groopman 2007: 5)

The following quotation reveals Groopman's (2007: 5–6) displeasure with any attempt to rely primarily on what he calls "evidence-based medicine," namely, allowing treatment decisions to follow " … statistically proven data". Groopman raises strong misgivings about evidence-based diagnostic reasoning and applying what he terms "algorithms" and statistical reasoning to clinical medicine. His doubts, while useful, may be overstated; evidence from epidemiological studies can be helpful if one understands their drawbacks. Evidence from clinical trials can also have drawbacks, but remain an essential source of data for clinicians despite the way many such trials have been appropriated by commercially motivated organizations.

An implicit issue in Groopman's remarks is: how to gather, analyze and present data from clinical practice in ways that can be generalized while acknowledging the limitations (but also usefulness) of a statistical analysis of numerical data? An issue that remains unclear is how are we to assess the relative validity of the different kinds of data, analyses, and inferences that exist across a broad range of studies on healthcare delivery and medical policy?

Groopman's focus on how doctors think remains challenging but not readily measured with traditional research strategies. As Groopman notes, clinical practice requires systematic observation of a patient's body surface, the patient's motor movements, responses to tactile activities, and verbal and nonverbal behavior and communication. But such details are not part of Groopman's presentation of cases in his book, but he no doubt takes note of the patient's body surface and the other conditions he references above.

I provide the reader with a brief example of a clinical medicine interview from a gastroenterology case I observed in a private practice. I address how physicians communicate and make inferences during healthcare delivery. Other sources of data (Cicourel 1974, 1982, 1992, 1995, 2000 and 2004) have relied on my observations and/or recordings of language use, and motor activities of physicians while engaged in clinical practice.

10.   Micro level evidence and inference

Searching for elusive invariance: science seeks invariant principles that can explain, except for error measures, most of the variation that is observed empirically. The following excerpts from a physician-patient-physician interview provide a few details not evident in Groopman's examples.

I = Interviewer; P = Patient
( ) = transcription problem
[ ] = author's observation
/ = overlap in speaking

1   I: (unclear) How are you?
2   P: Fine, thank you.
3   I: I'm Dr. Huntley [as door is closed] and uh thanks for [slight laugh]
4   undergoing your first interview. [sounds as if patient may have mumbled a
5   low-keyed acknowledgement] (pause)
6   Aas you know, uh and we're going ta re (slight pause) record this one
7   because we're trying to get better ways of getting medical facts from
8   patients (pause) in order to (slight pause) maybe get a more
9   systematized approach to medical interview.
10   P: Allright.
11   I: So we get more information and consequently help you and other
12   patients, better [P: low mumble like 'mmh'] and also we're teaching
13   medical students how to talk to (slight pause) patients, so this is
14   helpful too. That okay with you?
15   P: Yes, that's fine [in low voice that sounds quite 'agreeable']
16   I: Good (slight pause) great. (pause) Now let me have the history form
17   /you filled out.
18   /I haven't
19   I: That's alright, I'll go through it with you.
20   P: And, yah, because some of them, you know, I put a question mark
21   beside them, cause I'm [I: 'yah'] you know (pause)
22   I: Why don't you just sit over there, I can talk to you/better.
23   P: /You like
24   this one better [patient mumbling something here.]
25   I: Get a big pillow (pause, movement of objects heard) get out of the sun.

The above interview begins with some preliminary small talk, including an indirect remark by the physician to signal what had already been agreed to previously, namely, that we would record the patient's permission for the interview
to satisfy the Human Subjects Committee. We were seated in the office for the
interview and then moved to the examining room. The initial remarks by the
physician (lines 6–15) reiterated some earlier comments with the patient about
the purpose of the interview. In lines 16–21, the physician refers to the medical
history form previously given to the patient by the receptionist when she was
seated in the waiting room. In lines 21–25, the physician continues the small
talk, often viewed by patients as an indication that the physician is attentive and
polite rather than "cold" and overly formal.

The interview continued as follows:

26 I: Now just tell me your (slight pause) primary (slight pause) problem that
27   you want us to focus on. What is bothering you at the moment?
28 P: Well, Dr. B said I had high blood pressure. (pause)
29 I: And that was just uh found routinely, uh [P: 'Well'] in the course of an
30   exam (book?) [patient tries to say something like 'I was pregnant'] made
31   to see Dr. B (slight pause) [patient and Dr. talking simultaneously here]
32   You were pregnant.
33 P: That started it. I guess they thought it would go down (slight pause) and
34   un (pause) it didn't.
35 I: Now when was this first discovered? When were you pregnant?
36 P: Well, I delivered in uh, uh, in June (pause) I'd say [I: 'okay' said faintly]
37   I would say maybe, (slight pause) two and a half months before.
38 I: Two and a half months before or so perhaps [barely audible here]
39   sometime (unclear) in uh, uh time in March. And [cut off by patient]
40 P: Ohh about April [mumble afterwards]

The physician begins the clinical part of the interview (lines 26–28) by asking
fairly standard initial questions: "Now just tell me your (slight pause) primary
(slight pause) problem that you want us to focus on. What is bothering you at the
moment?" The patient seems to have ignored the question asking if anything
was bothering her "at the moment," but reported that at an earlier time, she was
told of having shown high blood pressure (lines 28–34) that did not go down
after a pregnancy. The two participants must supply missing details in order to
sustain coherency; a necessary feature of spontaneous exchanges.

Listening to a tape-recording 5, 6 or 10 times can alert the analyst to subtle
details neither participant may have heard at the time; perhaps I ignored essential details of the participants' understanding of the interview. The analysis of
the transcript, therefore, can mislead the reader if the researcher addresses particular aspects of an exchange that may or may not have communicated particular elements to the participants. I say all of this to give the reader a sense of what
I think usually happens in doctor-patient encounters that Groopman and others
seldom present to readers, often because such details are assumed to be irrelevant and/or known in common and taken for granted.

Some eleven minutes transpired before the "immediate problem" (lines
26–27) emerged. The physician's compressed medical history is presented in a
clear, concise manner, but readers of the history would not readily infer the real-
time details from reading the official summary. For example:

Immediate Problem. The patient was first told of modest blood pressure elevation at
age 31 when she consulted an American physician in Japan for palpitations and chest
discomfort. Apparently the palpitations were related to emotional stress. An EKG
was negative. Phenobarbital was prescribed. The physician noted that her blood
pressure was 'up a little'.

The interview had continued for some time before the physician discovered the patient's age and that her husband was in the military stationed in Japan when details about her symptoms emerged. The details about "palpitations and chest discomfort", the negative EKG, and taking Phenobarbital were assembled from disparate parts of an hour-long medical history. Not unexpectedly, the compressed written medical history is crafted for a healthcare (and legal) audience, and represents a physician who was a specialist with considerable clinical experience. The reference to "emotional stress" appears, as suggested by the physician's remarks, to be an inference based on his overall judgment of the patient's extensive remarks. The integration of information by the physician required assembling details scattered throughout the interview and also required considerable effort. The physician was perhaps gradually constructing his history from written notes at the time. I assume that his past clinical experiences and skilled expertise are evident here, and enabled him to produce a selective but highly coherent, real-time summary despite the extensive amount of spoken discourse that emerged. The compressed written history speaks to the information processing skills noted but not pursued by Groopman that a competent physician must acquire.

11.   Conclusion

The conceptual design of different research strategies are motivated by how to achieve documentation about healthcare problems, their content, their distribution, and the relevant conditions that appear to influence their emergence, treatment, and control. Common ground would allow each level of analysis to challenge and suggest modifications of the other, and improve our understanding of healthcare delivery practices, healthcare policy, and the distribution of healthcare problems.

The micro-level research that calls attention to language use and limited capacity cognitive processing can provide information about the limitations of macro-observational studies. Micro-level research, however, does not readily study sample sizes which permit statistical generalization, but can identify gaps in the use of macro observational studies, and clinical trial research vis-à-vis the elicitation, coding, and aggregation of information from surveys and clinical trials.

Public health professionals might react to the above remarks by noting that they are not expected to study micro-level activities, and that I am comparing "apples and oranges". But can the two levels be reconciled (Cicourel 2006)? Epidemiologists would have to clarify tacit assumptions about how the formulation of questions creates a frame of reference that can be linked to the everyday experiences of patients or respondents. One suggestion is to include clinicians in the design of a survey or when utilizing an existing cohort such as the

Framingham group. How would clinicians assess the questions and answers? A follow-up study could include a random sub-sample of the original respondents. Clinicians could conduct a medical history and physical examination of this group. The clinicians could also have asked the subjects about specific diseases or illnesses that were addressed in the original survey. For example, establishing links between micro and macro level studies by creating the conditions for new kinds of collaborative research on healthcare delivery.

References

Altmann, Jean
   1974   Observational study of behavior: Sampling methods. *Behaviour* 49: 227–267.
Anspach, Renee
   1993   *Deciding Who Lives: Fateful Choices in the Intensive Care Nursery.* Berkeley and Los Angeles: University of California Press.
Atkinson, Paul A.
   1981   *The Clinical Experience: The Construction and Reconstruction of Medical Reality.* Farnborough: Gower.
Atkinson, Paul A.
   (1995) Medical Talk and Medical Work. London: Sage.
Avendano, M., I. Kawachi, F. Van Lenthe, H. C. Boshuizen, J. P. Mackenbach, G. A. M. Van den Bos, M. E. Fay and L. F Berman.
   2006   Socioeconomic status and stroke incidence in the US elderly: The role of risk factors in the EPESE study. *Stroke* 37: 1368–1373.
Boshuizen, H. P. A. and H. G. Schmidt
   1992   On the role of biomedical knowledge by experts, intermediates and novices. *Cognitive Science* 16: 153–184.
Bosk, Charles
   1979   *Forgive and Remember: Managing Medical Failure.* Chicago: University of Chicago Press.
Bourdieu, Pierre
   1981   The specificity of the scientific field. In: Charles Lemert (ed.), *French Sociology*, 257–292. Cambridge: Cambridge University Press.
Burt, Ronald
   1992   *Structural Holes: The Social Structure of Competition.* Cambridge, MA: Harvard University Press.
Cicourel, Aaron V.
   1974   Interviewing and memory. In:Colin Cherry (ed.), *Aspects of Human Communication*, 51–82. Dordrecht: D. Reidel.
Cicourel, Aaron V.
   1982   Language and belief in a medical setting. In:H. Byrnes (ed.), *Contemporary Perceptions of Language: Interdisciplinary Dimensions*, 1–41. Georgetown: Georgetown University Press.

Cicourel, Aaron V.
  1992   The interpenetration of communicative contexts: Examples from medical encounters. In:Alessandro Duranti and Charles Goodwin (eds.), *Rethinking Context: Language as an Interactive Phenomenon*, 291–310. Cambridge: Cambridge University Press.
Cicourel, Aaron V.
  1995   Medical speech events as resources for inferring differences in expert-novice diagnostic reasoning. In:Uta. M. Quasthoff (ed.), *Aspects of Oral Communication*, 364–387. Berlin/New York: Walter De Gruyter.
Cicourel, Aaron V.
  2000   What counts as data for modeling medical diagnostic reasoning and bureaucratic information processing in the workplace. *Intellectica: Revue de l"Association pour la Recherche Cognitive* 30: 115–149.
Cicourel, Aaron V.
  2004   Cognitive overload and communication in two healthcare settings. *Communication and Medicine* 1(1): 35–43.
Cicourel, Aaron V.
  2006   Cognitive/affective processes, social interaction, and social structure as representational re-description: their contrastive bandwidths and spacio-temporal foci. Mind and Society 5: 39–70.
Cohen, I. Bernard
  2005   *The Triumph of Numbers: How Counting Shaped Modern Life*. New York: Norton.
Collins, Randall
  1980   *The Credential Society*. New York: Academic Press.
Coombs, Clyde
  1953   Theory and methods of social measurement. In:Leon Festinger and Daniel Katz (eds.), *Research Methods in the Behavioral Sciences*, 486–487. New York: Dryden.
Ellis, Richard H.
  1994   *The Case Books of Dr. John Snow*. London: Wellcome Institute for the History of Medicine.
Eng, P. M., E. B. Rimm, G. Fitzmaurice and I. Kawachi
  2002   Social ties and change in social ties in relation to subsequent total and cause-specific mortality and coronary heart disease incidence in men. *American Journal of Epidemiology* 155: 700–709.
Fauconnier, Gilles and Mark Turner
  2002   *The Way We Think: Conceptual Blending and the Mind's Hidden Complexities*. New York: Basic Books.
Fox, Renee C.
  1977   The medicalization and demedicalization of American society. *Daedulus* 106: 9–22.
Freidson, Eliot
  1970   *Profession of Medicine*. New York: Dodd-Mead.
Friedson, Eliot
  1975   *Doctoring Together: A Study of Professional Social Control*. New York: Elsevier.

Friedson, Eliot
    1988   *Profession of Medicine: A Study in the Sociology of Applied Knowledge.*
            (Republication of Friedson 1970.) Chicago: University of Chicago Press.
Goss, M. E. W.
    1961   Influence and authority among physicians in an outpatient clinic. *American
            Sociological Review* 26: 39–50.
Granovetter, Mark
    1973   The strength of weak ties. *American Journal of Sociology* 78: 1360–1380.
Groopman, Jerome
    2007   *How Doctors Think.* New York: Houghton Mifflin.
Harrah, David
    1973   The logic of questions and its relevance to instructional science. *Instruc-
            tional Science* 1: 447–467.
Hempel, Sandra
    2007   *The Strange Case of the Broad Street Pump.* Berkeley / Los Angeles: Uni-
            versity of California Press.
Johnson, Steven
    2007   *The Ghost Map: The Story of London's Most Terrifying Epidemic – and
            How it Changed the Modern World.* New York: Riverhead.
Kahneman, Daniel and D. T. Miller
    1986   Norm theory: Comparing reality to its alternatives. *Psychological Review*
            93: 136–153.
Kannel, William B. and Tavia Gordon (eds.)
    1968   *The Framingham Heart Study: An Epidemiologic Investigation of Cardio-
            vascular Disease.* Bethesda: National Heart, Lung and Blood Institute.
Kuipers, B. and Jerome P. Kassirer
    1984   Causal reasoning in medicine: Analysis of a Protocol. *Cognitive Science* 8:
            363–385.
Mechanic, David
    1978   *Medical Sociology.* New York: Free Press.
Mischler, Elliot G.
    1984   *The Discourse of Medicine: The Dialectics of Medical Interviews.* Nor-
            wood, N.J.: Ablex.
Newell, Allan and Herbert Simon
    1972   *Human Problem Solving.* Englewood Cliffs, N.J.: Prentice-Hall.
Parsons, Talcott
    1951   *The Social System.* New York: Free Press.
Peirce, Charles Sanders
    1960   *Pragmatics and Pragmatism.* Charles Hartshorne and Paul Weiss (eds.).
            Cambridge, MA: Harvard University Press.
Schluchter, Wolfgang
    1986   Modes of authority and democratic control. In:V. Meja, Nico Stehr &
            D. Thisgeld (eds.), *Modern German Sociology*, 291–323. New York: Col-
            umbia University Press.
Silverman, David
    1987   *Communication and Medical Practice: Social Relations in the Clinic.* Lon-
            don: Sage.

Starr, Paul
   1982   *The Social Transformation of American Medicine*. New York: Basic Books.
Styles, Margretta M.
   1982   *On Nursing: Toward a New Endowment.* St. Louis: Mosby.
Turner, Mark
   2006   *The Artful Mind: Cognitive Science and the Riddle of Human Creativity.* Oxford: Oxford University Press.
Tversky, Amos and Daniel Kahneman
   1981   The framing of decisions and the psychology of choice. *Science* 211: 453–58.
Waitzkin, Howard
   1991   *The Politics of Medical Encounters: How Patients and Doctors Deal with Social Problems*. New Haven: Yale University Press.
Weber, Max
   1968   *Economy and Society: An Outline of Interpretive Sociology.* Ed. by Guenther Roth and C. Wittich. New York: Bedminister.
Wohl, Anthony S.
   1983   *Endangered Lives: Public Health in Victorian Britain.* Cambridge, MA: Harvard University Press.

2. Applied linguistics in the legal arena

Roger W. Shuy

Abstract

Forensic linguistics is an integral part of applied linguistics. Those who do this work analyze statutes, legal procedures, courtroom language, and language used as evidence in criminal and civil court cases. One major difference from other types of applied linguistics is that there is no need to gather data because it is already provided. This means that the linguist has to work with data that already exists, using the major tools of linguistics, including phonetics, morphology, syntax, semantics, pragmatics, sociolinguistic variation, discourse analysis, language change, stylistics, lexicography, and graphemics. As in all applied linguistics, forensic linguists begin with the perspective of the legal context and audience and apply the appropriate linguistic tools to the legal issues. Linguists who testify at trials first have to meet certain legal standards in order to be accepted as experts. Throughout the process, the forensic linguist, like any applied linguist, has to teach lawyers, judges, and jurors the way linguistic analysis works in relation to the specific legal issues. The recent growth of forensic linguistics is a hopeful sign of the expansion of applied linguistics beyond its conventional focus on language learning, teaching and testing.

1. Background

One of the odd things about applied linguistics is that it took the field so long to discover that the legal arena is a fertile area in which to apply linguistic knowledge. Even though law is primarily about language, very little of the interaction between linguistics and law occurred until the past quarter century. Today, the interaction of linguistics and law, also known as forensic linguistics, is a flourishing and growing area of interest for both linguists and lawyers. A flurry of books and articles now represent the field, loosely held together by the International Association of Forensic Linguists and its journal, *The International Journal of Speech, Language and the Law*. Most contributions thus far have been from Europe and the United States, although interest in linguistics and law also is rising rapidly in the rest of the world, including Asia.

So why did it take so long for these two fields to begin to cross-pollinate? Both can share some of the blame but since lawyers were unaware of how linguists might offer help to them, most of the blame probably lies on the shoulders of linguists. Almost from the beginning, applied linguistics has placed its emphasis on educational issues, especially language learning, testing and teaching. Even today, these topics dominate applied linguistics conferences and journals. However, in addition to important issues in education, language is deeply involved in almost everything else in life, including such areas as law, medicine, advertising, politics, diplomacy, therapy, commerce, religion and bureaucracies. Linguists have held a rather myopic vision and they have not done a very good job of reaching out to these fields, offering our knowledge to them, or trying to see the world from the perspectives of other disciplines.

1.1.   What do forensic linguists do?

First it is useful to try to describe what is meant by *forensic linguistics*. As with most recently developed fields, it has been surprisingly difficult to define it narrowly. All practitioners seem to agree that it is an area of applied linguistics that works in the legal arena but there has been considerably less consistent agreement about what this work involves. From all appearances, practitioners seem to define it from their own perspective and their own involvement. For example, those who do authorship identification sometimes see the field as dealing with syntax, style, and lexicon, while those who analyze tape-recorded conversations think of forensic linguistics as a form of discourse analysis. Both are essentially right but the field is obviously larger than either of these areas. In fact, they embrace all of the tool areas of linguistics. Although forensic linguistics is still emerging, it would appear that on the basis of current work in this area, forensic linguistics uses these tools in five major areas. The following briefly describes these and cites some of the major book publications (not journal articles) in each.

1.1.1.   Analysis of statutes and legal procedures

One important focus is the effort to help the legal system from a more law-internal perspective. Those forensic linguists (some of whom are also lawyers and law professors with advanced degrees in linguistics) use their linguistic insights to describe the language issues of laws, statutes, and legal practice (Kurzon 1986; Levi and Walker 1990; Gibbons 1994, 2003; Tiersma 1999; Solan and Tiersma 2005; Heydon 2005; Schane 2006; Rock 2007). Considerable work also has been done in untangling legalese and clarifying such matters as jury instructions (Charrow and Charrow 1979).

1.1.2.   Analysis of courtroom language

Some forensic linguists analyze the written and spoken use of language by judges and lawyers in legal procedures (Solan 1993; Matoesian 1993, 2001; Philips 1998; Cotterill 2002; Heffer 2005). Others examine the cross-cultural issues involved in the legal process, especially those who speak languages other than the one used in the courtroom and including those whose cultural differences from the courts provide serious problems for them in legal procedures (O'Barr 1982; Conley and O'Barr 1990, 1998; Stygall 1994). In some cases, extensive linguistic analysis of individual trials is the focus, as in Matoesian's (2001) treatment of the William Kennedy Smith trial, Robin Lakoff's analysis of the Thomas/Hill hearings (2000), Cotterill's (2003) examination of the O. J. Simpson trial, and Coulthard and Johnson's (2007) treatment of the Harold Shipman trial.

1.1.3.   Analysis of written language evidence

Criminal cases in which the evidence is in the form of written threat messages, suicide notes, wills, or hate mail are probably the most common types of cases in which lawyers call on linguists for help (McMenamin 1993, 2002; Kniffka 1996; Olsson 2004). But written language evidence is also found in most civil cases, including those involving trademarks (Shuy 2002), product liability (Cushing 1994), and product liability hazard notices, contract disputes, discrimination, and deceptive trade practices (Shuy 2008).

1.1.4.   Analysis of spoken language evidence

It is common for linguists with strong backgrounds in phonetics to be asked to work on cases involving identification of speakers (Baldwin and French 1990; Hollien 1990, 2001; Rose 2002). Tape recordings of conversations, business meetings, police interviews, child sexual abuse interviews, and other speech events provide data in many criminal and civil cases (Shuy 1993, 1998b, 2005) in which the quality of such recording is not always the best, requiring linguistically trained ears and sophisticated listening equipment to produce jury-ready transcripts before providing other types of linguistic analysis. Cases in which more than one language is spoken require linguists who are experts in both languages (Berk-Seligson 1990). Linguists are also involved in analyzing the interviews of child victims of sexual abuse (Walker 1999), of sexual crime (Cotterill 2007), and police interviews where deception is suspected (Shuy 1998a; Galasinski 2000).

1.1.5.   Analysis of other areas

Much of the work done on the ambiguity and vagueness of laws, procedures, jury instructions and business contracts has an immediate relationship to other applied linguistics issues, such as the Plain English movement. Forensic linguists work with bureaucracies, such as the US Social Security Administration and Medicare, helping them send out clear and understandable documents to their beneficiaries (Shuy 1998a). Likewise, analysis of the language of television advertising (Geiss 1982) illustrates how forensic linguistics is applied to the Federal Trade Commission regulations and how language works in the media (Bell 1991). Much of forensic linguistics also has a direct relationship to determining fair and effective police interrogation techniques (Shuy 1998a; Heydon 2005; Rock 2007), in how to assess threat messages (Solan and Tiersma 2005; Kniffka 2007), and in ways of analyzing undercover police tape recordings (Shuy 1993; 2005).

2.   Forensic linguistics as applied linguistics

Now that forensic linguistics is coming into its own, it is timely to consider how working in this area is similar or different from other types of applied linguistics. On a broad scale, applied linguists address and try to help solve human problems, such as inequality, ignorance, and justice. Forensic linguists normally begin with language data, which is often difficult and time consuming to gather, then select the appropriate linguistic tools and apply what they know about linguistic theory, research and practice to those human problems. Finally, applied linguists communicate their findings to those in other fields in ways that they can understand and use. In these respects applied linguists and forensic linguists work in the same ways. The remainder of this section deals with the way forensic linguists have been working to accomplish these applied linguistics tasks in the context of the legal arena.

2.1.   Collecting data

In much of applied linguistics work, the linguist must first spend a great deal of time and effort collecting data appropriate to the applied task. In contrast, forensic linguists have most of the data gathered for them before they even begin their work. This is one major difference between forensic applied linguistics and virtually every other area of applied linguistics. The character of the language data used by forensic linguistics differs by types of cases.

2.1.1. Types of data in civil cases

In civil cases such as contract disputes, insurance policies, letters, memos, emails, articles, lectures, and speeches are provided as the evidence with which the linguist works. In trademark disputes, the names and slogans of the disputants are the primary data. In defamation cases, writings or speeches are where the work begins. In product liability cases, the data are usually the warning labels that linguists are called upon to analyze. In cases of deceptive trade practice, advertisements, letters and memos are the most common evidence.

2.1.2. Types of data in criminal cases

Criminal cases also provide linguists with the data to be analyzed. Undercover sting operations, fraudulent business practices, and sexual misconduct cases commonly provide tape-recorded conversations or email exchanges as the linguists' starting points. Cases of fraud and price fixing may offer both written and spoken data for analysis.

2.1.3. Advantages and disadvantages of these kinds of data

Unlike other applied linguistics research, the linguist is not responsible for assembling this written and spoken language database. The downside, of course, is that this evidence data is often not exactly what one would find ideal in a well-structured research project. However, in some cases it is possible to use electronic searches to augment the database with comparison evidence. For example, one can search electronic databases for trademark usage and advertisements to find data to compare with that in the trademark case at hand. One also can locate other documents that use the same or similar language, and one can even gather additional tape recordings or written texts of the client's language use to show that the patterns are the same or different. But even when the data corpus is extended, the forensic linguist is primarily bound to the language evidence in the law case and it cannot be ignored or changed.

This data limitation can prove troublesome, especially, for example, when linguists try to show similarities or differences in authorship identification cases. Many threat messages are very brief, yielding very few instances of language clues to an individual's style, gender, age, grammar, ethnicity, education, social status, or other background factors. This is one aspect that severely limits what the linguist can contribute at trial toward resolution of authorship controversies. On the other hand, such analysis can prove to be very useful to law enforcement in narrowing down lists of suspects. Although the linguistic analysis may not be adequate to prove guilt or innocence at trial, law enforcement officers sometimes have used it to narrow down suspect lists or to extract confessions from perpetrators.

In contrast, some cases may provide so much language data that the linguist can be overwhelmed with it. For example, in undercover sting operations, law enforcement agencies sometimes tape-record hundreds of hours of conversation between dozens of suspects, making the process of simply keeping track of themes and topics difficult to manage, especially within the narrow time limits of the case. In business fraud cases there may be thousands of pages of contracts, regulations, memos, deposition testimony, legal briefs, judicial rulings, and other documents to review and analyze. The linguist's task in such cases is to organize, select relevant passages, and assist the lawyers (and juries) to understand the data's trends and structure.

Whether the size of the database is small or large, linguists have to work with what the court cases give them and within the time limitations set by the court. With the exception of comparison corpus extension data that forensic linguists can sometimes gather, the evidence in the case normally dictates the universe of data to be used.

For researchers who have, in the past, spent months or even years gathering data in sociolinguistic and applied linguistic research projects, the fact that the data are handed them on a platter in law cases can come as something of a relief. One is not responsible for finding better evidence data. It is the *only* evidence and one has to make do with it. Based on that data one must always be vigilant to avoid making claims that this evidence does not substantiate.

3.   Marshalling linguistic theory, research and knowledge

As noted above, there are many types of law cases, each with their own particular language analysis needs. The competent linguist comes to each case with a full tool bag of analytical procedures. These tools include phonetics, phonology, morphology, syntax, semantics, pragmatics, speech acts, discourse analysis, sociolinguistics, lexicography, and knowledge of the processes of language change. And, in certain cases, the knowledge of languages other than English is required. First and foremost, forensic linguistics requires linguists to be trained and competent in all aspects of their field.

It is unwise, if not unethical, for linguists to agree to work on a case if they are deficient or weak in the tools needed to resolve it. Although linguists must be well trained in all of the above tools, one or more of them may be their linguistic specialization and this can help determine which cases they can feel comfortable enough to accept and which cases to leave for other experts. Phoneticians tend to specialize in speaker identification cases. Syntacticians and semanticists tend to take cases in which the structure and meaning of language is of foremost importance, such as trademark, contract, and defamation disputes. Discourse analysts tend to prefer cases in which the evidence consists of longer passages, such as conversations and longer written texts.

Some cases, such as speaker identification, call for knowledge and skills in of phonetics because it is often the sounds of language that can lead to matching individuals with talk. Other cases require application of knowledge of morphology and syntax, especially, for example, in contract disputes. Whatever the specialization preference, however, linguists inevitably call on virtually all the tools in their tool bag because, for example, doing syntax involves some phonology, doing semantics involves some syntax, and doing sociolinguistics involves most of these tools. Discourse analysis requires the most tools of all because the structure of discourse includes the sounds, grammar, and meanings found within it. In short, the applied linguist who works in the legal arena must know what the best-trained linguists know about their field.

4.   Applying linguistics to the human problems of law

The goal of applying linguistics to law may seem no different from the goal of applying linguistics to assist with human problems involved in the language education of children or in helping medical practitioners communicate effectively with their patients in order to achieve good health. But one difference is that educational and medical applications of linguistics deal with people who are at least somewhat motivated to learn in a context which often is not as immediately traumatic as the courtroom. The clients of forensic linguists are emotionally embroiled in intense legal battles with each other over issues of justice and fairness. Linguists cannot accomplish justice and fairness for law, of course, but they can aid in the legal process when the issues involve language.

4.1.   Matching cases with linguistic tools

In forensic linguistics work the law case itself is primary. In order to show the relevance of linguistic expertise to lawyers, linguists have to begin with lawyers where they are and to consider their perspectives on their types of law cases. This is similar to other types of applied linguistics, where it also is necessary to begin with the learners where they are. The following list shows some of the major types of law cases and the major linguistic tools that are commonly most relevant in them.

Case type (lawyer's perspective)	Tools (linguist's perspective)
Authorship identification	stylistics, syntax, discourse, lexicography, sociolinguistics
Speaker identification	phonetics, phonology, syntax, sociolinguistics
Trademark disputes	phonetics, phonology, semantics, syntax, lexicography
Product liability	syntax, semantics, discourse analysis
Discrimination	semantics, discourse analysis, sociolinguistics
Copyright infringement	syntax, semantics, discourse analysis
Child sexual abuse	phonetics, morphology, syntax, language acquisition, semantics
Adult sexual misconduct	semantics, syntax, sociolinguistics
Defamation	semantics, sociolinguistics, discourse analysis, syntax
Criminal offenses	all linguistic tools

The key for linguists is to start with the left column, where the lawyer is, and fig-ure out which linguistic tool can help that case most. Since many lawyers often do not know about the tools of linguists, we cannot expect them, for example, to seek out a semanticist simply because they have a product liability case. Their tendency is to flail about rather blindly for someone who can deal with the lan-guage in a case.

Obviously, there are likely to be additions and subtractions in each of the above listed tools, depending on the nature and data of each individual case. One point here, however, is to show that many tools can be relevant to each type of case and that the forensic linguist must be well versed and well prepared in all of them. The other point is that lawyers cannot be expected to know what these tools are or which linguistic tool can help them. Linguists have to begin with the lawyer's perspective of the problem, which is often the case type.

5.   Communicating linguistics to lawyers, judges and juries

A major problem in all types of applied linguistics is to communicate special-ized and technical knowledge to people who do not have such knowledge or, even worse, may even have false ideas that need to be overcome (Rieber and Stewart 1990). Forensic linguists are, therefore, teachers at virtually all levels of their work. First, they teach the lawyers with whom they work about the ways that linguistic analysis can help their cases. Eventually, they will also have to teach the opposing lawyers about their analysis. Next, they teach the Courts about what they plan to say at trial. Finally, they teach the jury about their find-ings in the case. These are equivalent to three different applied linguistics audi-ences, each with different beginning points and different expectations, moti-vations, and needs.

Intelligent lawyers learn new things in virtually every case they take on. They call on linguists because they think they might have something to tell them that will help them with their cases, making them highly motivated learners from the outset. As a result, teaching lawyers about language can be the easiest part of the forensic linguist's teaching task. But problems can arise when law-yers hold misguided or incomplete notions about linguistics that need to be cor-rected or amplified. However, there is a serious teaching complication since the experts not only teach linguistics to the lawyers they work with but at a later point they also have to teach the opposing lawyers, judges, and eventually the juries.

Lawyers talk about "preparing the witness" but in much of the work here it is actually the linguists who are preparing the lawyers. To be sure, lawyers pre-pare witnesses about court procedures and what is allowable and not allowable. Sometimes they also prepare the witnesses in strategies of testifying. But it is the linguist who prepares lawyers in the questions they can ask that will elicit the linguistic testimony clearly and appropriately. In many cases, linguists ac-tually write out the series of questions that lawyers can ask them in their direct examinations.

In most jurisdictions, linguistic experts in civil cases are first asked to write a report. In the USA there is an additional consideration, because the laws of dis-covery can require some experts, including linguists, to turn over all notes and drafts of their work to the opposing side if requested to do so. This severely handicaps the communication in writing between linguist and lawyer, especially when long distances are involved, because this communication has to be done by telephone or face-to-face in order to prevent the potential discovery of pre-liminary drafts. As in most research, the linguist may go down some blind alleys in the early stages, make errors of various types, misunderstand some of the facts of the case, and other matters. Revealing this to the other side can some-times be embarrassing at best.

In most law cases lawyers expect the scholars they call upon to be experts. This means that a forensic linguist normally needs to have obtained a doctor's degree in linguistics. In addition, lawyers expect their experts to have standing in their own fields. This means that other linguists also should be able to recognize a level of expertise that comes from their publishing academic articles and books. The reason that these standards are very high for a forensic linguist resides in the legal process itself. When lawyers request a linguist's services, they anticipate an eventual trial in which the expert is determined by the courts to be a highly qualified expert. Even though less qualified linguists might be able to come up with a useful linguistic analysis that would aid the lawyers, they may never be able to give testimony if they do not satisfy the requirement of being an expert.

Different jurisdictions within and across national boundaries have somewhat different standards that define what it means to be admissible as an expert. In the United Kingdom and many other countries, admissibility is rather loosely defined, with focus on the qualification of the experts themselves but not on the theory or methodologies they use. This was a little different in the USA where until 1993 the Frye test *(Frye v. United States)* was the standard measure of general acceptability. Like other countries, it required experts to be recognized in their fields but, in addition, *Frye* required evidence that the proposed testimony would be relevant to the issue in dispute and that the scientific theory or techniques proposed were accepted by the relevant scientific community (Solan and Tiersma 2005, 28–32). This general acceptability test was upgraded by a new standard set in 1993 *(Daubert v. Merrell Dow Pharmaceuticals, Inc.)*. This new reliability (rather than acceptability) assessment was soon adopted by all US federal court proceedings and by many state courts as well. *Daubert* contains four factors:

> Factor 1: Whether the theory or technique has been tested and therefore found to be sound.
> Factor 2: Whether it has been subjected to peer review and publication.
> Factor 3: Whether there is a high known or potential rate of error and whether there are standards controlling the technique's operation.
> Factor 4: Whether the theory or technique enjoys general acceptance within the relevant scientific community.

It is obvious, therefore, that in the USA at least, being considered an expert in forensic linguistics requires not only a PhD or equivalent and recognized stature in one's field, but also enough knowledge of the theory, research and techniques in that field to enable one to meet the recent *Daubert* standards. There is good reason to suspect that some version of this US standard eventually will be adopted by other countries and jurisdictions as well. Since the judge is the gatekeeper here, it is often necessary to teach the Court a great deal about linguistics.

Linguists have at least two opportunities to teach judges about what linguistics has to say in their cases. In US jurisdictions, lawyers with whom linguists work may first submit (written or oral) an offer of proof outlining the gist of the linguists' proposed contribution. If the forensic linguists have done a good job preparing the lawyers, the lawyers can describe the linguistic contributions accurately and effectively. Once this test is passed, the judge may get another opportunity to rule on the linguists' possible contributions during the *voir dire* (questioning) of the prospective expert witnesses at trial. This usually takes place after the lawyer who one works with has "qualified" the linguist first. This procedure brings out all the expert's academic and experiential good qualities and outlines which aspects of linguistics are relevant to the case. Then, the other side's lawyer gets a chance to *voir dire* the linguist, often trying to show that the linguist does not qualify as an expert, that linguistics is not a suitable discipline, and that whatever the linguist might have to say is not germane to the case at hand.

This experience is all for the judge's benefit, for it is the judge who must then make the decision about whether or not to permit the linguist's testimony at trial. Forensic linguists labor under a number of constraints that are uncommon in other types of applied linguistics work. They are challenged about their expertise, the relevance of their field, and what they are about to say in court. Even more difficult is that all of this happens in a very brief time with a limited opportunity to explain anything. Therefore, the linguist's preparation of the lawyer has to be concise and, as in all applied linguistics, suited to the judge's frame of reference. There is no margin for error but if the linguists are clearly experts in their field, this hurdle may be easy to overcome. Most witnesses have little trouble explaining the acceptability and status of linguistics in the academic community. The issue of relevance of linguistic analysis to the case can be troublesome, however. This must be thought out carefully in advance, with special care taken to show only the use of linguistics to the specific data. The possibility of being admitted to testify diminishes considerably if the linguist wanders outside the four corners of linguistic analysis. Judges' most common objections to proposed linguistic testimony are:

(1) that the testimony will go beyond the scope of linguistics;
(2) that the testimony will usurp the function of the jury;
(3) that the testimony is unnecessary because the proposed testimony could have just as easily been made by the lawyer.

Proper planning and teaching should enable the linguist to avoid the first objection and stay within the scope of linguistics. If the temptation is to delve even slightly into psychology or some other related area, it should be avoided.

The second objection is critical. There is often a temptation for the linguist to join with the lawyers that one works with but this should be avoided at all costs. Linguists should be objective and stay at arms length from advocacy at all times and never give the slightest hint of an opinion about guilt or innocence in criminal cases or about who is right or wrong in civil cases. Although linguists can aid greatly in the legal arena, the ultimate issues are always to be left to the jury or to the judge in the case of a bench trial.

The third objection can be the toughest to overcome. One of the paradoxes of applied linguistics in the legal context is that the linguist has to look like, to sound like, and to be an expert while, at the same time, communicating technical knowledge in ways that laypersons can understand. The requirement to simplify can easily backfire, making the expertise appear to be unneeded. Although in most cases the lawyer would never even have thought about what the linguist has to offer, when the analysis is explained in layperson's terms it can appear to be so obvious that the judge may say that the lawyers could have said it completely by themselves and without the assistance of a linguist.

Once linguists succeed in teaching applied linguistics to the lawyers they work with, to the opposing lawyer, and to the judge, the final task of teaching the jury begins. So far, there have been three different styles of teaching to three different audiences. Lawyers they work with are predisposed to learn and are highly motivated. The opposing lawyers are predisposed to not learn and are full of objections and challenges. The judges usually want to learn but are often unwilling to take the time to do it. They require crisp summaries and strong evidence in small packages.

Juries are usually willing to learn. In many cases they have been bored by the slow pace and predictability of the trial. Linguistics is something new to most of them. Most know little about it or have false conceptions of it. Teaching them is much like teaching an introductory linguistics course to undergraduates. One cannot take a lot of time teaching but if the examples speak to the jurors' own experiences and if technical terms are avoided (or at least are explained in ways jurors can understand), jurors can be very receptive students.

The linguist's common problem is trying to teach more than is required. There is only one opportunity – not like classroom teaching where there is always a second session or even a follow-up semester on the topic.

Teaching a jury is different from teaching a class because linguist expert witnesses are usually advised not to have notes with them on the witness stand. The reasoning comes from the fact that opposing lawyers have the right to inspect all notes that witnesses have with them and partly because witnesses are thought to be more competent without notes to guide their testimony.

Simple visual-aid charts usually help, largely because people remember what they see better than what they hear. For example, if the issue is one of comparing vowels or consonants, it can be instructive for juries to be shown a side view, cutaway drawing of the human head showing the oral and nasal cavities, along with the nose, mouth, tongue and upper teeth. Most have never seen such a chart, have never thought about how sounds are made, and are fascinated by it. By teaching such simple phonetics to the jury, linguists can make their points about differences between speakers in voice identification cases. In cases involving the analysis of conversations, linguists can use charts which can be used to show how their own transcripts of conversations are more accurate than those of the opposition.

Sometimes, the charts used to illustrate linguistic phenomena can be extremely simple. For example, in a case in which the prosecution claimed that a suspect said, "I would take a bribe, wouldn't you", the chart used by the linguist was no more than the words accompanied by marks to indicate 8 syllabic beats and a short pause. The tape was extremely hard to hear and it would have stretched the jury's believability to say simply that the government got it wrong. Instead, the linguist asked the jury to listen to two playings of the tape and to count "the beats and to notice where the slight pause comes." Two versions were charted for the jury, the prosecution's and the defense's, as follows.

First, the prosecution's version:

	I	would	take	a	bribe		would	n't	you?
Beat #	1	2	3	4	5		6	7	8
Pause						X			

Then, the defense's version:

	I	would	n't	take	a	bribe		would	you?
Beat #	1	2	3	4	5	6		7	8
Pause							X		

As with many difficult-to-hear tapes, contracted verb forms, like the "n't" in this case, are difficult to hear. But the jury did not need to be able to hear the words distinctly. All they had to do here was to find the place where the pause occurred. Once they heard that there were 6 beats before the final two syllables, they knew that the defense version was accurate and the prosecution's version had transported "wouldn't" from the front of the sentence to the end.

In undercover tape cases, charts are an efficient way to help the jury separate who said what to whom. Conventional transcription of speech takes the form of a play script, with speakers taking individual turns of talk. Placing the speech turns side by side separates different speakers more visually for jurors. The following is an example. A patient was trying to get her doctor to admit that he had sex with her during her recent visit to his office for an abortion. She begins by asking what she should tell her husband, who did not even know that she was pregnant:

Patient	Doctor
What do I say? What do I tell him?	
	Well, you might have miscarried you know.
What do you want me to tell him?	
	Well, just tell him that you started bleeding, you know.
He said I was talking to you yesterday.	
	You just tell him that you had a pain and that's why you were calling.
If he gets back to me, what do I do?	
	Okay, let me, I will call you back, okay?
What do you expect me to tell him?	
	You tell me.
When my husband leaves me, you will not be ready for me, is that right?	
	Why should I be?

At the time of the call, the doctor is busy with other patients and has no clue that the patient is tape-recording the call in the effort to elicit an apology from him for having sex with her and to get him to say that he will be her lover if she leaves her husband. There were five additional calls in which her strategy eventually backfired. The doctor had no idea what she was talking about and never offered a felicitous apology. He was acquitted at trial (Shuy 2005: 99–106).

Using charts during testimony also has the advantage of refreshing the linguist's memory when there are vast amounts of data to analyze in front of the jury. In criminal cases with many hours of tape-recorded conversation it is not easy to recall what was said by whom, to whom, and when. When the linguist and lawyer have prepared in advance of trial the sequence of questions with corresponding charts, this approach can be of great assistance to both.

6.   The future of applied linguistics in the legal arena

Predictions are always difficult to make, but it would appear that the application of linguistics in the field of law has a promising future. There are always lessons to be learned from past experience and the practice of forensic linguistics is no exception. First, like the field of linguistics on the whole, those who work in the area of language and law need to address and overcome the public's misperceptions about what linguistics is and what it can say. Secondly, like the more recently developed sub-field of sociolinguistics, forensic linguistics needs to continue to grow and mature. Third, like the sub-field of applied linguistics as it is currently practiced, forensic linguistics needs to identify more clearly the linguistic training that practitioners need to have in order for them to do this type of work.

A common lament among linguists of all types is that most non-linguists just do not have a clue about what the field of linguistics is. Are linguists the guardians of correct usage and grammar? Are they speakers of different languages? Are they analysts of the sounds, words, meaning, grammar, history, and discourse units of language, even in their native language? As all linguists know, being introduced as a "linguist" can be troublesome. In recent decades we do not seem to have seen much general improvement in this condition. Things are no different in the legal setting, where lawyers and judges, who themselves are experts at using language, often believe that they do not need help from anyone else about how it works in their law cases.

How can such misconceptions be overcome? Forensic linguistics has an advantage, perhaps, in that at least some of its leaders hold both linguistics and law degrees. This enables them to be considered "insiders" in the law field. They can speak the law's language, enabling them to be legitimized and heard. Meanwhile, forensic linguists without law degrees and status need to learn to frame their work using the perspective of lawyers and judges, starting with them where they are, not where linguists are, and carefully explaining technical terms and procedures in ways that are understandable.

It should also be mentioned that many in the media, like lawyers, also have misconceptions about language and linguistics, often reporting language errors as facts. The media that get it right (and there are some) need to be encouraged and the ones who produce linguistic nonsense should be responded to. But the temptation to remain above the fray, isolated in the ivory towers of academe, so common in the past, should be discouraged. Forensic linguistics attracts and invites media attention and the sooner linguists deal with it effectively, the quicker media accuracy will be likely to come.

Whatever misconceptions about the field of linguistics exist, they can be multiplied when it comes to forensic linguistics. Assisting lawyers defend clients who are tax frauds, murderers, or child abusers leads easily to the misperception that forensic linguists are mere "hired guns". Helping lawyers for one corporation extract money from another corporation can lead to the same accusation. This misconception about forensic linguistics grows naturally out of the adversarial nature of law. It is the work of defense attorneys, prosecutors, and lawyers on both sides of civil law cases to represent and advocate for their clients and positions. Forensic linguists are not advocates and they should never slip into such a role. They are outside, neutral analysts of the data in a given case. Their role is that alone. If their analysis helps the lawyers they work with, no matter which side, they are doing their jobs. If their analysis does not help these lawyers, there is little or no chance that they will be called to do anything more in that case. But even when this happens, most lawyers are grateful because the linguist has made an important contribution by showing the weaknesses of the lawyer's case. The best way to overcome this misconception of the role of the forensic linguist is for them to be totally neutral and objective at all times, both in any reports written and in any testimony given at trial. Unfortunately, such action will not be likely to remove the accusation of favoritism by opposing lawyers, but it is hoped that this situation will improve as the field grows and as the true role of linguistics expert becomes better recognized.

By academic standards, forensic linguistics is still in its infancy. Lessons can be learned from other recently developed specializations, such as sociolinguistics, in which some thirty years of development took place before comprehensive introductions to the field were ready to be written. It takes a field a while to figure out its own dimensions and proper scope.

One sign of a new field's maturation process is evident when introductory textbooks on that subject begin to appear. At the time of this writing, six introductions to forensic linguistics had been published (McMenamin 2002; Gibbons 2003; Olsson 2004; Turell 2005; Kniffka 2007; Coulthard and Johnson 2007). All are valuable in their own ways but they tend to focus on specific aspects of the field. It is only natural for writers of introductory texts to see the field from their own vantage points and activity. New fields need maturation time and it is very difficult to capture everything important in the early stages.

6.1.   Training programs

There appears to be considerable current discussion among practicing forensic linguists about how to go about training future forensic linguists to become competent in this field. Over past decades applied linguists have developed a spate of university training programs. Obviously this can be a good thing, since it is clearly useful for all linguists to know things about how linguistic theory and research can be applied to issues in education (where the majority of applied linguistics seems to take place). Whatever specialized or additional training is given to applied linguists, this should not be done in such a way that minimizes the basics of linguistic theory and research. Applied linguists are not (and should not be) marginal or second-class citizens. Some call it an even higher calling to know what all linguists know but, in addition, to be able to apply this to real-life problems and issues.

The development and growth of sociolinguistics, for example, has been a little different. Since the time it first began to emerge in university curricula in the 1960s, sociolinguistics has become an integral part of extant linguistics programs. In some cases, as at Georgetown, specialization in sociolinguistics was created within, and as an integral part of a linguistic department, but only with the assurance that the students also had a solid grounding in the major tools of linguistic theory and research. As William Labov argued from the onset, socio-linguistics is "real linguistics" that deals with actual language, using the theoretical knowledge of the field to do so.

So what does this signify for training in forensic linguistics? Some practitioners may argue that we need separate programs to train future forensic linguists. At the time of this writing, a few courses in forensic linguistics are offered at universities in the United Kingdom, Spain, and America and there are even a few (usually summer) programs in this field. But should these grow to become academic majors? One would hope not, for forensic linguistics is first and primarily linguistics and it would be disastrous to lose this mooring.

It may be sobering to realize that most of the senior forensic linguists in the world (see the books cited throughout this chapter) have never taken a single course in forensic linguistics. They are linguists who happen to use linguistics theory and research on the data and problems of law cases. Some of them teach individual forensic linguistics courses in which they show students how to do this but there appears to be no need to call it a separate field of study. To be sure, there are things to learn about how to write reports and testify in law cases but hardly enough to justify actually courses in these things. Books and articles are available to guide the learner. At any rate, working closely with an attorney usually provides much of the information and skills required to do this work.

7.   Conclusions

Since forensic linguistics began to arrive on the screen of applied linguistics, it has been developing at a rapid rate, dealing with linguistic aspects of statutory interpretation and legal procedures, courtroom language use, and the written and spoken language evidence of law cases. The relationship of language and law poses both some similar and some different issues for applied linguists. Sometimes the data are frustratingly sparse and sometimes overwhelmingly large, posing different challenges for the application of conventional linguistic tools. But one factor takes precedence: the forensic linguist must be, first of all, a well trained linguist who is able to preserve a neutral and objective stance in a field in which advocacy for one side or the other dominates the scene. Even the role, style, and content of teaching varies considerably with the "students" to be instructed (lawyers on opposite sides, judges, and juries). And many problems are yet to be resolved in forensic linguistic practice, primarily in the areas of public misperceptions, maturation, and ways to train future forensic linguists in this field.

References

Baldwin, John and Peter French
    1990   *Forensic Phonetics.* London: Pinter Press.
Bell, Allan
    1991   *The Language of News Media.* Oxford: Blackwell.
Berk-Seligson, Susan
    1990   *The Bilingual Courtroom: Court Interpreters in the Judicial Process.* Chicago: University of Chicago Press.
Charrow, Robert P. and Veda R. Charrow
    1979   Making legal language understandable: A psycholinguistic study of jury instructions. *Columbia Law Review* 79: 1306.
Conley, John and William O'Barr
    1990   *Rules Versus Relationships: The Ethnography of Legal Discourse.* Chicago: University of Chicago Press.
Conley, John and William O'Barr
    1998   *Just Words: Law, Language and Power.* Chicago: University of Chicago Press.
Cotterill, Janet (ed.)
    2002   *Language in the Legal Process.* Basingstoke: Palgrave Macmillan.
Cotterill, Janet (ed.)
    2003   *Language and Power in Court.* Basingstoke: Palgrave Macmillan.
Cotterill, Janet
    2007   *The Language of Sexual Crime.* Basingstoke: Palgrave Macmillan.
Cushing, Steven
    1994   *Fatal Words: Communication Clashes and Aircraft Crashes.* Chicago: University of Chicago Press.
Galasinski, Dariusz
    2000   *The Language of Deception.* Thousand Oaks, CA: Sage.
Geiss, Michael
    1982   *The Language of Television Advertising.* New York: Academic Press.
Gibbons, John (ed.)
    1994   *Language and the Law.* London: Longman.
Gibbons, John
    2003   *Forensic Linguistics: An Introduction to Language in the Justice System.* Oxford: Blackwell.
Heffer, Christopher
    2005   *The Language of Jury Trials.* Basingstoke: Palgrave Macmillan.
Hollien, Harry
    1990   *The Acoustics of Crime.* New York: Plenum.
Hollien, Harry
    2001   *Forensic Voice Identification.* New York: Academic Press.
Kniffka, Hannes (ed.)
    1996   *Recent Developments in Forensic Linguistics.* Frankfurt am Main: Peter Lang.
Kniffka, Hannes
    2007   *Working in Language and Law.* Basingstoke: Palgrave Macmillan.

Kurzon, Dennis
  1986   *It is Hereby Performed: Explorations in Legal Speech Acts.* Amsterdam: John Benjamins.
Lakoff, Robin.
  2000   *The Language War.* Berkeley: University of California Press.
Levi, Judith and Anne G. Walker (eds.)
  1990   *Language in the Judicial Process.* New York: Plenum.
Matoesian, Gregory
  1993   *Reproducing Rape: Domination through Talk in the Courtroom.* Chicago: University of Chicago Press.
Matoesian, Gregory
  2001   *Law and the Language of Identity: Discourse in the William Kennedy Smith Rape Trial.* Oxford: Oxford University Press.
McMenamin, Gerald
  1993   *Forensic Stylistics.* Amsterdam: Elsevier.
McMenamin, Gerald
  2002   *Forensic Linguistics: Advances in Forensic Stylistics.* Boca Raton: CRC Press.
O'Barr, William
  1982   *Linguistic Evidence: Language, Power and Strategy in the Courtroom.* New York: Academic Press.
Olsson, John
  2004   *Forensic Linguistics.* London: Continuum.
Philips, Susan U.
  1998   *Ideology in the Language of Judges.* New York: Oxford University Press.
Rieber, Robert and William A. Stewart (eds.)
  1990   *The Language Scientist as Expert in the Legal Setting: Issues in Forensic Linguistics.* New York: Annals of the New York Academy of Sciences.
Rock, Frances
  2007   *Communicating Rights: The Language of Arrest and Detention.* Basingstoke: Palgrave Macmillan.
Rose, Philip
  2002   *Forensic Speaker Identification.* London: Taylor and Francis.
Schane, Sanford
  2006   *Language and the Law.* London: Continuum.
Shuy, Roger W.
  1993   *Language Crimes: The Use and Abuse of Language in the Courtroom.* Oxford: Blackwell.
Shuy, Roger W.
  1998a   *The Language of Confession, Interrogation and Deception.* Thousand Oaks, CA: Sage.
Shuy, Roger W.
  1998b   *Bureaucratic Language in Government and Business.* Washington DC: Georgetown University Press.
Shuy, Roger W.
  2002   *Linguistics in Trademark Disputes.* Basingstoke: Palgrave Macmillan.

Shuy, Roger W.
   2005   *Creating Language Crimes: How Law Enforcement Uses (and Misuses) Language.* New York: Oxford University Press.
Shuy, Roger W.
   2006   *Linguistics in the Courtroom: A Practical Guide.* New York: Oxford University Press.
Shuy, Roger W.
   2008   *Fighting Over Words in Corporate Civil Cases.* New York: Oxford University Press.
Solan, Lawrence
   1993   *The Language of Judges.* Chicago: University of Chicago Press.
Solan, Lawrence and Peter Tiersma
   2005   *Speaking of Crime.* Chicago: University of Chicago Press.
Stygall, Gail
   1994   *Trial Language: Differential Discourse Processing and Discursive Information.* Amsterdam: John Benjamins.
Tiersma, Peter
   1999   *Legal Language.* Chicago: University of Chicago Press.
Turell, Teresa (ed.)
   2005   *Linguistica foresne, lengua y derecho: conceptos, metodos y aplicaciones.* Barcelona: Institut Universitari de Linguistica aplicada.
Walker, Anne G.
   1999   *Handbook on Questioning Children: A Linguistic Perspective.* Washington DC: ABA Center on Children and the Law.

3. Communication is not neutral: "Worldview" and the science of organizational communication

James R. Taylor

Abstract

This chapter is a chronicle of the efforts of the author to construct a theory of organization that would be based in the transactional dynamics of ordinary conversation and would support a relational view of identity. Choosing the relation as key premise, rather than the individual, the chapter argues, leads to a radically different view of organization from the widely accepted conventional image of organization. The chapter then contextualizes this approach in the historical development of the field known as organizational communication, a branch of communication studies dating from the 1960s. In the 1990s a shift of emphasis toward the examination of the role of discourse in the constitution of organization occurred. The work reported in this chapter represents a particular stream of research in that movement, one that emphasizes the role of applied linguistics in explaining organization. I describe the origins of one school in this trend, known as the "Montreal School", in my own initial exploration of the potential of linguistically based models of language, in particular that of "thematic relations", to explain transactions. From this analysis flows the concept of worldview, a consequence of the complementary character of communicative transactions. Worldview is seen as a property of relationship, not as a characteristic of individual or group ideology. The origins of worldview are further developed by an exploration of the seminal work of Algirdas Algirdas Greimas and John Austin on language as action. The implications for managerial practice are then briefly discussed.

1. Introduction: Bad management theory? (Or the wrong epistemology?)

Shortly before his death, Sumantra Ghoshal contributed an essay to the Academy of Management (*Journal of Learning and Education* 2005: 79) in which he wrote as follows: "Academic research related to the conduct of business and management has had some very significant and negative influences on the practice of management." The problem, according to Ghoshal, was as follows: taking the individual as the ultimate entity in a society. The cited phrase "individual as the ultimate entity in the society", he made clear, is taken verbatim, word for word, from the economist and neo-conservative icon Milton Friedman. "Why", Ghoshal went on to ask, "does the model of people as purely self-interested beings still so dominate management-related theories?" "The answer", he replied, "lies not in evidence but in ideology" (2005: 83). "Friedman's version of liberalism", he elaborated, "has indeed been colonizing all the management-related disciplines over the last half century" (2005: 84).

If we subscribe to Ghoshal's analysis (and even a cursory sampling of current management journals suggests he may not have been far off the mark) then we are obliged to come up with an alternative. If we are *not* to ground our research and practices on the assumption of the primacy of the individual as our unit of analysis, we need to specify what *other* basis is to be the preferred choice. In this chapter I will assume that the "ultimate entity in a society" (or an economy or an organization) is not the individual, but the situated *relationship* in which individuals are embedded and where they find an identity. This, I will argue, is a viable alternative to the Friedman choice. It is one that should have an immediate appeal to applied linguists, since its basis is in an investigation of the role of language in the construction of the organization and the relations that compose it, as I will try to show.

The study of circumstantially grounded relationships, and the role of language in constituting them, is precisely what defines the rapidly expanding discipline of organizational communication. I outline here some of the key assumptions that underpin current definitions of the field. I then point out some of the surprising and even disturbing consequences of adopting a perspective that is focused on relational bonds and not on "purely self-interested beings." The outcome of the shift is, however, not only richer conceptually but also offers the potential for a more realistic – and ultimately promising – understanding of the bases of organization.

2.   Organizational communication: A note on the history of the field

Organizational communication studies did not even exist as a formal discipline until the decade of the 1960s. When they began to flourish, as they then rapidly did, they borrowed the modes of practice current in mainstream social psychology and sociology at the time. The emphasis at the outset was on investigating such phenomena as the socialization of employees, supervisory practices, organizational "climate", and information flows. The focus stayed on the *individual*, much as Friedman advocated.

At the beginning of the 1980s, however, a "palace rebellion" of sorts occurred. The positivist models of research lifted from psychology and sociology had, after all, never been the *only* formative influence on the new field. Organizational communication, a uniquely U.S. field at the beginning, was also influenced by earlier American traditions of thought and inquiry, notably those of pragmatics (Charles Sanders Peirce, William James, John Dewey, Charles Horton Cooley, George Herbert Mead and others at the University of Chicago) and rhetoric (Kenneth Burke). Organizational communication thus grew up and was institutionalized as a field in the tradition of *speech* communication, not *mass* communication (unlike, for example, public relations studies).

In the decade of the 1960s, it will be recalled, pragmatism had enjoyed a revival. Schools of sociology, anthropology and analytic psychology were strongly rejecting the quantitatively driven social scientific approaches of a previous generation, and turning to an exploration of communicative practice. As is well known, Erving Goffman, Aaron Cicourel and others were focusing attention on the ordinary sensemaking practices of daily life, an approach generally subsumed under ethnomethodology. Harold Garfinkel, influenced by the phenomenological insights of Alfred Schutz and Edmund Husserl, emphasized the reflexive and indexical bases of social reality. In the same timeframe Peter Berger and Thomas Luckmann stressed the basis of social reality in sensemaking practices of ordinary people. Gregory Bateson and his disciples began to study the psychodynamics of family life, and the role of relationship abnormalities in mental illness. Claude Lévi-Strauss, Dell Hymes, John Gumperz, Joshua Fishman, Clifford Geertz and several others were pursuing an anthropology of communication, as exemplified in narrative and ceremony. William Labov, Rom Harré and Basil Bernstein recorded *in situ* language patterns in urban environments. Ray Birdwhistell, Edward Hall and Albert Scheflen developed an empirical study of non-verbal communication. Ludwig Wittgenstein had earlier turned attention to language-mediated activity as a form of life, based in a "language game". Speech act theory, although coming from a different tradition, developed this insight further, inspired by the reflections of John Austin, John Searle and Jürgen Habermas who all concentrated on language as action. Harvey Sacks, in collaboration with Emanuel Schegloff and Gail Jefferson, initiated the disciplined analysis of actual conversation (known as Conversation Analysis), discovering there its remarkable, but patterned complexity. European thinkers such as Hans-Georg Gadamer, Michel Foucault, Jacques Derrida, Roland Barthes and Pierre Bourdieu were becoming better known in North America: none of them positivistic in their modes of thinking. So when the young turks met in Alta, Utah, in 1981 to re-position their own field of organizational communication they had alternative models to draw on, both more interpretive and more critical than the mainstream researchers who had preceded them.

They also had two new heroes. The first was Karl Weick. Weick had published his revised version of the *Social Psychology of Organizing* only two years before Alta (he contributed a chapter to the group's 1983 manifesto, Linda

Putnam and Michael Pacanowsky's *Organizational Communication: An Interpretive Approach*). The other was Anthony Giddens, who would be a keynote speaker at the 1984 annual conference of the International Communication Association. Both left an indelible mark on the thinking of organizational communication scholars: Weick, through his concept of a world made sensible by its enacting; Giddens, by his refusal to take society as already pre-structured. Whatever "structure" means, Giddens argued, its origin cannot be found other than in the activities of ordinary actors, as they go about their daily business. Reflecting the influence of Garfinkel and Goffman, both Weick and Giddens, although coming from contrasting formations, psychology and sociology, were insistent on the reflexive, retrospective and recursive characteristics of sensemaking: the act and its meaning in a dialectic tension, linking the spaces of materiality and discourse through the medium of agency. Putnam in her contribution to the 1983 book (reprinted in Putnam and Krone [2006]) called this the "interpretive approach" and described the contrast with more conventional modes of inquiry as follows:

> Functionalists ... treat organizational charts as fixed, concrete structures ... Interpretivists ... view hierarchical structure as an outgrowth of sets of relationships that have real consequences on everyday interaction
> (Putnam and Krone 2006: 214).

The "interpretive turn" marked a significant transition in the development of the field, in that it introduced communication studies to ideas about the role of sensemaking and interpretation in organization. The shift of perspective was, however, more than conceptual. Privileging the interpretive activities that are operative in the construction of daily life meant opening the door to new methodologies, qualitative in kind. And it implied paying more attention to the role of language in the business of making sense. However, although the role of language in forming interpretations was recognized it was but little elaborated, empirically or theoretically. And there was still a tendency to revert to the individual as the default unit of analysis. To again cite Putnam in 1983 (reprinted in Putnam and Krone [2006: 214]), "Interpretivists ... treat society as constructed through the subjective experiences of its members".

Not surprisingly, even ten years later, Smith (1993) reported that she had found in her research an overwhelming tendency in organizational communication studies to treat organization as a container, and communication as what was contained (Taylor 1995; Putnam et al. 1996). Taking the individual as unit of analysis, as Friedman had assumed to be unproblematic, was still the mode. And how to link organization back to the self-organizing processes of communication intimated by Weick and Giddens remained as unclear as ever. It was hardly even recognized as an issue.

3.   Taking language as the building block: A new approach

Smith's (1993) report directly stimulated a sequence of articles and books originating in the communication program at the University of Montreal, beginning in 1995, focusing on the role of language. These form the background to the concepts developed in this chapter, which are grounded in the work of the so-called "Montreal school" (Taylor 1995; Taylor et al. 1996; Groleau and Taylor 1996; Taylor and Gurd 1996; Taylor and Lerner 1996; Cooren and Taylor 1997; Taylor and Cooren 1997; Taylor, Gurd and Bardini 1997; Cooren and Groleau 1999; Cooren and Taylor 1999; Robichaud, 1999; Taylor 1999; Cooren and Taylor 2000; Cooren 2000, 2010; Taylor 2000; Taylor and Van Every 2000, 2011).

The original stimulus for the approach I will be describing was based on a reading of the organizational implications of the generative-transformational grammar proposed by Noam Chomsky (1957, 1965). Chomsky, it will be recalled, had constructed his syntax using re-write rules that he hypothesized are what generate the syntactic structures that underlie ordinary sentences. The adaptation of this procedure proposed by James Taylor (1978), however, used a variation on this methodology proposed by Ray S. Jackendoff (1972). Jackendoff saw "thematic relations" as what constitutes the "deep structure" of a sentence. For example, the verb "buy" projects arguments that link an *agent* (the subject position in the sentence) via the verb to a *theme* (what is bought) and a *source* (from where it was bought), while optionally providing for a secondary theme (a *beneficiary,* for whom it was bought): "I found a great tie at Macy's for Dad."

You cannot, Jackendoff reasoned, buy without someone else selling, and vice versa. The verb "sell" thus links conceptually to another verb "buy," by an inversion. The "source" of the buying (Macy's, in my example) is now interpreted as the "agent" of the selling. The roles of seller and buyer complement each other – they make each of their activities meaningful by supplying a background for the figural preoccupation of the other.

To confirm his intuition that the basis of all organizing must be located in similar transactional exchanges, Taylor (1978) transcribed the conversations of subjects who were collaborating on an experimental task. From the resulting protocols of interaction he set out to trace the patterns of organizing that subjects exhibited in their interactive talk. Kenneth D. Mackenzie (1976, 1978) had earlier argued that the organizational charts which were then assumed to describe the command structure of an organization are in fact distortions of the real configuration of delegated roles and responsibilities that are actually operative in an organization. He, like Putnam, concluded that people who work together in practice spontaneously develop their own hierarchy, and for Mackenzie it was at best a distorted image of the official version. He therefore proposed to determine, empirically, through field research (observation and interview), the actual hierarchical pattern. Taylor's findings confirmed Mackenzie's self-organizing insight, using, however, conversational data as his source. He demonstrated that it was possible to identify, empirically, using conversation analysis, the emergence of roles, identities and distribution of authority – the relational patterns typical of organization, in other words.

It is important to understand the rationale for the spontaneous emergence of structure. First, tasks naturally concatenate to form means-end or head-complement chains. The lab technician produces the test results that the physician needs to perform a diagnosis or an operation. The film producer turns to a variety of sources (writers, camera operators, film laboratory technicians, actors, studio assistants) to get the film made. The surgeon needs an anesthetist and nurses. And so on. Second, the conversation of people in their roles itself generates as well as reflects a hierarchy or status ladder, as generations of research in CA have demonstrated. In practice, complementary roles emerge, it turns out, even where the role assignment has been deliberately left ambiguous (Linde 1988).

Jackendoff's grammar of thematic relations provides an insight into the syntactic/ semantic basis of such organizing. Jackendoff, in his analysis, distinguished between two primitive verbal attributions: CAUSE and CHANGE. Buying and selling, described above, illustrate the distinction. There is first a process of "change": an object undergoes a transfer of location from source to destination. Since the change is a material event involving transfer, it must be brought about by an actor. The act of transfer must then have been *caused* by agents, buyers and sellers. The "change" part has as its object something of value that is moving from one location to another. The "cause," however, has as *its* object not the thing itself, but the effecting of the *action* of changing location (and, by implication, ownership). A hierarchy of actions is therefore implied: CAUSE→CHANGE→OBJECT LOCATION. One level of agency is directed to the change itself, physically transferring the valued object from a source to a destination. A second, hierarchically superior level of agency is directed to motivating, directing and giving meaning to the change activity.

The two agencies may, of course, be embodied in a single person, and in conversational contexts they typically are. Communication, however, has as one of its enabling properties the splitting of agencies so that Agent 1 is then acting *for* Agent 2 (who thus becomes a *beneficiary*, to use a term for the logically indirect object preferred by M. A. K. Halliday [2002]). The physician *asks* the technician to do a test. The film producer *delegates* editing to an editor. The contractor *tells* the workers to lay the tile.

Jackendoff's formulation is sentence-oriented, and thus describes the two events, buying and selling, as separate, although complementary, *individual* acts. Communication ties those activities together, by making one actor an agent of the other, accomplished through a transfer of cause, from location *B* to location *A*. A relationship is established.

For Greimas (1987), the establishment of a CAUSE→CAUSE/CHANGE hierarchy of responsibility for an action defines the communication paradigm. He called the result a *schema of communication* or *structure of exchange*. He conceptualized the CAUSE→CAUSE/CHANGE delegation of responsibility as the transfer of a *modal* object, again utilizing a well established linguistic convention. (Austin [1962] used a different term, calling it the "perlocutionary effect" of a speech act). Greimas' proposal thus defined relationship as one action that is embedded within another: one that is communicative, in that it arises in a conversation (a *faire faire*, or a *cause to cause*); and one that is not (it is directed to an object of value: a *faire*, or a "doing"; a *cause to change*).

The ideas of both Jackendoff and Greimas, however, have this in common, that they imply a conjunction of actors, as in the case of buying and selling, since the change will not occur unless *both* parties are involved. It is this complementarity of role in the context of a communicative relationship that, as we shall see, defines worldview (Taylor and Cooven 2006).

In practice, Taylor (1978) found, this pattern of superimposing a cause agency on a change agency was reiterated in all of the conversations he recorded. It typically took the form of a question-answer sequence where one person raised the question of how to proceed, or suggested an action, and another took a decision. So, for example (Taylor, [1978: 243] translated from the original French), A says "Good, so what do we do now?" C follows up, "Uh, I guess we turn the answers in, right?" and L confirms "Yes, OK." Sequences such as this recurred in most groups: one person calls attention to the need for a standard procedure, a second person takes the lead in proposing a rule, and others nod assent. A pattern of precedence is established, from the bottom up.

In this process of deciding on what to do, repeated throughout the experiments, a hierarchy of CAUSE→CAUSE/CHANGE was in all cases established, equivalent to a bottom-up constitution of a circumstantial and tacit system of authority. Roles and responsibilities emerged. However, while each group evolved to its own preferred mode of problem-solving, with established procedures, roles and decision-making hierarchy, no two groups arrived at the *same* pattern. They each in effect internalized a script of their own making and, as they did so, organizing processes gradually dropped out of sight with the result that the efficiency of the group rapidly improved, to the point where in some groups no words needed to be exchanged at all. They just performed the task. This could also be interpreted, Taylor noted, as a finding that each group, taken as a unit, developed its own unique organization chart.

Taking the groups as a whole, however, there were evident disparities between their scripts. To project these results onto the larger sphere of a contemporary organization, with its many quasi-autonomous communities of practice, the need for a second-order *inter*-group organizing process to negotiate community-wide authority is evident – a "*meta*conversation" (Giroux and Taylor 1995;

Robichaud, Giroux and Taylor 2004). How this might be expected to unfold would remain for some time after 1978 an area of research yet to be addressed. It would, however, eventually become the topic of the sequence of articles mentioned earlier. It has subsequently developed into an area of intense concentration, engaging the field as a whole (Fairhurst and Putnam 1999; Miller 2002; Fairhurst and Putnam 2004; Putnam and Cooren 2004; Cooren, Taylor and Van Every 2006; Mumby 2007; Kuhn 2008; Nicotera 2008; Putnam and Nicotera 2009).

4.   Text versus conversation

It is one thing to study organizing processes in small groups. It is quite another to analyze the tangled webs of talk and text that are typical of any large contemporary organization. The essential difference is this. In conversational exchanges CAUSE and CHANGE are tightly coupled, both embodied by a person who is visibly talking and responding to you. In the larger arenas of the laminated layers of organizational discourse (Boden, 1994) CAUSE and CHANGE become uncoupled. It is different from when your boss addresses you in person than when you read on the bulletin board that "All employees are required to attend Friday's briefing, without fail." The change that is targeted, causing oneself to go to the meeting room, is the same. The cause/cause, however, is visibly located, in the first instance, in a live person who is speaking to you, here and now, face to face, with all that that implies in the immediate exercise of authority. In the blanket communiqué directed to "all employees" the agency embodying the cause/cause has seemingly vanished (Hodge and Kress 1993), skillfully disguised by the use of the passive voice ("are required"). As Cooren (2006) points out, the immediate agency of cause is materialized as a bulletin – a non-human medium.

The uncoupling of cause from its original source by its incorporation in an artifact defines what Paul Ricoeur (1991) called *distanciation* (Taylor et al. 1996). The written text carried by the bulletin board is *not* an "actor" because it is not human (Latour 1994). It is an "actant" (Greimas 1987). It nevertheless conveys, to use Greimas' term, an "anthropomorphic" intention to the reader – a CAUSE→CAUSE/CHANGE that can be understood as manifesting a motive that we would customarily take to be human.

Two immediate consequences of distanciation can be identified. As Robichaud, Giroux and Taylor (2004) observed, the organization literature manifests a schizophrenic tendency in this respect. On the one hand, it emphasizes the pluralistic character of organization: an array of individuals and groups loosely tied together by a more-or-less shared agenda but otherwise identifiable as a congeries of mixed and even contradictory purposes. On the other hand, we

freely attribute to organization intentions, emotions, attitudes and understandings that are the defining mark of an individual person. We all know perfectly
well that organizations are not human beings, and yet we treat them as if they
were – as if it were *they* who were making decisions, demanding, agreeing,
planning. Why do we do this? Clearly, the reason is because, to again refer to
Jackendoff, *changes must have causes*. So-called "primitive" societies, for
example, develop elaborate ceremonies, even to the point of a human sacrifice,
to mollify the gods, and thus, they hope, end a prolonged drought. Attributing
intention to organization is a modern instance of the same logic: lending to
every happening motives that account for what has just occurred. "Airbus is determined to regain market dominance", we say (or some such formulation), as if
Airbus were a person leaning back in his or her chair, somewhere in Toulouse,
issuing bulletins to calm the fears of the marketplace.

There is a second effect of distanciation, and it is also illustrated by the rain
dance. We freely attribute a malevolent intention to someone whose acts have
displeased us, even when it is unclear who is the source. It is the agency, we suspect (since it is not made explicit), that lies behind the outward sign of some
change. "The gods are angry." Except that in the circumstances of modernity the
veiled presence of an ulterior motive behind the sign is more usually given a
human face. Narrative enters. "What's the Friday meeting all about?" says one
employee to another, "What's going on?" "Hadn't you heard," replies the other,
"they hired a new district manager, and as usual with new people she thinks she
has to do the clean broom bit, and change everything." "Oh no," says a third,
"that's not what's happening; there's a power play involving the accounting department going on. They want to bring in a new system, and the development
people are not buying." "Whichever", says the first, "either way they win, we
lose."

The coffee machine magic is at work.

Before you know it, a story has crystallized, accurate or otherwise, that sets
the stage for the Friday event, unbeknownst to management, who are convinced
that they are the only ones who know the purpose of the meeting (they think
they are uniquely situated to speak for the organization). Imagine their surprise
at learning, if they ever do, that their briefing is given a totally different reading
than they had intended.

This is worldview at work.

5.   Worldview

The term "worldview" is borrowed from computer-based modeling of social
and economic activities. When programmers try to simulate a system of transactions, such as those of sales, they immediately confront the Jackendoff di-

lemma: there are *two* complementary perspectives on any bilateral transaction, so which do you privilege? Each partner to the transaction, seller and buyer, is embedded in their own socially defined space-time envelope. Each belongs to its own community of practice. Each has its own purposes, its own schedule and its own modes of sensemaking. Buying and selling are thus perceived by those involved through different lenses, coming from different experiential worlds. Simulators have to decide *whose* perspective – *which* social time and place – they are going to see the event from, that of the seller or that of the buyer.

Worldview is thus a *property of relationship*. There are *always*, and *only ever*, two worldviews exemplified *in any bilateral transaction*. The *relationship* establishes a distinction of worldview. To the extent that people enter into a transaction, they inherit a point of view that it, by definition, establishes. But of course, the converse is also true. As ethnomethodologists have consistently argued, it is the transaction that reflexively constitutes the roles of buyer and seller, and thus confers identity on the agents who embody those roles. There is thus an inherent tension in the enactment of organizational process. Communication is *not* neutral. True, *You* and *I* together compose a *we*: a fusion of two into one. But we err if we forget that every *we* is also decomposable into an *I* and a *you*. An organization is both a *we* and yet simultaneously a collection of *I*'s, *we*'s and *you*'s.

To imagine a whole organization as a configuring of harmonious complementary relationships, organized into neatly interlocking horizontal and vertical relationships, as management theory has sometimes done, is to subscribe to a dangerously mistaken view of human communication. Computer-based systems such as contemporary ERP's (Enterprise Resource Planning) are promoted on the same assumption. Not surprisingly, they frequently under-perform when measured against expectations (Beatty and Williams 2006; Taylor and Virgili 2008). What actually sustains the order of organization is (i) the link with the fictive person of the organization as a prime mover, and source of authority, and (ii) the development of grooves of routine. But beneath the tranquil surface of integration, the sharks of differentiation are at work – a relentless search for personal and group advantage, commonly masquerading as "turf wars".

It was Algirdas Greimas who furnished us with a model of communication that explicates best the principle of worldview. Like Jackendoff, Greimas saw communication as a recursive construction, composed of two kinds of act: CHANGE and CAUSE (*faire* and *faire faire*). Greimas, however, introduced a dimension that is lacking in Jackendoff: communication. The change of possession of an object from one location to another furnishes an *object of value* and a motive for communication (the object need not be material; it could, for example, be information). But the causing of it is itself an object, and the result of communication. "Bring the sample here, says the doctor", and if the sample is brought a material event – a *change* – has occurred, as the result of an assistant's action. But the material event has also been enfolded within a social event. There are now two causal agents, one to request, one to respond.

The communicative event involves a source and a destination, but that which is exchanged through communication is not information, or knowledge, but a *modal object*: an enabling of agency. That is why the attribution of anthropomorphic motives to the fictional entity we call an organization works. By creating the organization as a source of authority, employees thereby justify their own actions in carrying out its purposes. They are invested with an authority that originates in the intentions of their organization, and they thus acquire both prestige and enhanced power.

There is transmission from A to B, but what is transmitted is a motivation to act: a *cause* of action. That which is exchanged from source to agent, the "modal object," is a duty or obligation (*devoir*), a desire or motivation (*vouloir*), a knowledge or belief (*savoir*) and a know-how or the power to act (*pouvoir*). The communicative act, in other words, is enabling, in that it creates an agent (an actor), a motivation (located initially in the source and subsequently transferred to the destined agent), and a legitimacy on the part of the actual actor (because he, she or it is acting *for*, out of duty and/or conviction). Organization comes into existence. The transaction instantiates hierarchy, but it thereby also enables its agents.

There is, however, also a residual tension in all such transactions. The worldview principle guarantees that any transaction leads to *two* narrative trajectories, *two* potential accounts: one that of a subject; the other that of an anti-subject. The sensemaking, interpretive constitution of the organization ceases to be merely a neutral exercise in consensus building. There subsists a continuing struggle to institute the social order of the organization. The organization itself, because it is not really human (even when we treat it as if it were), cannot voice its own purposes. Someone must speak for it. What is now confirmed by an accumulation of empirical research is that, in any organization of even moderate complexity, many people make their voices heard, since each is persuaded that he or she, or their respective communities, are entitled to interpret the collective purpose. And since rarely do their perceptions align themselves easily, the determination of their organization's intention is contestatory.

Organizational communication research is no longer seen to be the study of how communication functions to transmit messages among members of the collectivity. It becomes, instead, a chronicle of how organizations, incorporating as they do multiple interests and ways of making sense, find (or fail to find) some kind of finality, establish a hierarchy of values and actors. The approach is *both* interpretive *and* critical in that it tries to understand how people live, and resolve (or fail to do so) their differences of worldview, and the divergences of power and legitimacy that result when they do so.

6.   Conclusion: Organizations on the edge of chaos?

Ghoshal's polemic, cited at the beginning, was motivated by his perception, as one of the world's outstanding specialists in the field, that the management of organizations is in crisis (his emphasis, it will be recalled, was on the "practices" of management). There is, indeed, more than a little evidence to suggest that organizations sometimes do become unmanageable: problems of governance, managerial malfeasance, instability at the top – all signs that management risks becoming alienated from its own domain of governance. What impressed me most, however, was that Ghoshal's response was not limited to a few nostrums intended to improve current managerial practices. Instead, he went back to first principles, to question the very foundation of management theory in its concentration on the individual.

I have argued here for a different starting point: the communicative transaction as the constitutive basis of organization. The consequences of such a shift, however, may seem to be more disturbing than comforting because, on close examination, every transaction carries with it the potential for misunderstanding, and conflict – an effect of worldview. The challenge of management is to accept the centrifugal pressure that arises from differentiation of knowledge bases, and the communities of sensemaking they support, and nevertheless find a principle of integration. Management deals not with ideal worlds, but possible ones.

In an earlier book (Taylor and Van Every 1993: 91) we cited Brunsson (1985: 4) as follows: "the main purpose and problem [of managers] are not to affect thinking and choice but to produce organized, co-ordinated actions". Rational decision-making, he observed, "is not after all the essence of good management" (1985: 3). Good management is "the ability to motivate people, to establish a good organizational climate, to create appropriate social networks, or to develop powerful organizational ideologies" (1985: 3).

Kauffman (1995) argues that all forms of organization, not just social, occur at a frontier between an excess of disorder – chaos – and an excess of order – immobility and stagnation. Because all transactionally-based communication is an encounter of worldviews it implies *differences*. Communication engenders *a*symmetric, complementary *relationships*. These are the real basis of organization. This means irreducibly contrasting – and often contradictory – perspectives and accounts. It means an unpredictable and always open-ended organizing process, in an effort to establish authority. The outcome of such a dynamic will be determined by how people, collectively, arrive at an account of their association – one that assures a measure of stability and continuity because it is sufficiently widely accepted. How that comes about, it seems to me, ought to be seen as a domain, not just of communication studies, but also of applied linguistics.

References

Austin, John. L.
1962   *How to Do Things with Words*. Oxford: Oxford University Press. Based on the William James Lectures at Harvard University [1955].
Beatty, R. C. and C. D. Williams
2006   ERP II: Best practices for successfully implementing an ERP upgrade. *Communications of the ACM* 49(3): 105–109.
Boden, Deirdre
1994   *The Business of Talk: Organizations in Action*. Cambridge: Polity Press.
Brunsson, Nils
1985   *The Irrational Organization: Irrationality as a Basis for Organizational Action and Change*. New York: Wiley.
Chomsky, Noam
1957   *Syntactic Structures*. The Hague: Mouton.
Chomsky, Noam
1965   *Aspects of the Theory of Syntax*. Cambridge, MA: MIT Press.
Cooren, François
2000   *The Organizing Property of Communication*. Amsterdam/ Philadelphia. John Benjamins.
Cooren, François
2006   The organizational world as a plenum of agencies. In: François Cooren, James R. Taylor and Elizabeth J. van Every (eds.), *Communication as Organizing: Empirical Explorations into the Dynamic of Text and Conversation*, 81–100. Mahwah, NJ: Lawrence Erlbaum Associates.
Cooren, François
2010   Action and Agency in Dialogue Amsterdam and Philadelphia. John Benjamins.
Cooren, François and James R. Taylor
1997   Organization as an effect of mediation: Redefining the link between organization and communication. *Communication Theory* 7: 219–259.
Cooren, Francois and James R. Taylor
1999   The procedural and rhetorical modes of the organizing dimension of communication: Discursive analysis of a Parliamentary Commission. *The Communication Re*view 3(1/2): 65–101.
Cooren, François and James R. Taylor
2000   Association and dissociation in an ecological controversy: The Great Whale case. In: Nancy W. Coppola and Bill Karis (eds.), *Technical Communication, Deliberative Rhetoric, and Environmental Discourse: Connections and Direction*, 171–190. Norwood, NJ: Ablex.
Cooren, François, James R. Taylor and Elizabeth J. Van Every (eds.)
2006   *Communication as Organizing: Empirical Explorations into the Dynamic of Text and Conversation*. Mahwah, NJ: Lawrence Erlbaum Associates.
Fairhurst, Gail T. and Linda L. Putnam
1999   Reflections on the organization-communication equivalence question: The contributions of James Taylor and his colleagues. *Communication Review* 3: 1–20.

Fairhurst, Gail T. and Linda L. Putnam
    2004   Organizations as discursive constructions. *Communication Theory* 14: 5–26.
Ghoshal, Sumantra
    2005   Bad management theories are destroying good management practices. *Academy of Management Learning and Education* 4(1): 75–91.
Giddens, Anthony
    1984   *The Constitution of Society: Outline of the Theory of Structuration.* Cambridge: Polity Press.
Giroux, Nicole and James R. Taylor
    1995   Le changement par la conversation stratégique. Colloque de l'AIMS. Paris.
Groleau, Carole and François Cooren
    1999   Understanding the distribution of enablements and constraints in computerized settings: A socio-semiotic analysis of interobjectivity. *Communication Review* 3(1/2): 125–164.
Groleau, Carole and James R. Taylor
    1996   Toward a subject-oriented worldview of information. *Canadian Journal of Communication* 21: 243–265.
Greimas, Algirdas Julien
    1987   *On Meaning: Selected Writings in Semiotic Theory.* P. Perron and F. H. Collins (trans.). Minneapolis: University of Minnesota Press.
Halliday, M. A. K.
    2002   *On Grammar.* London: Continuum.
Hodge, Robert and Gunther Kress
    1993   *Language as Ideology.* London: Routledge.
Jackendoff, Ray S.
    1972   *Semantic Interpretation in Generative Grammar.* Cambridge, MA: MIT Press.
Kauffman, Stuart
    1995   *At Home in the Universe: The Search for the Laws of Self-Organization and Complexity.* New York: Oxford University Press.
Kuhn, Timothy
    2008   A communicative theory of the firm. Talk presented to the international conference on "What is an organization: Materiality, agency and discourse," University of Montreal, May 21–22.
Latour, Bruno
    1994   On technical mediation – Philosophy, sociology, genealogy. *Common Knowledge* 3(2): 29–64.
Linde, Charlotte
    1988   Who's in charge here? Cooperative work and authority negotiation in police helicopter missions, 52–64. Proceedings of the Conference on Computer-Supported Cooperative Work, September 26–29, Portland, Oregon.
MacKenzie, Kenneth D.
    1976   *Theory of Group Structures.* New York: Gordon and Breach.
MacKenzie, Kenneth D.
    1978   *Organizational Structures.* Arlington Heights, IL: AHM Publishing.

Miller, Kathy
    2002   *Communication Theories: Perspectives, Processes and Contexts.* New York: McGraw-Hill.
Mumby, Dennis K.
    2007   Organizational communication. In: G. Ritzer (ed.), *The Encyclopedia of Sociology*, 3290–3299. New York: Blackwell.
Nicotera, Anne Maydan
    2008   Ontologizing organizational entities: Musings on communicative constitution. Talk presented to the international conference on "What is an organization: Materiality, agency and discourse", University of Montreal, May 21–22.
Putnam, Linda L.
    2006   The interpretive perspective: An alternative to functionalism. In: Linda L. Putnam and Kathy J. Krone (eds.), *Organizational Communication, Volume 1, Part 2*, 211–230. London/Thousand Oaks, CA: Sage.
Putnam, Linda L. and François Cooren
    2004   Alternative perspectives on the role of text and agency in constituting organizations. *Organization* 11: 323–333.
Putnam, Linda L. and Anne Maydan Nicotera (eds.)
    2009   *Building Theories of Organization: The Constitutive Role of Communication.* New York and London: Routledge.
Putnam, Linda L. and Michael E. Pacanowsky
    1983   *Organizational Communication: An Interpretive Approach.* Newbury Park, CA: Sage.
Putnam, Linda L., N. Phillips and P. Chapman
    1996   Metaphors of organization and communication. In: Stuart R. Clegg, Cynthia Hardy and Walter R. Nord (eds.), *Handbook of Organizational Studies*, 375–408. London: Sage.
Ricoeur, Paul
    1991   *From Text to Action: Essays in Hermeneutics, II*. Evanston IL: Northwestern University Press. First published Paris: Éditions du Seuil [1986].
Robichaud, Daniel
    1999   Interaction and textuality in organizing: Illustrations from a public discussion process. *Communication Review* 4: 103–124.
Robichaud, Daniel, Hélène Giroux and James R. Taylor
    2004   The meta-conversation: The recursive property of language as the key to organizing. *Academy of Management Review* 29(4): 1–18.
Smith, Ruth C.
    1993   Images of organization: Root-metaphors of the organization-communication relation. Paper presented to the annual conference of the International Communication Association, Washington, May.
Taylor, James R.
    1978   *A Method for the Recording of Data and Analysis of Structure in Task Groups*. Doctoral dissertation, Ann Arbor, Michigan: University Microfilms.
Taylor, James R. and Elizabeth J. Van Every
    1993   *The Vulnerable Fortress: Bureaucratic Organization and Management in the Information Age.* Toronto: University of Toronto Press.

Taylor, James R.
1995   Shifting from a heteronomous to an autonomous worldview of organiz-
        ational communication: Communication theory on the cusp. *Communi-
        cation Theory* 5(1): 1–35.
Taylor, James R., François Cooren, Nicole Giroux and Daniel Robichaud
1996   The communicational basis of organization: Between the conversation and
        the text. *Communication Theory* 6(1): 1–39.
Taylor, James R. and Geoffrey Gurd
1996   Contrasting perspectives on non-positivist communication research. In:
        Lee Thayer (ed.), *Organization <---> Communication: Emerging perspec-
        tives III*, 32–73. Norwood: NJ: Ablex.
Taylor, James R. and Loren Lerner
1996   Making sense of sensemaking: How managers construct their organization
        through their talk. *Studies in Culture, Organizations and Societies* 2:
        257–286.
Taylor, James R. and François Cooren
1997   What makes communication "organizational"? How the many voices of the
        organization become the *one* voice of *an* organization. *Journal of Prag-
        matics* 27: 409–438.
Taylor, James R., Geoffrey Gurd and Thierry Bardini
1997   The worldviews of cooperative work. In: G. Bowker, L. Gasser, S. L. Star
        and W. Turner (eds.), *Social Science Research, Technical Systems and Co-
        operative Work*, 379–413. Mahwah, NJ: Lawrence Erlbaum Associates.
Taylor, James R.
1999   What is "organizational communication"?: Communication as a dialogic of
        text and conversation. *The Communication Review* 3(1/2): 21–63.
Taylor, James R.
2000   What is an organization? *Electronic Journal of Communication / La Revue
        Électronique de Communication.* www.cios.org/www.ejc/v10n200.htm.
Taylor, James R. and Elizabeth J. Van Every
2000   *The Emergent Organization: Communication as its Site and Surface.*
        Mahway, NJ: Lawrence Erlbaum.
Taylor, James R. and Sandrine Virgili
2008   Why ERPs disappoint: The importance of getting the organizational text
        right. In: Bernard Grabot, Anne Mayère and Isabelle Bazzet (eds.), *A Socio-
        Technical Insight on ERP Systems and Organizational Change*, xx–xx.
        London: Springer Verlag.
Taylor, James R. and Elizabeth van Every
2011   The Situated Organization: Case Studies in the Pragmatics of Communi-
        cation Research. New York and London: Routledge.
Weick, Karl E.
1979   *The Social Psychology of Organizing.* Reading, MA: Random House.

Part III

4. Alignments and facework in paediatric visits: Toward a social choreography of multiparty talk

Karin Aronsson and Camilla Rindstedt

Abstract

This chapter concerns alignment and disalignments, focusing on paediatric visits, and the ways in which doctors, patients and parents overtly or covertly align with each other and the activities at hand. First, prior work in the area is reviewed, foregrounding detailed analyses of paediatric interactions. Second, social distance, which has been discussed as a background factor in work on facework is here discussed as an emergent phenomenon, negotiated in interaction. A model of social choreography is presented, where alignment is discussed with respect to the gradual emergence of social distance, upgradings, and resistance. Conversely, doctors recurrently exploit playful respectfulness, first naming, collaborative we-constructions, as well as other mitigations as ways of indexing increased alignment.

The multiparty paediatric visits constitute a rich arena for analyzing alignment in that parents' third party contributions recurrently disambiguate doctors' covert recommendations. Doctors and parents step by step covertly negotiate diagnostic matters as well as treatment recommendations through talk, pauses and other minute conversational resources. What is covert or overt is therefore to a large extent an accomplishment of interaction.

1. Introduction

This chapter concerns alignments and disalignments in paediatric settings, focusing on doctors, patients and parents, and the ways in which they can be seen to overtly or covertly align and re-align with each other and the activities at hand.

We begin with an excerpt from our most recent work (Rindstedt 2010), drawing on an ethnography of a child oncology unit, where it has been possible to follow individual children and parents in their encounters with a number of doctors, nurses and other staff members at the clinic during an extended period of time. All children are diagnosed with leukemia, and staff members outperform each other in making the hospital stay as child-friendly as possible; the atmosphere is warm and caring. In a number of ways, toys, games, colourful decorations, and child-adapted routines signal that the clinic is attending to the needs of children. There are both preschoolers and adolescents in the unit, and there are striking differences in the ways that adolescents participate in daily routines, compared to preschoolers. In Extract 1, we document the shape of greetings and problem presentation routines between doctors and an adolescent and her mother.

Extract 1

Katarina (17 years) is hospitalized in order to get chemotherapy. It is morning, and the physicians Dr Anna (A), Dr Cecilia (C) and a medical intern enter as part of the in-treatment medical round. The mother has spent the night at the hospital with Katarina.

1	Dr A	((knocks on Katarina's door at the ward))
2	Katarina	Come on in! ((sits up in bed, looks toward the door))
3	Dr A	He:llo.
4	Mother	Come on in!
5	Katarina	Hello.
6	M	Hello hello. (.) Shall I put- shall I put (.) ((the bed backrest))
7	Dr A	Yes hello.
8	M	=you up again?
9	Researcher	Hello.
10	Dr C	Hello hello.
11	Dr A	(.) So how are you?
12	Katarina	°Fine.°
13	Dr A	Goo:d.
14	Mother	A small thing here on here ((points to her own lip)) only on
15		the lip- there one of those ((points toward Katarina's lip))
16	Dr A	Should we turn on some light so that we can see?=
17	Mother	=That's all there is.
18	Katarina	It appeared yesterday.=
19	Mother	=It appeared yesterday. That is the only thing that is- has
20		changed since the last time.

The local etiquette of the oncology ward requires "the owner of the room" to show attention to the outsider who in turn should display respect. Katarina invites the doctor(s) to enter the room which can here be seen as a private setting (cf. Frake 1975). The room entering and greeting routine tends to occur as follows: (i) the doctor in charge knocks on the door; (ii) the patient acknowledges it by calling out, "come on in!", inviting him/her to enter; (iii) the doctor then greets the patient, and (iv) the patient then returns the greeting, followed by the doctors proceeding to ask questions about the patient's condition.

In this case, Dr. Anna asks a routine question about how Katarina is doing ("So how're you?", line 11), addressing her with a second person pronoun, "*du*", unambiguously selecting the girl patient (and not her mother or someone else) to answer the question. In contrast, our recent work on doctors and children (Rindstedt 2010) shows that doctors routinely address young patients and their parents in more ambiguous ways, e.g. "How are things?" (letting the child patients and their parents choose who is to respond, the child or the parent). In work on doctor-patient interactions, Díaz (2000) has shown that doctors' "how-are-you (HAY)-routines" are often ambiguous in that they can either be read as ritual questions (greetings) or as genuine questions about the patient's health. Our data show that the child oncology encounters with preschoolers often involve double ambiguities: both an ambiguity concerning *what* is said, and an ambiguity concerning *who* is addressed (child and/or parent).

In contrast, Katarina, who is in her late teens, takes charge of the situation from the very outset. She is the one who first answers the knock on the door, inviting the physicians to enter the room. She is also the first one to answer the question about how she is doing. Thereafter though, the mother also answers the question of how Katarina is doing; partly engaging in repair work on Katarina's part by telling the oncologist that a problem has indeed appeared since the last time they met, pointing toward Katarina's lip, indicating non-verbally that something about it is of medical concern. Katarina participates in this discussion and later on in the conversation (not shown) doctors, patient and parent jointly decide to put her on medication against herpes.

This case – involving an outspoken patient, engaging more or less on her own in dialogue with doctors without intermediaries – is quite different from the way that preschoolers and their parents engage with doctors. According to our child oncology data, such a multiparty routine generally takes quite a different shape if the patient is a younger child. The patient will then not be the one who invites the doctor to enter (a parent will do so), and the patient will generally not be the first one to return the doctor's greeting (a parent will). Moreover, one of the parents will be the first person to respond to the doctor's question about the patient's health status. In line with the predictions of Brown and Levinson's (1987) facework model, several factors will account for these patterns. For instance, young patients are more likely to speak to more familiar parties (parents) than less familiar parties (doctors) or to more familiar people in the clinic (nurses) rather than to less well-known members of the clinic (doctors).

Yet, even in the case of this outspoken and well-informed adolescent, there are asymmetries between the doctors and the patient. Katarina can only invite the doctors to enter her room; she cannot (except perhaps in exceptional cases) ask the doctors to leave. Moreover, she has acquired quite a lot of medical expertise, as is the case for most of the patients in our study. Yet, she naturally cannot match the expertise of the doctors, or of her mother, who is acutely alive to all minute changes in medication or medical regime. As can be seen, even in this case, mother and daughter do a bit of duetting, assisting each other in responding to the doctors.

2.   Relevant studies on alignment in multi-party healthcare encounters

In the following, we will discuss multiparty alignments and realignments. First, we will review some earlier work on paediatric interaction. Then we will present examples from our own work, showing ways in which multiparty paediatric encounters involve complex alignments and re-alignments.

Institutional discourse is rich in multiparty alignments in that such encounters often involve the presence of three or more participants. In clinical settings like paediatric visits, there are at least three parties, who may align with each other in various ways. In a classic paper, Georg Simmel (1902) discussed what constitutes a group, pointing out that any congregation of three or more persons constitutes a "group" in that the presence of three parties makes it possible to form alliances. As soon as three persons gather, two of them might align against the third one. In family therapy, a father may, for instance, position himself as something of a co-therapist, thereby aligning with the therapist (Aronsson and Cederborg 1994). In many ways, the micropolitics of much institutional talk is thus based on the presence of three participants, who position themselves either as allies (teams) or as opposing parties. Notably, two parties can cast a third party as a *bystander* (Aronsson 1991; Goffman 1981), which means that local alignments at times concern the design and re-design of participation frameworks.

2.1.   Footings and multiparty alignments

In a pioneer paper on paediatric discourse, Tannen and Wallat (1983) demonstrated that doctors delicately attune their language to different recipients. When interacting with a sick child, the doctors employed a style that had features of so called *motherese*, that is, a simplified register aimed at small children. In contrast, the doctors used a regular conversational style when interacting with the patient's parents. What is also quite striking in their data is how the doctors easily shifted between this informal intimate style and a more formal (institutional) reporting mode.

2.2.   Turn-taking and participation in paediatric encounters

The initial example documents an encounter in which an adolescent patient participates more or less seamlessly in the medical encounter. This example is somewhat extraordinary in that her mother does not appropriate her turns (but see lines 14–15 where she repairs her daughter's response). In contrast, a series of studies in paediatric settings have shown that parents tend to appropriate about every other turn allocated to the child. In his ethnography of paediatric interactions in Scotland and the US, Philip Strong (1979) identified various ways in which parents would position themselves as the children's spokesmen, and in which the patients, that is, the children, would become quite marginal parties in this multiparty setting. One of the first empirical studies to document such phenomena in sequential detail in an allergy clinic was Aronsson and Rundström (1988), who showed that on average, parents would appropriate 52% of all turns that doctors directed to a sick child (5–15 years of age). In a later study in the Netherlands, Tates and Meeuwesen (2000) showed that parents would appropriate 54% of all turns allocated to the child (4–12 years of age), and in a US study of who got to present the child's problem, Stivers (2001) showed that parents appropriated 41% of problem presentation turns allocated to their children. It can be noted that the figures are quite similar in the three studies undertaken in three different countries. In all these cases, the authors show that turn appropriations are linked to extended negotiations and various types of parent-child alignments: parents talk in order to back up children who are slow to respond or who offer answers that might be misleading or insufficient within a medical context. Similarly, parents and, at times, children recurrently engage in collaborative health accounts, filling in where the other party can be seen to miss some important aspect. Such parent-child collaborations seem rational in terms of the time rationality of medical encounters: the Dutch visits, on average, only lasted about 8 minutes, the Swedish about 20 minutes. Within such a restricted time period, parents may feel a strong urge to respond on their children's behalf in order to save precious doctor time for emergent questions or issues.

With regard to doctor-parent alignments, Aronsson and Rundström (1989) showed that Swedish doctors seem to create "think aloud" interactions, where they recurrently hint at various treatment recommendations (concerning delicate lifestyle issues), and where parents recurrently acknowledge and ratify these, and at times clarify and upgrade delicate implications. In detailed analyses of all phases of paediatric visits, Stivers (2007) has recently video-documented ways in which doctors and parents step by step covertly negotiate diagnostic matters as well as treatment negotiations through talk, gazes, pauses and minute conversational resources. Her work shows ways in which US doctors at first tend to deliver treatment recommendations in the form of relatively indirect constructions that gradually emerge across diagnostic trajectories and treatment plan trajectories, where there are series of pre-sequencing moves before the provisional diagnosis or treatment plan is spelled out. Her study documents that the doctors can be seen to orient to minute changes in parents' vocal and non-vocal stances, revealing a preference for patient elaborations of half-spoken recommendations. Such covert negotiations and doctor-parent alignments may have quite dramatic outcomes; Mangione-Smith and her collaborators (1999) have combined analyses of medical visits and interviews, suggesting that doctors tend to over-prescribe antibiotics in relation to their perceptions of the parents' covert demand for antibiotics. In fact, the doctors' perception of parental demands was a more important factor than the child's actual illness or other factors, and the chance of the child receiving antibiotics would increase dramatically (from 7% to 62%). Multiparty alignment phenomena are thus key elements of paediatric encounters.

In sum, the child's participation is intimately bound, not only to both his or her own initiatives, but also to doctor-parent and parent-child alignments that are partly shaped as the sequential outcomes of multiparty facework.

2.3.   Social choreography and positionings

Goffman's writing is replete with spatial metaphors for moving toward or away from someone in social space (Goffman 1955, 1979, 1981). In a series of ways, he has, for instance, analyzed how participants recurrently change their *positions* in conversations. In his early work, he discussed such changes in terms of the roles or *poses* that participants would choose. In his later writing, he discussed related phenomena in terms of position-*ings*, foregrounding the dynamic aspects of taking or shifting a position, the very activity of aligning with others or with specific stances toward something. Lately, Marjorie and Charles Goodwin (Goodwin 2006; Goodwin and Goodwin 1992) have discussed alignments in relation to inclusion and exclusion phenomena in social life.

We would argue that it is often difficult to identify "alignment", but that it is more feasible to identify *changes* in the direction of alignments or disalignments (Aronsson 1998), for instance shifts to address terms or formats that can be heard as more affiliative than candidate forms. Such changes may, at times, involve changes in *footings*, e.g. moving between serious and non-serious stances or positionings (Goffman 1979). When a doctor in a paediatric interview speaks in a jokingly stern way, he may still be able to get his serious message across, e.g. both to, for instance, an asthmatic child who is prescribed more exercise and to the child's over-protective mother (Aronsson 1991). Thereby, the doctor may align with the child *off-record* (Brown and Levinson 1987) without threatening the parent's face.

In a series of papers on social interaction in clinical settings, we have shown how multiparty talk often involves what we have called a *social choreography* of interaction (Aronsson 1998; Aronsson and Rundström 1989; Aronsson and Sätterlund-Larsson 1987). In these studies, we refer to how participants successively position themselves in novel ways as an outcome of talk-in-interaction. Choreographic analysis involves a perspective on talk, a choice of research strategy, rather than one restricted theory. Related empirical work has, for instance, concerned alignments and participation (Goffman 1981; Goodwin and Goodwin 1992), the step-wise delivery of bad news (Maynard 2003), and resistance (Heritage and Sefi 1992; Hutchby 2002; Stivers 2007). In a choreographic analysis of social space, we will focus on the ways in which participants move in interactional space: agreeing or disagreeing, aligning or disaligning, moving toward greater or lesser directness, to more mitigating or more aggravating moves, and between greater or lesser social distance. Such an analysis of positionings and moves in social space involves (i) a focus on directionality rather than preformed structures, and on (ii) theorizing in terms of continua rather than rigid dichotomies (Figure 1).

lesser social distance <————————————> greater social distance
downgradings <————————————> upgradings
non-resistance <————————————> resistance

Figure 1. Continua within a social choreography of discourse

The following analyses will focus on various types of sequential moves whereby doctors and patients might align and disalign: more specifically cases where doctors as well as patients and their parents can be seen to regulate social distance through various interactional resources such as first-naming, intimate forms of address (Swedish: *du*-pronouns), and collaborative we-pronouns. Moreover, the analyses will focus on downgradings and upgradings of doctors' recommendations in the multiparty setting of doctor-parent-child interaction. Lastly, the analyses will concern minimal acknowledgments and other ways of patients resisting doctors' treatment recommendations. What is important is that all positionings will be analyzed as interactional accomplishments, rather than as fixed structures (see also, Aronsson 1998; Maynard 2003; Stivers 2007).

3.   Data

This presentation primarily builds on sets of data where we have combined a systematic use of recorded data (video recordings and audio recordings) with field observations, including post-consultation interviews. A first set of data includes recordings of 20 first time visits by adult patients at a hospital unit of internal medicine (referred to below as "Internal Medicine Data"), and post-consultation interviews with both doctors and patients. A second data set in-

cludes audio recordings of 32 paediatric consultations, involving children between 5 and 17 years of age and their parents, and post-consultation interviews
with parents and children (Paediatric Visit Data). Moreover, the introduction includes data from an ongoing study involving one year's video ethnography at a
paediatric oncology unit (Rindstedt 2010).

4.   Alignments and social distance

Institutional encounters may vary between formal bureaucratic and informal
chatting or affiliative formats. Accordingly, participants may move in the direction of greater or lesser distance during a single conversation. In what follows, we
discuss doctors' deployment of playful respectfulness, first naming, collaborative
we-constructions and other types of pronoun choice in relation to doctor-patient
alignments in multiparty contexts. Institutional encounters, such as paediatric
consultations, involve parts that are at times affiliative (e.g. the physical examination which tends to be quite playful, particularly in the case of younger children –
cf. Aronsson and Rundström 1989; Stivers 2007; Tannen and Wallat 1983).This
in turn means that social distance may vary across phases of the encounter and
types of addressee. For instance, the motherese register tends to invoke other
types of alignments and distance than the bureaucratic medical register.

4.1.   Playful respectfulness in clinical settings

In Swedish paediatric visits, it can be noted that doctors (but not patients) at
times employ playful forms of respectfulness. For instance, the doctors jokingly
address the child patients with "sir" (Swedish *min herre*) or "little lady" (Swedish *lilla damen*), thereby downplaying the asymmetry or social distance of the
encounter (see also Aronsson and Rundström [1989]; or for US examples of
such address forms, see Stivers [2001], for instance, on "madam" as an address
form to an adolescent).

   Address terms, honorifics and other indices of respect are imbued with varying degrees of social distance, along a formal-informal continuum that may signal respect and/or different degrees of familiarity (Brown and Gilman 1989).
The French distinction between informal/familiar address (*tu*) and formal or
more distanced address forms (*vous*) is often seen as prototypical for what is
often referred to as the *tu-vous* distinction. Yet, languages differentiate between
formal and informal terms for address and reference in many subtle ways, including not only pronouns, but through honorifics (e.g. "sir", "madam") and
through choice of official or less official names (e.g. nicknames). Such choices
are related to familiarity and social distance, but also to affective distance
(Brown and Gilman 1989). In studies of facework and politeness (Brown and

Levinson 1987), social distance has traditionally been seen as a background variable that predicts degree of clarity in meaning. In contrast, the present choreographic analyses will focus on social distance as an outcome or accomplishment of social interaction.

4.2.   *Tu/Vous*-address forms and first naming in clinical settings

The institutional regulation of social distance can be seen quite neatly in the address patterns of medical visits. Drawing on American doctor-patient encounters, West (1984) has shown that doctors, but not patients, employ informal first-naming. Thereby, the doctors can be seen to align with patients, decreasing the asymmetry of doctor-patient talk (where patients, other things being equal, can be seen to be less powerful than doctors). In contrast, patients normally uphold social distance (respect) by employing formal types of address (family name or "doctor + family name"). The Swedish language provides yet another interactional resource for indexing social distance in that it offers a choice between a so called informal *tu*-form (Swedish: *du*) and a formal *vous*-form (*ni*). In Swedish internal medicine consultations, it can be seen that the doctors choose a more informal type of address than patients in that they generally used the intimate pronominal *tu*-form (85 % of all consultations), almost three times as often as patients who merely addressed doctors in this more intimate way in a minority of all consultations. Moreover, adult patients mostly chose to avoid pronominal address forms altogether (this was, in fact, their most common strategy in our data), thereby avoiding addressing the doctor in ways that could be seen as overly intimate or overly formal. As in the U.S. findings of West (1984), the Swedish data involve asymmetrical forms of address, where the less powerful party (the patient) recurrently can be seen to uphold this distance, whereas the more powerful party (the doctor) tends to reduce it. Again, it can be seen how patients can create social distance, whereas doctors can work toward alignments and greater proximity.

In doctor-patient data from Spain (Díaz 2000), it can similarly be seen that doctor-patient encounters involve asymmetries in two ways: first the doctor (but not the patient) makes polite inquiries about how the other party is. Second, the doctor uses more or less affiliative constructions such as first naming or endearment terms (e.g. "How are you Amelia? I saw you before out there. How are we, my child?"; Spanish: "*¿Qué tal Amelia? Ya la ha visto antes por ahí fuera¿Cómo estamos, hija?*"). A doctor may thus address his middle age patient as "my child" ("*hija*"; literally "daughter") in a type of friendly alignment. In contrast, the patients involved would address him as "doctor", positioning themselves as respectful patients.

With respect to alignment, it can be noted that doctor-patient talk is asymmetrical in terms of first-naming patterns. The doctors employ first names, whereas the reverse is not the case (cf West 1984; Aronsson and Sätterlund-Larsson 1987). In fact, doctors' first namings hardly ever involved the children's parents, but it was quite a common resource for greeting the child patients and for summoning their attention at strategic points. This is particularly the case when the doctors wished to formulate general health questions to the children or during the physical examination (for similar observations concerning US physicians, see Stivers [2007]). In multiparty paediatric encounters, first naming is apparently an important resource for addressing the child patients and securing their attention in a selective fashion.

In various ways, the child's and parent's voices are intertwined (see also Aronsson and Rundström 1988, 1989; Stivers 2001, 2007). Doctors routinely start to discuss health issues with the child, but parents then take over in different ways. In these cases, the doctor at times in turn selects the child as the next speaker, calling out his/her first name. Such first name summons can be seen to involve doctor-child re-alignments in that the doctor selects the child rather than the parent as the next speaker.

Extract 2
Paediatric Visit Data. Participants: Doctor, Victor (7 years) and his mother

```
1   Dr   →   Well, Victor. You've^du turned eight years old right?
2   C        [No:xx
3   M        [No: not yet
4   Dr       Not yet. No
5   M        Ninth Ju- ninth of July
6   Dr       Ninth of July. that's it well right uhm that's it i- you've^du started
7            school haven't you^du
8   C        Mhm:
9   M        Yea:h
```

→: arrow indicates address form

du: "you" as a second singular personal pronoun (familiar form)

Here, the doctor addresses Victor during the history taking phase. Victor's birth date is, of course, written down in the medical record, and the doctor asks about it not as a point of information, but as a way of aligning with the child, securing his attention and some kind of minimal rapport. Stivers (2007: 24–30) presents a related example of doctors' ways of first-naming children, as a way of summoning them for participation in history taking or in the physical examination. In Díaz's terminology, the doctor's question about Victor's birthday (line 1) is a ceremonial question, rather than a request for information. What can also be noted is that Victor's mother intervenes almost right away. She answers on her son's behalf, supplying his correct birth date (line 6). Then she goes on and rat-ifies her son's response about having started to go to school. Already, during the very first minutes of the paediatric visit, some parents answer on behalf of their children. Thereby, they can be seen to engage in distinct types of alignment work. On the one hand, they can be seen to align with their children (answering as a team as it were). Yet, on the other, they can simultaneously be seen to partly prevent the doctor from aligning with the child in that s/he does not get the chance of an uninterrupted dialogue with the patient. Yet, in both cases, parent interventions can be explained as rational moves in terms of economy of time of medical encounters.

4.3.   The collaborative we-form

A common interactional resource in medical talk is the collaborative we-form (cf. Brown and Levinson [1987] on orientations to recipients' positive face), i.e., the rhetorical use of "we"-forms in cases where the speaker is implicitly in-voking group alliances. In our data, it was found that doctors employed such forms of implicit alignments in about two thirds of all medical interviews. Thus, the doctor could be seen to project alignment on the part of the patient. At times, such an embedded form of address even caused some confusion on the part of the patient. In our paediatric data, collaborative we-form recommendations are, at times, associated with a lack of uptake on the part of the patient, as can be seen in the following extract.

Extract 3
Paediatric Visit Data. Participants: Dr; Dorotea, 6 years, and her mother.

1	Dr	→	Now *we're asking* you if *we may move* you a little
2	C		((does not move))
3	M		You may move yourself a little
			(Swedish: *får du flytta på dej lite*))
4	D1		My little miss. I think-
			((Swedish: *fröken lilla, jag tror-*))
5	C		((does not move))
6	M		Get moving! ((in Swedish: *flytta på dej*[DU]))
7	Dr	→	I think *we might* do- (.) that we place you here.
8	M		You can sit here

→ and italics: collaborative we-construction

In this episode, the doctor has not yet summoned Dorotea through first naming. In any case, she apparently does not see herself as someone implied through his "if *we may* move you a little" (lines 1–2). We do not know whether she has not heard him or whether she expects him to do the moving or whether she may even be resistant to moving. In any case, she does not move. The mother (M) then aligns with the doctor in his attempts to make the girl move, disambiguating his collaborative we-form, addressing her daughter with a second person reflexive construction (*dej*; derived from *du*), hearably pointing out that it is Dorotea, and no one else, who has to do the moving (line 3). At this point, the doctor employs a playfully formal address form (*fröken lilla* 'my little miss'). Yet, this is of no avail. The girl still does not move. Ultimately, the doctor and the mother align in placing Dorotea next to her mother, which, in fact, means that the collaborative plural could perhaps literally be read in terms of a doctor-parent alignment. But it can be noted that the mother reverts to "you", not "we".

In their work on problem presentations in US paediatric data, Clemente, Lee and Heritage (2008:1423), documented another type of collaborative we-construction. In one case, where a doctor addressed a boy and his mother, he, in fact, asked the two of them "Okay, I guess the purpose of *our visit* is to address the headaches. Is that – is that correct?" (italics added). Thereby, he can be seen to align with the two of them, foregrounding the interactional nature of a paediatric visit, presenting himself as someone who is in fact part of a collaborative patient-doctor "we".

The collaborative we-form is inherently collusive in that collaboration is taken for granted, whether we inspect parent-patient or doctor-patient talk. What is notable is that even preschool children at play do exploit this collusive feature of doctor-patient talk. When preschool and young school age peer dyads engaged in play, negotiating with a protesting child patient (played by the researcher), there was a significant difference between how children played at being the doctor and how they played the parent role (Aronsson and Thorell 2002). When playing doctor, the children employed the collusive we-form three times more often than if they played the sick child's parent. Apparently, the somewhat subversive we-form is seen as an intrinsic part of a doctor's voice.

5.   Mitigations, upgradings, and doctor-parent alignments

In the facework model of Brown and Levinson (1987), collaborative we-constructions constitute one of many resources for mitigating potentially face-threatening moves such as criticism or intrusive interrogations. Paediatric encounters, at times, involve a delicate interface between family privacy on the one hand, and institutional information requirements, on the other. For instance, children's asthma and allergic conditions invoke a series of lifestyle issues related to family hygiene (in the case of eczema or mite allergy), eating habits (food allergies), household cleaning routines, and the very presence – and survival – of family pets (in the case of allergy to furry animals). In many of these cases, doctors have to pose quite intrusive questions and, at times, they have to make prescriptions that put various inconvenient demands on family life. Such discussion can therefore become quite delicate. Also, they involve a type of dilemma in that doctors need to make unambiguous medical prescriptions, yet without trying to interfere or take over parental responsibilities (Aronsson and Rundström 1989). Doctors handle such delicate issues in various ways, negotiating with parents and patients in an intricate fashion.

During the physical examination of medical encounters, doctors recurrently offer what has been called *online commentaries* (Heritage and Stivers 1999). Thereby the patient, including patients' spokesmen, such as parents are implicitly invited to take part in the doctors' thinking. Such online commentaries are also very common in our Swedish medical data, e.g. in doctors' "think-aloud" interaction with patients (Aronsson and Sätterlund-Larsson 1987). During the physical examination and the prescription phase in our paediatric data, the parents recurrently produced sentence completions of doctors' recommendations, partial repeats, and emphatic acknowledgment tokens, signalling that they were listening to or aligning with the doctors' think-aloud contributions.

5.1.   Parents aligning with doctors, upgrading their recommendations

Moreover, the parents, at times, spelt out or ratified the doctors' treatment plans, disambiguating their recommendations, and, occasionally, they would even upgrade doctors' recommendations. Thereby, they could be seen to align with the doctors, positioning themselves as doctors' allies (e.g. Extract 4).

Extract 4
Paediatric Interview Data. Participants: doctor; patient, Max, 15 years, and his mother

1	Dr		No:, yes I know. How about your fitness then ((laughs))
2	C		((Laughs))
3	Dr		Are you in good shape or bad shape? Do you do any sports
4			in your spare time?
5	C		No:
6	Dr		You don't. Do you cycle?
7	C		Yes
8	M	→	Keep fit activities would be a good thing.
9	Dr		Yes ((laughing))

→: Arrow indicates parent's upgradings of doctor's recommendations (Extracts 4–8).

It can be seen that the doctor formulates a series of questions about this boy's physical fitness (lines 1, 3–4 and 6). His questions seem to have an underlying agenda, dealing with the boy's present lack of physical exercise. Yet, he does not directly spell out any recommendations. In contrast, the mother assumes the role of the one who spells out prescriptions, reading his thoughts (line 8). In any case, the multiparty format of the paediatric visit allows for a third party disambiguation of what has been said in a more covert way.

Parents in the Swedish paediatric encounters recurrently upgraded doctors' covert or half-spoken recommendations in the direction of greater clarity and aggravations (Aronsson and Rundström 1988). In doing so, they could be seen to live up to the norms of "ideal parents" (cf. Strong 1979). Parent-doctor alignments that involve aggravations can, at times, be seen as parent-child disalignments in that they put harsher demands on the child. This is what can be expected in terms of Brown and Levinson's (1987) reasoning on family life, where they refer to family life settings as arenas that will be rich in aggravated talk.

One way for doctors to handle the delicate issue of family life intrusion is to talk to the parent through the child as it were. A doctor may address a sick child in more direct ways than s/he may talk to the child's parents. What the doctor then undertakes is to talk in a playfully "stern" or joking way to the child, dealing with potentially intrusive demands without overtly speaking to the parent. Thereby the doctor exploits the ambiguity of veiled address for talking about sensitive family matters. What may seem as off-record criticism in the terminology of Brown and Levinson (1987) thus becomes a matter of sequential negotiation.

This analysis of doctors' indirect criticism of parents may seem somewhat speculative. However, the parents themselves recurrently seem to endorse such an interpretation in that they do respond to the doctor's recommendations to the children as if they were actually directed to the parents themselves. This occurs even in cases when the doctor hearably selects the child as next speaker, as when s/he employs the Swedish singular pronominal *du*-form (you) as in the following cases (Examples 4–8).

Extract 5
Paediatric Interview Data. Participants: Doctor; patient, Ernst, 12 years, and his mother.

1	Dr		So before you go there you*du* have to cut your fingernails
2			((rescheduled visit to specialist))
3	M	→	[That's what he must do
4	C		[that's what I must do

Extract 6
Paediatric Interview Data. Participants: Doctor; patient, Herbert, 13 years, and his father.

1	Dr		And you^{du} don't start smoking or anything crazy like that!
2	C		No.
3	Dr		No.
4	F	→	No, that's silly

Extract 7
Paediatric Interview Data. Participants: Doctor; patient, Max, 15 years, and his mother.

1	Dr		We:ell ((laughingly)) so smoking isn't exactly great,
2			you^{du} know that, don't youf?
3	C		Mhm, yes
4	Dr		You've heard it a few times.
5	M	→	Exactly downright crazy.

It can be noted that the parents routinely positioned themselves as the doctors' allies or team members. In these positions they ratified, clarified and amplified the doctors' instructions in such a way that there was not much remaining ambiguity or vagueness. As can be seen, the above three cases all involve increased clarity as a consequence of parent intervention. In the first case, Ernst's mother engages in clarifications in that she ratifies the doctor's recommendation (Extract 5). In the second and third cases, the parents both ratify and clarify or upgrade the doctor's recommendations (as in Extract 6 "no, that's silly", and in Extract 7; "exactly downright crazy"). The doctors' polite indirect requests are thus recast into unambiguous demands or into negative assessments. In all three cases, it can be seen that the parent, and not the child, responds to what the doctor says to the target patient.

Why do parents appropriate turns that doctors have allocated to the child? An obvious interpretation is, of course, that they feel that the doctor is, in fact, addressing them, the parents, and not only the child. By addressing the child in a playfully stern way, the doctor can, on an underlying level, tell the parents what they should do in order to improve their child's health. At the same time, the doctor succeeds in conveying this information without being imposing or overly intrusive. The parent could have chosen not to "understand" the message. Yet, in all the three extracts the parents apparently understand that something is at stake for the caretakers, and not only for the child. In line with the so called *proof procedure* of conversation analysis (Sacks, Schegloff and Jefferson 1974), they prove this interpretation by actually acting as if the doctors had indeed addressed them and not only the child.

Extract 8
Paediatric Interview Data. Participants: Doctor; patient Victor, 7 years, and his mother.

1	Dr		You^{du} do avoid them ((to Victor about furry animals))
2	C		Yes
3	Dr		So you^{du} are- uhm are not one of those who always have to
4			stroke every dog
5	C		No:
6	Dr		Well, that's good
7	C		Some of them- some of them [I can stroke
8	Dr		[↑ WHAT
9	C		Some of them- some of them I can stroke
10	Dr		Well, but that's [really not so smart ((in a restrained voice))
11	M	→	[You shouldn't do that you know
12	C		No
13	M	→	You SHOULD NOT do that

Victor is allergic to furry animals. Yet, he reveals (line 7) that he, at times, might stroke some dogs. The doctor responds with genuine surprise and, in what Brown and Levinson (1987) would call an indirect and mitigated recommendation, he tells him that that's really not so smart (line 10). At this point, Victor's mother intervenes and upgrades it in the direction of greater clarity in contrast to the doctor's mitigated recommendation. However, her son's uptake is a minimal one ("no"). In any case, she evidently thinks that she needs to upgrade the doctor's recommendation even more, repeating her admonition, without any kind of mitigation (dropping her aligning tag, "you know") and partly raising her voice into something that approaches shouting ("you SHOULD NOT do that"). Her recycled admonition is thus not only unmitigated, but also somewhat aggravated.

In line with what would be expected in terms of facework phenomena (Brown and Levinson 1987; Goffman 1955), the mother comes out as more outspoken than the less familiar doctor when addressing the child, spelling out his recommendations bold on record. Yet, what is not discussed in detail by Brown and Levinson is the sequential development of clarity (but see Aronsson and Rundström 1988, 1989; Aronsson and Sätterlund-Larsson 1987; Clemente, Lee and Heritage 2008; Díaz 2000; Stivers 2001, 2007). The present movements from covert to overt talk were generally achieved as the result of step by step multiparty upgradings.

6.   Resistance and disalignments

6.1.   Dispreference for open disagreement

What can research on multiparty paediatric talk tell us about the choreography of alignments and disalignments? In medical contexts, resistance often involves non-compliance with respect to medication or other prescriptions, e.g. life style advice (e.g. non-smoking regimes). Research on compliance shows that many patients do not follow medical prescriptions (Davies 1966; Ley 1982). Yet, neither child patients nor parents tend to verbalize open disagreement (Korsch and Negrete 1972; Stivers 2007; Strong 1979).

Stivers' (2007) analyses of paediatric visits richly illustrate the ways in which doctors delicately attune to patients' resistance, even when it is presented in the format of pauses, delays, hesitancies, and other more or less covert indices of resistance. In our Swedish data, there was similarly a dispreference for open disagreement. Yet it is clear that both doctors and patients recurrently engaged in various forms of covert disagreements. When carefully listening to the recordings, we found that non-compliant patients did express their disagreements, but in more or less indirect ways, drawing on a series of discursive resources: minimal feedback, *sotto voce*, low volume, pauses, outdrawn responses and other prosodic devices (Aronsson and Sätterlund-Larsson 1987:16).

6.2.   Minimal acknowledgments as indices of non-compliance

In line with prior observations on verbal disagreements (e.g. Strong 1979), the parents rarely voiced their disalignment or resistance in words. Instead, resistance was often marked through minimal responses. We can, for instance, see how a mother offered minimal responses in a case where she later (in post-consultation interview) divulged that she strongly disapproved of the doctor's "silly" recommendations of more physical exercise (football) for her son.

Extract 9
Paediatric Visit Data. Participants: doctor; Valentin, 11 years, and his mother.

```
1   Dr      Well, then you can get in touch with the football team
2           and we'll see how things go ((to the child)) the
3           important matter is [also ((to M))
4   M                           [Yes ((laughing voice))
5   Dr      What is important that that he should also warm up before
6           playing football [properly (xx)
7   M    →                   [mhm
8   C                        [mhm
9   Dr      He must not just inhale his spray and get going
```

10	M		No: no:
11	Dr		Instead he should take his sprays and then he could start
12			warming up and he will have to do a warming up programme of
13			his own before the others
14	M	→	Mhm. Yes
15	Dr		And I would like to say. One does not need to play outside right.
16			One can play full back. And possible even be a goalkeeper. Right
17	C		Mhm ((with enthusiasm))
18	M		There you are then ((laughingly))

→: indicates minimal acknowledgment

When the doctor recommends football, the parent responds with a series of non-committal "mhm" (e.g. lines 7 and 14). Such minimal responses are ambiguous in that they can either index agreement or merely that someone is listening. In many ways, the doctor's treatment recommendation (more exercise) was a disappointment to this mother who had hoped for a medical solution to her son's asthma. Yet, she never really voiced her misgivings openly during the consultation. As can be seen, her responses are designed in such a way that she neither commits herself, nor agrees to allow the boy to engage in football practice. During the post-consultation research interview, she told the interviewer that the doctor's recommendation was "silly". In this specific case, the doctor did not orient to the patient's silent opposition. On other occasions, though, the doctors routinely oriented to related series of minimal responses (cf. Aronsson and Sätterlund-Larsson 1987).

On the level of spoken consultation uptake this mother did not protest and did not really make any overt commitments about the doctor's treatment suggestions. Yet, her laughter (line 18) and happy voice (line 4) seem to index agreement with the doctor's recommendations. Another interpretation, though, is that she is merely indexing alignment as a listener, indicating that she is listening to the doctor and that he may continue talking (cf. Aronsson and Sätterlund-Larsson 1987). Thereby, she can simultaneously be seen to align with her son, who is responding with enthusiasm, endorsing the doctor's recommendation. In any case, she later revealed that there would be no football, as that would be too strenuous for her son.

7.   Concluding note on alignments and social choreography

Paediatric visits are multiparty events that involve various alignments and re-alignments between doctors and patients, and between doctors and parents. In this chapter, we have shown ways in which institutional conversations between professionals and clients involve shifts between alignment and disalignment. Medical professionals routinely exploit playful respectfulness, first person address forms, collaborative we-constructions, as well as pronoun shifts, or shift of address forms as ways of indexing increased or decreased alignment. Yet such shifts largely involve indirect moves.

Indirectness works in two ways. First, alignments and social distance are indexed through various indirect conversational resources. Second, participation frameworks are designed in indirect ways; it is often ambiguous who is addressed or who is not. In many ways, alignments and disalignments in institutional talk draw on various transformations of participation frameworks (Goffman 1981), where third parties are, for instance, transformed into addressees or, conversely, where participants are transformed into bystanders. It can be seen that such transformations involve a social choreography of covert and cautious moves. Covert disagreements about diagnoses or treatment plans are sequentially negotiated and some parents at times act as the amplifiers of doctors' veiled messaged to child patients. This means that social distance can be seen as a product of sequential multiparty negotiations, rather than as a background variable.

Appendix

Transcription symbols are mainly based on notations in conversation analysis (see also Stivers 2007).

[	Square bracket marks the onset of overlapping speech
Bold	Pronunciation differs from surrounding speech e.g. irony, theatrical
CAPITALS	Mark speech that is obviously louder than surrounding speech
° °	Quieter speech than surrounding talk
(.)	Micro pause
((Text))	Transcriber's comments
:	Prolongation of preceding vowel
< >	Slower talk
=	Immediate "latching" of successive talk
–	Utterance interrupted or ebbed away
(x)	Inaudible word
hehe	laughter

References

Aronsson, Karin
  1991   Facework and control in multiparty talk: A paediatric case study. In: Ivana
          Marková and Klaus Foppa (eds.), *Asymmetries in Dialogue,* 49–74. New
          York: Harvester.
Aronsson, Karin
  1998   Identity-in-interaction and social choreography. *Research on Language and
          Social Interaction* 31: 74–89.
Aronsson, Karin and Ann-Christin Cederborg
  1994   Conarration and voice in family therapy: Voicing, devoicing, and orches-
          tration. *Text* 14: 344–370.
Aronsson, Karin and Bengt Rundström
  1988   Child discourse and parental control in paediatric consultations. *Text* 8:
          159–189.
Aronsson, Karin and Bengt Rundström
  1989   Cats, dogs, and sweets in the clinical negotiation of reality: On politeness
          and coherence in pediatric discourse. *Language in Society* 18: 483–504.
Aronsson, Karin and Ullabeth Sätterlund-Larsson
  1987   Politeness strategies and doctor-patient communication: On the social chor-
          eography of collaborative thinking. *Journal of Language and Social Psy-
          chology* 6: 1–27.
Aronsson, Karin and Mia Thorell
  2002   Voice and collusion in adult-child talk: Toward an architecture of intersub-
          jectivity. In: Shoshana Blum-Kulka and Catherine E. Snow (eds.), *Talking
          to Adults: The Contribution of Multiparty Discourse to Language Acquisi-
          tion,* 277–293. Mahwah, New Jersey: Lawrence Erlbaum.
Brown, Roger and Albert Gilman
  1989   Politeness theory and Shakespeare's four major tragedies. *Language in So-
          ciety* 18: 159–212.
Brown, Penelope and Stephen C. Levinson
  1987   *Politeness: Some Universals in Language Usage.* Cambridge: Cambridge
          University Press.
Clemente, Ignasi, Seung-Hee Lee and John Heritage
  2008   Children in chronic pain: Promoting paediatric patients' symptom accounts
          in tertiary care. *Social Science & Medicine* 66: 1418–1428.
Davis, Milton
  1966   Variations in patients' compliance with doctors' orders. *Journal of Medical
          Education* 41: 1037–48.
Díaz, Félix
  2000   The social organization of chemotherapy treatment consultations. *Sociol-
          ogy of Health and Illness* 22: 364–389.
Frake, Charles O.
  1975   How to enter a Yakan house. In: Mary Sanches and Ben G. Blount (eds.),
          Sociocultural Dimensions of Language Use, 24–40. New York: Academic
          Press.
Goffman, Erving
  1955   On face work. *Psychiatry* 18: 213–231.

Goffman, Erving
    1979   Footing. *Semiotica* 25: 1–29.
Goffman, Erving
    1981   *Forms of Talk.* Oxford: Basil Blackwell.
Goodwin, Marjorie Harness
    2006   *The Hidden Life of Girls: Games of Stance, Status, and Exclusion.* Oxford: Blackwell.
Goodwin, Charles and Marjorie Harness Goodwin
    1992   Assessments and the construction of context. In: Alessandro Duranti and Charles Goodwin (eds.), *Rethinking Context: Language as an Interactive Phenomenon*, 147–189. Cambridge: Cambridge University Press.
Heritage, John and Sue Sefi
    1992   Dilemmas of advice: Aspects of the delivery and reception of advice in interactions between health visitors and first-time mothers. In: Paul Drew and John Heritage (eds.), *Talk at Work: Interaction in Institutional Settings*, 359–417. Cambridge: Cambridge University Press.
Heritage, John and Tanya Stivers
    1999   Online commentary in acute medical visits: A method of shaping patient expectations. *Social Science and Medicine* 49: 1501–1517.
Hutchby, Ian
    2002   Resisting the incitement to talk in child counselling: Aspects of the utterance "I don't know". *Discourse Studies* 4: 147–168.
Korsch, Barbara M. and Vida F. Negrete
    1972   Doctor-patient communication. *Scientific American* 227: 67–74.
Ley, Philip
    1982   Satisfaction, compliance and communication. *British Journal of Clinical Psychology* 21: 241–54.
Mangione-Smith, Rita, Elizabeth A. McGlynn, Marc N. Elliott, Paul Krogstad and Robert H. Brook
    1999   The relationship between perceived parental expectations and pediatrician antimicrobial prescribing behavior. *Pediatrics* 103: 711–718.
Maynard, Douglas W.
    2003   *Bad News, Good News: Conversational Order in Everyday Talk and Clinical Settings.* Chicago: The University of Chicago Press.
Rindstedt, Camilla
    2010   Conversational openings and multiparty disambiguations in doctors' encounters with young patients (and their parents). Manuscript.
Sacks, Harvey, Emanuel Schegloff and Gail Jefferson
    1974   A Simplest systematics for the organization of turn-taking for conversation. *Language* 50: 696–735
Simmel, Georg
    1902   The number of members as determining the sociological form of the group. *The American Journal of Sociology* 8: 1–46, 158–196.
Stivers, Tanya
    2001   Negotiating who presents the problem: Next speaker selection in paediatric encounters. *Journal of Communication* 51: 1–31.

Stivers, Tanya
    2007   *Prescribing under Pressure: Parent-Physician Conversations and Antibiotics*. Oxford: Oxford University Press.
Strong, Philip M.
    1979   *The Ceremonial Order of the Clinic: Parents, Doctors and Medical Bureaucracies*. London: Routledge and Kegan Paul.
Tannen, Deborah and Cynthia Wallat
    1983   Doctor/mother/child communication. Linguistic analysis of paediatric interaction. In: Sue Fisher and Alexandra Dundas Todd (eds.), *The Social Organization of Doctor-Patient Communication*, 203–219. Washington, D.C.: Centre for Applied Linguistics.
Tates, Kiek and Ludwien Meeuwesen
    2000   "Let mum have her say". Turn-taking in doctor-parent-child communication. *Patient Education and Counselling* 40: 151–162.
West, Candace
    1984   *Routine complications: Troubles with Talk Between Doctors and Patients*. Bloomington: Indiana University Press.

5. Peering inside the black box: Lay and professional reasoning surrounding patient claims of adverse drug effects*

Heidi E. Hamilton and Ashley M. Bartell

Abstract

Surveys and interviews of patients and physicians have strongly suggested that adverse reactions to prescription medications continue to be underreported despite a plea by Joyce (1976) decades ago for improved pharmaceutical surveillance methods aided by the collection and evaluation of such information by patients and their physicians. In this study, we focused on the interplay between lay and professional reasoning within 53 patient claims of adverse drug effects that surfaced in 129 video-recorded naturally-occurring physician-patient visits in the United States. Using interactional sociolinguistic methodology supported by insights from Chafe on evidentiality and Halliday and Matthiessen on functional linguistics, we were guided by the following questions: 1) How do patients' claims of adverse drug reactions surface within the institutional talk of physician-patient visits? 2) What is the linguistic nature of such claims? 3) How do physicians respond to these claims? Analyses revealed a great mismatch between physicians and patients in terms of level of conviction regarding the degree of purported connection between the adverse physical changes and the drug in question. In addition to distinctions in conviction levels, physicians and patients differed widely in the types of sources they cited to support their claims; most physicians either referred to published scientific studies or gave no supporting evidence whatsoever, in contrast with patients who overwhelmingly referred to sensory evidence.

1. Introduction

The physician-patient relationship, especially during the evaluation of treatment decisions, is predicated on a two-way flow of information between the patient and his or her physician as well as a mutual trust founded in the information supplied. The principle of informed consent, now a central tenet of medical practice, obligates physicians to inform their patients of possible risks associated with a given treatment, ethically binding a physician to contribute his or her knowledge of a specific treatment's effects to the dialogue. As illustrated in

Excerpt 1, the physician can take an active role in identifying potential consequences of a given medication:[1]

Excerpt 1
Doctor: Now have – have you considered going up to three times a day on
the medicine and maybe bring it [pain] down some? *And it would
be a safe thing to do. You're not having any problems with the
medicine, are you?*

Patient: No.

Doctor: *No upset stomach or black stool, blood in the stool or swelling in
the legs?*

Patient: No.

The potential adverse effects presented by physicians practicing evidence-based
medicine (Sacket et al. 1996) are usually the result of extensive clinical studies
drawn from medical journals and supplied by regulatory agencies aimed at protecting prospective patients, such as the references to upset stomach, blood in
the stool, or swelling in the legs seen in Excerpt 1 above. Recent studies have
shown, however, that serious adverse drug reactions, warranting the ominous
black box label from the Food and Drug Administration (FDA), are commonly
accepted years after the prescription medication has cleared FDA trials and
been made available to patients (Lasser 2002). Increased patient contributions
to conversations with their physicians regarding possible effects of medications
in their own bodies may well uncover additional adverse effects and thereby improve the efficacy of current pharmaceutical surveillance efforts, as Joyce proposed more than thirty years ago:

> Despite extensive clinical trials before drugs are put before the prescribing doctor,
> side effects cannot be entirely anticipated or eliminated, and indeed many are not
> harmful. However, it is important … for information to the doctor from the patient
> and from the doctor to the manufacturer to be collected and evaluated. Only in this
> way can effects of drugs other than those intended be drawn to the notice of the
> manufacturer.
> (Joyce 1976: 112)

There has been renewed expression of the need for patients to act as their own
advocates, as misrepresentations and omissions from both physicians and
patients have been shown to contribute to misunderstandings during treatment
evaluation (Britten et al. 2000). Commitment to patient advocacy and a dialogue of care requires patient efforts to report suspected side effects as they appear and for physicians to respond to these claims, supporting a model of "phar-
macovigilence" that has yet to gain prevalence in the field (Lyles 2006).

Probing further into the dual concepts of patient report and physician response, Golomb et al. (2007) used a survey-based approach to ascertain whether or not physicians were acknowledging patient claims of adverse drug reaction within a single drug class. Less than half of respondents reported that the physician endorsed their claims of adverse drug reactions, indicating a possibility of underreporting in market surveillance efforts. This study exemplifies the need for further research into the nature of patient claim and physician response on a microscopic level in order to shed light on the processes at work and identify how they might better facilitate the detection and dissemination of adverse drug reaction information.

In order to gather more detailed data on the communication of treatment effects, it is necessary to observe doctor-patient interaction within the physician's office with analytical tools sensitive both to the minutiae of interactional discourse as well as to the more macroscopic features of text structure, such as phases of the consultation (ten Have 1989; Byrne and Long 1976). At the critical juncture in the doctor-patient visit when treatment decisions are being evaluated and reformulated, the voices of medicine and of the lifeworld first described in Mishler's (1984) seminal work are engaged in a conversation with potentially serious implications for the patient's health.

The voice of medicine has been well studied, especially as it relates to the institutional and professional contexts shaping it (Sarangi and Roberts 1999), and to the co-constructed asymmetry (ten Have 1991: Ainsworth-Vaughn 1998) and functional phases (ten Have 1989; Byrne and Long 1976) of the physician-patient visit. As a scientific institution, the professional work of medicine encourages the treatment of patients as data sources, creating pressures for physicians to orient to the established organization and objectives of the visit and deemphasizing patient theories in favor of professional algorithm (Gill and Maynard 2006:147). Specific focus on the medical perspective within the treatment phase (Roberts 1999; Stivers 2006) indicates that potential adverse effects typically entertained by physicians originate in the professional sources of medical information that comprise medical "truth" (Atkinson 1995; Cicourel 1992) according to evidence-based medicine (Sackett et al. 1996). This collection of information directs the physician's evaluation of a given treatment, as a physician probes for evidence of common side effects with a variety of linguistic devices, including but not limited to open-ended, colloquial questions and statements as well as specific inquiries to symptoms reported in the scientific literature. Excerpt 2 illustrates such a precipitating remark by the physician (lines 1–2):

Excerpt 2
1. Doctor: Uh, but I know you called this morning and said you were not
2.   feeling well.

3. Patient: But, uh, uh, and I just haven't felt good. And last night, I don't
4.   know what it was. I don't know really what it was. I've never –
5.   it I was – I was sitting on the couch and *had taken the – that new*
6.   *medication you gave me, that Q--? … And I had taken it and*
7.   used it about 9 o'clock and about 9:30 *all of a sudden, I just got*
8.   *real fainty.* I had – I had all the week. I'd taken it. I hadn't felt
9.   it *… felt real numby, and I don't know. I got to thinking well*
10.   *maybe I had -- you know.*

Without the knowledge of, or vested interest in, the complaints of others on similar regimens, the lifeworld voice of the patient exemplified in Excerpt 2 speaks from personal experience, providing crucial insight into the patient's life outside the four walls of the examination room as well as the internal sensations of his or her own body (Hamilton 2003; Mishler 1984). The personal account of the patient represents a subjective experience of illness that may or may not coincide with the literature on a given treatment or categorically defined disease (Helman 1984), creating a situation in which medical and lifeworld voices may sound in dissonance, as seen when the interaction represented in Excerpt 2 continues.

Excerpt 3
Doctor: *I don't think it's the Qvar.*

Patient: It wouldn't have been that?

Doctor: No because it's just a cortisone inhaler.

If conflicts exist between the two voices, as with disagreements in a conversation, they must be negotiated to facilitate the continuation of a productive dialogue. A considerable body of linguistic study exists on the subject of symmetricality, or lack thereof, in such doctor-patient interactions (see ten Have 1991; Ainsworth-Vaughn 1998; Heritage 1997). Co-constructed asymmetricality (ten Have 1991) and resulting power differentials in favor of physicians can pose formidable obstacles in the process of attunement (Becker 1995; Hamilton 2004) of patients' and physicians' points of view. If patients' lifeworld concerns are minimized or dismissed in this process, patients may not receive the medical attention they require or think they require. As a consequence, patients may be left to their own devices to claim power through noncompliance, with some choosing, say, not to take prescribed medications or even to fill prescriptions in the first place (see also Britten et al. 2000). On a public health level, potentially important information contained in such patient claims may never leave the four walls of the doctor's office to be considered by the greater medical community, including the FDA, the pharmaceutical industry, and other physicians (see also Golomb et al. 2007).

This chapter aims to illuminate the language of patient claims pertaining to adverse drug reactions and associated physician responses by examining 53 such claims drawn from 128 physician-patient visits centered on a wide range of health concerns in the United States. Section 2 provides relevant information regarding the interactions examined, the theoretical approach taken, and the analytical decisions regarding definitions and units of analysis. Section 3 responds to the following research questions: 1) How do patients' claims of adverse drug reactions surface within the institutional talk of physician-patient visits? 2) What is the nature of such claims? 3) How do physicians respond to these claims? Finally, Section 4 considers the implications of this work for discourse analysts who study physician-patient communication as well as for healthcare professionals who think that a more nuanced understanding of communication practices may result in better medical care, on both the individual and societal levels.

2.   Methodology

In order to examine the interplay between lay and professional reasoning within physician-patient encounters, this study uses interactional sociolinguistic methodology (Gumperz 1999; Schiffrin 1994) supported by insights from Chafe (1986) on evidentiality, as well as Halliday and Matthiessen (2004) on functional linguistics, to focus on discussions regarding purported side effects of prescription medication as they surface in talk between patients and their physicians. The analysis is based on 53 excerpts drawn from transcribed video-recordings of 128 physician-patient visits conducted within approximately fifty different primary care and specialty medical practices in the United States. Diseases and conditions at the center of these visits included Alzheimer's disease, anti-platelet therapy, diabetes, lung cancer, lymphoma, metastatic breast cancer, osteoporosis, pain/inflammation, pediatric and adult Attention Deficit Hyperactivity Disorder (ADHD), pediatric and adult asthma, rheumatoid arthritis, and seasonal allergy (see Table 1). Most frequently named side effects in our interactions had to do with the digestive system (e.g., appetite, thirst, nausea, diarrhea, constipation). These side effects were followed in frequency by those having to

Table 1. Treatments and side effects found in doctor-patient visit transcripts organized
by condition (n=53)

Disorder/Condition	Treatment	Side Effect
ADHD	medication change	dizziness
	Adderall	cough, tick
	Dexedrine	loss of appetite
	Adderall	cough, tick
	Concerta	insomnia
	medications	insomnia
	medications	picky eating
	medications	thirsty, strange feelings
	Risperdal	ticks
	Melatonin	drowsiness
	Strattera	suicidal ideations
Allergy	Claritin	kidney damage
Alzheimer's disease	Seroquel	drowsiness
	"memory medicine"	constipation
Antiplatelet therapy	Plavix	pink blood
	Coreg	sleepiness, tiredness
	Coumadin	increased urination
Asthma	Rocephin shot	fever, dots
	prednisone	swelling
	prednisone	nervousness
	Allegra-D	digestive problems
	naproxen	nasal swelling
	anesthesia	hair loss
	nicotine patches	nightmares
	Spiriva	fear
	albuterol	shakiness
	"Z-packs and stuff"	cramps
	Qvar	feeling "fainty"

Disorder/Condition	Treatment	Side Effect
Diabetes	Avandia	nausea
	"new medication"	diarrhea
General PCP Visit	Ambien	bizarre dreams
Oncology	eye drops	nasal drips
	Zaroxolyn	cramps
	"one pill"	dizziness, nausea
	Kytril	constipation
	chemotherapy	constipation
	Percocet	"spacey" feeling
	steroids	stomach bleeding
	Phenergan	blurred vision
Osteoporosis	shot	red spots
	Pravachol	rash
	Actonel	rash
	Lipitor	stomach cramps
Pain/inflammation	Percocet	constipation
	heart medication	"made me sick", swelling
	Cnelebrex/Vioxx	weight gain
Rheumatoid arthritis	Humira	difficulty breathing
	Skelaxin	digestive issues
	Remacide	morning stiffness
	Plequenil	eye problems
	Methotrexate	"dizziness or something"
	"stuff I'm taking"	cramps in hands and ankles
	prednisone	weight gain
	niacin	flushed skinte

do with cognitive processes (e.g., "spacey", dizzy, "fainty", suicidal thoughts), muscular systems (ticks, shakiness, cramps, stiffness), sleep-related problems (drowsiness, insomnia, strange dreams), and dermatological issues (rashes, swelling). Our transcripts and recordings were part of individual physician-patient communication studies with which the first author was involved over the past eight years in her role as linguistic consultant for MBS/Vox, a large healthcare communication company in the northeastern United States. Transcripts of post-visit interviews with all participants served as a source of supplementary information regarding patient treatment plans.

Each of the 53 excerpts allowed exploration of the emergent discourse that was centered on a patient's[2] assertion or question positing a connection between a recent physical problem (e.g., nausea, diarrhea, cramping, thirst) and a recent change in medication. Because our focus was on adverse drug reaction claims *brought up* by patients, we did not include any patient claim that immediately followed a physician's query that named possible specific side effects (as in Excerpt 1). In contrast, any patient claim that immediately followed a physician's *general* inquiry into the patient's health or progress on given medication was admitted, since any subsequent mention of a specific side effect by the patient would not have been directly influenced by the physician's words. In order to remain faithful to the medical motivation of this work, only negative side effects of medication treatments were considered; unintended positive effects of medications and treatments not involving a drug, such as surgery or radiation, were excluded from analysis.

3.   Analysis

Several patterns surrounding patients' claims of adverse drug effects emerged from the data that have possible significance for discourse studies as well as for medical practice. Section 3.1 investigates the ways in which these claims surfaced in medical encounters. Section 3.2 characterizes patients' claims in relation to different periods in their lifetime and describes the linguistic presentation of the claims. Section 3.3 focuses on physicians' responses to purported connections between medications and symptoms that constitute adverse drug reaction claims. These observations collectively illustrate the complexity of the interplay between lay and professional voices during the process of treatment negotiation within physician-patient interactions.

3.1.   How do patients' claims of adverse drug reactions surface within the institutional talk of physician-patient visits?

Before focusing our attention on the nature of patients' claims of adverse drug reactions, we turn first to an examination of the environment in which such claims are realized. The utterances preceding a specific claim are of particular theoretical importance in that they provide a discourse context that may facilitate or hinder the introduction of the claim. Claims that must be introduced into the conversation unilaterally by the patient could be expected to be constructed with different linguistic features and to display additional degrees of patient agency when compared with those claims whose relevance is established when the physician opens up an adjacency pair (Schegloff and Sacks 1973) by uttering the "first pair part" in the form of a question or other directive, such as a command. The power-claiming function of questions has been well documented within the doctor-patient interaction (see, for example, Ainsworth-Vaughn 1998) due to the fact that a question not only sets up an expectation that an answer will follow (the "second pair part" in the terminology of Schegloff and Sacks [1973]; see also Schegloff 1968; Goody 1978), but that a specific topical agenda has been thereby established for the next speaker (Mishler 1984; Boyd and Heritage 2006). This interactional power arguably accounts at least partially[3] for the fact that patients have been consistently observed to ask far fewer questions than their physicians during their interactions with one another (Ainsworth-Vaughn 2001; Frankel 2002; West 1983; Wodak 1996). In Brown and Levinson's (1987) politeness framework, such question-asking behavior may well be a threat to a patient's own positive face (in that the patient would be seen as doing something untoward) even while it threatens the physician's negative face (in that the physician needs to adjust his or her plans to meet the needs of the patient).

In our set of 53 claims of adverse drug effects, 40 % (i.e., 21) were uttered as "second pair parts" immediately following a specific or general prompt ("first pair part") by the physician. Seventeen of these 21 prompts (81 %) were specific directives in the form of commands or questions that explicitly proposed the topic of medication as illustrated in the following excerpt by the physician's questions regarding Adderall (lines 1 and 3) during a visit with an 11-year-old patient centered on the treatment of ADHD.

Excerpt 4
→   1. Doctor: So any side effects, Kelsey, that you notice?
    2. Patient: Umm.
→   3. Doctor: Problems with the medicine?
    4. Patient: I'm very thirsty.

The balance of the 21 prompts (i.e., 4 or 19 %) were general directives that did not focus explicit attention on medication or side effects, as illustrated by the physician's directive in line 1 of excerpt 5 taken from an oncology visit.

Excerpt 5
→   1. Doctor: OK. Tell me how you are feeling today.

    2. Patient: Ah, actually, I had a lot of leg cramps and I'm a little tired with it,
    3.   because it kept me up most of the night – not just in the legs
    4.   either. – arms, everything else. I don't know what it's from. –

As mentioned above, claims that followed general inquiries arguably required more agency on the part of the patients than those that followed specific questions, as the patients had to specify the scope of their responses and supply enough context into which to insert their claims. This kind of discursive work, evidenced in Excerpt 5 by the use of the sentence-modifying adverb *actually* and temporal orientation information (*most of the night*), contrasts clearly with the much simpler *I'm very thirsty* uttered in response to the specific question posed in Excerpt 4.

Even more challenging than managing to bring up a claim of adverse drug reaction in response to one of these general directives (rather than a more specific one) was when there was no such directive issued by the physician that provided a slot for a second pair part of an adjacency pair. Despite this challenge, 60 % (i.e., 32) of the 53 patient claims of an adverse drug reaction in our study occurred outside a context of conditional relevance – coming up "out of the blue" as changes in topic during physical examinations or discussions of the patient's relative state of wellness. Excerpt 6, taken from a visit centered on the treatment of metastatic breast cancer, shows a patient introducing a problem with bloating (line 2) immediately following her physician's statement in line 1 on a completely different topic, i.e., the scheduling of her next PET CT.

Excerpt 6
1.   Doctor: So uh probably in November or December we'll do another PET CT.

→ 2.   Patient: I always kind of get kind of bloated right here.

3.   Doctor: Mmhmm.

4.   Patient: I mean=

5.   Doctor: =I don't think that that's from anything that's going on
6.   with the cancer.

→ 7.   Patient: But could it just be my reaction to the – or like my gastrointes-
8.   tinal workings are slowed down, so=

9.   Doctor: =It's possible. I mean, the
10.   chemotherapy could – can cause diarrhea and sometimes it
11.   causes constipation. So, yes. It's possible.

→ 12. Patient: Cause I always feel like it's paralyzed right after I have the Ab-
       raxane.

It is clear from the doctor's initial response in lines 5–6 (*I don't think that that's from anything that's going on with the cancer*) to the patient's observation that he had not yet understood that the patient was proposing an adverse reaction to a medication rather than talking about a symptom that was directly related to her cancer. Once he heard the term *reaction* in line 7, he understood the causal link she was making between the bloating and the chemotherapy. After the doctor allowed for a possible connection between the two, the patient then provided more specific detail by naming the chemotherapeutic agent, Abraxane, in line 12.

3.2.   What is the nature of patient claims of adverse drug reactions within physician-patient visits?

Having characterized the environments in which patients' claims of adverse drug reactions emerged in physician-patient visits, we turn now to an examination of the nature of such patient claims. Observations relate to the time period in the patient's life in which the purported side effect was situated (section 3.2.1) and the linguistic presentation of the claim (section 3.2.2).

3.2.1.   *Relationship of patient claims to time periods in the patients' life*

Patients in these interactions referred to 53 purported side effects as related to three different time periods in their lifetime: past, present, and future. Table 2 shows the distribution of these types of problems as referenced within the 53 excerpts along with illustrations from the transcripts.

Table 2. Time periods referenced in patient claims of adverse drug reaction

Reference Period	Prevalence	Example of Patient Claim
Past	19% (n=10)	"He started putting me on a heart medication, or actually it's a high blood pressure medication? I forgot what it was called? And it actually made me sick. Actually, that's when I started noticing the swelling happen. This was over a year ago"
Present	60% (n=32)	"Um – no, but I – the last group of painkillers I took, the uh – what's it called? The last one (looks at paper), OK … Percocet, yeah, OK? Um – it, it's constipating me, OK? and – not that that's any big deal."
Potential	21% (n=11)	"It [the package insert] said it could cause blurred vision. And I thought 'I don't want blurred vision.'"

The largest group (32 of 53 or 60 %) of claims represented side effects that were being dealt with at the time of the visit (present) and were purported to be related to some aspect of a current treatment plan. These 32 claims fulfilled two major functions within the physician-patient visit. The overwhelming majority of these (26 of 32 or 81 %) were secondary concerns of the patient that were framed linguistically as a non-critical curiosity about a medication (e.g., *[laughs] This may sound strange but – have you ever known any – any patients with problems digesting it, where the medication didn't digest?*). By using a variety of hedges and other minimizing phrases, patients backgrounded these claims in terms of their relative importance. The other 19 % of claims (6 of 32) functioned as chief complaints or primary concerns of the patient within the current visit. The exchange represented in Excerpt 7 occurred at the beginning of a visit for the treatment of rheumatoid arthritis and illustrates the primacy of the patient's concerns in her mind (note the use of intensifiers *very* and *really* in addition to the adjective *terrible* in lines 4, 7 and 8).

Excerpt 7
1. Doctor: Good morning [Name]. How are you this morning?

2. Patient: Not too good.

3. Doctor: You look tired. What's going on?

→ 4. Patient: I'm having trouble breathing at times. I – I get out of breath
5. very easy. I'm still having pressure on my chest like I tol – told
6. you before.

7. Doctor: Uh huh.

8. Patient: And, also, I've been getting – I had *terrible* pain in the top part
9. of my leg. Well, last night, it went down the side of my leg.
10. And my legs are *really* weak.

11. Doctor: Okay.

12. Patient: Seems like –

13. Doctor: Let's start with the difficulty breathing. How long have you no-
14. ticed that?

→ 15. Patient: Uh, it starts right after I take the Humira. It seems as soon as
I take the Humira it starts, and it'll last for maybe about 7
days.

At the patient's first mention of the breathing problem in line 4, the physician did not yet know that the patient understood her symptoms in terms of the pattern she noticed with a medication she had been taking. They were presented as chief complaints and possible reasons for the visit itself. Only after the physician asked a specific question focusing on the breathing problem in lines 13–14 did it become clear that the patient understood this important symptom as a possible adverse reaction to the drug, Humira.

The balance of the claims (21 of 53) were divided nearly equally between those that referred to problems in the past and those that brought up potential problems in the future. Ten of these 21 (or 19 % of all 53 claims) reported symptoms that had been experienced by the patient in the past and were unrelated to the current treatment plan. These references to past purported adverse drug reactions functioned in two ways during the medical visits. Seven of the ten claims were introduced during the history-taking phase to provide potentially important medical information for the patient's record (e.g., *I did buy the patches once and I had serious nightmares*); the other three instances were brought into the treatment discussion near the end of the visit (e.g., *We tried Adderall and he got a cough – he got a tick from doing that.*) as potentially useful information when the physician was considering possible drug recommendations.

The additional 11 of the 21 (or 21 % of all 53 claims) brought up adverse drug reactions that might occur in the future as part of a treatment plan. Just over half of these instances (i.e., 6) were introduced during the discussion of the patient's present state of health or the physical examination when patients inquired about or asserted the possibility of a side-effect to a current treatment that they had not actually experienced (e.g., *Umm, but what I wanted to tell you is, I stopped taking the Paquenil because you said that it could cause some problems with your eyes*). The other five instances were brought up during the treatment recommendation phase of the visit when patients constructed a hypothetical future involving a possible side-effect and the physician had to decide whether or not to indulge this concern (e.g., *And they don't make you get fat, right? Please just tell me they don't make you get fat*).

3.2.2.   Linguistic presentation of patient claims

Having characterized the environment in which patient claims of adverse drug reactions surfaced in the physician-patient visit, we turn now to an examination of the actual presentation of these claims. In this effort, we are interested not only in understanding possible distinctions between lay and professional reasoning related to the possibility of drug reactions, but in identifying linguistic evidence of these differences. To this end, we draw first on Chafe's (1986) work on evidentiality with its four modes of knowing (belief, induction, hearsay and deduction) linked to four sources of knowledge (see Table 3). We then follow

Table 3. Taxonomy for relative certainty in patient claims (n=53)

Degree of certainty	Prevalence	Example of patient claim
1: no connection made	5 % (n=3)	"I don't know what it's from."
2: not likely	4 % (n=2)	"And they don't make you get fat, right?"
3: possible connection	34 % (n=18)	"I don't know if there was a correlation, but it's just really.."
4: likely connection	15 % (n=8)	"I felt it was affecting my umm digestive system."
5: certain of connection	42 % (n=22)	"I can't take that. It makes me cramp."

this up with insights related to the six "process types"[4] of Hallidayan functional grammar (Halliday and Matthiessen 2004) that differentiate ways in which speakers voice their experiences.

Following Chafe, all 42 patients who claimed adverse drug reactions in the past or present grounded these claims in personal experiences and cognition rather than basing these on external sources of information, such as public media or other individuals including health professionals or family and friends. These claims were supported by beliefs in the form of personal understanding of their health status, induction related to evidence gathered through the senses, and deduction evidencing cognitive reasoning. In Excerpt 8, taken from a visit centered on the treatment of asthma, the patient used sensory evidence of her swollen nose to induce a claim and then deduced a connection between her medication and the physical symptom.

Excerpt 8
1. Patient: Yeah. So, when you look in my nose, you're gonna see it's swollen.

2. Doctor: [examines nose] Oh, you have the polyps right back.

4. Patient: It's that ummm – my nose swells whenever I take that medi-
5.   cation= for ummm my female problems.

6. Doctor: Oh okay.

7. Patient: It's uhh – I forgot the name of it.

The patient later added the health belief that the adverse effect only arose after stopping the medication (i.e., *My nose is totally clear once I'm taking it. It's once I quit it starts growing*).

In contrast to the claims of experienced adverse drug effects, external evidence was drawn upon in the form of spoken and written information ("hearsay" as the mode of knowing) as the basis for 5 of 11 (45 %) claims of *potential* adverse effects. This external evidence included pharmaceutical package inserts (as illustrated in Excerpt 11 below) or other persons (e.g., *My aunt is a nurse and she said that my hair might fall out.*) The remaining six patient claims lacked any linguistically observable knowledge source whatsoever, evidencing instead an underlying health belief system or personal concerns regarding specific side effects, as illustrated in Excerpt 9 taken from a visit centered on the treatment of Alzheimer's disease.

Excerpt 9
1. Doctor: Well, if, if I have some samples of medicine for your memory,
2.　　　　 would you be willing to try it for a month?

→ 3. Patient: Is it constipating?

4. Doctor: No, it's not constipating [laughs]

In Hallidayan terms, of the 42 patients who had physically experienced symptoms, nearly three-fourths (31 of 42 or 74 %) represented these in "material" clauses, in which the purported side effect was expressed as an external "doing-and-happening" (Halliday and Matthiessen 2004: 179) in the outside world. These clauses described changes in the body in size, shape, surface, color, etc., as illustrated by the reference to swelling in Excerpt 8 above. The other 11 patients (of 42 or 26 %) who had physically experienced symptoms represented them in "mental" clauses, where the purported side effect was linked explicitly either to the patient's thought process (cognition) or perception via the senses (seeing, hearing, feeling, tasting, or smelling),[5] as illustrated in excerpt 10 from a visit centered on the use of the muscle relaxant, Skelaxin, in the treatment of rheumatoid arthritis.

Excerpt 10
1. Doctor: And what happened?

2. Patient: Uh nothing. Three weeks I was on it. The only thing that was
3.　　　　 happening was – is I – *I felt it was affecting my umm*
4.　　　　 *digestive system.*

Of the 11 patients who had not experienced the symptoms (future time category), three represented their concerns about potential side effects in "mental" clauses, as illustrated in Excerpt 11 where we see the patient's thinking reported in lines 2–3 and again in lines 5–6.

Excerpt 11

1.	Patient:	I haven't taken it [Phenergan] cause it [the package insert] said
→ 2.		it could cause blurred vision. *And I thought "I don't want*
→ 3.		*blurred vision."* And this Thursday if it's okay which is – you
4.		have to tell me I have this standing appointment for my eye doc-
→ 5.		tor and *I thought "I don't want to mess up my eyes before I go*
→ 6.		*to the eye doctor."*
7.	Doctor:	I've not – I 've not had anybody complain of blurred vision.
8.		That's strange. I've taken the medicine myself a lot too.

An additional three patients represented their concerns in "verbal" clauses (e.g., *I stopped taking the Paquenil because* <u>you said</u> *that it could cause some problems with your eyes*) that provided insight into selected portions of conversations with others via directly or indirectly reported speech (see also Clark and Gerrig 1990; Chafe 1994; Tannen 1989). In the five remaining cases, patients asked their doctors questions about the likelihood of a specific adverse reaction to a drug (e.g., *Is that bad on the stomach? Is it constipating?*) in "relational" clauses that zeroed in on a particular (possible) attribute of the drug, as contrasted with information that came from experience in the outside world ("material" clause) or through their own processes of cognition or perception ("mental" clause).

In addition to these differences in evidentiality and process type that shed light on patients' thinking regarding the connections between symptoms and medications, differences existed on the level of conviction speakers displayed linguistically regarding the likelihood of these connections. As shown in Table 4, 22 of the 53 patients (42 %) expressed absolute certainty that the drug in question was the cause of adverse physical change in their body; eight additional patients (and additional 15 %) thought a connection was likely. Approximately one-third of the patients (i.e., 18 or 34 %) were unsure but entertained a possible connection. A small minority thought a connection was unlikely or claimed not to know a possible cause of their symptoms.

With this characterization of lay reasoning regarding adverse drug reactions – including the modes of knowing and sources of knowledge (Chafe 1986) that underlay their claims, the process types (Halliday and Matthiessen 2004) they used to represent these experiences linguistically, and the level of certainty they displayed toward these connections, we turn now to an examination of the professional reasoning displayed by physicians in their responses to these patients' claims.

Table 4. Modes of knowledge as given in Chafe (1986) as applied to the sources of knowledge exemplified in patient claims of adverse drug reactions

Modes of Knowing	Sources of Knowledge	Example
Belief	Personal understanding of health and illness	"At first I had a little diarrhea, <u>but my body seemed to adjust</u>. So, Monday, I started taking two and I'm experiencing diarrhea now, but it's not like the Glucophage."
Induction	Sensory evidence	"I don't know why these <u>little red spots have turned up</u>, but they're sort of where, where the shots have been"
Hearsay	Spoken and written information	"<u>started to read it</u>, and I haven't taken it cause it said it could cause blurred vision ..."
Deduction	Hypothesis or causal connection	"The <u>prednisone made me</u> really really nervous and jittery"

3.3.   How do physicians respond to these claims by patients?

Though the nature and structure of patient claims are central to the discussion of side effects, physician responses can be expected ultimately to determine the fate of the patient's complaint, either by accepting or rejecting its validity. Various factors can affect the process of accomplishing this task and the level of certainty exhibited by the resulting stance. The symptoms expressed by the patient, physical evidence supporting the patient's claim, and the impact of the patient's condition on his or her life may help formulate the physician's perception (Hamilton 2004). Institutional knowledge (Heritage 1997) and professional vision (Goodwin 1994) also have an effect, tempering or heightening the physician's level of concern. Due to the multitude of influences on the physician's reasoning, responses by the physicians in our study to their patients' claims ranged from full agreement to outright invalidation (or even apparent ignoring) of the patient's claim (see Table 5).

Table 5. Taxonomy for physician's degree of certainty regarding the patient's claim (n=53)

Degree of certainty regarding the patient's adverse drug reaction claim	Prevalence (n=53)	Example of physician's response
1: ignores the claim of a drug connection	15% (n=8)	Patient: "It's constipating me, OK? and – not that that's any big deal." Doctor: "Does it help the pain?"
2: clearly disagrees with the connection	9% (n=5)	"Well you are not allergic to it for sure."
3: doubts the connection	15% (n=8)	"Well Avandia isn't typically associated with nausea."
4: allows for a possible connection	25% (n=13)	"He may or may not have a rash with that Rocephin."
5: thinks the connection is likely	19% (n=10)	"Well it could be from the new medication – the Zaroxolyn."
6: clearly agrees with the connection	17% (n=9)	"Yes, it'll do that."

As the numbers in Table 5 indicate, slightly more than one-third of the physicians either agreed completely with the patient's claim connecting an adverse drug reaction to a particular medication or thought the connection was likely, as illustrated in line 3 of Excerpt 12 connecting weight gain to the steroid Prednisone.

Excerpt 12
1. Patient: When I got back on the Prednisone it seemed like I started blow-
2.   ing up again. My weight went 'ffsh'

3. Doctor: Yes, it'll do that.

One-fourth of the physicians thought the connection was possible, as illustrated in line 10 (*He may or he may not*) of Excerpt 13 regarding the connection of a child's rash to the drug Rocephin.

Excerpt 13
1. Mother: And it wasn't that high but it – but it did kind of come back,
2.   umm, the next day after – you know, we were here on Thursday
3.   and so then, umm, Thursday night and Friday he had like these
4.   red dots--

5. Doctor: Oh, yeah, I know (indiscernible), yeah.

6. Mother: All over; it was really weird and then, umm, it started – sort of
7.   spreading into like this big red – like these big red blobs and
8.   then they finally went away, but with that he had a little bit of a
9.   fever. It was like 100.

       ...... [deleted lines]

→ 10. Doctor: He may or he may not have a rash with that Rocephin. It – it may
                havebeen actually even, umm, illness.

An additional one-fourth of the physicians either doubted their patients' claims of adverse reactions or expressed outright disagreement with them. Since the face-threatening act of disagreement is socially difficult to accomplish, it is useful to examine in some detail two such excerpts from our transcripts. Excerpt 14 illustrates one of the eight physicians who doubted their patients' claims, in this case a diabetic patient's connection between nausea and the drug Avandia.

Excerpt 14
1. Patient: I didn't feel well in the beginning was the nausea when I was
2.   beginning with the Avandia.

3. Doctor: Uhhuh.

4. Patient: And frankly, I felt better on the Rez.. on the uh on the um
5.   Rezulin. I really did. I know we don't want to go back to it
6.   because of the liver, but I ha- I felt personally better on Re-
7.   zulin. Is there anything else besides the Avandia that we could
8.   try?

9. Doctor: Well, *Avandia isn't typically associated with nausea.* I mean,
10.   that's number one. *It doesn't usually cause any problems in*
11.   *terms of stomach upset* or anything like that. It's really supposed
12.   to be safe that way. Um, Glucophage does that. You know, Glu-
13.   cophage clearly is associated with a lot of problems with upset
14.   stomach.

Excerpt 15 illustrates one of five physicians who displayed complete disagreement with their patients' claims, in this case a patient on the anticoagulant Coumadin who blamed the drug for ongoing troubles with equilibrium and somewhat unspecified "bathroom" issues.

Excerpt 15
1. Patient: Just seems to knock my equilibrium off. I'm having trouble
2.   walking in a straight line going to the bathroom. One thing
3.   with the Coumadin, I have to have a facility available every
4.   hour and a half, something like that. Makes it kind of a mess
5.   if you happen to be driving. I think I'm allergic to it be-
6.   cause=

7. Doctor: = well *you are not allergic to it for sure. Those are*
8.   *not allergic things.* In fact, I have a *great deal of difficulty mak-*
8.   *ing any connection with Coumadin* medicine with those kinds
9.   of symptoms. Now the *bruising for sure* or something like that
11.   but the *bathroom* and stuff like that, *there should be no connec-*
12.   *tion* there.

Consideration of Excerpts 14 and 15 reveals an intriguing phenomenon that was also evidenced in the other physician responses that expressed skepticism or outright disagreement with the patients' claims of adverse side effects. Following a mini-series of utterances that denied the purported connection (e.g., *isn't typically, doesn't usually* in Excerpt 14; *not allergic for sure, not allergic things* in Excerpt 15), physicians stated what *is* or *could be* the case – either by choosing a different medication that could have caused the side effect in question (*Glucophage clearly is associated with a lot of problems with upset stomach*) or by choosing a different side effect that could have been caused by the medication in question (*Now bruising for sure or something like that*). These disagreeing responses were clearly much longer and more involved than, say, the outright agreement illustrated in Excerpt 12 (*Yes, it'll do that*) and provided a good deal of insight into the specifics of drug knowledge and character of medical reasoning on the part of the physicians.

The amount of discourse work involved in disagreeing may well have influenced some physicians to avoid the negative response entirely. Indeed, 15 % of physicians (8 of 53) seemed to evidence their disregard for the patients' claims by ignoring them with a shift in topic or an unrelated follow-up question on the same topic as illustrated in line 4 of Excerpt 16.

Excerpt 16
1. Patient: Um – no, but I – the last group of painkillers I took, the uh –
             what's it called? The last one (looks at paper), OK …

2. Woman: Percocet

3. Patient: Percocet, yeah, OK? Um – it, it's constipating me, OK? and –
             not that that's any big deal.

→ 4. Doctor: Does it help the pain?

In fact, seven of the eight physicians who ignored the patients' claims were responding to patients who displayed the highest degree of certainty regarding these claims. It seems quite possible that the physicians might have chosen to ignore the claim rather than having to construct the relatively detailed responses that would have had a chance of convincing the patients of their alternate explanation or view.

When comparing patient claims and physician responses using the taxonomies represented in Tables 4 and 5, we first noted a stark contrast between the 42 % (22 of 53) of patients and the 17 % (9 of 53) of physicians who expressed absolute certainty regarding the connection between the drug and symptom in question. Further investigation of responses at all levels of certainty revealed that only one-fifth (19 % or 10 of 53) of patient-physician pairs were matched in their relative certainty of the connection between the patient's health problem and the medication. In nearly three-fourths (32 of the 43 or 74 %) of the mismatched pairs, the physician was more skeptical of the connection than the patient was; the physician was more certain of the connection than the patient was in only 11 of the 43 mismatched pairs (26 %). These findings would seem to be a clear illustration of the epistemic caution typical of professionals as identified by Heritage (1997) in his work on institutional discourse.

In addition to the differences in certainty levels between physicians and patients regarding these claims of adverse drug reactions, physicians and patients differed greatly in the types of sources they cited in support of their understanding of the situation (see Table 6). Most physicians either referred to published scientific studies (n=18) or gave no supporting evidence whatsoever (n=24) to back up their positions, in stark contrast with patients who overwhelmingly based their claims on sensory evidence.

Table 6. A comparison of knowledge sources presented by patients and physicians

Type of evidence	By patient	By doctor	Totals
Own perception	42	2	44
Other people	4	9 (patient in focus as well as other patients)	13
Scientific studies/texts	1	18	19
None displayed	6	24	30
Totals	53	53	106

Table 7. Process types (Halliday and Matthiessen 2004) used by patients and physicians in utterances supporting or denying adverse drug reactions, separated according to experienced symptoms vs. potential symptoms (*total number of physician responses excludes eight instances that ignore the claim and 11 instances of follow-up questions that display implicit acceptance of the claim, but do not respond to it explicitly)

Process Type	Experienced symptoms		Potential symptoms		Totals
	Patient	Doctor	Patient	Doctor	
Material	31	1	0	0	32
Behavioral	0	0	0	0	0
Mental	11	5	3	1	20
Verbal	0	1	3	3	7
Relational	0	12	5	6	23
Existential	0	4	0	1	5
	42	23*	11	11	87

When we applied the Hallidayan framework of process types to the physicians' responses[6] and placed these next to the previous analysis of patient claims (see Table 7) from Section 3.2.2, several distinctions between professional and lay reasoning came into clear relief. Focusing first on claims related to symptoms experienced by the patient in the past or present, we noted that only one physician of 23 (4%) used a "material" clause in which evidence for or against the purported side effect was expressed as an external "doing-and-happening" in the real world in contrast to the nearly three-fourths (31 of 42 or 74%) of patients who did so. Further, nearly 70% (16 of 23) of the physicians used "relational" or "existential" clauses to base their understanding of the reasonableness of specific adverse reactions on attributes or classes of drugs; not a single patient out of 42 did so. Similar percentages of physicians and patients highlighted mental processes (either cognition or perception) as the basis for their perspective (26% of patients and 22% of physicians) on the experienced side effect, although of course it would be expected that the content of the mental processes indexed could be quite different from each other.

Secondly, looking at the clauses that topicalized symptoms that had not (yet) been experienced by the patient, but functioned within the physician-patient interaction to clarify potential problems in the future, we noted much greater similarity between lay and professional perspectives. Approximately half of both groups (5 patients and 6 physicians) used "relational" clauses to focus attention on attributes of drugs; mental and verbal clauses were used by both physicians and patients. This greater alignment between the two groups that showed such disparity when discussing *experienced* side effects can arguably be accounted for as follows: when patients had no personal experience with the symptoms, they needed to get their information from outside sources, such as published materials (that included information on drug attributes) and other persons (whose ideas and experiences could then be cited), some of the sources drawn upon by physicians as well.

4.   Conclusion

In closing, we return to the guiding voice of Joyce who identified the need thirty years ago for the collection and evaluation of information to the doctor from the patient on potential drug side effects:

> Despite extensive clinical trials before drugs are put before the prescribing doctor, side effects cannot be entirely anticipated or eliminated, and indeed many are not harmful. However, it is important … for information to the doctor from the patient and from the doctor to the manufacturer to be collected and evaluated. Only in this way can effects of drugs other than those intended be drawn to the notice of the manufacturer.
> (Joyce 1976: 112)

Surveys and interviews of patients and physicians have strongly suggested that side effects are being underreported in market surveillance efforts, as Golomb et al. (2007) have shown in their recent survey-based approach to the acknowledgement of patient claims of adverse drug reactions within a single drug class, HMG-CoA reductase inhibitors. What had yet to be done was to peer inside the black box of individual physician-patient visits to see the actual words used (i) as patients attempted to bring their notions of causal connections between a personal health problem and a specific medical drug to the attention of their physicians; and (ii) as physicians responded to these claims. The careful conversation analytic study by Gill and Maynard (2006) of patients' proposals regarding their illness and physicians' responses to these proposals provided sound analytical insights regarding ways in which Mishler's (1984) notions of the voices of medicine and the lifeworld can be put into practice as both parties attempt to understand the *primary* concern of the patient. To our knowledge, however, ours is the first in-depth, nuanced study to characterize naturally-occurring language used by physicians and patients on the specific topic of a connection between health problems and medications that are purported to be causing those problems.

   In our investigation of 128 physician-patient visits, we identified and characterized 53 such patient claims of a wide variety of purported side effects. As shown in Table 1, these health problems were almost exclusively those that are directly experienced by the patient rather than the relatively invisible problems that are identified by clinical instruments, such as MRIs and blood tests (see also Hamilton 2004). As acknowledged by Joyce (1976), most of the named adverse drug reactions reported in these visits were not particularly harmful, but instead were burdensome hindrances to patients' quality of life, although some were potentially life-threatening (e.g., breathing difficulties and suicidal thoughts). What is clear from our analyses, however, is that even relatively minor side effects can have potentially major consequences for patient health. We noted, for example, that some patients were taking medical decision-making into their own hands, either by stopping a medication that they determined was the cause of aggravating side effects or, in some cases, not even starting treatment in the first case, if they were concerned about potential side effects of a medication in question. Lack of knowledge about such patient non-adherence can have dramatic effects on subsequent treatment decisions by the prescribing physician, if it is unclear, for example, why the patient is not responding as expected to the medication (see Britten et al. 2000).

This situation highlights the importance of physicians allowing for the patients' perspectives regarding possible adverse drug reactions to come up in each visit: (i) during the past-oriented history-taking phase in order to gain potentially important information regarding drug allergies or patient preferences; (ii) during present-oriented discussions of current health, especially in situations where there has been a change in medication, either in terms of type or dosage, in order to allow for important discussions related to adherence to treatment plans; and (iii) during future-oriented discussions of treatment changes in order to facilitate decisions regarding prescription medications.

Based on our study where we saw 60 % (32 of 53) of patients having to figure out a way to get information regarding purported side effects to the physician by carrying out potentially face-threatening and agentive acts such as changing the topic or asking questions (rather than being able to respond to a physician's question), we propose that physicians ask questions about specific medications (e.g., *How are you doing on X? Any bad effects?*) before going through the typical list of expected side effects (e.g., *Any problems with nausea?*). This is in line with recommendations by Maynard (1991) that physicians elicit patients' views by what he calls "perspective display series" (PDS) before a specific diagnosis is given.

We hope that our characterization of the nature of these 53 patient claims (including what counted as evidence for the connection between the health problem and the medication in question and how certain the patient was regarding this causal connection), how they emerged within physician-patient visits, and how they were responded to by physicians may help to shed light on elements of physicians' and patients' cognition and logical frameworks at work within institutional discourse. By examining the linguistic realization of these phenomena, the nature and degree of dissonance or agreement experienced between lay and professional participants may begin to be understood on both linguistic and cognitive levels. Further, we are hopeful that this nascent understanding will spark an interest on the part of other linguistic and medical researchers to continue this line of investigation into patient claims of adverse drug reactions.

A concerted effort must be made by researchers, health care professionals, pharmaceutical companies, regulatory organizations, and individual patients to address the issues inherent in bringing adverse drug reaction reports into a productive dialogue. The preliminary recommendations of our probative study are twofold. Primarily, we encourage public health initiatives that inform patients of their rights and responsibilities to communicate all potential concerns to the professionals involved in their care. Through this work, we also promote current efforts within the medical profession to develop pedagogy in the art of medical communication both in the medical training and continuing education settings. Future interdisciplinary work (focused, for example, on side effects related to specific drugs or the shaping influences of different models of health-care delivery) within this intriguing area of application of linguistic discourse analysis is almost certain to illuminate a topic that has high stakes for society at the intersection of lay and professional spheres, requiring cooperation between these groups to stimulate progress. As the medical community continues to increase its emphasis on cooperative discourse as central component of patient care, studies focusing on the language of medicine will shape the innovations in the least invasive of patient interventions, effective communication.

Notes

* We are grateful to Chris Candlin and Srikant Sarangi for their numerous insightful comments on our paper.
1. Here we see the physician asking the questions in an optimized way, assuming a best-case scenario (see Boyd and Heritage 2006), rather than asking, say, *Are you having some problems with the medicine?* or *You're having problems with the medicine, aren't you?*
2. Parents' utterances were also included in cases of pediatric visits, as were utterances by adult children accompanying elderly parents with Alzheimer's disease.
3. Interactional power is, of course, not the entire story. Physicians need to use questions in order to learn about their patients and patients come to the visit with expectations that this will be the case. Thus, institutional and professional constraints as well as cognitive schemas and scripts also contribute to the asymmetry in question-asking by physicians and patients within their interaction.
4. See especially Chapter 5 of Halliday and Matthiessen (2004) for an in-depth introduction to the three primary process types (material, mental and relational) and the three subsidiary process types (behavioral, verbal and existential).

5. Note here that perceptual evidence gathered via the senses (a mental process type by Halliday and Matthiessen [2004]) can be used as source of knowledge in the process of induction (Chafe 1986) to identify a pattern that leads to a claim of adverse drug reaction.

6. The total number of physician responses in this Table excludes eight instances that ignore the claim and 11 instances of follow-up questions that display implicit acceptance of the claim, but do not respond to it explicitly. The total number is, therefore, 23 instead of 42.

References

Ainsworth-Vaughn, Nancy
    1998   *Claiming Power in Doctor-Patient Talk*. Oxford: Oxford University Press.
Ainsworth-Vaughn, Nancy
    2001   The discourse of medical encounters. In: Deborah Schiffrin, Deborah Tannen, and Heidi E. Hamilton (eds.), *The Handbook of Discourse Analysis*, 453–469. Oxford: Blackwell.
Atkinson, Paul
    1995   *Medical Talk, Medical Work*. London: Sage.
Becker, A. L.
    1995   Attunement: An essay on philology and logophilia. In: A. L. Becker, *Beyond Translation*, 369–403. Ann Arbor, MI: University of Michigan Press.
Boyd, Elizabeth and John Heritage
    2006   Taking the history: Questioning during comprehensive history-taking. In: John Heritage and Douglas W. Maynard (eds.), *Communication in Medical Care: Interaction between Primary Care Physicians and Patients*, 151–184. Cambridge: Cambridge University Press.
Brown, Penelope and Stephen Levinson
    1987   *Politeness*. Cambridge: Cambridge University Press.
Britten, Nicky, Fiona A. Stevenson, Christine A. Barry, Nick Barber and Colin P. Bradley
    2000   Misunderstandings in prescribing decisions in general practice: Qualitative study. *British Medical Journal* 320: 484–488.
Byrne, Patrick S. and Barrie E. L. Long
    1976   *Doctors Talking to Patients: A Study of the Verbal Behaviours of Doctors in the Consultation*. London: Her Majesty's Stationery Office.
Chafe, Wallace
    1994   *Discouse, Consciousness, and Time*. Chicago: University of Chicago Press.
Chafe, Wallace
    1986   Evidentiality in English conversation and academic writing. In: Wallace Chafe and Joanna Nichols (eds.), *Evidentiality: The Linguistic Coding of Epistemology*, 261–72. Norwood, NJ: Ablex.
Cicourel, Aaron V.
    1992   The interpenetration of communicative context: Examples from medical encounters. In: Alessandro Duranti and Charles Goodwin (eds.), *Rethinking Context*, 291–310. Cambridge: Cambridge University Press.

Clark, Herbert H. and Richard J. Gerrig
    1990   Quotations as demonstrations. *Language* 66: 764–805.
Frankel, Richard M.
    2002   The (socio)linguistic turn in physician-patient communication research. In:
            James E. Alatis, Heidi E. Hamilton and Ai-Hui Tan (eds.), *Linguistics, Lan-*
            guage, and the Professions: Education, Journalism, Law, Medicine, and
            Technology (GURT 2000). Washington, D.C.: Georgetown University Press.
Gill, Virginia Teas and Douglas W. Maynard
    2006   Explaining illness: Patients' proposals and physicians' responses. In: John
            Heritage and Douglas W. Maynard (eds.), *Communication in Medical*
            Care: Interaction between Primary Care Physicians and Patients,
            115–150. Cambridge: Cambridge University Press.
Golomb, B., J. McGraw, M. A. Evans, and J. E. Dimsdale
    2007   Physician response to patient reports of adverse drug effects: Implications
            for patient-targeted adverse effect surveillance. *Drug Safety* 30(8):
            669–675.
Goodwin, Charles
    1994   Professional vision. *American Anthropologist* 96(3): 606–633.
Goody, Esther
    1978   Towards a theory of questions. In: Esther Goody (ed.), *Questions and Pol-*
            iteness, 17–43. Cambridge: Cambridge University Press.
Gumperz, John J.
    1999   On interactional sociolinguistic method. In: Srikant Sarangi and Celia Ro-
            berts (eds.), *Talk, Work and Institutional Order: Discourse in Medical,*
            Mediation and Management Settings, 453–471. Berlin / New York: Mouton
            de Gruyter.
Halliday, M. A. K. and Christian M. I. M. Matthiessen
    2004   *An Introduction to Functional Grammar*, 3rd edition. London: Hodder Edu-
            cation.
Hamilton, Heidi E.
    2003   Diabetic patients' accounts of noncompliance: Self-identity as roadblock.
            In: Deborah Tannen and James E. Alatis (eds.), *Linguistics, Language, and*
            the Real World (GURT 2001). Washington, D.C.: Georgetown University
            Press.
Hamilton, Heidi E.
    2004   Symptoms and signs in particular: The influence of the medical concern
            on the shape of physician-patient talk. *Communication & Medicine* 1(1):
            59–70.
Have, Paul ten
    1989   The consultation as a genre. In: Brian Torode (ed.), *Text and Talk as Social*
            Practice, 115–135. Dordrecht: Foris Publications.
Have, Paul ten
    1991   Talk and institution: A reconsideration of the 'asymmetry' of doctor-patient
            interaction. In: Deirde Boden and Don Zimmerman (eds.), *Talk and Social*
            Structure, 138–163. Cambridge: Polity Press.
Helman, Cecil G.
    1984   *Culture, Health and Illness*. Oxford: Butterworth-Heinemann.

Heritage, John
    1997   Conversation analysis and institutional talk: Analyzing data. In: David
              Silverman (ed.), *Qualitative Research: Theory, Method and Practice*,
              161–182. London: Sage.
Joyce, C.R.
    1976   "Side"-effects: a misnomer. *Journal of Medical Ethics* 2(3): 112–117.
Lasser, K. E., P. D. Allen, S. J. Woolhandler, D. U. Himmelstein, S. N. Wolfe, and
    D. H. Bor
    2002   Timing of new black box warnings and withdrawals for prescription medi-
              cations. *The Journal of the American Medical Association* 287: 2215–2220.
Lyles, A
    2006   Postmarketing drug surveillance and death by committee. *Clinical Thera-
              peutics* 28(6): 962–3.
Maynard, Douglas W.
    1991   The perspective display series and the delivery of diagnostic news. In:
              Deirdre Boden and Don H. Zimmerman (eds.), *Talk and Social Structure*,
              165–192. Cambridge: Polity Press.
Mishler, Elliot G.
    1984   *The Discourse of Medicine*. Norwood, NJ: Ablex.
Roberts, Felicia
    1999   *Talking about Treatment: Recommendations for Breast Cancer Adjuvant
              Therapy*. Oxford: Oxford University Press.
Sacket, David L., William M. C. Rosenberg, J. A. Muir Gray, R. Brian Haynes, and
    W. Scott Richardson
    1996   Editorial: Evidence based medicine: What it is and what it isn't. *British
              Medical Journal* 312: 71–2.
Sarangi, Srikant and Celia Roberts (eds.)
    1999   *Talk, Work and Institutional Order: Discourse in Medical, Mediation and
              Management Settings*. Berlin / New York: Mouton de Gruyter.
Schegloff, Emanuel
    1968   Sequencing in conversational openings. *American Anthropologist* 70:
              1075–1095.
Schegloff, Emanuel and Harvey Sacks
    1973   Opening up closings. *Semiotica* 8: 289–327.
Schiffrin, Deborah
    1994   *Approaches to Discourse Analysis*. Cambridge: Cambridge University Press.
Stivers, Tanya
    2006   Treatment decisions: Negotiations between doctors and patients in acute
              care encounters. In: John Heritage and Douglas W. Maynard (eds.), *Com-
              munication in Medical Care: Interaction between Primary Care Physicians
              and Patients*, 279–312. Cambridge: Cambridge University Press.
Tannen, Deborah
    1989   *Talking Voices*. Cambridge: Cambridge University Press.
West, Candace
    1983   "Ask me no questions ..." An analysis of queries and replies in physician-
              patient dialogues. In: Sue Fisher and Alexandra Dundas Todd (eds.), *The
              Social Organization of Doctor-Patient Communication*, 75–106. Washing-
              ton, DC: Center for Applied Linguistics (CAL).

Wodak, Ruth
    1996   "What pills are you on now?" Doctors ask, and patients answer. In: Ruth
            Wodak, *Disorders of Discourse*, 35–62. London: Longman.

6. Institutional bodies and social selves: The discourse of medical examinations in hospital settings

Per Måseide

Abstract

This chapter focuses on discourse in medical examinations conducted in hospital settings. The kind of examinations in question differs significantly from the medical examinations focused on in traditional studies of doctor-patient interaction. The analysis concentrates on one case of bronchoscope examination. This is a major examination that is regularly conducted in thoracic wards. The bronchoscope examination is conducted by a doctor assisted by nurses and a radiographer. The patient is the object of the work conducted and all participants collaborate to accomplish the examination. The examination is an instrumental task requiring professional competence, experience, collaboration and use of technology; but it is essentially also a socio-moral encounter between the patient and the professionals. As such it has communicative characteristics of different kinds. This chapter looks at the various discursive forms enacted during the examination and suggests that the examination is an instrumental activity conducted within institutionalized frames, but tensions arise since the professionals during their work have to attend to what is simultaneously an objective body and a social subject. Hence, communicative formats must be established to manage adequate footing and shifts of frame during the examination.

1. Introduction

Preparations are made for a bronchoscope examination with full narcosis. Two nurses talk in low voices and communicate very gently with the patient. The doctor who will do the examination arrives together with an anesthetist. They greet the patient and also act in a gentle and deferential manner. An atmosphere of quiet respectfulness, kindness and professionalism characterizes the situation. Once anesthetics is administered and the patient falls asleep, however, the tone changes. The professionals start talking in normal voices, jokes are shared, also with reference to the patient, and sometimes they laugh loudly. Before the bronchoscope is passed down the patient's throat, his head is brusquely moved into an instrumentally adequate position. The doctor's professional attention is singularly on what he observes through the bronchoscope. Otherwise the atmosphere is jocular and lively throughout the whole examination. When the examination is finished and the machine is removed, the mouthpiece that is plastered in the opening of the patient's mouth is roughly removed. The way it is done would have been painful if the patient were awake. While this takes place, the doctor makes some notes about the examination and leaves the room saying goodbye to the nurses.

The scenario above refers to the kind of medical examinations where health professionals collaborate. The case is uncommon in the sense that the professionals initially relate to a social subject, but once anaesthesia is administered the patient as social subject is taken out of the situation and the physical body becomes the central target. In what follows the common form of bronchoscope examinations will be described. In these examinations the patient is fully conscious and an important part of professional discourse has to do with the management of moral tension: shifts of footing become a necessity as the examination proceeds.

Medical examinations within the hospital constitute "activity systems" (Goodwin 1994). They are professionally designed, follow institutionalized schedules and represent distinct social events. For the professional participants the patient is an objective body, but also a "social object" (Mead 1972 [1938]: 190) with meanings beyond the strictly medical. This "dualism" of the medical object is a critical element that affects professional discourse and the roles enacted by participants in conducting medical work. The major topic of this chapter is the integration of the various communicative forms embedded within a bronchoscope examination, how these forms of communication interconnect to mediate the relationship between patients and professionals, to organize the professional work that is done, and manage the practical distinction between the patient as a medical body and as a social subject.

2.   Communication and medical examinations

Much literature on medicine and discourse has concentrated on doctor-patient communication in general practice settings (Fisher and Todd 1983; Heritage and Maynard 2006), often with a focus on strategies employed by doctors to exercise discursive control in the encounter (Waitzkin 1989; West 1984). However, Mishler (1984) has rightly concluded that the discourses of medical consultations are not singularly professional or institutional. The documented complexity of medical discourses (Candlin and Candlin 2003) makes them occasions of what Sarangi and Roberts (1999) have termed "discursive hybridity". Medical communication has been studied in hospitals and other specialist settings (Fagerhaugh and Strauss 1977; McIntosh 1977; Davis 1979; Iedema 2007) and the role of language and discourse in collaborative practice has been studied, among others, by Atkinson (1995, 1999), Cicourel (1990) and Måseide (2003, 2006, 2007). An early contribution to studies of medical examinations is Emerson's (1970) article on the interactional tactics used to maintain a medical definition of the situation in gynecological examinations. Some studies of doctor-patient interaction have been undertaken focusing on the integration of gaze, talk, body movements and touch to sustain professional frames during physical examinations (Frankel 1983; Heath 1986, 2006). Even if Emerson's study is from specialist medicine and the others from general practice, they all refer to interaction between a single practitioner and his or her patient when the physical examination is one segment of a medical encounter. This chapter focuses on examinations with technology and with several professional practitioners involved. These examinations are accomplished at specific sites and constitute distinctive parts of the distributed system of medical problem-solving. Literature on this kind of medical work is scarce. Studies exist on collaboration among professionals in anesthetics and their communicative management of the front stage-back stage divide while the patient is still conscious (Hindmarsh and Pilnick 2002). Contrary to this kind of work, however, the patient in bronchoscopic examinations is usually a conscious participant during the whole event.

3.   Theoretical framework

The bronchoscope examination is an institutional "activity type" (Levinson 1979). As an activity type it is both verbal and non-verbal. It is connected to other activity types distributed spatially and temporally within the hospital system. The bronchoscope examination involves different phases of activities characterized by instrumental activities and "sentimental work" (Strauss et al. 1982): on the one hand, it is instrumental "body work" (Wolkowitz 2006) involving medical technology; and on the other, the practices of the participants are symbolically loaded and the examination represents a socially occasioned "focused gathering" (Goffman 1971).

The examination is framed and characterized by shifts, transformations and negotiations of frames. A "frame", according to Goffman (1974), is a meaning generating system. An utterance may be located within different frames and understood or meant differently by different participants in a given situation. Contextual elements or features not necessarily controlled by single participants may also affect the meaning-framing connection. Usually we routinely move in and out of interpretative frames during an activity. In many cases interaction takes place within multiple frames organized as laminations of meaning systems.

In an institutional setting such as the hospital, participant statuses include those of patients, nurses and doctors. They constitute the production format of institutional discourse. During medical work, however, the same participants may enact other participant statuses than the institutional ones and the production format of discourses will thus change. Change of participant status takes place during social intercourse. The concept of "footing" (Goffman, 1981) refers to the change of alignment between participant statuses that may take place during an encounter. Participant statuses may be self-ascribed, as in self-presentations, or be ascribed by others. The potential of participant statuses to be enacted, attributed, or changed in a medical examination is extensive. Shifting of frames affords new participation statuses and vice versa. During an institutionally or professionally framed activity a participation status that is not particularly relevant within such frames may be enacted or ascribed by one or more of the participants. This kind of footing may provide an interpersonal slack that may be useful for the structuring of the specific activity. The concept "participant framework" refers to the constellation of participant statuses involved in an activity at any time. A participant framework represents what Erickson (2004: 4–5) has termed "the social ecology of mutual adaptation within the interactional environment". Such ecologies are constantly generated, regenerated and changed during social discourse.

Several analysts of "the social body" (Crossley 2001; Shilling 2003) use Merleau-Ponty's (1962) distinction between the "objective body" and the "lived body". The objective body is the biomedical body. It is a professional and institutional "thing", a body without self or subjectivity. The lived body differs from the objective body in that we experience our world as bodies. Our bodies are our selves and the concept of "self" refers to the concept of "embodiment". The body is always a vehicle of meaning, and it is impossible for us to escape from it. We attend to our selves and the selves of others by attending to bodies. Hence, it is difficult to sustain a distinction between objective bodies and lived bodies. But for instrumental reasons it is sometimes done during medical examinations.

4.   Data presentation and analysis

Data for the following analysis come from fieldwork observation in the thoracic ward of a Norwegian teaching hospital. Discursive data come from field notes and not from electronic recordings.

4.1.   The bronchoscope examination

The bronchoscope examination is conducted on a special location in the thoracic ward. A resident physician usually conducts the examination assisted by two nurses and sometimes by a radiographer. When the examination starts, a thin flexible tube, the bronchoscope, is passed through the mouth, down the patient's air duct and into the bronchia. Through the tube it is possible to observe, make video recordings, take biopsies or cell samples, and administer anaesthetics. Patients have to fast before the examination. They are dressed in a hospital gown, put to bed and given a mild sedative and medication to reduce coughing. The fasting, the hospital gown, being put to bed and the medication indicate the institutionalization of the patient's body before the patient arrives in the examination unit. The examination may be divided into three phases, the pre-examination, the examination and the post-examination phases, which are detailed below.

4.1.1. The pre-examination phase

When the patient arrives medication is administered in order to diminish the production of mucus, reduce coughing and diminish the vomiting reflex as the bronchoscope is passed down the patient's throat. The anaesthetic regime transforms the body into a professionally adequate and collaborative medical object. A docile patient with few expressions of discomfort also contributes to maintaining a socially appropriate situation for the professionals.

In the following case the patient is a middle-aged male with a suspected lung tumor. The purpose of the examination is to locate the tumor, extract biological material from it and identify it pathologically. When I arrive, two female nurses and the patient are exchanging small talk and jokes while asthma medication is administered and a cannula is fastened to one of the patient's hands. Jocular relations between patient and professionals are very common during the pre-examination phase. With male patients and female nurses the interaction also has an element of playful flirtation. The jokes and the jokers' relations are highlighted and the examination frame fades away. Keeping this kind of jocular relationship going seems to be a mutual and moral responsibility for all participants.

The nurse informs the patient why she fastens a cannula (for possible blood transfusion), "but usually we don't need it" she adds. She also tells the patient that he must not make her laugh while she fastens the cannula. The second nurse asks what he has got for pre-medication. "Two Valiums" he answers. "That's a lot for you" the nurse responds with a smile. A participant framework is established where the patient is not only a medical body and the nurses act outside of their professional statuses. They might be understood as "acting out of frame"; but while their small talk and jokes create distance from the institutional frame of the examination, their verbal activity implicitly also makes reference to this frame. Personally, the patient and the nurses are strangers; they meet solely for this particular institutional event. The humorous conversational style is part of an institutional ceremony rather than personal talk. The talk is both informal and institutional.

The arrival of a young male doctor points to the forthcoming examination. He too exchanges jokes with the nurses. The verbal style of the initiating phase is in general light-hearted and jocular. The doctor puts on a green dress and hat, surgical gloves and mouth protection; then he turns to the patient. They shake hands; the doctor gives his name and indicates that he will conduct the examination. Since the ward nurse has informed the patient about the examination, nothing more is said about it now. The doctor articulates ordinary politeness that corresponds to general principles of an "interaction order" (Goffman 1983); but his behavior is also part of the institutional order that regulates the relationship between health professionals and patients. The doctor soon turns to medical matters and makes the patient inhale local anaesthetics. He informs that the next dosage of anaesthetics will not taste good and sprays anaesthetics into the patient's throat through a thin tube. While this is done, the patient says "*ahhh*" as he is instructed to. The patient admits it did not taste good, but that he has drunk worse liquor. The others laugh. One of the nurses says, "*that was nice*". Then the doctor starts swabbing the patient's throat with another type of anaesthetics. One of the nurses pats the patient's hand whenever she passes. The patient contributes with more jokes and the doctor and nurses laugh. These sequences of informal verbal exchange make the participants appear as a friendly and informal group.

After the initial preparations the patient is moved into the examination room and over to an examination bench. All of us put on lead aprons, hats and mouth protection. We become anonymous as persons. This is our institutional front. X-ray equipment is moved into position with some noise. The patient's bodily position is adjusted so as to fit the requirements of the x-ray equipment. The patient is attached to the technical equipment to monitor vital physiological processes. He is told by one of the nurses that she will attach a measuring device for his blood pressure, "*just to take care of you*" she adds. They also attach a measuring device for oxygen. They show him a thin tube that they put up on his nose and tell him it will provide him with enough air. Before the examination starts, a mouthpiece is plastered to the opening of the patient's mouth to pass the bronchoscope through. A nurse has some trouble fastening the mouthpiece; the patient sets his teeth hard. She asks him to relax and the doctor asks him to breathe normally in and out. A screen shows that his heartbeat that has been high goes down a little bit. The patient's emotional state is measured as a physical reaction and is visualized on a monitor. It becomes an externalized institutional fact. Oxygen saturation, rate of heart beat, and blood pressure level are similarly made visible on screens. Vital internal bodily processes are now externalized. When the mouthpiece is fastened the patient is unable to speak. This implies a strong restriction on the opportunity to enact social subjectivity.

Then the patient starts coughing. The doctor addresses one of the nurses in a low voice, "*exactly, not good*". Implicitly the utterance ascribes a certain participant status to the patient; he sounds like a "difficult case". The distinction between front stage (including the patient) and back stage (for professionals only) is not spatial but discursive. While the patient coughs, the doctor continues in a low voice that they have to wait; but if the patient continues coughing like this, the examination will be difficult. The professionals exclude the patient through their quiet talk.

As the preparations proceed, the atmosphere in the room gradually changes. The activities become calmer; the health professionals speak in lower voices and deploy a new form of respectfulness toward the patient. They become distinctly more involved in the professional and instrumental parts of their work. As the institutional frame becomes more dominant, professional and institutional participant statuses become privileged. However, the moral dimension of the activity is not completely replaced by institutional instrumentalism. By the nurse's patting of the patient's hand and her touch of his skin his subjective and moral identity is indicated while he is gradually transformed into a medical object conforming to the examination frame. To use Latour's (2005) expression, the medical equipment attached to the patient together with the doctor's and nurses' professional activities "enrol" the patient into the medical activity.

4.1.2.   The examination phase

When the examination starts, the patient as social subject is medically superfluous. But the patient is still there as a conscious social subject. During much of the examination an "awareness context" (Glaser and Strauss 1964) is recognized in which the principles of deference and demeanor (Goffman 1967) are enacted in relation to the patient and his body. A subtle balance is attempted between professional and institutional forces and demands, constituting the patient as medical object, and the communicative moves needed to recognize the patient's social and moral participant status. During long sequences of the examination process one of the nurses holds the patient's hand. The patient's subjective identity is literally drawn into to the medical situation by the nurse's hand.

Before the examination starts, the doctor has a brief look into the patient's journal. Then he turns to the patient: "*Are you ready Olsen (name anonymised)? Bend your head a bit backwards and breathe calmly. Don't forget to breathe.*" This marks the beginning of the examination phase. The patient is addressed as a person who will collaborate to make the examination physically possible. The doctor passes the tube through the mouthpiece, down the patient's windpipe and into his bronchia. The patient immediately starts coughing. Passing the bronchoscope tube down the patient's throat and air duct and into his bronchia is an act of medical "invasion" and "objectivation" of the patient's body. As the terms are used here, they are not morally intended. They refer to an essential part of the medical job to be done.

Coughing is very common during bronchoscope examinations. It may obstruct the examination; it is uncomfortable for the patient; it expresses discomfort; and the discomfort expressed may be heard as a sign of suffering inflicted upon the patient by the professional work. This may be experienced as morally charging by the professionals. Extract 1 captures the sequence of talk that follows after the patient starts coughing. All extracts of talk are translated from Norwegian. As the talk is not audio-recorded the transcription conventions are simple. Short pauses are indicated by (.), sometimes by (,) and by (pause) to signal approximate length; exclamations are marked by (!) and rising tone by (?).

Extract 1
1. *Doctor (to the patient): The coughing is not dangerous*
2. *we just touch your mucous membrane (.) breathe calmly*
3. *(nothing is said while the tube is moved further)*
4. *Doctor: We are down (turns to the nurses)*
5. *we'll take it easy till he calms down (.) give him a bit more*
6. *anaesthetics (to the patient) we will give you some more*
7. *anaesthetics.*
8. *(Anaesthetic is provided by one of the nurses through*
9. *the tube. Nothing is said while it is done)*
10. *Doctor (to the patient): We have given you some more*
11. *anaesthetics and we will wait till it starts having effect (.)*
12. *just you relax*
13. *(After a short break the doctor continues*
14. *the examination while he talks to the nurses*
15. *about what he observes)*
16. *Doctor (to the patient): We are talking a little bit*
17. *here about what we see (.) it is nothing important*
18. *to you (.) you don't listen to us (.) just you relax (.)*
19. *everything goes just fine now*

The doctor's first utterance expresses a concern for the patient's well-being while it also requests the patient to collaborate. After that, nothing is said while the doctor moves the tube till he declares, "*we are down*". The plural "we" refers to an institutional accomplishment. Then the doctor addresses the nurses about the patient's coughing in a lowered voice (lines 5–6). The doctor's statement indicates a back stage comment because of his explicit turning to the nurses and his lowered voice. When he turns to the patient to inform him about the anaesthetics, a front stage situation is again established by the doctor's bodily movement while he addresses the patient verbally. The patient is informed that more anaesthetic has been provided. This utterance marks the ascribing of a subjective participant status for the patient. During the shifting phases of the examin-

ation, the professionals considered inclusion of the patient's subjective participant status to be more or less relevant or desirable. As part of the inclusion, the
doctor also informs the patient about how they will proceed and concludes with
the statement, "*just you relax*". Inclusion means cooperation. But the final appeal to relaxation is also an appeal to subjective withdrawal from the examination. The doctor continues examining the patient's bronchia while he talks to
the nurses. After a while he asks the patient not to listen to them because what
they talk about is not important to him (lines 16–19). By this move the doctor
asks the patient to withdraw from the discursive event he has previously been
included in. As a co-present addressee, the patient is physically unable to move
out of the discursive site, yet he is urged to adopt the status of a non-ratified bystander in the encounter.

The patient is told that the professional talk is not important to him, although
he is the object of the professional activity. The professional talk is important
with reference to the patient's physical body, but not to the patient as a lived
body. Is it a transcendental or disembodied "owner" of a body that is addressed?
The patient is asked not to listen to their talk even if this is physically unavoid-
able. Again, is a transcendental ego being addressed here? Finally, the patient is
told to relax because everything is going okay. The examination has hardly
started; the doctor's remark is uttered to control the patient's emotions and thus
also the medical activity. But everything is not okay for the patient. The doctor
is trying to locate a malignant tumor in one of his lungs. All the participants
know that. But examination talk in general does not refer explicitly to the purpose of the examination.

The patient has stopped coughing and lies completely still and quiet. As the
doctor moves the bronchoscope he explains to one of the nurses where in the patient's bronchia the instrument is positioned. He works systematically and
examines first the right side of the bronchial tree and then the left. On the right
side no anomalies are mentioned in the X-ray description. The bronchoscope
observation confirms this. Then the bronchoscope is partially extracted and
moved down the left main bronchus. Here the doctor observes much mucus,
which he draws out through the tube; he asks for more anaesthetics. This sequence excludes the patient's subjectivity totally, but after a while the doctor addresses him again. "*Are you okay Olsen? I think this goes just fine.*" The doctor's question is ceremonial; it cannot be answered, but for a moment it "enrols"
the patient into the examination as a social subject; he is also assured about the
ordinariness of the activity.

The inside of the bronchus is visible on the monitor. It looks red and inflamed. The doctor comments on this to the nurse who assists him. The observed
mucus membrane does not look normal and indicates that something is wrong in
this area. Shortly after, however, the doctor addresses the patient and states, "*It's
okay, it looks good. Just relax.*" This remark may sound contradictory to the

doctor's previous comment to the nurse. But these remarks are addressed to different participants for different purposes. To the patient the utterance is not professionally descriptive; it is a verbal act that in Searle's (1969) terms represents a "constative". To the patient the constative form may sound convincing and make the situation ordinary.

When the bronchoscope reaches the area where the suspect tumor has been spotted, the mucus membrane does not look as red any more; however, it does appear a little more swollen. The doctor says something inaudible to the nurse before they continue as follows:

Extract 2
Nurse: Would it be an idea to brush there?
Doctor: Yes I think so
Nurse: Couldn't we use a thin needle here?
(The doctor observes something white further down in the
bronchus, he tries to reach it with the tube but doesn't
succeed. Turns to the nurse): Could you call the chief
physician?
(The nurse tries to call the chief physician but
doesn't get any answer).
Doctor (to the nurse): Could you go to the chief
physician's office and notify him?
Nurse: Can I do that?

In the above episode the nurse and the doctor talk specifically about their concrete professional work. The nurse makes suggestions about what to do. She acts as a collaborator in the joint medical accomplishment. The doctor agrees to her first suggestion but ignores the second; he has seen something white further down in the bronchus, which may be the tumor. He tries to reach it with the tube but does not succeed. The bronchoscope examination is connected to a wider network of experts and the doctor asks the nurse to call the chief physician for assistance. The nurse tries to call on the phone but gets no answer. The doctor then asks her to go to the chief physician's office and ask him to come. The chief physician's authority is a barrier for the nurse. She is uncertain if she can just go to his office and ask him to come. It would be an intrusion into an institutional site she never enters. This kind of institutional and professional hierarchy is not manifest in the examination situation. The problem of intrusion is obviously smaller by a phone call than by personal invasion of the chief physician's office. But the chief physician is part of the medical apparatus that may be "plugged-in", to use Latour's (2005) term, when medically required. But to the nurse this kind of institutional plugging-in may be experienced as socially challenging. The doctor urges the nurse to do this. She leaves, and shortly afterwards the chief physician arrives.

The doctor expresses politeness and deference when the chief physician appears and excuses for disturbing the chief physician; the chief physician answers ceremonially, *"No, that's okay when it's you."* His answer is a personal recognition of the doctor's personal and professional standing. The doctor shows the white spot to the chief physician. It is now barely visible. The doctor explains that it is too narrow for the tube. The chief physician does not seem to engage much with the problem presented. He tells the doctor to brush the area he can reach; then he leaves. The doctor is involved in the practical task of extracting biological material; the chief physician, however, seems more intent on making an institutionally accountable attempt as to whether the examination is successful or not.

The doctor makes several attempts to get samples out with a thin needle, but with little success. He talks to the nurses about it; the bronchoscope is visually right on the spot and technically everything should function well. The doctor sends for the chief physician again, who is still busy with a meeting. Again the doctor excuses himself and again the chief physician answers that it is okay; they are welcome to come for him if they have problems. The doctor wants the chief physician himself to try to get samples out, but the chief physician is reluctant. He does not have time and suggests that the doctor makes one more attempt with a thin needle. After that he should try to brush. The chief physician is refraining from direct involvement in the examination; instead he authorizes the doctor to continue as he has been doing. This procedure is exactly the one that has failed to this point and what it was that the doctor asked for help about. The visit by the chief physician has no practical consequence, but he provides institutional approval of what is done. The chief physician focuses only on the restricted area of the patient's body highlighted by the doctor. The patient is not involved or addressed as a social subject.

Shortly afterwards the patient starts coughing. The doctor only extracts what the nurse describes as *"tiny, tiny, tiny bits"*. This material is of no value for the pathologist and the examination is by now not successful. The doctor continues and now he ignores the patient's coughing. The focal point now is to obtain adequate samples. The patient is thus transformed into a complete medical object. After a while, however, the doctor talks to the patient again and explains, *"we try to get out enough cells."* Again, the patient is afforded participant status as a "body-subject", one who is informed. The doctor does not go into further detail about their practical difficulties with the procedure. This kind of professional information is obviously considered irrelevant for the patient and most of the time the patient is included in the participant framework of the examination only as a biomedical body.

The professional team stops trying to obtain biopsies. Instead, they go for sampling cells by brushing the surface of the bronchial wall. The patient can see them take out the brushes. One of the nurses says to the patient, *"it is like a small bottle brush"*. This is an explanation about the new tool, but it is also a kind of euphemism. It is hardly important to the patient what the tiny brushes look like; the information draws the attention away from the object of examination and refers to something insignificant, the means used for examining. A distance is kept between the patient's mind and the examination activities.

When the first brush is taken out, the nurse states that now there is at least material. Another brush is taken, again with plenty of material attached. After the second brush, the doctor turns to the patient and says, "*We will soon be finished.*" Again the subjective patient is addressed. The doctor then addresses the nurses: "*let us try once more with a thin needle because now the scope is so nicely located*". They try again but the nurse describes what comes out as "*something very tiny*". After that a last brush is taken. The nurse says to the doctor: "*The last sample from the thin needle was so sparse that it is nothing to send, they will laugh at us, don't send it.*"

The professional participants have to relate to a problem-solving system beyond the site of the bronchoscope examination. When the nurse says, "*they will laugh at us*", "they" refers to those working in the pathology laboratory. The pathology laboratory is part of the expanded problem-solving system. The participants in the bronchoscope examination make their professionalism apparent outside of the examination room on the basis of the quality of the samples they send to another site. But the words, "*they will laugh at us*", indicate more than professional failure. Being laughed at is a moral affair. Consideration of their social and professional reputations or local statuses is a regulating principle for their practical interaction with other parts of the problem-solving system. As a consequence, they do not send the thin needle biopsies.

4.1.3.   The post-examination phase

The doctor starts removing the bronchoscope. Before it is completely out he asks the patient so say "*aaa*" and "*eee.*" Then he takes the bronchoscope out and the mouthpiece is carefully removed by one of the nurses. The doctor addresses the patient and a short exchange follows with one of the nurses included:

Extract 3
  Doctor: Finished! That was it, Olsen
  Nurse: Have we been awful to you?
  Patient: No, I wouldn't say that, I have experienced worse

The removal of the tube and the mouthpiece marks a significant change of the patient's participant status. So does the doctor's remark. The nurse's inquiry is excessively empathic; from a professional point of view they have done no harm to the patient. The enquiry is part of the institutional "empathy game". With the stated minimization of his discomforts, the patient demonstrates composure and moral character. With his regained ability to talk, the patient has also more of a potential for enacting his social subjectivity. Some small talk follows as all equipment is removed. The patient is further praised for being brave and one of the nurses tells him that he deserves a nap now. The professionals know the examination is uncomfortable and they communicate this to the patient. The doctor turns to the patient again as follows.

Extract 4

> Doctor: I cannot see any obvious tumors in your
> air duct (.) we have tried to punctuate where the spot is
> (.) but we do not get anything out (.) and we do not see
> anything localized
> Patient: Is that positive?
> Doctor: It is positive by itself yes.

This extract is taken from the final sequence of talk between the doctor and the patient. The doctor informs the patient about what he has seen, although his message is ambiguous. It may be heard as stating that they have not found anything, which implicitly weakens their suspicion of a malignant disease. The patient's subsequent question indicates such an interpretation. The doctor's response is again ambiguous. As a direct response it indicates that his message is positive, but the second part, "*by itself, yes*" restricts the meaning of it. In other words, his message is incomplete. The patient is given restricted medical information. But this is the site of an examination, and the demand for comprehensiveness of information delivered here is limited. Within the confined context of the examination the doctor may talk like a strict empiricist, referring exactly to what is seen, and not to how it might be interpreted. Besides, nothing should be explicated before the results from the pathology laboratory are available. But the patient is informed and the information is situationally adequate. The doctor's use of the pronouns "I" and "we" in Extract 4 is also noteworthy. The doctor first refers to what he has not seen. And he is the individual professional agent who has observed the insides of the patient's bronchia. Following the medical ethos that the doctor should see the patient, his professional vision is communicated. Then he turns to what the institutional collective "we" have done. "We" includes the medical apparatus, consisting of professional agents and technical devices that have conducted the examination. The doctor reports what this institutional collective has done and gives an account of a shared vision that conforms to his own individual observations.

After the patient is taken away the doctor and one of the nurses look at the samples. They throw away those with least material. The nurse repeats that they should not look ridiculous to the pathologists. She restates the importance of their "local identities" (Cook-Gumperz and Messerman 1999).

4.2.   Discussion

A bronchoscope examination is a medically oriented instrumental activity, but it is also an activity mediated with social, moral and interpersonal challenges. For the professional participants the examination is a routine affair, even if doctors who often conduct such examinations describe it as professionally challenging. The professional team members know each other and know how to collaborate. For the patient the situation is different. Most patients undergo this examination for the first time. They are anxious about the examination and what may be disclosed by it; for most patients the experience of being practically defined and treated as a physical object is special and uncomfortable. It is difficult for patients to enact subjectivity and the professionals' display of subjectivity in relation to the patient is limited. This constitutes an essential quality of the bronchoscope examination and its production format.

To conduct the examination, talk is used to instruct and encourage patients to collaborate and to achieve professional collaboration. Even those parts of the examination that are not linguistically grounded may require communicative efforts by the professionals for social and moral reasons. The nurse's patting and holding the patient's hand or stroking his forehead together with the doctor's small talk to the patient during the examination indicate this. Language and communication marks the difference between the purely instrumental activity in relation to a physical object and the examination as a social occasioned encounter between social subjects.

The bronchoscope examination is characterized by shifting participant frameworks and local ecologies. The patient is essentially and often manifestly ascribed a participant status as medical body or object. In certain sequences and moments of the examination, however, a local ecology is generated where the patient is ascribed a social and subjective participant status. But even these statuses are institutionally prescribed or constructed. Goffman (1961) describes the difference between enacting the statuses ascribed by institutions and institutional structures and the individual expression that articulates subjectivity. To enact subjectivity situational opportunities and conditions for producing recognizable expressions of individual identity and character are needed. Goffman (1971) describes how participants in diverse kinds of social activities regularly do this. He terms the process "role distancing". Medical examinations limit the opportunity for patients to perform that process.

A striking characteristic of the bronchoscope examination is that apart from the pre-examination and post-examination phases, the patient does not contribute discursively. One very good reason for this is that the patient cannot talk during the examination. Coughing, a bodily reflex, is the only way of communicating during the examination phase. For the professionals, this coughing is not just a physical reflex without meaning. The physical reflex does not represent a "thin description", a signal with no meaning, as such reflexes may do in Ryle's (1971) account; in the examination setting a bodily reflex is often loaded with professional and moral meanings. As we have seen, communication with the patient takes place verbally and non-verbally entirely initiated by the professional staff. The patient cannot initiate communication. In the post-examination phase, verbal interaction between professionals and the patient is again possible, but it is the professionals who initiate talk with the patient. It is not the other way round. The examination and the post-examination phases are totally professionally orchestrated.

Talk between the patient and nurses in the pre-examination phase takes on a jocular, informal and friendly style, with the patient as an active participant. The patient acts out of his institutional patient role. He flirts and jokes and the nurses respond approvingly. To generate a frame for the patient's subjective participation is a collaborative accomplishment, and the patient's enacted subjectivity is possible only as long as the nurses respond accordingly. The exchange takes place within an institutional frame. To the nurses this is a routine working frame. For the patient it is not. Even if the patient implicitly or explicitly recognizes that he is part of an activity that is medically and institutionally framed, he does not share the nurses' frame. This lack of sharing makes a difference. The nurses' responses are enacted within a frame that is different from the patient's frame. Hence, the patient's individuality or subjectivity is never really recognized. He is afforded an institutionalized subjectivity generated through routine and ritualized forms of "informal" interaction.

In spite of this, a central aspect of the examination for the professionals has to do with their practical and professional relationship with a body that is their medical object; but for cultural and moral reasons the body is to be recognized as a social subject. During the examination the patient is variously ascribed participant statuses as social subject and medical object; however, when the status as a social subject seems highlighted, it is always grounded in the institutional practice. The individuality of the patient is always represented by a ceremonially generated social image. The patient is provided with the kind and extent of individuality or subjectivity that the medical institution can afford.

During the pre-examination phase, the patient is gradually transformed into an institutional object appropriately suited for those activity types which belong to the medical frame. Nonetheless, awareness of the patient's cognitive or subjective presence is occasionally also displayed during the instrumental work of the examination. At certain times, however, the professionals act discursively as if the subjective and mindful patient is not present. They generate back stage discussions or discursive time-outs to exchange information that are not meant for the patient to hear; they practice ignorance of the patient's subjective presence; they concentrate on medical activities; they avoid addressing the patient. During the examination, boundaries are generated between the patient and his body and between the professionals and the patient as social subject.

In the bronchoscope examination the medical discourse is characterized by hybridity with certain particular characteristics. Much of the talk and communicative action is about the patient's body or a restricted part of it, about diverse tools, about biological samples, anaesthetics and other medical "things". Collaborative talk between the professionals about the patient's body and about how to proceed with the medical work is also accomplished. To the extent that talk and action are directed toward the patient as a Self, the communicative forms belong to the ceremonial practices of the examination. In this sense, the medical discourse is to a large extent institutionally grounded body talk.

Discourse is also needed to expand the examination activity beyond the physical examination site. In the case presented above the professionals refer verbally to the pathology laboratory; they talk about how to provide this institution with adequate biological material and how to maintain their local professional reputation in relation to the professional expertise and authority of the laboratory. The biological material they deliver becomes a symbolic representation of their professional standing. The doctor also has to call the chief physician for assistance and he asks one of the nurses to do it. These sequences show the hierarchical structure of the collaborative activity.

5.   Conclusion

Within certain activity types, such as bronchoscope examinations, the professionals face dilemmas when trying to meet institutional, professional, social and moral demands. Dilemmas are problems that cannot be solved and in certain kinds of medical examinations it is not easy to see how such dilemmas should be dealt with professionally; yet they have to be managed. The dilemmas are at once ethical and discursive. Arthur W. Frank (1997) has written about similar dilemmas in medicine. He demands that medical practitioners should allow their patients "to stand up to the occasion" of their diseases. In bronchoscope examinations that might mean to loosen the institutional grip and allow patients a more personal role. While that might in principle be possible within the examination's discursive context, it is hard to see how that could be realized within the examination's institutional and professional contexts and restraints.

Linking back to the initial scenario, the critical distinction in the bronchoscope examination between the body as physical object and the body as social subject becomes obvious. In the discussion above it is shown how the professionals attempt to handle this distinction. The extreme case of a patient in full anesthesia generates a back stage region for the professionals completely cut off from the patient's subjectivity while the examination is conducted. It simplifies the collaborative professional work and discourse; as an activity type it has more in common with that seen in surgery and anaesthesiology than in ordinary bronchoscope examinations. Medical activities like the bronchoscope examination will always invoke dilemmas such as those suggested above. While the technology used and the professional body work conducted may be steadily improved, and this would also be in the patient's best interest, managing the moral relationship with the patient as a social subject is a communicative concern. This represents a particular challenge to professional practitioners as there are no communicative techniques or scripts that will dissolve the dilemma. However, professionals are at least implicitly aware of the dilemma and try to find adequate ways of managing it. It means that they have to develop professional practices that involve the patient as a social subject, while they also generate a context for instrumental medical work.

References

Atkinson, Paul
   1995   *Medical Talk and Medical Work: The Liturgy of the Clinic.* London: Sage.
Atkinson, Paul
   1999   Medical discourse, evidentiality and the construction of professional responsibility. In: Srikant Sarangi and Celia Roberts (eds.), *Talk, Work and Institutional Order: Discourse in Medical, Mediation and Management Settings*, 75–107. Berlin/New York: Mouton de Gruyter.
Candlin, Christopher N. and Sally Candlin
   2003   Health care communication: A problematic site for applied linguistics research. *Annual Review of Applied Linguistics* 23: 134–154.
Cicourel, Aaron V.
   1990   The integration of distributed knowledge in collaborative medical diagnosis. In: Jolene Galegher, Robert E. Kraut and Carmen Egido (eds.), *Intellectual Teamwork. Social and Technological Foundations of Cooperative Work*, 221–242. Hillsdale, NJ: Lawrence Erlbaum.
Cook-Gumperz, Jenny and Lawrence Messerman
   1999   Local identities and institutional practices: Constructing the record of professional collaboration. In: Srikant Sarangi and Celia Roberts (eds.), *Talk, Work and Institutional Order: Discourse in Medical, Mediation and Management Settings*, 145–181. Berlin/New York: Mouton de Gruyter.
Crossley, Nick
   2001   *The Social Body: Habit, Identity and Desire.* London: Sage.
Davis, Alan (ed.)
   1979   *Relationships Between Doctors and Patients.* Westmead: Teakfield Limited.
Emerson, Joan
   1970   Behavior in private places: Definitions of reality in gynecological examinations. In: Hans Dreitzel (ed.), *Recent Sociology, No 2*, 74–97. London: Macmillan.

Erickson, Frederick
    2004   *Talk and Social Theory: Ecologies of Speaking and Listening in Everyday Life.* Cambridge: Polity Press.
Fagerhaugh, Shibutani and Anselm Strauss
    1977   *Politics of Pain Management: Staff-Patient Interaction.* Menlo Park CA: Addison-Wesley.
Frank, Arthur W.
    1997   Illness as moral occasion: restoring agency to ill people. *Health* 1: 131–147.
Frankel, Richard M.
    1983   The laying on of hands: Aspects of the organization of gaze, touch and talk in a medical encounter. In: Sue Fisher and Alexandra Dundas Todd (eds.), *The Social Organization of Doctor-Patient Communication*, 19–54. Washington DC: Center for Applied Linguistics.
Fisher, Sue and Alexandra Dundas Todd (eds.)
    1983   *The Social Organization of Doctor-Patient Communication.* Washington DC: Center for Applied Linguistics.
Glaser, Barry G. and Anselm Strauss
    1964   Awareness context and social interaction. *American Sociological Review* 29: 669–678.
Goffman, Erving
    1961   *Asylums: Essays on the Social Situation of Mental Patients and other Inmates.* New York: Doubleday.
Goffman, Erving
    1967   The nature of deference and demeanor. In: Erving Goffman, *Interaction Ritual: Essays on Face-to-Face Behavior,* 47–95. New York: Doubleday Anchor.
Goffman, Erving
    1971   *Encounters: Two Studies in the Sociology of Interaction.* Indianapolis: Bobbs-Merrill.
Goffman, Erving
    1974   *Frame Analysis: An Essay on the Organization of Experience.* Harmonsworth: Penguin.
Goffman, Erving
    1981   Footing. In: Erving Goffman, *Forms of Talk*, 124–159. Philadelphia: University of Pennsylvania Press.
Goffman, Erving
    1983   The interaction order. *American Sociological Review* 48: 1–17.
Goodwin, Charles
    1994   Professional vision. *American Anthropologist* 96: 606–633.
Heath, Christian
    1986   *Body Movement and Speech in Medical Interaction.* Cambridge: Cambridge University Press.
Heath, Christian
    2006   Body work: The collaborative production of the clinical object. In: John Heritage and Douglas W. Maynard (eds.), *Communication in Medical Care: Interaction between Primary Care Physicians and Patients,* 185–213. Cambridge: Cambridge University Press.

Heritage, John and Douglas W. Maynard (eds.)
2006   *Communication in Medical Care: Interaction between Primary Care Physicians and Patients.* Cambridge: Cambridge University Press.
Hindmarsh, Jon and Alison Pilnick
2002   The tacit order of teamwork: Collaboration and embodied conduct in anesthesia. *The Sociological Quarterly* 43: 139–164.
Iedema, Rick (ed.)
2007   *The Discourse of Hospital Communication: Tracing Complexities in Contemporary Health Care Organizations.* Basingstoke: Palgrave Macmillan.
Latour, Bruno
2005   *Reassembling the Social: An Introduction to Actor-Network Theory.* Oxford: Oxford University Press.
Levinson, Stephan C.
1979   Activity types and language. *Linguistics* 17: 356–399.
McIntosh, Jim
1977   *Communication and Awareness in a Cancer Ward.* London: Croom Helm.
Mead, George Herbert
1972   *The Philosophy of the Act: Works of George Herbert Mead. Vol. 3.* Charles
[1938] W. Morris (ed.). Chicago: The University of Chicago Press.
Merleau-Ponty, Maurice
1962   *Phenomenology of Perception.* London: Routledge.
Mishler, Elliot
G. 1984 *The Discourse of Medicine: Dialectics of Medical Interviews.* Norwood, NJ: Ablex.
Måseide, Per
2003   Medical talk and moral order: Social interaction and collaborative clinical work. *Text* 23: 369–403.
Måseide, Per
2006   The deep play of medicine: Discursive and collaborative processing of evidence in medical problem solving. *Communication & Medicine* 3(1): 43–54.
Måseide, Per
2007   The role of signs and representations in the organization of medical work: X-rays in medical problem solving. In: Rick Iedema (ed.), *The Discourse of Hospital Communication: Tracing Complexities in Contemporary Health Care Organizations,* 201–221. Basingstoke: Palgrave Macmillan.
Ryle, Gilbert
1971   The thinking of thoughts: What is "le penseur" doing? In: Gilbert Ryle, *Collected Papers: Collected Essays 1929–1968. Volume 2,* 480–496. London: Hutchinson.
Sarangi, Srikant and Celia Roberts
1999   The dynamics of interactional and institutional orders in work-related settings. In: Srikant Sarangi and Celia Roberts (eds.), *Talk, Work and Institutional Order. Discourse in Medical, Mediation and Management Settings,* 1–57. Berlin/New York: Mouton de Gruyter.
Searle, John
1969   *Speech Acts: An Essay in the Philosophy of Language.* Cambridge: Cambridge University Press.

Shilling, Chris
    2003   *The Body and Social Theory,* 2nd edn. London: Sage.
Strauss, Anselm, Shibutani Fagerhaugh, Barbara Suczec and Carolyn Wiener
    1982   Sentimental work in the technologized hospital. *Sociology of Health and Illness* 4: 254–278.
Waitzkin, Howard
    1989   A critical theory of medical discourses. *Journal of Health and Social Behavior* 30: 220–239.
West, Candance
    1984   *Routine Complications: Troubles with Talk between Doctor and Patients.* Bloomington: Indiana University Press.
Wolkowitz, Carol
    2006   *Bodies at Work.* London: Sage.

7. Uncomfortable moments in speech-language therapy discourse

Dana Kovarsky and Irene Walsh

Abstract

We examined uncomfortable moments that surfaced as speech-language pathologists (SLPs) were engaged in therapy. Their clients were adults with aphasia and traumatic brain injury. The uncomfortable moments involved instances when positive rapport was threatened by challenges to the professional face of the SLPs. Such moments did not occur frequently and were of interest because of the premium placed on avoiding them. Analysis revealed that when therapy participants competed over the interpretation of communicative actions and events, the construal and evaluation of meaning was dominated by a clinical logic rooted in traditional, impairment-based therapy. Here, an underlying conduit metaphor of communication (Reddy 1979) and oracular reasoning (Mehan 1990) contributed to the construction of uncomfortable moments. Implications are discussed in terms of alternative models of intervention that are evolving.

1. Introduction

We examine uncomfortable moments – when interlocutors appear ill at ease about the unfolding interaction – that surface as speech-language pathologists (SLPs) are engaged in therapy. The clients are adults with aphasia and traumatic brain injury. Similar to Erickson and Shultz's (1982) ground-breaking analysis of advising sessions involving junior college counselors and students, instances of discomfort manifest themselves in the referential content of the talk itself and/or through a combination of "intonation cues, sudden postural and proxemic shifts, facial expressions, eye contact, and other aspects of communicative performance, [like turn interruption]" that often disturb the conversational synchrony or the flow of the interaction (Erickson and Shultz 1982: 109). These sorts of contextualization cues not only help frame how individual utterances are to be interpreted, they also have the potential to signal when longer stretches of communicative interaction have gone awry (Gumperz 1982).

The following uncomfortable moment occurred at the beginning of a group therapy session involving adults with traumatic brain injury (TBI) when a woman (Paula) complained that goals established by the speech-language pathologist (SLP) were not addressing her individual needs (transcription conventions are in the Appendix).

1. SLP: We discussed why we were up here and some of our goals.

2. Wilbur: Yeah.

3. SLP: And we need to be tolerant of that. So (pause) okay what I want to do "toda[y ((rubs mouth with fingers))

4. Paula: [Can I disagree with you now with what we talked about on Friday. ((P looking straight ahead and not at the SLP, while SLP looks at P)) Because I don't think we are working on the goals that I need to work on for me ((P raises and lowers eyebrows)).

5. SLP: Okay? ((slight vertical head nod))

6. SLP: [We can't address all your goals in this group (pause) [that's correct.

7. Paula: [No   [I don't think you're working on my goals at all.

In turns 4 and 7, Paula interrupts and proclaims in a very articulate manner that the SLP is not "working on my goals at all". When a more extended version of this episode and others are examined in greater detail, analysis will reveal how and why these uncomfortable moments emerge, and the nature of therapy practice. Before examining actual excerpts, some general characteristics of traditional speech-language therapy discourse are discussed.

1.1.   Speech-language therapy discourse

Although much has been written about interactions between professional experts, like physicians and psychiatrists, and individuals who are diagnosed with particular medical and/or psychological problems (Ferrara 1994; Labov and Fanshel 1977; Ainsworth-Vaughn 1998; Duchan, Kovarsky and Maxwell 2005), we focus on clinical encounters between SLPs and their clients. Speech-language therapy discourse bears a close resemblance to traditional classroom lessons involving teachers and pupils. Like classrooms (Cazden 1988; Sinclair and Coulthard 1975), one hallmark of speech-language therapy is the three-part, quiz question sequence where the clinician makes a request for known information, the client responds, and then the clinician evaluates that response (Prutting et al. 1978; Ripich et al.1984). When the response is deemed inappropriate, repair work is initiated by the therapist. These correctional sequences can extend over a number of turns as the SLP provides a series of hints and clues until the desired response is produced by the client (Kovarsky 1989). In other words, quiz questions, coupled with any remedial work considered necessary by the SLP, constitute the "interactional substrate" through which clients are held accountable for their performance (Maynard and Marlaire 1999).

Behaviors targeted for repair by the clinician reveal that a conduit metaphor of communication (Reddy 1979) underlies traditional therapeutic practice. Through this metaphor, communication is depicted as consisting of a sender, a receiver and a prepackaged message that travels along the conduit. As long as clear, intelligible information can be conveyed through the pipeline, successful communication is achieved. Miscommunications occur when there are distortions in the message, including "problems of articulation, lexical choice [and] syntactic form" (McTear and King 1991: 197). When difficulties do take place, the therapist's task is to evaluate and fix client problems of expression or comprehension along the conduit by initiating repair work.

Without repairables that can be construed as errors on the part of the client, there is no therapy (van Kleeck and Richardson 1986; Kovarsky and Maxwell 1992). Referred to as the "inherent paradox of therapy" (Simmons-Mackie and Damico 1999), the idea is to help clients improve their communicative abilities by constructing contexts where they are more likely to perform incompetently so that their errors can be fixed via repair work (Kovarsky, Kimbarow and Kastner 1999).

This traditional approach to intervention is dubbed "impairment-focused" because it revolves around remediating those cognitive, linguistic and/or communicative deficits that are located within the client. Here, it is the therapist who sets the goals of intervention, selects therapy materials and activities, controls the introduction of new topics into the discourse, and regulates access to the interactional floor (Bobkoff and Panagos 1986; Kovarsky and Duchan 1997; Prutting et al. 1978).

When taken together, studies of traditional, impairment-based intervention discourse reveal a number of interactional asymmetries. By virtue of their professional expertise, therapists control the introduction and termination of therapy activities and tasks, and decide who will participate and in what manner (Panagos 1996). When client performance is deemed problematic, repair work is initiated until the clinician is satisfied that an appropriate response has been provided. It is the communicative appropriateness of the client and not the SLP that is scrutinized for the purpose of evaluation and correction.

The negotiation of all these interactional asymmetries can be a delicate issue because of the premium SLPs place on the establishment and maintenance of rapport during clinical encounters (Hand 2003). While clinicians focus their evaluative lenses on closely regulating and interpreting the communicative participation of clients, as professionals, they are expected to do so in a way that promotes positive interpersonal relationships between all interactants (Meitus and Weinberg 1983). However, even though "the relative harmony and smoothness of relations between people" may be the ideal, individuals "can hold differing types of rapport orientations towards each other" (Spencer-Oatey 2005: 96) – orientations that range from enhancing and maintaining, to neglecting and even challenging interpersonal relationships.

The uncomfortable moments to be discussed involve instances when positive rapport is threatened by challenges to the professional face (or public self-image, Brown and Levinson [1987]) of the SLPs. Such moments do not occur frequently in therapy and are of interest precisely because of the premium placed on avoiding them. Their analysis provides an opportunity to explore and evaluate aspects of clinical practice that might otherwise go unnoticed.

Our examination of these uncomfortable moments reveals that when participants compete over the interpretation of communicative actions and events, the construal and evaluation of meaning is dominated by a clinical logic rooted in traditional, impairment-based therapy. This type of clinical reasoning does not adequately account for the viable, contrastive points of view expressed by clients, or their communicative abilities, and contributes to the construction of uncomfortable moments where rapport is threatened. Reflecting on these findings, alternative communicative practices for conducting therapy are discussed. However, before presenting specific uncomfortable moments and how they are accomplished interactionally, a brief description is provided about the sources of data from which these moments are drawn.

2.   Sources of the data

The uncomfortable moments to be presented were taken from two different sources. First, we re-examined Simmons-Mackie and Damico's (1999) previously published analysis of conflict in a therapeutic encounter between an SLP and a woman with aphasia and apraxia of speech where a carefully transcribed record of the interaction was provided. We then analyzed a therapy session involving an SLP working with a group of adults with TBI. This session was part of a larger data set that had been collected over a five-week period (Kovarsky, Kimbarow and Kastner 1999).

In the extracts to be presented, uncomfortable moments manifested themselves in different ways. In the session involving the woman with aphasia and apraxia of speech, some of the discomfort appeared to result from the fact that her speech was difficult to understand. That is, referring back to the previously discussed conduit metaphor, part (though not all) of the problem was due to a lack of message transmission clarity caused by limitations in the articulatory, syntactic and lexical abilities of the client. Although both parties realized that there was a problem and sought to repair it, their continued miscommunication led to an inability to sustain a therapeutic agenda. In the second set of examples involving adults with traumatic brain injury, there were no problems with spoken intelligibility. That is, the uncomfortable moments could not be attributed to a problem with the conduit of communication. Rather, uncomfortable moments manifested themselves when the professional face of the clinician was threatened, and when a particular topic of discussion raised by the client was resisted by the clinician.

3.   Miscommunication and uncomfortable moments during aphasia therapy

Simmons-Mackie and Damico (1999) describe a highly unusual session when a client becomes so upset that she pointedly removes herself physically from therapy before it is finished. While sessions typically lasted from 30 to 60 minutes, the client left after participating for only 11 minutes.

During the session, the therapist (L) wanted the client (C) to produce grammatically complete sentences that described picture cards. The trouble began when L directed C to write a sentence.

Extract 1
47. L: If I can give you a tablet here. ((putting a tablet and pencil before C))

48. L: All right. I want you to write that sentence for me.

49. C: hhhhhh ((audible sigh)) ((clears her throat)) (pause) ((downward gaze, shakes head no))

50. C: I don know ((quiet voice, rapid, clipped rate))

51. L: (hhhhh) ((hissing laughter sound))

52. L: You can do it. You can do it. You can do that.

53. C: ((Writes)) hhhhhh (sighs loudly) ((stops writing))
        (pause) ((writes then drops pencil))
        ((C pushes the tablet toward L and lifts eyes to L))
        ((looks down; leans back with downward gaze))

54. L: Goo:d. Very good.

55. L: Can you read that sentence for me now? Read that whole sentence.

Starting in turn 49, the contextualization cues framing C's responses were very different from how she typically replied to a request. Her use of eye gaze, audible sighs, lateral head shaking, and quiet clipped voice, coupled with dropping her pencil and leaning back, all functioned communicatively to signal that she was reluctant to comply with the therapist's directive. In turn, L oriented to the fact that something was amiss by responding with a hissing laughter sound and encouragement in turns 51–52.

Even though both participants signaled that something atypical and problematic was occurring, L continued by initiating another 3-part, quiz question sequence in turn 55. However, C did not comply and called instead for a change, something "new".

Extract 2

55. L: Can you read that sentence for me now? Read that whole sentence.
56. C: (pause) ((downward gaze, leans forward))
         ((clears throat, eyes closed))
57. C: Is NE:::W please ((lifts "sleeping card))
         ((looks at L, then down, then up and down rapidly))
58. L: New? [What ya mean?
59. C: [Yeah, plea::se ((tense voice)) is is alu ((gestures stop)) ((writes "enough")) ((loudly drops pencil))
60. C: PLEA:::SE
61. L: Enough?=
62. C: Yeah.
63. L: =What ya mean?
64. C: Isy ((pointing to "sleeping" card)) is is is good ((speaks rapidly, points to tablet then to card)) is NE:::W ((points to L))
65. L: What's new? What ya [mean it's new?
66. C: [Is is too ((leans forward and sweeps hand across cards on L's side of table))

67. L: You want anoth[er one?
68. C: [Yeah, plea::se.

In retrospect, it became apparent that C's call for something "new" was a desire for a different set of pictures or a different task. However, at this point in time, L was uncertain about what was being requested and an extended repair sequence ensued. Finally, L interpreted C's comments as a request for a new card within the pre-existing set of pictures (turn 67).

Instead of taking C's request at face value and simply presenting her with a new card, L construed C's discomfort as symptomatic of her difficulty understanding the task instructions and then launched into another explanation of the therapy activity (turn 69). In response, C began to express her frustration again (turns 70, 71 and 73).

Extract 3
69. L: What I'd like you to do is go through and
        [reread it after you've written it.
70. C: [I know (pause) I don kno::w ((gaze down))
71. C: O::h o:h no::: ((grabs head))
72. L: Too frustrating today?
73. C: Yeah – ((clipped, terse))
74. L: Okay. The couple is sleeping in bed. That was good. Perfect sentence.
75. L: Nothin' wrong with it ((singsong intonation)).

Turns 71 through 74 were key to understanding how this series of uncomfortable moments would eventually escalate to the point where C decided to opt out
of therapy altogether and leave the session before it was finished. That is, L interpreted C's upset as resulting from her inability to successfully produce grammatically correct sentences using this particular set of cards. However, C was
frustrated with L's inability to comprehend that a change in course was being
called for: C wanted a new therapy activity altogether that, at the very least,
would involve a different set of picture cards that had not been used in a previous session.

   After a few more of these question sequences, C's frustration continued to
mount and she began to cry.

Extract 4
102. C: I don know is is ((crying, looking down at lap, body turned to side))

103. L: Is it frustrating today? (pause) C----, it's okay (pause) all right?
         ((said in soft voice))

104. L: ((pause)) Just take each day as it comes ((places a box of tissues
         directly in front of C)) and we just do as much as you can do, okay?

105. C: ((turns to L, leans forward)) So::rry.

106. L: So[rry?

107. C: [Yeah.

108. L: Don't apologize.

109. L: No need to apologize.

110. L: [No reason to say you're sorry.

111. C: [((C grabs tissue box, abruptly puts it aside, looks down))

112. L: Okay? (pause) Want to skip the writing part today?

113. L: You tell me what you feel up to [doing, okay?

114. C: [NO IS IS ((leaning forward,
     speaking loudly, rapidly)) IS IS IS NEW ((gestures writing))
     PLEA:::SE ((holds up picture card)) CARD IS (pause) [I don know isy

115. L: [Mhm

116. C: Is PLEA::SE NE:W (pause) ah CARD ((pleading intonation)).

117. L: Oh you want different [pictures?

118. C: [PLEA:SE! YES ((nods)).

119. L: O:::::H. Oh. Okay.

In turn 105, C actually apologized for crying, even though, as would become
evident in subsequent turns, it was L's failure to understand her desire for something "new" in therapy that was the root of the problem.

Eventually, C held up a picture card and made a dramatic effort to repair L's
faulty perception by stating that she did not take exception to writing; rather, she
wanted a new card (turn 114). Even though L finally realized that something beyond
the current set of pictures was being called for (turn 119), this SLP went on to defend her decision to stick with this particular set of therapy materials by invoking
an agreement both parties had reached in a previous session (turns 120 and 122).

Extract 5

120. L: Well, remember last time we talk[ed=

121. C: [hhhhhhhhh ((sigh and downward
     gaze))

122. L: =and we went through the pictures and I just picked 10 out and said
     we'd [work on these a few times?

123. C: [I know I know ((looking away shaking head "no"))
     ((raises hand as in stop gesture)) No I don know is ((hand to forehead)).

124, L: I know ((soft voice)).

125. C: Isy I don know ((hand up)) where I don know.

126. C: Bye-bye ((looking down, waves bye, nodding no)) is me ((points to
     self)) [isy ((looking at L))

127. L: [Well I'll try to find some different pictures but remember when I
     found some that wer- had more to them and it got you frustrated 'cause
     you tried to write so much? (pause)

128. L: Ya remember that?

C signaled her opposition to L's desire to maintain the status quo through the highly expressive use of gestures, suprasegmental cues, and words (turns 121 and 123). However, it was only when C actually threatened to leave (126) that L finally indicated her willingness to "find some different pictures" – although L continued to defend her position by recalling how "frustrated" C became with new pictures that taxed her speaking abilities and that required her "to write so much" to make herself understood.

In response to L's continued desire to press ahead with old pictures, C threatened to leave again and appeared to argue that simply repeating the same picture task was not a good use of the money she spent to attend therapy.

Extract 6

129. L: So we said we'd back up and try these again.

130. C: ((looking down, looks up and then down)) Isy, I don know isy.

131. C: Is bye bye.

132. C: Is MONEY ISY ((gestures grasping money to self))

133. C: BYE BYE ((waves)).

134. L: About money?

135. C: YEAH::: IS ME.

136. C: IS NEW ((leans forward; stares at L))

137. L: OKAY OKAY.

138. L: IT'S AWRIGHT

139. L: I'll find some new ones.

140. L: Can we use these today then [since I haven't picked any new ones out?

141. C: [hhhhhh ((sighs, gazing down)) ((puts hand to head over left eye))

142. C: (pause) ((points to video camera)) is bye bye ((stop gesture)) isy ((points to camera)) please ((low voice, quiet and terse; chin resting on fist)).

143. L: I'm not understanding.

144. L: You want me to turn that off?

145. C: Yes please.

Realizing that L still intended to continue with exactly the same activity because there were no alternative materials, C requested that the video camera be shut off. Soon after, C left the therapy room, even though L pleaded with her to stay.

Given the value therapists place on establishing and maintaining positive rapport, it was remarkable that L allowed this series of uncomfortable moments to escalate by continuing to champion an activity that made C so visibly upset that she eventually removed herself from the room. We will argue that at least three interrelated aspects of the situation accounted for this unfortunate circumstance: (i) adherence to a planned agenda with a client deemed linguistically and communicatively incompetent; (ii) the interactional substrate; and (iii) miscommunication.

Adhering to a planned agenda, L had developed a set of picture cards for eliciting mistakes in communicative performance. There was a strong desire to keep using this particular activity because, as a therapeutic task, it was a very efficient way of making grammatical errors visible. Therefore, when C requested something "new" in therapy (Extracts 2, 4 and 6), L resisted.

Another aspect of the situation that made the picture card activity attractive was the interactional substrate of therapy itself. Through the use of quiz questions, C could be held accountable for her performance. When her performance was deemed inappropriate, repair work was initiated. The pictures and quiz questions existed in a symbiotic relationship because with each new card, a fresh quiz question cycle could emerge; and with every cycle, there were more opportunities to do the work of therapy, fixing client mistakes, through picture cards.

Uncomfortable moments became visible when C refused to participate in these quiz question sequences. Much of L's time was then taken up with trying to get C to re-enter the pre-established interactional substrate (Extracts 1–3) so that therapy could continue. L's inability to coax C back into this typical therapeutic participation structure was exacerbated by the fact that L had difficulty understanding the nature of C's escalating complaint. While C repeatedly sought to convey her disapproval with the kind of therapeutic activities being provided by L (Extracts 1–6), especially since she was a paying customer (Extract 6), L believed that C was frustrated simply because she did not have the linguistic competence to produce grammatically correct sentences. L's efforts to console C only added fuel to the fire because it underscored the fact that C had not been successful in conveying her upset over the therapy task itself.

These uncomfortable moments were, in part, the result of a miscommunication caused by C's expressive aphasia and dysarthria. That is, in keeping with the aforementioned conduit metaphor, there were difficulties caused by C's lack of intelligible speech and language. Beyond the transmission of a clear message, however, there was another problem at work here. A more recent email communication from one of the original authors of this investigation, Simmons-Mackie, revealed a kind of interpretive resistance to the perspective being conveyed by C.

I spent lots of time (hours and hours) with the client before and after that session doing interviews and participant observations . . . . The client was extremely worried about her finances and was worried about how long insurance and her own funds would allow her to participate in therapy, so she wanted to get the most out of it. She did say that she did not want to go back to that therapist because she did the same tasks over and over . . . . The gist of her dissatisfaction was clearly that of a consumer evaluating the "cost benefit" of therapy . . . . Regarding the client's verbal limitations, most of her friends and family were able to have conversations with her because they paid close attention to context and body language, as well as her words. To me, one of the interesting parts of this whole interaction was the fact that watching it from outside, you could read her meanings much more clearly than the therapist who was intent on her own agenda at the time.

(Simmons-Mackie, personal communication, October 30, 2007)

While the researcher realized that C was expressing her concerns as a consumer for the benefits of intervention, it was never really clear that the SLP fully understood this. Miscommunications can be particularly problematic during therapy because when they arise, there is a tendency to place the onus for such communicative nonsuccesses primarily on the impaired linguistic and communicative abilities of the client, and not on the therapist's role in constructing misunderstandings (Kovarsky and Maxwell 1992). In this case, C's complaint about the nature of the therapy task was taken as further evidence of her own internal deficits and struggles with using language, and not as a criticism about how intervention was being practiced by the SLP. Put another way, the idea that C's dissatisfaction was symptomatic of the repeated use of the same activity was resisted by the therapist in favor of an interpretation that located the problem in the intrinsic ability of the client to convey a message.

One thing that is striking about the awkward moments to be described subsequently, involving a woman with TBI, is that this client is not limited in grammatical or articulatory ability. The concerns she expresses are delivered in a clear and unambiguous manner. In other words, there is no problem with the conduit of message transmission that contributes to the following uncomfortable moments.

4.   Uncomfortable moments during therapy for adults with traumatic brain injury

In the next examples, the professional face of an SLP was threatened when a client goes on record publicly during group therapy to argue that the clinician was not addressing goals appropriate to her individual needs. The excerpt was taken from a group therapy session involving the SLP working with 5 survivors of TBI in a rehabilitation hospital setting. Among other things, individuals with TBI, especially those treated soon after their injuries in this hospital, have difficulty remembering events and activities. In an effort to stimulate their memories, the SLP began by recounting a previous session when she had led a discussion about the reasons for, and goals of, therapy. The participants (all fictitiously named) are seated around a rectangular table and Paula is adjacent to the SLP.

Extract 7

1. SLP: We discussed why we were up here and some of our goals.

2. Wilbur: Yeah.

3. SLP: And we need to be tolerant of that. So (pause) okay what I want to do today[(rubs mouth with fingers)

4. Paula: [Can I disagree with you now with what we talked about on Friday. ((P gazes straight ahead and not at the SLP, while SLP looks at P)) Because I don't think we are working on the goals that I need to work on for me ((P raises and lowers eyebrows)).

5. SLP: Okay? ((slight vertical head nod))

6. SLP: [We can't address all your goals in this group (pause) [that's correct.

7. Paula: [No (pause)   [I don't think you're working on my goals at all.

The uncomfortable moment is initiated by Paula in turn 4 when she interrupts the SLP by stating that the group's therapeutic goals are not directed toward her personal needs. For an individual with a cognitive-communication disorder, one of the striking things about this example is the communicative competence displayed by Paula. For instance, note the oppositional use of pronouns between these two participants. The SLP starts by using "we" to speak on behalf of all participants and "our" to indicate that therapy goals have been discussed in a previous session (turn 1) and that "we" (all members of the group) "need to be tolerant" of these goals (turn 3). Paula counters this by using pronouns in a dramatic way to highlight her conflicting position ("I") from the SLP's claim ("you") and the idea that the group ("we") is addressing her needs (turn 4). These comments not only challenge the appropriateness of any prior goals established by the SLP, they also question the right of the SLP to speak on behalf of the entire group.

The SLP then counters by saying that "we" (the group) "can't address all your goals in this group". Through the continued contrastive use of pronouns, Paula then issues an even stronger challenge by stating that the SLP is not working on her goals "at all" (turn 7). In response to this escalating threat to professional expertise, the SLP subsequently argues that Paula and the group do share a common goal (turn 8).

Extract 8
8. SLP: Okay one of your goals is to be sure that you're um paying attention?
           ((nodding head up and down))

9. Paula: Yeah? ((nods head up and down once))

10. SLP: And [you

11. Paula: [That's not that's not ((nods head sideways)) one of my goals.
           That's one of YOUR goals ((dipping head toward SLP and pointing
           at SLP with index finger while hands are clasped)). I ((moves index
           finger away from SLP to point forward)) don't think you're doing
           what I need. ((looks at SLP)) But I: ((swiveling head away from SLP,
           head and eyes up)) can talk to you about that later.

12. SLP: Okay? ((looking down at paper)) That sounds good. We can do that.
           Um but paying attention is the one that's generally universal because
           people ((leaning head toward table and then looking sideways at
           Jim)) have difficulty paying attention.

13. Jim: ((cheek down on table resting on his hand)) Um hm.

14. SLP: Um hm. Okay ((smiling and looking across table toward Harold)). So
           this ((smiling)) (pause) next activity I want to do or this first activity
           of the day I wanna do is gonna really FORCE you to pay attention or
           you're not gonna be able to DO it ((spoken rapidly while looking
           around the table pointing her pen at Jim then Paula)). And some of
           you may have done this. It's a good car game (pause) car activity.

Paula interrupts the SLP again (turn 11) and states that paying attention is one
of the SLP's goals, but not one of her goals. Paula emphasizes her position by
stressing the word 'your' while clasping hands and pointing both index fingers
at the SLP. In an effort to cut off any further discussion, she looks away from the
SLP and states this topic can be discussed at a later time. Typically, it is the
therapist and not the client who decides when and how topics are discussed.
Paula's commentary, delivered in a very eloquent manner, functions as a serious
threat to the professional face of the SLP – not only is she criticizing the selection of therapeutic goals, Paula is also assuming interactional rights usually accorded to the clinician when she seeks to terminate discussion.

Paula does not, however, have the final word regarding what constitutes an
appropriate therapy goal. Instead, the clinician explicitly states that "paying attention" is a "universal" goal for all individuals with TBI (turn 12). To support her
contention, the SLP leans toward the table, turns her head to the side and looks at
Jim whose head has been down on the table during this exchange. In other words,
Jim's physical position (head down, not gazing at any of the group participants)

serves as a warrant for the SLP's claim that paying attention is an appropriate goal for this group and Jim ratifies this claim by saying "um hm". Interestingly, Jim's response is produced in a pragmatically appropriate manner within this unfolding sequence, indicating that, in fact, he is attending to the interaction.

Finally, the SLP builds upon this pronouncement of what constitutes an appropriate goal to launch into a description of what the first group therapy activity of the day will be: "a good car game". At this point, there is no further counter argument from Paula and, after some brief explanation, the participants begin to play the game.

In sum, there are, at least, three facets of these uncomfortable moments that are notable: (i) the communicative competencies of Paula; (ii) the relationship between face and rapport; and (iii) the reasoning practices of the SLP. First, for an individual with TBI whose cognitive-communicative abilities are deemed impaired, Paula does a powerful job communicatively of disagreeing with the SLP and expressing her concerns. Among other things, her use of pronouns, gestures and the manner in which she seeks to terminate discussion of the entire topic are all indicative of communicative competence, not incompetence. Ironically, while this uncomfortable moment constitutes a threat to the establishment of positive rapport and is not a preferred manner of therapeutic interaction, the incident itself actually provides a context for the client to display real communicative proficiency – a primary reason for doing therapy in the first place.

Second, Paula's articulately delivered claim that her therapeutic needs are not being addressed and her effort to terminate the entire topic of discussion in front of the group before the SLP can even offer a rebuttal to this claim (turn 11) function communicatively as threats to the professional face of the SLP.

Additionally, by challenging the professional face of the SLP, the positive rapport that is supposed to characterize a good interpersonal, therapeutic relationship is also being endangered. In response to the challenge, the SLP seeks to manage this threat to face and rapport simultaneously by agreeing to meet with Paula privately to discuss her concerns, and by indicating that the goal of "paying attention" is relevant to all members of the group (turn 12). Thus, while acquiescing to Paula's request to meet privately, this response also reasserts the SLP's authority as the arbiter of what constitutes an appropriate therapeutic goal. The interactional rights of the therapist-as-professional-expert are reinforced even further in turn 14 when the SLP informs the group about what the first official therapeutic activity of the day will be ("a good car game") and why it is important (because it will "force" them to "pay attention").

Finally, the reasoning practices used by the SLP to re-establish her expertise and manage the face threat are of interest. When Paula states that the goals of the group are not meeting her individual needs, the SLP responds to this challenge by claiming that the therapeutic agenda is appropriate because all people with TBI have difficulty paying attention. As evidence of this difficulty, the SLP publicly points to Jim whose head is literally down on the table. In response, Jim agrees with her assessment about the difficulty in paying attention (turn 13) and the SLP positively evaluates Jim's agreement by saying "um hm, okay" and smiling (turn 14). This difficulty then becomes a warrant for the first therapeutic activity of the day, the car game.

On one level, the internal logic of the SLP's argument appears to be flawed. Based upon this excerpt and the rest of the therapy session, it is clear that Paula has no difficulty attending to, and participating in, an ongoing interaction. In addition, Jim's agreement with the SLP's position about the "universal" problem of paying attention indicates that he too is tuned in to the conversation at hand. In other words, there is nothing in the SLP's rebuttal that provides firm proof to counter Paula's claim that group goals are not addressing her needs. On another level, however, there is a logic of practical action. Irrespective of whether or not Paula's concerns for the goals of therapy are addressed in a credible way, a warrant for a specific course of therapeutic action is presented. More specifically, the argument that the group's needs are being met through the goal of paying attention functioned as both a reason, albeit a questionable one, and an introduction for the first therapeutic task of the day. Here, clinical reasoning practices that support moving forward into the work of therapy override the internal logic of the argument being made about the appropriateness of an intervention goal.

More insight into the nature of Paula's unmet personal needs surfaced during another uncomfortable moment as the SLP was introducing a different game to be played by the group. While the therapist was focused on goals like paying attention and playing games according to a prespecified set of rules, Paula was upset about the fact that she was not being allowed to return to her job as a school teacher because of her brain injury. In the subsequent example, Paula was asked to explain how to play a game called Hangman.

Extract 9

1. SLP: Okay. Well Paula would you explain it to Jim since then since he hasn't played it.

2. Paula: No. School teacher's days they tell me are over now. I'm not allowed to explain it anything anymore.

3. SLP: You're allowed to explain somethin' in here.

4. Paula: No I'm super serious. I would really prefer not to=

5. SLP: =Alright=

6. Paula: =I'm still kind of upset that I can't go back to teaching.

7. SLP: Okay then Bobby would you explain to Jim how this is played.

Paula disclosed that she would not explain how to play this particular game because of her deep personal concern over a lost career as a teacher (turn 2). Unlike the previous examples where Paula interrupted the SLP, this uncomfortable moment was not characterized by interactional asynchrony. Rather, through a series of closely latched utterances (turns 4–6), Paula not only reiterated that she was unwilling to comply with the SLP's directive (turn 1), she again raised her upset over an inability to return to teaching.

Rather than pursuing a topic now raised more than once by Paula about her damaged sense of self after receiving a TBI, the SLP merely released her from the obligation to explain the game and elected another individual to take her place, and all in the space of one conversational turn (7). After the rules were finally explained, intervention was directed toward playing this psycholinguistic guessing game (Hangman) so that client errors in message production and reception along the conduit could be repaired when they occurred. Why were Paula's legitimate worries as a TBI survivor ignored and not considered an appropriate topic for therapy? Part of the answer lies in the perceived nature of Paula's problems.

As part of a larger investigation (Kovarsky, Kimbarow and Kastner 1999), this uncomfortable moment was reviewed with the head SLP of the unit where the session was video taped. This individual had a number of years of experience working with adults with TBI, and with all the therapists in this particular unit. When he viewed this particular segment, he stated that one of the problems experienced by many of those with TBI was that they tended to "confabulate". That is, some clients would state things that they believed were true when, in fact, they had never occurred. In other words, there was a sense that Paula could have been reporting a situation about an inability to return to teaching that was simply false or somehow misrepresented. In this way, Paula's complaint was just another symptom of her underlying problem, a traumatic brain injury. As a result, this particular concern was not to be taken at face value and treated as a bona fide topic of therapeutic discussion. Even though Paula expressed herself in an articulate and compelling manner, the focus on treating the conduit of communication independent of identity, the drive to keep moving from one clinical activity to the next, and the way her complaint could be transformed into a symptom of her own underlying pathology all helped motivate the SLP's decision to ignore her concerns and get on with the therapeutic business at hand, playing another game.

5.   Discussion

Across both sessions, the SLP's clinical gaze was fixed, almost exclusively, on moving from one task to the next, and repairing receptive and expressive conduit problems of message transmission believed to be caused by deficits intrinsic to the impaired client. However, the conduit model of communication underlying therapy was problematic in two ways. First, even when prepackaged messages were transmitted clearly, communicative success was not assured. Although Paula argued clearly and competently about her concerns for the goals of group therapy (Extract 8), her interpretation was forcefully discounted by the SLP. It was not surprising that the SLP felt compelled to resist the client's interpretation given that Paula's complaint was delivered in a way that constituted a serious threat to professional face. The point is, however, that the conduit metaphor was inadequate as a way of capturing the nature of communication – even though both parties communicated their positions articulately along the conduit, communication itself is still problematic. Instead of relying on a conduit metaphor that focuses on the delivery of prepackaged messages, the communication of meaning can be better characterized as something that occurs in retrospect, where understandings are negotiated and potentially finalized through the give and take of interaction (Hanks 1996).

Second, a singular focus on fixing lexical and grammatical pieces of messages being passed along the conduit can lead to an overly narrowed evaluative perspective for interpreting the appropriateness of clients' utterances (Extracts 1–6). In this way, problems in the social life-world where clients may have to confront issues of identity transition caused by a brain injury can be divorced from helping someone with a communication problem through speech-language therapy (Extract 9) (Kovarsky, Shaw and Adingono-Smith 2007).

Finally, oracular reasoning (Mehan 1990) – whereby client complaints are not interpreted at face value and, instead, are construed as symptoms of their own underlying internal deficits – may have been at work in both sessions. The SLP believed that the woman with aphasia was complaining solely about her own lack of capacity to successfully complete a clinical task, instead of the therapist's ability to provide appropriate activities. Similarly, the experienced SLP who reviewed the taped TBI session speculated that Paula's expressed concerns and criticisms were symptomatic of confabulations resulting from brain injury. In both sessions, client grievances were transformed into symptoms of intrinsic underlying pathologies.

Irrespective of the degree to which clients struggled to convey their dissonant versions of reality during these uncomfortable moments, it was the interpretive perspective of the therapist that dominated. As Hanks (1996: 236) noted in his discussion of communicative practices where differences in power, authority and legitimacy are realized as part of the interactional context, whether it is "a representative of the court, a grammar school teacher, a religious specialist, a doctor, or anyone else with the power to call the shots … authorized speakers make social reality when they speak."

6.   Conclusion

It would be convenient simply to end here because the negotiation of these uncomfortable moments was consistent with previous accounts in the literature regarding the nature of traditional speech-language therapy – clinicians tend to dominate these speech events in ways that, even with the best of intentions, do not always encourage and support the communicative perspectives and abilities that clients bring to the therapeutic process. More recently, however, in response to concerns like those raised in this chapter, alternative models of intervention have been evolving. It is toward some of these contrasting therapeutic practices that our brief concluding comments are directed.

There are, are least, two key features that distinguish these alternative practices from traditional, impairment-based intervention: discourse equality (Simmons-Mackie et al. 2007) and attention to the relationship between language and the social life-worlds experienced by clients (Duchan and Black 2001; Elman 2005; Marshall 1993; Simmons-Mackie 2001). Discourse equality is likened to Goffman's (1981) characterization of ordinary conversation:

> … everyone is accorded the right to talk or listen without reference to a fixed schedule; everyone is accorded the status of someone whose overall evaluation of the subject matter at – whose editorial comments as it were – is to be encouraged and treated with respect; and … differences of opinion [are] to be treated as unprejudicial to the continuing relationship between the participants.
> (Goffman 1981: 14)

Because communicative parity is a primary feature of intervention, the interactional substrate of therapy is changed. There is an absence of quiz question-repair sequences where the SLP controls the flow of information and judges what constitutes appropriate performance. Here, the focus is on more equal participation in the construction and evaluation of meaning, as opposed to simply fixing the grammatical, lexical and syntactic errors of message transmission and reception caused by deficits located within the individual. Clients are not expected to adhere to a pre-planned clinical agenda and they share more responsibility for initiating and managing topics of discussion. In an effort to follow the communicative leads of clients, the work of therapy is done by supporting their efforts to participate in talk and interaction through the use of language, gesture and other available resources. In their analysis of group therapy for individuals with aphasia, Simmons-Mackie, Elman, Holland, and Damico (2007) describe how all these communicative practices manifest themselves in this alternate form of intervention.

Along with the concern for discourse equality, attention is also paid to the social life-world experiences and expressed needs of individuals with communication difficulties. Marshall (1993), for example, describes an approach to therapy designed around the concerns for communication in everyday life voiced by clients. In this type of a person-centered approach (Duchan and Black 2001), issues of identity and identity management are integrated into, and not separated from, the therapeutic process. Instead of viewing communication and social life as entities that can be divorced from one another for therapeutic purposes, the focus is on recognizing how the two are mutually constitutive of one another (Walsh 2007). In closing, we are not claiming that uncomfortable moments will disappear by adopting these alternative discourse practices – indeed there may even be times when traditional, impairment-based models of intervention are appropriate. Hopefully, however, when therapy is geared more toward discourse equality and how communication and social life are related to one another, uncomfortable moments can become actual learning opportunities for clinicians who seek to support the communicative abilities and perspectives of their clients.

Appendix

Transcription conventions

=	indicates no gap and no overlap between adjacent utterances
(( ))	nonverbal information and information about tone of voice placed within double parentheses
.	indicates end of an utterance
[	marks point of overlap between utterances
hh	refers to exhalation of breath
:	indicates sound elongation
CAPS	upper case letters mark increased stressed on words spoken

References

Ainsworth-Vaughn, Nancy
    1998   *Claiming Power in Doctor-Patient Talk.* Oxford: Oxford University Press.
Bobkoff, Karen and John Panagos
    1986   The "point" of language intervention lessons. *Child Language Teaching and Therapy* 2: 50–62.
Brown, Penelope and Stephen Levinson
    1987   *Politeness: Some Universals in Language Use.* Cambridge: Cambridge University Press.
Cazden, Courtney
    1988   *Classroom Discourse.* Portsmouth, NH: Heinemann.
Duchan, Judith and Marion Black
    2001   Progressing toward life goals: A person-centered approach to evaluating therapy. *Topics in Language Disorders* 22(1): 37–49.

Duchan, Judith, Dana Kovarsky and Madeline Maxwell
    2005   *Diagnosis as Cultural Practice*. Berlin/New York: Mouton de Gruyter.
Elman, Roberta
    2005   Social and life participation approaches to aphasia intervention. In: Larry
              LaPointe (ed.), 39–50. *Aphasia and Related Neurogenic Language Dis-
              orders*, 39–50. New York: Thieme.
Erickson, Fred and Jeffrey Shultz
    1982   *The Counselor as Gatekeeper*. New York: Academic Press.
Ferrara, Kathleen
    1994   *Therapeutic Ways with Words*. Oxford: Oxford University Press.
Goffman, Erving
    1981   *Forms of Talk*. Philadelphia, PA: University of Pennsylvania Press.
Gumperz, John
    1982   *Discourse Strategies*. Cambridge: Cambridge University Press.
Hand, Linda
    2003   *Discourses in the Professional Practices of Speech Pathology Interviews*.
              Unpublished Ph.D. Dissertation, Department of Linguistics, Macquarie
              University, Sydney.
Hanks, William
    1996   *Language and Communicative Practices*. Boulder, CO: Westview Press.
Kovarsky, Dana
    1989   *An Ethnography of Communication in Child Language Therapy*. Unpub-
              lished Ph.D. Dissertation, University of Texas, Austin.
Kovarsky, Dana and Judith Duchan
    1997   The interactional dimensions of language therapy. *Language, Speech, and
              Hearing Services in Schools* 28: 219–230.
Kovarsky, Dana, Michael Kimbarow and Deborah Kastner
    1999   The construction of incompetence during group therapy with traumatically
              brain injured adults. In: Dana Kovarsky, Judith Duchan and Madeline Max-
              well (eds.), *Constructing Incompetence: Disabling Evaluations in Clinical
              and Social Interaction*, 291–312. Mahwah, NJ: Erlbaum.
Kovarsky, Dana and Madeline Maxwell
    1992   Ethnography and the clinical setting: Communicative expectancies in clini-
              cal discourse. *Topics in Language Disorders* 12(3): 76–84.
Kovarsky, Dana, Allen Shaw and Maureen Adingono-Smith
    2007   The construction of identity during group therapy among adults with trau-
              matic brain injury. *Communication and Medicine* 4(1): 53–66.
Labov, William and David Fanshel
    1977   *Therapeutic Discourse*. New York: Academic Press.
Marshall, Robert
    1993   Problem-focused group treatment for clients with mild aphasia. *American
              Journal of Speech-Language Pathology* 2(2): 31–43.
Maynard, Doug W. and Courtney L. Marlaire
    1999   Good reasons for bad testing performance: The interactional substrate of
              educational testing. In: Dana Kovarsky, Judith Duchan, and Madeline Max-
              well (eds.), *Constructing (In)Competence: Disabling Evaluations in Clini-
              cal and Social Interaction*, 171–198. Mahwah, NJ: Erlbaum.

McTear, Michael and Florence King
    1991   Miscommunication in clinical contexts: The speech therapy interview. In: Nikolas Coupland, Howard Giles and John Wiemann (eds.), *"Miscommunication" and Problematic Talk*, 195–214. Newbury Park, CA: Sage Publications.
Mehan, Hugh
    1990   Oracular reasoning in a psychiatric Exam: The resolution of conflict in language. In: Allen D. Grimshaw (ed.), *Conflict Talk: Sociolinguistic Investigations of Arguments in Conversation,* 160–177. Cambridge: Cambridge University Press.
Meitus, Irving and Bernd Weinberg
    1983   *Diagnosis in Speech-Language Pathology.* Austin, TX: Pro-Ed.
Panagos, John M.
    1996   Speech therapy discourse. In: Michael Smith and Jack L. Damico (eds.), *Childhood Language Disorders*, 41–63. New York: Thieme Medical Publishers.
Prutting, Carol, Nancy Bagshaw, Howard Goldstein, Susan Juskowitz and Ilene Umen
    1978   Clinician-child discourse: Some preliminary questions. *Journal of Speech and Hearing Disorders* 43: 123–139.
Reddy, Michael
    1979   The conduit metaphor: A case of frame conflict in our language about language. In: Andrew Ortony (ed.), *Metaphor and Thought*, 284–297. Cambridge: Cambridge University Press.
Ripich, Danielle, Georgia Hambrecht, John Panagos and Patricia Prelock
    1984   An analysis of articulation and language remediation discourse patterns. *Journal of Childhood Communication Disorders* 7: 17–26.
Simmons-Mackie, Nina
    2001   Social approaches to the management of aphasia. In: Robin Chapey (ed.), *Language Intervention Strategies in Aphasia and Related Neurogenic Communication Disorders*, 246–268. Philadelphia, PA: Lippincott, Williams and Wilkins.
Simmons-Mackie, Nina and Jack L. Damico
    1999   Social role negotiation in aphasia therapy: Competence, incompetence, and conflict. In: Dana Kovarsky, Judith Duchan and Madeline Maxwell (eds.), *Constructing (In)Competence: Disabling Evaluations in Clinical and Social Interaction*, 312–342. Mahwah, NJ: Erlbaum.
Simmons-Mackie, Nina, Roberta Elman, Audrey Holland and Jack L. Damico
    2007   Management of discourse in group therapy for aphasia. *Topics in Language Disorders* 27(1): 5–23.
Sinclair, John and Malcolm Coulthard
    1975   *Towards an Analysis of Discourse: The English Used by Teachers and Pupils*. Oxford: Oxford University Press.
Spencer-Oatey, Helen
    2005   (Im)Politeness, face and perceptions of rapport: Unpackaging their bases and interrelationships. *Journal of Politeness Research* 1: 95–119.

van Kleeck, Anne and Alice Richardson
  1986   What's in an error? Using children's wrong responses as language teaching
            opportunities. *National Student Journal of Speech-Language Pathology*
            14(1): 25–50.
Walsh, Irene
  2007   Small talk is "big talk" in clinical discourse. *Topics in Language Disorders*
            27(1): 24–36.

8. Speaking for another: Ethics-in-interaction in medical encounters

Ellen Barton

Abstract

An emerging area of research in discourse studies analyzes how medical deci-sion-making is imbued with ethical dimension, describing the linguistic means by which ethical matters emerge for clinicians and patient/families in the inter-action of medical encounters. The actual language of medical decision-making with such ethical dimensions has rarely been studied directly in the literature, and a discourse perspective on ethics as an interactional accomplishment has the potential to make important contributions to the interdisciplinary literature on medical ethics and bioethics. This chapter lays out descriptive, methodologi-cal, theoretical, and ethical questions for investigating ethics-in-interaction and then presents research from two types of medical encounters with ethical di-mensions – end-of-life discussions and enrollment on clinical trials.

1. Introduction

Consider the following sequences from two types of medical encounters:[1] Extract A is from an end-of-life discussion between a physician (Ph) and the family (Fam) of a terminal patient in an Intensive Care Unit (ICU); and Extract B is from an offer to participate in a clinical trial from a physician (Ph) to a patient:

Extract A
(1) Ph: And this has gone on for a few days now and she's shown no im-provement at all, zero. [...] [W]e can very confidently say that we don't think she's ever going to get better. We can keep her body alive on the machine for a very long period of time, but==
(2) Fam: ==but she is going now.
(3) Ph: And it sounds like that's not what she would want.
(4) Fam: No.
(5) Ph: Everybody is in agreement with that [...] Based upon what every-body said, her to her doctors and all of you to me, it sounds like it's not what she would want.
(6) Fam: No.

Extract B

(1) Ph: But we don't know whether it [experimental medication] is going
          to truly help Stage II patients right now. And that's why we're doing
          this study. You might say-- you could definitely-- some people may
          say you're not comfortable with this. There's a chance that even if I
          go on the study that I won't get the pill.
          [...]
(2) Ph: Again I am just mentioning that. It is a little bit early.

These excerpts are both linguistically interesting and ethically significant. Linguistically, the clinician in each excerpt uses what Schiffrin (1994: 107) calls
"speaking for another". In Extract A, the physician uses the medical *we* (turn 1)
to speak for the profession in his prognosis, and in turn 3, he speaks for the patient in articulating a candidate end-of-life decision that reflects her wishes (Barton 2005). In Extract B, the physician uses the pronoun *you* (turn 1) to speak for
the patient in articulating a candidate reason to refuse an offer to participate in
medical research, specifically a clinical trial in cancer medicine (Barton 2007a).

In terms of the ethical significance of these excerpts,[2] another linguistically
interesting feature is present. Peräkylä (1998) argues that physicians sometimes
index the medical basis for their diagnosis. The sequences above similarly show
that clinicians sometimes index the ethical basis of decision-making with patients and families. The clinicians in each excerpt can be seen to speak ethically
by indexing their accountability to the traditional Hippocratic ethics of the profession of medicine (Jonson, Siegler, and Winslade 2006). In Extract A (see turn
1), the physician indexes the professional standard of medical futility as the
basis for an ethical end-of-life decision (*we can keep her body alive*) (AMA
1997). In turn 3, he puts into place the process of surrogate decision-making in
end-of-life care by indexing the patient's wishes as the basis for the decision
(AMA 2001). In Extract B (see turn 1), the physician indexes the voluntary nature of participation in medical research by offering a reason why the patient
may refuse (*you're not comfortable with this*), consistent with the principles and
regulations of IRB (Institutional Review Board) review of research in the
United States (*Belmont Report* 1979; 45 CFR 46 2005/1991).

In the excerpts above, the responses from patients and family members are
also linguistically interesting and ethically significant, especially with respect
to the decisions made in the encounter as a whole. In Extract A (see turn 2), the
family member takes up the physician's inference about the futility of further
treatment by latching onto and repeating the pivotal term *but*, continuing with a
cliché to express her understanding of the contrast between an artificially prolonged life and a natural death. In turn 4, the family member provides simple
agreement to the physician's articulation of the patient's wishes as the end-of-
life decision, and the patient was then removed from life support and allowed to

die. In Extract B (see turn 1), the patient and his accompanying family member did not respond at all to these particular utterances within a lengthy physician monologue that continued to offer participation in a clinical trial. The physician may have interpreted this lack of uptake as implying a reluctance to participate because he deferred an immediate decision to a future discussion in turn 2.

These excerpts and their brief analysis above are from an emerging area of research in the discourse analysis of medical encounters, one that investigates ethics-in-interaction, defined as the linguistic means by which ethical matters emerge for clinicians and patients/families in the interaction of medical encounters, particularly with respect to decision-making. Ethics is most often thought of as an abstract system of principles underlying moral reasoning, and contemporary bioethics is similarly considered the set of ethical principles that should normatively underlie medical decision-making (Beauchamp and Childress 2001). Medical decision-making with ethical dimensions, however, most often takes place in interaction among real people, in real time, in (semi-)ordinary language, and in complex contexts that are often institutional and asymmetrical. Further, ethical matters are most often addressed indirectly rather than directly by both clinicians and families in medical encounters, as shown in the excerpts above. But the actual language of medical decision-making with ethical dimensions has rarely been studied directly in the literature, and a perspective on ethics as interactional is only beginning to emerge in discourse studies, a discourse perspective that has the potential to make important contributions to the increasingly interdisciplinary literature on medical ethics and bioethics.

The key research questions in the investigation of ethics-in-interaction are descriptive, methodological, theoretical, and ethical:

–   What are the linguistic means by which ethical matters are raised, explored, negotiated, justified, and settled (or not) in medical decision-making? How does the discourse of medical encounters thereby construct and reflect ethics-in-interaction?
–   What are the methodological approaches available for the investigation and analysis of ethics in interaction?
–   What are the theoretical concepts and frameworks available to underpin the investigation and interpretation of ethics-in-interaction?
–   What are the ethical issues for discourse researchers investigating ethics-in-interaction in medical settings?

In this chapter I consider the ethics-in-interaction of two types of medical encounters: end-of-life care and communication (Section 2), and offers to participate in clinical trials (Section 3). In each section, I briefly introduce the multiple ethical dimensions of these encounters and then review research on two specific communicative events – end-of-life discussions and offers to participate in clinical trials in cancer medicine. I first introduce the theoretical frameworks and methodological approaches being used to investigate ethics-in-interaction, and then briefly present some of the key empirical and theoretical findings. In Section 4, I discuss the possibilities for further research in this area, paying particular attention to the question of how discourse researchers can work ethically in this area.

2.   End-of-life care and communication

Since the 1970s, with the well-known case of Karen Quinlan in the United States, the public, the media, and the American healthcare establishment have paid considerable attention to the end of life as a medical, ethical, and social issue. End-of-life care may be the most publicly visible topic in medical ethics, with well-known comparisons of this century's idea of a good death – a death with dignity, defined as physically pain-free and emotionally meaningful for the patient and family, a death preferably at home – vs. this century's idea of a bad death – a death without dignity, defined as technologically excessive and emotionally unsatisfying, perhaps for the patient but certainly for the family, often a death in an impersonal institution (Battin 1994; Cassell 2005; Christakis 1999; Kaufman 2005; Last Acts Coalition 2002). In the medical literature, the end-of-life is widely recognized as one of the most ethically complicated aspects of medical care, from the provision of palliative care to chronically ill patients to the decision to change the goals of treatment from aggressive therapeutic care to comfort care in hospital ICUs (Cimino 2003; Curtis and Patrick 2001; SUPPORT 1995).

To use the terms of the current theoretical model of biopsychosocial healthcare (Engel 1977; Borrell-Carrió, Suchman, and Epstein 2004), the ethical issues related to end-of-life care are both biomedical and psychosocial. The AMA (1994) identifies a wide variety of biomedical issues, including making a determination of medical futility; deciding to withhold or withdraw life-sustaining treatment, including food and fluids; using appropriate treatments such as terminal sedation for symptom control, particularly control of pain; participating in physician-assisted dying; practicing euthanasia; and more. The AMA also identifies a number of psychosocial issues, such as quality of life and quality of dying for the patient and the family; securing and applying advance directives for end-of-life care; using a surrogate decision-making process; and allocating scarce resources such as ICU beds. Addressing many of these psychosocial issues crucially involves communication, including disclosure of prognosis to patients and families, cultural sensitivity in end-of-life communication, and consistent communication with patients and families in the context of an attentive clinician-patient relationship that does not abandon the patient at the end of life. Studies on end-of-life communication regularly show that families rate good communication as highly as good clinical care at this critical juncture (Hickey

1990; Shannon 2001). Turning to end-of-life care and communication in the acute care setting of hospital ICUs, the recommendations of the Ethics Committee of the American Society of Critical Care Medicine describe end-of-life care primarily in terms of communication, specifically the need for shared decision-making toward a consensus to shift the goals of treatment from aggressive therapeutic care to comfort care within a broad context of care that meets the needs of the family at this difficult time (Truog et al. 2001; Kirchoff, Song, and Kehl 2004).

End-of-life care in the ICU involves a wide variety of communicative events, including bedside communication with many different clinicians and nurses (Cassell 2005). One recognized and important communicative event in end-of-life care is the end-of-life discussion (sometimes called the family conference) in which a negotiated consensus about the move from therapeutic care to comfort care is established among clinicians, typically the attending physician(s), and the family. There is a small research literature in medicine on the end-of-life discussion, but much of this literature is retrospective, primarily using survey, interview and focus group methods with general qualitative analysis if discursive data is collected at all (Abbott, Sago, and Green 2001; Azoulay et al. 2003; Heyland et al. 2003; Hickey 1990; Kirchoff, Walker and Hutton 2002). There is, however, one research program in medicine that looks at prospective data from actual end-of-life discussions.

In this project, J. Randall Curtis and his colleagues collected and transcribed 50 end-of-life discussions in ICUs. As is typical in current studies of communication in medicine, qualitative methods of open coding were used to develop a content and style analysis of physician communication (Curtis et al. 2002; Curtis et al. 2001). Data consisted of physician contributions only. Using some of the features identified by Roter and Hall (1992), physician style was described in terms of using direct language, practicing active listening, and providing emotional support. Content was analyzed into six domains: openings, information exchange, discussions of the future, decision-making, explicit discussions of dying and death, and closings. Curtis (2004) suggests using these categories and stylistic features as a framework for an end-of-life discussion. From a discourse perspective, the importance of this research program in medicine is in its use of data from actual end-of-life encounters, what medical researchers call prospective data, and what we call naturally-occurring data. In setting an agenda for further research, Curtis et al. (2002: 157) specifically call for more research using empirical data on how end-of-life communication actually occurs, particularly in the end-of-life discussion.

Barton and colleagues have conducted research on a corpus of 20 end-of-life discussions from a surgical ICU using the methods of discourse analysis (Schiffrin, Tannen, and Hamilton 2001; Sarangi and Roberts 1999). The data for the study consisted of both physician and family contributions, under the standard assumption in discourse analysis that it is in interaction that speakers co-construct communicative events, including institutional ones (Drew and Heritage 1992). Barton et al. (2005) developed a structural-functional analysis of the phases of the end-of-life discussion, describing the internal structure and functional contribution to the overall discussion of four phases: the Opening (Phase 1), Description of Current Status (Phase 2), Holistic Decision-Making (Phase 3), and Logistics of Dying (Phase 4).

Barton (2005) described the emergence of ethical dimensions in the interaction of end-of-life discussions using Sarangi and Robert's (1999) theoretical framework of communication in the workplace as constructing and reflecting both an institutional order and an interactional order. Briefly, institutional orders seek to regulate professional practices, including decision-making and communication, to achieve accountability to the policies of the institution. Interactional orders are the discourses of particular communicative events in which decision-making actually takes place. In medicine, there is often a conflict between institutional and interactional orders: Barton (2005) argues that clinicians often seek accountability primarily in terms of their profession's standards and ethics, in part by controlling the interactional order.

In the United States, the institutional order of end-of-life care is manifest in hospital policies written in terms of the four principles approach of contemporary bioethics (Beauchamp and Childress 2001). Respect for autonomy is the first of the four principles, defined as a person's right to make choices based on his/her personal values and beliefs (the other three principles are non-maleficence, beneficence, and justice). In bioethics, autonomy has an important communicative component: Beauchamp and Childress (2001: 63) see medical communication as a process whereby clinicians enable autonomy in patient or surrogate decision-making using very strong terms: "Respect for autonomy is not a mere *ideal* in health care; it is a professional *obligation*" (authors' emphasis).

However, Barton (2005) argues that in the interactional order of end-of-life discussions, clinicians (sometimes deliberately) do not foreground patient autonomy within explicit surrogate decision-making, at least as normatively set out in the bioethics literature. As exemplified in Extract A, the discourse analysis showed that physicians focus on medical futility as the medical and therefore ethical basis of end-of-life decision-making. In what could be seen as problematic with respect to autonomy and surrogate decision-making, end-of-life decision-making interactionally is more of a trajectory toward consensus than an explicit process of decision-making (Barton 2006). In traditional medical ethics, such consensus with the family is regarded as an ethical responsibility in providing what clinicians call caring for the family (Kirchoff, Song, and Kehl 2004; Truog et al. 2001), and physicians frequently index consensus upon the patient's wishes as the ethical basis for shared decision-making, as shown in Extract A (see turns 5–6).

As evident in Extract A, what the family provides in many end-of-life discussions is simple agreement to establish alignment to the terminal status of the patient in Phase 2 of the discussion and the decision to withdraw life support in Phase 3, raising questions about the considerations and contributions of the family in decision-making. However, in a second discourse analysis, Barton (2007b) argues that Phase 4 of the discussion is the place where the family considers the ethical dimensions of end-of-life decision-making. Phase 4 typically begins with a description of the logistics of dying in the ICU, with an explanation of the withdrawal of life support under terminal sedation. But it is in Phase 4 where families review the decision and index a different ethical frame, not the medical frame that physicians use to index their decision as medically and ethically responsible, as in Extract A, but in a lay frame. To use Mishler's (1984) well-known terms, physicians index "the voice of medicine" to situate end-of-life decision-making as ethical in Phases 2 and 3, but families index an ethics of personhood within "the voice of the lifeworld" to do the same in Phase 4.

In describing the process of dying, physicians typically emphasize the logistics of end-of-life care, as in turn 1 (Extract C), keeping the patient comfortable, that is, pain free and fully sedated, until death:

Extract C
(1) Ph: [after a description of the withdrawal of life support] But I can tell you that we can do this keeping her comfortable.
(2) Fam: Yeah, yeah. We want her being comfortable. It doesn't make sense when we know she is not going to be here any more.
         [...]
(3) Fam: If she's not in any pain, if she's not struggling with-- if I'm standing there I don't want to see her going through this because that would make me feel that I made the wrong choice if she's trying to catch on. You know what I'm saying?
(4) Ph: Right. We will keep her pain free. [...] Right. I can guarantee you. Right now she's perfectly comfortable.
(5) Fam: Right.

In turn 2, the family goes beyond agreement that the patient should be kept comfortable to review the end-of-life decision, indicating that any other decision *doesn't make sense* since their loved one is *not going to be here any more*. This review of the decision often indexes an ethical framework that defines death as the irretrievable loss of human consciousness, as shown in turns 3–5. In turn 3, the family member explicitly specifies what would be the *wrong choice* ethically – a decision carried out to withdraw life support if the patient has any human awareness (*trying to catch on*); the physician reassures the family that the patient will be *comfortable* in (turn 4); and the co-construction of this consensus is indexed with multiple alignment tokens of *right*, as in turns 4–5.

The interaction in end-of-life discussions thus suggests that consideration of the ethical dimensions of decision-making is distributed across the encounter. Physicians index their ethical responsibilities for end-of-life decision-making earlier in Phase 2 of the discussion when they indicate that medical futility is the basis for the decision to withdraw life support. Families, in turn, index their ethical responsibilities later in Phase 4 of the discussion when they indicate that loss of human consciousness is the basis for their consensus on the decision as a shared one both medically and ethically.

Most recently, the United States issued an apology for unethical syphilis research it conducted in Guatamala in the 1940's by one of the Tuskegee physicians (Reverby, 2011), and a new best-selling book entitled *The Immortal Life of Henrietta Lacks* (Skloot, 2010) tells the story of cancer cells taken by researchers from a poor African-American woman without her knowledge or consent and made into an important cell-line for medical research over the past 60 years.

3.   Offers to participate in clinical trials

Another type of medical encounter fraught with ethical issues is an offer to participate in clinical trials. Bringing clinical research into an encounter reverses the typical communicative dynamic of a medical encounter from a (more or less) definitive diagnosis and treatment plan based on the scientific expertise and best clinical practices of the profession to a diagnosis and an experimental treatment plan based on an open question in the scientific and clinical literature.

Alongside the near daily coverage of the progress of medical research in the media, particularly in the American media, the scandals of unethically conducted research are covered widely as well. In the United States in the 1970s, there was extensive coverage of the Tuskegee scandal: in a longitudinal U.S. Public Health Service study, a cohort of poor and illiterate rural African-American men were left untreated for a virulent form of syphilis in order to chart the course of the disease, long after penicillin was known to be a safe and effective cure. More recently, ethical lapses in research have again been in the news: the 2002 TIME Magazine cover story entitled "How Medical Research Has Turned Millions of Us Into Human Guinea Pigs" (Lemonick and Goldstein 2002) prominently features research shut-downs in major universities for lack of compliance with federal regulations concerning IRB (Institutional Review Board) review of research. Arguably, this ambivalent perception toward participation in medical research has had an impact on the progress of medical science: clinical trials, defined as the comparative investigation of an experimental therapy, are the gold standard in medical research leading to evidence-based best practices of clinical care ("ClinicalTrials" 2007). But in cancer research, for example, fewer than 5 % of patients enter clinical trials nationwide in the United States, a number that is even lower for certain population groups such as older patients and patients from minority groups, and many trials are delayed or even discontinued due to low enrollment ("Boosting" 2007).

Although the ethics scandals of medical research may be generally known to some extent, the reactive development of law, policy, and the regulation of research by IRBs may be less well-known, even though offering participation in medical research is one of the most regulated interactions in medicine today, particularly in the United States. In medicine worldwide, the seminal document of research ethics is the *Nuremberg Code* (1949), which set out the bedrock principle of voluntary participation in research: no individual should participate in medical research without his/her knowledge and informed consent. In the United States, the *Belmont Report* (1979) sets out the bioethics framework for the protection of human subjects based on the principles of respect for autonomy, beneficence, and justice. The *Belmont Report* is the basis for the current U.S. federal regulations that mandate the review of research by Institutional Review Boards (IRBs) in American universities (45 CFR 46 2005/1991). In the federal regulations, the principle of autonomy is operationalized in IRB review of the process of informed consent as the basis for voluntary participation in research; informed consent, in turn, is operationalized in the form of a written consent that provides information about the purpose, procedures, risks, benefits, and other aspects of a study. Beneficence is operationalized in the assessment of risks and benefits of participation in research, which is the basis of IRB review. Justice is operationalized in the review of subject selection to ensure the equitable distribution of the risks and benefits of research across individuals and groups (that is, study populations such as minority or underprivileged groups should not be selected as convenient populations to bear the risks of research, especially if they do not stand to benefit from the results of the research).

The American Medical Association (1998) identifies a wide variety of ethical issues related to the design, conduct, and dissemination of clinical research: for example, to enroll patients in a clinical trial ethically, clinicians must be in a state of equipoise, defined as true uncertainty with respect to the research question of the study. Some of the most important ethical issues are related to communication: for example, if a physician enrolls his/her own patients in a clinical trial, there may be a conflict of interest between the role of a clinical provider, who is obliged to provide the best care possible to his/her patient, and the role of a clinical investigator, who wants to conduct the best research possible, in part by enrolling sufficient numbers in the study (AMA 2000). Also important as an ethical issue is the language of the offer itself: to enable autonomy and voluntary participation, the AMA (1998) recommends that "Physicians should be completely objective in discussing the details of [the trial] ... and should not use persuasion to obtain consent", especially since persuasion can merge imperceptibly into undue influence and coercion. Most important, perhaps, is that offers to participate in clinical trials do not create what is called the therapeutic misconception, that is, that patients hold the idea that participation in research provides treatment known or assumed to be beneficial (Miller and Brody 2003). Bioethicists note, however, that both pressure to enroll and the therapeutic misconception seem widespread: Beauchamp and Childress (2001: 96) point to a study that reports patients' "feeling severe pressure to enroll in clinical trials" (Kass et al. 1996), and Miller and Brody (2003) cite a study that reports that up to 70 % of patients enroll in trials with a belief or expectation of therapeutic benefit (Appelbaum et al. 1987).

In research on participation in clinical trials in cancer medicine, retrospective research regularly identifies physician-patient communication as a key factor in the decision to enroll or not enroll in a clinical trial (Fleming, Schain and Mansour 1994; Gotay 1991; Jenkins and Fallowfield 2000; Roter and McNeilis 2003; for a brief review, see Albrecht, Franks, and Ruckdeschel 2005). Two research programs in medicine look at prospective data from actual encounters with an offer to participate in clinical trials. Eric Kodish and his colleagues look at the relationship between ethnicity and socio-economic status with respect to information-giving and rapport in informed consent encounters for pediatric leukemia trials (Miller et al. 2005; Simon and Kodish 2005). Both studies found, perhaps not surprisingly, that parents from lower socio-economic and/or minority groups received less information and participated less in the informed consent discussion, which is consistent with other research (Fisher 2005).

Terrance Albrecht and her colleagues collected prospective data from medical oncology encounters where adult patients were offered participation in clinical trials. Working within the biopsychosocial framework, Albrecht et al. (1999) found that strategic communication leading to clinical trial enrollment is both informational and supportive. The informational dimensions include content about the particular study, defined in terms of the elements of informed consent (purpose and procedures of a study specifically identified as research, risks, benefits, alternatives to participating in the research (e.g., standard treatment), confidentiality, compensation and continued medical care, contact information for questions, and voluntary participation). The supportive dimensions of strategic communication about clinical trials include the features of patient-centered communication (Roter and Hall 1992), such as active listening and expressions of understanding, as well as attention not only to the patient's motivation for enrollment (such as hope for direct benefits or altruism) but also to the logistical needs patients may have while participating in a clinical trial (such as alleviating the potential burden for a caregiver). In another study from this project, Eggly et al. (2008) found that most offers to participate in a clinical trial include explicit recommendations to participate and that these direct recommendations were associated with trial enrollment. These findings enter a controversial area since bioethicists suggest that offers to participate in trials should be objective and informational, not directive or persuasive.

In discourse studies, Barton (2007a) looks at ethics-in-interaction in a small pilot study of seven medical oncology encounters with offers to participate in clinical trials in cancer research, again using the theoretical framework of the institutional and interactional orders to argue that the institutional order of bioethics is in conflict with the interactional order of physicians offering participation in trials in terms of traditional medical ethics. In this work, Barton used the methodological framework of what Roberts and Sarangi (2005) call theme-oriented discourse analysis of medical encounters. Briefly, this methodological framework includes the following steps:

- identifying key interactional events within the context of interest (record and transcribe)
- identifying structural phases of the interactional event
- analyzing interaction within and across phases in terms of analytical themes (linguistic features, patterns, and conventions) and focal themes (functional actions such as decision-making)
- connecting the findings to outcomes

This methodological framework defines context broadly as a communicative ecology encompassing participants, settings, content, and influencing factors such as values and beliefs.

Barton (2007a) found that offers to participate in trials typically begin with an eligibility statement, as in turn 1 and turns 2–3 (Extract D):

Extract D
(1) Ph: There's a possibility that I might be able to enroll you on a clinical trial.

(2) Ph: Now what I'd like to propose for you is that you're eligible for something called a clinical trial that I'd like to tell you about because it may work for you and it's worth considering.
         [...]
(3) Ph: There is a new drug, kind of experimental drug, but a drug that has a track record that's been given to literally thousands of people.

The use of eligibility statements indicate that the development of the topic will be persuasive rather than objective, as it positions both the patient and the trial positively. The eligibility statement stands alone in turn 1, but in turn 2, it is accompanied by a mention of direct benefits that might allow the therapeutic misconception (*it may work for you*) and what may be the beginning of a direct recommendation (*it's worth considering*). In turn 3, the physician provides information about the drug as *experimental*, with a brief mitigation (*kind of*), but he then goes on to position the drug positively and persuasively by referring to its *track record*, perhaps reflecting a lack of true equipoise with respect to the trial. In terms of traditional medical ethics, however, an offer like this might be seen to indicate that the physician sees participation in the trial as the best possible treatment for the patient. In this view, the reference to the track record of the drug in turn 3 as well as the physician's candidate explanation for not participating in a trial presented earlier (Extract B, turn 1) – *There's a chance that even if I go on the study that I won't get the pill* – refer to the possibility of receiving cutting-edge treatment, reflecting the importance of the Hippocratic principle to provide the best care possible for a patient (Jonson, Siegler, and Winslade 2006).

Interestingly, Barton (2007a) also found that bringing up the topic of trial participation often did not end in explicit decision-making to enroll or not enroll in the trial. Instead, physicians frequently deferred the enrollment decision, as shown in Extract B (turns 1–2) above. Physicians sometimes seemed to defer enrollment when there were signs of interactional trouble, but they also deferred decision-making even when patients and families seemed interested in participating in the trial. Barton (2007a) suggests that deferring explicit decision-making is a way of managing the tension between the institutional and interactional orders of participation in clinical research and the conflict of interest in the clinician/investigator role. In effect, physicians separate the communicative events of recruiting to participating in research and providing informed consent. With this separation, the physician can interactionally construct the recruitment informally and persuasively in line with traditional medical ethics, while turning over informed consent to research staff, who conduct a formal informed consent encounter following the principles of bioethics and IRB review. Physicians thus manage the conflict of interest of the clinician/investigator roles because formal decision-making takes place within the institutional order of informed consent. Arguably, however, actual decision-making may take place during the interactional order of research recruitment, thereby finessing bioethics with traditional medical ethics. In offers to participate in medical research, then, physicians speak for themselves as clinicians and researchers, but also sometimes speak for another in the voice of the patient making an ethically charged decision based not only on expertise but also on trust.

4.   Further research

In the Introduction, the key research questions for investigating ethics-in-interaction in medical encounters called for descriptive, methodological and theoretical research. Obviously, there remains a tremendous amount of descriptive research to be done. End-of-life discussions and offers to participate in clinical trials are just two communicative contexts that are complex linguistically and ethically, and there are hundreds more: almost every kind of medical decision-making has ethical dimensions, from relatively simple treatment recommendations to ethics consults when there is conflict within or among hospital administrators, medical staff, patients, or families. Of great importance in the development of descriptive research in this area is the need to look at ethics-in-interaction in encounters involving participants from different social, cultural, and linguistic groups (Candlin and Candlin 2003). Most of the studies described above collected data primarily from white, middle-class families in encounters with white male specialist clinicians, no doubt a reflection of the academic research hospitals where the studies took place. Further, these studies mostly collected data in English. There is a pressing need to begin to understand ethics-in-interaction in a wider variety of medical encounters, including different languages, non-Western settings, encounters in translation, intercultural encounters, medical encounters in the community, encounters in complementary medicine, and more.

Methodologically, describing ethics-in-interaction is a challenge, complicated by the indirect ways in which both medical professionals and lay patients and families orient to the ethics of their decision-making. For many clinicians, ethical issues are worked out relatively unself-consciously in the action and interaction of everyday work: making particular decisions, guiding patients and families to ethical decisions, etc. – most often without conscious or reflective attention to the ethical dimensions that are nonetheless an important part of decision-making (Jonson, Siegler and Winslow 2006). Constructing an argument in a discourse study is thus necessarily within what Sarangi (2007) calls "the analyst's paradox" in the interpretation of discourse data: the problematics of developing sufficient contextual knowledge, best acquired, Sarangi argues, through "thick participation". Although a number of methodological frameworks were mentioned above, including interactional sociolinguistics, discourse analysis, and theme-oriented discourse analysis, other frameworks such as conversation analysis and critical discourse analysis could certainly be added to the repertoire. There is a great need for more meta-methodological scholarship on the best design of a research program investigating ethics-in-interaction.

Theoretically, too, we are only beginning to work in discourse studies on the concepts and frameworks for investigating ethics-in-interaction. As with methods and methodologies, some of our existing theoretical concepts and frameworks, such as Sarangi and Roberts' (1999) distinction between the institutional and interactional orders, seem to work well in interpreting how ethical matters are interactionally negotiated in medical encounters. But Sarangi (personal communication) has also set out an even more challenging meta-theoretical question that is relevant to the interdisciplinary literature on ethics: what does an interactional perspective on ethics reveal about ethics in theory and practice? This is an important question that should be systematically addressed in further research on ethics-in-interaction (Barton, 2008).

Finally, discourse researchers working in medical settings have ethical obligations of their own, as pointed out by Hamilton (1993: 207), who formulates the central ethical question for discourse researchers as "How can I make sure that patients are getting the best care possible whenever language is concerned?" This question is not always easy to answer, especially in the application of discourse research, which can sometimes be seen to serve the interests of the profession over the interests of the patient. But the discourse analysis of medical encounters has a long tradition of "speaking for" the patient (see, especially, Ainsworth-Vaughn 1998), so Hamilton's question reminds us that our ethical obligations as linguists are similar to the ethical obligations of clinicians – contributing to the best care of the patient.

Notes

1. To save space, the transcriptions in this chapter are presented in broad form, using the following conventions:

Falling intonation	.
Rising intonation	?
Continuing intonation	,
Incomplete utterances	--
Latching	==
	==
Deleted material	[...]
Contextual information or editing	[ ]

Excerpts in the text are in italics. To preserve confidentiality, contributions from clinicians are labeled as Ph (physician); contributions from patients are labeled Pt, and from family members, Fam. Following usage common in medicine (Institute of Medicine 1997), I use the term family here to include individuals with close relationships with the patient, even if they are not relatives. Also following current usage, I use the term clinicians to encompass the variety of professionals in healthcare, although I continue to use the term physician when describing communicative events in which they typically take the lead role.

2. To introduce ethical issues in medicine, I use the Current Opinions of the AMA (American Medical Association) because these policies are in wide circulation in the US and similar to policies in the UK. This chapter draws upon research conducted primarily in Western contexts, an issue I take up in Section 4.

References

45 CFR 46
2005/1991   Code of Federal Regulations Title 45 Public Welfare Part 46 Protection of
             Human   Subjects.   http://www.hhs.gov/ohrp/humansubjects/guidance/
             45cfr46.htm (accessed December 14, 2007).
Abbott, Katherine, Joni Sago, and Catherine Green
   2001   Families looking back: One year after discussion of withdrawal or with-
             holding of life-sustaining support. *Critical Care Medicine* 29: 197–201.
Ainsworth-Vaughn, Nancy
   1998   *Claiming Power in Doctor-Patient Talk.* Oxford/New York: Oxford Uni-
             versity Press.
Albrecht, Terrance, Christina Blanchard, John Ruckdeschel, Michael Coovert and Re-
             becca Strongbow
   1999   Strategic physician communication and oncology clinical trials. *Journal of
             Clinical Oncology* 17: 3324–3332.
Albrecht, Terrance, Melissa Franks, and John Ruckdeschel
   2005   Communication and informed consent. *Current Opinions in Oncology* 17:
             336–339.
Aldridge, Matthew and Ellen Barton
   2007   Establishing terminal status in end-of-life discussions. *Qualitative Health
             Research* 17: 908–918.
AMA [American Medical Association]
   1994   E-2.20 Withholding or withdrawing life-sustaining medical treatment.
             AMA Code of Medical Ethics Current Opinions. http://www.ama-assn.org/
             ama/pub/category/2498.html (accessed December 14, 2007).
AMA [American Medical Association]
   1997   E-2.037 Medical futility in end-of-life care. AMA Code of Medical Ethics
             Current Opinions. http://www.ama-assn.org/ama/pub/category/2498.html
             (accessed December 14, 2007).
AMA [American Medical Association]
   1998   E-2.07 Clinical investigation. AMA Code of Medical Ethics Current
             Opinions. http://www.ama-assn.org/ama/pub/category/2498.html (accessed
             December 14, 2007).
AMA [American Medical Association]
   2000   E-8.0315 Managing conflicts of interest in the conduct of clinical trials.
             AMA Code of Medical Ethics Current Opinions http://www.ama-assn.org/
             ama/pub/category/2498.html (accessed December 14, 2007).
AMA [American Medical Association]
   2001   E-8.081 Surrogate decision-making. AMA Code of Medical Ethics Current
             Opinions. http://www.ama-assn.org/ama/pub/category/2498.html (accessed
             December 14, 2007).
Angus, Derek, Amber Bonato, and Walter Linde-Zwible et al.
   2004   Use of intensive care at the end of life in the United States: An epidemi-
             ologic study. *Critical Care Medicine* 32: 638–643.
Appelbaum, Paul, Loren Roth, Charles Lidz, P. Benson, and W. Winslade
   1987   False hopes and best data: Consent to research and the therapeutic miscon-
             ception. *Hastings Center Report* 17: 20–24.

Azoulay, Elie, Sylvie Chevret, Ghislaine Leleu, Frederic Pochard, Michel Barboteu, Christophe Adrie, Pierre Canoui, Jean Roger Le Gall, and Benoît Schlemmer
    2000   Half the families of intensive care unit patients experience inadequate communication with physicians. *Critical Care Medicine* 28: 3044–3049.

Barton, Ellen
    2005   Institutional policies, professional practices, and the discourse of end-of-life discussions in American medicine. *Journal of Applied Linguistics* 2: 249–267.

Barton, Ellen
    2006   Trajectories of alignment and the situated ethics of end-of-life discussions in American medicine. In: Maurizio Gotti and Françoise Salager-Meyer (eds.), *Advances in Medical Discourse Analysis: Oral and Written Contexts*, 23–42. Bern /New York: Peter Lang.

Barton, Ellen
    2007a   Institutional and professional orders of ethics in the discourse practices of research recruitment in oncology. In: Rick Iedema (ed.), *The Discourse of Hospital Communication: Tracing Complexities in Contemporary Health Care Organizations*, 18–38. New York: Palgrave Macmillan.

Barton, Ellen
    2007b   Situating end-of-life decision making in a hybrid ethical frame. *Communication & Medicine* 4: 131–140.

Barton, Ellen
    2008   Further contributions from the ethical turn in composition/rhetoric: Analyzing ethics in interaction. *College Composition and Communication* 59: 596–632.

Barton, Ellen, Matthew Aldridge, Thomas Trimble, and Justin Vidovic
    2005   Structure and function in end-of-life discussions in the surgical intensive care unit. *Communication & Medicine* 2: 3–20.

Battin, Margaret
    1994   *The Least Worst Death: Essays in Bioethics on the End of Life*. Oxford/ New York: Oxford University Press.

Beachamp, Tom and James Childress
    2001   *Principles of Biomedical Ethics*. (5th edn.) Oxford /New York: Oxford University Press.

The Belmont Report
    1979   http://www.hhs.gov/ohrp/humansubjects/guidance/belmont.htm (accessed December 13, 2007).

Boosting cancer trial participation
    2007   http://www.cancer.gov/clinicaltrials/digestpage/boosting-trial-participation (accessed December 14, 2007).

Borrell-Carrio, Francesca, Anthony Suchman, and Ronald Epstein
    2004   The biopsychosocial model 25 years later: Principles, practice, and scientific inquiry. *Annals of Family Medicine* 2: 576–582.

Candlin, Christopher N. and Sally Candlin
    2003   Health care communication: A problematic site for applied linguistics research. *Annual Review of Applied Linguistics* 23: 134–154.

Cassell, Joan
    2005   *Life and Death in Intensive Care*. Philadelphia: Temple University Press.
Christakis, Nicholas
    1999   *Death Foretold: Prophecy and Prognosis in Medical Care*. Chicago: University of Chicago Press.
Cimino, James
    2003   A clinician's understanding of ethics in palliative care: An American perspective. *Critical Reviews in Oncology/Hematology* 46: 17–24.
Clinical Trials
    2007   http://clinicaltrials.gov (accessed December 14, 2007).
Curtis, J. Randall
    2004   Communicating about end-of-life care with patients and families in the intensive care unit. *Critical Care Clinics* 20: 363–380.
Curtis, J. Randall, Ruth Engelberg, Marjorie Wenrich, Elizabeth Nielsen, Sarah Shannon, Patsy Treece, Mark Tonelli, Donald Patrick, Lynne Robins, Barbara McGrath, and Gordon Rubenfeld
    2002   Studying communication about end-of-life care during the ICU family conference: Development of a framework. *Journal of Critical Care* 17: 147–160.
Curtis, J.Randall and Donald Patrick
    2001   How to discuss dying and death in the Intensive Care Unit. In: J. Randall Curtis and Gordon Rubenfeld (eds.), *Managing Death in the Intensive Care Unit*, 85–102. Oxford/New York: Oxford University Press.
Curtis, J. Randall, Donald Patrick, Sarah Shannon, P. Treece, R. Engelberg, and G. Rubenfeld
    2001   The family conference as a focus to improve communication about end-of-life care in the intensive care unit: Opportunities for improvement. *Critical Care Medicine* 29: N26–N33.
Drew, Paul and John Heritage (eds.)
    1992   *Talk at Work: Interaction in Institutional Settings*. Cambridge /New York: Cambridge University Press.
Eggly, Susan, Terrance Albrecht, Felicity Harper, Tanina Foster, Melissa M. Franks, and John C. Ruckdeschel
    2008   Oncologists' recommendation of clinical trial participation to patients. *Patient Education and Counseling* 70: 143–148.
Engel, George
    1977   The need for a new medical model: A challenge for biomedicine. *Science* 196: 129–136.
Fisher, Celia
    2005   Commentary: SES, ethnicity and goodness-of-fit in clinician-parent communication during pediatric cancer trials. *Journal of Pediatric Psychology* 30: 231–234.
Fleming, Irvin, Wendy Schain, and Edward Mansour
    1994   Barriers to clinical trials. *Cancer* 74: 2662–2675.
Gotay, Carolyn
    1991   Accrual to cancer clinical trials: Directions from the research literature. *Social Science and Medicine* 33: 569–577.

Hamilton, Heidi
  1993   Ethical issues for applying linguistics to clinical contexts: The case of speech-language pathology. *Issues in Applied Linguistics* 4: 207–224.
Heyland, Daren, Graeme Rocker, Christopher O'Callaghan, Peter Dodek, and Deborah Cook
  2003   Dying in the ICU: Perspectives of family members. *Chest* 124: 11–12.
Hickey, Mairead
  1990   What are the needs of families of critically ill patients? A review of the literature since 1976. *Heart and Lung* 19: 401–415.
Institute of Medicine
  1997   *Approaching Death in America*. http://www.nap.edu/readingroom/books/approaching/ (accessed December 14, 2007).
Jameson, Patricia, Marjorie Schiebmier, and Frances Bott et al.
  1996   The experiences of families with a relative in the intensive care unit. *Heart and Lung* 25: 467–474.
Jenkins, Valerie and Lesley Fallowfield
  2000   Reasons for accepting or declining to participate in randomized clinical trials for cancer therapy. *British Journal of Cancer* 82: 1783–1787.
Jonson, Albert, Mark Siegler, and William Winslade
  2006   *Clinical Ethics: A Practical Approach to Ethical Decisions in Clinical Care*. 6th edn. New York: McGraw-Hill Medical.
Kass, Nancy, Jeremy Sugerman, Ruth Faden, and Monica Schoch-Spana
  1996   Trust: The fragile foundation of contemporary biomedical research. *Hastings Center Report* 25–29.
Kaufman, Sharon
  2005   *… And a Time to Die: How American Hospitals Shape the End of Life*. New York: Scribner.
Kirchoff, Karin, Lee Walker, and Ann Hutton
  2002   The vortex: Families' experiences with death in the intensive care unit. *American Journal of Critical Care* 11: 200–209.
Kirchoff, Karin, Mi-Kyung Song, and Karen Kehl
  2004   Caring for the family of the critically ill patient. *Critical Care Clinics* 20: 453–466.
Last Acts Coalition
  2002   *Means to a Better End: A Report on Dying in America Today*. http://www.rwjf.org/newsroom/feature.jsp?id=20938&typeid=151 (accessed December 14, 2007).
Lemonick, Michael and Andrew Goldstein
  2002   How medical testing has turned millions of us into human guinea pigs. *TIME Magazine* (22 April): 46–56.
Miller, Frank and Howard Brody
  2003   A critique of clinical equipoise: Therapeutic misconception in the ethics of clinical trials. *Hastings Center Report* 33: 19–28.
Miller, Victoria, Dennis, Drotar, Christopher Burant, and Eric Kodish
  2005   Clinician-parent communication during informed consent for pediatric leukemia trials. *Journal of Pediatric Psychology* 30: 219–229.
Mishler, Elliot G.
  1984   *The Discourse of Medicine*. Norwood, NJ: Ablex.

The Nuremberg Code
1949   http://www.hhs.gov/ohrp/references/nurcode.htm (accessed December 14, 2007).
Peräkylä, Anssi
1998   Authority and accountability: The delivery of diagnosis in primary health care. *Social Psychology Quarterly* 61: 301–320.
Reverby, Susan
(2011)   Normal exposure and inoculation syphilis: A PHS 'Tuskegee' doctor in Guatamala. 1946–1948 *Journal of Policy History* 23: 6–28.
Roberts, Celia and Srikant Sarangi
2005   Theme-based discourse analysis of medical encounters. *Medical Education* 39: 632–640.
Roter, Deborah and Judith Hall
1992   *Doctors Talking to Patients / Patients Talking to Doctors: Improving Communication in Medical Visits*. Westport, CT: Auburn House.
Roter, Deborah and Kelly McNeilis
2003   The nature of the therapeutic relationships and the assessment of its discourse in routine medical visits. In: Teresa Thompson, Alicia Dorsey, Katherine Miller and Roxanne Parrott (eds.), *Handbook of Health Communication*, 121–140. Mahwah, NJ: Lawrence Erlbaum.
Rothman, David
1991   *Strangers at the Bedside: A History of How Law and Bioethics Transformed Medical Decision Making*. New York: Aldine de Gruyter.
Sarangi, Srikant
2007   The anatomy of interpretation: Coming to terms with the analyst's paradox in professional discourse studies. *Text and Talk* 5: 567–584.
Sarangi, Srikant and Celia Roberts
1999   The dynamics of interactional and institutional orders in work-related settings. In: Srikant Sarangi and Celia Roberts (eds.), *Talk, Work and Institutional Order: Discourse in Medical, Mediation and Management Settings*, 1–60. Berlin / New York: Mouton de Gruyter.
Schiffrin, Deborah
1994   *Approaches to Discourse*. Oxford/Cambridge, MA: Blackwell.
Schiffrin, Deborah, Deborah Tannen, and Heidi Hamilton (eds.)
2001   *Handbook of Discourse Analysis*. Oxford/Malden, MA: Blackwell.
Shannon, Sarah
2001   Helping families prepare for and cope with a death in the ICU. In: J. Randall Curtis and Gordon Rubenfeld (eds.), *Managing Death in the ICU*, 168–182. Oxford/New York: Oxford University Press.
Simon, Christian and Eric Kodish
2005   "Step into my zapatos, Doc": Understanding and reducing communication disparities in the multicultural informed consent setting. *Perspectives in Biology and Medicine* 48: S123–138.
Skloot, Rebecca
2010   The Immortal Life of Henrietta Lacks. New York: Random House.
Solomon, Mildred
2005   Realizing bioethics' goals in practice: Ten ways "*is*" can help "*ought*". *Hastings Center Report* 35: 40–47.

SUPPORT Principal Investigators
> 1995   A controlled trial to improve care for seriously ill hospitalized patients: The study to understand prognoses and preferences for outcomes and risks of treatment (SUPPORT). *JAMA [Journal of the American Medical Association]* 274: 1591–1598.

Truog, Robert, Alexandra Cist, Sharon Brackett, Jeffrey Burns, Martha Curley, Marion Danis, Michael DeVita, Stanley Rosenbaum, David Rothenberg, Charles Sprung, Sally Webb, Ginger Wlody, William Hurford
> 2001   Recommendations for end-of-life care in the intensive care unit: The Ethics Committee of the Society of Critical Care Medicine. *Critical Care Medicine* 29: 2332–2348.

9. Psychological and sociomoral frames in genetic counselling for predictive testing*

Srikant Sarangi, Lucy Brookes-Howell,
Kristina Bennert and Angus Clarke

Abstract

Psychosocial and moral/ethical debates pervade the genetic counselling litera-ture – focusing on clients and professionals respectively – but there are very few discourse-based, empirical studies dealing with their manifestation in the actual clinical encounter. Routinely, genetic counsellors initiate reflective frames early on in the counselling process in order to explicitly seek the client's orientation towards decisions about testing and their readiness to disseminate (or not) the testing process and the test results. The extent to which clients do (not) align with the counsellor's non-directive, reflective agenda in facilitating informed decisions is open to interactional negotiation. In this chapter we focus on how clients' broad spectrum of psychosocial concerns are accomplished interaction-ally in real-life genetic counselling sessions through "psychological" and "sociomoral" frames, by drawing specific attention to the familial roles and re-sponsibilities that go with individual actions and their consequences. Adopting a discourse analysis approach we examine extended data extracts taken from the preliminary coding of 24 counselling sessions involving 12 clients in the con-text of predictive testing for Huntington's disease (HD). Our main findings are that genetic counsellors create the opportunity for clients to engage actively with decision-making – in relation to the testing process and disclosure of test results – by strategically interweaving psychological and sociomoral frames throughout the counselling activity without necessarily compromising the pro-fessional ethos of non-directiveness.

1. Introduction

Most genetic conditions run in the family. In some cases family members may already have been affected by the condition, while others may be at risk or may simply be of carrier status. In order to know if they or any of their offspring are likely to develop the genetic condition in the future, at-risk individuals may decide to undergo a predictive genetic test. Consider the following extract where a young woman (CL), at risk of Huntington's Disease (HD) – which is an incurable degenerative neuropsychiatric disorder with a highly variable age of onset – is discussing with the genetic counsellor (GC) her prime reasons for undergoing predictive testing (see Appendix 1 for transcription conventions).

Example 1

```
01  GC:  and within yourself (.) is it- is it something you want to know
02  CL:  yeah it is um (..) I've never really been (…) bothered about the Hunt-
         ington's um (..) I mean I've- I've grown up with it in my life
03  GC:  mm
04  CL:  =so it's- it's always something that's been there um (..) and it's never
         really (.) sort of deeply upset me erm (.) so I've never (..) until- until
         recently I've never really wanted to know (.) it hasn't bothered me
         either way
05  GC:  mm
06  CL:  um (..) but since we've been married and we've been talking about
         having kids and (.) you know (.) I'd like to know
07  GC:  that's why a lot of people want (it)
08  CL:  =yeah 'cause I- I've seen my sister and she's had three kids and then
         she had the test done (.) and then I've seen my older brother (.) he's
         had the test (.) um and then they had each embryo tested (1.0) so I've
         seen how (.) how it works either side (.) and I think I'd rather (.) rather
         know before I decide to have children
[a few turns omitted]
14  CL:  you know knowing I would be able to stop the gene and and not (.)
         sort of carry it on through the family
```

At the outset, the genetic counsellor (GC) emphasises CL's inner feelings ("and within yourself") to open up discussions of the client's (CL) decision about testing. CL then goes on to describe how Huntington's disease is in her mind ("it's always something that's been there"), but she quickly foregrounds her ability to cope ("it's never really sort of deeply upset me" and "I've never really wanted to know"). However, in turn 06, CL shifts from her own concerns and positions herself in her role as wife ("since we've been married") and as potential mother ("we've been talking about having kids") as she foregrounds her responsibilities in relation to her reproductive decision. In turn 07, GC provides supportive feedback by alluding to the routine practice of others, which allows CL to work through her moral dilemma (turn 14).

All clinical encounters are essentially moral encounters (Goffman 1961) involving facework and character work. In a seminal paper, Engel (1977) talked of biomedicine and the uncoupling of the "biopsychosocial". Since then, many researchers within social psychology and social anthropology have drawn attention to the significance of the psychosocial dimensions of illness experience (Kleinman 1988; Good 1994; Frank 1995). With regard to communication/discourse-based studies, the work of Silverman (1987, 1994), Fisher (1991, 1995), Bergmann (1992, 1998), White (2002) and Måseide (2003, 2006) has explored the tacit moral order as an integral part of healthcare encounters. For instance, Bergmann (1992) and Silverman (1994) have shown how morality is exercised by constructing particular conversational topics as "delicate". In other words, issues are not "psychosocial" or "moral" *per se*, but are formatted as such through interactional devices, as can be seen from our opening extract.

Genetic counselling as a hybrid activity type (Sarangi 2000) is invariably underpinned by clients' psychological as well as moral, ethical concerns. In this chapter our main focus is to examine how psychosocial concerns are often articulated either within a "psychological" frame (with a focus on the individual and their personal feelings) or within a "sociomoral" frame (with a focus on interpersonal relationships and their accompanying obligations) in the setting of the genetic counselling clinic. We examine the extent to which maintenance of, and/or shifts between, such frames can display the clients' coping strategies in relation to their current and future genetic status. We use the notion of "frame" in Goffman's (1974) sense to characterize the interactional dynamics of the communication system. In interpersonal, interactional settings, framing consists of "principles of organisation which govern events – at least social ones – and our subjective involvement in them" (Goffman 1974: 10). First, we review how researchers have treated psychological and moral issues in the context of counselling for genetic disorders. In Section 3, we discuss our data corpus and our analytic framework. Following from an overview of psychological and sociomoral frames in Section 4.1, in Section 4.2 we present a discourse analysis of two extended data extracts in order to demonstrate the complex ways in which differentiated roles are formulated and legitimated vis-à-vis psychological and sociomoral modes of reasoning. Finally, we link our discussion to genetic counselling practice vis-à-vis nondirectiveness.

2.   The psychosocial and moral dimensions of genetic counselling

Weil (2000, 2003), among many others, stresses that psychosocial adjustment should be a central feature of genetic counselling and that genetic counsellors as gatekeepers have to balance attention to genetic science and the psychosocial concerns of the counselees. Psychosocial concerns cover a range of topics and are seen to vary across conditions and timing of counselling. Based on a small-scale study of outcome measures involving both counselling professionals and clients, Bernhardt, Biesecker and Mastromarino (2000) identify immediate and long-term psychosocial support as significant indicators of successful counselling.

Given the complexity of genetic conditions, a number of researchers have addressed factors such as anxiety, distress, anger, emotions and affection, as a way of accounting for particular social behaviours and actions. This psychoso-cial research tradition is mainly based on interview and/or questionnaire data. A majority of these studies focus on scenarios of decision-making arising from the contexts of prenatal screening and diagnosis (Green and Statham 1996; Kenen et al. 2000; Marteau and Dormandy 2001; Van Berkel and van der Weele 1999; and Williams, Alderson and Farsides 2002) and predictive testing for late-onset disorders (Evers-Kiebooms and Decruyenaere 1998; Evers-Kie-booms et al. 1989; Huggins et al. 1992; Codori and Brandt 1994; Decruyenaere et al. 1997). Such work has largely, although not invariably, focused on quanti-tative measures of knowledge, attitudes and mental state in relation to testing. Rather few studies have encouraged research participants to elaborate upon their thoughts, feelings and decision-making processes (e.g. Dudok deWit et al. 1997; Chapman 2002a, 2002b; Richards 2004).

Within the genetic counselling literature, ethical and moral issues have been addressed primarily in terms of professional ethics and their implications for counselling practice. Following Beauchamp and Childress (1994 [1974]), a number of theoretically oriented papers discuss how ethical principles might apply to concrete problems (most famously, the Georgetown mantra of "benefi-cence, non-maleficence, autonomy, and justice"). Not surprisingly, such ab-stract principles come into conflict with each other and thus offer little guidance as to how particular situations should be responded to by counsellors (e.g. Wüstner 2003; Huibers and van't Spijker 1998). There may be multiple reasons for professionals to adhere to specific principles, such as non-directiveness, and these may serve personal and professional functions other than the profes-sional's explicit application of code of ethics (Clarke 1997; Sarangi 2010). For example, in the context of genetic counselling for prenatal testing, van Berkel and van der Weele (1999: 159) claim that genetic counsellors are reluctant to re-spond to the moral issues raised by patients for fear of compromising their non-directive stance.

Some researchers take the view that ethical guidance needs to become an in-tegral part of genetic counselling and that, if performed in the right manner, such guidance will enhance rather than threaten client autonomy. Stone and Miles (1999), using an HD prenatal testing scenario, speculate what such moral guidance would look like. They state that clients are often unable to articulate the embedded ethic that informs their decision-making. It then becomes the responsibility of the counsellor to support clients by offering them methods for moral decision-making. Stone and Miles go on to advise genetic counsellors to become aware of how their own values influence the course of the counselling they provide, then to tell clients outright what they think rather than opt for subtle manipulation. They also recommend that counsellors actively use ques-tions raised in similar situations with others to alert clients to the full spectrum of issues that could be considered.

These are very strongly worded directives, without any analysis of what actually happens in the counselling encounter. Several researchers (Arribas-Aylllon, Sarangi and Clarke 2008a, 2008b; Downing 2005; Forrest et al. 2003; Hallowell 1999; Hallowell et al. 2003, 2006) have examined themes such as responsibility, blame and guilt – which cut across the psychological and moral aspects – based on research interview data. However, to our knowledge, there are very few attempts at examining the psychological and moral dimensions of the clinical interaction as they unfold in the genetic counselling setting (see Sarangi 2005, 2010, forthcoming; Pilnick 2002a, 2002b).

3.   Data and Methodology

Participants for the study were recruited through the All Wales Medical Genetics Service. Following standard ethics committee approval, the procedure for recruitment of clients involved the genetic nurse specialist introducing the background to the research project to the client during their home visit. If the client was interested, the nurse gave the client letters of introduction and invitation and a consent form. Clients were then able to decide over a period of time whether they wished to participate in the study by giving written consent and thus allowing their clinic sessions to be audio-recorded. Sessions were transcribed following standard procedure for anonymisation. Most clients were also interviewed about their experiences of the genetic counselling process once they had received a test result.

The genetic counselling provided for the predictive testing for HD follows a formal, although not completely inflexible, protocol (see Appendix 2). There are three clinic sessions before the test result is given. The first session is referred to as the "Preliminary Interview" (PI). This is followed by "Appointment 1" (A1) and "Appointment 2" (A2) where further discussions take place and blood samples are taken. The test result will then be given at a further meeting. A follow-up appointment is normally offered to the client, regardless of the test result.

Our analysis in this paper is based on a sub-corpus of 24 counselling sessions involving 12 clients undergoing testing for HD, selected purposively from a larger data corpus to consist of 8 each of the pre-result sessions (PI, A1 and A2). The clients (7 female, 5 male) represent different family circumstances and in most cases attended clinics with their partners (17 out of 24 sessions), or occasionally with their mothers or friends (4 out of 24 sessions). Only in 3 sessions did the client attend alone. Two of the counsellors were female and one male.

In examining the psychosocial concerns we limited ourselves to two categories of reflective questions (from a total of six main categories identified in Sarangi et al. 2004). These were questions about clients' "decision about testing" (DAT) and questions exploring their "decision about disclosure" (DAD), i.e., who to tell about the testing process and the test result. These two categories of questions were chosen because they represent two of the key items on the counsellor's agenda and are reiterated across all three stages of the counselling process.

Two members of the research team (LBH and KB) identified and coded all instances of psychosocial concerns in the sub-corpus. Instances of initiation-response sequences were coded in terms of "psychological" and "sociomoral" frames. Appendix 3 provides an illustrative list of psychological and sociomoral frames based on clients' statements in the counselling encounter. Our use of the term "sociomoral" does not suggest that moral issues can be reduced to social or vice versa; instead we restrict our discussion to those moral issues that have a social character, especially in terms of role-responsibilities. On the basis of emerging patterns, two extended data extracts were then examined more closely using discourse analysis (for a discourse analytic approach to genetic counselling, see Sarangi 2000, 2002; Sarangi and Clarke 2002a, 2002b; Sarangi et al. 2003, 2004, 2005).

4.   Data analysis

4.1.   Coding of initiation-response sequences as psychological and sociomoral frames

Since reflective questions (e.g., "if I were to ask you"; "what would you do if"; "who would you tell") are easily identifiable through use of the subjunctive mood and other features, we took such questions as the basis for identifying initiation-response sequence in our sub-corpus. We identified a total of 126 initiation-response sequences spanning the three pre-result counselling sessions (PI, A1 and A2). When initiating sequences concerning decisions about testing (DAT) or decisions about disclosure (DAD), counsellors can formulate their questions either in an open frame (O) to allow clients to pursue their own agenda, in a psychological frame (PY) or in a sociomoral (SM) frame to elicit clients' responses that align with the counsellor's agenda.

We initially devised three categories for coding the responses – principle-based (explicitly deontological, drawing upon ethical, legal or religious principles); psychological (focusing on the mental, and especially the emotional, welfare of the particular individual under consideration); and sociomoral (basing decisions upon the mutual, often reciprocal, obligations between relatives and friends, and so taking into account the welfare of others as much as oneself when making decisions). The deontological category turned out to be empty, so categories could be restricted to the self-focused "psychological" and the other-focused "sociomoral".

While coding of psychological frames was relatively easy, coding of socio-moral frames proved more complex. There are at least three different meanings of moral: good-bad; right-wrong; responsibility/duty/obligation (see Hare 1964). We chose to adopt a role-relational perspective (Sarangi forthcoming) in our characterisation of the sociomoral frame. We agree with Fletcher (1967: 235) when he says: "In every situation the probing question is not so much, What shall I *do*? As What shall *I* do?". This signals a shift of emphasis from making choices based on available alternatives to reflecting on available choices based on one's role-relations and responsibilities vis-à-vis others. In other words, informed choice is premised upon other-orientation. This perspective is also endorsed in Emmett's (1966: 15) claim that "what people think they ought to do depends largely on how they see their roles, and (most importantly) the conflicts between their roles". Such conflicts, or the moral dilemma, following Campbell (1984 [1972]), can be characterised in terms of alternative choices, neither of which provides a satisfactory solution to the problem. For instance, a parent requesting childhood testing may foreground his/her parental responsibility ahead of the child's right (not) to know. This role-relational dimension is inherently social, so our notion of "sociomoral" may help to capture how clients define and legitimise their role-specific actions in relation to testing and disclosure of testing process and test results. Many of the factors to be considered as the consequences of decisions about genetic testing relate to people's social lives, especially their family relationships, which are constituted as a system and maintained through communication patterns and interactional trajectories.

Our coding produced the following frequency of initiation-response sequences for decisions about testing (DAT) and decisions about dissemination (DAD) (see Table 1).

Table 1. Frequency of psychological (PY) and sociomoral (SM) frames in DAT and DAD initiation-response sequences

Sequence	DAT	DAD	— TOTAL
O-SM	3	–	3
O-PY	3	1	4
SM-SM	19	18	37
PY-PY	9	2	11
SM-PY	2	–	2
PY-SM	2	–	2
TOTAL	38	21	59

The first set of initiation-response sequences (O-SM and O-PY) involves open questions by counsellors followed by either sociomoral or psychological responses from clients. Consider the following examples:

Example 2 (O-SM)/DAT

GC: um, if I were to ask you are there any particular reasons um for you wanting to have the test? I mean (.) is there any particular reason that comes above any other?
CL: um well (.) there are a few (.) a number of reasons (.) I think the most important one is that I've got a son who's two and a half um
GC: okay
CL: it's the whole illness that's been, um has been a bit of a shock to my wife and to the other women who've married in to the family who weren't told of the situation (.) weren't given the information that was available (.) and obviously we'd like to have more children

Example 3 (O-PY)/DAD

GC: What's changed in that time do you think?
CL: I don't know (.) I just think I've changed (.) It's just that your knowing the tests are there (.) and you see it on telly and programmes and all that (.) it's something I know if I got I got (.) and if I you know I'm living with it whether I got it

In Example 2, in response to GC's open frame question, CL chooses to foreground children, family and reproduction decision making among the reasons for wanting to have the test. Note that she also alludes to her commitment to sharing information and repairing past mistakes of nondisclosure. In Example 3, a similarly open frame question elicits a different set of concerns: the need to know and the trigger behind CL's desire to know.

The second set of initiation-response includes specific frames – psychological (PY) or sociomoral (SM) – initiated by the counsellor, followed by responses aligned to the counsellor's orientation. Consider Examples 4 and 5.

Example 4 (SM-SM)/DAD

GC: So in terms of um your result, were you planning to say anything to your father or brother anything (.) whatever happens?
CL: Whatever happens as far as we're concerned is (.) this is done for our family

Example 5 (PY-PY)/DAT

GC: If you say it is <u>such a background issue</u> for you and you have so many other <u>daily</u> concerns that occupy you (.) is what <u>is</u> the need to know? I mean why (.) in what sense (.) what would knowing change for you?

CL: I don't know (.) I just think I need to know now

MO: For peace of mind

CL: Yeah (.) I just think I really need to know now (.) Whether I have or haven't got it

In Example 4, GC uses the sociomoral frame to topicalise the issue of disclosure of test results to family members. CL's response stays within the sociomoral frame, although she signals her preferred familial circumference ("<u>our</u> family") which excludes her father and brother. In Example 5, we see CL (and her mother) extending the psychological frame initiated by GC in talking about need to know and "for peace of mind".

It is worth noting here the prevalence of alignment of SM-SM or PY-PY initiation-response sequences (Table 1). Moreover, we see that the SM-SM alignment is more frequent in DAD (making up 86 % of all DAD instances compared to 50 % of all instances in DAT). On the other hand, PY-PY alignment is more frequent in DAT (making up 24 % of instances compared to 10 % in DAD). We will return to these patterns in our Discussion (Section 5).

The initiation-response alignment as suggested above is not always present in the data corpus. We have identified possible misalignment sequences. Consider the following:

Example 6 (SM-PY)/DAT

GC: what was their response when you told them? (…) and your daughter?

CL: not too happy about it I don't think (.) But they know I'm a pretty determined person and if I make up my mind to do something (.) I will do it

Example 7 (PY-SM)/DAT

GC: why move from this sort of sitting on the fence (.) everything's balanced and it's a long way off and things could happen in between anyway (.) to the <u>possibility</u> of living with a certainty (.) with an inevitable?

CL: mm (.) I would say (.) I think I said last time it's more it's more really (.) for my daughter

In Example 6, CL initially aligns herself to the GC-initiated sociomoral frame, but quickly moves to a psychological framing of herself as "a pretty determined person". In Example 7, although GC initiates a psychological frame to talk about coping with an inevitable certainty, CL shifts attention to her daughter as the main reason for her decision to have the test.

It is also possible to identify instances where SM or PY frames are extended beyond the immediate initiation-response sequence. Two particular patterns of three-part sequences can be identified. Firstly, the genetic counsellor might initiate a question in one frame, to which the client responds in a different frame. The genetic counsellor might then follow up with a further attempt by reinforcing the original frame. The second pattern occurs when the client's response falls within the genetic counsellor's chosen frame, but the genetic counsellor then follows up a certain aspect of the client's response by resorting to a different frame.

Table 2. Frequency of three part initiation-response sequences in DAT and DAD

PATTERNS	DAT	DAD	— TOTAL
SM-SM-PY	3	–	3
SM-PY-SM	2	1	3
PY-SM-PY	1	1	2
PY-PY-SM	4	–	4
TOTAL	10	2	12

It is the identification of such complex variations as signalled in Table 2 which led us to examine extended extracts from our sub-corpus.

4.2.   The interplay of psychological and sociomoral frames in extended extracts

In our discussion so far we have maintained a distinction between "psychological" and "sociomoral" frames. In extended sequences, however, we can anticipate a continuous interplay of such frames. In what follows, we consider the scenario of decisions about disclosing the test process and the test results.

The following example is taken from an A1 session. This is the second time that the client (CL) has met the Genetic Counsellor (GC). This extract occurs halfway through the session, after about 15 minutes. CL attends the clinic with her husband (MP).

Example 8

01	GC:	so who who sort of have you sort of told about the sort of fact that you're coming here today or who knows about the test and that if anybody (.) your <u>son</u>
02	CL:	my son and my friend?
03	MP:	yeah
04	GC:	right (.) so that's er (.) um=
05	CL:	=and my husband of course
06	GC:	I think that's er (.) it's er that sounds good it's a sort of a balance I think some people want to tell everybody what's going on and then (.) it can sometimes be a bit difficult afterwards telling the test 'cause other people don't know quite how to respond to something that might happen in the future rather than something now (.) but also one needs support and it sounds like well you've got your husband and your friend so that's er (.) that's the support (.) um (.) so it sounds like the only sort of tricky sort of situation is perhaps your (.) your daughter but she (.) she wouldn't find out until you told her I take it (.) your son wouldn't (.)
07	CL:	no he won't tell her
08	GC:	okay
09	CL:	((to MP)) it slipped out with you yesterday didn't it
10	GC:	((laughs)) (.) I mean that can (.) that can happen
11	CL:	you don't want it (.) oh what for she says (.) oh you're going down the ((hospital)) (.) mum's seeing a professor (.) oh what for? oh er her leg ulcer's playing up he just realised what he'd said (.) I didn't know what to say (.)
12	GC:	yeah no it's er (.) it it can be
13	MP:	you've only got to say something and she's got it
14	CL:	she's got it the next day it's crazy
15	GC:	okay
16	CL:	we we had a medical book (.) we hid it from her
17		((laughter))
18	GC:	alright well that can that may prove a little bit difficult I suppose over the sort of next few weeks and er (.) I suppose you could play it by (.) by ear
19	CL:	mm
20	GC:	see how it how it goes (.) um do you think afterwards she'll feel um (.) she'll feel sort of left out or feel (.) um sort of upset that you [kept] =
21	CL:	[no]
22	GC:	= it from her or she'll sort of understand does she know that she's quite anxious about these things does she sort of have an [insight to that]

23 CL: [I wouldn't] tell her anyway
24 GC: right (.)
25 CL: if (0.5) the thing is if I am carrying it then (.) I dread telling her (.)
          'cause she'll have it the next day
26 GC: mm
27 CL: she'll be down the surgery oh my god I can picture it (1.0)
28 GC: well I mean if that (.) if that did occur [(.)] then of course she could =
29 CL: [mm]
30 GC: = have the go through the whole process and it's actually for sort of
          often for people like your daughter who (.) have a lot of and have
          all sorts of things that this kind of process where we can go over
          things is actually very helpful for them (.) so um (.) if if that did occur
          we would obviously be able to see her and and and talk to her about
          it

The extract starts with GC initiating the sociomoral frame in turn 01 to invite
CL to elaborate on her decision about disclosing the testing process. GC appeals
to what is jointly known, i.e., the son is told, as a trigger for CL to disclose who
else she has already told about her decision to have the test. CL's response aligns
with this sociomoral frame, as she provides, in turns 02 and 05, a list of names
that are already aware of her decision to test: her son, friend and husband. GC
responds to this in a supportive manner, by framing it psychologically, as she
stresses the need to share the decision to have the test with others ("you've
got your husband and your friend so … that's the support"). She considers CL's
position to be "a sort of balance" (turn 06) by offering a contrast to indiscrimi-
nate disclosure by some people without realising others' inability to deal with
"risks of knowing". GC then approaches the more sensitive issue of differential
disclosure, i.e., the choice of CL to tell her young son, but not her older
daughter. Towards the end of turn 06, GC introduces this concern in a hedged
and hesitant manner: "so it sounds like the only sort of tricky sort of situation is
perhaps your your daughter". In turn 07, CL emphatically asserts her belief that
her son is reliable and that he will not disclose anything to the daughter. This is
followed by a brief side sequence where CL enacts, using constructed dialogue,
the occasion of accidental disclosure involving her partner. GC immediately
latches on to this in turns 10 and 12 in order to underscore the possible leakage
of such sensitive information which can have consequences for familial relations. In turns 09–16, CL offers a robust account to justify her decision not to
involve her daughter in the testing process based on character work – the
daughter as someone who is too anxious to be able to deal with the situation.
This is how we notice the interplay of sociomoral and psychological frames:
the daughter's current psychological status is invoked to justify the responsible
parental decision for non-disclosure in order to protect the daughter from a po-

tential nervous breakdown. GC attempts to introduce the delicate issue prospectively, with a combination of face work and character work, in turn 20 ("do you think afterwards she'll feel … left out or feel um sort of upset that you kept it from her"). Once again GC draws attention to the psychological predisposition of the daughter, while articulating the mother's actions in a sociomoral frame, which is resisted by CL in turns 23 and 25. This resistance is recognised finally by GC who then reasserts her professional role and the genetic counselling protocol which is geared towards providing the necessary psychosocial support for the daughter in the event of a positive test result.

Our final example is taken from an A2 session, the third visit for the client to the clinic. The extract occurs as the interaction nears the half-way point, 13 minutes in to a 34 minute appointment. The client (CL) attends the clinic with a female friend. CL has been describing the distress her brother has felt at being diagnosed as having the HD gene and the strain it has put on her mother.

Example 9

01 CL: but I think it's a cruel thing, isn't it? (.) to have- I mean I think it's cruel to my mother as well (..) you know?
02 GC: well I was going to ask you about her actually (.) I was going to ask you about (…) what your thoughts are about telling her
03 CL: oh she's coming as well?
04 GC: she's coming as well (.) [(so she'll be here)]
05 CL: [no problem] ((laughs))
06 GC: *no problem*
07 CL: yeah (1.0)
08 GC: a- are you planning the- the (..) that they will wait and and you'll come in for [your results]
09 CL: [no] I'll just (.) (get in here) ((laughs)) *he he he he*(..) that's what she wants anyway and that's what [((brother))] wants
10 GC: [mm] mm
11 CL: you know (.) I'd just have done it with either a phone call or whatever and (..) but- don't bother me? I mean they want to be here (.) that's [fine] =
12 GC: [mm]
13 CL: = in fact that's quite nice (.) really
14 GC: *mm* (.) 'CAUSE THERE ARE TWO WAYS OF PLAYING that. there is the way by which (..) 'cause as you said in one in- one sense (..) you'd have done it (..) differently if left just to yourself?
15 CL: mm
16 GC: and I think you have to bear in mind that ultimately this is your result

17 CL: yeah (.) [yeah? but er-] you know (.) that's my family innit you know
           (.) =
18 GC: [and]
19 CL: = the ones I love(.) so I'm not going to let that affect- I'm not going to
           let anything like that affect (…) you know it's there (..) it's going to
           happen whatever the result is it's going to be
20 GC: mm
21 CL: told(.) read out or whatever [the way] you do it(.) and um
22 GC: [yeah]
23 CL: it's just something? (..) that's in my body [or isn't]
24 GC: [*mm] right*
25 CL: you know? (..) doesn't change the fact that how much I love my
           family
26 GC: mm
27 CL: and it won't change it that either whatever(.)
28 GC: no (.) no. I mean the options are to have everybody altogether and (.)
           give the result just sort of (..) en masse (.) in a sense we're then
           breaking it to lots of people all at the same time
29 CL: yeah (..)
30 GC: the other option is for you and (..) ((friend)) to come in (.) together and
           for us to tell you the result first if you just had that fraction of space
31 CL: I think I'd rather come in on my own
32 GC: mm

In turn 02, GC initiates a sociomoral frame to facilitate discussion about CL's
decision about disclosure, i.e., how she feels about telling her mother her test
results. The opportunity to explore CL's decision making process is cut short as
CL responds by simply stating that her mother and her brother will accompany
her to the clinic when the test results are made available. In turn 08, GC shifts to
the more practical aspect of the decision about disclosure, by outlining exactly
how the result giving will take place. CL retains the sociomoral frame by signalling her family ties, in turns 9–13, as she accounts for her decision from the
perspective of her mother and brother ("that's what she wants anyway and that's
what ((brother)) wants"). She contrasts this with her own preference to take responsibility to give the test result to her mother and brother at another time ("I'd
just have done it with either a phone call or whatever"), but follows this up
quickly with her decision to adhere to the wishes of her mother and brother and
act as a "dutiful" daughter/sister with the following assessment: "that's fine";
"in fact that's quite nice (.) really". In turn 14, GC picks up on the tension between CL's responsibility to her close family members and to herself ("you'd
have done it (..) differently if left just to yourself"). She then re-frames the decision about disclosure as, ultimately, her own individual responsibility ("you

have to bear in mind that ultimately this is your result"). This psychological orientation to the decision about disclosure is juxtaposed to the sociomoral stance taken up by CL in turn 17 ("yeah? but er-] you know, that's my family innit") and in turns 25–27 ("doesn't change the fact that how much I love my family"). In turns 28 and 30, GC attempts to return to the procedural routine surrounding test results giving, by explaining to CL her options and the possibility of hearing her test result alone first to give her a "fraction of space" away from her familial role-responsibilities. In turn 31, CL responds to GC's options and we notice a shift in her preferred choice of action regarding receipt of test results and thus monitoring subsequent disclosure ("I think I'd rather come in on my own").

5.   Discussion and conclusion

The detailed analyses of the above extracts show that psychosocial concerns are distinctly manifest as psychological and sociomoral frames in longer stretches of interaction. There are shifts back and forth between these two frames, in overlapping and flexible ways, by both genetic counsellors and clients. Individual clients may carry differential role-relational burdens when it comes to decisions about testing (DAT) and disclosure of the testing process and test results (DAD). They will usually know more about family members and relationships, and hence the moral ethos, while the counsellor may be more aware of ethical (and perhaps legal) principles and the clinical facts, and may wish to ensure that these awkward topics have been thought through rather than glossed over.

Our analysis suggests that there are variations across the topic areas of DAT and DAD. In general, sociomoral frames are used frequently in both DAD and DAT initiation-response sequences. This may be explained by the fact that clients often arrive at the clinic determined to go ahead with testing. They may not feel the need to elaborate on emotional issues and therefore tend to adopt a more pragmatic approach, including a sociomoral stance. Bernhardt et al. (2000) point out how clients routinely expect counsellors to provide factual information rather than engage actively with psychosocial concerns. The opportunity to elaborate on their decision about testing in a sociomoral frame remains restricted. However, the issue that is still open for clients and genetic counsellors to engage with is how, when, and to whom to disclose the testing process and the test result. This is supported by our ethnographic interviews with clients following the genetic counselling process, who drew attention to the need to talk about the delicate process of how and when to disclose about the testing process and the test result to family members.

A major focus of our argument is the distinction between the duty to disclose one's decision to test and the obligation to disclose their genetic status following the test to family members who have a *prima facie* reason to know. The client's "right not to disclose" can be based upon either his/her prospective assessment of the recipients' emotional ability to cope (i.e., their vulnerability and therefore the need to shield them, as in Example 8, the extent of the familial proximity and involvement, their anticipation of an excess of blame or anger being directed at the messenger and the misaligned nature of family relations (Arribas-Ayllon, Sarangi and Clarke 2008a, 2008b). Decisions about disclosure have to weigh up these factors against the recipients' right to know, as in Example 9, including clinical need or legal right. We can see from our analysis that the psychological and sociomoral frames overlap and are flexible. The shifting of frames depends on the interactional trajectories, particular clients, the timing of testing and the specific condition. In Example 8, for example, we saw how the sociomoral frame can be elaborated upon and can eventually come to a dead end, in which case the psychological frame might be taken up as a way forward. While the client's psychological interests might seem under some circumstances to differ from their sociomoral obligations to kin, the interweaving of these two domains in real life will usually prevent a narrow sense of autonomy (in effect, egotism) from sabotaging family relationships because such relationships are inseparable from most people's sense of identity (Hallowell et al. 2003).

A basic premise of this study is that the factors involved in making and justifying decisions in genetic counselling, especially DAT and DAD, can be identified and accounted for within the counselling activity. Therefore, the findings based on our discourse analytic approach have implications for practice. Counsellors might want to re-think when and how to frame psychosocial issues in relation to testing and disclosure protocols. We could ask whether moral concerns should be explicitly framed in DAT and DAD scenarios. The interactional management of moral issues may lie beyond the scope of professional codes of practice based upon abstract principles whose potential applications may be difficult to specify.

The debate on how genetic counsellors might best be equipped to deal with the moral issues that arise during genetic counselling is intricately linked to broader questions regarding counsellors' self-understanding. Researchers who advocate a more involved approach to the discussion of moral issues in the clinic usually also stress the need for a more experiential counselling style that puts clients' psychosocial needs first and information transfer second (Wolff and Jung 1995; Weil 2003; Biesecker and Marteau 1999; Biesecker 2003). However, some researchers believe that the current position of genetic counsellors as employed and situated within the medical setting already constitutes such a substantial bias (in terms of an implicit preference to respond to psychological or sociomoral problems with biomedical solutions) that they advocate moving genetic services out of the medical realm into an independent set-up more akin to social or pastoral services (van Berkel and van der Weele 1999). This study does not provide a simple way of resolving this debate but we hope that we have contributed to clarifying the frames of reference underpinning the debate about the non-directive ethos of genetic counselling.

Appendix 1: Transcription Conventions

We have used the following simplified transcription conventions:
GC: genetic counsellor
N: genetic nurse
CL: adult female/male client
F/MP: female/male partner
MO: mother of client

(.): micropause;
(..): pauses up to one second;
(…): pause exceeding one second;
((gap)): an interval of longer length between speaker turns and an approximation of length in seconds;
.hhh: inhalation;
hhh: exhalation;
word: decreased volume;
underlining: increase emphasis as in stress;
question mark [?]: rising intonation;
–: cut-off of prior word or sound;
[text in square brackets]: overlapping speech;
((text in double round brackets)): description or anonymised information;
(text in round brackets): transcriber's guess;
=: a continuous utterance and is used when a speaker's lengthy utterance is broken up arbitrarily for purposes of presentation.

Appendix 2: Diagram of counselling protocol

Preliminary Interview	Appointment 1	Appointment 2	Result Session	Follow-up

Appendix 3

Articulation of the psychological
–   It'd put my mind to rest
–   It's the thought of easing the pain
–   We've got to live with it
–   It's an emotional thing and a lot of these things are even psychological
–   I still got an irrational emotional sort of thing because my cousin died from
    BC at 30
–   [one mammogram before fifty] would give me more confidence and reas-
    surance
–   It almost sets up a little panic button in me
–   it gives me the space to think
–   I'm the only one who knows about me

Articulation of the sociomoral
–   It's not an option, I won't tell her [mother]
–   I'm the black sheep of the family
–   He [father] didn't want to know, he just wasn't interested … they are the
    type who will if they can brush it under the carpet until it's hitting them in
    the face.
–   We're loners … we get on with everyone but we're not the type for mingling
–   [when my mum was diagnosed' I first thought 'Oh … the daughter is the
    first thing I think about 'I hope she hasn't got it oh for goodness sake'
–   I would be able to stop the gene and not sort of carry it on through the family
–   I think I'd rather know before I decide to have children
–   I haven't really wanted to know, it hasn't bothered me … but since we've
    been married and we've been talking about having kids … I'd like to know
–   I can understand about resources and one figure or another, I mean in an
    ideal world every woman would have one [mammogram] every year
–   Also at the time my children were small and I thought "oh fancy having to
    leave them without a mother"

Note

*   This paper is based on the project titled "Communicative Frames in Counselling
    for Predictive Genetic Testing", funded by the Wellcome Trust (Award Reference:
    057179, 2000–2004).

References

Arribas-Ayllon, Michael, Srikant Sarangi and Angus Clarke
    2008a   Managing self-responsibility through other-oriented blame: Family ac-
           counts of genetic testing. *Social Science & Medicine* 66: 1520–1532.
Arribas-Ayllon, Michael, Srikant Sarangi and Angus Clarke
    (2008b)   Micropolitics of responsibility vis-à-vis autonomy: Parental accounts of
           childhood genetic testing and (non)disclosure. *Sociology of Health and Ill-
           ness* 30(2): 255–271.
Beauchamp, Tom L. and James F. Childress
    1994   *Principles of Biomedical Ethics,* 4th edn. New York: Oxford University
    [1979]   Press.
Bergmann, Jörg R.
    1992   Veiled morality: Notes on discretion in psychiatry. In: Paul Drew and John
           Heritage (eds.), *Talk at Work: Interaction in Institutional Settings,*
           137–162. Cambridge: Cambridge University Press.
Bergmann, Jörg R.
    1998   Introduction: Morality in discourse. *Research on Language and Social In-
           teraction* 31: 279–294.
Bernhardt, Barbara, Barbara B. Biesecker and Carrie Mastromarino
    2000   Goals, benefits, and outcomes of genetic counselling: Client and genetic
           counsellor assessment. *American Journal of Medical Genetics* 94: 189–197.
Biesecker, Barbara B.
    2003   Back to the future of genetic counselling: Commentary on Psychosocial
           genetic counselling in the post-nondirective era. *Journal of Genetic Coun-
           selling* 12(3): 213–217.
Biesecker, Barbara B. and Theresa M. Marteau
    1999   The future of genetic counselling: An international perspective. *Nature
           Genetics* 22: 133–137.
Campbell, Alastair V.
    1984   *Moral Dilemmas in Medicine,* 3rd edn. Edinburgh: Churchill Living-
    [1972]   stone.
Chapman, Elizabeth
    (2002a)   Ethical dilemmas in testing for late onset conditions: reactions to testing
           and perceived impact on other family members. *Journal of Genetic Coun-
           selling* 11(5): 350–367.
Chapman, Elizabeth
    2002b   The social and ethical implications of changing medical technologies: the
           views of people living with genetic conditions. *Journal of Health Psychol-
           ogy* 7(2): 195–206.
Chapple, Alison, Carl May and Peter Campion
    1995   Parental guilt: The part played by the clinical geneticist. *Journal of Genetic
           Counselling* 4(3): 179–91.
Clarke Angus
    1997   The process of genetic counselling: beyond non-directiveness. In: Peter S
           Harper and Angus Clarke (eds.), *Genetics, Society and Clinical Practice,*
           179–200. Oxford: Bios Scientific Publishers.

Codori Ann-Marie and Jason Brandt
  1994   Psychological costs and benefits of predictive testing for Huntington's dis-
          ease. *American Journal of Medical Genetics* 54(3): 174–184.
Decruyenaere, Marleen, Gerry Evers-Kiebooms, Andrea Boogaerts, Trees Clooster-
          mans, Jean Jacques Cassiman, Koen Demyttenaere, René Dom, Jean Pierre
          Fryns and Herman Van den Berghe
  1997   Non-participation in predictive testing for Huntington's Disease: Individual
          decision-making, personality and avoidant behaviour in the family. *Euro-
          pean Journal of Human Genetics* 5: 351–363.
Downing, Claudia
  2005   Negotiating responsibility: Case studies of reproductive decision-making
          and prenatal genetic testing in families facing Huntington Disease. *Journal
          of Genetic Counselling* 14(3): 219–234.
Dudok de Wit, Christine A., Aad Tibben, Petra G. Frets, E.J. Meijers-Heijboer,
          P. Devilee, J.G.M. Klijn, J.C. Oosterwijk and M.F. Niermeijer 1997 BRAC1
          in the family: a case description of the psychological implications. *Ameri-
          can Journal A Medical Genetics* 71: 63–71.
Emmett, Dorothy
  1966   *Rules, Roles and Relations*. London: Macmillan.
Engel, Gerald L
  1977   The need for a new medical model: A challenge for biomedicine. *Science*
          196: 129–136.
Evers-Kiebooms, Gerry and Marleen Decruyenaere
  1998   Predictive testing for Huntington's disease: A challenge for persons at risk
          and for professionals. *Patient Education & Counselling* 35:15–36.
Evers-Kiebooms, Gerry, A. Swerts, Jean Jacques Cassiman and Herman van Den Berghe
  (1989) The motivations of at-risk individuals and their partners in deciding for or
          against predictive testing for Huntington's disease. *Clinical Genetics* 35:
          29–40.
Fisher, Sue
  1991   A discourse of the social: Medical talk/power talk/oppositional talk? *Dis-
          course & Society* 2(2): 157–182.
Fisher, Sue
  1995   *Nursing Wounds*. New Brunswick, NJ: Rutgers University Press.
Fletcher, John
  1967   *Moral Responsibility: Situation Ethics at Work*. Philadelphia: The West-
          minster Press.
Forrest, Karen, Sheila A. Simpson, Brenda J. Wilson, Edwin R. van Teijlingen, Lorna
          McKee, Neva Haites and Eric Matthews
  2003   To tell or not to tell: Barriers and facilitators in family communication
          about genetic risk. *Clinical Genetics* 64: 317–326.
Frank, Arthur W.
  1995   *The Wounded Storyteller: Body, Illness and Ethics*. Chicago: The Univer-
          sity of Chicago Press.
Gert, Bernard, Edward M. Berger, George F. Cahill, K. Danner Clouser, Charles M.
          Culver, John B. Moeschler and George H. S. Singe
  1996   *Morality and the New Genetics: A Guide for Students and Health Care Pro-
          viders*. Sudbury, Mass: Jones and Bartlett Publishers.

Goffman, Erving
    1961   *Asylums: Essays on the Social Situation of Mental Patients and Other Inmates*. Garden City, NY: Doubelday.
Goffman, Erving
    1974   *Frame Analysis*. New York: Harper & Row.
Good, Byron J
    1994   *Medicine, Rationality and Experience*. Cambridge: Cambridge University Press.
Green, Josephine and Helen Statham
    1996   Psychosocial aspects of prenatal screening and diagnosis. In: Theresa Marteau and Martin Richards (eds.), *The Troubled Helix: Social and Psychological Implications of the New Human Genetics*, 140–163. Cambridge: Cambridge University Press.
Hallowell, Nina
    1999   Doing the right thing: Genetic risk and responsibility. *Sociology of Health and Illness* 21: 597–621.
Hallowell, Nina, Audrey Arden-Jones, Ros Eeles, Claire Foster, Anneke Lucassen, Clare Moynihan, and Maggie Watson
    2006   Guilt, blame and responsibility: Men's understanding of their role in the transmission of BRCA1/2 mutations within their family. *Sociology of Health and Illness* 28(7): 969–988.
Hallowell, Nina, Claire Foster, Ros Eeles, Audrey Ardern-Jones, Victoria Murday and Maggie Watson
    2003   Balancing autonomy and responsibility: The ethics of generating and disclosing genetic information. *Journal of Medical Ethics* 29: 74–83.
Hare, Richard
    1964   *The Language of Morals*. London: Oxford University Press.
Huggins, Marlene, Maurice Bloch, Sandi Wiggins, Shelin Adam, Oksana Suchowersky, Michael Trew, Marylou Klimek, Cheryl R. Greenberg, Michael Eleff, Louise P. Thompson, Julie Knight, Patrick MacLeod, Kathleen Girard, Jane Theilmann, Amy Hedrick and Michael P. Hayden
    1992   Predictive testing for Huntington disease in Canada: Adverse effects and unexpected results in those receiving a decreased risk. *American Journal of Medical Genetics* 42(4): 508–515.
Huibers, Alex K. and Adriaan van 't Spijker
    1998   The autonomy paradox: predictive genetic testing and autonomy: Three essential problems. *Patient Education & Counselling* 35: 53–62.
Kenen, Regina, Ann C. M. Smith, Carolee Watkins and Carol Zuber-Pittore
    2000   To use or not to use: the prenatal genetic technology/worry conundrum. *Journal of Genetic Counselling* 9(3): 203–217.
Kleinman, Arthur
    1988   *The Illness Narratives: Suffering, Healing and the Human Condition*. New York: Basic Books.
Marteau, Theresa and Elizabeth Dormandy
    2001   Facilitating informed choice in prenatal testing: How well are we doing? *American Journal of Medical Genetics* 106: 185–190.

Måseide, Per
  2003   Medical talk and moral order: Social interaction and collaborative clinical work. *Text* 23(3): 369–403.
Måseide, Per
  2006   The deep play of medicine: Discursive and collaborative processing of evidence in medical problem solving. *Communication & Medicine* 4(1): 43–54.
Pilnick, Alison
  2002a   What "most people" do. Exploring the ethical implications of genetic counselling. *New Genetics & Society* 21: 339–350.
Pilnick, Alison
  2002b   "There are no rights and wrongs in these situations": Identifying interactional difficulties in genetic counselling. *Sociology of Health and Illness* 24(1): 66–88.
Richards, F
  2004   Couples' experiences of predictive testing and living with the risk or reality of Huntington's Disease: A qualitative study. *American Journal of Medical Genetics* 126A: 170–182.
Sarangi, Srikant
  2000   Activity types, discourse types and interactional hybridity: the case of genetic counselling. In: Srikant Sarangi and Malcolm Coulthard (eds.), *Discourse and Social Life*, 1–27. London: Pearson.
Sarangi, Srikant
  2002   The language of likelihood in genetic counselling discourse. *Journal for Language and Social Psychology* 21(1): 7–31.
Sarangi, Srikant
  2005   Activity analysis in professional discourse settings: the framing of risk and responsibility in genetic counselling. *Hermès* 41: 110–120.
Sarangi, Srikant
  2010   Professional values in interaction: Non-directiveness, client-centredness and other-orientation in genetic counselling. In: Stephen Pattison, Ben Hannigan, Roisin Pill and Auw Thomas (eds.), *Emerging Values in Healthcare*. London: Jessica Kingsley: 163–185.
Sarangi, Srikant
  forth-   Owning responsible actions/selves: Parental accounts in the context of
  coming   childhood genetic testing. In: Jan-Ola Östman and Anna Solin (eds.), *Responsibility in Discourse and the Discourse of Responsibility.*
Sarangi, Srikant and Angus Clarke
  2002a   Constructing an account by contrast in counselling for childhood genetic testing. *Social Science & Medicine* 54: 295–308.
Sarangi, Srikant and Angus Clarke
  2002b   Zones of expertise and the management of uncertainty in genetics risk communication. *Research on Language and Social Interaction* 35(2): 139–171.
Sarangi, Srikant, Kristina Bennert, Lucy Howell and Angus Clarke
  2003   Relatively speaking: Relativisation of genetic risk in counselling for predictive testing. *Health, Risk and Society* 5(2): 155–169.

Sarangi, Srikant, Kristina Bennert, Lucy Howell, Angus Clarke, Peter Harper and
        Jonathan Gray
    2004   Initiation of reflective frames in counselling for Huntington's Disease pre-
            dictive testing. *Journal of Genetic Counselling* 13(2): 135–155.
Sarangi, Srikant, Kristina Bennert, Lucy Howell, Angus Clarke, Peter Harper and
        Jonathan Gray
    2005   (Mis)alignments in clients' responses to reflective frames in counselling for
            Huntington's Disease predictive testing. *Journal of Genetic Counselling*
            14(1): 29–42.
Silverman, David
    1987   *Communication and Medical Practice: Social Relations in the Clinic.* Lon-
            don: Sage.
Silverman, David
    1994   Describing sexual activities in HIV counselling: the cooperative manage-
            ment of the moral order. *Text* 14(3): 427–453.
Stone, Howard W. and Rebekah Miles
    1999   Moral direction in genetic counselling: Prenatal testing and Huntington's
            Disease. *Families, Systems and Health* 17(1): 75–87.
van Berkel, Dymphie and Cor van der Weele
    1999   Norms and prenorms on prenatal diagnosis: New ways to deal with moral-
            ity in counselling. *Patient Education & Counselling* 37: 153–163.
Weil, Jon
    2000   *Psychosocial Genetic Counselling.* Oxford: Oxford University Press.
Weil, Jon
    2003   Psychosocial genetic counselling in the post-non-directive era: a point of
            view. *Journal of Genetic Counselling* 12(3): 199–211.
White, Susan
    2002   Accomplishing the case in paediatrics and child health: medicine and
            morality in interprofessional talk. *Sociology of Health and Illness* 24(4):
            409–435.
Williams, Clare, Priscilla Alderson and Bobbie Farsides
    2002   Dilemmas encountered by health practitioners offering nuchal translucency
            screening: A qualitative case study. *Prenatal Diagnosis* 22: 216–220.
Wolff, Gerhard and Christine Jung
    1995   Nondirectiveness and genetic counselling. *Journal of Genetic Counselling*
            4(1): 3–25.
Wüstner, Kerstin
    2003   Ethics and practice: two worlds? The example of genetic counselling. *New
            Genetics & Society* 22(1): 60–87.

10. Theoretical vocabularies and moral negotiation in child welfare: The saga of Evie and Seb*

Susan White and David Wastell

Abstract

This chapter examines the social processes taking place as a group of child welfare professionals attempt to make sense of complex circumstances and ambivalent relationships affecting the members of a family, which has been referred to the Child and Adolescent Mental Health Service (CAMHS) of a UK health service. The chapter illustrates the interactional and rhetorical processes involved in professional sense-making in morally contentious domains. Versions of psychological theory and accounts of observed behaviours work to legitimate moral judgements and render ambiguous behaviours amenable to available child welfare "technologies". It is argued that moral judgements are essential to professional work and that patients/clients are not passive recipients of these. Rather, they are rational, motivated actors who come to services with their own moral tales to tell. Professional work in morally contestable realms is accomplished through elaborate moral-discursive dances which take place within institutional contexts which are laden with taken-for-granted short-cuts. The chapter concludes that the close examination of institutional talk is vitally important for humane professional practice.

1. Introduction

> Evelyn has presented a picture of increasing pressure and tension to such an extent that she feels unable to cope with the children's behaviour and loses control … She feels she often does not want Seb around and regularly tells him so. She has admitted to hitting the children, pulling their heads back by their hair and shouting in their faces. Evelyn has stated she is frightened she may completely lose control and injure one of them.

The extract above is taken from social work records relating to a family, "the Hatters", who have been referred to the Child and Adolescent Mental Health Service (CAMHS) of a UK health district as a result of concerns about Seb's behavioural problems, which include bed-wetting, aggressive outbursts and high risk activities such as fire setting and running away. The Hatters, Evie (mother), Seb (6) and Abel (7), are causing the professional network from a range of statutory agencies considerable concern. In the extracts we analyse, we follow the action leading up to a child protection conference, and a subsequent review several months later. A child protection conference is a standard UK multi-agency forum in which recommendations are made about future professional activity in cases involving children at risk

We use the deliberations about the Hatters to illustrate some conceptualizations about the interactional and rhetorical processes involved in professional sense-making in morally contentious domains. We shall see how versions of psychological theory and accounts of observed behaviours, work to legitimate moral judgements and render ambiguous behaviours amenable to available technologies, such as therapy services or child protection systems. We also examine the mother's spirited narration of a moral self in a situation where, in order to keep the services she wants *and* keep other interventions at bay, she must, at one and same time, confess responsibility *and* exonerate herself for various aspects of her parenting. She must construct herself as caring *about* "not caring adequately" for her children. We argue that moral judgements are essential to professional work, but they are highly consequential, conferring favour or misfortune in what are often contested and ambiguous situations, where attributions of error, or indeed success, may be assigned only retrospectively (cf. Horlick-Jones 2003).

2.   Making the case in child welfare

Professionals are involved in acts of meaning-making, which are often collaborative, bound by available linguistic repertoires of interpretation, and take place in particular social and organizational contexts. To get their job done, professionals must package their opinions for consumption by others. They must be able to justify and "perform" their judgements (*inter alia,* Atkinson 1995; Hall 1997; Sarangi and Candlin 2003; White and Stancombe 2003), either for the patient or client, or for colleagues, or in some other arena of accountability or judgement-making, like the courts. They must also "work-up" a written synopsis of their thinking for case files, reports and other records. Although the processes of professional judgement involve recasting client histories in a form consistent with specialist knowledge and theoretical edifices, they are often more than technical descriptions. They embody a "folk logic", legitimating and normalising culturally shared, moral attributions of blameworthiness and creditworthiness.

> [The] cultural system provides members with a logic of action … for what is right, moral, or at least acceptable. What counts as "right", "smart", or at least "passable" conduct depends on the group's (culture's) system of beliefs, values and ideologies – a folk logic. … [F]olk logic is not simply a set of implicit rules and shared beliefs, but includes the *practice of using* these rules and beliefs through blames and accounts. (Buttny 1993: 49)

That is, professionals working in the domain of human relationships draw also on vernacular moral logics, which intersect with the theoretical vocabularies in complex ways. Thus, it is very important that the processes of professional sense-making in both frontstage and backstage are opened up for examination. Studies of institutional sense-making in child welfare have shown that practitioners frequently invoke theory or institutional categories to authorize *ex post-facto* judgements made on other grounds (*inter alia,* Firkins and Candlin 2006; Taylor and White 2006). Moreover, patients/clients themselves are not passive; they are rational, motivated actors who come to services with their own moral tales to tell. Horlick-Jones (2003: 224) talks of the "complex discursive 'dance' of categorization" involving professionals and clients, a quadrille we shall see for ourselves in the case study.

In our analysis, we will give particular attention to the role of emotions. Perspectives on the role of emotion in reasoning carry a number of appellations, for example, the "sentimental rules hypothesis" (Nichols 2004) or "social intuitionism" (Haidt 2001). The latter approach is particularly apposite for child welfare work. Based on evidence from experimental psychology, Haidt demonstrates that *reasoning* follows moral judgement not the other way round. Nussbaum (2001) also argues that verbal reasoning is often the postscript to judgements made on other grounds, and cognitive neuroscience has also shown that moral judgements rely substantially on affect, with "reasoning" added *ex post facto* (e.g. Damasio 1994).

Although emotions are integral to decision-making, they are conventionally portrayed as murky, fallible contaminants to reason. Moral judgements have to be made and managed in contexts where professional neutrality must be displayed (Stancombe and White 2005). This leads to two potential problems: (i) affective/moral judgements are justified using other warrants and therefore are concealed and not debated; (ii) positive emotional responses, such as compassion, can be bracketed out by technological vocabularies, procedure, habit, rule and routine (White forthcoming). Moreover, rather than destabilise judgements, group discussion tends to solidify them, since affective judgements generate group (or indeed institutional) norms.

> Because moral positions always have an affective component to them, it is hypothesised that reasoned persuasion works ... by triggering new, affectively valenced intuitions in the listener ... Because people are highly attuned to the emergence of group norms ... the mere fact that friends, allies and acquaintances have made a moral judgement exerts a direct influence on others, even if no reasoned persuasion is used.
> (Haidt 2001: 819)

It is for this reason that the close examination of institutional discourses and practices is so important. The elaborate moral-discursive dances take place within heavily camouflaged institutional contexts impregnated with taken-for-granted short-cuts. But before illustrating our arguments empirically, we must summarise the literature on the moral nature of "case tellings" in child welfare.

3.   The good, the bad and the could do better: Moral judgements in child welfare

Ethnographic work has shown that child welfare takes place in a moral context where children are generally exonerated from blame and parents constructed as potentially culpable for problems exhibited by the child (for a similar account in the context of childhood genetic testing, see Arribas-Ayllon, Sarangi and Clarke [2008a, 2008b]). This may be summarized in the tacit rule: "identify those features of the parent that have produced the troubled child" (White and Stancombe 2003: 103). In their study of accident and emergency departments, Dingwall and Murray (1983) noted that children routinely appear to breach conventional criteria of the category "good patient" (Jeffrey 1979) and yet are still assigned to that category. For example, they frequently injure themselves whilst undertaking some form of irresponsible act, such as leaping from a tree. They often "overreact" to their injuries by crying, screaming and being uncooperative. Yet, children do not seem to receive moral censure. Dingwall and Murray distinguish between *theoretic agents* (deemed responsible for their own behaviour) and *pre-theoretic agents*, who legitimately lack this capacity. Children are classified as pre-theoretic and are hence exempt from classification as "bad patients". The concept of theoreticity (McHugh 1970) can also apply to adults. Thus, moral judgements may be affected by the extent to which actors produce adequate moral accounts which may mitigate, explain or excuse their actions. So, we must pay attention to how moral adequacy is enacted and how it is judged in clinical work.

This is particularly apposite when applied to judgements about parenting (usually mothering). For example, the literature on parent-professional interaction in medical encounters provides compelling evidence of parents' awareness that they may be blamed by clinicians in some way. Parents, and particularly mothers, must present their actions in the context of canonical versions of responsible parenthood (Strong 1979; Heritage and Lindstrom 1998; White 2002). For instance, in his work in a paediatric diabetic clinic, Silverman (1987) notes that moral evaluations of parenting depended on the ability of parents to show that they managed and took responsibility for the child's medical condition. Decisions became more complex with older children, for whom parents also had to demonstrate that they were encouraging responsible degrees of autonomous behaviour.

Stancombe's work on family therapy comes to a similar conclusion (White and Stancombe 2003). Analysing accounts which therapists treat as persuasive, he shows that the successful production of a moral account by a parent involves the use of one of the following two schemata: (i) Parents may present themselves as a "good" parent who has done their very best to ensure the welfare of their child and are continuing to do so by seeking expert help for their child; or (ii) they may admit to blame, seek absolution and accept guidance, in the form of expert help to ensure that they become "better" parents. Similarly Hall, Slembrouck and Sarangi (2006) demonstrate how "character work" in child protection case conferences accomplishes categorisation and blame attribution for professionals. Storytelling and evaluative claims about a mother's appropriateness and help-seeking are seen to shift a case formulation from *poor parenting* to *mother's poor self esteem*, hence making the mother both responsible and "caring, but not coping" (Slembrouck and Hall 2003). We shall see a similar process in the production of both the professionals' and the mother's own version of herself in our saga below. We shall argue that these moral accounts trigger affective judgements on the part of professionals, which are frequently authorised by phrases derived from popularized versions of psychological theory. The concealed "emotional dog" (Haidt 2001) is thus manifested by his rational tale (*sic*).

4.   The saga of Evie and Seb: A ballet in two acts

The data for the case study are part of a corpus produced from an ethnographic study of an integrated child health service situated in a district general hospital in "Erewhon", a fictitious metropolitan borough in the North of England. The service comprised paediatric inpatient and outpatient services, a child and adolescent mental health unit (CAMHS), together with child development (CDS) and social work services. A single case study design was used, with the first author as sole researcher. The fieldwork took place between July 1999 and October 2000. In the analysis we have made use of a number of concepts derived from conversation analysis, such as Sacks' work on membership categorisation analysis (e.g. 1972, 1992) and Pomerantz's work on blamings (1978, 1986). However, these have been used as part of an approach more associated with applied linguistics and professional discourse studies, focusing on how "factual" accounts are assembled successfully or unsuccessfully to persuade (Smith 1978).

Table 1 shows the key actors in the drama, most of whom play "speaking parts" in the ensuing account. The material for the first Act of our drama is drawn entirely from the case notes of the Erewhon CAMHS. The Second Act is based on the transcribed dialogue of a subsequent meeting.

Table 1. Dramatis Personae

Dramatis Personae	
John Solomon (JS)	Consultant Child Psychologist, Erewhon Child and Adolescent Mental Health Services (CAMHS)
Jeremy Bentham (JB)	Team Manager Erewhon Social Services and Chair of the Child Protection Conference
Evelyn "Evie" Hatter	Mother (25 years)
Damian Young	Estranged father of Seb
Seb Hatter	Primary subject of investigation (6 years old boy)
Abel Hatter	Seb's half brother (7 years old)
"Jethro"	Evie's new boyfriend
Florence Black (FB)	Nurse Specialist, Erewhon CAMHS
Angela White (AW)	Staff Nurse, Erewhon CAMHS
Ruth Benedict (RB)	Social Worker (Case notes)
Jenny Taylor (JT)	Social Worker (Meeting)
Regan West (RW)	NSPCC Worker

4.1.   Act One: Making the case

The period covered by Act One runs from the initial referral to CAMHS of the primary subject (Seb Hatter) on the 19th May (1999) through to the Child Protection conference held six months later in early November. The case notes were multi-disciplinary, with all professionals able to document pertinent observations. The notes were hand-written, jotted during the session and immediately afterwards. They display aspects of the routine practical reasoning of practitioners, and thus reveal a great deal about the kinds of issues that discrete professional groups consider relevant. Case notes have long been examined in ethnomethodologically inspired ethnographic work, for what they reveal about the tacit relevances and explanatory schemata in use in organizations and professions (e.g. Garfinkel 1967; Hak 1992; White 2003).

The opening observations of John Solomon (JS, Consultant Child Psychologist) included the following comments on Seb's "challenging" behaviour:

> Problem: Lighting fires, no respect for authority, no access to matches now, no recent events but still fascination ... Very aggressive to others – not always when thwarted, lashes out ... always been very clingy, bed wetting. Mother has thought inheritance difficulties. Seb is stubborn / temper like mother. Other explanations: moves, indulgent relationship with father. Mother finds it hard to be consistent. Mother uses smacking, threat of smacking, realises no long term benefit use ...

We can see John has attended to the immediate risk of fire lighting. The rest of the account contains various paraphrases of mother's reported speech, including candidate explanations for Seb's behaviour. Subsequently, the first meeting with the family (7 June 1999) was held at the CAMHS offices, Erewhon District Hospital. It was manifestly a highly fraught affair, vividly reflected in JS's entry in the notes:

> Horrendous meeting. Had to abandon complete family history. Seb and Abel at war. Seb had an almighty tantrum. Mum had to hold to prevent physical harm to her. Lasted for three quarters of an hour, even with support, Seb refused to calm down.

The entry with its extreme case formulations (Pomerantz 1986) established this as a serious case and following this meeting; a number of actions were set in train. It was agreed that specialist assessments would be undertaken by both Erewhon social services and the National Society for the Prevention of Cruelty to Children (NSPCC). These would afford a "comprehensive assessment of risk … to provide a holistic view of the family". It was also resolved to engage the CAMHS Day Unit based in Erewhon District Hospital to provide a mix of family support, individual counselling and further assessment.

4.1.1.   Family sessions at the day case unit

Four sessions were arranged, with two CAMHS nurses involved in all of these sessions (AW and FB). The first meeting took place on the 8th September. Evie and Seb attended, and the session seemed to go well. AW observed:

> Seb came across as a pleasant little boy who was very helpful when it came to making a cup of tea and getting biscuits ready … All his play was age appropriate and during this time he was quite chatty answering any questions posed. No problems when Mum left the room, continued playing happily.

We see two emergent characterisations of Seb, the one who refused to calm down from his "almighty tantrum" and the "pleasant little boy" who displays "age appropriate behaviour". The nature of AW's notes also clearly shows the orientation of these sessions to developmental psychological assessment, albeit implicit. The oblique reference to the spontaneous "Strange Situation" scenario (the mother leaving the room) is especially noteworthy. A child's ability to cope with a parent leaving is taken by child welfare professionals to be diagnostic of the presence or absence of a range of "attachment disorders" (Howe et al. 1999). This is a leitmotif to which we will return. On this occasion, no alarm is raised for AW.

FB's notes below clearly bring out Evie's ambivalent relationship with Seb, and some planned actions to address this. Her concluding thoughts also underscore the importance of implicit behavioural observations in the diagnostic process and are again exonerative of Seb. Here we also see the first stages of a candidate formulation of the case as one involving "parental rejection" and "attachment problems".

> A plan was agreed including for Evie and Seb to make a point of spending time together to play and interact more positively. Evie feels that even when Seb's behaviour is acceptable, she cannot overcome her negative feelings to enjoy time with him ... Following this session, Seb and his mother challenged staff to a game of giant Connect. Seb was very appropriate and warm towards his mother, able to take turns and remedy his action when he mistakenly took mum's go. Also coped well with losing.

The second family session began well, with significant progress seemingly underway. However, all was not what it first seemed, as FB's notes reveal:

> Initially on arrival at the unit, both seemed relaxed, positive and both said they had a good week. However as soon as Seb left the room to make a drink with AW, Evie became tearful and informed me that things were awful ... she said there had been no change in Seb's behaviour, nor in her view of him and at present she doesn't want to be around him at all.

Evie's strong ambivalence towards Seb and her overly-controlling attitude were conspicuous features of the following session, on the 29th September. Evie and the boys had been away on a short holiday during the intervening period. Whereas Seb appeared very enthusiastic, talking animatedly about "the weather, the water slides and the coach", FB's notes use Evie's reported speech to recount an altogether more stress-laden version, describing the holiday as "horrendous and no pleasure". Noteworthy in this session was Evie's apparent adoption of proto-professional terminology with reference to herself. At one point, Seb flicked paint at her (during a painting activity). FB offered praise for having ignored this: FB records Evie's response in the notes as follows:

> Evie said "it depended what 'child' I'm in". She went on to explain that in group therapy at NSPCC she has learnt that she has a spoilt stroppy child side and a withdrawn sad child side. She is very aware that which phase she is in determines how she responds to the children, particularly Seb and this can vary from minute to minute.

Evie then went on to express her fears for the future, offering further insights into her ambivalent feelings for Seb:

> [She] became tearful and said her worst fear is that he will go into care. However can foresee times when she would wish for both boys, but particularly Seb, to live somewhere else. Started to cry and said the trouble is I wanted Abel and I had Seb for Gary[former partner]. Talked about feeling resentful towards Seb because his existence forced her to stay with Gary and by this time he was being very abusive

It was decided that the final family session should also include Abel. The same themes of helpless ambivalence emerge in the notes but now with even greater force, reinforced by "psychodynamic" insights regarding Evie's childhood, invoked for the first time. The following extract is from FB's notes.

Evie very dependent and low. States that she has reached a point of awareness in her therapy. Now believes that when she is with Seb and Abel, she feels and behaves like a child ... Relayed an incident where she had bought 6 cakes. The boys had theirs, and she decided to leave her cakes. However the cakes disappeared and the boys blamed each other. Evie reports instantly becoming furious ... she grabbed both boys by the hair and banged their heads together until they told the truth. Feels guilty for hurting them, but cannot fully accept responsibility for this ... Reports feeling that her own life events have damaged her irreparably. Talked about life as a child, never able to show any feelings or naughty behaviour because Mum would retire to bed with a migraine. Even when recalled abuse by step-grandfather struggled to tell mother in case she got upset and became unwell.

Whilst FB talked to Evie, AW spent time with both boys – at one point instigating a game of snakes and ladders. Seb's behaviour was apparently exemplary compared to his brother. We thus see the progressive formulation of Evie as "needy and dependent", inconsistent and sometimes ineffectual in her parenting, and of Seb's behavioural problems the result of confusing and contradictory parenting. All are complicit in the production of this diagnostic schema, including Evie herself. Various forms of mitigation for Evie complete the moral narrative. She *cares* that she can't care and invokes a repertoire of proto-professional language to explain her behaviours.

4.1.2.   The child protection conference

These and a series of other concurrent events involving the children being "out of control" (including a fire-setting incident in which Abel was injured) resulted in a child protection case conference being arranged for early November. In the following sections, we present extracts from several key reports which formed important inputs to the Conference. These are followed by a synopsis of the Conference itself.

Erewhon Social Services' investigation was led by RB and drew in part on evidence from the family sessions; the following quote summarises her professional opinion:

Evelyn [Evie] has presented a picture of increasing pressure and tension to such an extent that she feels unable to cope with the children's behaviour and loses control ... She feels she often does not want Seb around and regularly tells him so. She has admitted to hitting the children, pulling their heads back by their hair and shouting in their faces. Evelyn has stated she is frightened she may completely lose control and injure one of them. The conclusion of the assessment is ... that Evelyn is able to understand parent management strategies with but has difficulty putting them into practice in a consistent way ... However concerns now appear to have increased and as a result we would question Evelyn's attachments specifically to Seb and her motivation and ability to focus on this to improve the children's situation.

Though measured, RB's report is explicitly normative in tone, describing a series of "unhappy incidents" (Pomerantz 1978) and casting Evie as the prime cause of Seb's problems. Evie has entered a deviant sub-category "abusive mother", and the report recommends the need for a child protection plan "to reduce the harm and future risk for both Abel and Seb". The conclusions explicitly re-invoke attachment theory recommending that "Evelyn undertake work on her attachment. This work would need to be very structured and focussed on the children".

The second report was submitted by the NSPCC. Following some general comments on Evie's parenting difficulties and the escalating history of events, the report then related one short paragraph summarising "the present situation". Its concluding comments are conspicuous for their moral tone and theoretical vocabulary. They even cast doubts on Evie's worthiness as a recipient of support.

> Evie has found the process of risk assessment challenging, but is beginning to understand and accept the seriousness of their situation and her responsibility to make changes in her relationships with the children and others. It is recognised by the group therapists that although Evie has received considerable therapeutic input it is only now that she may be ready to receive this. Primary to Evie's difficulty in accepting intervention there are problems with attachment which we believe stem back from insecure attachments in childhood.
>
> One possibility of any continuing therapeutic work with Evie and her relationship with her children is that she or others may at some stage conclude that she is unable to care for them appropriately. We would hope to avoid this and will be working with her to improve the situation for the children and herself as soon as possible.

The final report for the Case Conference to be considered here is that of JS. Despite the gestured acknowledgement of uncertainty, JS's accountabilities in the high risk, high blame child protection arena lead him to the clear conclusion, expressed as a direct paraphrase from the Children Act 1989 [shown in italic]

> I would argue that the precise formulation of the case remains equivocal. However the fact remains that both boys, Seb in particular, are presenting with signs of significant emotional and behavioural disturbance of which their mother is finding it increasingly difficult to cope. In my view unless there is a fairly significant change in the social and psychological environment for both boys, but particularly Seb, I envisage they are both *likely to suffer significant and/or psychological harm* which could have serious implications for their long term adjustment.

The Child Protection Conference itself was held on 9th November. In the minutes of the meeting the version of Evie as "caring about not coping" was replayed. As would be expected, there was a clear consensus that the children were at serious risk, and that they would need to be entered on the Child Protection register. However, the exact nature of their registration provoked some animated discussion. The lengthy "categorisation debate" (using criteria and terms derived from the 1989 Children Act) borders on the pedantic if not the comic.

JB says he feels that in the case of Seb, registration should be for *emotional abuse actual* and for Abel *emotional abuse likely* because Abel is not currently suffering *significant harm* ... RB [social worker] said she agreed with what had been said but the children should be registered with *physical abuse* actual in view of the information that Miss Hatters herself had given. She would suggest registration *physical abuse actual*, registration for *emotional abuse paramount*. JS said he agreed there was a need for registration but he felt that the category of *physical/emotional abuse* actual should apply to both boys because they have both suffered *significant harm* ... Detective Constable H said that she agreed with everything that had been said and echoed the same urgency with regard to Seb.

4.2.   Act Two: Moral tussles: Competing versions of Evie

In Act Two, the action has moved on four months. We drop in on a meeting at the Day Unit, Erewhon CAMHS (April 2000) convened to prepare for a Child Protection review conference to be held the following month. The meeting was tape-recorded and transcribed. Present were John Solomon (Chair), Evie, Jenny Taylor (ESS), Regan West (NSPCC) and Florence Black (Nurse Specialist) (see Table 1).

JS began by inviting Evie to give her view on how things had gone, and we see her working up an "improving" version of events referring to a recent crisis and apparent epiphany for Abel. Notably, John also invites Evie to present herself as a grateful and appropriate candidate for professional help – a position she had occupied somewhat precariously before the conference, as we saw.

Evie: Abel. and Seb are getting on a lot, lot better lately as well, they're not looking to me to solve their arguments as much, you know they're not shouting at me every two minutes .... What I think it is, is a fortnight ago we were at my mum's and a couple of days beforehand Abel had kept running off ... then a couple of days later Seb did the same, only he didn't come back and I went looking for him ... In the end I had to get the police and Abel was with us and we were all really worried about him and Abel said I hope we find him because I really love him ... I think maybe it gave Abel a bit of a shock

JS: So this last 2 weeks then there was an improvement down to this sort of shock ... Certainly the main concern at the last meeting was about how the boys were getting on wasn't it? And you feeling that no matter what you tried you couldn't sort of help them to get on better and there were some quite dangerous things happening weren't there? So where do you think your new found patience has come from?

EVIE: These new tablets for one thing ... but I'm happier as well, you know, I feel ... I'm really happy in my relationship ... I'm really happy with Jethro, he treats me nice, he makes me happy, we don't argue ...

JS: Anything that I have missed out that you think is important that you think has changed since we last met?

EVIE: Yes, having like Liz and Cathy [family support workers] come in – because when I moved into the house there's no carpet, no wallpaper or anything … it needed them to say, you know, the boys need their rooms doing, you need to change Seb's bed in the morning not leave it till you're coming home.

Here Evie proffers a reformed version of herself as a moral parent whose changing circumstances are allowing her to begin to address problems, but she signals that she is still in need of support. However, the reformed version of Evie meets a sceptical challenge from Regan, the NSPCC worker, who uses the euphemism "interesting" to signal her doubts. She reports that Evie has failed to complete her diary, to which Evie responds rather lamely:

RW: Going on to the first session, things seemed OK but after that it kind of went downhill … So it's *interesting* to hear you say that things are so much better … It's *interesting* that you say that it's been positive because I think we felt it might not have been very positive because there have been things that haven't happened the way we've wanted them to, you know when the two friends came to play so we just had to do a very brief session then, then we gave you some diaries and you didn't feel able …

EVIE: I've done a couple but … I don't know because when I write it down it just seems insignificant but I think it's because it's seeing it, but the actual feelings that are going on while it's happening you can't get them down on paper …

Evie is rescued at this point by JS, who invites her to reiterate her claim that things have *really* changed.

JS: It was in the last couple of weeks, but you feel that there is a real change in your approach again?

EVIE: Yes, because I'm not getting all worked up and thinking he's got to walk up the side of me to school, I'm just thinking well, he's going to run off whether I shout him or not, he's going to do it so I might as well let him do it as long as he's doing it safely which he does.

JS's intervention operates as a candidate response initiation, that is, it suggests to Evie what an appropriate answer may be and successfully produces a moral account by Evie of her reformed parenting practices. Next the social worker (JT) enters the fray also displaying scepticism about Evie's version of events, invoking the original state of the house to buttress her case. Notably, she uses the more formal address "Evelyn". JT refers explicitly to the enduring risk and harm to the boys from "fire setting" and from Evie's propensity to "lose it". She uses another euphemism "surprise" at Evie's claim that things have improved, an example of a persuasive device addressing an issue of delicacy (cf. Suoninen and Jokinen 2005; Silverman 1997)

JT: ... Obviously I appreciate that Evelyn had not long moved into the house and we don't expect ideal homes but I think in terms of the kids' bedrooms particularly it really struck a chord ... Evelyn took all that on board anyway and she's made a start with that ... actually trying to move things on with the basic clearing out and changing things in the house just for it to be more warm for the kids, more a home for them ... The other things we were concerned with – fire-setting, both of them have been doing that which is why we talked about matches in the house ... I was quite *surprised* really at you saying that things were so positive in the last two weeks, because we've been going out to visit you and you've been saying, you're still losing it with them and still getting angry, shouting and hitting them, so obviously this is a very new thing isn't it?

Evie is again rescued by John Solomon referring to the recent improvements, which this time receives a qualified endorsement from RW.

RW: And I suppose from my point of view ... I do feel the last few weeks Evie is working hard. I think she's engaged emotionally now, whereas I think before a lot of people were attempting to sort of be around, but we weren't getting anywhere really, but I feel like we're getting some-where now and so it's ...

As the meeting reaches its denouement, it turns to practical matters and the possible outcome of the forthcoming review conference. Evie shows she is ex-plicitly aware of the precariousness of her situation.

EVIE: Is the meeting in May the one ... the child protection one? I'm worried about that, that if there's a big improvement that they're going to cut off the support, you know if they think the children don't need to be on the register anymore, I'm going to lose all the support and I'm really concerned about that because I don't want that to happen and I know that it can do.

In this extract Evie accomplishes a version of herself in which she is "better", whilst also heading off the possible reading that she is "really better", which may jeopardise the support she has carefully gathered about her. She produces an artful moral account which literally allows her to "play" the system.

As we reflect back on Act Two, what stands out is Evie's performance of a moral self as an "ideal service recipient", a delicate performance which requires careful balancing in a moral mine-field. It is noteworthy that despite the initial competing versions of Seb, the notion that he may be intrinsically difficult to parent rapidly withers. In contrast not only must Evie confess *responsibility,* she must also *exonerate and excuse* herself. She must show *positive change*, *yet retain eligibility for services*. She must construct herself as *caring* about *not caring adequately* for her children and she must at all costs avoid blaming the child. She is by no means a passive stooge, she contributes in full part to the decision-making process and its shifting categorisations.

5.   Coda: Emotion and rhetoric in child welfare

In this chapter, we have been moved to ask, how do the professionals apparently "know their own minds" in what is self-evidently highly contested terrain? Throughout the case, we have seen a strong tendency for professionals to move from the idiographic and nuanced discourse to an impoverished discourse of crude categorisations, furnished either by favoured psychological theories or administrative fiat. Rather than ascend to the particular, to borrow Marx's phrase, collective professional categories are seen to create simplistic epistemic objects out of the complexity of lives in the living. Borrowing the vivid phraseology of Feyerabend (1999), abundance is conquered; singular instances are annihilated by tyrannical universals, namely the general categories formed by attachment theory and the top-down dispensations of welfare legislation on the one hand and commonsense moral reasoning on the other.

Professional judgements are highly consequential, but they seem to be made with disquieting ease. We seem to see equivocation only in the written words and utterances of John Solomon; others show a strong preference for certitude. Such doubts, and indeed humility, are important. Standardised formulations, as we have seen, are sometimes accompanied by implicit and occasionally explicit references to specific theories. Here, it is the highly malleable and virtually incorrigible lexicon of attachment theory (Howe et al. 1999). In the slippery world of relationships and interaction, professionals seem to suspend disbelief. Whilst the law of requisite variety (Ashby 1956) urges rich description and the nuanced crafting of remedies to grapple effectively with the complexities of real-life dilemmas, the necessarily reductionist vocabularies of behavioural theory offer only the comforting simplicities of standard solutions.

To understand why these generic prescriptions have such a potent hold, let us awake our sleeping emotional dog. In all professional work engaged with human distress, anxiety is an omnipresent psychic force, especially in settings such as child welfare where the consequences of misjudgement are likely to incur massive social sanction. In a range of professional contexts from nursing to software engineering, the power of anxiety to configure behaviour, especially collective behaviour, has been recognised (Wastell 1999).[1] Seemingly rational task-oriented activity, such as conforming to rules or following procedures, functions primarily as a social defence for containing the anxiety evoked by the imperative for accountable control over complex, dynamic processes that are inherently risk-laden, uncontrollable and unpredictable. Yielding ourselves to the higher institutional authority of the organisation, or some pet theory or technology, confers ontological security, to borrow a handy phrase from Giddens (1984). Not the whole emotional story perhaps, but anxiety certainly plays a big part.

"What counts as professional knowledge … is intricately tied up with bureaucracy and government policies – in short with the state" (Sarangi and Roberts 1999: 8).

In a world where the institutional order profoundly and illiberally shapes the metaphysics of professionals, and anxiety (putatively) wags the tale of reason, what can be offered up as a prescription for hope? Reflective practice and an attitude of humility would seem to be part of any salvation. Liking institutions to megalomaniac computers, Douglas (1986: 92) avers that "the hope of intellectual independence, and the first step in resistance is to discover how the institutional grip is laid upon our mind". Moreover we should note that neither professionals nor clients are simply hapless instruments plucked and played by the institutional hand, like the gods of antiquity. Within the apparent "iron cage" of institutional categories, Evie precariously manages to perform Stancombe's second category of moral worthiness, noted at the commencement of this chapter, that is that parents "may admit to blame, seek absolution and accept guidance, in the form of expert help to ensure that they become 'better' parents". To continue our balletic analogy, professionals (as well as their clients) are dancers and can be helped toward virtuosity (or even virtue) given the right reflexive tools, of which the ability to analyse their own talk as text is assuredly one (Taylor and White 2000; Sarangi and Candlin 2003; White and Stancombe 2003; Firkins and Candlin 2006; Sarangi 2007).

Notes

* This research referred to here was supported by the Economic and Social Research Council, award number R000 222892.
1. Lest the reader be misled, no totalizing theory of human behaviour and emotionality is intended here, any more than our advocacy of reflexive practice should be taken as a standard "one size fits all" panacea.

References

Arribas-Ayllon, Michael, Srikant Sarangi and Angus Clarke
   2008a   The micropolitics of responsibility vis-à-vis autonomy: Parental accounts
            of childhood genetic testing and (non)disclosure. *Sociology of Health & Ill-
            ness* 30(2): 255–271.
Arribas-Ayllon, Michael, Srikant Sarangi and Angus Clarke
   2008b   Managing self-responsibility through other-oriented blame: Family ac-
            counts of genetic testing. *Social Science & Medicine* 66: 1521–1532.
Ashby, W. Ross
   1956   *An Introduction to Cybernetics*. London: Chapman & Hall.
Atkinson, Paul
   1995   *Medical Talk and Medical Work*. London: Sage.
Bruner, Jerome
   1990   *Acts of Meaning*. Cambridge, MA: Harvard University Press.
Buttny Richard
   1993   *Social Accountability in Communication*. London: Sage.
Dingwall, Robert and Topsy Murray
   1983   Categorisation in accident departments: "good" patients, "bad" patients and
            "children". *Sociology of Health and Illness* 5(2): 127–148.
Douglas, Mary
   1986   *How Institutions Think*. New York: Syracuse University Press
Erickson, Fredrick
   2004   *Talk and Social Theory: Ecologies of Speaking and Listening in Everyday
            Life*. Cambridge: Polity Press.
Feyerabend, Paul
   1999   *Conquest of Abundance: A Tale of Abstraction versus the Richness of
            Being*. (Bert Terpstra ed.) Chicago: University of Chicago Press.
Firkins, Arthur and Christopher N. Candlin
   2006   Framing the child at risk. *Health, Risk and Society* 18(3): 272–291.
Fleck, Ludwik
   1979   *Genesis and Development of Scientific Fact*. Chicago: University of Chi-
            cago Press.
Garfinkel, Harold
   1967   *Studies in Ethnomethodology*. Englewood Cliffs, NJ: Prentice-Hall.
Giddens, Anthony
   1984   *The Constitution of Society. Outline of the Theory of Structuration*. Cam-
            bridge: Polity Press.
Hak, Tony
   1992   Psychiatric records as transformations of other texts. In: Graham Watson
            and Robert M. Seiler (eds.), *Text in Context: Contributions to Ethnometho-
            dology*, 138–55. Newbury Park, CA: Sage.
Hall, Christopher
   1997   *Social Work as Narrative: Storytelling and Persuasion in Professional
            Texts*. Aldershot: Ashgate.
Hall, Christopher, Stefaan Slembrouck and Srikant Sarangi
   2006   *Language Practices in Social Work: Categorization and Accountability in
            Child Welfare,* London: Routledge.

Heritage, John and Anna Lindstrom
  1998   Motherhood, medicine and morality: Scenes from a medical encounter. *Research on Language and Social Interaction* 31(3/4): 397–438.
Horlick-Jones, Tom
  2003   Managing risk and contingency: Interaction and accounting behaviour. *Health, Risk and Society* 5(2): 221–228.
Howe, David, Gillian Schofield, Marian Brandon and Diana Hinings
  1999   *Attachment Theory, Child Maltreatment and Family Support.* London: Palgrave.
Jeffrey, Roger
  1979   Normal rubbish: Deviant patients in casualty departments. *Sociology of Health and Illness* 1(1): 90–107.
McHugh, Peter
  1970   A common-sense conception of deviance. In: Jack D. Douglas (ed.), *Deviance and Respectability: The Social Construction of Moral Meanings*. New York: Basic Books.
Pomerantz, Anita
  1978   Attributions of responsibility: Blamings. *Sociology* 12: 115–121.
Pomerantz, Anita
  1986   "Extreme case formulations: A new way of legitimating claims. *Human Studies* 9: 219–230.
Sacks, Harvey
  1972   On the analyzability of stories by children. John Gumpertz and Dell Hymes (eds.), *Directions in Sociolinguistics: The Ethnography of Communication*, 325–345. New York: Holt, Rinehart and Winston.
Sacks, Harvey
  1992   *Lectures on Conversation.* (Gail Jefferson ed.) Oxford: Blackwell.
Sarangi, Srikant
  2007   The anatomy of interpretation: Coming to terms with the analyst's paradox in professional discourse studies. *Text & Talk* 27(5/6): 567–584.
Sarangi, Srikant and Celia Roberts (eds.)
  1999   *Talk, Work and Institutional Order: Discourse in Medical, Mediation and Management Settings.* Berlin / New York: Mouton de Gruyter.
Sarangi, Srikant and Christopher N. Candlin
  2003   Categorization and explanation of risk: A discourse analytical perspective. *Health, Risk and Society* 5(2): 115–124.
Silverman, David
  1987   *Communication and Medical Practice: Social Relations in the Clinic.* London: Sage.
Silverman, David
  1997   *Discourses of Counselling: HIV Counselling as Social Interaction.* London: Sage.
Slembrouck, Stefaan and Christopher Hall
  2003   Caring but not coping: Fashioning a legitimate parent identity. In: Christopher Hall, Kirsi Juhila, Nigel Parton and Tarja Poso (eds.), *Constructing Clienthood in Social Work and Human Services*, 44–61. London: Jessica Kingsley.

Smith, Dorothy
　　1978　　K is mentally ill: The anatomy of a factual account. *Sociology* 12: 23–53.
Stancombe, John and Susan White
　　2005　　Cause and responsibility: Towards an interactional understanding of multi-partiality in family therapy. *Journal of Family Therapy* 27: 331–352.
Strong, Philip
　　1979　　*The Ceremonial Order of the Clinic.* London: Routledge
Suoninen, Eero and Arja Jokinen
　　2005　　Persuasion in social work interviewing. *Qualitative Social Work* 4(4): 469–487.
Taylor Carolyn and Susan White
　　2000　　*Practising Reflexivity in Health and Welfare: Making Knowledge.* Buckingham: Open University Press.
Taylor Carolyn and Susan White
　　2006　　Knowledge and reasoning in Social Work: Educating for humane judgement. *British Journal of Social Work* 35: 1–18.
Wastell, David
　　1999　　Learning dysfunctions in information systems development: Overcoming the social defences with transitional objects. *MIS Quarterly* 23: 581–600.
White, Susan
　　2003　　The social worker as moral judge: Blame, responsibility and case formulation. In: Christopher Hall, Kirsi Juhila, Nigel Parton and Tarja Poso (eds.), *Constructing Clienthood in Social Work and Human Services,* xx–xx. London: Jessica Kingsley.
White, Susan
　　forth-　　Fabled uncertainty in social work: A coda to Spafford et al. *Journal of*
　　coming　*Social Work* 9(2)
White, Susan
　　2002　　Accomplishing the case in paediatrics and child health: Medicine and morality in interprofessional talk. *Sociology of Health and Illness* 24(4): 409–435.
White, Susan and John Stancombe
　　2003　　*Clinical Judgement in the Health and Welfare Professions: Extending the Evidence Base.* Buckingham: Open University Press.

11. Interrogation and evidence: Questioning sequences in courtroom discourse and police interviews

Sandra Harris

Abstract

The role of language in eliciting, establishing, presenting, and ultimately assessing the validity of evidence in both police interviews and criminal trials is a crucial one. After a brief review of literature, this chapter focuses on questioning sequences in both contexts and identifies a number of problems and issues, i.e., a built-in asymmetry of power and knowledge in the institutional participant roles, how conflicting goals generate different interactional strategies, the tensions which result from the attempt to present evidence in both factual and narrative modes of discourse. A selection of data extracts from the trial of Harold Shipman (UK, 2000) and from the police interrogations of Shipman are analysed in detail in order to explore these issues and also to mark some of the differences between the questioning of defendants and suspects. This is followed by a brief discussion of the accessibility of both trial and police interview data to researchers in applied linguistics and some of the changes which have taken place in the past decade or so, particularly in the UK and the USA. The conclusions stress the importance of authentic language data, the need for making it more available to applied linguists and the desirability of greater collaboration between linguists and lawyers/police authorities. Lastly, more research needs to focus on how linguistic evidence is interpreted and transformed both previous to and throughout a judicial trial.

1. Introduction: Evidence as "talk"

It is probably impossible to overestimate the importance of "evidence" in the legal process at almost every stage. One of the leading textbooks for students and practitioners in the UK, *Murphy on Evidence* (2003), is probably typical in contending both that "evidence underlies the whole practice of law in every field of litigation" and that "it is not the product of theory but rather of the need to solve practical problems in trials" (Murphy 2003: 21). Murphy goes on to elaborate further that:

> ... for legal purposes, the nature of evidence can best be understood by reference to the nature of the judicial trial. A trial is an inquiry into past events, the main purpose of which is to establish to an acceptable degree of probability those past events which it is claimed entitle the court to grant or deny some relief in accordance with law. From a scientific viewpoint, evidence may be defined as any material which would aid the court in establishing the probability of past events into which it must inquire.
> (Murphy 2003: 2)

Thus it is perhaps not surprising that legal discourse has been of paramount interest to applied linguists, especially over the past four decades or so, since the majority of this evidential "material" must necessarily be presented or negotiated or disputed by means of the "talk" (often comprising evidence in itself, along with the texts generated by such "talk") which takes place not only in the courtroom but also in the police station. Murphy goes on to identify two of the most crucial characteristics which distinguish judicial trials from other types of enquires. These are that:

> (1) Trials are not objective inquiries into past events, but adversarial contests, in which parties, who have an interest in the outcome, not only decide what evidence they wish to present and prevent from being presented, but also present the evidence in as persuasive a manner as possible, a manner calculated to win them the sympathy and support of the court. Each party also seeks to persuade the court, by means of partisan, persuasive argument, to interpret the evidence in a light favourable to his case.
> (Murphy 2003: 3)

And:

> (2) A judicial trial is not a search to ascertain the ultimate truth of past events inquired into, but to establish that a version of what occurred has an acceptable probability of being correct. It is in the nature of human experience that it is impossible to ascertain the truth of past events with scientific or mathematical certainty.
> (Murphey 2003: 4)

If, as Murphy argues, evidence underlies the whole of the legal system, then the role of language in the process of eliciting, establishing, negotiating, presenting, disputing and, ultimately, assessing the validity of evidence is a crucial one which is clearly within the domain of applied linguistics.

2.   Brief review of literature

As a consequence of the importance of language in the legal process, for the past four decades or so, interrogations, i.e., lengthy sequences of questions and responses which comprise the major portions of judicial trials, have been a rich source of research for linguists working in different cultures, languages and legal systems, using a variety of theoretical frameworks and methodologies, e.g., conversation analysis, pragmatics, critical discourse analysis, sociolinguistics, social psychology, forensic linguistics. More recently, a number of researchers have also been working very fruitfully on police interviews from several different perspectives (see Shuy 1998, 2005; Komter 2002; Rock 2004, 2007; Heydon 2005; Johnson 2005; Haworth 2006, 2010).

Atkinson and Drew (1979) are among the first researchers to produce a full-length book focussing on the close analysis of questioning sequences in the courtroom. As sociologists writing within an ethnomethodology/conversation analysis perspective, they, predictably, describe their main emphasis as being on the contrast between courtroom interaction and ordinary conversation. Thus *Order in Court* concentrates on such topics as turn-taking, the "management" of accusations, "accomplishing silence" etc., using as evidence the official transcripts of the Scarman Trials in Northern Ireland, presumably because they had no access to audio or video recordings of British courtroom discourse. In a subsequent edited book, *Talk at Work* (Drew and Heritage 1992), both Drew and Atkinson contribute chapters which exemplify some of the developments within conversation analysis in the intervening period as a methodology for the analysis of questioning sequences in the courtroom by making use of actual recorded data rather than official transcripts. Drew's chapter concerns the "contested evidence" in cross-examinations in the context of a rape trial and how both attorneys and witnesses attempt to subvert the other's account, and it is worth noting that in the 1990s issues of sexual identity and power become a dominant theme in a number of studies of courtroom interaction.

An example of this is the work of Matoesian on "talk" in the courtroom, which has also been influenced by conversation analysis in the context of trials involving rape (see Mateosian 1993, 2001). However, in both books, and particularly *Law and the Language of Identity: Discourse in the Kennedy Smith Rape Trial*, Matoesian is concerned with issues of gender and ideologies of power which go well beyond Drew's CA generated account. Matoesian investigates how agency "functions, at crucial moments in the trial, as a covert method of naturalizing domination through the linguistic and ideological constitution of sexual identity" (2001: 6) and, more specifically, the ways in which courtroom participants strategically accomplish particular interactional tasks in a trial through the mobilization of "sexually ordered oppositions".

Although Stygall's (1994) *Trial Language: Differential Discourse Processing and Discursive Formation* is not specifically concerned with sexual identity, it is, crucially, concerned with power and justice, and "seeks to bring legal language in use in the trial court before a jury under the scrutiny of critical language analysis in combination with social theory" (Stygall 1994: 3), taking as its data an audio recording of an entire trial from an American civil court. On the basis of such evidence, she attempts convincingly to demonstrate how legal discourse practices are used to regulate lay citizens, silence, and interrupt them and, ultimately "deny them access to the mechanisms of their regulations" (1994: 201). Her book is exemplary in demonstrating how social and critical theory can generate a methodology which depends on close linguistic analysis.

O'Barr (1982), writing a decade earlier, also focuses on issues of power and gender, but in conjunction with the style witnesses adopt in courtroom interrogation sequences. O'Barr attempts to correlate these "styles" with his version of powerful and powerless speech, based on Robin Lakoff's early work on women's language, now, rightly, regarded as highly problematic for a number of reasons (see Lakoff 1975, 1989). As a social psychologist, O'Barr sets out to "transform" his original recorded trial data into "constructed" testimony which is ultimately read by actors to student subjects who are asked to evaluate the witnesses in this now simulated data on the basis of their competence and social dynamism. It is interesting that O'Barr's later book *Just Words* (Conley and O'Barr 1998), though still concerned with gender and power, takes a very different approach in attempting primarily to integrate the methodologies of sociolinguistics with those of law and society (sociological and legal studies), making the case for an "even deeper collaboration in the future" between the two.

Another identifiable strand of research concentrates mainly on the way questions are used strategically in courtrooms in both direct- and cross-examination and how their function and effectiveness relates in a significant way to their syntactic form. (See Harris 1984; Woodbury 1984; Phillips 1987.) These studies explore, mainly in terms of pragmatics, the different strategic functions of polar and "wh" type questions in the exercise of power and control over witnesses. Such studies tend to concentrate on the predominant use of polar questions, especially in cross-examination where the aim is for the attorney to put forward questions mainly as propositions for confirmation by the witness so as to maximise control by allowing the witness minimal scope for propositions of his/her own or for resistance (see Harris 1989). Harris (2001, 2005) examines further how attorneys make use of question and answer sequences, especially in adversarial Anglo-American judicial systems, in order to fragment possible narrative accounts of witnesses, particularly in conjunction with cross-examination, and to subvert the coherence of potentially hostile witnesses from the "other side". Komter (1994) provides a significantly different perception of accusation and defence in courtroom interaction, working within a Dutch inquisitorial legal system. Lastly, there are a number of studies which look at how questioning sequences in court can exploit and disadvantage members of minority cultures and languages (see Eades 1994, 1996 and 2002).

Studies based on police interviews as data are also diverse in terms of their methodologies and theoretical frameworks. Shuy (1998, 2005) writes mainly as a forensic linguist on the basis of his experience of many years as an expert witness in American criminal trials, where his role has been to assess and evaluate the evidence put forward by the prosecution and the police. Heydon (2005), working with Australian data, draws initially on Goffman's participation frameworks and, following this, on a combination of conversation analysis (for the close analysis of data) and critical discourse analysis to provide a critical account of police discursive practices as they represent the exploitation of the existing interactional structure in order to construct a police version of events. She maintains that though it is not possible for suspects to "hijack" this structure or subvert participant roles, they can resist police questioning at particular points (Heydon 2005: 146). Rock (2004, 2007), Johnson (2005) and Haworth (2010) have obtained police interviewing data in a British context, and it is interesting to note that there are several instances in Haworth's data (taken from the Shipman trial) where the suspect not only resists police questioning but also manages both to "hijack" the question/answer sequencing structure and to subvert the role of the police interviewer as questioner. Komter (2002) explores the authenticity of suspects' written statements made to the police in the context of their later use in courtroom interaction in the context of the Dutch legal system. (See Section 5 "Interrogation in police interviews and judicial trials" of this chapter.)

Probably the most comprehensive and important recent study is Cotterill's (2003) analysis of the O J Simpson trial. What Cotterill says of her own work also applies to many of the studies previously mentioned, namely, that:

> The approach to data analysis adopted … is deliberately eclectic. In allowing the data to speak for itself, I have employed a range of theoretical and methodological models and principles. In each case, the choice of approach has been motivated by a data-driven assessment of what type of analysis would best elucidate the particular aspect of courtroom language under scrutiny.
> (Cotterill 2003: 3)

Cotterill's is an important methodological point, and what links all of those researchers cited above is the use of actual language data for purposes of analysis. (Atkinson and Drew [1979] are exceptional in adopting a straightforward conversation analysis approach.) Like Cotterill, nearly all the work on questioning sequences both in courtrooms and police stations is very much data driven and takes an eclectic approach to methodology.

3.   Problems and issues

This chapter will attempt to explore briefly, and primarily from the perspective of applied linguistics and pragmatics, some of the problems and issues raised by Murphy's definition of evidence, its nature and relationship to the interaction which takes place in the evidential portions (those involving the questioning of witnesses and defendants) of judicial trials (and, to a lesser extent, police interviews) mainly within the adversarial system of law which obtains in the UK and certain other countries, including the United States and Australia. I shall identify, initially, some of the most significant of these issues and problems and then illustrate them with reference to data extracts taken from the trial of Harold Shipman for murder, which took place in the UK in 2000. I shall also very briefly compare two extracts from the police interviews with one from the judicial trial of Harold Shipman.

Firstly, there is a significant and built-in asymmetry of power and knowledge in the institutional participant roles in both judicial trials and police interviews which cast the institutional member (lawyer, judge, police interviewer, etc) as the questioner and the non-institutional member (witness, defendant, suspect, etc) as the respondent, and this asymmetry affects the manner in which evidence is elicited and dealt with linguistically in important ways. As Thornborrow (2002) points out in her book on "power talk" in institutional discourse, "One of the principal means of exercising power discursively is through institutionally grounded rights to take certain actions in the talk, and, in unequal status encounters, those rights are not held equally by all participants." (Thornborrow 2002: 58) Nowhere, perhaps, are these prescribed interactional roles more marked (and generally enforced) than in a courtroom. This makes it possible for lawyers most frequently to be the initiators in the process of the inquiry as well as the evaluators of witness responses, a powerful position which severely limits the witnesses' interactional options. (See also Adelsward et al. 1987; Sarangi and Slembrouck 1996; Cotterill 2003: 103–106). In addition, the fact that information must be elicited in the form of questioning sequences also necessitates a more complex relationship between the "knower" of that information (who is usually the witness or defendant) and the "teller" (who is often the lawyer, who frequently puts forward propositions containing information for witnesses to confirm rather than allowing witnesses merely to "tell" what they know). How the relationship between "knowing" and "telling" is negotiated in both the evidential portions of trials and in police interviews is a particularly interesting process and crucial to Murphy's version of a trial as an "adversarial contest" rather than an "objective inquiry into past events" (Murphy 2003: Section 1 "Introduction").

Secondly, the adversarial legal system ensures that in judicial trials there are a series of conflicting goals, as also is the case in the vast majority of police interviews. Because, as Murphy argues, trials are "not objective inquiries into past events" (2003: 3) and do not seek "to ascertain the ultimate truth of past events" (2003: 4) but only to establish a version of what occurred as having an "acceptable probability of being correct" (2003: 4), such trials inevitably consist of highly strategic language which is primarily oriented to winning or losing a case. This is particularly evident in the contrasting strategies employed in examination-in-chief (or direct examination) and cross-examination, as a number of researchers have already pointed out (see Woodbury 1984; Philips 1987; Stygall 1994; Harris 2001, 2005). In a similar way, police interviews can be said to be oriented towards establishing evidence which will lead to a conviction rather than to the "ultimate truth" of what actually happened. (See Harris [1995] for how this can be related both to the conversational maxims of Grice and the validity claims of Habermas as proponents of universal pragmatics.)

Thirdly, the object of both the judicial trial and the police interview is an inquiry into past events, i.e., what happened and who was responsible, which raises a number of further interesting and problematic questions. Murphy (2003) states clearly that "evidence may be defined in general terms as any material which has the potential to change the state of a fact-finder's belief with respect to any factual proposition which is to be decided and which is in dispute" (2003: 2). The emphasis here is on the factual nature of the trial as an inquiry and the construction of the jury as a body of "fact-finders". If the nature of evidence in a trial is to be characterised as "factual", the manner of presenting it effectively and persuasively in relation to events which have happened in the past is highly dependent on narrative forms. This leads not only to the inevitable fragmentation of narratives which must be related through sequences of questions and responses but also to the hybridisation and intermingling of narrative and non-narrative modes of discourse in the testimony of these same witnesses and defendants. At the same time, the adversarial system puts pressure on prosecution lawyers, in particular, to construct witness narratives as a powerful and persuasive way of achieving the kind of discourse coherence which will persuade a jury of the "probable correctness" of the events it describes.

4.   Analysis of data

The trial of Harold Shipman was a very high profile case, in which a British doctor was convicted in January 2000 of murdering fifteen of his patients, with a further inquiry concluding that he may have murdered as many as 260 patients over the course of his long professional career. Transcripts A, B and F below involve extracts from Day 32 of the Shipman trial, and transcript C is an extract taken from Day 34. In all of the transcripts quoted in the chapter, Shipman is being questioned either by his own lawyer, Miss N. Davies, QC, in the case of examination-in-chief (Transcript A) or by the prosecuting lawyer, Mr R. Henriques, QC, in the case of cross-examination (Transcripts B, C and F). Hence, for purposes of clarity, I have identified the two lawyers respectively as ND or RH and the defendant merely as S. The material enclosed in quotation marks in the transcripts refers to Dr Shipman's notes, records and earlier testimony which have been previously submitted to the court as evidence. (I have presented the transcripts exactly as they appear in the source. See the Appendix for a key to the transcription of the police interrogation data.)

Extract A (examination-in-chief) Transcript from Day 32 of the trial

ND: N Davies (lawyer for the defence)
S: Harold Shipman (defendant)

ND: When did you last see the deceased alive? "About 30 minutes". What is that a reference to?
S: Before she died.
ND: Is that a reference to your visit to her home?
S: Yes. I mean, that could have been 60 minutes.   5
ND: "8(a)" (reference to previous evidence) How soon after death did you see the body? About 4 hours?
S: Yes, it was after 6 o'clock when I got there.
ND: What examination of it did you make? You have there signed "complete external". You have told the Court by reason of the information   10
given to you by the paramedics you did not carry out an examination?
S: No, it was just the modified look and checking who the patient was and having the asystole trace in front of me.
ND: Then we see that there you recite that in "box 11" that the lady was found by a neighbour collapsed and I have to confess I can't actually   15
read the first word of the second line there "Neighbour found her?"
S: Neighbour found her collapsed and dead.
ND: And that is what you wrote and so certified on the next page, a Dr Fitton has completed form C. Can I ask this, prior to Dr Fitton's completion of form C did he raise with you any queries relating to the death   20
of Pamela Hillier?
S: Dr Fitton isn't a doctor that I often use for a second part cremation. The undertakers who were handling the affair rang me and told me that Dr Fitton normally did the second part. I rang him, spoke to him, it seemed a long time because I took him back through the history.   25
I explained what had happened on the day and he seemed content with that. I don't think he offered, sorry, I don't think he asked other questions.
ND: On the 9th February 1998 did you administer to Pamela Hillier morphine or diamorphine?   30
S: No I did not.
ND: On the 9th February 1998 did you murder Pamela Hillier?
S: No I did not.
ND: My Lord, that concludes the questioning ......

Extract B (Cross-examination of defendant) Transcript from Day 32 of trial

RD: R Henriques (lawyer for the prosecution)
S: Harold Shipman (defendant)

RD: And then "Renata Overton: This woman was a patient of the defend-
      ant. The records show that the defendant visited her on the 18th
      February 1994 when she was seriously ill with chest pain. After as-
      sessment the defendant administered 10 milligrams of diamorphine
      intravenously. He admits that he was carrying the drug with him. 5
      There was no prescription issued in her name in relation to this dia-
      morphine." You see that, bottom of page 3?
S: Yes thank you.
RD: Where did you get that diamorphine?
S: I got it out of my bag.   10
RD: Yes, where did you get the diamorphine that was in your bag?
S: I don't know.
RD: You had a stock, hadn't you?
S: No
RD: Well, if you hadn't got a stock how did you get it?   15
S: You mean how did it get into my bag?
RD: That is the meaning of my question.
S: Thank you. All I can assume is that the patient had given my drugs
      back and there was an ampoule of diamorphine in it and it all got
      thrown into the bag and that when I took the drugs out it got missed. 20
RD: A variation on the Arundale (reference to previous case) explanation,
      is that what you are saying?
S: I believe it is almost the same explanation.
RD: Well, it is a variation in the amount of drugs involved, isn't it?
S: In the mechanism of it being there it is the same.   25
RD: We will look at one more before our break at the conventional time.
      Would you look at the top of page 4. "Mary Smith. This woman was a
      patient of the defendant. On 17th May 1994, 10, 100 milligram am-
      poules of diamorphine were dispensed in her name from the Norwest
      Coop Pharmacy, Market Street, Hyde following the presentation of 30
      a prescription issued by the defendant. The only other record of her
      being prescribed morphine during 1994 was in the form of tablets.
      The diamorphine was never apparently administered. She never
      required a syringe driver." Now there we have 1,000 milligrams of
      diamorphine. What happened to that diamorphine?   35
S: I have no idea.
RD: Finally, would you just please answer the question that I asked you a little
      while ago, that related to Marion Gilchrist, the only thing you had

done wrong was not arranging for Mrs Grundy to be cremated. The
question was what had you done wrong?   40

S: I had done nothing wrong.

RD: Why were you saying that to Mrs Gilchrist?

S: I put it to her as a black joke. At that time I obviously was under an
enormous amount of pressure but I had intended it as a joke and I
think she took it as a joke.   45

RD: But what was funny about that?

S: I am not being funny with you, sir, you can't dig up ashes.

RD: You cannot dig up ashes you said?

S: Yes.

RD: That was what was behind your thought process, wasn't it?   50

S: No.

RD: Has it crossed your mind that in fact you had successfully got away
with the other 14 deaths we are looking at in this case?

S: I'm not aware that I have got away with anything.

RD: You had done, hadn't you, but for Mrs Grundy?   55

S: Since I didn't do any of this then the answer has to be no.

(End of this session)

In both of these extracts, one involving the defendant being questioned by his
own lawyer (A) and one in which he is questioned by the prosecuting lawyer
(B), the asymmetry in terms of the interactive roles of the participants is a
relatively clear one, with the lawyer in both instances acting as the questioner
and the defendant as the respondent as a part of a lengthy interrogation, though
there is one point in each extract when either the lawyer (Extract A, ll. 14–17) or
the defendant (Extract B, ll. 15–17) momentarily breaks the question-response
sequencing to ask for a clarification. It is also clear in both extracts that it is the
lawyer as the questioner who initiates the topics and controls the progress of the
underlying argument. Both transcripts, as I have said, involve references to
documentation produced previously and submitted to the court, i.e., Shipman's
notes and records kept on the various cases, along with his earlier testimony.
This is significant, since both the defence and the prosecution lawyers incorporate this material into their questions as information specifically for confirmation
(or denial) as a crucial part of the examination of the defendant. Consequently,
Shipman's written notes, records and the transcripts of his previous testimony
become re-incorporated into the trial itself and specifically called to the attention of the jury.

However, there are some revealing and significant differences between the
examination-in-chief (Extract A) and the cross-examination (Extract B). Both
lawyers attempt to maintain a high degree of control over the witness, but since
they have clearly conflicting goals and adversarial roles, their strategies are very

different ones. This is most evident in the use of particular types of questions, and, especially, in their coercive nature and intent. Though both lawyers use predominantly "yes/no" question forms, the putting forward of a hostile proposition accompanied by a coercive "tag form" occurs only in the cross-examination (see B, ll. 13, 24, 51 and 55). Moreover, the questions asked by the lawyer for defence (Extract A), though also restrictive, provide the defendant with more scope to put forward his own account of what happened. ND, as the defence lawyer, is much less inclined to put forward information propositions merely for the defendant to confirm or deny, and she willingly accepts responses which elaborate a "yes" or "no" response (see A, ll. 5, 8, 12, and, especially, 22, where the response to a "yes/no" question involves a longer narrative account).

"Yes/no" questions put by the prosecuting lawyer (RH) are more likely to receive merely a simple confirming response without elaboration. (See B, ll. 14, 49, 51.) It is interesting that both lawyers conclude their respective interrogating sessions with explicit questions involving the charge that Dr Shipman murdered one or more of his patients but in very different ways. In Extract A, ND, by asking overtly whether Dr Shipman has administered diamorphine (the cause of the victim's death) to Pamela Hillier followed by a question referring directly to the murder of the victim, provides the defendant with a clear opportunity explicitly to deny both charges (A, ll. 31, 33), while the prosecuting lawyer's concluding questions in Extract B contain built-in accusations of guilt in a coercive form which tend to prohibit a simple "yes/no" denial (B, ll. 52–56) and are intended to provoke a defensive response.

This pattern of a series of questions which climax in an assertion of guilt is even more clear in Extract C, taken from Day 34 of the trial.

Extract C (Cross-examination of the defendant) Day 34 of the trial.

RH: R Henriques (lawyer for the prosecution)
S: Harold Shipman (defendant)

RH: When you saw Mrs Mellor was there any sign of drug abuse?
S: Not that I came across.
RH: Anything about her that indicated she had been taking drugs?
S: Not that I am aware of.
RH: Any suspicion when you had seen her anytime during the day?   5
S: No.
RH: She had between 0.7 and 0.9 micrograms of morphine per gram of
      thigh tissue.
      Can you explain how she came to have that volume of morphine
      within her body?   10
S: I cannot even tell you how she got any morphine into her body.
RH: You say that she was at your surgery at 4 o'clock?

S: I do say that.

RH: We know that she was dead with morphine in her body by 6.30 at the
      very latest don't we?   15

S: Yes.

RH: Have you any explanation as to how she could have got such a level
      of morphine within her body?

S: I have already said I cannot explain the amount in her body, I cannot
      even explain how she got morphine in her body.   20

RH: There is a very simple explanation, Dr Shipman, isn't there? It was
      placed there by you between 3 o'clock and 3.20 when Mrs Ellis saw
      you.

S: No it wasn't.

(End of session)

Here, once again, propositions are built into a series of questions which lead to
an inevitable assumption of the guilt of the defendant. This cross-examination
extract is a good illustration of Murphy's (2003) contention that the purpose of a
judicial trial is "not a search to ascertain the ultimate truth of past events" but
rather "to establish that a version of what occurred has an acceptable probability
of being correct". There is a clear division between the "knower" (Shipman) and
the "teller" (the prosecutor), who puts forward most of the questions which contain propositions enabling construction of a coherent argument premised on
the guilt of the defendant. "Truth" becomes negotiable, a matter of getting the
defendant to agree with the propositions put forward (or to demonstrate to the
jury that he has explicitly failed to explain facts which then lead up to the accusation of guilt). "Truth" is the logical conclusion of the build-up of "factual" information, i.e., Mrs Mellor was not a drug addict and had no access to drugs;
Mrs Mellor had a lethal amount of morphine within her body which was the
cause of her death; Mrs Mellor attended Dr Shipman's surgery at 4.00 on the
day of her death and was dead by 6.30 at the latest; Mrs Ellis witnessed Dr Shipman with Mrs Mellor between 3.00 and 3.20, the only possible logical explanation being that Dr Shipman deliberately injected Mrs Mellor with the morphine which resulted in her death. The defendant is not permitted to narrate his
own version of these events but only to confirm or explain certain "facts" put
forward by the prosecutor. The guilt of the defendant becomes the only possible
explanation and the "truth" which the series of factual propositions establishes.
Though the defendant ultimately resists accepting the prosecution's version of
the "truth" (l. 24), he has not been able to contradict it convincingly or even to
deny the validity of the "facts" which lead up to it, nor has he been permitted to
put forward any alternative form of "truth".

5.   Interrogation in police interviews and judicial trials

It is extremely interesting to compare the questioning of Harold Shipman by the police when he was arrested and interviewed in the police station with the cross-examination in his judicial trial which followed. Much of the case, as I have stated, turned upon Dr Shipman's use of diamorphine and other dangerous drugs, since the jury ultimately accepted that these provided the means for Shipman to bring about the deaths of a number of his patients without, at least for a very lengthy period, arousing suspicion. Thus, both the police interrogators and the prosecuting lawyer concentrate on Shipman's access to and use of such drugs. However, the way questions are employed strategically by the respective interrogators and their discursive force is markedly different. Here are two extracts (D and E) from the police interviews with Dr Shipman (cited in Haworth [2006:748,751) and a further extract from the cross-examination by R Henriques, the lawyer for the prosecution on Day 32 of the Shipman trial (Extract F).

Extracts D and E

P: Police interrogator
S: Harold Shipman

Extract D

P: 'kay (.) erm (.) where d'you (.) access dangerous drugs (.) for (.) say the
    treatment say of terminally (.) ill patients
S: I would issue a prescription ... and deliver the drug (.) directly to the
    house. (.) and that's the only time I would touch them ...
P: mhm (-) what happens say (.) if (-) one of your patients (.) dies from a   5
    terminal illness, you're aware that they have (.) whatever it is the
    [dangerous drugs what happens (.) to those drugs]
S: [.hh hh   ]   [well' the drugs are usually destroyed by the
    district nurse ... I would never take drugs away.

Extract E

P: ... if you're really suggesting that. to us (.) [then-]
S: [may] I ask whether the
    house was searched?
P: yes. (.) no drugs whatsoever (.) that could cause a fatality (.) (are) the
    findings that we've got [from-]   5
S: (wh-) when was it searched
P: I haven't got the date to hand that it was searched (.)

S: well that's quite important. (.)
P: are you suggesting though doctor, (.) [?]
S: [I'm not suggesting] anything I'm 10
    just telling you my fears and worries of this lady (.) er at that time.

As Haworth (2006) points out, in Extract D the police interrogator asks only in-
formation-seeking questions, with no element of accusation built into them.
Even when Shipman answers both questions defensively (as if they had contained accusations), P does not follow these questions up with requests for
further detail, even though such details later become crucial to the case against
Shipman. The police interrogator appears merely to accept Shipman's responses
at face value and allows him to put forward his own account of his behaviour.

    Extract E is even more markedly different from the cross-examination (or
even the examination-in-chief) which takes place in Shipman's trial. In this
extract, Shipman effectively takes over the role of questioner, not only forcing
the policeman into the role of respondent but also implicitly criticising his professional behaviour. It is the policeman who becomes defensive here (l. 7–11)
and Shipman as the suspect who takes on the dominant role. Both of these
extracts contrast sharply with the cross-examination of Shipman on the same
topic, as can be seen below.

Extract F (cross-examination of Harold Shipman) Day 32 of the trial.

RH: R Henriques (the prosecution lawyer)
S: Harold Shipman (the defendant)

RH: From which patient had you borrowed drugs?
S: From no patient that I know of.
RH: Well, where had you borrowed the drugs from?
S: I had found them on the mat behind the door of my surgery.
RH: You had found some diamorphine on a mat in your surgery?   5
S: That's what I have said.
RH: Did you notify anybody about finding dangerous drugs on a mat in
     your surgery?
S: Well, no.
RH: Could you imagine anything more irregular than some dangerous   10
     drugs being on a mat in a doctor's surgery?
S: I would have thought that was one of the safer places for it to go.
RH: Which mat are you talking about, inside the front door on Market St?
S: Yes.
RH: Somebody had put some drugs through your front door?   15
S: Yes.
RH: Did you ever find out who put them through the front door?

S: No.

RH: What enquiries did you make as to who might have put them through
      your front door?   20

S: I activated the computer and looked who had received drugs, diamor-
      phine from me in the past couple of months.

RH: Did it cross your mind to inform the Dangerous Drugs Inspectorate?

S: No

      .... (utterances left out)   25

RH: Please answer the question. Did you inform your partners that drugs
      had been pushed through the letter box?

S: I am not quite sure what you are asking me.

RH: I think the question is clear. Please answer.

S: I have already said.   30

Clearly, in the cross-examination extract, the prosecutor retains absolute control, both in the role of questioner and over the topic. The questions are very
specific ones which do not allow Shipman to elaborate or to put forward an alternative narrative. When he does attempt to pose a contradiction to the prosecutor's line of questioning (l. 12), RH ignores his answer and proceeds to ask a
series of very specific questions (ll. 13, 15, 17, 19) as a follow-up. When Shipman asks for clarification of the prosecutor's question (ll. 27–28), he is told
sharply that the question is clear and he must answer it.

It is interesting to speculate on the possible reasons for the marked contrast
between the police interviews and the interrogation of Harold Shipman in the
subsequent trial, especially as the contrast reverses the usual stereotype of the
police interview as an example of one of the most obvious, coercive and unequivocal exercises of institutional power. Certainly, in terms of their institutional roles, the balance of discursive power is massively with the police, and
the power inequality generally between the participants is on the face of it
greater than in the courtroom, where the presence of the judge and jury play
a crucial role in imposing certain limits on the discursive power of lawyers. Although I have only been able to quote two brief extracts, Haworth (2006), who
is familiar with the entire sequence of police interviews, suggests that the level
of discursive resistance that Dr Shipman manages is throughout the sequence
"quite remarkable" (2006: 755). Her explanation is, in part, that the fact that
Shipman is a doctor and a professional in his own right has a strong influence
on the interaction which takes place in the police station. She suggests that Dr
Shipman "uses his professional status to bolster his discursively weaker position and place himself on a more equal footing with P. He also constantly undermines P's status, both an investigative officer and as questioner" (2006: 755).

However, as Haworth also suggests, it may be misleading to look too closely
at the immediate context of the police interview in isolation from the entire judi-

cial process and that the "weak" questioning of Shipman must be considered in the light that the police have other kinds of damning evidence, i.e., the evidence of a witness who saw him removing drugs after the death of a patient and the discovery of diamorphine in his own home. She further argues that "given the overall aim of building a case against S, it has been seen that P in fact gains the most when S does take discursive control" and that allowing Shipman to put forward his own explanation for his behaviour may be a discursive strategy in itself. Hence, the police tactic of "making a very open request for comment and giving up his powerful discursive position in order to allow S to speak freely" (2006: 755) is actually effective in that it highlights Shipman's failure to put forward a convincing explanation for his own actions. This would undoubtedly be considered an exceptionally risky strategy by a prosecuting lawyer and one that even a defence lawyer would be likely to employ much more judiciously, if at all. However, it is surely right to argue that it is essential to look beyond the immediate context of the police interview and to consider such interviews in the light of the judicial process as a whole, inasmuch as this is possible. Certainly, more research needs to be done on current practices of police interviewing, and Haworth is also right in suggesting that applied linguists (and other researchers) should exercise a measure of caution when posing analytic judgements, especially on isolated data extracts.

6.   Access to courtroom and police interview data

During the past thirty years or so, there have been substantial changes in the access which linguists have had to both courtroom and, to a much lesser extent, police interview data. It was probably the televising of the O J Simpson trial in 1995 in the United States which did more to heighten public awareness and interest in the judicial process and courtroom procedure than any other single event, and one which was watched worldwide. The transcripts which were subsequently published on the internet in conjunction with this trial, followed by numerous others, have provided a rich and fascinating source of data for applied linguists interested in courtroom discourse, and made it relatively easy to download real language material which can be used either for research purposes or for teaching. The vast majority of this courtroom material has in the past been American, and access to the language of judicial trials has been much more restricted in the UK, where it is still not possible to record or televise the courts. Recently, however, the whole of the Shipman Trial has become available on the internet, which has been particularly useful to me in writing this chapter, though there are obviously also limitations and difficulties involved in making use of internet data.

The accessibility of police interviews to researchers has also recently changed quite substantially. Recorded police data has typically been more readily available in the United States (see Watson 1990 and Shuy 1998) than in the UK in the past, though even in the US there has been no widespread accessibility, and relatively little research has been done compared to that on courtroom interrogations. European comparisons, under inquisitorial rather than adversarial legal systems, are more difficult to make, given the different roles (and goals) of the participants. It was The Police & Criminal Evidence Act 1984 (PACE) that brought about a radical transformation in police interviewing practice in the UK, not only in terms of how the police currently conduct interviews with suspects but also for applied linguists who wish to gain access to police data. Most significant is Section 60 of PACE, which specifies, with some exceptions, that all interviews with suspects must be audio recorded, and this section of PACE acts as the basis of current police interviewing practice. Haworth (2007) argues further that "it is interesting to note that the requirement for audio recording was initially met with some resistance from the police, but is now widely regarded within the force as, among other things, a vital safeguard to protect the police themselves from accusations of malpractice" (2007: 3).

It is widely believed that the requirement to audio-record police interviews has radically transformed the nature of those interviews, as well as providing a much more reliable and tangible form of evidence which can be produced if and when a case comes to trial. Heydon (2005) constructs a similar argument for the required audio recording of police interviews in Australia. It is indeed arguable that analyses of police/suspect interviews before 1992 may now be relevant in a very much more limited way to current police practice. For example, Fairclough (1995), Harris (1995) and Thornborrow (2002) make substantial use of the BBC documentary made in 1980, in which the Thames Valley police were recorded during a series of interviews conducted with suspects/witnesses that became controversial in themselves. Indeed, one of these, with a rape victim, resulted in a change in the law prescribing that rape victims were henceforth to be interviewed only by women police officers (see also Candlin 1987).

Clearly (and fortunately), the type of extremely coercive interaction revealed in this particular recording would be much less likely to occur at the present time, and the use made of these documentary interviews by a number of linguists is largely the result of data involving unrecorded police interviews at that time being almost impossible to obtain. Indeed, it is still difficult to gain access to police interview data, but there is now a body of work (in addition to Heydon's research in Australia) based on the cooperation and trust between applied linguists in the UK and various police authorities, and the police have recently been much more confident in allowing, with certain specifications and restrictions, linguists access to substantial numbers of audio recordings (see Rock 2004, 2007; Johnson 2005; Haworth 2006, 2010).

7.   Conclusions

In summary, it is first of all important to re-iterate that it is almost impossible to overestimate the crucial role that language plays in the process of eliciting, establishing, negotiating, presenting, disputing and, ultimately, assessing the validity of evidence in the judicial procedure at all stages (including the gathering of evidence by the police), though I have been concerned in this chapter specifically with interrogations. Just as evidence underlies the whole legal system, so applied linguistics has an important role to play in helping to determine the nature of that evidence, its definition and the role it plays, particularly in the "adversarial contests" which characterise the judicial trials held in the USA, the UK and other countries which adhere to an adversarial system. Secondly, considerable research has already been undertaken during the last thirty years or so, based on actual language data, in order to enhance our understanding of the power dynamics and built-in asymmetry prevalent in the courtroom, the prescribed nature of the interactional roles of the various participants, and the characteristic types of strategic communication which play such a significant role in the winning or losing of actual cases.

Following on from this, there is a need to increase still further the accessibility of such data to researchers and for collaboration between lawyers and linguists. The cooperation and trust which is beginning to be established between some linguists and individual police authorities has proved productive and suggests a way forward which will generate further research and enhance understanding on both sides. Lastly, although it often proves difficult, more research needs to focus on how linguistic evidence is interpreted and transformed both previous to, and throughout, the process of a judicial trial, something which is of particular concern to legal professionals. Both Rock (2004) and Haworth (2006) comment perceptively on this process in the light of their own research on police interviews. Rock demonstrates clearly how the spoken accounts of witnesses can be transformed by those involved in the legal process when such accounts are subsequently produced as written statements and in the preparation for their presentation as evidence in a trial. Haworth (2006) argues, also in relationship to police interviews, that "through the judicial process the interview data is transformed and 'interpreted' to an extent which goes entirely unnoticed in legal circles but which is of great significance from a linguistic perspective" (Haworth: 756). That there is much still to be done perhaps establishes, once again, the truth of Gibbons' (2003) contention that "it is not only the law that permeates our lives, but the language of the law" (2003: 1)

Appendix

Key to transcription of police interrogation data (cited in Haworth [2006]):

(.)	small pause
(-)	longer pause
.	stopping fall in tone
,	"continuing" intonation
?	rising/questioning inflection
!	animated/emphasis
" "	reading/quoting tone
[ ]	overlapping talk
.hh	audible in-breath
hh	audible out-breath
(guess)	unclear fragment – best guess
(?)	unintelligible fragment

References

Adelsward, Viveka, Karin Aronsson, Linda Jonsson and Per Linell
    1987   The unequal distribution of interactional space: Dominance and control in courtroom interaction. *Text* 7(4): 313–346.

Atkinson, J Maxwell and Paul Drew
    1979   *Order in Court: The Organisation of Verbal Interaction in Judicial Settings*. London: Macmillan.

Candlin, Christopher
    1987   Explaining moments of conflict in discourse. In: Ross Steele and Terry Threadgold (eds.), *Language Topics: Essays in Honour of Michael Halliday (Vol 2)*, 413–429. Amsterdam: John Benjamins.

Conley, John M and William M O'Barr
    1998   *Just Words: Law, Language and Power*. Chicago: Chicago University Press.

Cotterill, Janet
    2003   *Language and Power in Court: A Linguistic Analysis of the O J Simpson Trial*. Basingstoke: Palgrave Macmillan.

Drew, Paul
    1992   Contested evidence in courtroom cross-examination: The case of a trial for rape. In: Paul Drew and John Heritage (eds.), *Talk at Work: Interaction in Institutional Settings*, 470–520. Cambridge: Cambridge University Press.

Drew, Paul and John Heritage (eds.)
    1992   *Talk at Work: Interaction in Institutional Settings*. Cambridge: Cambridge University Press.

Eades, Diana
    1994   A case of communicative clash: Aboriginal English and the legal system. In: John Gibbons (ed.), *Language and the Law*, 234–264. London: Longman.

Eades, Diana
    1996   Verbatim courtroom transcripts and discourse analysis. In: Hannes Kniffka, Susan Blackwell and Malcolm Coulthard (eds.), *Recent Developments in Forensic Linguistics*, 241–254. Frankfurt am Mein: Peter Lang.

Eades, Diana
    2002   Evidence given in unequivocal terms: Gaining consent of aboriginal young people in court. In: Janet Cotterill (ed.), *Language in the Legal Process*, 162–179. Basingstoke: Palgrave Macmillan.

Fairclough, Norman
    1995   *Critical Discourse Analysis: The Critical Study of Language*. Harlow, England: Longman.

Gibbons, John
    2003   *Forensic Linguistics: An Introduction to Language in the Justice System*. Oxford: Blackwell.

Harris, Sandra
    1984   Questions as a mode of control in magistrates' courts. *International Journal of the Sociology of Language* 49: 5–28.

Harris, Sandra
    1989   Defendant resistance to power and control in court. In: Hywel Coleman (ed.), *Working with Language: A Multidisciplinary Consideration of Language in Use in Work Contexts*, 131–164. Berlin / New York: Mouton de Gruyter.

Harris, Sandra
    1995   Pragmatics and power. *Journal of Pragmatics* 23: 117–135.

Harris, Sandra
    2001   Fragmented narratives and multiple tellers: Witness and defendant accounts in trials. *Discourse Studies* 3(1): 53–74.

Harris, Sandra
    2005   Telling stories and giving evidence: The hybridisation of narrative and non-narrative modes of discourse in a sexual assault trial. In: Joanna Thornborrow and Jennifer Coates (eds.), *The Sociolinguistics of Narrative*, 215–238. Amsterdam: John Benjamins.

Haworth, Kate
    2006   The dynamics of power and resistance in police interview discourse. *Discourse & Society* 17(6): 739–759.

Haworth, Kate
    2010   Police interviews as evidence. In Malcolm Coulthard and Alison Johnson (eds) The Routledge Handbook of Forensic Linguistics. London: Routledge (pp 169–185).

Heydon, Georgina
    2005   *The Language of Police Interviewing*. Basingstoke: Palgrave Macmillan.

Johnson, Alison
    2005   "Ask me a story" police interviews: Pragmatic effects of questions in elicited narratives. Unpublished Ph.D. dissertation, Department of English, University of Birmingham.

Komter, Martha
    1994   Accusations and defences in courtroom interaction. *Discourse & Society* 5(2): 165–87.

Komter, Martha
  2002   The suspect's own words: The treatment of written statements in Dutch courtrooms. *International Journal of Speech, Language and the Law* 9(2): 168–192.
Lakoff, Robin
  1975   *Language and Women's Place*. New York: Harper and Row.
Lakoff, Robin
  1989   The limits of politeness: Therapeutic and courtroom discourse. *Multilingua* 8(2/3): 101–129.
Matoesian, Gregory
  1993   *Reproducing Rape: Domination through Talk in the Courtroom*. Cambridge: Polity Press.
Matoesian, Gregory
  2001   *Law and the Language of Identity: Discourse in the Kennedy Smith Rape Trial*. Oxford: Oxford University Press.
Murphy, Peter
  2003   *Murphy on Evidence*. 8th Edition. Oxford: Oxford University Press.
O'Barr, William M
  1982   *Linguistic Evidence: Power and Strategy in the Courtroom*. New York: Academic Press.
Philips, Susan U
  1987   The social organisation of questions and answers in courtroom discourse. In: Leah Kedar (ed.), *Power through Discourse*, 83–113. Norwood, NJ: Ablex. *The Police and Criminal Evidence Act 1984*. London: Home Office.
Rock, Frances
  2004   Recontextualisation in the police station. Unpublished Ph.D. dissertation, Department of English, University of Birmingham.
Rock, Frances
  2007   Communicating Rights: The Language of Arrest and Detention. Basingstoke: Palgrave.
Sarangi, Srikant and Stefaan Slembrouck
  1996   *Language, Bureaucracy and Social Control*. London: Longman.
Shuy, Roger W
  1998   *The Language of Confession, Interrogation, and Deception*. Thousand Oaks, CA: Sage.
Shuy, Roger W
  2005   *Creating Language Crimes: How Law Enforcement Uses (and Misuses) Language*. Oxford: Oxford University Press.
Stygall, Gail
  1994   *Trial Language: Differential Discourse Processing and Discourse Formations*. Amsterdam: John Benjamins.
Thornborrow, Joanna
  2002   *Power Talk: Language and Interaction in Institutional Discourse*. Harlow, England: Longman.
Watson, D R
  1990   Some features of the elicitation of confessions in murder interrogations. In: George Psathas (ed.), *Interaction Competence*, 263–295. Lanham, MD: University Press of America.

Woodbury, Hanni
   1984   The strategic use of questions in court. *Semiotica* 48(3/4): 197–228. http://
                www.the-shipman-inquiry.org.uk/trialtrans.asp. Shipman trial website.
                Accessed April 2007.

12. Judging by what you're saying: Judges' questioning of lawyers as interactive interpretation

Pamela Hobbs

Abstract

Although scholars in the fields of sociolinguistics and discourse analysis have written extensively about courtroom questions over the past thirty years, few studies have examined the questions that judges pose to lawyers; instead, the study of questions in legal discourse has focused on lawyers' questioning of witnesses. Yet judges' questioning of lawyers is both ubiquitous and consequential, for through these questions judges seek lawyers' input, not only in the framing of the issues and the furnishing of authority, but also in formulating the interpretations by which they apply the law to the specific facts and issues that are before them. This chapter describes four questioning strategies that judges use to engage lawyers in interactive interpretation of the issues presented: taking candidate positions on the facts or law; displaying confidence or doubt in their own interpretations; posing "exam" questions that engage lawyers in Socratic dialogue; and using humor or displays of virtuosity to challenge lawyers' interpretations. Through the analysis of examples of judges' questioning of lawyers in trial and appellate courts, I demonstrate how judges use these strategies to both clarify and challenge lawyers' positions, and to resolve questions relating to those positions prior to making their rulings.

1. Introduction

Although scholars in the fields of sociolinguistics and discourse analysis have written extensively about courtroom questions over the past thirty years, few studies have examined the questions that judges pose to lawyers. Instead, the study of questions in legal discourse has focused on lawyers' questioning of witnesses. This focus is mirrored in the approach of law school texts on trial advocacy and lawyers' practice manuals, which provide foundational knowledge to law students and practical advice to lawyers that is framed primarily in terms of what to say (see, e.g., McElhaney 2005, 1995; Haydock and Sonsteng 2004; Tigar 1999; Mauet 1980; Younger 1976). Even handbooks on appellate practice (e.g., Hornstein 1984), which devote considerable attention to oral argument, including how to deal with questions from the court, rarely discuss the questions themselves in any detail.

However, in a book geared to assisting lawyers to respond effectively to judges' questions, Lavine, a trial court judge, lists five common reasons that judges ask questions of lawyers: to gather information; to test the limits of the lawyer's argument; to elicit the lawyer's opinion; to induce the lawyer to commit to a position; and to demonstrate their own knowledge, proficiency and expertise (Lavine 2004: 10–11). Questions that request information seek specific facts that are relevant to the issue(s) before the court, while those that elicit a lawyer's opinion, probe the contours of the lawyer's argument, or press him or her to commit to a particular position engage the lawyer's advocacy, inviting dialogue and discussion (Lavine 2004: 33–34). Judges' questions thus create an interactional space in which the factual and legal issues of a case can be examined, challenged and debated (cf. Hobbs 2007a: 196).

For example, in this excerpt from an oral argument before a federal appellate court in one of the cases that will be examined here, after the lawyer for the state (Woods) answered a question posed by one member of the appellate panel (Judge 1), another judge (Judge Kozinski) interjected a series of apparently facetious questions:

15   JUDGE 1: Do you agree with Professor Tribe that this is de novo on the
16   law review, or should this be abuse of discretion?
17   WOODS: Your Honor, the law, the law of this circuit, the law of the land
18   is that this is an abuse of discretion (.) review. There – there is not a single –
19   JUDGE KOZINSKI: – Even if we're convinced that the district court got
20   the law wrong?
21   WOODS: There – there is not a si:ngle legal point (.) in the district
22   court's decision that is in dispute.
23   JUDGE KOZINSKI: We – maybe that's right, but that's a different
24   question. That – that's a different question. The question is, do w:e look at
25   whether he got the law right, or do we sort of say, "Close enough"?
26   ((inbreath))
27   WOODS: Your Honor –
28   ((laughter in background))
29   WOODS: No –
30   JUDGE KOZINSKI: We are government workers, –
31   WOODS: --No, Your Honor. This Court – this Court is entitled to look
32   at whether he got the law right. I submit that he did; plaintiffs do not –
33   JUDGE KOZINSKI: He sort of missed it on the Voting Rights Act, right?
34   Just between us.
35   ((raucous laughter in background))
36   JUDGE KOZINSKI: I – I won't tell if you won't tell.
37   ((more laughter))

The topic introduced by Judge 1 is the appropriate "standard of review", the level of legal scrutiny to be applied in determining whether the original ruling was in error. Two competing standards of review were asserted by the parties: the "*de novo*" standard, which grants the appellate court broad power to address the issue presented, and the more deferential "abuse of discretion" standard. In this excerpt, Judge Kozinski's questions are triggered by Woods' emphatic rejection of the *de novo* standard of review proposed by his opponent, "Professor Tribe". Tribe, who is arguing for reversal of the ruling, has reason to endorse the *de novo* standard, and Woods would benefit from the abuse of discretion standard in arguing for its affirmance. Judge Kozinski pointedly alludes to this fact by interrupting him in mid-sentence to ask if the abuse of discretion standard would be applicable "[e]ven if we're convinced that the district court got the law wrong?" (lines 19–20).

Judge Kozinski's remarks signal their humorous intent by their extreme departure from the expected speech register of a federal judge. The marked informality of his speech is strikingly at odds with the imposing setting of the federal courtroom, where black-robed judges sit behind a raised dais flanked by ceremonial flags and an armed federal marshal, while his casual deprecation of the court ("We are government workers") and the situationally-ludicrous suggestion that any portion of the proceedings could be reclassified as private communications create the incongruity that is "an essential and persistent feature of humor" (Mulkay 1988: 35; cf. Fry 1963: 141). Yet Judge Kozinski's questions in this excerpt are not mere humorous asides; they are direct, aggressive challenges to Woods' position: By asking, "do w:e look at whether he got the law right", he implies that the lower court was wrong; and when Woods concedes that it is appropriate to address the correctness of the ruling, he explicitly identifies a legal error: "He sort of missed it on the Voting Rights Act, right?" Through such questions, a judge can stimulate a lawyer's advocacy and sharpen the focus of debate by inviting him or her to refute the judge's formulations, thus assisting in the decision-making process.

This chapter describes four questioning strategies that judges use to engage lawyers in interactive interpretation of the issues presented: taking candidate positions on the facts or law; displaying confidence or doubt in their own interpretations; posing "exam" questions that engage lawyers in Socratic dialogue; and using humor or displays of virtuosity to challenge lawyers' interpretations. Through the analysis of examples of judges' questioning of lawyers in trial and appellate courts, I demonstrate how judges use these strategies to both clarify and challenge lawyers' positions, and to resolve questions relating to those positions prior to making their rulings.

2.   The role of questions in legal settings

Questions play a central role in legal discourse. This is due to the law's requirement that, prior to the entry of judgment, evidence must be presented and the
facts of the case determined. Whether this determination is made by a judge or
jury is dependent upon the legal system involved. There is also variation among
legal systems as to who asks questions of witnesses – the judge, the lawyers, or
both. In the Anglo-American system, the lawyers ask questions of the witnesses,
and the examination takes place before an audience of non-speaking over-
hearers, the judge and jury (Drew 1992: 475; Bülow-Møller 1991: 39–40). In
inquisitorial systems, where the judge asks the questions, the questioner is also
the adjudicator; thus the judge controls both the scope of the testimony and the
weight that it will be accorded. In other legal systems the presiding judge and
prosecutor are both actively involved in the questioning of criminal defendants.

Nevertheless, most studies of courtroom questioning in the fields of sociolinguistics and discourse analysis have focused on lawyers' questioning of witnesses in the context of the Anglo-American adversarial system (see, e.g., Ehrlich 2006; Pascual 2006; Heffer 2005; Matoesian 2005; Cotterill 2004; Hobbs
2003, 2002; Luchjenbroers 1997; Drew 1992, Atkinson and Drew 1979). A far
less extensive body of work has examined the questioning of defendants or witnesses by judges. Thus Chang (2004) examines the questioning practices in
Chinese criminal trials, in which the presiding judge is actively engaged in the
questioning of witnesses, and identifies five strategies that are used to obtain
confessions and expressions of remorse from defendants. Similarly, Komter
(1994) examines the accusations implied in questions posed by judges to Dutch
criminal defendants, which are designed to induce defendants to confess to (at
least some of) the charged offenses.

However, few discourse analytic or sociolinguistic studies have examined
judges' questioning of lawyers (but see Hobbs 2007c). One reason for this may
be that the predominant focus of research on Anglo-American trials acts to concentrate attention on "frontstage" presentations to the jury, while judges' questioning of lawyers occurs primarily outside the jury's presence, at motions, pre-
trial hearings and appellate oral arguments. Yet these proceedings, in which
judges make their legal rulings, are of great importance to the outcomes of
cases. A judge's application of the law to a particular set of facts necessarily involves interpretation; however, the concept of the law as a set of fixed, external
rules implies that some interpretations are correct while others are erroneous.
Accordingly, judicial decision-making is the process of discovering correct interpretations through the operation of reasoning and analysis. This process involves not only the review of the parties' written submissions but the judge's
questioning of the lawyers at hearings. This questioning enacts a process of interactive interpretation through which judges seek to clarify the lawyers' posi-

tions, to challenge their reasoning and analysis, and to resolve any questions regarding their positions, the facts, or the applicable law prior to making their rulings (Hobbs 2007a: 195; Levison 1979: 277). It thus plays an important, though underappreciated, role in shaping the decisions that result.

3.   Data and methodology

This chapter applies the methodology of discourse analysis to the examination of judges' questioning of lawyers during courtroom argument. My data are drawn from three cases: *Lucero v. Donovan, et al.*, United States District Court for the Southern District of California, Central Division; *Wisconsin v. Tran*, Kenosha (Wisconsin) County Circuit Court; and *Southwest Voter Registration Education v. Shelley, et al.*, United States Court of Appeals for the Ninth Circuit. The *Lucero* data are taken from the official transcript of the proceedings; the *Tran* data were transcribed from a videotape accessed via the *CourtTV* website; and the *Southwest Voter Registration* data were transcribed from an audiotape accessed via the Ninth Circuit's website. These data were selected in order to illustrate the effects of differences in setting and judicial attitude on judges' questioning and lawyers' responses, and are representative, although not exhaustive, of the range of questioning styles of American judges in state and federal courts.

In analyzing this material, I draw upon the work of scholars in the fields of sociolinguistics and discourse analysis, and upon my 15 years' experience as a personal injury litigator in the Midwestern United States. During that time, I learned how to talk to judges and to answer their questions, applying techniques acquired by experimentation, observation of other lawyers, and the reading of bar journal articles and practice manuals, including those written by America's most requested speaker on trial advocacy, James W. McElhaney (1995: 284–287), whose pithy and practical advice on talking to judges, as summarized in his paragraph headings, is reproduced here:

"Know Who You Are Talking To"
"Watch the Clock"
"Keep a Civil Tongue"
"Do Not Make Faces"
"Do Not Interrupt the Judge"
"Help the Judge Save Face"
"Know When It Is Over"
"Be Prompt"
"Be Scrupulously Honest"
"Do Not Cave In"
"Confront Injustice"

As the following analysis illustrates, lawyers would do well to heed this advice.

4.   Judges' questioning strategies

In what follows, I examine judges' questioning of lawyers on legal issues at hearings held outside the jury's presence. The purpose of such hearings is to re-solve issues of law prior to trial, or to review on appeal claims that legal error occurred in the course of a trial. Because these hearings are preceded by the fil-ing of the parties' briefs (formal written presentations), which should be suffi-cient to support the submitting party's position without further argument, it is clear that the purpose of hearings is to provide an opportunity for interactive discussion – subject, of course, to the formal rules of courtroom interaction as to topic initiation, turn-taking, etc. Judges have differing attitudes about both the value of such hearings and the manner in which the time allotted should be spent, and may also come to the hearing with differing levels of preparation and differing attitudes towards particular lawyers or cases. All of these factors may influence the types of questions that a judge will ask at a given hearing.

The four question types identified in this chapter are among the most com-mon question types used by American judges. Moreover, given the inherent complexities of legal topics, most or all of these question types may be used in the course of a given hearing, as is demonstrated in the present data.

4.1.   Lucero v. Donovan

The case is a civil action for police misconduct. The plaintiff, Irene Lucero, was in her apartment giving her two young children a bath when her brother, Frank Lucero, entered the apartment accompanied by two police officers. The officers had picked Frank up on the street,[1] questioned him, and asked him if he would consent to a search of his home. Frank allegedly consented and led the officers to his sister's apartment, where a search of the kitchen cupboards yielded a brown plastic bottle containing two pills and a capsule. Following this dis-covery, Irene Lucero was arrested and taken to jail where she was forcibly dis-robed by four police officers, two of whom were male, and underwent a body-cavity search by a female officer. She was released from custody following the search and was never charged with any crime. The suit requested compensation for the embarrassment and humiliation that she sustained as a result of being strip searched in the presence of male officers. Among the contested issues in the case was whether or not the search of the apartment was an illegal search that tainted with illegality everything that resulted from it.

The argument examined here took place prior to jury selection, and concerns the scope of the evidence to be presented at trial. The issue presented by plain-tiff's counsel ("Mr. Chodos" in the transcript) was whether the search of his client's apartment was an illegal search, based on the testimony of the officer who conducted it. Chodos argued that although the officer stated that Frank

Lucero consented to the search, the consent was coerced, and therefore invalid, because Frank was in custody at the time. Following a brief response by defense counsel, the judge requested clarification of Chodos' argument:

32   THE COURT: Yes. Now, I don't understand the point that Mr. Chodos is
33   making. Did you say that based on the deposition of the peace officer
34   involved? Conrad?
35   MR. CHODOS: Yes, your Honor.
36   THE COURT: As a matter of law, that the search was illegal?
37   MR. CHODOS: That's correct.
38   THE COURT: I haven't read his deposition, but from all the contentions
39   here, it appears that there will be some questions of fact that will have to be
40   determined.

Here the prefatory remark, "I don't understand the point that Mr. Chodos is making", allows the judge to request the lawyer to endorse the reformulated version of his argument that the judge presents. Once obtained, the endorsement stakes Chodos to the position that the evidence demonstrates that the search was illegal "as a matter of law", that is, that there is no conflicting evidence that would permit the opposite conclusion. The judge now challenges this position by asserting the candidate position that "it appears there will be some questions of fact" (line 39), which would make the issue an issue for the jury. This signals that Chodos has failed to make his case, and invites him to supplement his argument. However, he merely repeats the points that he has made. The judge then responds with a series of "exam questions" that are based upon information contained in the parties' briefs:

52   THE COURT: Well, doesn't Conrad contend that he had the consent of
53   Lucero?
54   MR. CHODOS: Your Honor, he does contend that Frank Lucero said,
55   "Yes, you may go and search my sister's apartment." Yes, he does contend
56   that.
57   However, he also states that, number one, he picked Lucero up on the
58   street and he was in custody and probably under arrest at the time that the
59   consent was allegedly given.
60   THE COURT: You say as a matter of law that that vitiates the consent?
61   MR. CHODOS: Under the cases that I cited in my brief, your Honor –
62   THE COURT: Well, they cite some on the other side. I haven't read them
63   yet, but they cite them on the other side.
64   MR. CHODOS: Well, I understand that –
65   THE COURT: What case in particular do you rely on?
66   MR. CHODOS: Well, I was relying, your Honor, on the case of People v.

67 Shelton, which is practically four-square. However, as I mentioned –
68   THE COURT: That's on appeal.
69   MR. CHODOS: Yes, that is correct.
70   THE COURT: Has the Supreme Court taken it over?
71   MR. CHODOS: I understand last Tuesday that the Supreme Court granted
72 review in the case. I do not know on what ground, or whether it applies to the
73 aspect of the case which is relevant here. * * *

The judge's initial question, "doesn't Conrad contend he had the consent of
Lucero?" (lines 52–53), points to the discrepancy between this contention and
Chodos' argument that the consent was invalid, implying that this gives rise to a
question of fact. However, Chodos continues to assert both arguments without
addressing the judge's inference. The judge then presses him with the question,
"You say as a matter of law that vitiates consent?" (line 60), which challenges
him to provide authority for his claim. When Chodos responds with a nonspe-
cific reference to the cases cited in his brief (line 61), the judge interrupts him
with the tart observation, "Well, they cite some on the other side" (line 62),
which rebukes him for the vagueness of his answer while acting to inform him
that the judge has read his brief, and that of his opponent. The judge then
tempers his remark by adding, "I haven't read them yet, but they cite them on
the other side" (lines 62–63), which signals that he is still open to persuasion.
However, when the lawyer continues to vacillate, the judge signals that he is
out of time, firing off a series of questions that force him to admit that the legal
decision that he relies on is currently being reviewed by the California Supreme
Court, thus calling the authority on which his position is based into serious question. The judge's rapid-fire questions and rejoinders ("What case in particular
do you rely on?" "That's on appeal." "Has the Supreme Court taken it over?")
reveal his meticulous preparation in a display of virtuosity that orchestrates the
collapse of Chodos' argument, while his initial questions on the issue demonstrate that the lawyer has been given ample opportunity to support his position.

The judge is confident, competent and well prepared, in command of the
case and his courtroom. By his adroit use of candidate positions and exam questions, he efficiently demolishes an argument constructed on shaky grounds, thus
clarifying the issues for trial, while retaining a professional, impersonal style, a
demeanor that is in marked contrast to that of the judge in the following case.

4.2.   Wisconsin v. Tran

This is a criminal case in which the defendant Trang Tran, a 23-year-old University of Wisconsin student, was charged with second-degree reckless homicide in the death of her 21-year-old sister Bao Tran. Following an evening of
drinking and dancing, the two sisters and Trang's boyfriend, Jacob Karras, re-

turned to the off-campus apartment that they shared. While Karras was in the bathroom, Trang, who stated that she was "playing *Charlie's Angels*"[2] with her sister, took Karras' handgun from the drawer in which he kept it, pointed it at her sister and pulled the trigger (Associated Press 2006; Pordum 2006). Trang testified that she did not believe that the gun was loaded, and it was undisputed that she did not intend to cause her sister's death.

An accidental killing is "excusable homicide" according to Wisconsin law; however, acts which, while not intentional, are criminally reckless or negligent do not meet the definition of "accidental". Given the undisputed facts, a key question that arose was whether there was a basis to allow the jury to find that Bao's death was accidental from a technical legal standpoint.

The data examined here are excerpted from a colloquy regarding jury instructions, the purpose of which is to determine the final version of the judge's instructions to the jury. The dispute centers upon the inclusion of the phrase "but rather that what happened was an accident" and, specifically, the meaning of the word "accident" in this context. The leading Wisconsin case on the subject, *Watkins v State*,[3] holds that in order to establish that a killing was accidental, the absence of both an intent to kill and criminal negligence must be proved. It is the latter requirement that is at issue here, since Trang undeniably pointed a gun at her sister and pulled the trigger without checking to see if the gun was loaded. However, the judge does not appear to be familiar with or, alternatively, does not appear to understand, the rule.

5   JUDGE: It – it's in there. Everything is in there. Every word of the
6   accident instruction is there except for the words "but rather that what
7   happened was an accident." Because there's no dispute it was an accident.
8   If it were other than an accident (.) it would be (.) intentional. (0.3) As I
9   sa::y, the para – the civil law (.) says – and I think, not just the civil la:w, but
10   ordinarily – ordinary conversational English (.) is (.) that an accident is
11   something that was neither intended nor expected (.) by the actor. (0.2) Or by
12   anyone else, I guess, but –. Ahhhhm, I mean, Mr. Zaph, do you dispute the
13   s – proposition that what happened in this case was accidental? In terms of
14   the charges you're presenting?
15   ZAPH: Yes. We don't believe it was accidental.
16   JUDGE: ((slaps bench and looks up at the ceiling))(0.3)
17   JUDGE: H – how do you me::an the word "accidental"? I – if I use the
18   definition of accident to mean something (.) other than what is expected (.) or
19   intended (.). I – I – I – where am I goin' wrong here?
20   ZAPH: That's what the defense is claiming – Uhh, you've asked me if
21   I –(.) That's what their defense is. Are you asking if I (.) believe that that's
22   what the evidence is?

These data are unusual for the extent and the openness of the confusion that the judge displays. Throughout the exchange, he makes no attempt to hide his hesitancy and doubt, and the candidate positions that he takes are undisguised attempts to obtain direction and guidance from counsel which, however, is not forthcoming. He begins by defending his decision to exclude the contested phrase, "but rather that what happened was an accident" (lines 6–7), which was requested by defense counsel Valerie Karls, but objected to by the prosecutor, Robert Zaph. He offers the candidate position that the phrase constitutes an unnecessary explanation because "there's no dispute that it was an accident" (line 7) and because not only the law but "ordinary conversational English" defines an accident as "something that was neither intended nor expected (.) by the actor" (lines 9–11). However, his delivery is punctuated by hesitations, pauses and restarts. Moreover, having stated this definition, he appends to it, after a pause, the phrase, "Or by anybody else, I guess" (lines 11–12), thus calling his formulation into question by the use of this markedly unjudicial qualifier.

He then interrupts himself and, after a prolonged "Ahhhhm", poses a specific question to Zaph, "do you dispute. . .that what happened in this case was accidental?" (lines 12–13), attempting to obtain Zaph's concession that the shooting was an accident, as it clearly was in the sense that Trang did not intend to kill her sister. However, Zapf responds with the explicit contradiction, "We don't believe it was accidental" (line 15). The clear implication of his response is that the legal definition of the term makes its use problematic here. This is exactly the issue that the judge is struggling with, and his question was a clear invitation to Zaph to provide a definition that would assist him. Upon Zaph's failure to do so, he slaps the bench in frustration and gazes despairingly at the ceiling. After a pause, he repeats his proffered definition of accident and then dissolves into confusion, stammering, "I – I – I – where am I goin' wrong here?" (lines 17–19). Zaph responds by pointing out that this candidate position aligns with the position of the defense, and then poses the rhetorical question, "Are you asking if I (.) believe that's what the evidence is?" (lines 20–22), a response that is implicitly disdainful of the judge's predicament.

72   JUDGE: I think it would be, uhhh, an acceptable legal statement, and also
73   one that could be made in ordinary discourse, uhhh, by non-lawyers, that they
74   – thee – death of D – Bao Tran was due to an accident. (.) An accidental
75   shooting. (.) But that she (.) was (.) criminally reckless (0.1) that the d – the
76   defendant was criminally reckless (.) in (.) bringing about that accident.(0.2)
77   Where am I going wrong?
78   ZAPH: I don't think that's the state of the law. I can understand the
79   Court's (.) general understanding of the term "accide" –
80   JUDGE: --What am I missing?
81   ZAPH: --in the context, but, in light of *Watkins* I – I – I can't accept the

82 Court's position.
83 (0.5)
84   JUDGE: Well, what do you think?
85 (0.1)
86   KARLS: I think-- ((overlap))
87   JUDGE: On the subject of the language which I have italicized
88   KARLS: I think it should stay in. I used a pattern jury instruction. Uh,
89 didn't do any changes (.), used right out of seven seventy-tw::o, nothing
90 unusual about it, uh, and – I don't think that *Watkins* fits this case very well,
91 because the court made clear that that was, ahh, an application to an
92 intentional cri::me, with self-defense wa::s (.) one of thee, I think, two (.)
93 defenses, so –. (0.1) So I used the pattern jury instruction and (.) we just
94 request that it be (.) given, as such.
95 (0.6)
96   JUDGE: Let's go on to the next issue.

His opening gambits having failed, the judge has now changed tacks, taking the
candidate position that the "accident" language could be included, because an
accident could result from criminal recklessness; however, he admits to his continuing confusion by appending the question, "Where am I going wrong?" (line
77). When Zaph responds with the statement, "I don't think that's the state of
the law" (line 78), the judge's impatience explodes, and he interrupts yet another unhelpful answer to ask, "What am I missing?" (line 80). By this time his
discomfort with the possibility that the law might not allow the jury to be told
that the shooting was accidental is clear, and he essentially entreats the defense
lawyer's assistance (line 84). However, Karls, who has been remarkably silent
throughout the exchange, responds mechanically and does not directly address
the point at issue (lines 88–94). After a slight pause, the judge admits defeat,
and defers ruling on the issue (line 96).

This exchange is striking for both the uncertainty expressed by the judge and
its ultimate failure to resolve the issue addressed. Here the judge's tacit admission of his failure to grasp the applicable legal principles serves to reverse the
ordinary institutional asymmetries between lawyer and judge (cf. Mertz 1998:
154), acting to solidify the lawyers' divergent positions. Thus by positioning
himself as a supplicant who cannot proceed without assistance (cf. Holmes,
Stubbe and Vine 1999: 367), the judge severely limits his ability to obtain the
assistance that he requests.

4.3.   Southwest Voter Registration Education v. Shelley

This case arises out of the ultimately successful effort to recall California Gov-
ernor Gray Davis in 2003. After the recall election had been scheduled, but before

it took place, a lawsuit was filed in federal court on behalf a coalition of voter education and civil rights organizations, alleging that the planned use of "punch-card" voting machines in some (but not all) counties violated the Equal Protection Clause of the Constitution and Section 2 of the federal Voting Rights Act, 42 U.S.C. §1973, because the machines' error rate in tabulating and counting votes was almost twice that of other voting technologies, a fact that had led the California Secretary of State to decertify punch-card machines for use in elections held subsequent to March, 2004. The plaintiffs sought an injunction (order of the court) to delay the election until the punch-card machines could be replaced by the counties still using them. The district court denied the injunction on August 20, 2003. On September 15, 2003, following an expedited appeal, a three-judge panel of the Ninth Circuit Court of Appeals reversed the order of the district court and granted the injunction, ordering that the election be delayed. However, the state requested and was granted a rehearing "en banc" (by the entire court), in which the full court agreed to stay the effect of the ruling in order to reconsider the question of whether the order denying the injunction was erroneous.

A key issue on appeal was whether the plaintiffs had established a strong likelihood that they would succeed in proving that the use of punch-card ballots in some but not all California counties violated Section 2 of the Voting Rights Act, which prohibits the use of voting qualifications or prerequisites to deny or abridge the right to vote on the basis of race or ethnicity. The plaintiffs had alleged that because greater numbers of minority voters reside in counties using punch-card ballots, the machines' error rates prejudiced the rights of minority voters.

These data are taken from an exchange between Assistant Attorney General Douglas J. Woods and Judge Alex Kozinski during oral argument before the federal Ninth Circuit Court of Appeals sitting "en banc". Appellate oral argument differs from the trial-court colloquies examined here in two obvious respects: the lawyers' presentations are sequential (i.e., a specific period is allotted to each side), and there is more than one judge. Accordingly, the exchanges are not between one judge and two or more lawyers, but between one lawyer and one or more members of the appellate panel. Here the argument was convened before the entire court, resulting in a panel of eleven judges. The issue presented was the same issue that was presented to the original three-judge panel: Did the trial judge correctly apply the law or did he commit legal error?

The exchange began with the sequence examined in the introduction to this chapter, in which the judge attacked Woods' position on the applicable standard of review in a series of humorous questions and asides that threatened to derail his argument. Judge Kozinski, who is well known in legal circles for his use of humor in his written opinions (see, e.g. Hobbs 2007b; Editors 1992; Golden 1992), appeared to treat this sequence as a "warm-up exercise" for, immediately upon its completion, he abandoned both the topic and his humorous tone to embark upon a discussion of the substance of the district judge's ruling:

42 JUDGE KOZINSKI: – You think his c – analysis is consistent with *Salt*
43 *River* and *Farakkan*? ((inbreath)) I – I realize he didn't have *Farrakhan*, but
44 he did have *Salt River* (.) and – and, I – I mean, it – th – th – th – th – the
45 evidence seems to be in the record, and the, y'know, the district court didn't
46 resolve the dispute so we have to take ((inbreath)) plaintiffs' case ((inbreath))
47 that (.) there is a greater error rate for punch card ballots th'n for other
48 methods, first. Second of all, that ((inbreath)) counties that u:se punch card
49 ballots are more heavily ((inbreath)) minor – uh, have, uh, greater minority
50 populations than other (.) counties. And, third, there is evidence, as I read the
51 affidavit, ((inbreath)) that, the (.) number of residual votes, the votes rejected
52 by the machines, is greater in minority districts than in – than in other
53 districts. ((inbreath)) Th – those are the facts, more or less, th't the plaintiffs
54 rely on for their – for their Section Two claim. ((inbreath)) Wh::y isn't (.) the
55 district court's analysis, application of the Section Two ((inbreath)) uhh,
56 uhhh, law in this area simply wrong?
57   WOODS: What – what Judge Wilson said (.) w:as that (.) the allegations
58 that plaintiffs make about what has happened in the past that guess as to what
59 may happen in the future might be sufficient to satisfy the liberal pleading
60 standards in the federal court, and to stay in the case. But that's a far
61 different proposition (.) from demonstrating a likelihood of success in a
62 preliminary injunction setting.=

Here the judge asks Woods if he believes that the district judge's reasoning "is
consistent with *Salt River* and *Farakkan*",[4] opinions of the Ninth Circuit that
constitute binding authority on the subject, and that the district judge would thus
be required to follow. Without waiting for Woods to reply, he then delivers a
concise but detailed summary of the relevant issues, punctuated by a series of
inbreaths and restarts which forestall interruption by signaling his continuing
claim to the floor. He completes his performance by stating, "Th – those are the
facts", and then asking, "Wh::y isn't (.) the district court's analysis, application
of Section Two. . .law in this area simply wrong?" (line 52–55). In this excerpt,
Judge Kozinski displays virtuosity by engaging in what appears to be an extended episode of extemporaneous thinking out loud, his breathlessness resulting from the fact that his words cannot keep pace with the rapid forward motion
of his thoughts. Woods responds with a succinct summary of his position (lines
56–61), which appears to satisfy the judge, for he immediately proceeds to another question, now asking what the attorney thinks of an Eighth Circuit opinion
on the subject, *Roberts v. Wamser*:[5]

63   JUDGE KOZINSKI: =What – what do you make of *Roberts v. Wamser*?
64 The St. Louis case that in 1989 hail – held there was a Section Two violation?
65 ((inbreath)) This was twelve years before *Bush v. Gore*? ((inbreath))

66   WOODS: Yeah –
67   JUDGE KOZINSKI: --held that because of the use of punch card ballots
68   ((inbreath)) uh precisely in a situation very c – similar to ours? ((inbreath))
69   WOODS: Y – your Honor, I – I don't rem –
70   JUDGE KOZINSKI:--I realize the Eighth Circuit reversed it on – on
71   --on other grounds, but there was a finding by a district court on the merits.
72   ((inbreath)) Y – you're familiar with the case?
73   WOODS: Yes, I'm familiar with the case –
74   JUDGE KOZINSKI: --it's in the books.
75   WOODS: --and – and, in the circumstances of that case, it may have been
76   sufficient to – to state a claim. But in terms of a preliminary injunction to
77   stop an ongoing or even imminent election, that wasn't at issue in that case.
78   And – and in – in *Wamser* –

The judge begins to describe the case, noting that it was decided twelve years
before *Bush v. Gore*,[6] and that the factual situation of the case as "very c – similar to ours" (line 67), thus framing his initial question, "what do you make of
Roberts v. Wamser?", as requesting the lawyer to commit to a position on
whether that case is in fact similar to the present case. However, it is clear that
he is continuing to think aloud, and that his questions ("Y – you're familiar with
the case?") serve primarily to confirm that Woods is following him. Thus although Woods continues to attempt to press his point that there is a difference
between a claim and the evidence that is needed to prove it (lines 74–77), the
judge again interrupts him:

79   JUDGE KOZINSKI: But – but we have to feel a lot worse abou:t – I
80   mean, we can go to the balancing of the equities, and we can look at a lot of
81   other things, but if we think the district court ((inbreath)) got the law wrong
82   as to Section Two--. But again, I'm – I'm not looking at *Bush v. Gore* right
83   now; I'm looking at the – at the Voting Rights Act. ((inbreath)) That itself is
84   a basis f:or, would be a basis for granting an injunction if the court weighed
85   the equities correctly, the public harm and so on. And if he got the law right.
86   WOODS: Uh, your Honor, e – even if Judge Wilson got – got the law
87   incorrect (.) by – by considering the totality of the circumstances, in the
88   absence of a demonstration of the totality of the circumstances, ((inbreath))
89   even if he got the law incorrect in doing that, the – the public interest is still a
90   required element in consideration of – of A, a preliminary injunction, and –
91   and, B, equitable relief on a Voting Rights Act claim by itself, even
92   outside –

Signaling a shift of focus by his use of the word "But", the judge returns to the
Voting Rights Act and the question of whether the district judge "got the law

right" (line 82–85). Woods responds by arguing that, even if he "got the law incorrect", the public interest would support an order for injunctive relief in the circumstances of the case (line 86–92), thus indexing the legal rule that an appellate court should not reverse the ruling of a trial court where the court reached the right result, albeit for the wrong reason. The exchange is then brought to a close by a question from another member of the panel.

In this excerpt, Judge Kozinski's insistent questioning of Woods is illustrative of the practices of appellate courts, in which oral argument, particularly in important cases or at higher levels of appeal,[7] produces an extremely sophisticated explication of the issues as members of appellate panels press lawyers to confirm or refute the candidate positions that the judges take. Moreover, the questions judges pose at appellate oral argument are addressed not only to the lawyers, for members of appellate panels, through these questions, seek to recruit their colleagues to their point of view. And although this may be frustrating to appellate lawyers who view oral argument as an additional opportunity to persuade the court, it is consistent with the purpose of oral argument, as explained by United States Supreme Court Justice Byron White:

> As for oral argument in our court, it is much more than a ritual extension of due process to the parties. Although we now hear most cases for only one-half hour on a side, oral argument remains an important step in the decision-making process. It is then that all of the Justices are working on the case together, having read the briefs and anticipating that they will have to vote very soon, and attempting to clarify their own thinking and perhaps that of their colleagues. Consequently, we treat lawyers as a resource rather than orators who should be heard out according to their own desires. (White 1982: 383)

5.   Conclusion

In an adversarial legal system where either of two opposing results is always a possibility (Mertz 1998: 158), the lawyers' obligation to painstakingly research and vigorously argue the issues in dispute, and to bring all relevant authority to the court's attention, ensures that the arguments that support each party's position will be fully developed (Hobbs 2007a: 194). Thus Hornstein states:

> The great advantage of oral argument is the opportunity to engage the mind and attention of the court, to be able to determine and to deal directly with those aspects of one's position found troublesome by the court. It is a great advantage to learn whether one's position has been understood, what portions of it need further clarification, what difficulties have not been dealt with adequately and to be able to attempt to cure the deficiencies and resolve the doubts. Yet it is only when the court talks back that this can be effectively undertaken. Thus, oral advocacy at its best is not a monologue by the advocate, but a dialogue with the court's colloquy rather than a soliloquy. (Hornstein 1984: 281–282)

Hornstein's observations serve to emphasize the importance of judges' questions in stimulating this dialogue; and, although he presents the lawyer's point of view, the benefits that he describes are equally applicable to the judge's perspective. Given the structuring of Anglo-American law, judges' questioning of lawyers plays a key role in the decisional process by providing an interactional space in which judges can attempt to both delineate and clarify the considerations that are essential to the adjudication of the issue(s) presented (Levison 1979: 277).

As illustrated in the data examined in this chapter, judges actively seek the input of lawyers, not only in the formulation of the issues and the furnishing of authority, which are properly the province of the lawyer and not the court, but also in formulating the interpretations by which they apply the law to the specific facts and issues that are before them. In so doing, they frequently engage in displays of stance that are calculated to stimulate lawyers' advocacy and thus sharpen the focus of debate. Judges take candidate positions on the facts or law that invite lawyers to refute some aspect of an opponent's argument, or to explain why the court should or should not rule in a certain way. They display confidence or doubt in their own interpretations, thus signaling how the lawyers' arguments should be presented, including the specific points to be argued, their degree of elaboration, and how the issues should be framed.

Judges also engage lawyers in Socratic dialogue by posing "exam questions" that test the lawyer's knowledge, preparation and endurance with their relentless efforts to force the lawyer to clarify or concede a particular point. Such questioning usually involves the judge's own displays of knowledge and expertise, including an intimate familiarity with the facts of the case, and an encyclopedic knowledge of the applicable law, and may at times include a generous dollop of humor, which serves to drive a point home. These displays of virtuosity are most common in appellate settings, but occur in other courts as well, and may index the judge's appreciation of the fact that the stakes and the level of advocacy displayed are high or, alternatively, may be a power play – a form of intimidation. Such displays may also serve to clarify the judge's thoughts or to attempt to persuade other members of the appellate panel.

Discourse analysis can contribute to the understanding of these complex interactions by combining a "thick description" (Geertz 1973) of their discursive processes with a fine-grained analysis – informed by "thick participation" (Sarangi 2007: 573) – of how these practices are deployed by judges to actively produce both the institutional categories in which they are embedded ("motion", "pretrial hearing", "oral argument") and the resulting legal outcomes. It can thus be of benefit to both lay and professional audiences by providing insight into how judges decide cases. It is hoped that this analysis will spur further research on this important subject.

Appendix

Transcription Conventions
(.)	Pause of less than one second
(0.2)	Two-second pause
–	Dash indicates incomplete or cut-off utterance
_____	Underlined word indicates intonational emphasis
::	Mid-word colons indicate a drawn-out syllable
(( ))	Double parentheses enclose a description of speech, etc.
=	Equal signs indicate latching

Notes

1. It appears that Lucero was picked up for "loitering" in an area where drugs were known to be bought and sold.
2. *Charlie's Angels* was a popular American television series aired in the late 1970s depicting the fictional adventures of three attractive and often provocatively-attired young women employed by Charles Townsend, the owner of a private investigation agency bearing his name. Each episode featured an assignment via speakerphone by "Charlie" to the three "angels" which required them to go undercover to perform their investigations.
3. 255 Wis.2d 265; 647 NW2d 244 (2002).
4. *Smith v. Salt River*, 109 F.3d 586 (9th Cir. 1997); *Farakkan v. Washington*, 338 F.3d 1009 (9th Cir. 2003).
5. 883 F.2d 617(8th Cir. 1989).
6. 531 U.S. 98 (2000). The case, as is well known, pivotally involved the use of punch-card voting machines in the 2000 presidential election in Florida.
7. That is, in state supreme courts, federal appellate courts, and the United States Supreme Court.

References

Associated Press
    2006   Kenosha college student guilty in sister's shooting death. *La Cross Tribune*, December 21.
Atkinson, J. Maxwell and Paul Drew
    1979   *Order in Court: The Organisation of Verbal Interaction in Judicial Settings*. London: The Macmillan Press Ltd.
Bülow-Møller, Anne Marie
    1991   Trial evidence: Overt and covert communication in court. *International Journal of Applied Linguistics* 1: 38–60.
Chang, Yanrong
    2004   Courtroom questioning as a culturally situated persuasive genre of talk. *Discourse & Society* 15: 702–722.

Cotterill, Janet
  2004   Collocation, connotation, and courtroom semantics: Lawyers' control of witness testimony through lexical negotiation. *Applied Linguistics* 25(4): 513–537.
Drew, Paul
  1992   Contested evidence in courtroom cross-examination: The case of a trial for rape. In: Paul Drew and John Heritage (eds.), *Talk at Work: Interaction in Institutional Settings*, 470–520. Cambridge: Cambridge University Press.
Editors
  1992   The *Syufy* Rosetta Stone. *Brigham Young University Law Review* 1992: 457–477.
Ehrlich, Susan
  2006   "I think that's not an assumption you ought to make": Challenging presuppositions in inquiry testimony. *Language in Society* 35(5): 655–676.
Fry, William F., Jr.
  1963   *Sweet Madness: A Study of Humor.* Palo Alto, CA: Pacific Books.
Geertz, Clifford
  1973   *The Interpretation of Cultures.* New York: Basic Books.
Golden, David A.
  1992   Humor, the law, and Judge Kozinksi's greatest hits. *Brigham Young Law Review* 1992: 507–548.
Haydock, Roger and John Sonsteng
  2004   *Trial Advocacy Before Judges, Jurors and Arbitrators, 3rd edition.* St. Paul, MN: West Publishing Company.
Heffer, Chris
  2005   *The Language of Jury Trial.* Basingstoke: Palgrave Macmillan.
Hobbs, Pamela
  2002   Tipping the scales of justice: Deconstructing an expert's testimony on cross-examination. *International Journal for the Semiotics of Law* 15(4): 411–424.
Hobbs, Pamela
  2003   "You must say it for him": Reformulating a witness' testimony on cross-examination at trial. *Text* 23(4): 477–511.
Hobbs, Pamela
  2007a   Extraterritoriality and extralegality: The United States Supreme Court and Guantánamo Bay. *Text & Talk* 27(2): 171–200.
Hobbs, Pamela
  2007b   Judges' use of humor as a social corrective. *Journal of Pragmatics* 39(1): 50–68.
Hobbs, Pamela
  2007c   Lawyers' use of humor as persuasion. *Humor: International Journal of Humor Research* 20(2): 123–156.
Holmes, Janet, Maria Stubbe and Bernadette Vine
  1999   Constructing professional identity: "Doing power" in policy units. In: Srikant Sarangi and Celia Roberts (eds.) *Talk, Work and Institutional Order: Discourse in Medical, Mediation and Management Settings*, 351–385. Berlin: Mouton de Gruyter.

Hornstein, Alan D.
    1984   *Appellate Advocacy in a Nutshell.* St. Paul, MN: West Publishing Company.
Komter, Martha
    1994   Accusations and defences in courtroom interaction. *Discourse & Society*
                5(2): 165–187.
Lavine, Douglas S.
    2004   *Questions from the Bench.* Chicago: American Bar Association.
Levison, Gayle Lewis
    1979   The rhetoric of the oral argument in The Regents of the University of Cali-
                fornia v. Bakke. *Western Journal of Speech Communication* 43: 271–277.
Luchjenbroers, June
    1997   "In your own words …": Questions and answers in a Supreme Court trial.
                Journal of Pragmatics 27: 477–503.
Matoesian, Gregory M.
    2005   Nailing down an answer: Participations of power in trial talk. *Discourse
                Studies* 7(6): 733–759.
Mauet, Thomas A.
    1980   *Fundamentals of Trial Techniques.* Boston: Little, Brown & Company.
McElhaney, James W.
    2005   *McElhaney's Trial Notebook, 4th edn.* Chicago: American Bar Association.
McElhaney, James W.
    1995   *McElhaney's Litigation.* Chicago: American Bar Association.
Mertz, Elizabeth
    1998   Linguistic ideology and praxis in U.S. law school classrooms. In: Bambi B.
                Schieffelin, Kathryn A. Woolard and Paul V. Kroskrity (eds.), *Language
                Ideologies: Practice and Theory*, 149–162. New York: Oxford University
                Press.
Mulkay, Michael
    1988   *On Humour: Its Nature and Its Place in Modern Society.* Cambridge: Polity
                Press.
Pascual, Esther
    2006   Questions in legal monologues: Fictive interaction as argumentative strat-
                egy in a murder trial. *Text & Talk* 26: 383–402.
Pordum, Matt
    2006   Jury convicts woman of homicide for fatally shooting her younger sister.
                CourtTVNews, December 20. http:www.courttv.com/trials/tran/122006_
                verdict_ctv.html/. (Last accessed February 28, 2007.)
Sarangi, Srikant
    2007   Editorial. The anatomy of interpretation: Coming to terms with the analyst's
                paradox in professional discourse studies. *Text & Talk* 27(5/6): 567–584.
Tigar, Michael E.
    1999   *Persuasion: The Litigator's Art.* Chicago: American Bar Association.
White, Byron
    1982   The work of the Supreme Court: A nuts and bolts description. *New York
                State Bar Journal* 54: 346–383.
Younger, Irving
    1976   *The Art of Cross-Examination.* Chicago: American Bar Association.

13. Professional discourses in contact: Interpreters in the legal and medical settings

Giuliana Garzone

Abstract

This chapter looks at the discourse associated with the interpreting profession (in particular "dialogue interpreting" or "liaison interpreting"), taking special account of the sociolinguistically oriented strand of enquiry that has taken shape in this specific area in the last few years. The focus is on two major domains considered to be representative of the profession, the healthcare and the legal domain, using case studies as a starting point.

As the interpreter's professional discourse is by definition routinely intertwined with the discourses of those professionals being assisted, the mutual relationship between them in the interpreter-mediated encounter is explored, examining forms of mutual conditioning and the impact of interpreter-mediation on discursive dynamics. The chapter also addresses variation in the interpreter's discursive role in different settings and institutional contexts.

Important insights can be gained from a systematic study of the interpreter's relationship with the professional discourse communities s/he serves, providing a basis for the training of dialogue interpreters.

1. Introduction: Professional discourses in contact

Some types of professional discourse are routinely intertwined with the discourses of other professions, and can only be analysed in combination with them. One such type is that associated with the interpreting profession, and in particular with "dialogue interpreting", which – in Mason's (1999: 147) definition – "includes what is variously referred to in English as Community, Public Service, Liaison, Ad Hoc or Bilateral Interpreting – the defining characteristic being interpreter-mediated communication in spontaneous face-to-face interaction".

This interplay between professional discourses is clearly observable in the following two extracts taken from interpreter-mediated encounters from legal and medical settings, respectively, which will be used as case studies in this chapter. Extract 1 occurs in the early stages of an interview involving an Italian suspect in a Police Station in England (for a discussion of the whole interview cf. Section 2.1 below).

Extract 1. PC = Police Constable; Int = Interpreter

83	*PC*	you were arrested in the early hours of this morning
84	*Int*	lei è stato <u>detenuto</u>* nelle prime ore di stamattina
		you were detained in the early hours of this morning
85	*PC*	for an offence of possession with intent to supply
86	*Int*	<u>in reato di possesso con l'intenzione di fornire</u>*
		in offence of possession with the intention to supply
87	*PC*	before we begin I would like you to tell me your account
88	*Int*	prima di iniziare io vorrei chiedere <u>da lei</u>* di dare la sua versione
		before starting I would like to ask from you to give your version
89	*PC*	of what you did
90	*Int*	di ciò che ha fatto
		of what you did
91	*PC*	last night prior to your arrest
92	*Int*	ieri sera prima di <u>essere detenuto</u>*
		last night before being detained

Extract 2 is the opening of a medical consultation involving an English woman and her seven year old daughter in an Emergency Ward for Tourists in Italy (for an extensive discussion of this consultation cf. §3.1 below).

Extract 2. Doc = Doctor; Int = Interpreter; Moth = Patient's Mother

5	*Doc*	allora ha avuto febbre secrezioni
		so has she had a temperature discharges
6	*Int*	so did she have problems with fever or=
7	*Mot*	=no [pain]
8	*Int*	[discharge↑] in the ear
9	*Mot*	no discharge[pain
10	*Int*	[no
11	*Moth*	= in it
12	*Int*	no ha solo un dolore no [febbre
		No she has only pain no fever↑
13	*Doc*	[solo dolore
		only pain
14	*Int*	non ha avuto secrezioni solo dolore anche esterno
		she has had no dischargess only pain also external

In both cases the outcome of the encounter depends critically on the successful interplay between the two professional discourses in contact – that of the interpreter and that of the Police Constable or the Doctor.

This is a peculiarity of interpreted encounters, making it necessary for any research to give adequate consideration to the mutual relationship between the two professional discourses involved. In particular, forms of mutual orientations and the impact of interpreter-mediation on discursive dynamics need to be explored. A further issue raised by this close relationship is whether the interpreting profession can be said to have its own autonomous form of professional discourse, i.e. whether a construct such as "interpreters' professional discourse" is viable.

A further issue arising from a comparison of the two extracts is that of substantial differences emerging in the interpreters' roles and behaviours in terms of their involvement, communicative performance, and translating technique. In the police setting the succession of turns is more systematic and there is closer textual rendering, while the overall organization of the healthcare interaction is much less orderly. These elements suggest that interpreter's roles vary in different settings and situations. This chapter explores this variation from an essentially data-driven perspective, identifying the critical factors that determine it.

The methodological framework of this study reflects those sociolinguistically oriented discursive approaches that have characterized Interpreting Studies, and in particular dialogue interpreting research (e.g. Wadensjö 1998; Roy 2000; Angelelli 2004; Hale 2007), over the last decade or so. Conversation Analysis and pragmatics research provide additional analytical tools. In particular, the chapter draws upon concepts developed in what Hall, Sarangi and Slembrouck (1999: 296) call "socially-oriented pragmatic research".

2.   Interpreting in the legal setting: The police interview

The label "legal interpreting" embraces a number of communicative events (like investigative procedures at the police station, cross-examinations, courtroom hearings, witnesses' statements, etc.), each characterized by varying degrees of formality and privacy, and involving different participant roles (cf. Berk-Seligson 2000: 214). I focus here on the interpreter-mediated police interview, exploring those traits that are distinctive of interpreting in the legal setting in general.

The police interview is a highly formalised communicative event, which in the UK must be carried out under caution, being subject to the *Police and Criminal Evidence Act 1984* and its *Codes of Practice* (2002). In conformity with the *Codes* (and in particular with *Code E*: 117–129), nowadays all police interviews are audio tape-recorded and subsequently transcribed *verbatim* (Russell 2004: 111–112), a measure aimed at preventing the police officer who drafts the official transcript from "editing" it, as was often the case in the past (cf. Coulthard 2004: 20; Hale 2007: 74).

The legal setting has attracted considerable attention in interpreting research in the last two decades. A number of studies have been published focusing on each of the various sites where legal interpreters operate, or discussing specific issues, e.g. the effects that the interpreter's intervention may have on some aspects of the interview, in particular on the pragmatics of questions (Rigney 1999); on the rendering of the "caution" (Cotterill 2000; Russell 2000); and on the unintended consequences of the employment of untrained interpreters (e.g. Berk-Seligson 2000). There are a few book-length studies, some with a practical or professional focus (e.g. Laster and Taylor 1994; Colin and Morris 1996), others taking a more specifically discursive approach (Berk-Seligson 2002 [1990]; Cotterill 2004; Heydon 2005; Hale 2007; Rock 2007), and all of them featuring a chapter on the interpreter-mediated police interview.

From a discursive perspective, the police interview is subject to very strict constraints. In particular, its initial and final sections – including, respectively, party identification, reminder of entitlement to free legal advice, caution, and the final request of any possible addition to information given, recapitulation of facts ascertained, etc. – are subject to detailed procedural rules, with a determined script allowing no deviation. Specifically overarching the event is the characteristically marked power inequality (e.g. Fairclough 1989: 18–20; Heydon 2005), due not only to the institutional order in which it is set, but heightened by the interaction order applying specifically to it (cf. Sarangi and Roberts 1999: 3–4). For example, the interviewer usually exploits his/her position of power discursively to leave the suspect very little possibility of making his/her version of the facts prevail. In this respect, research has identified recourse to coercive questioning as possibly the main device (e.g. Berk-Seligson 1999; Newbury and Johnson 2006; Harris, this volume). In the case of interpreter-mediated encounters, power inequality is exacerbated by the inherent asymmetry characterizing all cross-linguistic exchanges where the various participants do not have the same command of the language used in communication (cf. Garzone 2002: 249–251).

2.1.   The interpreter's role in the police interview

The interpreter-mediated interview drawn on here, of which Extract 1 above is part, was recorded in a police station in England and concerns the arrest of an Italian young man – with low proficiency in English – charged with possession of controlled drugs with intent to supply.

The discovery of a quantity of pills and hashish on him provides evidence of the offence (*actus reus*). The interview, comprising 405 turns, has the main purpose of proving the suspect's *mens rea*, i.e. his knowing intention to commit the alleged offence, in order to obtain a conviction. Thus, according to a distinction made in the U.S. system, it would qualify as an "interrogation", mainly aimed at collecting supporting evidence or "securing a confession" when a person's guilt is reasonably certain, rather than as an "interview", simply aiming to "gather facts" (Shuy 1998: 8; Berk-Seligson 2000: 233).[1]

The provision of a professional interpreter[2] (in this case, quite unusually, a man) in compliance with *PACE Code C*, in itself a guarantee of fair and equitable conduct of the interview, has the effect of altering the dynamics of the interaction, including the participants, the two main interlocutors – Police Constable and suspect – and a female solicitor.

During the interview, the interpreter's role in the communicative exchange changes over time, with a varying impact on the discursive dynamics. In some phases, he merely provides a "voice-over text" (Pöchhacker 1994: 177), as for instance in the early stages of the interview when the PC states all details concerning the situation and the participant (turns 1–49) or illustrates the charges against the interviewee (cf. Extract 1 in § 1 above). Each single contribution is broken down into chunks – usually incomplete clause segments – for the interpreter to translate, a common practice in institutional contexts where there is great concern for accuracy and exact transposition of details.

It comes as no surprise that a specific study (cf. Perez and Wilson 2007: 84) concluded that experienced police officers identify "conversation flow" as one of the main difficulties in interpreter-mediated interviews. Discourse segmentation also makes it difficult for the interpreter to focus on syntactic cohesion and sequentiality; he even translates the denomination of the offence incorrectly, rendering it literally from English ("*possesso con l'intenzione di fornire*", lit. 'possession with the intent to supply') rather than using the specific term contained in the Italian Criminal Code, "*detenzione e spaccio di sostanze stupefacenti*" (lit. 'detention and pushing of narcotic substances').

These inaccuracies result from the fact that the organization of the conversation in the interview leaves the interpreter no choice of the interpreting technique to adopt. The only possible option for him is the so-called "short consecutive" or "semi-consecutive (cf. Pöchhacker 2004: 18–19) mode of interpreting, which entails a *mot-à-mot* (or word-by-word) transposition, or *transcodage*. Instead, if the interpreter were put in the position of translating complete conversation turns, he would have the option to adopt an "interpretive" approach, i.e. an approach based on the reformulation of the meaning of complete textual units independently of the surface organization of the source text (cf. Seleskovitch and Lederer 1986 [1984]: 105), an approach which usually leads to a more effective translation. In spite of the existence of a prescribed formula indicated in the *PACE Codes*, even the "caution" (or "Miranda warning") is broken down into small phrases. This makes it hard for the interpreter to control cohesion, collocations and grammar patterns across turns, and also contributes to making the caution even more difficult to understand for non-native persons under arrest (cf. Berk-Seligson 2004).

Fortunately, these problems are slightly less disturbing in the central phases of the interview, mainly consisting of short complete questions and answers, as the parties involved tend to stop at the end of each meaningful semantic unit. As we see in the following extract, at this stage the interpreter is directly involved in the questioning sequence, standing in between the two main interlocutors, although never intrusively.

Extract 3. PC = Police Constable; Int = Interpreter; Det = Detainee

147 *PC*   how much money did you have with you sir↑
148 *Int*   lei aveva con sé quanti soldi↑*
          you had with you how much money
149 *Det*   sixty pound
150 *PC*   and where did you get that from
151 *Int*   e da dove* aveva ottenuto questi soldi
          and from where had you obtained this money
152 *Det*   every week we send my father
153 *PC*   your father sent you the money
154 *Int*   suo padre manda questa somma ogni settimana
          his father sends this amount every week
155 *Det*   non questa somma manda diversi soldi
          not this amount he sends some money
156 *Int*   not that amount of money
157 *PC*   where does your father live
158 *Det*   in Rome
159 *PC*   in Rome
[…]
169 *PC*   last night who were you with when you went to the club
170 *Int*   ieri sera lei era con chi* quando è andato al night
          last night you were with whom when you went to the night club
171 *Det*   with nothing
172 *PC*   with nothing or with no one?
173 *Int*   con nessuno
          with no one
174 *Det*   con nessuno sì with no one
          with no one yes with no one
175 *PC*   lovely

Concerning turn-taking, it is interesting that there are no meaningful instances of overlaps or interruptions, a matter which on the contrary has been shown to be a potential problem in interpreted-mediated interviews (cf. Roy 2000; Russell 2004: 118–120). A comparison to the way the turn-taking system works in the medical setting (cf. Section 3.1 below) suggests that in the police interview this orderliness could result from its highly structured and formalized nature, as well as from the recording requirements it is subject to.

The impact of the interpreter's presence on the profoundly unequal power relations characterizing the police interview is also crucial, even in cases – as here – where the PC does not adopt an openly face-threatening stance. His linguistic behaviour does manifest certain attributes – loudness, variation in intonation, absence of hesitation and of vocalized pauses – usually included among those that make the speaker appear more powerful to hearers (cf. Gibbons 2003: 88–89). But it is evident that he takes care to make the detainee feel reasonably at ease, minimising the potential for open confrontation. He avoids coercive or "lead" questions as well as technical language, although at some points he cannot refrain from "copspeak" (Gibbons 2003: 85–87) (e.g. "… *prior* to your arrest", " … where do *these items* come from?", etc.). He also checks regularly that the suspect can understand what is going on, and concludes each sequence with some kind of supportive backchanneling ("OK" or – oddly enough – on seven occasions "lovely": cf. turn 175 in Extract 3 above). The interpreter's rendition reflects this avoidance of aggressiveness by using general words and expressions, which also contribute to mitigating the pressure on the interviewee.

All the questions asked by the PC are *wh*-questions, i.e. questions with a typically informative focus, except for one prosodic question (e.g. a rising-intonation statement) and two yes/no polar questions. One of the latter approximates a lead question, consisting of a cleft sentence with the demonstrative pronoun *that* as a focusing element, obviously aimed at eliciting a positive reply to confirm the hypothesis that the Italian guy regularly sells drugs in the night club where he was arrested (in turn 106: "*is that* a regular place where you go to↑"). The interpreter maintains the original textual organization as far as possible ("*questo* è un posto che lei frequenta regolarmente↑", lit. "is *this* a place you attend regularly↑"). He never aligns with either party, a line of conduct also made possible by the word-by-word translating technique used, enabling him to transpose contributions across languages without having to interpret meaning or make discretionary choices.

The detainee mostly gives his replies in segments, adjusting to the system adopted by the PC, but in complete syntactic units, so the interpreter's rendition is still very close but can be more effective. It is noteworthy that at different times the suspect tries to answer questions directly in English, possibly because of the vexation caused by the inherent indirectness of communication in an interpreted discourse, or out of diffidence towards the interpreter due to his non-alignment. When on two occasions he produces an incorrect or incomprehensible answer in his poor English, the PC either corrects him immediately (cf. turns 152 and 153) or starts an other-initiated other-repair sequence (Schegloff, Sacks and Jefferson 1977: 364–365, cf. turns 171–174). Quite interestingly, on one occasion it is the detainee who rectifies the inaccurate Italian rendition given by the interpreter (turn 155, Extract 3).

An advantage of the *mot-à-mot* approach is that it reduces the cases of zero-rendition (i.e. omission) to a minimum, although there are a few such omissions

at crucial points. For instance, one occurs when the PC uses a *so*-prefaced statement to move on to the next step of the interrogation, summarizing the sequence
of facts that has emerged in the previous stage in order to make the suspect confirm the police's reconstruction, as is made clear by means of a metalinguistic
device – "we can establish":

Extract 4. PC = Police Constable; Int = Interpreter; Det = Detainee
220 *PC*   so we can establish that the gentleman went to the club by himself
221 *Int*   si può stabilire che <u>il gentiluomo</u>* è andato al club da solo
             it can be established that the gentleman went to the nightclub alone
222 *PC*   and that he did have with him
223 *Int*   e che aveva con sé
             and that he had with him
224 *PC*   and knowing that he had with him the
225 *Int*   cioè sapendo che aveva con sé
             that is to say knowing that he had with him
226 *PC*   thirty-three pills on him
227 *Int*   trentatre pillole <u>su di lui</u>*
             thirtythree pills on him
228 *Det* Yea

In omitting to translate the word *so* the interpreter fails to transpose a discursively crucial element (cf. Johnson 2004), an error which is reinforced by the
switch from a first person plural verb form to an impersonal one in the translation of *we can establish* ("si può stabilire", lit. 'it can be established'). Similarly, in the final recapitulation at the end of the interrogation, the omission to
translate another metadiscursive element – "*I believe* that you were there to sell
them" translated as "Ø lei era lì per vendere" (lit. 'you were there to sell': turns
394 and 395) – on the one hand leads to a decreased illocutionary impact of the
PC's assertions, and on the other states in absolute terms what the police officer
formulates as a personal hypothesis.
    In the very final section of the interrogation the disadvantage caused to the
interviewee by his inadequate knowledge of English, in spite of the assistance
of the interpreter, becomes manifest. When the police officer summarizes the
results of the interview, drawing his conclusions which are likely to lead to
incrimination, the suspect does not even try to insist on his version of the facts.
He only repeats "no, no" weakly a few times, and although in legal terms his
position is compromised, the impression is that the discourse dynamics of the
interpreter-mediated encounter in the end prevents him from defending himself
adequately.

2.2.   The impact of interpreter-mediation on discursive dynamics

The analysis of the dynamics of the interaction shows that the interpreter is not perceived as a participant in his own right by the other actors, and in particular by the interviewee. Presumably this is because he does not make any original personal contribution, but mostly limits himself to relaying utterances between the other participants, and refrains from any attempt to facilitate the interaction in any other way. This behaviour complies with the principles laid out in most codes of ethics for the interpreting profession, but is in contrast with the diverging views put forth by many researchers in Interpreting Studies who critique the "invisible conduit" metaphor often used to represent interpreters and assert the interpreter's visibility, agency and non-neutrality (cf., among others, Barsky 1994; Wadensjö 1998; Roy 2000; Bolden 2000; Angelelli 2004).

Concerning the discursive impact of the interpreter's mediation, this seems to alter to some extent the pragmatics of statements and questions – thus confirming findings in the literature (e.g. Rigney 1999; Berk-Seligson 2000) – and leads to an overall effect of attenuation of the coerciveness of the interrogation. This is due not only to the interpreting technique adopted but also to small variations and to occasional inappropriateness in lexical and syntactic choices in Italian. In the overall economy of the interaction these inaccuracies do not have a disruptive effect, as the situational context provides sufficient clues and prosodic elements serve to clarify meaning. Nevertheless, the lack of directness in communication seriously disadvantages the suspect.

Which of the features observed are characteristic of the interpreted-mediated police interview, and which on the contrary apply also to other interpreted professional encounters, will emerge in the next section dealing with medical interviews.

3.   Interpreting in healthcare settings

In spite of its institutional nature, the healthcare setting is generally not as tightly regulated as are judicial and courtroom settings, neither is the role assigned to interpreters, with, however, substantial differences across various medical specializations. As in most countries, in Italy there is no statutory obligation for medical institutions to provide professional interpreting services. The practice of using untrained *ad hoc* interpreters is quite widespread, although subject to heavy criticism (e.g. Cambridge 1999; Valero Garcés and Downing 2007).

In the medical consultation the role of the interpreter is all the more critical as communication between physicians and patients is not problem-free (see among others, Mishler 1984; Ainsworth Vaughn 1998; West and Frankel 1991;

cf. also the general overview in Candlin and Candlin [2003]), an aspect also highlighted in studies by doctors lamenting difficulties when working with the assistance of an interpreter (e.g. Putsch 1985).

Among the issues discussed – parallel to those debated in other areas of community interpreting – is the general question of the interpreter's status within the medical interview as only "a talking head between two main interlocutors" or as an active social agent (cf. e.g. Davidson 2002; Angelelli 2004). The notion that medical interpreters should also act "as cultural brokers, mediators and advocates", in contrast with the impartiality and neutrality prescribed in the profession's code of ethics, has both supporters and detractors (cf. e.g. Meyer et al. 2003; Gentile, Ozolins and Vasilakakos 1996; Roberts 1997: 11–14). In this section, specific attention will be given to the impact of the interpreter's mediation on discursive dynamics.

Medical encounters are goal-oriented, like police interviews, with the difference (already noted by Kaufert and Putsch [1997] in the comparison with the courtroom; cf. also Hale 2007: 41) that in legal interrogations the process is argumentative, as the police constable has a case to argue. In the medical setting, in contrast, the interview has the ultimate purpose, shared by doctor and patient, of reaching a diagnosis and finding therapy. How this purpose is achieved is relatively unimportant, in contrast to the police interview which needs to follow clear rules, subject as it is to recording-and-transcription requirements. This differential weighting of the formal and procedural aspects of the interview in the two types of encounter is a prominent factor conditioning the interpreter's performance in each case.

3.1.   The interpreter's role in the medical interview

The discussion that follows is based on a corpus of medical interviews[3] set in the Accident and Emergency Ward for tourists (*Ambulatorio di Medicina Turistica*) functioning in the Summer months in the hospital of a popular seaside resort in northern Italy, where two onsite interpreters operate.[4] While the general discussion draws upon the whole corpus, more detailed analysis will focus on some significant examples.

As indicated above, in this type of medical interviews the role assigned to the interpreter is not strictly regulated on an institutional level as it is in legal settings. This emerges clearly in the example discussed below, involving a Polish mother and her child who has fever. After examining the little boy, the doctor goes on to produce a tentative diagnosis and prescribes treatment:

Extract 5. Doc = Doctor; Int = Interpreter; Moth = Patient's Mother

64 Doc diciamo che non ci s- non c'è un quadro non ci sono placche le ton-
         sille sono un po' gonfie sì le tonsille sono gonfie ma non
         Let's say that there a- there is no picture there are no plaques the ton-
         sils are a bit swollen yes the tonsils are swollen but not

65 I: (there isn't plaques) in the throat ok↑ is just a little inflamed ok

66 Doc: allora io direi che adesso gli continua a dare l'ibuprofene solo ibupro-
         fene per la temperatura
         then I should say that now she continues to give him ibuprofen only
         ibuprofen for the temperature

67 I: ibuprofen   [for the temperature]

68 D: [solo quello per   ] la temperatura poi se domani
         il bambino quindi oggi cos'è il secondo giorno o il terzo secondo
         only that for the temperature then if tomorrow the kid so what is it
         today the second or the third day

69 I: oggi è il secondo perché è da ieri
         today is the second because it is since yesterday

70 D: ecco quindi aspettiamo tre giorni (.) sc domani va avanti anche do
         mani con
         [l'ibuprofene=

71 I: [mhm

72 D: =se dovesse persistere oltre domani la temperatura gli diamo l'anti-
         biotico
         perché le tonsille sono [infiammate=
         = should the temperature persist after tomorrow we'll give antibiotic
         because the tonsils   [are inflamed

73 I: [hm

74 D: =c'è un po' di infiammazione anche nelle orecchie però (.) al mo-
         mento aspetterei ancora un giorno dopo il terzo giornata se continua
         la febbre gli dà l'antibiotico va bene↑
         there is some inflammation also in the ears but at the moment I should
         still wait a day after the third day if the fever persists you give him the
         antibiotic ok↑

75 I: give him ibuprofen↑=

76 M: =yes=

77 I: =and if the temperature persists after three days probably he needs an
         antibiotic therapy [ok↑]

78 M: [so] now now I shouldn't give him antibiotic now↑

79 I: [no not now

80 D: [not now not

81 M: [not now]

82 I: [not now] you can continue the therapy with ibuprofen

83	M:	yes
84	I:	and then if the temperatures persists after three days=
85	M.	=mhm=
86	I:	=with this therapy=
87	M:	=mhm=
88	I:	=then you have to give him=
89	M:	=mhm
90	I:	antibiotic
91	M:	if he has a te- a high temperature after three days from now

An even superficial look at Extracts 2 (in Section 1 above) and 5 reveals that interactions in healthcare settings tend to be far less orderly than in the interpreter-mediated police interview, with often incomplete utterances and frequent back-channeling. The turn-taking pattern is clearly less regular than in the police station setting where no overlaps at all were recorded. Here 18.87 % of the turns are overlapped in some way, with the interpreter being involved in most of the cases. These overlaps are predominantly collaborative, including confirmatory intrusions and repetitions for approval. Only in about a quarter of the cases do they affect the interpreting procedure, with the interpreter starting her translation as soon as she grasps what the interpretee is saying, without letting him/her finish the utterance, or with the interpretee adding a new statement before the interpreter has completed her translation – a potentially disruptive behaviour (cf. Garzone 2002: 254–255) which however in this case is relatively undisturbing.

Another difference with the orderly progress of the police interview, where the interpreter is in all cases the point of exchange and negotiation of information, is that in some cases in healthcare consultations pieces of information are negotiated between only two of the participants (mainly Interpreter – Doctor or Interpreter – Patient), a tendency which in Extract 5 is particularly marked. For a few turns (68–74) the doctor illustrates the diagnosis and the recommended treatment addressing only the interpreter, and she interacts with him without providing any translation for the mother's benefit until the end of the exchange. This kind of behaviour, not unusual in ordinary three-party conversations (cf. Sacks, Jefferson and Schegloff 1974: 712), may be especially disturbing in medical interviews if it contributes to inducing a sense of exclusion in the patient (or in the patient's relatives). In Extract 5 this is partly attenuated by the fact that it is followed by a sequence of turns where the interaction is exclusively between interpreter and patient, with only one short intervention – quite curiously in English – by the doctor (turn 80).

With regard to the interpreting technique adopted, in medical settings the less rigidly regulated institutional order leaves the interpreter wide scope for discretion. In general, preference is given to an interpretive approach (cf. Section 2.1 above) which involves translating full statements at the end of each complete turn, so that reformulation of meaning is possible. But, as Extracts 2 and 5 show, this is not unproblematic because in medical interviews the natural flow of the interaction is often fragmentary and disorderly: in contrast to police interviews, they are not governed by a formalized "speech-exchange system" (Sacks, Schegloff and Jefferson 1974: 701). This lack of regularity often induces the interpreter to concentrate on the successful progress of the interaction rather than on accuracy of rendition. Sometimes she waits two or more turns before translating, as is the case for turns 68–74 in Extract 5 above, for which a translation is provided in turns 75 and 77, and very concisely, giving only a "summarized rendition" (cf. Wadensjö's 1998: 107–108) which synthesizes the contents of a sequence of two or more short utterances. In the same episode there are also "reduced renditions" which contain "less explicitly expressed information than the preceding original utterance", and, more noticeably, "zero renditions", i.e. total omissions of the translation of some part of the utterance, albeit sometimes important (*ibidem*). In her translation the interpreter talks about an "inflamed throat", while the doctor had specified "inflamed *tonsils*" (turns 64 and 72), and does not include the prevention of ear inflammation (mentioned by the doctor in turn 74) among the reasons why the antibiotic should be given. Although in some cases reductions and omissions may be justified, if perceived by the clients they can undermine their confidence in the interpreter, with a disruptive effect on the professional relationship. This probably happens with the Polish mother in Extract 5: she seeks confirmation of the diagnostic and therapeutic indications repeatedly, checking them with questions and rehearsing them several times until the end of the interview, mostly negotiating clarifications with the interpreter rather than with the doctor.

In the corpus there are several other cases where the interpreter omits translating important information, or reduces it substantially, providing evidence that she perceives selection of relevant information as part of her mandate. This appears particularly problematic when the omitted information is part of the diagnostic and/or therapeutic indications. For instance, in the case of an English woman reporting swollen ankles, when the interpreter translates the doctor's tentative diagnosis she only mentions the possibility that the swelling may be caused by an insect bite, but omits the doctor's suggestion that high blood pressure may play a role. Similarly, for another patient there is a very serious tentative diagnosis of retinal detachment and she is referred urgently to a main hospital, but all the information she receives is that she should see a specialist (without even specifying an ophthalmologist).

There could also be the suspicion that under the time constraints typical of emergency wards the interpreters may occasionally have problems retrieving specific lexical items from memory, or may not even try to do so, a shortcoming which is all the more objectionable for onsite staff. However, Merlini (2007) argues that this kind of gatekeeping behaviour is more likely to be due to the interpreters' desire not to upset patients with potentially alarming technical words, giving them only a vague idea of the diagnosis and treatment prescribed.

This would confirm that in this context the interpreters see their role as going well beyond that of "linguistic experts", as is indicated also by other aspects of their conduct. For instance, they sometimes act as "patient-substitutes", answering the doctor – probably on the basis of information gathered during the admission procedure – instead of translating his questions for the patient to answer. Thus in Extract 5 in turn 69 the interpreter does not relay the doctor's question to the patient's mother (turn 68: *what is it today the second or the third day*), but answers directly (*today is the second because it is since yesterday*). In other episodes the interpreter provides unsolicited information trying to orient the doctor's attention, as in the case of the English patient with swollen ankles when the interpreter suggests that the complaint may be due to excess walking, a hypothesis the patient herself contradicts immediately.

On the whole, these elements suggest that in medical consultations interpreter mediation does not involve the addition of a participant in the interaction as a mere "overhearer" or "animator" (Goffman 1981: 144) who simply duplicates each turn by repeating it in another language, but rather entails a complete restructuring of the overall discursive dynamics, although the interpreter's role varies greatly especially as a function of institutional rules and procedures. Furthermore, utterance reformulation in a different language inherently involves some degree of alteration, to which small and not so small changes introduced by the interpreter are added, thus to some extent compromising the integrity of provider-patient communication, with a more problematic impact in the case of diagnostic statements.

3.2.   The impact of interpreter-mediation on discursive dynamics

In light of the discussion above it is evident that in interactional terms, the interpreter-mediated medical consultation cannot be seen simply as a modified version of same-language interviews. The interpreter's presence by definition deeply alters discourse dynamics with a potentially problematic impact on the way the interaction functions, leading to a number of shortcomings that may to some extent affect the patient's ability to follow satisfactorily a conversation of which in theory s/he is the addressee and the main object at the same time.

These elements are in line with Davidson's (2000: 380, 400) contention that in medical settings resident interpreters tend to see themselves not only as active social agents and participants – a status which has by now been largely recognized – but also as gatekeepers who have to keep the interview "on track". In actual fact, in the episodes included in the corpus it often appears that the interpreters – more than the doctors – feel responsible for the successful communication with patients, while in the police interview this responsibility falls obviously on the police officer himself/herself. It is evident that the interpreters feel part of the hospital community, as is confirmed by their occasional recourse to inclusive *we* when translating the doctors' statements (e.g.: "what *we* can do now is a therapy against the fever", although the doctor's statement in Italian was "*the only thing to do* is give her an anti-fever therapy").

This mutuality results in a strongly collaborative perception of their role, sharply in contrast with the interpreter's non-involved position in the police interview, and leads them to evaluate the quality of their work more in terms of the final outcome of the medical encounters than in terms of the linguistic accuracy and the overall quality of their professional performance. This is confirmed by their rather informal attitude, their occasional interferences in the therapeutic interaction and their gatekeeping action in information transmission. Incidentally, these factors may to some extent compromise the viability of the doctor-patient relationship and trigger a sense of frustration and exclusion in the patient.

As in the police interviews, the medical consultation is characterized by an unequal power relationship between the actors involved, but here a doctor's power essentially stems from the knowledge differential between him and his patient, giving rise to a typical "asymmetry of initiative" (ten Have 1991) between them. This is not comparable, however, to the absolute (discursive) power vested in the police officer within the police interview. Of course, it may happen that a doctor takes advantage of his control of the questioning process (e.g. Frankel 1990), and uses it to exercise power (e.g. Fairclough 1989; Wodak 1997), but in general the consultation has a constructive finality: even when s/he uses leading questions (cf. Hale 1997: 38), by eliciting information, summarising patients' utterances and giving positive feedback, ideally a doctor can build a viable therapeutic relationship giving the patient a sense of inclusion and involvement in the decision-making process and choice of therapy (Cicourel 1999).

4.   Conclusions

The main distinctive trait emerging from the discussion of two different types of interpreter-mediated encounters in public services, representing two extreme examples in the spectrum of possible interpreters' roles and interpreting techniques, is the characteristically "derived" or "secondary" nature of the discourse of the interpreting profession. If translating is re-writing, interpreting is "saying (nearly) the same thing" (Eco 2003). In fact, interpreters' professional discourse is typically a form of metadiscourse, based in each single case on the discourse of the professional community being served.

The analysis has shown that the interpreter's role and position within the professional communicative interaction, far from being constant, varies greatly as a function of the institutional context and the type of encounter. His/her role is sometimes subject to specific conventions or constraints and the professional profile of the interpreter him/herself.

Concerning the discursive dynamics of professional encounters, the impact of interpreter mediation is not negligible, often resulting in less effective communication and occasionally in information loss. In the police interrogation, interpreter mediation occasions an inevitable slowing down of the interviewing process and a fragmentation of the syntactic integrity of linguistic exchanges, varying according to the interpreting technique used. These factors contribute to making questions less coercive for the suspect, but at the same time puts him/her in the position of being less articulate in his/her line of defence. In contrast, in Emergency Ward consultations, the interpreter, being subject to less stringent constraints, has more freedom of action, enabling her to participate more effectively in the interaction. She does not always succeed in refraining from an excessively collaborative attitude, however, going beyond the limits of her role, and sometimes acts as a filter selecting the information to be relayed. This goal-orientedness also occasionally prevents her from giving sufficient attention to accuracy of rendering, above all when technical vocabulary is involved.

The problem of terminological accuracy also emerges in the police interview, indicating that under the time constraints and the pressure of the interpreting process insufficient attention tends to be given to the exact and correct use of specific terminology, although this ought to be a *sine qua non* for professional interpreters if they are to render an adequate service to the professionals they work for.

From the point of view of the "user" of the public service (in the case studies discussed, the detainee or the patient), the interpreter's assistance makes communication possible, but does not always succeed in completely offsetting the linguistic asymmetry inherent in the situation. Sometimes it even contributes to making the original power inequality even worse on account of occasional inaccuracies and omissions.

Of course, by definition, any translation – if only because of typological differences between languages – involves a degree of alteration in utterance meaning at different levels. But some of the problems discussed here could be partly prevented if in interpreter recruiting and training more emphasis was laid on the specific aspects of the discourses of the professional communities where interpreters are called upon to operate. Today this is more frequently achieved in the case of legal interpreters, for which in various countries (as in the U.K.) there are rigorous accreditation procedures, and much less so for other areas of public service interpreting, and especially for medical interpreters, who are often recruited only on the basis of a good grasp of the languages involved and the ability to translate some medical terms (cf. Davidson 2000: 400).

In this respect, applied linguistics can offer useful insights which, if introduced in the interpreter training process, would lead to more appropriate behaviour and greater caution on the part of the interpreter in handling some crucial aspects of communication. Those same insights could lead to an increased awareness by professionals and organizations of the issues involved in interpreter mediation and could contribute to promoting interprofessional collaboration. Interpreters' performance would certainly improve if the other actors took account of the discursive space they need, and behaved accordingly.

These are important challenges for applied linguistics-oriented research, which still has considerable work to do to bring satisfactorily into focus all the peculiarities of the interpreter's role within the professional situations and communicative events where s/he serves, both generally and with specific reference to each single setting. In particular, it would be desirable for researchers engaged in the systematic study of the interpreter's relationship with the professional discourse communities s/he serves to explore critical issues from a problem-driven perspective. This would be a step towards the development of an ecology of professional discourse in the sector of public service interpreting, combining – as advocated in Candlin and Candlin (2003: 146) – disciplinary reflexivity and practical relevance.

Appendix

Transcription conventions

In the Extracts, the text in italics provides the interlinear translation of the previous line; an asterisk indicates that the underlined section of the preceding phrase contains either an incorrect translation or inappropriate use of Italian.

Abbreviations
Int   Interpreter
PC   Police Constable
Det   Detainee
Doc   Doctor
Pt   Patient

Symbols

Symbol	Meaning
(1.5)	Pause timed in 10th's of seconds.
(.)	Micro-pauses of less than 0.2 seconds.
((information))	Relevant contextual information added by the transcriber.
:::::	Lengthening of a sound; the number of colons shows the relative stretch of sound.
CAPITAL LETTERS	Utterance/word enunciated more loudly than surrounding speech.

°word°	Decrease in volume
(word)	Transcriber's guess
↑	Rising intonation.
>words<	Speech delivered at a markedly quicker pace, relative to surrounding talk.
=	Latched speech.
[text in square brackets]	Overlapping speech.
{*sic*}	Linguistic mistake, which the transcriber has checked to be actually present in the original utterance.

Filler		*Meaning*
English	*Italian*	
Umm	umm	Doubt
Mhm	mhm	Expression or request of agreement
Ah	Ah, eh	Emphasis
Eh	eh	Query
Uh	ehm	Staller
Oh	oh	Surprise

Notes

1. In this chapter the word "interrogation" will be used as a hyponym for "interview".
2. Most police forces in the U.K. maintain some kind of register of accredited inter-preters; cf. Colin and Morris (1996: 26–30).
3. The corpus, consisting of 850 turns in all, comprises medical examinations recorded in the course of one month in the Summer of 2004, and was originally collected by Raffaela Merlini through a student interpreter for a dissertation project. For a more de-tailed description cf. Merlini (2007: 435–437); Merlini (forthcoming). I thank Merlini for generously granting me permission to use the corpus.
4. The two onsite interpreters were recruited by the hospital for the tourist season on a five-month contract. Their position included the administrative duties involved in the admission of non-Italian speaking patient ("administrative assistants-interpreters").

References

Ainsworth Vaughn, Nancy
    1998   *Claiming Power in Doctor-Patient Talk.* New York: Oxford University Press.
Angelelli, Claudia
    2004   *Medical Interpreting and Cross Cultural Communication.* Cambridge: Cambridge University Press.
Barsky, Robert
    1994   *Constructing a Productive Other.* Amsterdam/Philadelphia: John Benjamins.

Berk-Seligson, Susan
  1999   The impact of court interpreting on the coerciveness of leading questions. *Forensic Linguistics* 6(1): 1350–1771.
Berk-Seligson, Susan
  2000   Interpreting for the police: Issues in pre-trial phases of the judicial process. *Forensic Linguistics* 7(2): 211–236.
Berk-Seligson, Susan
  2002 [1990]   *The Bilingual Courtroom. Court Interpreters in the Judicial Process.* Chicago: The University of Chicago Press.
Berk-Seligson, Susan
  2004   The Miranda Warnings and linguistic coercion: The role of footing in the interrogation of a Limited-English-Speaking murder Suspect. In: Janet Cotterill (ed.), *Language in the Legal Process*, 127–143. Basingstoke: Palgrave Macmillan.
Bolden, Galina B.
  2000   Toward understanding practices of medical interpreting: Interpreters' involvement in history taking. *Discourse Studies* 2(1): 387–419.
Cambridge, Jan
  1999   Information loss in bilingual medical interviews through untrained interpreters. *The Translator* 5(2): 201–219.
Candlin, Christopher N. and Sally Candlin
  2003   Health care communication: A problematic site for applied linguistics research. *Annual Review of Applied Linguistics* 23: 134–154.
Cicourel, Aaron V.
  1999   The interaction of cognitive and cultural models in health care delivery. In: Srikant Sarangi and Celia Roberts (eds.), *Talk, Work and Institutional Order: Discourse in Medical, Mediation and Management Settings*, 183–224. Berlin / New York: Mouton de Gruyter.
Colin, Joan and Ruth Morris
  1996   *Interpreters and the Legal Process.* Winchester: Waterside Press.
Cotterill, Janet
  2000   Reading the rights: A cautionary tale of comprehension and comprehensibility. *Forensic Linguistics* 7(1): 4–25.
Cotterill, Janet (ed.)
  2004   *Language in the Legal Process.* Basingstoke: Palgrave Macmillan.
Coulthard, Malcolm
  2004   Whose voice is it: Invented and concealed dialogue in written records of verbal evidence produced by the police. In: Janet Cotterill (ed.), *Language in the Legal Process*, 19–34. Basingstoke: Palgrave Macmillan.
Davidson, Brad
  2000   The interpreter as institutional gatekeeper: The social-linguistic role of interpreters in Spanish-English medical discourse. *Journal of Sociolinguistics* 4(3): 379–405.
Davidson, Brad
  2002   A model for the construction of conversational common ground in interpreted discourse. *Journal of Pragmatics* 34: 1273–1300.

Eco, Umberto
  2003   *Dire quasi la stessa cosa. Esperienze di traduzione.* Milano: Bompiani
          (English edition: *Experiences in Translation.* Toronto: University of Toronto
          Press, 2001).
Fairclough, Norman
  1989   *Language and Power.* London: Longman.
Frankel, Richard M.
  1990   Talking in interviews: A dispreference for patient-initiated questions in
          physician-patient encounters. In: George Psathas (ed.), *Interaction Com-
          petence,* 231–262. Washington D.C.: University Press of America.
Garzone, Giuliana
  2002   Conflict in linguistically asymmetric business negotiations: The case of
          interpreter-mediated encounters. In: Maurizio Gotti, Dorothee Heller and
          Marina Dossena (eds.), *Conflict and Negotiation in Specialized Texts,*
          249–271. Bern: Peter Lang.
Gentile, Adolfo, Uldis Ozolins and Mary Vasilakakos
  1996   *Liaison Interpreting: A Handbook.* Melbourne: Melbourne University Press.
Gibbons, John
  2003   *Forensic Linguistics. Introduction to Language in the Justice System.* Ox-
          ford: Blackwell Publishing.
Goffman, Erving
  1981   *Forms of Talk.* Philadelphia: University of Pennsylvania Press.
Hale, Sandra Beatriz
  2007   *Community Interpreting.* Basingstoke: Palgrave Macmillan.
Hall, Christopher, Srikant Sarangi and Stefaan Slembrouck
  1999   The legitimation of the client and the profession: Identities and roles in
          social work discourse. In: Srikant Sarangi and Celia Roberts (eds.), *Talk,
          Work and Institutional Order. Discourse in Medical, Mediation and Man-
          agement Settings,* 293–322. Berlin / New York: Mouton de Gruyter.
Heydon, Georgina
  2005   *The Language of Police Interviewing: A Critical Analysis.* Basingstoke:
          Palgrave Macmillan.
Johnson, Alison
  2004   *So …?* Pragmatic implications of *so*-prefaced questions in formal police in-
          terviews. In: Janet Cotterill, *Language in the Legal Process,* 91–110. Bas-
          ingstoke: Palgrave Maamillan.
Kaufert, Joseph M. and Robert W. Putsch
  1997   Communication through interpreters in health care: ethical dilemmas aris-
          ing from differences in class, culture, language and power. *The Journal of
          Clinical Ethics* 8(1): 71–87.
Laster, Kathy and Veronica Taylor
  1994   *Interpreters and the Legal System.* Sydney: The Federation Press.
Mason, Ian
  1999   Introduction: *The Translator. Special Issue. Dialogue Interpreting* 5(2):
          147–160.
Merlini, Raffaela
  2007   L'interpretazione in ambito medico. Specialità di lessico o di ruolo? In: Diego
          Poli (ed.), *Lessicologia e metalinguaggio,* 433–452. Roma: Il Calamo.

Merlini, Raffaela
    2009   Interpreters in emergency wards: An empirical study of doctor-interpreter-
              -patient interaction. In: Raquel de Pedro, Isabelle Perez and Christine Wil-
              son (eds.), *Breaking down the Barriers in Public Service Interpreting and
              Translating*. Manchester: St. Jerome: 89–114.
Meyer, Bernd, Birgit Apfelbaum, Franz Pöchhacker und Alexandra Bischoff (eds.).
    2003   Analysing interpreted doctor-patient communication from the perspectives
              of Linguistics, Interpreting Studies and Health Sciences. In: Louise Brunette,
              Georges L. Bastin, Isabelle Hemlin and Heather Clarke (eds.), *The Critical
              Link 3. Interpreters in the Community*, 67–79. Amsterdam: John Benjamins.
Mishler, Elliot G.
    1984   *The Discourse of Medicine: Dialectics of Medical Interviews*. Norwood,
              NJ: Ablex.
Newbury, Philip and Alison Johnson
    2006   Suspects' resistance to constraining and coercive questioning strategies in
              the police interview. *The International Journal of Speech, Language and
              the Law* 13(2): 213–240.
Perez, Isabelle and Christine Wilson
    2007   Interpreted-mediated police interviews. Working with a professional team.
              In: Cecilia Wadensjö, Birgitta Englund Dimitrova and Anna-Lena Nilsson,
              (eds.), *The Critical Link 4. Professionalisation of Interpreting in the Com-
              munity*, 79–94. Amsterdam: John Benjamins.
Pöchhacker, Franz
    1994   Simultaneous interpretation: "Cultural transfer" or "voice-overtext"? In:
              Mary Snell Hornby, Franz Pöchhacker and Klaus Kaindl (eds.), *Translation
              Studies: An Interdiscipline*, 169–178. Amsterdam: John Benjamins.
Pöchhacker, Franz
    2004   *Introducing Interpreting Studies*. London: Routledge.
Police and Criminal Evidence Act 1984. Codes of Practice. Revised edition 2002. Lon-
              don: HMSO.
Putsch, Robert
    1985   Cross-cultural communication: The special case of interpreters in health
              care. *Journal of American Medical Association* 254: 3344–3348.
Rigney, Azucena C.
    1999   Questioning in Interpreted Testimony. *Forensic Linguistics* 6(1): 1350–1371.
Roberts, Roda P.
    1997   Overview of community interpreting. In: Silvana E. Carr, Roda Roberts,
              Aideen Dufour and Dini Steyn (eds.), *The Critical Link: Interpreters in the
              Community*, 7–26. Amsterdam: John Benjamins.
Rock, Frances
    2007   *Communicating Rights: the Language of Arrest and Detention*. Basing-
              stoke: Palgrave Macmillan.
Roy, Cynthia
    2000   *Interpreting as a Discourse Process*. Oxford: Oxford University Press.
Russell, Sonia
    2000   Let me put it simply …: The case for a standard translation of the police
              caution and its explanation. *Forensic Linguistics* 7(1): 26–48.

Russell, Sonia
    2004   "Three is a crowd": Shifting dynamics in the interpreted interview. In: Janet
            Cotterill (ed.), Language in the Legal Process, 111–126. Basingstoke: Pal-
            grave Macmillan.
Sacks, Harvey, Emanuel A. Schegloff and Gail Jefferson
    1974   A simplest systematics for the organization of turn-taking in conversation.
            Language 50(4): 696–735.
Sarangi, Srikant and Celia Roberts
    1999   The dynamics of interactional and institutional orders in work-related set-
            tings. In: Srikant Sarangi and Celia Roberts (eds.), *Talk, Work and Institu-
            tional Order: Discourse in medical, Mediation and Management Settings*,
            1–57. Berlin / New York: Mouton de Gruyter.
Schegloff, Emanuel A., Harvey Sacks and Gail Jefferson
    1977   The Preference for self-correction in the organization of repair in conver-
            sation. *Language* 53(2): 361–382.
Seleskovitch, Danuta and Marianne Lederer
    1986 [1984]   *Interpréter pour traduir.* Paris: Didier erudition.
Shuy, Roger
    1998   *The Language of Confession, Interrogation and Deception.* Thousand
            Oaks, CA: Sage.
ten Have, Paul
    1991   Talk and institution: A reconsideration of the asymmetry of doctor-patient
            interaction. In: Deirdre Boden and Don H. Zimmerman (eds.), *Talk and So-
            cial Structure*, 138–163. Cambridge: Polity Press.
Valero Garcés, Carmen and Downing, Bruce
    2007   Modes of communication between suppliers of services and non-native
            English-speaking users: Doctor-patient interaction. In: Giuliana Garzone
            and Cornelia Ilie (eds.), *The Use of English in Institutional and Business
            Settings: An Intercultural Perspective,* 313–330. Bern: Peter Lang.
Wadensjö, Cecilia
    1998   *Interpreting as Interaction.* London: Longman.
West, Candace and Frankel, Richard M.
    1991   Miscommunication in medicine. In: Nikolas Coupland, Howard Giles
            and John M. Wiemann (eds.), *"Miscommunication" and Problematic Talk*,
            166–94. Newbury Park, CA: Sage.
Wodak, Ruth
    1997   Critical discourse analysis and the study of doctor-patient interaction. In:
            Britt-Louise Gunnarsson, Per Linell and Bengt Norberg (eds.), *The Con-
            struction of Professional Discourse*, 173–200. London: Longman.

14. Enabling bids: Occupational practice and "multi-modal" interaction in auctions of fine art and antiques*

Christian Heath and Paul Luff

Abstract

In this chapter, we consider how social interaction is central to the performance of highly specialised activities that underpin occupational and organisational culture. We examine an occupation where a turn-taking organisation is deployed to systematically specify and allocate the contributions of others. We draw primarily on audio-visual recordings of auctions of art, antiques and objet d'art to reveal how the accomplishment of an auctioneer's activities is not only dependent upon talk, but also on visible conduct – body orientation, gestures and the like – and the use of various material artefacts. In particular we consider how an interactional organisation is deployed that enables the price of goods to be systematically escalated until they are sold to the highest bidder; how auctioneers elicit a first, and then a second bid, and thereby establish an order of action that serves to transparently distribute opportunities to particular participants at successive stages of the proceedings. We further suggest that the interactional organisation of the auction not only enables an extraordinary economy of behaviour, allowing the most simple of visible actions to significantly advance the price of the goods, but also serves to legitimise the valuation and exchange of goods worth in some cases many millions of pounds.

1. Introduction

A: Lot <u>Forty</u> <u>Fi</u>:ve:: the Ludovico Carra<u>cci</u> (5.5) Five hundred and fifty thou-
    sand pounds (.) to open it
    (0.8) [Bid] Six hundred thousand pounds, I see already. (0.4) At six h<u>und</u>red
    <u>thous</u>and p<u>ound</u>s::
    (0.3) [Bid] Six hundred and fifty thousand
    .
    .
A: Last chance (0.6) Anywhere (0.5) at six million (0.2) six hundred (0.2) thou-
    sand pounds (0.3) {knock} <u>Sol</u>:d
    [*Applause*]

Lot 45 was one of sixty seven lots sold at the evening sale of Old Master Pictures at Christie's in 2007. Widely considered the star lot of the sale there was significant interest in the painting before the auction and an adjoining room was opened to allow a hundred people or so to attend the sale and arrangements were made for more than twenty sales staff to man the telephones. At the sale, the painting generated intense competition and after only a couple of minutes sold at more than ten times its starting value, setting a record price for a Ludovico Carracci.

The auctioneer knew there was interest in the picture but had little idea what people might be willing to pay, or even with any certainty who was planning to bid. As with any other lot, the auctioneer needs to encourage people to bid and coordinate those contributions, whether they are from buyers in the room, over the telephone or now increasingly through the Internet. He has to provide an orderly, ascending sequence of bids that progressively and transparently escalates the value of the goods until the highest possible price, for all practical purposes, is achieved. To maximise price, the auctioneer must establish, and in some cases encourage, competition between potential buyers and on occasions enable the price to be successfully escalated well in excess of expectations. At its most basic, the auctioneer, in cooperation with bidders, has to implement an organisational arrangement whereby the potential contributions of multiple participants, many of whom might wish to bid if the price is right, are organised through an orderly sequence of turns, where those turns, to corrupt Sacks, Schegloff and Jefferson (1973), are "valued", literally in this case.

In this chapter, we would like to address the ways in which auctioneers of fine art and antiques, deploy an organisation that enables the price of goods to be systematically escalated until they are sold to the highest bidder. In particular, we examine how auctioneers elicit a first, and then a second bid, and thereby establish an order of action that serves to transparently distribute opportunities to particular participants at successive stages of the proceedings. Underpinning this arrangement is an organisation that specifies the action undertaken by bidders and provides alternating opportunities for the production of bids until only one buyer remains. In other words, we are concerned with revealing an occupational practice that entails the deployment of a turn-taking system that economically and efficiently enables the transfer of the ownership of goods to the highest bidder.

It has long been recognised that social interaction is central to the performance of highly specialised activities and underpins occupational and organisational cultures. In this regard, the ethnographic studies, emerging in part through the initiatives of Hughes (1958), have had an important influence on our understanding of occupations and the interactional foundation of the practice and procedure, the tacit knowledge and skills that inform the performance and organisation of work. With the growing interest in discourse and talk, we have witnessed the emergence of a burgeoning corpus of studies of work and organisational environments; a corpus of studies that unlike the more conventional ethnographic tradition places social interaction at the heart of the analytic agenda and examines in fine detail the ways in which occupational and work-place activities are accomplished in and through talk. Conversation analysis, in particular, has made a profound contribution to our understanding of the ways in which talk, and its sequential and interactional organisation, forms the foundation to and enables the production of range of highly specialised activities and events.

In this regard, the turn-taking organisation of talk has proved particularly significant and a range of studies have powerfully demonstrated how occupational and professional activities rely upon, and are accomplished through, special or particular turn-taking organisations. These include, for example, studies of courtrooms (Atkinson and Drew 1979), health care and medical consultations (Frankel 1990; Perakyla 1995; Silverman 1997; Heritage and Maynard 2006) and news interviews (Greatbatch 1988; Clayman and Heritage 2002). In this regard, auctions and auctioneering raise one or two interesting issues. First and foremost, unlike other occupations, the role of the auctioneer is primarily concerned with deploying a turn-taking organisation that systematically distributes the opportunities to bid amongst potential buyers. It should be noted, that in many cases, especially in the field of fine arts and antiques, auctioneers are themselves highly specialised experts in particular fields whether this is in ceramics, contemporary art or early vernacular furniture. Nevertheless, in an auction, the principal aim of auctioneers is to organise the interaction of others so that the price can be escalated and the goods sold. Moreover, many of the actions that form an important element of the auction, including almost all the contributions of buyers and potential buyers, namely bids, are not accomplished though talk but rather nonverbal or visible conduct. Indeed, visible conduct not only informs the production of "turns" by bidders, but is a critical aspect of the ways in which auctioneers allocate turns, opportunities to bid, to particular participants. In addressing auctioneering and the organisation of auctions, therefore, we need to consider the characteristics of an interactional arrangement that involves the interdependence of talk and visible conduct and the deployment of a particular turn-taking system that is primarily concerned with specifying and allocating the contributions of others.

There is a substantial corpus of research within economics and econometrics concerned with auctions and auction mechanisms and it is argued that the significance of this research reflects the "importance of auctions to many of the world's most significant markets and the ways in which auction theory bears upon various areas of economics" (see, for example, Klemperer 2004; Menzes and Monteiro 2005; Krishna 2002). In economics it is recognised that different auction mechanisms can produce significantly different outcomes and yet, within the framework of particular models, the contingent accomplishment of the auction and the social and interactional arrangement on which it relies remains disregarded, or at least epiphenomenal. As Geismar (2004) suggests, despite their academic and social significance there is a "dearth of sociological writing about auctions" and yet it is clear that highly sophisticated economic models of auctions and auction mechanisms rely upon the routine deployment, by auctioneers, of a largely un-explicated body of practice and procedure that successfully organises the interaction of participants, whoever they might be, and whatever interests they may have in the goods in question.

There are however, a number of important exceptions (see, for example, Cassady 1967; Boeck 1990) and it is worthwhile mentioning two in particular. Smith's (1990, and also see 1991, 1993) wide ranging ethnography of auctions, whilst not concerned with auctioneering or interaction at auctions *per se*, demonstrates how auction mechanisms and price construction derive from, and arise through, social processes that are concerned with establishing the legitimacy of valuation and exchange. Smith considers the ways in which a range of practices, procedures, organisational arrangements and the like serve to establish and sustain trust in auctions and their ability to determine the price of goods and enable exchange; "the communities faith in and the fairness of the process". In rather a different vein, the work of Kuiper (1992, 1995) and Kuiper and Haggo (1984) examines proto-English auction speech and the word patterns and discourse rules that underpin the performance of auctioneers in different settings. This includes, for instance, analysis of the "chant", a characteristic feature of the talk of auctioneers that involves the rapid repetition of particular words or phrases, and is seen as a consequence of the "processing pressures on the speaker"; a way of coping with "cognitive complexity". In very different ways, these studies provide important insights into auctions and auctioneering and raise a number of issues that are central to understanding how auctions efficiently establish the price and enable the exchange of goods. They include, for example, matters of order and how auctioneers identify and juxtapose bids, questions of trust and legitimacy and how auctioneers preserve neutrality, and the significance of performance and curious characteristics of the auctioneer's talk – largely the only speaker at auctions. We believe that the answer to some of these questions and more generally understanding the characteristics of auctions and auctioneering can be found by taking the interaction seriously and considering the ways in which the accomplishment of the various activities is dependent upon the interplay of talk, visible conduct and the use of various material artefacts.

The data on which this paper is based consist of audio-visual recordings of auctions of art, antiques and objet d'art augmented by fieldwork and discussions as well as interviews with auctioneers, sales room staff and buyers. In many cases recording involved using three cameras, one primarily focused on the auctioneer, the other two encompassing potential buyers in the room and sales assistants manning the telephones. The data were gathered at a range of auction houses, in the UK, elsewhere in Europe, and North America, including those that specialise in sales of art and antiques, as well as provincial rooms that hold a fine art sale every few months. All of these auction houses use the Roman or English model of auction characterised by an ascending sequence of bids until the goods are sold to the highest bidder (see for example Learmount 1985; Cassady 1967). The fall of the hammer on the rostrum, the "knock", marks the moment, and the price at which, the object is sold to a particular bidder. The auction house receives ordinarily between 12 and 20 percent of the selling price from the purchaser and between 12 and 25 percent of the selling price from the vendor. It is in the auctioneer's interest therefore, that goods reach their reserve, the minimal price at which they can be sold, and achieve a good price.

2.   Securing an initial bid

Sales of fine art and antiques may include up to eight hundred lots that, in some cases, are sold in one day. The sale of each lot typically takes little more than thirty seconds, but within that time, the price may rise more than five times the starting value. The auctioneer has to rapidly encourage and secure bids from interested parties and yet, it is not unusual to find that potential buyers are reluctant to bid at first – waiting to see how things develop before literally showing their hand. The auctioneer has to encourage people to bid and to bid with dispatch and to establish competition between interested parties so that the price of the goods may be escalated to the point at which they can be sold.

Consider the following fragment. It involves the sale of a Crown Derby dinner service with a catalogue estimate of 80 to 120 pounds. For convenience, we simply represent bidding by [B bids] numbering particulars bidders [B.1. bids] in the order in which they first join the bidding.

Fragment 1
A: Quantity of Royal Crown Derby, Lot Four Five Six. Bid a hundred pounds?
       (0.6) Eighty? (1.0) Fifty to start me off if you want this lot.
B1:   Forty
A: Forty bid, forty, got forty pound.
       [B.2 bids]
A: Forty five
       [B.1 bids]
A: Fifty
       (0.4) [B.2 bids]
A: Five:
       (0.5) [B.1 bids]
A: Sixty

Following a brief description of the goods and the lot number, the auctioneer attempts to initiate the bidding, inviting bids at one hundred pounds. He simultaneously turns from the right to the left hand side of the assembled audience looking to see whether anyone is prepared, or preparing, to bid. Receiving no response, he tries eighty, then fifty, and finally secures a bid at forty pounds. The de-escalation of the price to a figure significantly below the anticipated value of the object serves to encourage a potential buyer to bid. On receiving the first bid, the auctioneer announces the figure and then repeats the bid. As he produces "forty bid, forty, got forty pound" he turns and looks at people gathered in different areas of the room, turning from his right to his left. As the auctioneer orients towards the left of the room, a hand is raised and the auctioneer announces "forty five". Irrespective of the price that the potential buyer may have in mind, in receiving the second bid, the auctioneer specifies the bid that has been made. A price of forty-five is announced and at that moment the bidder discovers the price he has bid.

Having secured one bidder the auctioneer secures a second. He then juxtaposes their successive bids and rapidly escalates the price of the goods until one of the two bidders withdraws. The announcement of the second bid by the auctioneer establishes an incremental structure, each bid advancing the price by five pounds. The incremental structure remains stable and the dinner service is sold to the highest, the remaining, bidder, at two hundred and forty pounds, more than five times its starting price.

Each turn at bidding is specified by the auctioneer and allocated to a particular participant. Save for the first bid, where the amount is volunteered by one of those gathered in the sales room, the auctioneer specifies the amount that each participant bids. The incremental structure projects, as least for a series of prices, what constitutes the value of each bid. In this way, participants bid with some certainty against the current value anticipating that the increment is likely to remain the same. At any point during the proceedings, potential buyers, and all those in the room, know what it will take to bid and advance the price of the object. The incremental structure provides a vehicle through which the auctioneer transparently and rapidly escalates the value of the goods despite (unknown) variations in the price that people may be willing to pay.

It will be noticed that in Fragment 1, the serial escalation of price does not involve numerous bidders, but rather the successive contributions of two participants. In receiving a first bid, the auctioneer identifies a second potential buyer, takes a bid at the projected next increment, and then turns to the original bidder and invites a next bid. Fragment 1 involves three exchanges in which the bids of two potential buyers are juxtaposed and the price escalated until the dinner service is sold. The escalation of price at auctions of fine art and antiques is based upon what is known as a "run". The auctioneer establishes, or seeks to establish, *two bidders and no more than two bidders at any one time*. The prin-

ciple is applied irrespective of the value of the object or the scale of the increments that escalate the price, whether they are five pounds, five thousand, or
five hundred thousand. With stable incremental scales, the run forms a corner-
stone of the turn-taking organisation through which auctions are accomplished
in an orderly manner.

Establishing two bidders and no more than two bidders at any one time, provides the auctioneer with a way of establishing direct competition between two
principal protagonists. It also provides a resource for disregarding the potential
or actual contributions of others that, if acknowledged, would disrupt the flow
and rapid escalation of the price. The participation of further bidders is post-
poned until one bidder withdraws. At that place, the auctioneer undertakes a
search to identify a new bidder to replace the participant who has withdrawn.
When the auctioneer fails to find a new bidder then the goods are sold, that is, if
they have reached the reserve – the lowest price that the vendor is prepared to
accept for the goods in question. The transition of bidders at auction therefore is
localised to places in the run where one bidder withdraws and the auctioneer
identifies and accepts a bid from a new potential buyer.

Fragment 1 suggests one or two of the difficulties that arise in establishing
bidding. As a way of tempting potential buyers to bid, the auctioneer has to reduce the starting price of the lot to well below its expected value before a willing participant is prepared to bid. Starting an auction in this way can unduly extend the time it takes to sell lots and the length of the overall sale. Secondly, it is
not that unusual for auctioneers to receive no bids at all for particular lots, or to
only receive bids well below the reserve, despite having reduced the price well
below expectations. The absence of bids or weak bidding can depress competition for the lot in question (and other lots in the sale) and undermine negotiations that might take place after the auction, if the goods fail to sell, with potential buyers.

Aside from the potential buyers in the room, those on the telephone represented by sales assistants, and increasingly, those on the Internet, there are two
other sources of bids at auctions. Buyers who are unable to attend the auction
leave commission bids with the auction house, the maximum price that they
willing to pay for a particular lot. The commission bids are listed alongside the
lot number in the sales sheets or the "book" that is usually placed the podium
and accessible only to the auctioneer. A second source of "absentee" bids are
those placed by the auctioneer on behalf of the vendor. It is not necessarily well
known, at least outside the trade, that auctioneers and the auction houses assume
the right, to bid on behalf of the vendor up until one increment below the reserve, the minimum price at which vendor has specified that the goods may be
sold. Many of the leading international auction houses detail this convention in
the rear of their sale catalogues and in United States it is formally announced at
the start of the auction.

Commission bids and bids on behalf of the vendor provide an important resource in auctions. They enable the auctioneer to initiate bidding for a particular
lot, even create an impression of interest and competition, whilst only having
to find one active bidder say in the room and in some cases, where there is no
bidder at all.

In the following example commission bids are represented by "[A. bids]"
that is the auctioneer bids on behalf of the absentee buyer.

Fragment 2

A: Lot Thir:ty Nine: (.) is the, Batoni portrait (1.4) Showing here (0.3) And
    I have interest here with my commission bids (0.2) of eighty thousand
    pounds, [A. bids] to open it. (.) >At eighty thousand pounds commission bid
    against the room. (0.2) At eighty thousand pounds (.) now (0.2) At eighty
    thousand pounds
    [B.1 bids]
A: Eighty five thousand
A: [A. bids] Ninety thousand with me. At ninety thousand pounds. (0.4) At ni-
    nety thousand pounds
    (1.0) [B.2 bids]
A: Ninety five thousand
    [A. bids]
A: One hundred thousand
    [B.2]
A: One hundred and ten thousand
    [A. bids]
A: One hundred and twenty thousand.
    [B.2]
A: One hundred and thirty thousand.

The auctioneer initiates bidding by announcing a bid off commission. He then
invites contributions from the room rapidly repeating the current increment, as
if beginning a chant, whilst looking for someone willing to bid. Turning towards
the left hand side of the room he announces a bid of eighty five thousand. The
auctioneer immediately takes a second bid from commission and once again
looks for a contribution in the room. B.2 raises his hand and the auctioneer announces the increment, namely ninety five thousand. The auctioneer establishes
a run between the buyer in the room and the absentee bidder, the commission,
until the painting is sold for two hundred and twenty thousand pounds to B.2.

By decomposing the commission, the maximum price left by the absentee
buyer, the auctioneer is able to create a series bids, turns within this particular
turn-taking organisation, that enable him to rapidly escalate the price of the
good in juxtaposition with contributions from a willing participant in the room.

Eighty five thousand   Ninety thousand with me   Ninety five thousand

Fragment 2. Figure 1.

Initiating bidding with the commission at a relatively low, some hundred thousand pounds less than the price left on commission, enables the auctioneer to not only create a sense of "spirited bidding", rapidly escalating the price of the painting so that it can reach its reserve and be sold, but also to play fair, and be seen to play fair, for the absentee buyer, that is for example, not using the ceiling price of the commission to start the proceedings. Moreover, in taking successive bids from commission, the auctioneer goes to some trouble to display the 'turn' is with him, as the representative of the absentee bidder, rather than simply created or taken from the reserve to rapidly escalate the cost of the painting for the buyer in the room. In creating and sustaining the run the auctioneer displays the source of bid and thereby establishes, or seeks to establish, the integrity of each successive contribution.

In principle, the minimal requirement to enable the price to be escalated at auction is for two potential buyers to be willing to bid and compete for the goods in question. Auctioneers have to systematically and transparently juxtapose the contributions of potential buyers to achieve the reserve, establish a price and enable the exchange of goods. In this regard decomposing a commission into a series of bids is an important resource in establishing bidding and escalating the price. It provides the auctioneer with the opportunity to juxtapose bids and establish competition in circumstances where there is only one willing participant in the room. Moreover, given the reticence of potential buyers to bid before they have a sense of who else might be interested and what they may be willing to pay, only having to find one active bidder in the room (be the buyer present, represented by a sales assistant, or connected via the Internet) can simplify the initiation of bidding for the auctioneer. It may also be the case that the very revelation of interest in the goods, a potential buyer, who at least is willing to bid, if only through the auctioneer, may serve to encourage others to show their hand.

In this regard, it is worth mentioning that it is not uncommon to find auctioneers beginning the sale of a lot by announcing a rapid series of bids, ordinarily three but in some five or seven, and thereby increasing the price of the goods by the relevant number of increments. The announcement is routinely preceded by an invitation for anyone to bid, and in receiving no response the series of bids are called out. It is only following these "preliminary" bids that the auctioneer will attempt to more extensively pursue a bid from the room. It is believed, and there is some evidence to suggest, that these rapid preliminary "runs" encourage, and facilitate bids in the room, not only providing an immediate sense of interest in, and competition for, the goods in question, but providing an opportunity during the announcement of the bids for the auctioneer to see if anyone is preparing or willing to bid. The bids are taken against a commission(s) or in some cases against the reserve and are produced and displayed as if they are actual bids that are ordered with regard to the turn-by-turn organisation that informs sales by auction. Whilst such practices are legitimate and formally declared, one can begin to see what those new to auctions may fear being 'run up' by the auctioneer, that is that the auctioneer may be taking bids "off the wall" or "from the chandelier" to create competition, and a sense of competition, to encourage people to bid and to bid with dispatch.

The integrity of bids, that they are actual bids on behalf of potential buyers, is critical to the ability of auctions to determine the value of goods and enable their exchange. Indeed, as Smith (1990) and others suggest, issues of trust and fairness pervade auctions and underpin their ability to establish price and value and the legitimate exchange of goods. In this regard we can see that an incremental structure coupled with turn allocation arrangements creates successive competition between two bidders and no more than two bidders, at any time, and can serve to contribute to the transparent escalation of price. Moreover, in announcing bids, auctioneers go to some trouble to display the source of those bids, not simply to the active participants but all those within the room. For example, an invitation to bid and its announcement is often accompanied by a bodily orientation – sometimes a gesture – that is directed towards the bidder and reveals his or her location within the sales room. The entry of new bidders is often accompanied by explicit reference to their location, and in the case of sales room assistants, their first names. Even in taking bids from commission, auctioneers frequently point to the sales sheets or themselves when announcing the bids, and in some cases go to some trouble to reveal the independence of the bid, that represents at absentee buyer.

In deploying an interactional arrangement to order bidding and escalate price, auctioneers also differentiate the sources of bids. All things being equal, the auctioneer will begin by taking bids from commission (in some cases the reserve) and juxtaposing those bids with potential buyers in the room, prior to seeking interest from the sales assistants, or finally the internet. Various reasons are put forward for this ordering procedure, and certainly it does enable auctioneers to steer a relatively clear path on occasions where there may be some eagerness to bid from a variety of sources. One issue should however be mentioned in particular. In taking bids from commission or even the reserve at the beginning of the sale of each lot, the auctioneer can be seen to expose right from the outset, contributions from absent parties and thus avoid the suspicion that might arise if he were to proffer a bid on behalf of a commission buyer (or even against the reserve) at seemingly convenient moments during the proceedings. The ordering, selection and attribution of bids to particular sources renders visible – witnessable – a process that might otherwise be called into question.

3.   An alternating sequential organisation

The organisation of "first" bids, that is "first" bids by a particular participant, differs from the organisation that informs the production of subsequent bids, second, third or nth bids within runs. A first bid is produced with regard to a generalised invitation to bid by the auctioneer. The auctioneer seeks a bid by virtue of announcing and, in some cases, repeating a figure, and undertaking a search to find a participant willing to bid. In contrast, bids within a run are organised rather differently, and enable a pace and economy of action that rapidly and transparently escalates the price of the lot.

Consider the following fragment that involves the sale of a Genoese bureau cabinet. We join the action during a run between a sales assistant representing a telephone bidder and a buyer in the room. The opening price is four thousand five hundred and the goods finally sell at fourteen thousand pounds; much of the action involves a run between these two principal protagonists.

Fragment 3
A: Six thou:sand
    (2.2) [SA.1 bids]
A: Six thousand five hundred
    (0.6) [B.1 bids]
A: Seven thousand
    (1.2) {SA.1 bids]
A: Seven thousand^ five hundred
    (0.6) [B.1 bids]
A: Eight thousand
    (1.4) [SA. 1 bids]
A: Eight thousand five hundred
    (0.3) [B.1 bids]
A: Nine:: thousand
    (1.8) [SA.1 bids]
A: Nine thousand five hundred

    ....
A: For the last time (0.3) selling in the room at fourteen thousand:: (1.6)
    {knock}

Seven thousand   thousand^ five hundred   Eight thousand

Fragment 3. Figure 1.

Consider the voicing of the bid "seven thousand". The bidder in the room begins to nod at approximately 0.3 of a second during the prior pause. At the onset of the nod, the auctioneer begins to turn his upper body towards the sales assistant who is located on his extreme right. As he begins to utter the word "seven", he turns and looks at the sales assistant, his visual orientation arriving at the beginning of the word "thousand". His visual and bodily orientation are retained towards the sale room assistant until approximately one second into the ensuing pause where she gestures towards the auctioneer. At that moment, he begins to turn bodily towards the bidder in the room, located on his left of centre, and with the voicing of the word "seven", turns and looks at the under-bidder. Whilst bodily he progressively aligns towards the bidder throughout the utterance, his visual orientation arrives during the word "thousand". Roughly 0.4 of a second into the ensuing pause, the bidder nods and once again, whilst beginning to announce the increment bid, the auctioneer turns bodily and visually towards the sales assistant, now the under-bidder.

The way in which the auctioneer articulates each bid enables the principal protagonists as well all those within the sales room to know who has bid and at what price. It renders the bid and its attribution to a particular participant visible, witnessed and witness-able. Indeed, the very announcement of each increment is in part voiced to the room, whilst the onset and completion of the announcement is directed towards particular bidders whose location is accessible to all. The announcement of the current increment, coupled with the accompanying bodily and visual orientation implicates a sequentially relevant next action for a particular participant, that is, to accept or decline, with dispatch, the invitation to bid at the next increment.

The announcement of the bid and the accompanying realignment of bodily orientation not only serves, prospectively, to invite a bid at the next increment, but retrospectively to acknowledge a bid has been received. The sequential import of the auctioneer's actions enables a simple bodily movement such as a nod of the head to constitute a "turn" within this turn-taking organisation, an acceptance or declination, of the invitation to bid. The incremental structure and the alternation between two principal protagonists in a "run" enables an extraordinary economy of behaviour; allowing the most simple of visible actions to significantly advance the price of the goods. In other words, we find an alternating sequential organisation through which auctioneers, by virtue of announcing the current bid and bodily orienting towards a particular individual, serves to rapidly, efficiently and transparently escalate the price of goods and secure their sale to the highest bidder.

It is interesting to add that in inviting a next bid, the auctioneer retains his orientation on the bidder or the sales room assistant throughout the ensuing pause until the bid is issued. In some cases, his bodily and visual orientation (without a change of visual orientation or blinking) may be held for up to a few seconds as he awaits a response. Awaiting a response in this way maintains the demand on the participant to bid and to bid with dispatch, though of course for the sales room assistant, the pressure under which she is placed has to be communicated to the caller. In various ways, this action, an action that demands an immediate response from a specific participant, contrasts with the general invitation for anyone to bid that arises at the start of the auction or during a break in a run when one bidder withdraws and the auctioneer looks for a replacement.

The ways in which auctioneers establish bidding and create competition between potential buyers raises interesting issues with regard to how participants orientate to the psychology of behaviour at auctions. For example, auctioneers believe that it is easier to encourage a participant in the room to bid following a first bid, even when that first is taken from the book, rather than to make the first bid. It is also believed that a first run can serve to encourage others to enter the bidding once a participant withdraws. Moreover, it is often suggested in both the general and specialist press that "spirited bidding" can serve to encourage others and escalate the price of objects beyond all expectations. For example, in the press coverage of the Sotheby's sale of the contents of the Pharmacy and associated Damian Hirst paraphernalia a few years ago the headline of the London Evening Standard was: "What are they on? £11 million is raised for Damian Hirst's Pharmacy cast-offs. Even the pill cabinet went for over £1,100,000." (Evening Standard 19/10/2004, p.3). To corrupt Keynes (1936), we have a sense of the ways that the conduct of others can serve to engender a "state of confidence". In contrast lacklustre bidding on particular goods when they are put up for sale can significantly depress the price they achieve and even affect the price of similar goods in the same sale. In this regard, we can begin to see how the organisation deployed by auctioneers to establish bidding and create, even animate, competition by the rapid juxtaposition of bids, can serve to engender confidence and excitement. It is not surprising, therefore, that it is believed that particular auctioneers are able to create excitement, animate competition, and encourage bidding and make a significant contribution to the value that goods achieve.

4.   Encouraging bids: Differentiating the chant

One of the characteristic features of the auctioneers' speech that has received some attention in both academic and the more popular press is the chant; the rapid repetition of particular phrases primarily, but not solely, prices or increments, that pervades sales by auction. It is argued that the chant sustains the illusion of activity during lapses of bidding and establishes and maintains a pace and rhythm despite the temporary absence of bids (Kuiper 1995). As one would suspect, chants ordinarily arise at the beginning of the sale of a particular lot, or at a place where a bidder withdraws from a run and the auctioneer is looking for a willing participant. The role that these seemingly idiosyncratic behaviours play in attempting to discover and engender bids has received less attention, in part perhaps, by virtue of the focus on the speech and discourse at auctions without regard to the visible aspects of the conduct of auctioneers and others within the sale room.

It is worthwhile considering the following example. It is drawn from the sale of a lot in which the auctioneer receives no bids from participants in the room and eventually has to sell the goods, a fine solitaire ring at the opening price, to a bid from commission. In this, as in many cases, the chant is primarily concerned with inviting, even encouraging bids, while the auctioneer searches the sales room for a willing participant.

Fragment 4.

A: Four five two ladies and gentlemen, the solitaire ring seems to have captured everybody's imagination? I've got three thousand two hundred pounds bid on this lot straight away. [A bids]. Three thousand two hundred. (0.3) Three three is it now? Three three anywhere do I hear? Three three. Three thousand three hundred pounds. (0.2) Three three? (.) Three three with me now? (.) Three three (0.4) Three three (.) Three three (0.3) Three thousand two hundred pounds. It's the maiden bid this solitaire is going to be sold make no mistake. (.) At three thousand two hundred pounds all parties done. At three two (.) {Knock}

The chant consists of the successive re-iteration of (versions of) the current increment and the price of the next bid, coupled, in two instances with phrases, "is it now?" and "anywhere do I hear". The chant is accompanied by the auctioneer looking for a potential buyer willing, or preparing, to bid. The search for a willing participant does not however consist of a continual, undifferentiated

sales sheets	right	left	right
↓	↓	↓	↓

hundred---Three three is it now? Three three anywhere do I hear? At three

Fragment 4. Figure 1., transcript 2 (with images)

"scan" of the room, but rather successive looks that co-occur with components of the chart. It is worthwhile considering one or two instances.

The auctioneer looks up from the sales sheets and begins to search for a willing participant as he announces the current bid, taken from commission. He turns first to his right, then to the extreme left and returns to the right hand side. His gaze passes rapidly, without hesitation, over the centre of the room. As he invites a bid with "three three is it now?" he looks directly towards, and momentarily holds his orientation at two or three individuals that are gathered on the far right hand side of the sale room (for him). They volunteer no bid. As he begins to turn to the far left of the room he produces "Three three anywhere do I hear?" and with the invitation looks at, and again momentarily holds his orientation towards, a small gathering of four individuals standing towards the back of the room. While the two invitations provide an opportunity for anyone present to (attempt to) bid, in the ways in which they are produced, vocally and visibly, they are directed towards, and addressed to, particular individuals. The two invitations are differentiated by virtue of the auctioneer's visual and bodily orientation: they provide an open opportunity for anyone to bid if they so wish, whilst simultaneously encouraging a bid from particular individual(s) within a specific area of the room. In this way, whilst the chant appears to consist of a largely undifferentiated repetition of increments, particular utterances or units of the chant have particular sequential significance for certain individuals in the room.

Elsewhere we have discussed the difference between a display of availability and a display of recipiency where, in the one case a participant provides an open, undifferentiated opportunity for another to produce a response, and in the other, the realignment of bodily and visual orientation encourages a response from a particular individual (Heath 1986). The way in which (re)iterations of the increment, components of the chant are visibly addressed suggests that certain individuals can be subject to the demand for a response by virtue of the bodily con-

Fragment 4. Figure 2. (.) Three three (0.4) Three three (.) Three three (0.3)

duct that accompanies the general invitation to bid. Following "Three thousand with me now." the auctioneer repeats the increment to bid "(.) Three three (0.4) Three three (.) Three three (0.3)". By virtue of the accompanying bodily and visual orientation, the same figure, the general invitation to bid, has very different sequential significance for different people in the room. Whilst the first iteration is addressed to those in the centre of the room, with the second, the auctioneer turns and looks at the sales assistant manning one of the phones to his right. His gaze arrives towards the end of "three?" and is momentarily held.

The sales assistant turns slightly away offering no bid or indication that he is preparing to bid, yet seemingly sensitive, at that moment, to the auctioneer's invitation. With the third reiteration, the auctioneer turns and once again looks towards the left of the room. Not unlike, for example, the way in which a teacher might ask a question of all the class, and yet by virtue of her bodily comportment encourage a particular pupil to answer, the chant does not simply consist of a series of repetitions but rather invitations that specifically encourage particular individuals to respond.

Segments of the chant therefore are interactionally differentiated by virtue of the auctioneer's bodily and in particular visual orientation. The rapid repetitions of the increment discriminate participants, identifying particular members of the audience as the principal recipients of the invitation to bid whilst excluding others from responding at particular moments. The chant does not simply consist of a rapid repetition of particular phrases, but is rather a series of distinct actions that have different sequential import for particular individuals or gatherings of individuals. It should be added that in cases where bids are forthcoming during a chant, they routinely arise as the auctioneer's orientation is directed towards the area of the room where the individual bidder is located.

These re-iterations of increments coupled with small shifts in orientation therefore are not simply matters of performance or theatricality, though they can certainly serve to sustain some interest in the auction as it proceeds over many hours. Rather, they are critical interactional-organisational aspects of the ways in which auctions are accomplished. They are designed to identify potential buyers, to encourage bidding and create competition to enable the price of the object to be systematically and collaboratively escalated. They also serve to display the auctioneer's efforts to encourage and elicit bids, to provide all those present with the opportunity to participate in the sale of the lot if they so wish. In this way, when the hammer falls, the value of the lot determined and ownership transferred, the auctioneer can be seen, and seen to be seen, to have made every effort to achieve a fair, reasonable and accountable price.

5.   Discussion

> My concern over the years has been to promote acceptance of this face to face domain as an analytically viable one, a domain which might be titled, for want of any happy name, the interaction order.
> (Goffman 1983: 2)

One, if not the, principal responsibility of auctioneers is to organise and undertake auctions – to enable the value of numerous goods and services to be determined and sold on the fall of the hammer. The occupational skills, the practice of auctioneers, is primarily concerned with facilitating the interaction of potential buyers and deploying an organisation that efficiently escalates the price of goods so that they can be legitimately sold to the highest bidder. Matters of trust and integrity are critical to the ability of auctions and auctioneers to determine the value of goods and enable their exchange. Indeed, notwithstanding some cynicism concerning the conduct of auctions and auction houses, disputes are rare and seem to have little effect on the growing significance of auctions both traditional and electronic. Auctions rest upon an interactional arrangement, a social organisation that auctioneers deploy, in concert and collaboration with buyers and sales room staff, to rapidly, repeatedly and contingently sell numerous lots, often more than eighty an hour that may consist of different types of goods, with differing values, and involving a diverse range participants with differing interests, commitments and resources. This same organisation can serve to sell numerous lots of little value, a few pounds each, or highly important works of art at outstanding prices, be they a Warhol, a Riesener Commode, or as in our earlier example, a rare Ludovico Carracci.

The organisation relies upon the auctioneers' ability to initiate the sale of each lot in an appropriate and timely fashion. First and foremost, a first and a second bid need to be established at a value that encourages participation without unduly extending the time it takes to sell the goods. The first and then the second bid establish an incremental structure that enables the transparent projection of values and provides potential buyers and all those present with the ability to know where they and others stand at any moment during the rapid escalation of price. The initiation of bidding involves establishing a turn-taking organisation that successively distributes opportunities to bid to two principal protagonists, with an alternating sequential arrangement that invites successive bids, with dispatch, at the projected next increment. This organisation enables the slightest visible actions to constitute a turn, to accept or decline an increment, and thereby to support the rapid and systematic escalation of price. Whilst showing no favour to particular individuals, the organisation orders contributions from different sources – the book, the room, the telephone and the Internet – and thereby provides opportunities for all those present and all interested parties to bid at some place during the sale of a single lot. Indeed, the close of sale is foreshadowed by the auctioneer providing successive opportunities to any remaining interested parties to bid and to bid with dispatch. In these and other ways, auctioneers deploy an organisation that establishes an order of interaction; forms of participation that enable the demand for goods to be rapidly exposed, ordered, and transparently sold to the highest bidder.

In considering auctions and auctioneering, we can begin to see the ways in which an occupational activity is not simply mediated through interaction, but rather interaction forms the foundation to a significant aspect of the work and work's accomplishment. In the case of auctioneers, and one suspects for a number of other occupations, a specialist occupational skill consists of the systematic deployment and management of an interactional arrangement; a particular turn-taking organisation that is repeatedly and contingently applied to constitute the value and sale of particular goods. Auctions are accomplished, accountable and recognisable by virtue of the auctioneer's abilities to structure the interaction of others in a particular fashion and thereby transparently and legitimately sell goods and services some of which are worth many millions of dollars. In contrast therefore to certain forms of ethnographic studies of work and occupation, social interaction is not simply a vehicle through which work is accomplished and occupational culture sustained, but rather constitutive of the principal task for which they are responsible: the work, or at least an important part of the work, is managing the interaction of others, in this case potential buyers. In other words, prioritising the social interactional organisation of the event provides the resources through which we can begin to address and understand occupational performance and the characteristics of work and organisations.

A further point should be mentioned. Despite the significant contribution of studies of talk and discourse to our understanding of work and the professions, we can begin to see the importance of visible and material conduct to the accomplishment of organisational activities. Auctions are perhaps exemplary in this regard, since the very production of actions throughout the event, both by auctioneers and potential buyers, relies upon visible conduct be it gestures, head movements, changes in visual orientation and the like. It is interesting to note that the structure of auctions relies upon a systematic transformation of the turn-taking organisation of talk in conversation with turns of particular participants, namely bidders, accomplished visibly rather than through talk. However, auctions do powerfully reveal the ways in which even seemingly simple occupational activities are accomplished through the interplay of talk, bodily conduct and use of material artefacts. Now we have such a powerful methodological and substantive foundation for the analysis of talk at work, it is worthwhile to begin to consider the range of resources that are brought to bear by participants themselves in the accomplishment of organisational activities. "Multi-modal" is an unfortunate term, perpetuating an impression of different channels of communication that has undermined studies of nonverbal behaviour, but at least it serves to direct attention to the ways in which many, if not most occupational and professional activities, are dependent upon the interplay of the visible, the spoken and the use of various tools and technologies.

The robust and pervasive organisation that underpins auctions, an organisation that enables the contingent contributions of numerous participants to be specified, juxataposed and ordered, provides the foundation to price determination and the legitimate exchange of goods. It produces the regular and reliable outcomes upon which economists formulate and build models and, in the case of art and antiques, enables goods worth some billions of dollars to be exchanged each year. It is in one sense a very simple interactional arrangement, an arrangement that minimises the actual contributions of participants, to no more than, for example, a gesture, and enables those contributions to be unambiguously and efficiently elicited and juxtaposed. There is, as we have suggested, a remarkable economy to the organisation of the event – an economy that not only serves to order the contributions of particular participants but to systematically display those contributions to all who are present. Indeed, the very presence of others and the clarity and efficiency of the procedure, the way in which the participation is both witnessed and witness-able, serves to legitimate the sale of particular goods, and more generally sales, by auction. It is hardly surprising therefore that one of the most successful internet sites, namely eBay, attempts to reproduce an organisation, an organisational arrangement, that as Reitlinger (1982) suggests, has informed the sale of goods of uncertain value since the 17th century and undoutedly a great deal longer.

Note

* We would like to thank all those, auctioneers, assistants and buyers who so willingly allowed auctions to be observed and recorded and who more generally helped with the research. Anthony Morris, Menisha Patel and Robin Meisner, provided invaluable support, assisting with data collection and editing. We would also like to thank Jon Hindmarsh, Dirk vom Lehn, Howard Gospel and Stephen Pratten for their very help-

ful comments and ideas concerning the observations and issues discussed here and Christopher Candlin and Srikant Sarangi for their very helpful comments on an earlier version of this paper. The research of which this paper forms part is undertaken as part of an EPSRC funded project namely UTIFORO.

References

Atkinson, J. Maxwell and Paul Drew
    1979   *Order in Court: The Organisation of Verbal Interaction in Judicial Settings.* London: Macmillan.
Boeck, George A
    1990   *Texas Livestock Auctions: A Folklife Ethnography.* New York: AMS Press.
Cassady, Ralph. Jr.
    1967   *Auctions and Auctioneering.* California: University of California Press.
Clayman, Steven and John Heritage
    2002   *The News Interview: Journalists and Public Figures on the Air.* Cambridge: Cambridge University Press.
Dargan, Amanda and Steven Zeitlin
    1983   American talkers: Expressive styles and occupational choice. *The Journal of American Folklore* 96(379): 3–33.
Evening Standard
    2004   What are they on? £11 million is raised for Damian Hirst's Pharmacy cast-offs. Even the pill cabinet went for over £1,100,000. 19 October 2004 edition, p. 3. London.
Frankel, Richard M.
    1990   Talking in interviews: A dispreference for patient initiated questions in physician-patient encounters. In: George Psathas (ed.), *Interaction Competence*, 231–262. Washington D.C.: University Press of America.
Geismar, Haidy
    2004   What's in a price? An ethnography of tribal art at auction. In: Ash Amin and Nigel Thrift (eds.), *The Blackwell Cultural Economy Reader*, 289–306. Oxford: Blackwell.
Goffman, Erving
    1983   The interaction order. *American Sociological Review* 48: 1–17.
Greatbatch, David
    1988   A turn taking system for British news interviews. *Language and Society* 17(3): 401–430.
Heath, Christian
    1986   *Body Movement and Speech in Medical Interaction.* Cambridge: Cambridge University Press.
Heritage, John and Douglas W. Maynard (eds.)
    2006   *Communication in Medical care: Interaction between Primary Care Physicians and Patients.* Cambridge: Cambridge University Press
Hughes, Everett
    1958   *Men and Their Work.* Glencoe: Free Press.

Klemperer, Paul
    2004   *Auctions: Theory and Practice.* Oxford: Princeton University Press.
Krishna, Vijay
    2002   *Auction Theory.* London: Academic Press.
Kuiper Koenraad
    1992   The English oral tradition in auctions speech. *American Speech* 67: 279–289.
Kuiper Koenraad
    1995   *Smooth Talkers: The Linguistic Performance of Auctioneers and Sports-*
            casters (Everyday Communication: Case Studies of Behavior in Context).
            Mahwah: NJ: Lawrence Erlbaum.
Kuiper, Koenraad and Frederick Tillis
    1986   The chant of the tobacco auctioneer. *American Speech* 60: 141–149.
Learmount, Brian
    1985   *The History of the Auction.* Ivers, England: Barnard and Learmount.
Menzes, Flavio M. and Paulo K. Monteiro
    2005   *An Introduction to Auction Theory.* Oxford: Oxford University Press.
Peräkylä, Ansi
    1995   *Aids Counselling: Institutional Interaction and Clinical Practice.* Cam-
            bridge: Cambridge University Press.
Reitlinger, Gerald
    1982   *The Economics of Taste. The Rise and Fall of Picture Prices 1760–1960,*
            Volume II. New York: Hacker Art Books.
Sacks, Harvey, Emanuel A. Schegloff and Gail Jefferson
    1973   A simplest systematics for the organization of turn-taking in conversation.
            Language 50(4): 696–735.
Silverman, David
    1997   *Discourses of Counselling: HIV Counselling as Social Interaction.* Lon-
            don: Sage.
Smith, Charles W.
    1990   *Auctions: The Social Construction of Value.* California: California Univer-
            sity Press.
Smith, Charles W.
    1991   Comment on Siegelman's review of auctions. *American Journal of Sociol-*
            ogy 96(6): 1539–1541.
Smith, Charles W.
    1993   Auctions: From Walras to the real world. In: Richard Swedberg (ed.), *Ex-*
            plorations in Economic Sociology, xx–xx. New York: Russell Sage.

15. Argumentation across Web-based organizational discourses: The case of climate change

Graham Smart

Abstract

The chapter investigates a common yet little-studied discursive phenomenon – the collective formation of argumentation across networks of texts produced by various professional organizations as they engage in public debates over major social issues. A case study of argumentation produced by organizations active in the debate over climate change serves to illustrate this phenomenon. The case study draws on the work of James Gee and Maarten Hajer as well as on scholarship in Science Studies in analyzing a corpus of Internet-published texts gathered from a range of organizations involved in the climate-change debate. Using Hajer's 'argumentative discourse analysis' approach, the study identifies two 'discourse coalitions' – clusters of organizations sharing a common position on an issue – one labeled the 'climate-change crisis discourse coalition' and the other the 'climate-crisis skepticism discourse coalition'. While these two clusters of organizations are diametrically opposed in their positions on climate change and clearly not attempting to establish mutual understanding through an authentic deliberative dialogue, they are nevertheless highly engaged with one another discursively. The case study also reveals that science, as appropriated rhetorically in argumentation on climate change, is represented in multiple ways across different instances of argumentation – with each particular representation of science cast in either a positive or a negative light for persuasive effect, depending on which of the two discourse coalitions is employing it to advance or counter an argument.

Introduction

Below we see two highly divergent characterizations of the same individual, Dr. James Hansen, widely considered one of the world's leading climate scientists. The two depictions of Hansen convey very different claims about the reality of human-driven climate change and its potentially catastrophic impacts.

James Hansen: The World's Leading – and Most Politically Outspoken – Climate Researcher

James Hansen is sitting in his cluttered corner office on the seventh floor of the NASA Goddard Institute for Space Studies, just blocks from the Columbia University campus in upper Manhattan. ... A wiry scientist who looks young for his 65 years, Hansen speaks with a distinct Midwestern accent; as he talks, he gazes off into space ... If he has a lot on his mind, it's no surprise: Hansen is the number one scientist in America – and perhaps the world – who has been publicly speaking out about our looming climate catastrophe. And in so doing, he has shattered some long-held convictions in the scientific community, ones overdue for a challenge. Hansen believes, as did Albert Einstein, that speaking out politically at key moments is part of a scientist's responsibility. (Chris Mooney, *New Scientist*, March 11, 2009)

Bogeymen of the C02 Hoax Losing Ground

James Hansen, head of NASA Goddard Institute of Space Studies ... made statements clearly designed to frighten people. [He is] politically active in climate change and at the forefront of the attempt to convince the world that CO2 is a problem. [His] remarks are intended to scare people by threatening impending doom – nothing new – except there is increasing urgency and fear because [his] message is failing. Hansen increases urgency for action, claiming we are on the verge of a tipping point. ... We're reaching a tipping point, but it's not the one Hansen anticipates. We're close to the point where the public and politicians realize they have been totally deceived about the nature and cause of climate change. (Timothy Ball, *Canada Free Press*, March 29, 2009)

What are we to make of these two contrasting characterizations of Hansen? As we will see later in the chapter, although each of the two accounts is credited to a single author, each also reflects a position, or macro-argument (Toulmin, 1959), that is widely propagated across the network of Internet-published texts produced by professional organizations active in the public debate over climate change. At the same time, we will also see that each of the two depictions of Hansen can be viewed as an appropriation of science for partisan rhetorical ends.

This chapter discusses a common yet empirically under-examined aspect of organizational discourse – the collective formation of argumentation across the discursive networks of Internet-published texts produced by different professional organizations as they engage in public debates over major social issues such as abortion, assisted dying, evolution/creationism, same-sex marriage, and the state of the global environment. The first part of the chapter reviews literature in organizational discourse studies relevant to this topic. This is followed by an illustrative case study of Internet-published texts created by organizations engaged in the current debate over climate change.

Studies of organizational discourse and collective argumentation

In tune with the 'discursive turn' across the social sciences (Fischer, 2003), many researchers investigating life and work in professional organizations in recent decades have focused their inquiry on organizational discourse – indeed the trend has reached the point where the study of organizational discourse 'has become a veritable cottage industry' (Mumby, 2004: 237). In the main, this research on organizational discourse has been social constructionist in orientation, reflecting a belief in the constitutive nature of discourse and its central role in the ongoing creation of social reality within organizations (Grant, Hardy, Oswick and Putnam, 2004). In a widely quoted passage, Mumby and Clair (1997: 181) articulate this ontology:

> When we speak of organizational discourse, we do not simply mean discourse that occurs *in* organizations. Rather we suggest that organizations exist only as their members create them through discourse. This is not to claim that organizations are 'nothing but' discourse, but rather that discourse is the principle means by which organizational members create a coherent social reality that frames their sense of who they are.

Applying various constructivist and critical discourse-analytic methods to spoken and written texts, researchers have described, analyzed and theorized previously unexamined organizational phenomena. Aspects of organizational reality brought to light and investigated through the discourse-analytic approach include, for example, identity formation, ideology, gender roles, control and resistance, innovation and change, and the dialectic between social structure and agency (Grant, Keenoy and Oswick, 1998). In exploring the discursive dimension of organizational reality, researchers have examined different genres of spoken and written discourse – narratives, conversations, meetings, vision statements, and speeches, for example – as well as other features of discourse such as speech acts, rhetorical strategies, metaphors, synecdoche, intertextuality and argumentation (Clegg, Hardy, Lawrence and Nord, 2006).

The last in this list of discourse features, argumentation, is the topic of this chapter. While the occurrence of argumentation within organizations has long been recognized, research has typically focused on micro-level interaction between individuals, as between managers and union representatives or supervisors and their employees (e.g., Zanoni and Janssens, 2003). As Sillince (1999: 795) observes, 'very little research has been undertaken into the organizational setting, institutionalization and use of argumentation. Argumentation is still considered to be undertaken between isolated individuals ...'. Not surprisingly, Sillince immediately moves to occupy this research space with his concept of the 'argumentation repertoire': '[O]rganizations institutionalize very specialized repertoires of arguments, which constrain what their members can say, and which are discourse resources which are subject to appropriation and manipulation by organization members to increase their power and influence' (p. 795).

While Sillince approaches organizational argumentation from the macro-level of the organization as a whole, his gaze remains confined to the individual organization. To find scholarship on the formation of argumentation beyond the bounds of a single organization, we need to look outside organizational discourse studies – to the field of argumentation theory. The area of argumentation theory most relevant to our purposes focuses on the collective dimension of argumentation – specifically, on the argumentative norms existing across organizations within different sectors of the social world. Most influentially, Toulmin (1959) introduced the concept of the 'argument field', suggesting that certain features of arguments are field-specific, while other features are identical across all fields. Toulmin, together with Rieke and Janik (1979), further developed this theory in identifying field-specific characteristics of arguments in science, law, management, and the arts. Goodnight (1982) elaborated on this idea with his notion of 'argument spheres' – he identifies three: personal, technical, and public – each with its own conventions for what constitutes legitimate evidence and valid arguments. For Goodnight, argumentation in the public sphere is a form of deliberative discourse, arising out of uncertainty, involving 'probable knowledge', and usually featuring predictions of future events. While Toulmin and Goodnight shed light on certain aspects of argumentation as it occurs on a collective level, it remains that their concern is with arguments viewed as artifacts or constructs rather than with the discursive processes at work as argumentation is collectively formed in networks of texts produced by organizations engaged in public debates, our concern in this chapter. The next section presents a case study that takes up this latter theme.

The debate over climate change: A case study

After providing historical background for the current debate on global warming and climate change, this section describes the collection of data for the case study, presents the research questions guiding the study, outlines the analytical framework used to interpret the data, and reports the findings.

Science and Politics of Global Warming and Climate Change

Contemporary debate over climate change has its roots in 19th-century European science, primarily in the work of Joseph Fourier (1824) in France, John Tyndall (1860) in England and Svante Arrhenius (1896) in Sweden. The cumulative outcome of this work was the theory that certain atmospheric gases, including carbon dioxide (CO_2), combine to create a 'greenhouse effect' (Arrhenius) that could potentially increase the surface temperatures of the Earth. In the 1930s, British engineer Guy Callendar (1938) revived this earlier science with his claim that the observed rise in global temperatures in the early years of the 20th century was due to rising levels of atmospheric CO2 resulting from the growing use of fossil fuels, particularly coal.

In the 1960s, Charles Keeling (1970) of California's Scripps Institute of Oceanography empirically linked rising levels of atmospheric CO2 to increasing annual temperatures; and in the next decade Stanford's Stephen Schneider (1976), coining the term 'global warming', argued that higher concentrations of atmospheric CO2 could produce a dangerous rise in the Earth's average surface temperature. The late 1970s and the 1980s saw growing concern among climate scientists in many countries that global warming could cause 'climate change' – severe and worsening disruptions in weather patterns around the world such as heat-waves, droughts, desertification, storms and widespread coastal flooding (Weart, 2003). (For succinctness, hereafter the pair of terms 'global warming' and 'climate change' is referred to as 'climate change'.)

A political response to the science began to develop in the 1980s. In North America, the policy debate began in earnest in 1988 when James Hansen, chief climate scientist at the U.S. National Aeronautics and Space Administration (NASA), testifying before a U.S. Senate committee, declared that anthropogenic, or human-caused, global climate change was clearly a reality, predicting a significant increase in global temperatures over the next two decades (Hansen, 1988).

On the international political scene, in the early 1980s supra-national organizations initiated a series of conferences where climate scientists and environmental activists voiced increasing alarm over the threat of anthropogenic climate change. A key outcome of these conferences was the founding in 1988 of the United Nation's Intergovernmental Panel on Climate Change (IPCC). The IPCC was given the mandate of monitoring peer-reviewed scientific publications on climate change, assessing the risks for the biosphere and humankind, and reporting periodically on its work to policy-makers from the IPCC's 194 members.

The IPCC released major reports in 1990, 1995, 2001 and 2007, each including a lengthy scientific component along with a 'Summary for Policymakers'. *Fourth Assessment Report: Climate Change 2007* was the most dramatic to date, featuring the widely reported assertion that 'warming of the climate system is unequivocal [and] most of the observed increase in globally averaged temperatures since the mid-20th century is *very likely* due to the observed increase in anthropogenic greenhouse gas concentrations' (pp. 4, 8; italics in the original).

Each of the four IPCC reports has been the focal point of animated debate over the reality and consequences of anthropogenic climate change as well as, most intensely, over the mitigation of climate change through the reduction of

CO2 emissions from fossil fuels, particularly oil, gas and coal. As Hulme (2009) argues, with climate change having become a prime issue of contestation in public and policy forums, the 'idea of climate change' has circulated throughout the various spheres of discourse constituting the social world – Hulme specifically mentions the discourses of science, economics, psychology, media, development, and governance – so that in any given instance of argumentation, the meaning of climate change is framed within one or more of these discourses, a point to be taken up later in the chapter.

Data collection and research questions

For the last six years I have been monitoring the public debate over climate change on a regular basis as it has played out in Internet-published organizational discourse on the Web. Using Google 'alerts' with customized search terms, on-line subscriptions to electronic texts from various professional organizations (e.g., newsletters, reports, press releases), as well as frequent visits to the websites of organizations active in the climate-change debate, I have collected a corpus of approximately 14,000 texts. Over this period of inquiry, my effort to learn more about the way in which argumentation is collectively formed across the field of discourse jointly created by organizations participating in the debate has crystallized into three research questions:

– What types of discourses appear most frequently in argumentation produced by professional organizations engaged in the climate-change debate (e.g., scientific, economic, legal)?
– What recurrent themes and claims appear in this argumentation?
– What patterns of congruence and contradiction occur across instances of climate-change argumentation?

Discourse-analytic framework

As public and policy debates over the global environment have intensified in recent years, researchers in a number of disciplines – Geography, Communication, Sociology, Urban Planning, and Political Science among them – have turned to discourse analysis in the Foucauldian constructivist tradition (Sharp and Richardson, 2001; Waitt, 2005) to investigate how environmental issues are represented and contested within the discourses of professional organizations (e.g., Carvalho and Burgess, 2005; Livesey, 2002; Rydin, 2003). Runhaar, Dieperink and Driessen (2006: 47–48) describe this approach as follows: '[Foucauldian] discourse analysis explores patterns in written or spoken statements as well as related practices in order to identify the representations of reality that are employed ... ... [It] focuses on the ways in which [social] actors give meaning to particular phenomena ...'. According to them, this mode of discourse analysis is particularly useful for examining scientific and political controversies:

> [A] strength of the [Foucauldian] tradition of discourse analysis is that it can [inves-tigate] complex scientific or political debates [and] shed light on controversies about certain issues. ... What meanings, arguments, and lines of reasoning [do] the various (groups of) actors involved bring forward? [And why is it that] a particular under-standing of a problem at some point gains dominance and is seen as authoritative, while other understandings are discredited ...? (pp. 48–49)

Seeking a constructivist analytical framework for the case study, I turned to the work of two neo-Foucauldian theorists: James Gee and Maartin Hajer. Gee's (2005: 21) approach to discourse analysis begins with a distinction between 'discourse' – spoken or written utterances used in particular social contexts – and 'Discourses' (capitalized for distinction) – 'ways of combining and inte-grating language, actions, interactions, ways of thinking, believing, valuing, and using various symbols, tools, and objects to enact a particular sort of so-cially recognizable identity'. Discourses, according to Gee, do not operate in isolation; rather they 'always [exist] in relationships of complicity or contes-tation with other Discourses'. Taking this idea to a broader plane, Gee points to the regular occurrence of what he terms 'Conversations' among opposing Dis-courses:

> [Conversations] are long-running discussions in our society ... between and among Discourses, not just among individual people (1996: 35). ... Most of us today are aware of the societal Conversations going on around us about things like abortion, creationism, global warming, terrorism, and so on ... ... To know about these Con-versations is to know about the various sides one can take in debates about these is-sues and what sorts of people are usually on each side. (2005: 22)

While Gee's image of Conversations among opposing Discourses provides a panoramic view of the discursive dynamics of public debates over controversial social issues, Hajer (1995: 59) offers a more finely focused analytical perspec-tive on such debates, which he views as 'struggle[s] for discursive hegemony in which [social] actors try to secure support for their definition of reality'. Hajer's discourse-analytic approach is anchored in his own definition of discourse – one quite apt for an investigation of the discourses comprising environmental de-bates: '[A discourse is] an ensemble of ideas, concepts and categorizations through which meaning is given to social and physical phenomena, and which is produced, reproduced, and transformed in a particular set of practices' (2005: 447).

Moving to a broader plane, as with Gee, Hajer's discourse-analytic ap-proach, which he terms 'argumentative discourse analysis', offers a conceptual frame for investigating the collective formation of argumentation by 'discourse coalitions' of social actors engaged in a battle for 'discursive hegemony' in public and policy debates. Hajer (1995: 45) explains:

> [I]n the struggle for discursive hegemony, coalitions are formed among [social] actors ... that for various reasons are attracted to a specific set of story-lines. Discourse-coalitions are defined as an ensemble of (1) a set of story-lines; (2) the [social] actors who utter these story-lines; and (3) the practices in which this discursive activity is based. Story-lines are seen as the discursive cement that keeps a discourse-coalition together.

Hajer (1995: 62) describes story-lines as 'narratives on social reality [in which discourses] from many different domains are combined [to] provide [social] actors with a set of symbolic references that suggest a common understanding'. For Hajer (1993: 47), '[s]tory-lines are the medium through which actors try to impose their view of reality on others, suggest certain social positions and practices, and criticize alternative social arrangements'.

Hajer also points to different possible outcomes in a 'struggle for discursive hegemony'. When a discourse coalition succeeds in projecting its discursive version of reality into the social world so that large numbers of other actors incorporate it into their own discourse, the coalition has achieved what Hajer refers to as 'discourse structuration'; and then if this version of reality is sanctioned in policies and laws, the coalition has achieved 'discourse institutionalization' – and its discourse has become 'dominant'.

In addition to the work of Gee and Hajer, the analysis in the case study draws on concepts from Science Studies, a field of interdisciplinary scholarship that emerged in the 1970s. Science Studies couples sociological, rhetorical, anthropological and historical perspectives with empirical inquiry to challenge the traditional philosophical view of a Science that exists 'everywhere and nowhere' (Golinski, 2005) – an abstract epistemic enterprise, occurring 'in a world outside human space and time' (Traweek, 1988, cited in Golinski, 2005) – producing objective truths of universal validity about the natural world. What Science Studies offers instead is an empirically grounded and more complicated view: science is portrayed as a historically, socially and institutionally situated activity in which groups of disciplinary specialists, operating in specific locales and using distinctive repertoires of material, social and literary practices, collaborate to produce contingent, contestable 'facts' and causal explanations that, repeatedly recontextualized (Berkenkotter, 2001), are communicated through ever-broader networks of experts, eventually to be conveyed to society as achieved knowledge available for material application and policy-making (Knorr Cetina, 1999; Latour, 1987; Lynch and Woolgar, 1990; Shapin, 1998).

Findings

An analysis of the approximately 14,000 Internet-published texts that I have collected from 2003 to the present (October 2009) leads to a number of findings regarding the collective formation of argumentation across the discourses of organizations engaged in the debate over the reality, impacts and remediation of climate change. This section of the chapter first identifies organizations and discourse coalitions active in the climate-change debate and discusses the argumentation collectively produced by two opposing discourse coalitions. The section then considers the ways in which representations of science are used for rhetorical effect within this argumentation.

Organizations, discourse coalitions and macro-arguments

Eight types of organizations appear to be the most active in the Web-based public debate over climate change: environmental NGOs, international political organizations, government agencies, business corporations, organized groups of scientists, media organizations, policy think-tanks, and religious organizations.[1] The argumentation on climate change produced by these organizations incorporates a range of discourses, including those of science, politics, economics, law and ethics.

Analysis of Internet-published texts produced by organizations active in the climate-change debate reveals two clusters of discursively aligned organizations, or 'discourse coalitions' in Hajer's (1995) terms. The two discourse coalitions advance radically opposed story-lines – or what I will refer to as macro-arguments (Toulmin, 1959) – regarding climate change. The macro-argument collectively formed by texts produced by the first of these discourse coalitions, referred to hereafter as the 'climate-change crisis' coalition, can be expressed as follows:[2] 'Anthropogenic climate change threatens the world with impending catastrophe, and policy-makers must act without delay to counteract this danger'. Below we see this macro-argument presented in a text from the David Suzuki Foundation, a Canadian environmental NGO. Unlike most texts in the corpus, which typically present only part of the macro-argument, this text contains the full version.

Solving Global Warming

Climate change is considered by many scientists to be the most serious threat facing the world today. ... Solutions include phasing out coal plants, expanding renewable energy sources and public transit, and creating new efficiency standards for vehicles and buildings.

Science

The pollutants we pump into our atmosphere are changing its composition and preventing heat from escaping the earth's surface. Today's atmosphere contains 32 per cent more carbon dioxide, one of the main greenhouse gases, than at the start of the industrial era. The result is climate change: altered long-term weather patterns. Global warming, a rise in the average global temperature, is one measure of climate change. And it has already begun – global average temperature has risen by 0.6 degrees Celsius since 1900, and the northern hemisphere is substantially warmer than at any point during the past 1000 years.

Burning fossil fuels such as coal, oil and gas is largely responsible for climate change. Deforestation and modern intensive farming methods also contribute to the problem.

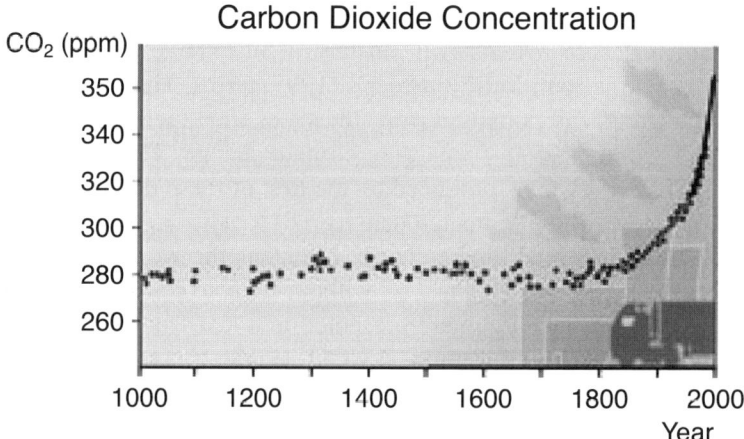

Impacts

Climate change is already having a significant impact on ecosystems, economies and communities. Rising average temperatures do not simply mean balmier winters. Some regions will experience more extreme heat, while others may cool slightly. Flooding, drought, and intense summer heat could result. Violent storms and other extreme weather events could also result from the increased energy stored in our warming atmosphere.

The world's leading scientists report that to prevent dangerous levels of global warming governments should act to limit global warming to less than 2°C by taking concerted action to reduce greenhouse gas emissions. The sooner we act to reduce greenhouse gases, the less severe future impacts will be.

Solutions

Greenhouse gas emissions can be greatly reduced many different ways. Most of the solutions involve increasing the efficiency of our energy use to reduce fossil fuel demand, while maintaining – or improving – our lifestyles.

Many of the potential solutions have benefits beyond greenhouse gas reduction, such as increased employment, stimulation of the green technology manufacturing sector, and reduced urban air pollution. A combination of public interest and government sponsored programs can make these solutions a reality.

(Anonymous, website of David Suzuki Foundation, http://www.davidsuzuki.org, accessed on January 10, 2008)

Taken as a composite whole, the texts produced by the cluster of organizations comprising the second discourse coalition, which I will refer to as the 'climate-crisis skepticism' coalition, form a sharply contrasting macro-argument:[3] 'The theory of anthropogenic climate change is false, and we must avoid misguided remedial governmental policies that would undermine our economies and way of life'.[4]

We see this macro-argument presented in the text below, a manifesto released following the March 2008 International Conference on Climate Change, a three-day international gathering of climate-change skeptics in New York City attended by several hundred scientists, engineers, economists, politicians, lobbyists, business leaders, policy analysts and citizens. The manifesto was published on the Web by the Heartland Institute, the Chicago-based conservative policy think-tank that organized the conference. Again, unlike most of the texts in the corpus, this text contains a full version of the macro-argument.

Manhattan Declaration on Climate Change
"Global Warming" Isn't a Global Crisis

We, the scientists and researchers in climate and related fields, economists, policymakers, and business leaders, assembled at Times Square, New York City, participating in the 2008 International Conference on Climate Change,

Resolving that scientific questions should be evaluated solely by the scientific method;

Affirming that global climate has always changed and always will, independent of the actions of humans, and that carbon dioxide (CO_2) isn't a pollutant but rather a necessity for all life;

Recognising that the causes and extent of recently-observed climatic change are the subject of intense debates in the climate science community and that oft-repeated assertions of a supposed 'consensus' among climate experts are false;

Affirming that attempts by governments to legislate costly regulations on industry and individual citizens to encourage CO_2 emission reduction will slow development while having no appreciable impact on the future trajectory of global climate change. Such policies will markedly diminish future prosperity and so reduce the ability of societies to adapt to inevitable climate change, thereby increasing, not decreasing human suffering;

Noting that warmer weather is generally less harmful to life on Earth than colder:

Hereby declare:

That current plans to restrict anthropogenic CO_2 emissions are a dangerous misallocation of intellectual capital and resources that should be dedicated to solving humanity's real and serious problems.

That there is no convincing evidence that CO_2 emissions from modern industrial activity has in the past, is now, or will in the future cause catastrophic climate change.

That attempts by governments to inflict taxes and costly regulations on industry and individual citizens with the aim of reducing emissions of CO_2 will pointlessly curtail the prosperity of the West and progress of developing nations without affecting climate.

That adaptation as needed is massively more cost-effective than any attempted mitigation, and that a focus on such mitigation will divert the attention and resources of governments away from addressing the real problems of their peoples.

That human-caused climate change isn't a global crisis.

Now, therefore, *we recommend:*

That world leaders reject the views expressed by the United Nations Intergovernmental Panel on Climate Change as well as popular, but misguided works such as "An Inconvenient Truth".

That all taxes, regulations, and other interventions intended to reduce emissions of CO_2 be abandoned forthwith.

Agreed at New York, 4 March, 2008.

(Heartland Institute, http://www.heartland.org, accessed on May 8, 2008)

Each of the two macro-arguments discussed above can be seen to comprise a logical progression of claims, a feature typical of deliberative discourse. The table below places detailed versions of the macro-arguments side by side in order to display the sequence of claims in each macro-argument while at the same time showing the contrast between the two macro-arguments.

'Climate-change crisis' discourse coalition: the macro-argument	'Climate-change skepticism' discourse coalition: the macro-argument
1) Global warming is occurring: the temperatures of the atmosphere and the oceans have been steadily increasing since the industrial revolution of the early 19th century.	1) Cycles of global warming and cooling have occurred throughout geological time, and it appears that during the 20th century the Earth was in a phase of slight global warming as it emerged from the Little Ice Age.[5]
2) The scientific consensus is that global warming is primarily caused by human activity – specifically, by fossil-fuel emissions adding CO2 to the greenhouse gases in the Earth's atmosphere.	2) Scientific studies show that the recent global warming is primarily due to natural causes, such as solar activity and oceanic conditions, rather than human-induced increases of atmospheric CO2.
3) CO2-driven global warming has already begun to produce climate change – repeated severe disruptions to the Earth's climate – and this will intensify in the coming years.	3) It is far from certain that global warming is disrupting the Earth's climate in any way at present, and it is virtually impossible to predict future effects.
4) If global warming isn't curbed, the future impacts of climate change will be catastrophic, causing widespread physical, social, and economic damage, with the poor in developing nations most vulnerable to these threats.	4) The negative consequences of global warming for the planet and human life will be minimal; indeed, humankind will benefit, as for example, from higher crop yields and fewer deaths from excessive heat.
5) Policy-makers around the world must make immediate efforts to mitigate climate change by reducing the use of fossil fuels and promoting a move to carbonless energy sources. While this effort may require changes in our way of life, a shift to 'green' technologies and practices is not only necessary but will also bring overall economic benefits.	5) Efforts to counter climate change by restricting the use of fossil fuels will undermine economic growth, lower global standards of living, and take up resources that could be used to address serious problems such as disease, starvation, air pollution, and water shortages. Any attempts by governments to remedy climate change by imposing regulatory policies must be resisted.

As mentioned earlier, argumentation on climate change typically draws on a number of different discourses (Hulme, 2009; Scollon, 2007), and we have an illustration of this above. In the first macro-argument, we see that the first four claims draw on scientific discourse, with the fourth claim also reflecting economic discourse and the final claim reflecting both political and ethical discourses. In the second macro-argument, we see that the first four claims draw on scientific discourse, with the last two points including political and economic perspectives. This recalls Hajer's (1995: 62) point that 'story-lines', or macro-arguments as we refer to them here, combine meanings from discourses of 'many different domains … [to] provide [social] actors with a set of symbolic references that suggest a common understanding'.

Another key finding from the case study is that the two opposing discourse-coalitions described above are highly engaged with one other, discursively, in that each of the coalitions appears to be very aware of the other's evolving position, or macro-argument, regarding climate change, and very alert to any emerging claims or new evidence for older claims. One can see this intense mutual engagement in the rapidity – sometimes it is only a matter of hours – with which new claims published on the Web by one discourse coalition are followed by the appearance of countering texts from the other coalition. In a similar indication of the discursive engagement of the two discourse coalitions, one frequently sees in texts published by each coalition descriptions and analyses of the ideology, motives and rhetorical strategies of the opposing coalition, along with proffered discursive tactics and counter-arguments for use in opposing it. Below is an example: the first part of 'How to Talk to a Climate Skeptic' (Beck, nd.), a primer intended to help climate-change activists anticipate and counter the claims of skeptics. The text was originally published in *Grist*, an on-line environmental magazine, and subsequently turned up on the websites of various organizations associated with the 'climate-change crisis' discourse coalition.

How to Talk to a Climate Skeptic: Responses to the Most Common Skeptical Arguments on Global Warming

Below is a complete listing of the articles in "How to Talk to a Climate Skeptic," a series by Coby Beck containing responses to the most common skeptical arguments on global warming.

There are four separate taxonomies; arguments are divided by:
- Stages of Denial,
- Scientific Topics,
- Types of Argument, and
- Levels of Sophistication.

Stages of Denial

1. There's nothing happening
   a.   Inadequate evidence
   - There is no evidence
     - Objection: Despite what the computer models tell us, there is actually no evidence of significant global warming.
     - Answer: Global warming is not an output of computer models; it is a conclusion based on observations of a great many global indicators. By far the most straightforward evidence is the actual [historical] surface temperature record.

(Coby Beck, How to talk to a climate skeptic. Grist website, http://gristmill. grist.org/skeptics, accessed on March 22, 2009)

Below we see a similar commentary on the motives and rhetorical strategies of the opposing discourse coalition, although this time the account comes from the 'climate-crisis skepticism' coalition. It is an excerpt from the audio file of a presentation given at the 2009 International Conference on Climate Change along with excerpts from the accompanying PowerPoint. The text was published on the Heartland Institute website (Murray, 2009). The speaker's presentation was titled 'The Paradigm of Alarmism'. He began as follows:

> One of the things I discovered when writing my book was that, time and time again, whatever the issue was, the environmental movement used the same methodology for promoting their scare in the first place, getting done what they needed done, and once they've got it done making sure they have absolutely no blow-back at all. So I've defined this as a paradigm.

In the accompanying PowerPoint, the speaker described the tactics of environmentalists in this way:

The Roots of the Alarmist Movement – Their Tactics:

- Legal maneuvering
- Reliance on regulation
- Intimidation
- Mass protests
- Disdain for humanity
- The paradigm of alarmism

The PowerPoint expanded on the final point in the list as follows:

The Paradigm of alarmism:

- Identify your cause and the laws you want enacted (use syllogism)
- Create an apocalyptic scenario
- Claim there's a threat to children

- Don the mantle of science and decry those who disagree as anti-science
- Create a clamor that rules out rational debate, using intimidation if necessary
- Once your measures have been adopted, defend them ruthlessly

The PowerPoint then applied the paradigm specifically to the issue of climate change:

> The Paradigm in Action – Global Warming:
> - Earth warming; fossil fuels cause earth to warm; so ban fossil fuels
> - A-Z of apocalyptic scenarios
> - All scenarios take place 50–80 years out
> - An Inconvenient Truth, IPCC, "consensus"
> - $300m ad budget …

The speaker ended his talk with a word of warning:

> They call us "deniers," "delayers," and "climate criminals." They *will not* let us go. The whole point of their [rhetoric] is to go against the cultural movement they call 'skeptics'. There's no way they will allow us any breathing room if they can help it. That's what we are up against.
> (Murray, The paradigm of alarmism, 2009)

Rhetorical Representations of Science

While, as we have seen, collectively formed argumentation on climate change draws on a variety of discourses that are incorporated in a single macro-argument, the analysis indicates that the discourse of science is the most prevalent, as one would expect given the physical basis of climate change and the authority accorded science in our culture for explaining the natural world. Accordingly, the next part of the chapter focuses on another finding from the case study – that science, as appropriated for rhetorical ends in debates over climate change, is represented in multiple ways across different instances of argumentation. Here the analysis takes its inspiration from Science Studies, drawing both on that field's depiction of science as a historically, socially and institutionally situated set of practices for constructing knowledge and on the older philosophical view of Science that this depiction is set against (Golinski, 2005; Knorr Cetina, 1999; Latour, 1987; Shapin, 1998).

Analysis of the references to science found in the Internet-published texts in the corpus revealed that science is represented, in any particular instance of argumentation on climate change, in one of ten ways, as:
- An institution personified in an individual scientist.
- An institution embodied in a group of experts.

- An institution with a history reaching back, in the West, to the early 17th century.
- Knowledge about the natural world that is objective, certain, and universally valid.
- Knowledge about the natural world that is socially constructed, provisional, and consensus-seeking.
- An activity that serves society as its primary source of understanding of the natural world and thus an essential resource for material production and policy-making.
- An amoral and uncontrolled activity that has repeatedly created major risks for the planet and human society.
- An activity that, from its inception in the 17th century, has operated freely, beyond the influences of politics and finance.
- An activity dependant on funding from either government or business, a relationship that can distort its aims and practices.
- Techno-science – a nexus of science, engineering, and finance.
- A normative dichotomy of 'junk science' (their degraded science) versus 'sound science' (our authentic science).

Each of these eleven representations of science, when deployed for rhetorical purposes in climate-change argumentation, is shown in either a positive or a negative light, depending on which of the two discourse coalitions discussed earlier is using it to advance or counter a claim.

While there is insufficient space here to discuss the rhetorical appropriation of each of these ten representations of science, I will describe three cases where a particular facet of science is cast very differently by the two discourse coalitions. The first case concerns the representation of science as a body of experts, in this instance the Intergovernmental Panel on Climate Change. As represented by the 'climate-change crisis' discourse coalition, the IPCC is portrayed as comprising hundreds and sometimes thousands of the world's leading climate scientists and vaunted as *the* unquestioned authority on the reality and impacts of climate change, a status seen to have been confirmed when the IPCC was awarded the 2007 Nobel Peace Prize. Here is an example of such a positive depiction of the IPCC taken from the website of the Sierra Club of Canada, an environmental activist organization: '[The IPCC] is a body of over 2000 scientists and experts from around the world who gather periodically to review the existing peer-reviewed literature of the relevant science. … The IPCC's methods are rigorously fair to dissent, and incomparably thorough'.

Contrastingly, as depicted by the 'climate-crisis skepticism' discourse coalition, the IPCC is a highly politicized organization, including in its membership only a small number of actual climate scientists, along with a host of non-scientific specialists such as economists, engineers and statisticians, as well as political representatives from the 194 participating nations – with all these actors seen to be biased by their own particular career, financial and/or ideological interests. *Nature, Not Human Activity, Rules the Climate*, a 2008 report edited by skeptic scientist Fred Singer and published on the website of the Heartland Institute, the conservative policy think-tank mentioned earlier, describes the perceived bias of the IPCC as follows:

> The IPCC [has been] an activist enterprise from the very beginning. … Its agenda [has been] to justify control of the emission of greenhouse gases, especially carbon dioxide. … [The organization is] a political rather than scientific entity, with its leading scientists reflecting the positions of their governments or seeking to induce their governments to adopt the IPCC position. (iv)

Another facet of science that is represented quite differently, depending on which discourse coalition is employing it for rhetorical purposes, is the technical practice of using computer-run climate models to simulate the global climate system and predict future climatic trends. These climate models play a key role in the IPCC's assessment of the risks associated with climate change. The 'climate-change crisis' discourse coalition consistently portrays climate models as wholly credible in their simulations of the climate system and predictions of future climatic conditions, an assumption reflected in this description taken from the website of the Union of Concerned Scientists:

> [Climate models] are the reference standard for global change research. These models incorporate the latest understanding of the physical processes at work in the atmosphere, oceans, and the Earth's surface. [They] are constantly being enhanced … as our understanding of climate improves and as computational power increases, enabling additional components of the Earth-ocean-atmosphere system to be dynamically linked.

In contrast, the 'climate-crisis skepticism' discourse coalition represents the same climate models as technically flawed and incapable of adequately simulating the Earth's present climate system, let alone of making viable predictions, and also as highly susceptible to ideological influence. An example of a negative characterization of this kind comes from the website of the Friends of Science, a Canadian group advocating the view that climate change is primarily driven by variations in solar activity, not by CO2 emissions:

> [Climate] models assume that CO2 is the primary climate driver, and that the Sun has an insignificant effect on climate. You cannot use the output of a model to verify or prove its initial assumption – that is circular reasoning and is illogical. Computer models can be made to roughly match the 20th century temperature rise by adjusting many input parameters and using strong positive feedbacks. They do not "prove" anything.

A third case in which science is represented very differently by the two discourse coalitions when appropriated for rhetorical ends is the personification of science in a particular individual. We see below how James Hansen, climate scientist and director of NASA's Goddard Institute of Space Studies, is depicted as either hero or villain, depending on the source. In the first example, taken from the website of The Nation Institute, a progressive U.S. policy think-tank, a positive image of Hansen is used to buttress the claim that if emissions of CO2 are not curtailed, the Earth's climate could change very abruptly, with catastrophic consequences:

> A few weeks ago, our foremost climatologist, NASA's Jim Hansen, submitted a paper to *Science* magazine with several co-authors. The abstract attached to it argued – and I have never read stronger language in a scientific paper – "If humanity wishes to preserve a planet similar to that on which civilization developed and to which life on earth is adapted, paleoclimate evidence and ongoing climate change suggest that CO2 will need to be reduced from its current 385 [parts per million] to at most 350 ppm." Hansen cites six irreversible tipping points – massive sea level rise and huge changes in rainfall patterns, among them – that we'll pass if we don't get back down to 350 soon; and the first of them, judging by last summer's insane melt of Arctic ice, may already be behind us. (Bill McKibbon, "The World at 350: A Last Chance for Civilization").

In the second example, below, we see a much different characterization of Hansen in an editorial from the website of the *Washington Times*. Here a negative depiction of Hansen is used in arguing that predictions of sudden catastrophic climate events are baseless and should not be taken seriously.

> Climatologist James Hansen's article "The Threat to the Planet" is featured on the front page of the July 13 *New York Review of Books*, which carries the label "Fiction Issue." How appropriate. In his review of three alarmist books on global warming and of Al Gore's documentary "An Inconvenient Truth," Mr. Hansen stresses all kinds of catastrophic consequences of higher temperatures. Echoing the horror movie "The Day After Tomorrow," he has sea level rising 20 feet by 2100, inundating most of Florida and a good many East Coast cities. The main problem with Mr. Hansen, and others like him, are [sic] not the wild claims of coming disasters. No one in his right mind pays attention to these anyway. No, it is the fact that nowhere does he demonstrate that the current, rather modest warming trend is human-caused. He just assumes it. ... Sorry, that's not good enough. Not when he calls for far reaching policies that would throttle energy use and the national economy. (*Washington Times*, editorial, "The Climate of Fear", 2006)

These rhetorically employed representations of science resonate strongly with Wenden's (2005) claim that

> modes of representation will vary depending on the perspective from which they are constructed, whether biographical, historical, sociocultural [or] ideological. ... Moreover, inasmuch as linguistic representations determine the way in which we think about particular objects, events, situations and, as such, function as a principle of action influencing actual social practice ... there will be competition among groups over what is to be taken as the correct, appropriate, or preferred representation. (p. 90)

Conclusion

This chapter has attempted to illuminate the discursive processes at work in a frequent yet little examined occurrence in organizational discourse: the collective formation of argumentation across discursive networks of Internet-published texts produced by professional organizations engaged in public debates over major social issues. I will conclude by proposing a methodological model derived from the study that could be used to empirically explore the collective formation of argumentation within and across organizations engaged in any public debate over a highly contested social issue:

- First, within an individual organization: the discourse genres and rhetorical strategies employed inside the organization to develop a common understanding of a particular issue, to construct a set of shared arguments regarding it, and to consolidate a consensus position.
- Second, within a discourse coalition: the collaborative process of argument-building that occurs across a group of discursively aligned organizations as they exchange compatible perspectives, pertinent 'facts', and mutually useful claims and evidence.
- And third, between discourse coalitions: the argument-building that occurs through the discursive interactions of opposing discourse coalitions as they monitor and respond to one another's arguments.

If other researchers, for their own ends, were to take up this methodological model, as I plan to do myself in future research, perhaps together we might be able to describe in greater depth the broad and complex fields of discourse and argumentation jointly created by organizations participating in public debates over major social issues.

Notes

1. Two examples of each of the eight types of organizations: Environmental NGOs (Greenpeace, World Wide Fund for Nature); international political organizations (United Nations Environment Program, Asia-Pacific Partnership on Clean Development and Climate); government agencies (U.S. Environmental Protection Agency, European Climate Change Programme); business corporations (Peabody Energy, Munich Re); groups of scientists (Union of Concerned Scientists, Friends of Science); media organizations (*The Guardian*, *The Washington Times*); policy think-tanks (Competitive Enterprise Institute, Pembina Institute); and religious organizations (Evangelical Climate Initiative, Cornwall Alliance).
2. The organizations that comprise the 'climate-change crisis' discourse coalition include, for example, the World Wide Fund for Nature, the Union of Concerned Scientists, *The Guardian*, Munich Re, the Pembina Institute, the U.S. Environmental Protection Agency, and the Evangelical Climate Initiative.

3. Organizations comprising the 'climate-crisis skepticism' discourse coalition include, for example, the Fraser Institute, The Friends of Science, the U.S. Chamber of Commerce, Peabody Energy, *The Washington Times*, and the Cornwall Alliance.
4. I am not suggesting that there are only two discourse coalitions involved in the debate over climate change – there are certainly others as well. For example, the organizations in a third discourse coalition identified from my analysis of Internet-published texts share the following macro-argument: 'Climate change is human-caused and poses a real threat to the planet, and to counter this threat nations around the world must continue to expand their economies in order to create the additional wealth required for investment in the 'green' technologies needed to deal with the problem'.
5. The Little Ice Age was a period of planetary cooling lasting approximately from 1600–1850. In the Northern Hemisphere, where the impact appears to have been greater, the Little Ice Age forced Norse settlers to abandon Greenland and repeatedly froze the River Thames in England.

References

Arrhenius, Svante
    1896   On the influence of carbonic acid in the air upon the temperature of the ground. *Journal of Science* 41: 237–275.
Ball, Timothy
    2009   Bogeymen of the C02 hoax losing ground. *Canada Free Press*, March 30, 2009. (retrieved April 4, 2009, from http://www.canadafreepress.com/index.php/article/9746).
Beck, Coby
    n.d.   How to talk to a climate skeptic. Grist. (retrieved March 22, 2009, from http://gristmill.grist.org/skeptics).
Berkenkotter, Carol
    2001   Genre systems at work: DSM-IV and rhetorical recontextualization in psychotherapy paperwork. *Written Communication* 18: 326–349.
Callendar, Guy
    1938   The artificial production of carbon dioxide and its influence on climate. *Quarterly Journal of the Royal Meteorological Society* 64: 223–240.
Carvalho, Anabela and Jacquelin Burgess
    2005   Cultural circuits of climate change in UK broadsheet newspapers, 1985–2003. *Risk Analysis* 25: 1457–1469.
Clegg, Stewart, Cynthia Hardy, Thomas Lawrence and Walter Nord (eds.)
    2006   *The Sage Handbook of Organizational Studies*. London: Sage Publications.
David Suzuki Foundation
    n.d.   Climate change: Impacts and Solutions (retrieved January 10, 2008, from www.davidsuzuki.org/climate change).
Fischer, Frank
    2003   *Reframing Public Policy: Discursive Politics and Deliberative Practices*. New York: Oxford University Press.

Fourier, Joseph
    1824   Remarques générales sur les températures du globe terrestre et des espaces planétaires. *Annales de Chemie et de Physique* 27: 136–67.
Friends of Science
    n.d.   Common misconceptions about climate change. (retrieved June 10, 2007, from www.friendsofscience.org).
Gee, James
    1996   *Social Linguistics and Literacies: Ideology in Discourses.* London: Taylor and Francis.
Gee, James
    2005   *An Introduction to Discourse Analysis: Theory and Method.* New York: Routledge.
Golinski, Jan
    2005   *Making Natural Knowledge: Constructivism and the History of Science.* Chicago: University of Chicago Press.
Goodnight, Thomas
    1982   The personal, technical, and public spheres of argument: A speculative inquiry into the art of public deliberation. *Journal of the American Forensic Association* 18: 214–227.
Grant, David, Cynthia Hardy, Cliff Oswick and Linda Putnam (eds.)
    2004   *The Sage Handbook of Organizational Discourse.* London: Sage Publications.
Grant, David, Tom Keenoy and Cliff Oswick (eds.)
    1998   *Discourse and Organization.* London: Sage Publications.
Hajer, Maarten
    1993   Discourse coalitions and the institutionalization of practice. In Frank Fischer and John Forester (eds.) *The Argumentative Turn in Policy Analysis and Planning*, 43–76. Durham: Duke University Press.
Hajer, Maarten
    1995   *The Politics of Environmental Discourse: Ecological Modernization and the Policy Process.* Oxford: Oxford University Press.
Hajer, Maarten
    2005   Rebuilding Ground Zero: The politics of performance. *Planning Theory & Practice* 6: 445–464.
Hansen, James
    1988   The greenhouse effect: Impacts on current global temperature and regional heat waves. Testimony to U.S. Senate, Committee on Energy and Natural Resources. Washington, DC.
Heartland Institute
    n.d.   Manhattan declaration on climate change: "Global warming" isn't a global crisis. (retrieved May 8, 2008, from www.heartland.org).
Hulme, Mike
    2009   *Why We Disagree about Climate Change.* Cambridge: Cambridge University Press.
IPCC
    2007   *Fourth Assessment Report: Climate Change 2007.* Cambridge: Cambridge University Press.

Keeling, Charles
  1970   Is carbon dioxide from fossil fuel changing man's environment? *Proceedings of the American Philosophical Society* 114: 10–17.
Knorr Cetina, Karin
  1999   *Epistemic Cultures: How the Sciences Make Knowledge.* Cambridge: Harvard University Press.
Latour, Bruno
  1987   *Science in Action: How to Follow Scientists and Engineers through Society.* Cambridge: Harvard University Press.
Livesey, Sharon
  2002   Global warming wars: Rhetorical and discourse analytic approaches to ExxonMobil's corporate public discourse. *Journal of Business Communication* 39: 117–146.
Lynch, Michael and Steve Woolgar (eds.)
  1990   *Representation in Scientific Practice:* Cambridge: The MIT Press.
McKibbon, Bill
  2008   The world at 350: A last chance for civilization. (retrieved June 3, 2008, from www.nationinstitute.org).
Mooney, Chris Mooney
  2009   James Hansen is the world's leading   and most politically outspoken – climate researcher. *New Scientist*, March 11, 2009. (retrieved June 5, 2009, from http://seedmagazine.com/content/article/the_new_scientist).
Mumby, Dennis
  2004   Discourse, power and ideology: Unpacking the critical approach. In David Grant, Cynthia Hardy, Cliff Oswick, and Linda Putnam (eds.), *The Sage Handbook of Organizational Discourse*, 237–258. London: Sage Publications.
Mumby, Dennis and Robin Clair
  1997   Organization discourse. In Tuen van Dijk (ed.) *Discourse as Social Interaction*, 181–205. London: Sage Publications.
Murray, Iain
  2009   The paradigm of alarmism. Conference on Global Warming, New York City, March 2009. (retrieved June 3, 2009, from http://www.slideshare.net/ismurray/heartland09)
Runhaar, Hens, Carel Dieperink and Peter Driessen
  2006   *International Journal of Sustainability in Higher Education* 7: 34–56.
Rydin, Yvonne
  2003   *Conflict, Consensus, and Rationality in Environmental Planning: An Institutional Discourse Approach.* New York: Oxford University Press.
Schneider, Stephen
  1976   *The Genesis Strategy: Climate and Global Survival.* New York: Plenum Press.
Scollon, Ron
  2007   *Analyzing Public Discourse: Discourse Analysis in the Making of Public Policy.* New York: Routledge.
Shapin, Stephen
  1998   *The Scientific Revolution.* Chicago: University of Chicago Press.

Sharp, Liz and Tim Richardson
    2001   Reflections on Foucauldian discourse analysis in planning and environ-
              mental policy research. *Journal of Environmental Policy and Planning* 3:
              193–209.
Sillince, John
    1999   The organizational setting, use, and institutionalization of argumentation
              repertoires. *Journal of Management Studies* 36: 795–830.
Singer, Fred (ed.)
    2008   *Nature, Not Human Activity, Rules the Climate.* Chicago: Heartland Insti-
              tute.
Toulmin, Stephen
    1959   *The Uses of Argument.* Cambridge: Cambridge University Press.
Toulmin, Stephen, Richard Rieke and Allan Janik
    1979   *An Introduction to Reasoning.* New York: MacMillan.
Traweek, Sharon
    1988   *Beamtimes and Lifetimes.* Cambridge: Harvard University Press.
Tyndall, John
    1860   *Glaciers of the Alps.* London: John Murray.
United Nations Framework Convention on Climate ChangeSecretariat
    1997   Kyoto protocol.
Union of Concerned Scientists
    n.d.   Global warming science and impacts. (retrieved August 10, 2007, from
              www.ucsusa.org).
Waitt, Gordon
    2005   Doing discourse analysis. In Iain Hay (ed.) *Qualitative Research Methods
              in Human Geography,* 163–191. New York: Oxford University Press.
Weart, Spenser
    2003   *The Discovery of Global Warming.* Cambridge: Harvard University Press.
Wendon, Anita
    2005   The politics of representation: A critical discourse analysis of an Aljazeera
              special report. *International Journal of Peace Studies* 10: 89–112.
Washington Times editorial
    2006   Fear factor. (retrieved August 9, 2006, from http://www.washingtontimes.
              com/news/2006/jul/31/20060731-085007-4855r).
Zanoni, Patrizia and Maddy Janssens
    2003   Deconstructing difference: The rhetoric of human resource managers' di-
              versity discourses. *Organizational Studies* 25: 55–74.

16. E-mail messaging in the corporate sector: Tensions between technological affordances and rapport management*

Maria do Carmo Leite de Oliveira

Abstract

Understanding the influence of information and communication technologies (ICT) is a challenge for research on organizational communication. Corporations often adopt ICT tools such as e-mail to improve performance and increase productivity. However, the opposite may also occur. In this chapter I analyze the case of a Brazilian company facing internal communication dilemmas six years after privatization to an international consortium. I draw upon Hutchby's (2001) view that the interaction between the social and the technical is based on the notion of affordances (Gibson 1979) to explain why, how, and when the use of e-mail may become a problem. The analysis revealed strong tension between e-mail communicative affordances and rapport management: first, even though e-mail facilitated access to a larger number of colleagues, it also contributed to keep co-workers physically apart, weakening ties of trust in a cultural context in which personal relationships are highly valued; second, affordances such as the ability to transform exchanges into documents and to share information with visible and invisible audiences encouraged professionals to use e-mail to "tell on colleagues" or to protect themselves from accusations, generating hostility. This seriously compromised the efforts to engage professionals in a common project and develop a sense of community, one of the major aims of internal communication.

1. Introduction

An announcement published in the technology section of a Brazilian newspaper draws attention to the unexpected: every Friday 150 engineers working at Intel have to rely on old-fashioned means of communication and talk to workmates face-to-face or by telephone. Using e-mail is not allowed; the idea is to encourage professionals to interact among themselves without using a computer ("Technology Section", *O Globo*, 22 October, 2007).

What types of risks can a corporation perceive in e-mail messaging to discourage its use? To what extent are internal communication problems a result of computer mediation as suggested by Intel's initiative?

Understanding the influence of information and communication technologies (ICT) is still a challenge for current research on organizational communication, as recognized by researchers from various fields, such as Business Administration (Jones et al. 2004) and Linguistics (Bargiela-Chiapini, Nickerson, and Planken 2007: 49). Nevertheless, investment in communication technologies in corporate organizations has been largely motivated by technological determinism. From a deterministic perspective (Hutchby 2001), technologies trigger change in social life. Influenced by a transmission model of communication (Shannon and Weaver 1949), corporations have neglected the role of participants in the communicative process, assuming that technological innovations may, in and of themselves, increase efficiency and effectiveness and yield positive changes in organizational culture. In turn, Business Administration studies focusing on the role of ICT have inquired on the transforming power of technology by investigating its use in relation to several aspects, such as adoption of management practices geared toward modernizing corporations (Spanos, Prastacos, and Poulymenakou 2002); implementation of the knowledge management concept (Cabrera and Cabrera 2002); the process of decision-making in groups (Scott et al. 1998); transformation of organizational culture (Silva 2000); efficiency and efficacy (Vries and Diana 2005; Vihera and Nurmela 2001); and improvement in performance and productivity (Mahmood, Hall, and Swanberg 2001; Oliveira and Barbosa 2002; Oliveira 2004).

A similar scenario is observed in Linguistics. When describing the state of the art in computer-mediated discourse (CMD), Herring (2001) cites among the most active research areas those whose main focus is to investigate how computer mediation affects language and communicative exchanges. Examples include studies investigating the impact of computers on communication genre (oral or written) (Murray 1988; Herring 1999; King 1996; Daft and Langel 1984; Baron 1984), studies on the structural properties of messages in terms of typography, orthography, word choice, and grammar (Baron 1984; Herring 1998; Murray 1990; MacKinnon 1995; Chafe 1982: Ko 1996); on the coherence of the text; and on the management of virtual interactions, vis-à-vis face-to-face exchange parameters (Cherny 1999; Lunsford 1996; Murray 1989; Baym 1996; Herrring 1996; Severinson Eklundh and Macdonald 1994).

A literature review by Herring (2001: 614) underscores the notion that the properties of computer messaging systems are crucial in shaping CMD. The author cites studies addressing the impact of variations in the medium on transmission type (Cherny 1999) (one way, such as e-mail, and two way, such as instant messaging and participation structure [Kiesler, Siegel, and McGuire 1984], synchronous, as in chats, vs. asynchronous, such as in e-mail). Other studies discuss the implications of a wide range of physical properties in messaging systems, from limiting the message size 'up' (Cherny 1999) to providing additional channels of communication, such as audio, video or graphics (Yates and Graddol 1996).

An alternative approach to think about the way technologies affect the social world is offered by Hutchby (2001). Hutchby's view on the interaction between the social and the technical is based on Gibson's (1979) notion that human beings and animals, insects, birds and fish orient themselves toward objects based on affordances, i.e., guided by the possibilities for action offered by each object. His study of the different forms of "technologized interaction" aims to assess how our ordinary conversation practices may be shaped by and/or shape the affordances of communication technologies. This perspective can help us reflect on the use of e-mail in professional settings. From this stance, technology will be viewed both as a medium that introduced a new form of interpersonal communication and also as a work tool interacting with the quality of professional relationships.

Having this in mind, I will move on to discuss the need to investigate what professionals *do* in this kind of "technologized interaction", giving examples of how the affordances provided by e-mail as a technological tool as well as by the context guide professional practices and help answer the questions of why, how, and when the use of e-mail may become a problem.

In Section 2, I will focus on communicative affordances of e-mail shaping written (typed) communication and the possibilities of interaction. In Section 3, to illustrate this discussion, I present a case study dealing with how e-mail is perceived by professionals working for a corporation undergoing structural changes. In Section 4, I identify the actions perceived as problematic for rapport management – and consequently for productivity – in the work environment. In Section 5, I propose contextual factors that are likely to contribute to the way rapport management deals with the impact of e-mail's communicative affordances.

2.   Together and apart

One of the claims about electronic media is that it is radically changing our ways of thinking about authors, readers, information and text (Johnstone 2002: 178). In the same way, CMD research claims that e-mail has changed the nature of written and oral communication genres (Herring 2001: 614). On the one hand, it is undeniable that e-mail is a written genre, and as such it promotes, similarly to old-fashioned corporate letters, distance communication (Oliveira 1992). On the other, e-mail differs from traditional letters because its associated technological features afford a peculiar combination of oral and written communication. For example, two features of written genres have been modified in e-mail communication: asynchronicity and the recording and storage of information. In non-computer mediated writing, the time available for editing and formatting of text favors the production of relatively planned discourse (Tannen

1982; Chafe 1982). However, as pointed out by Herring (2001), e-mail exchanges are typically faster than most other types of written exchanges, making it "less synchronous", with less planning and editing and more contact.

With regard to the recording of information, e-mail messaging has reinforced the documental character of written text. The simple act of sending a message originates a document, whether or not the message is read. In addition, storage is more flexible: e-mail messages can be stored as paper or electronic files. Not only do these properties enhance the conditions of access to an organizational memory (Spanos, Prastacos, and Poulymenakou 2002: 661), but they also increase the vulnerability of interaction. In this medium there is always a record, the risk of recontextualization is higher, and the communicative act is highly visible.

Therefore, e-mail is unmistakably a written genre; but it also has unquestionable affinity with spoken genres. Just like spoken exchanges in face-to-face interaction, e-mails allow others to take part in the conversation. Resources such as "copy" and "forward" grant access to other participants (who may be visible or invisible), invited or uninvited. Also, as in face-to-face interactions involving multiple participants, e-mail can be sent to one participant but targeted at a different one. However, in the case of e-mail, the sharing of information is not (always) accidental or invasive (Goffman 1981) – it results from an invitation made by the sender through features such as "copy" or "forward".

"Carbon copies" are a well-known resource of traditional corporate letters. However, the ease of producing an electronic "copy" has transformed virtual conversations into staged events (Goffman 1981). The resource made it easy to expand the audience and allowed for the presence of both visible and invisible guests. Another possibility of the "copy" resource is, in certain contexts, attributing to a specific member of the audience the status of communication target. Similarly, the "forward" resource allows non-invited participants to have access to the conversation. Thus, differently from what is observed in some spoken and written exchanges, e-mailing has the potential to make public interactions of a private nature, at least apparently addressed to those visually designated as interlocutors in the "To" and "From" fields.

Therefore, e-mail as a communication genre is shaped by technological properties that afford simultaneous distance and proximity and great visibility to the communicative action. In the following section I present a case study that illustrates how people manage the impact of these technological features.

3.   Case study

The interviews to be discussed in this section are part of a larger research /consulting project, undertaken in partnership with a management specialist to assess the quality of internal communication carried out at a Brazilian company that provides electrical infrastructure services. The study began in 2002, approximately six years after the company's privatization and acquisition by a consortium formed by several Brazilian and foreign private and state-owned companies. Currently, the company is run by the Consortium's controlling shareholders (a European company specializing in the same business).

After the first years of privatization, the predominant feeling among employees was that the company was going through a phase of stabilization or maturation of its new profile as a private corporation aiming to be competitive. The corporation's top management was focused on trying to consolidate a management model that would promote individual and team commitment and thus increase the chances of success. One of the greatest challenges faced by the corporation was the improvement of internal communication processes, especially considering the heavy personnel turnover rate and the many services being provided by the company through third parties.

Our tasks as consultants were: to diagnose the state of internal communication and to identify the aspects favoring or hindering the construction of an integrative culture; to provide support for the preparation of an Internal Communication Plan including the definition of a strategic focus for communication; and to develop a training program for all management levels (directors, middle management, team leaders) to prepare them to lead the implementation of the new communication strategy.

Data were collected through (i) a set of semi-structured interviews with 20 professionals from several hierarchical levels and ranks, from different areas and working at the company for different lengths of time; (ii) observation of routine practices, such as meetings involving one or more departments; (iii) focus-group discussions with workers engaged in different communicative practices; (iv) compilation of electronic communication, institutional communication (e.g. newsletters), and the Internal Communication Plan produced at the European headquarters as a reference for the local company.

To illustrate the present discussion, excerpts from the interviews with eight professionals who had at the time been working for the company between 1 and 29 years are presented. The main criterion for the selection of this material was the spontaneous mention of e-mail. Of the eight employees whose interviews are examined, two were hired before the privatization process: João and James. João had been with the company for 24 years. In the years after privatization, he had been moved around as manager of four different areas, and was currently product distribution manager. His statements reveal a concern with loss of team productivity due to e-mail misuse. James had been working at the company for 29 years, and at the time was managing the industrial area, which was going to be deactivated relatively soon. As observed by other old-time employees, James' criticisms referred to the loss of personal relationships, of the family spirit within the company.

Six post-privatization employees were also selected: Fábio, from the technical area, had been an employee for five years; Silvina, initially hired on a contract basis, had been with the corporation for four years and was currently in the purchasing/contracts area; Alex, also initially a contractor, had been employed for four years at the time of the interview, and was working with in-house publications and documentation; Taís, in charge of the marketing team, had been with the company for three years; Hugo, who worked in an area that explored a new commercial niche, had been with the company for two years; and Rose, from customer support, had been with the corporation for one year and a half.

4.   Management of technological affordances and rapport

One of the challenges of professionals in charge of managing internal communication is to develop a sense of community, reinforcing integration among the members of the corporation and their commitment to a common project. One of the expectations associated with communication technologies such as e-mail is that they will bring people closer together, fostering relationships and consequently improving productivity. This straightforward relationship, however, does not match the perceptions of the professionals interviewed. Rather, their interviews suggest that the quality of rapport management is directly linked to the management of technological affordances, which may in the end produce the opposite effect: isolation, less collaboration, and fewer results.

4.1.   Talking to strangers

As Bauman (2004 [2003]: 81) points out, proximity and distance are two sides of the same coin. When the company under study adopted electronic communication as the main tool for interpersonal communication, it also made a choice to keep people physically apart.

Excerpt 1

Não, eu ... atualmente antigamente a gente tinha mais assim diálogo com as pessoas, hoje tá muito assim via note, via note, qualquer coisa é via note, é tudo correio eletrônico correio eletrônico ... então o correio eletrônico se tornou um negócio assim é ao meu ver muito frio, entendeu, então você não tem de repente aquele elo de comunicação com a pessoa em si até o próprio contato telefônico, né, agora é tudo via note, via note via note e-mails ... via note o negócio é ... às vezes fica difícil, porque a gente se comunica com pessoas e não sabe nem quem é a pessoa. qualquer coisa senta lá no computador e pá pá pá pá pá pá ... quem é a pessoa? passa por você e você não sabe, tá entendendo? então eu acho que isso aí (James)

'no ah I ah no, we used to well talk to people more, now it's a lot like through notes, through notes[1], anything is through notes, everything electronic mail electronic mail ... so electronic mail became a thing like what I see is it's real cold, you know, so you don't have like that link of communication with the person himself and even a phone call, you know, now it's all through notes, through note through note e-mails ... using notes is ... sometimes it's hard, since we communicate with people and don't know even who they are. You just sit there at the computer and tac tac tac tac tac ... who is the person? Goes by you and you don't know, you see? So I think that's it' (James)

The feeling of these professionals is that they no longer know their fellow workers. Relationships are marked by a lack of long-term commitment and by weak ties of trust: the features of relationships with strangers. Giddens (2000 [1998]), citing Simmel, states that in urban settings, in modern societies, a stranger is someone that we do not know well, whom we have never met, but with whom we interact on a rather regular basis. For the interviewees, the preferential use of e-mail in detriment of other forms of communication made the corporation become a community of strangers.

The fact that contacts are only virtual makes professionals somewhat suspicious about what they do not see/hear. One of the interviewees calls attention to the advantages of knowing somebody personally, of physical contact, when the communicative exchange involves asking somebody to do something for you, or interpreting the delay of a colleague in doing what was requested:

Excerpt 2

Aí quando chegar ali, "pô, tô vendo ... a Renata tá num esforço tremendo, né, realmente o caso do meu amigo não é tão prioritário. Ih! ela teve outro ali que é mais prioritário ..." (Fabio)

'Then, when I get there, "yes, I see ... Renata is working really hard, you know, really the case of my friend is not such a priority. Oh my! She had something else come up that is of higher priority ..."' (Fabio)

In other words, it is easier to understand the needs of those whom we see/know than the needs of those we only meet virtually. Personal contact is relevant to cooperation. Knowing people orients the inference of the meaning of an action.

The lack of physical contact contributes to the construction of formal, more distant, relationships:

Excerpt 3

é a mesma coisa eh você tá lidando com uma pessoa que você não tem não tem contato, não tem nunca viu de repente, aí você fica "prezado fulano pá, pá, pá" tudo bonitinho e quando chega no final saudações atenciosamente ponto. aí mandou pra lá e o cara manda de volta pra você mas você nunca viu a pessoa e a pessoa nunca te viu (James)

'it's the same thing uh you you're dealing with a person that you have no contact with, don't have never saw and all of a sudden you go "dear sir da, da, da" all nice and when you get to the end yours truly period. then you send it and the guy sends it back to you but you never saw the person and the person never saw you' (James)

Excerpt 4

são poucas as pessoas são poucas as pessoas que eu boto assim bom dia boa tarde, normalmente é assim "preciso disso nanan" quando muito quando muito bota SDS e o nome. ou então até logo, tá entendendo, não tem aquela (James)

'there are only a few there are a few people that I put like this good morning good afternoon, usually it's like "I need this dadad" the most you get the most you get is Sincerely and a name. or goodbye, you see, there isn't' (James)

Especially old-timers perceive e-mail as a turning point between the old and the new company. In a nostalgic discourse, they reject the present, idealizing a past when people mattered:

Excerpt 5

Todo mundo gosta de ser bem tratado, né, Você pedir o que você quer, o serviço e depois botar, né, Apareça, Estou com saudades. Ou alguma coisa assim. Acho que pode, não custa nada, né? (Alex)

'Everyone likes to be treated well, right, You state what you want, the job you want done, and then you add, well, pop in some day, I miss you. Or something like that. You could do it, it's not hard, right?' (Alex)

So, it seems that the way people manage distance and proximity has confined the relationship to its professional dimension, resulting in an inappropriate balance between instrumental and social goals.

4.2.   Living with competitors

A major characteristic of organizations is a sense of community, which implies, among other aspects, mutual engagement to build a project desired by all and undertaken as a personal responsibility by each of the persons involved. The quality of the relationships between the parts involved reflects – and is reflected in – a shared sense of community. In the company under study, the professionals realize that the affordances of the technological tool are being managed in a way that makes colleagues feel more like competitors than partners.

4.2.1.   Affordances: A matter of record

One of the affordances of e-mail that is managed for competition is the recording of information. Many workers recognize that they do not trust their partners. They send e-mail not because it is necessary to send a message, but because it is necessary to document an action:

Excerpt 6

Então o note eu mando pra ficar registrado. É um documento que eu vou imprimir e deixar registrado que eu entrei em contato com aquela pessoa, porque eu não tenho como gravar por telefone. (Rose)

'So the note, I send it for the record. It is a document that I am going to print out and keep a record that I contacted that person, since I don't have a way of recording a telephone conversation.' (Rose)

Excerpt 7

as vantagens que eu vejo no note, a nível de, vamos dizer assim de rapidez, vamos dizer uma eficiência e aquele negócio, um documento que você tem porque a palavra na verdade você diz que disse mas pode não ter dito, né. Disse mas não disse (...) e ali ela já fica, quer dizer, ela seria, vamos dizer assim, uma autenticação do que você realmente pediu, do uma confirmação, né (na realidade) quer dizer, por esse lado eu vejo que é realmente importante você ter o coisa. agora, que tira um pouco do relacionamento porque o cara (James)

'the advantages that I see in a note (...) in terms of let's say speed, let's say efficacy and what not, a document that you have because a word actually you say that you said it but maybe you didn't say it, right. Said it but can't prove it ... (...) and it stays there, that is, it would be like, let's say like, an authentication of what you really asked for, of a confirmation, right (in fact) I mean, in this sense I see that it is really important having the thing. Now, you can't deny it takes away a bit of relationships because you' (James)

Both the new (Rose) and the old (James) employees draw attention to the recording of e-mail messages as a defensive practice. Sending e-mail to remind, inform or request something may be motivated by the need to generate a proof, to hold the other responsible.

Another use of the affordance of register as a defensive practice is the use of e-mail to get rid of responsibility:

Excerpt 8

(…) eu acho que essa teoria de que "passei um note pra fulano" e me eximi da responsabilidade, em termos isso funciona (…) as pessoas entendem muito assim passei um note pra Sonia, pronto, me eximi da responsabilidade. (Silvina)

'(…) I think that this theory that "I sent a note to someone" and I am no longer responsible, this sort of works (…) people see it like that I sent a note do Sonia, that's it, it's not my responsibility anymore' (Silvina)

Excerpt 9

É eu acho que ela (a comunicação via correio eletrônico) não cumpre o objetivo da comunicação, ela é, ela só libera um peso na consciência de quem tem que comunicar (Taís)

'I guess that it (communicating via e-mail) does not ensure communication, it's, it's only a weight off the shoulders of whoever has to communicate' (Taís)

Excerpt 10

teoricamente o cara mandou um note lá pra você e tirou (…) tirou aquele degrau … já mandei, minha obrigação já foi então agora hhh tô livre, entendeu? (James)

'In theory, the guy sent you a note and got rid (…) he has moved up one step … I sent it, my duty is done, so now hhh I'm free, you see?' (James)

In the three excerpts, both old-timers and new employees draw attention to the misuse of e-mail. Communication is seen as a unilateral process: none of the parts involved are committed to the final result. They do not see themselves as sharing the responsibility for the solution of a problem. They only want to protect themselves from future accusations.

4.2.2. Affordances: You see what you get

Another communicative affordance of e-mail emphasized in the interviews is that of making interactions visible and public. The way the professionals in this corporation managed this affordance characterizes a competitive relationship.

As the example shows, use of "cc" is more significant when the audience is comprised of people from higher hierarchal levels and the topic of the message involves professional performance. In these cases, "cc" may be used to construct or threaten the image or challenge efficiency:

Excerpt 11

eu recebo cerca de trinta e cinco notes por dia ... notes tolos, notes que vêm eh cópia pra mim e não deveriam vir, como eu também evito mandar pro diretor, eu não mando qualquer notes pro diretor ... né, notes em que eu percebo que só tão querendo me mostrar que tão trabalhando ... não me interessa isso, né (João)

'I get about thirty-five notes every day ... silly notes, notes uh copied to me and that shouldn't have been, they type I try not to send to the director, I don't send just any note to the director ... right notes where I see that they're only trying to show that they are working ... none of this doesn't interest me right' (João)

Thus, using the "cc" resource may be seen as an aggressive face-work practice (Goffman 1967, 2001), rather than as a means of keeping a third person informed. Within this frame, the status of participation is also altered – the copied participant recognizes him/herself as the target participant (Levinson 1988), with a right to take part in the conversation.

Excerpt 12

eh a própria empresa tem que controlar isso exemplo se eu como gerente recebo ou um diretor recebe um notes entre um subordinado seu e um de outra área e vejo que o outro foi agressivo eu já entro no meio e digo oh vamos assim, assim, assado, vamos trabalhar direito ... (João)

'the company itself has to control this for example if I as a manager receive or a director receives a note sent by one of his employees to an employee from another area and I see that the other one was aggressive I get involved and say c'mon, let's do this or that, let's do things right ...' (João)

The "cc" resource helps build contextual presuppositions (Gumperz 1982) that may frame the topic of the message, the sender's goal, the role of the participants, and the type of illocutionary act being performed:

Excerpt 13

porque às vezes jogando no ar que uma determinada obra está atrasada, ou que um determinado serviço ... está dependendo do outro de uma forma leviana, eu diria que leviana porque o notes ele fica exposto até a uma resposta dura ... né, e às vezes tem que ser dura.porque você tá lidando com profissionais né (João)

'because sometimes spreading the word that a particular job is late, or that a certain service ... is depending on the other person in a thoughtless manner, I would say thoughtless because the notes the person is exposed to reactions that may be harsh ... right, and sometimes they must be harsh. Because you are dealing with professionals right' (João)

In other words, publicizing certain information may serve personal strategic objectives, including indirectly accusing a colleague of being incompetent or not responsible. There may also be the perception that the threat is intentional, produced deliberately and consciously, contributing to the feeling of hostility that orients the rapport management:

Excerpt 14

Às vezes eu acho que ele é usado de maneira intencional. Como quem diz assim, se você não quiser já vou lhe avisando que o teu chefe tá sabendo também. Serve até de ameaça, serve até de ameaça, você sabia? (Hugo)

'sometimes I think that it (e-mail) is used intentionally. Like someone saying, if you don't want to do it, I'm warning you that your boss is aware of it. It works even for threats, works even for threats, you know?' (Hugo)

Excerpt 15

domingo mesmo uma pessoa me ligou e disse que ia me mandar um e-mail se eu não ... com cópia, se eu não fizesse determinada coisa, com cópia pro diretor, pro gerente. Você pode ficar a vontade, eu vou fazer aquilo que tem que ser feito. Ele até hoje não mandou (Alex)

'this very Sunday someone called me and said that he was going to send me an e-mail if I didn't ... and he would copy the director, the manager, if I didn't do a particular thing. Until now he hasn't done it' (Alex)

As Goffman (1974) points out, frames include assumptions, knowledge and expectations expressed symbolically through language. The professionals reveal a tacit knowledge of the conventional use of the affordances of e-mail for recording information and creating an audience. It is based on this knowledge that messages are framed as defensive and aggressive face-work practices that signal hostile, competitive behavior in the work environment.

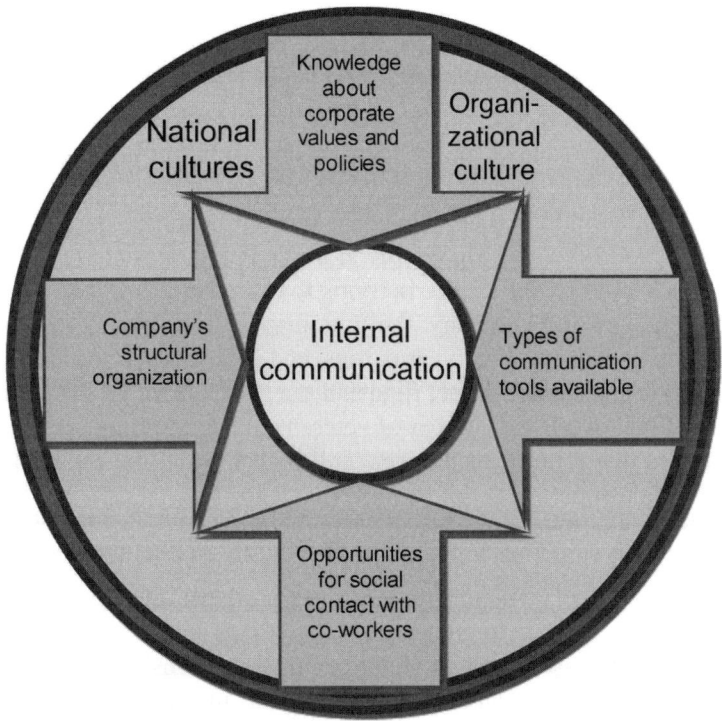

Figure 1. Main aspects influencing internal communicative practices

5.   Sociocultural context and rapport management

The analysis of interviews revealed that one of the most negative effects of e-mail is the failure to promote integration between members of an organization. This effect was perceived as being related to the strategies used to manage technological affordances such as creating distance/proximity, recording information and making communicative actions visible.

However, as proposed by Oliveira and Silva (2009), there are many aspects in communication management that must be taken into account for the understanding of internal communication practices.

As shown in Figure 1, the main aspects influencing internal communicative practices, identified in the broader project at the company under study, are: the organizational/ national culture; the degree of knowledge about the organization (including a company's mission, strategy, values, politics etc.); the employees' knowledge about the company's structure (hierarchical, horizontal); types and uses of communication tools available (upward, downward or horizontal communication tools); and the opportunities of social contact with co-workers (opportunities for socializing).

Some of these aspects were highly relevant to explain how people managed the impact of the communicative affordances of e-mail.

The quality of interpersonal relationships shaped and was shaped by the changes happening at the company after the privatization process. The implementation of a management model focused on results (rather than on people) and achievement, which underscores competitiveness between people/sectors more than collaboration, has encouraged a spirit of hostility.

Similarly, the move to keep people at arm's length was also influenced by decisions made after privatization. In trying to erase the indulgence that characterized the state-owned company, the new management abandoned fraternization programs, such as end-of-year parties, and closed down spaces of interaction/integration such as the soccer field and the gym. On top of that, employees saw the dismissal of a large number of veteran colleagues, high personnel turnover, practices that reinforced the weakening of ties and the establishment of low trust relationships.

Another relevant factor to explain the way e-mail was used may be the conflict of cultural patterns of communication. According to Barros and Prates (1996), hierarchy and personalism, two characteristics of Brazilian-style administration, are important to maintain social cohesion. Personalism means that individuals are ranked according to their personal relationships. The attitude towards people depends on whether they are seen as members of the in-group or of the out-group. The practice of personalism was left aside by the foreign management team and the excessive use of one form of distance communication prevented professionals from recognizing in-group members. This had a negative impact on productivity and on the quality of relationships. Therefore, the use of e-mail shaped and was shaped by the type of interactional ethos that was established in the company.

6. Concluding remarks

I opened this discussion with a question: how can a communication tool such as e-mail, implemented to facilitate dialogue and cooperation, be perceived as a risk? The review of the literature about computer mediation shows that in both Business Administration and Linguistics there are many studies that are strictly oriented toward the discipline's interests and theoretical frameworks. Business Administration has privileged the study of CMD from the perspective of organizational efficacy, whereas Linguistics has turned its attention to the way the medium shapes discourse and interaction. Therefore, each academic discipline has produced some insights on the issue, while missing many others.

Whenever issues involving CMD emerge in the real world (as in the use of e-mail in organizations) a need for new theoretical and methodological approaches becomes evident. In terms of theories, these issues deserve to be studied with a greater degree of interdisciplinarity – interdisciplinarity meaning not merely the adoption of concepts and methodologies of a given discipline, but the establishment of interdisciplinary teams composed of linguists and management specialists (Oliveira 2007). The effort of matching and exchanging rationales, concepts and tools can shed light on the understanding of e-mails as a medium and as a work tool.

In methodological terms, the proposal made by Sarangi (2006) of a collaborative research approach with dense investigator participation is appealing. Each corporation has its own forms of life, often recognizable only by its members. Understanding that universe as an outsider and producing knowledge that may be of practical relevance for its members require both intense socialization in the environment under study, as well as an effort to integrate the employee's lay knowledge and the researcher's technical expertise about human communication.

Concerning the relationships between technology and professional interaction, as the present discussion illustrates, the role of the subject and the context cannot be neglected. While technological properties may increase the vulnerability of mediated interaction, it is the system of beliefs that orients the deployment of the communicative affordances of e-mail messaging. As our case study shows, the relational affordances merely reflected – and reinforced – an interactional ethos characterized by low confidence and highly competitive, formal and task-oriented relationships. This shows that the context helps to frame what people *do* with e-mail, and also the meanings attributed to communicative actions.

From an applied perspective, I believe that the present discussion may help organizations to rethink the use of technology by providing a closer look at its limits. If corporations want to promote a stronger identification of employees with the company or stimulate greater integration among the members of the corporation, people must be able, first of all, to align the discourse of integration with other practices that provide the context for their everyday actions. My reflection also underscores the importance of organizations being sensitive to cultural differences in the implementation of technological solutions. In cultures that value seeing others at an arm's length, as is the case of the Brazilian culture, the abusive use of a communication model characterized by high technology and low contact should be counterbalanced with other, more efficient means to encourage interpersonal communication and consequently group cohesion.

Finally, I hope that the evidence I have presented will encourage organizations to rethink programs aimed at teaching professionals how to use e-mail. For full participation in a networking environment, professionals must have a better understanding of language-context relationships, interaction and the construction of intersubjectivity. Understanding the complexity of technological mediation and the communication process is not enough to resolve the problems of communicating via e-mail in the work environment, but serves as a starting point for the search for reasons and solutions for this dilemma.

Notes

* Acknowledgment: I would like to acknowledge the financial support of Conselho Nacional de Desenvolvimento Científico e Tecnológico – CNPq – for my ongoing study of New Professional Identities, New Communicative Abilities (306928/2006–0).
1. "Note" is the word used to refer to the company's e-mail system.

References

Bargiela-Chiappini, Francesca, Catherine Nickerson and Birgitte Planken
  2007   Challenges in the future. In: Bargiela-Chiappini, Francesca, Nickerson, Catherine and Planken, Birgitte (ed.), *Business Discourse*, 39–76. New York: Palgrave Macmillan.
Baron, Naomi S.
  1984   Computer mediated communication as a force in language change. *Visible Language* XVIII(2): 118–41.
Barros, Betania T. and Marco Aurélio S. Prates
  1996   *O Estilo Brasileiro de Administrar* [*The Brazilian Way of Running a Business*]. São Paulo: Atlas.
Bauman, Zygmunt
  2004   *Amor Líquido: sobre a Fragilidade dos Laços Humanos* [*Liquid Love: On*
  [2003]   *the Frailty of Human Bonds*, translated into Portuguese by C. A. Medeiros]. Rio de Janeiro: Jorge Zahar.
Baym, Nancy
  1996   Agreements and disagreements in a computer mediated discussion. *Research on Language and Social Interaction* 29(4): 315–45.
Cabrera, Angel and Elizabeth F. Cabrera
  2002   Knowledge-sharing dilemmas. *Organization Studies* 23: 687–710.
Chafe, Wallace
  1982   Integration and involvement in speaking, writing, and oral literature. In: Deborah Tannen (ed.), *Spoken and Written Language: Exploring Orality and Literacy*, 35–54. Norwood: Ablex.
Cherny, Lynn
  1999   *Conversation and Community: Chat in a Virtual World*. Stanford: CSLI Publications.
Daft, Richard L. and Robert H. Langel
  1984   Information richness: A new approach to managerial behavior and organizational design. In: B. M. Staw and L. L. Cummings (eds.), *Research in Organizational Behavior*, 191–233. Greenwich, CT: JAI Press.
Gibson, James J.
  1979   *The Ecological Approach to Perception*. London: Houghton Mifflin.

Giddens, Anthony
  2000   Entrevista 4 e entrevista 5. In: Anthony Giddens and Christopher Pierson
  [1998]   (eds.), *Conversas com Anthony Giddens: O Sentido da Modernidade* [*Con-versations with Anthony Giddens: Making Sense of Modernity*, translated into Portuguese by L. A. Monjardim], 73–110. Rio de Janeiro: Fundação Getúlio Vargas.
Goffman, Erving
  1967   *Interaction Ritual: Essays in Face-to-Face Behavior Garden*. New York: Doubleday.
Goffman, Erving
  1974   *Frame Analysis: An Essay on the Organization of Experience*. New York: Harper and Row.
Goffman, Erving
  1981   *Footing*. In: Goffman, E., *Forms of Talk*, 124–159. Philadelphia: University of Pennsylvania Press.
Goffman, Erving
  2001   *A Representação do Eu na Vida Cotidiana* [*The Presentation of Self in Every-*
  [1975]   *day Life*, translated into Portuguese by M. C. S. Raposo]. Petrópolis: Vozes.
Gumperz, John J.
  1982   *Discourse Strategies*. Cambridge: Cambridge University Press.
Herring, Susan C.
  1996   Two variants of an electronic message schema. In: Susan C. Herring (ed.), *Computer-Mediated Communication: Linguistic, Social and Cross-Cultural Perspectives*, 81–106. Amsterdam: John Benjamins.
Herring, Susan C.
  1998   Le style du courier électronique: variabilité et changement. *Terminograme* 84(5): 9–16.
Herring, Susan C.
  1999   Interactional coherence in CMC. *Journal of Computer-Mediated-Communication* 4(4). Special issue. *Persistent Conversation*. T. Erickson (ed.). http://jcmc.indiana.edu/vol4/issue4/herring.html (accessed 2009 may 04).
Herring, Susan C.
  2001   Computer-mediated discourse. In: Deborah Schiffrin, Deborah Tannen and Heidi E. Hamilton (eds.), *The Handbook of Discourse Analysis*, 612–634. Oxford: Blackwell.
Hutchby, Ian
  2001   *Conversation and Technology: From the Telephone to the Internet*. Cambridge: Polity Press.
Johnstone, Barbara
  2002   Discourse and Medium. In: Johnstone, B. (ed.), *Discourse Analysis*, 168–195. Oxford: Blackwell.
Jones, Elizabeth, Bernadette Watson, John Gardner and Cindy Gallois
  2004   Organizational communication: Challenges for the new century. *Organizational Communication* 54: 722–749.
Kiesler, Sara, Jane Siegel, and Timothy W. McGuire
  1984   Social psychological aspects of computer-mediated communication. *American Psychologists* 39: 1123–1134.

King, Storm
  1996   Researching Internet communities: Proposed ethical guidelines for the re-
            porting of results. *Information Society* 12(2): 119–127.
Ko, Kwang-Kyu
  1996   Structural characteristics of computer-mediated language: A comparative
            analysis of InterChange discourse. *Electronic Journal of Communication/
            La revue électronique de communication* 6(3). http:www.cios.org/www/
            ejc/v6n396.htm (accessed 2009 may 04).
Levinson, Stephen
  1988   Putting linguistics on a proper footing: Explorations in Goffman's concepts
            of participation. In: Paul Drew and Anthony Wootton (eds.), *Erving Goff-
            man: Exploring the Interaction Order*, 161–227. Cambridge: Polity Press.
Lunsford, Wayne
  1996   Turn-taking organization in Internet relay chat. Unpublished manuscript,
            University of Texas at Arlington.
MacKinnon, Richard
  1995   Searching for the Leviathan in Usenet. In: S. Jones (ed.), *Cybersociety:
            Computer-Mediated Communication and Community*, 112–137. Thousand
            Oaks, CA: Sage.
Mahmood, Mo Adam, Laura Hall and Daniel Leonard Swanberg
  2001   Factors affecting technology usage: A meta-analysis of the empirical litera-
            ture. *Journal of Organizational Computing and Electronic Commerce* 11:
            107–130.
Murray, Denise E.
  1988   The context of oral and written language: A framework for mode and
            medium switching. *Language in Society* 17: 351–73.
Murray, Denise E.
  1989   When the medium determines turns: Turn-taking in computer conversation.
            In: Hywel Coleman (ed.), *Working with Language,* 251–66. Berlin / New
            York: Mouton de Gruyter.
Murray, Denise E.
  1990   CmC. *English Today* 23: 42–46.
Oliveira, Maria do Carmo Leite
  1992   Polidez, uma estratégia de dissimulação. Análise de cartas de pedido de em-
            presas brasileiras [Politeness, a deceit strategy. Analysis of request letters
            in Brazilian companies]. Unpublished Ph.D. Dissertation, Pontifícia Uni-
            versidade Católica do Rio de Janeiro.
Oliveira, Maria do Carmo Leite
  2004   Language, technology and late modernity: a study of interaction in a call
            center. In: Carlos A. M. Gouveia, Carminda Silvestre and Luísa Azuaga
            (eds.), *Discourse, Communication and the Enterprise: Linguistic Perspec-
            tives*, 65–78. Lisbon: University of Lisbon.
Oliveira, Maria do Carmo Leite
  2007   The language specialist as organizational consultant. Plenary paper at IV –
            DICOEN-Discourse, Communication and Organization, Nottingham, UK,
            September 12.

Oliveira, Maria do Carmo Leite and José Roberto Gomes da Silva
2009   The composition of a participative view for the management of organizational communications. In: Fernando Ramalho, Anxo M. Lorenzo Suárez, Xoán Paulo Rodríguez-Yánez and Piotr Cap. (eds.). New Approaches to Discourse and Business Communication, 190–211. Great Britain: Palgrave Macmillan.

Oliveira, Maria do Carmo Leite and Begma Tavares Barbosa
2002   Novas tecnologias e novos padrões de interação: um estudo da fala em uma central de atendimento telefônico [New technologies and new interaction standards: Talk in interaction in a call center]. *Palavra* 8: 155–168.

Sarangi, Srikant
2006   The conditions and consequences of professional discourse studies. In: Richard Kiely, Pauline Rea-Dickins, Helen Woodfield and Gerald Clibbon (eds.), *Language, Culture and Identity in Applied Linguistics*, 199–220. London: Equinox.

Scott, Craig R., Laura Quinn, C. Erik Timmerman and Diana M. Garett
1998   Ironic uses of group communications: evidence from meeting transcripts and interviews with group decision support system users. *Communications Quarterly* 46: 353–374.

Severinson Eklundh, Kerstin and Clare Macdonald
1994   The use of quoting to preserve context in electronic mail dialogues. *IEEE Transactions on Professional Communication* 37(4): 197–202.

Shannon, Claude and Warren Weaver
1949   *The Mathematical Theory of Communication*. Urbana: University of Illinois Press.

Silva, José Roberto Gomes da
2000   A implementação do correio eletrônico e a tentativa de promover um novo modelo de interações em uma empresa brasileira [The e-mail implementation and the attempt to promote a new model of interactions in a Brazilian company]. *Arché Interdisciplinar* 9(28): 61–83.

Spanos, Yannis E., Gregory Prastacos and Angeliki Poulymenakou
2002   The relationship between information and communication technologies, adoption and management. *Information and Management* 39: 659–675.

Tannen, Deborah
1982   *Spoken and Written Language: Exploring Orality and Literacy*. Norwood: Ablex.

Vihera, Marja Lisa and Juna Nurmela
2001   Communication capability as an intrinsic determinant for information age. *Futures* 33: 245–265.

Vries, Sjoerd de and Italo de Diana
2005   Implementation of networked organization communication. *Corporate Communications: An International Journal* 10: 117–128.

Yates, Simeon and David Graddol
1996   "I read this chat is heavy": The discursive construction of identity in CMC. Paper presented at the 5th International Pragmatics Conference, Mexico City, July 8.

17. Gatekeeping discourse in employment interviews

Celia Roberts

Abstract

The employment interview is shot through with contradictions, facing Janus-like both out to the organisation and the candidates' past experience and in to the interview itself. The competency-based selection procedure is now standard practice in the English-speaking world and reflects the new work order in which all employees are expected to buy into the corporate ideology, be flexible and self-managing. However, ironically, this competency framework which is designed to be objective and create equality of opportunity constructs a "linguistic penalty" for just those groups it is designed to help. The selection interview, with its interactional constraints, hidden assumptions and co-constructed and subjective nature disadvantages all those unfamiliar with its institutional requirements, particularly those from Black and ethnic minority groups (BMEs). The detailed interactional processes of the job interview have been analysed, using Interactional Sociolinguistics, pragmatics and critical discourse analysis, combined with ethnography, at four interlocking levels: the culturally specific nature of interview discourse; assumptions about purpose, role and allowable content; interactional norms and structuring of responses; and communicative style at micro-level interaction. The empirical analysis in this chapter is based on seventy real video recorded interviews and associated feedback data. This research shows that successful candidates seamlessly blend the institutional discourses of impartiality and discretion with the personal discourses of narrative and emotional aspects of the self. The practical relevance of research on the selection interview is clear and can encompass both evidence for challenging the fairness of job interviews and, in the short term, research-based training interventions for both job-seekers and interviewers and designers of interviews.

1. Introduction

It is estimated that over 99 % of all job recruitment, and most promotion and selection for training and membership of professional colleges, involves a face to face gatekeeping interview. Janus, the god of doors, gates and thresholds in Roman mythology, is usually represented as facing two ways, both outward and inward. And the selection interview is Janus-like in several ways: interviewers look out to the candidate but also back to their own organisations, since interviews are also one site for the production of institutional order. Candidates have to present their past but in ways that are aligned to the organisation where there future may lie. Also the talk-in-interaction of the interview is a two-way process with the candidates' contributions constructed by the heavy traffic of interviewers' questions, evaluations and follow-ups. Facing two ways simultaneously creates an interactional dilemma and sums up the tensions and paradoxes of the selection interview.

The Janus-like quality of job interviews is illustrated in two extracts from an interview for a low-paid job – packing coat hangers in a Scottish factory. Paula, a redundant factory manager, has to downskill to an unskilled job as there is very little work in the area.

Example 1. Paula: White British, Successful

1. I: So (.) you were really (.) in charge of production there what- what tell me what that involved
2.   (twenty seconds of talk deleted)
3. C: What else I do in a day in that is (.) I mean if you've ever worked in a small company Brenda (.) thing about when you start up something like that (.) I mean there's a lot of peaks and troughs (.)
4. I: Yes=
5. C: =Because these they put (.) would customers would just come on and it would literally just be a couple of days notice ((low pitch and falling tone))
6. I: Right
7. C: Right (.) so again I could work every single machine I could do every single job in the contract packing I had to ken (.)
8. I: Yes
9. C: Because if somebody was off or something or s- a customer came on and there was things to be done
10. I: You just had to get on and do it
11. C: That's the name of the game yeah get on and do it and get it done um I didn't mind it to be honest (.)
12. I: So you would do all the lifting and the standing and the=
13. C: = Oh God yeah
14. I: Running about and all the rest of that
15. C: Oh yeah oh yeah
16. I: Ok so
17. C: No problem with that

(Roberts and Campbell 2006: 50)

To mitigate her perceptions that her past experience makes her over-qualified, Paula carefully crafts her position in relation to Brenda, the interviewer and human resources manager. In terms of social positioning she calls up a shared set of assumptions at turn 3, looking forward to a possible social relationship with Brenda, but she is careful not to come across as over-bearing or managerial. She presents herself as a hands-on person (turns 9–11), working alongside colleagues. Interactionally and stylistically, Paula manages a mix of solidarity and deference. She aligns herself to Brenda's "get on and do it" assumption and uses low pitch and falling tone (turn 5) and pausing to present herself as more worker than manager. This careful re-presenting of her past to fit the requirements of the present job pays off, as is illustrated in turns 10–17 where Brenda's interventions serve to construct her as able to meet all the physical requirements of the coat hanger factory.

In the second extract from Paula's interview, she reflects back to Brenda the reputation of the company in the community. This "why do you want the job?" question, if answered with a preferred response, as in this case, helps to produce and reproduce the institutional order of the organisation.

Example 2. Paula: White British, Successful

1. I: what made you (.) think of applying here as opposed to [anywhere else
2. C: well] firstly because I've got <u>no</u> doubt I can do the job
3. I: Mhmm
4. C: Secondly because shifts don't bother us
5. I: Right
6. C: Right (.) and thirdly because you've got quite a secure reputation (X company) has fo:r employment

(Roberts and Campbell 2006: 47)

2.   Current conceptualisations of the job interview

The employment selection interview is perhaps the most conspicuous of all gatekeeping encounters (see Erickson this volume) and yet it has been relatively under-researched by applied linguists. There is a lack of evidence-based studies using substantial data bases of naturally occurring recruitment and selection interviews. The obvious reason for this is that neither interviewers nor candidates are over-enthusiastic about being recorded in such a high-stakes event. In addition, the world of human resources, colonised by occupational psychology, has not oriented to the detailed discourse processes of the selection interview and this has led at best to indifference and, more commonly, to resistance to the idea of opening up the selection interview beyond the usual general requirements of validity and reliability.

The current concerns of those who design the selection interview are how to make it more standard in overall design and methods of elicitation (Campion et al. 1988; Campion et al. 1994; Palmer and Campion 1997; Latham 1989; Tetlock and Boettger 1989). While many interviews still typically rely on more biography based interviews, assessing motivation and using role play and hypothetical situations to judge workplace attitudes and skills (see Komter [1991] for an overview of this structure), in the English-speaking world competencey-based selection is increasingly dominant (Wood and Payne 1998). The use of a competency framework, with standard questions and training is designed to lead to the holy grail of objectivity, reliability and equality of opportunity. This chapter charts some of the ways in which applied and sociolinguists have critiqued the assumption that this is possible, or indeed justifiable.

A typical list of competencies for both low-paid work and management level posts will include team working, communications, customer focus, adaptability and flexibility and self-management. The latter two in particular reflect the "new work order" (Gee et al. 1996) in which workers, however low their status in the workplace, are expected to buy into a corporate ideology. The view that successful candidates should embody the organisation's values is evident in the move towards an "accountancy" (Miller 1994) or "enterprise" culture whereby individuals are required to become "autonomous, productive and self-regulating" (du Gay 1996, 2000). One aspect of this is the ability to manage boring, repetitive work, as in the following example of an interview for entry-level work in a large delivery company:

Example 3. Ire: Nigerian, Candidate born abroad, Borderline Successful

1. I: right what would you tell me is the advantage of a repetitive job (1)
2. C: advantage of a
3. I: repetitive job (1)
4. C: er I mean the advantage of a repetitive job is that er:m it makes you it it
         keeps you going(.) er it doesn't make you bored(.) you don't feel bored
         you keep on going and(.) I mean I me= a – and also it it puts a smile on
         your face you come in it puts a smile on your face you feel happy to
         come to the job the job will (trust) you
5. I: you don't get to know it better
6. C: sorry
7. I: you don't get to know it better
8. C: yeah we get to know the job better we I mean we learn new ideas lots of
         new ideas as well
9. I: right what is the disadvantage of a repetitive job

10. C: well, disadvantage er:m er disadvantages (1) you may you may f-offend customers you may f- offend our customers in there that's a disadvantage of it
11. I: you don't find it boring
12. C: yeah it could also be boring, to be boring and you- and you (.) yet by being bored you may offend the customers
13. I: how how would you offend them by being bored
14. C: by not putting a smile on your face

(Roberts and Campbell 2006: 39)

The competency question at turns 1 and 9 is based on a set of conventionalised expectations that repetitive jobs are boring, but that enterprising, self-managing candidates will recognise this and find ways of dealing with the boredom which will maintain their identity as motivated workers. The opening section of this example gives some evidence of perturbation, with a one second pause after the opening question, a partial repetition by the candidate, a further pause after the interviewer's completion of his utterance and then several "fillers" and vocalised pauses. He then produces an unconventional or dispreferred response which the interviewer indirectly rebuts at turn 5 ("You don't get to know it better") and again at turn 11 with his second unlooked for response. This lack of a shared perspective about boring work is reinforced by what we call "the immigrant story" (Roberts and Campbell 2006) in which Black and minority ethnic (BME) workers, aware of the "ethnic penalty" (Heath and McMahon 1997) faced by many from these groups, strive to present themselves as positively as possible in all circumstances: "you feel happy to come to the job" (turn 4). Such positive assertions are often conveyed in "extreme case formulations" ("I can do anything; I never have problems") in an attempt to sell oneself. But they are often used by interviewers as evidence of over-claiming and untrustworthiness (see Kerekes [2003] on trust in the interview).

So, this short extract exemplifies many of the themes of the selection interview: its interactional constraints and expectations; the hidden assumptions which serve to construct inequality when there is no shared definition of the interview, and its joint accomplishment. It also illustrates the permeability of the encounter with corporate discourses and prejudices leaking into talk and its evaluation.

3.   Research themes in the selection interview

As a particular "activity type" (Levinson 1979), the selection interview instantiates many of the features of institutional discourse (Agar 1985; Sarangi and Slembrouck 1997) and talk at work in institutional settings (Drew and Heritage

1992; Thornborrow 2002; Sarangi and Roberts 1999). So, a major theme is the asymmetrical power relationships of the "interview orthodoxy" (Button 1992) and the interview as a site for the production and maintenance of institutional and social order (Auer and Kern 2000; Mäkitalo and Säljö 2002; Silverman and Jones 1975). Unsurprisingly, the selection interview, like other gatekeeping encounters, is not an objective or neutral activity (Heritage 1985) but is "rigged ... in favour of those individuals whose communication style and social background are most similar to those of the interviewer with whom they talk" (Erickson and Shultz 1982: 193). Understanding the discourse processes and interactional environment of these encounters has been the major focus of enquiry by those, relatively few, discourse analysts, sociolinguists and applied linguists interested in the production and reproduction of inequality in employment and other "people sorting" interviews (Adelswärd 1988; Auer and Kern 2000; Gumperz 1992; Komter 1991; Roberts and Campbell 2006; Sarangi and Roberts 1999). The relevant literature falls into two broad categories: studies concerned with the general social order of interviews and those concerned with cultural and linguistic diversity in ethnically stratified societies, although several themes cut across both.

3.1.   The "interaction order" of the selection interview

The interview genre contains certain inherent contradictions (Auer and Kern 2000; Komter 1991; Linell and Thunquist 2003). While the interview is presented as an objective sorting process, as a social encounter it is shot through with subjectivities. Issues of personality, social class or ethnicity remain "unmentionables" and only conveyed implicitly (Komter 1991; Birkner 2004:298) and yet personal liking and co-membership (Erickson and Shultz 1982) are at the hidden heart of decision-making. The rationalisations that interviewers make are designed to mask these contradictions as the "quiet sorting" process is carried out:

> ... deciders ... can employ an open-ended list of rationalisations to conceal from the subject (and even from themselves) the mix of considerations that figure in their decision and, especially, the several weight given to these determinants.
> (Goffman 1983: 8)

Similarly, there is a tension between the superficial egalitarianism of the western job interview, with friendly conversation masking the subordinated position of candidates as objects of evaluation (Auer and Kern 2000; Fairclough 1992). Adelswärd (1988), in her study of interviews for graduate level positions, emphasises the importance of an ironic stance in which candidates can play on some of the tensions between personal and official definitions of the interview situation to foster empathy with the interviewers. In the same vein, Scheuer

(2001: 23) argues that the ability to display meta-consciousness about the interview game, for example in knowing jokes, helps develop shared understandings with interviewers.

The paradoxes and tensions of the interview often lead to a lack of shared definition of the interview situation. Shared inferential processes depend upon "socially constructed knowledge of what the interview is about" (Gumperz 1992: 303) but there are few explicit clues to this. If candidates have not been socialised into the "institutionalised networks of relationships" (Gumperz 1996: 401) where the language games of middle class life are routinely acted out, then there is little chance that they will be able to infer from the interactional sequences of the interview what their roles and modes of communicating should be. A further complication is that the interviewers' definition of the situation is not entirely fixed or pre-determined. The ability to read covert signals and move between institutional frames has particular significance in the job interview where transition points are marked indirectly (Linell and Thunquist 2003). So a candidate's social identity and status are both brought along and brought about in the interview, reflecting some of the current arguments about the relationship between agency and structure in the construction of social and institutional life:

> Today [the interview] has grown into a key situation where social inequality is ritually dramatized, where basic differences in class, ethnicity, access to power and knowledge, and culturally specific discourse conventions mediate the interaction between participants.
> (Akinnaso and Ajirotutu 1982: 120)

Adelswärd's (1988) study illustrates how social class becomes linked with what Jenkins (1986) calls "acceptability criteria" to exclude more working class candidates from job offers (see also Silverman and Jones 1975). The ability to move between different styles is a crucial resource for the successful candidate. The "recontextualisation" of different aspects of one's work, education and private life into the interview setting helps candidates to present themselves as flexible and rounded individuals (Scheuer 2001). The capacity to recontextualise styles and move between them with ease, as Scheuer points out, is not equally distributed among members of different social groups and this is particularly problematic for Black and minority ethnic (BME) groups (see below). However Auer (1998) and Erickson and Shultz (1982) argue that roles and identities cannot be automatically attributed to participants by virtue of their social backgrounds but depend upon how these are made relevant by both sides in the interaction.

Drawing on conversation analytic insights, the interview as a joint production is a central theme in many studies. Candidates are routinely blamed for the interviewers' own poor performance (Gumperz, Jupp and Roberts 1979; Button 1992; Roberts 1985; Roberts and Campbell 2006). But this is a matter of institutional requirements and norms, as much as, or often more than, individual interviewers' lack of competence. And as the interview is as paradoxical for the interviewers as for the candidate, they are subject to some of the same communicative dilemmas. The interview is controlled almost entirely by the interviewers who govern the interactional norms, allocation of turns and speaking roles (Komter 1991; Birkner 2004). But where the interview is highly structured or conforms to the demands of equal opportunity legislation, there is little or no opportunity for repair or negotiation sequences (Birkner 2004; Button 1992) by either side. So, ironically, the very design of the interview intended to address issues of subjectivity and inequality produces a regime which prevents misunderstandings from being repaired. And it is often the most disadvantaged groups who are most likely to misunderstand and misalign to the interviewers' assumptions (Roberts and Campbell 2006).

3.2.   Ethnicity and linguistic diversity in the job interview

Job interviews are specific "communicative cultures" which "pre-structure what can or should be talked about" (Auer 1998: 280) and what styles are acceptable. So this sorting process, like many other aspects of institutional life, can systematically disadvantage certain groups and help to reproduce inequality (Bourdieu 1991). In our increasingly globalised economies, cities are characterised by ethno-linguistic diversity, and so issues of discrimination in employment have taken on a new urgency as minority ethnic groups continue to be disadvantaged both in terms of recruitment and promotion. Weber's (1947) arguments for objective and rational forms of work were in part designed to cater for such diverse societies and the goal of fair and objective procedures in selection interviews has led to a vast literature both on the recruitment interview and, in turn, its potential for both direct and indirect discrimination.

The psychological literature has looked at three key areas in analysing what aspects of the selection interview are prone to bias against minority ethnic groups: the extent to which interviews are structured; type of questions – whether past experience or hypothetical are more likely to introduce bias; and the ethnic make-up of interview panels (Palmer and Campion 1997; Hubbock and Carter 1980; Huffcutt and Roth 1998). However, no clear picture emerges from these studies. This is hardly surprising since the social dynamics of the interview, based on recordings of real interviews, has not been addressed within the psychological literature (Posthuma, Morgeson and Campion 2002: 13). It is only in discourse analysis, informed by pragmatics and sociolinguistics, that the detailed interactional processes have been considered. These studies have examined the social and cultural dynamics of the job interview at four interlocking levels: the culturally specific nature of interview discourse; assumptions about purpose, role and allowable content; interactional norms and structuring of responses; and communicative style at micro-level interaction. The ways in which these four levels are realised differentially by interviewers and candidates can be summed up in the notion of "Crosstalk" (Gumperz, Jupp and Roberts 1979).

Despite attempts to make interviews culturally and ideologically neutral, current workplace ideologies leak into the interview at all points (Murray and Sondhi 1987; Sarangi 1994; Auer 1998; Birkner 2004). Birkner, in her study of contrasts between West and East German job interviews, shows how West German interviewers made relevant their assumptions about East German interviews, thus commenting implicitly on the apparently universally valid presuppositions about western interviews. The misunderstandings which arose over how much to display personal agency and decision-making (Auer and Kern 2000) also illustrate the source of many cross-purposes related to interview definition, role relationships and allowable content.

The extent to which candidates talk up their personal strengths and show their individual agency through narratives of action is a crucial component of relative success. Some of the more general cross-cultural literature compares groups in terms of their willingness to "sell themselves" (Fitzgerald 2003; Hawthorne 1992; Scollon and Scollon 1995; Young 1994). In the communications literature, similar broad differences have been identified in comparing national groups. For example, Longmire (1992) discusses the negative judgements of Cambodian candidates who defined themselves in terms of hierarchies and group membership. And, similarly, Chinese candidates were perceived as overly deferential and oriented to a collective identity (Wong and Poo-Ching 2000). However, interaction based research suggests a more complex picture with many minority ethnic candidates over-interpreting the recently acquired nostrum to "sell themselves", and aware of the potential for discrimination, producing what are perceived as over-assertive and unmitigated claims of ability and willingness (see Example 3 above, Roberts and Campbell 2006; Roberts, Campbell and Robinson [2008] for more examples of the "immigrant story").

Interactional norms and preferred structuring of responses also present conditions for indirect discrimination. Gumperz and his associates have identified patterns in turn taking between South Asian candidates and white interviewers in which silence is interpreted differently. After interviewer silence, white British candidates tend to take the floor again, to elaborate their initial comments and put themselves in a favourable light, while foreign-born South Asian candidates remain silent, waiting for the next question (Gumperz, Jupp and Roberts 1979; Gumperz 1992). Similarly, foreign-born candidates from a variety of ethnic and language backgrounds tend to misinterpret follow-up questions because of their location in a particular sequence. So, questions which are intended as requesting expansion are frequently treated as confirmatory questions and are answered with minimal response tokens (Roberts and Campbell 2006). The rhetorical and narrative structuring of candidates' answers may also deviate from interviewers' expectations. The Labovian, "Anglo" narrative structure used in some American and UK interviews to structure candidates' answers and record them on the appropriate forms (Roberts and Campbell 2005, 2006) constructs a particular teller identity which does not necessarily accord with candidates' own ways of narrating (Chafe 1980; Zimmerman 1998; Linde 1993). For example, Akinnaso and Ajirotutu (1982) argue that African-American candidates with little job interview experience tend to use an associational style which contrasts with the western problem-centred or teleological style (Auer 1998) expected by interviewers, in which the narrative is a goal-oriented exposition of skills.

Finally, communicative styles at the micro level can create miscommunication. These features of conversation such as rhythm, pitch and stress are unconsciously processed but function to cue the local context at any point. These "contexutalisation cues" (Gumperz 1982b, 1992) signal what is to be expected in the encounter, flag the transition between stages of the interview, convey satisfaction or the opposite and initiate clarification or repair sequences (Gumperz 1996: 396–7; Kerekes 2006; O'Grady and Millen 1994; Roberts and Sayers 1987). The misreading of contextualisation cues can lead to both interactional discomfort and negative evaluation of candidates. For example, the matching of pitch and tempo between white candidates and interviewers contrasted with the mismatches among South Asian candidates. Despite their relevant experience, they were perceived as unresponsive and slow to infer meaning (Gumperz 1992). Similarly, interviewers failed to interpret many of the features of African-American communicative style such as vowel lengthening and rhythmic patterning and so misjudged candidates' intent and motivation (Akinnaso and Ajirotutu 1982); while an Italian-American candidate became increasingly disfluent as the interview failed to give him the expected active listening behaviour (Erickson 1986).

These four interlocking levels of analysis identify some of the dynamics and discourse processes which lead to the systematic disadvantaging of BME candidates. Those with less "linguistic capital" (Bourdieu 1991), however experienced or well-qualified they are, and whatever the distance between the communicative demands of the job interview and the job itself, are more likely to be exposed to increasingly stringent institutional requirements. Their answers are more likely to be controlled, whereas those whose self-presentation is bureaucratically processable are allowed to transgress the institutional frame and to contribute to a more informal and conversational tone. Those who cannot "fit their stories" into the interviewer's "boxes" are labelled as "poor English speakers" and suffer a "linguistic penalty" constructed by the interview as an institutional event (Roberts and Campbell 2005 and see below).

4.   Some methodological considerations

The bulk of discourse analytic studies of employment interviewing can be located within the Interactional Sociolinguistics tradition. Drawing on the ethnography of communication, pragmatics, Goffman's notions of interaction and frame (Goffman 1981), and conversation analysis, John Gumperz developed a qualitative sociolinguistic analysis tuned to linguistic and cultural diversity and oriented to understanding how inequality could be communicatively produced (Gumperz 1999). Macro concerns related to urbanisation, institutionalisation and discrimination and sociological notions of ethnicity, social identity, networks and gatekeeping are linked to micro issues of interactional conduct. The routine small scale evaluation of others in institutional life feeds into the larger societal forces which construct a racially and culturally stratified society. These social evaluations are based on judgements of how candidates present themselves and manage the interactional requirements of the job interview.

The conventionalised means whereby interviewers and candidates interpret each other, what Gumperz calls "conversational inference" (1982b), are not linked in any stereotyping way with a particular ethnic group. Rather, inferential practices are the result of participation in similar "networks of relationships" which may or may not be ethnically based. So, any candidate may bring to the interview a range of communicative styles, some clearly influenced by their early socialisation and others the result of more recent communicative experiences. As Auer and Kern assert (2000), because interactants come from different ethnic groups, this does not make the interview necessarily intercultural. It is only if differences are attended to or made relevant either implicitly or explicitly in the interaction and subsequent evaluation that it can be called intercultural (see also Sarangi 1996).

While the detailed sequential analysis of Interactional Sociolinguistics owes much to traditional conversation analysis, the latter cannot account for those elements of the interview that are suppressed. These "unsayables" (Komter 1991) range from aspects of social identity such as class, ethnicity and gender through to face-threatening evaluations of a candidate's contribution. For example, unsuccessful candidates were given as many perceived positive feedbacks such as "good" and "thank you" as unsuccessful ones in junior management interviews (Roberts, Campbell and Robinson 2008). But without the additional ethnographic knowledge that these candidates were judged negatively, reliance on such overt markers could be used to argue that the candidate's contribution was well received. For this reason, studies of recruitment interviews often combine interactional discourse analysis with ethnography both to establish the accepted discourses of human resources management and, more specifically, to document how candidates and interviewers comment on the interview and how the latter come to decisions in the "wash-up" sessions when final judgements are made.

Ethnographic studies of organisational discourse give insights into managers' and interview designers' ideals of worker identity which are so central to the judgement of candidates (Jupp, Roberts and Cook-Gumperz 1982; Komter 1991; Roberts and Campbell 2006). In particular, critical organisational discourse analysis relates gatekeeping and other workplace events to the wider discourses of the new capitalism or "new work order", as was briefly mentioned above. This relationship demands a close identification between the individual and the culture of the organisation that employs them (du Gay 1996; Gee, Hull and Lankshear 1996; Iedema 2003; Iedema and Scheeres 2003). The seamless integration of workplace and personal identity has to be artfully performed in the interview to produce a convincing synthetic personality which embodies certain competencies and dispositions (Fairclough 1992; Wodak 1996). This artful performance calls up Wittgenstein's notion of language games, Goffman's (1981) "expression games" and Bourdieu's (1991) notion of the "feel for the game". Candidates without this "feel" for the delicate blending of the institution and the self required by corporate discourses are rapidly dismissed as either over-personal or not being their real selves, and so untrustworthy (see example below). Since, the employment interview is as much about constructing the institution as it is about the fair selection of the best candidate, methodologies for its study need to include ethnographic and organisational discourse analysis as well as the detailed micro analysis afforded by Interactional Sociolinguistics.

There have been some criticisms of Interactional Sociolinguistics that it has been over-zealous in hunting down misunderstandings and establishing too close a connection between intercultural communication and misunderstanding. For example, Kerekes (2006) found that minority ethnic groups did as well as white local speakers in her study of employment agency interviews. From a different perspective, Rehbein (2000) argues that intercultural negotiation can be marked not by misunderstanding but by "co-operative opposition". It is not that either side misunderstands the other but that they disagree with each other and use different culturally influenced styles to oppose each other without the encounter breaking down. However, while there are some exceptions, the overriding picture is one in which BME groups in particular, but also other social groups who have not been socialised into "the game", are more likely to be judged negatively. And although misunderstandings may not be overt, these judgements are based on the observable features of interaction, linked to wider organisational and societal discourses, which Interactional Sociolinguistics as a methodology is designed to document.

5.   Empirical Analysis

This section is based on data from two studies already referred to, and from which the earlier data example also comes, which look at language, ethnicity and the job interview in the UK (Roberts and Campbell 2006; Roberts, Campbell and Robinson 2008). On the analogy of the "ethnic penalty" (Heath and McMahon 1997) in which ethnicity is rated as a negative factor in its own right to partially account for racial disadvantage, these studies argue that there is a "linguistic penalty" experienced by candidates born, and with their early socialisation, outside the UK. This penalty is faced by anyone who has not developed the "linguistic capital" (Bourdieu 1991) of the particular institutional sub-field of the job interview. The discourses required of this genre, and the ability to move between them and blend them into a convincing synthetic whole, interactionally construct the ideal candidate. The fact that this "linguistic capital" is taken for granted by employers as a matter of individual competence or merely a question of adequate preparation masks its power in reproducing structural inequalities. Failed candidates "just don't have the skills".

The main data example analysed here (Example 5) illustrates what happens to one BME candidate, Sara, who fails to produce the synthesised, authentic self as required by the interview. In this case, it is a promotion interview from acting manager to a permanent junior management position in a large delivery company.

Before considering the data in detail, some of the theoretical background will be discussed. Drawing on a distinction between institutional and personal discourses made in a comparable medical setting (Roberts and Sarangi 1999; Roberts et al. 2000), this analysis traces some of the features that lead to the catastrophic evaluation of Sara. The institutional discourses of the job interview reflect the new work order ideology, realised in a standard set of competencies, and shaped by features of "impartiality ... decency and discretion" (Bourdieu 1991). So institutional discourse is characterised by analytic framing of talk, more employment of technical or sub-technical vocabulary, more abstract formulations and certain types of modality (Auer 1998; Iedema 2003; Morales-Lopes et al. 2005). Paula, in example two above, shows how lists (often of three items) is a rhetorical device to produce an impersonal and analytic stretch of discourse which aligns her to the institutional demands of the job interview. Interactionally, interviewers take on strict participation roles, such as reading questions verbatim from a sheet, minimising conversational features, and doing more overt controlling.

"Personal discourses" are used to display aspects of the self either in settings that are not strictly work-related or to reveal emotional and interpersonal elements that tell the interviewer what the candidate is "really like". Candidates have to show that they are personally invested in the organisation and to do this in ways that corresponds to the Foucauldian "confession" (Foucault 1978). As with institutional discourses, micro-linguistic, rhetorical and interactional features all contribute to the performance of the personal. Vivid narratives with detailed self-commentary, conversational relationships with interviewers, co-membership (Erickson and Shultz 1982) and humour are routine in the successful mobilising of personal discourses.

The candidates who are most successful are those that synthesise institutional and personal discourses, moving seamlessly between them. For example, Jim, a local white candidate, talks about implementing institutional procedures in a vivid personalised way: "So I made myself a little sheet up so I could put it in my wallet ... just have a check". In this way the institutional and personal identity of the candidate appear fused together in a homogenised ideal employee.

By contrast, unsuccessful candidates were perceived as disfluently juxtaposing the institutional and personal. They were often criticised for "rehearsed answers" or for being overly emotional or by contrast not personally engaged enough. Candidates born abroad were less likely to have access to the discursive skills required of the job interview than other groups. Many in our studies were unemployed or working in backstage jobs in ethnic work units where there is scant opportunity to be socialised into such skills. And, as Sheuer (2001) argues, people in low paid jobs are unlikely to use their work to form their identity. So there is a wider gulf between the personal discourses they use to talk about themselves and those they use to talk about the institution.

In the following example, Tahir is being interviewed for a receptionist post in a college. As with other unsuccessful candidates, his lack of blending of institutional and personal discourses leads to criticisms of inconsistency and doubts about his trustworthiness (see also Kerekes 2003).

Example 4. Tahir: British Bangladeshi, Unsuccessful

1. Int 1: can you tell me about any experiences you have of cash handling
2. C: obviously you have to do the recon-reconciliation and I've done we do <u>that</u> well in: my current job and (.) before when I've worked as a sales assistant I've worked on tills like operated the g- s like as a cashier so:
        (.) [credit card cash] ... my current job we do like I was saying we do the reconciliation and petty cash and things that I buy to buy tea coffees and (4)
        I buy the flowers as well ((rising intonation))
3. Int 2: You buy the [flowers] ((laughs))
4. C: [for reception] yeah but I get refunded though (ten seconds of talk
5.   deleted) If you see our reception

[and um]
6.   I2:   [Yeah]
7.   C: I chose some really nice flowers and then get refunded I chose the
           flowers ((laughs)) but they give you a budget (five seconds of talk de-
           leted)
8.   The girls really like it like the flowers they come and pinch it though
           i- i-it
           doesn't last more than like a couple of hours the new ones
9.   I1:   ((laughs))
10. C: But they all come and pinch it and they take it ((Laughs))
11. I1:   Ok (.) the next one is I've got a nice scenario for you

Here, in a pattern which is repeated throughout the interview, Tahir presents a list of administrative tasks in a relatively impartial style (turn 2), followed by a more personal narrative which is only loosely connected topically to the question about cash handling. This second part of the answer is more animated with rising tone and laughter and it positions him as having fun with the girls who "pinch" the flowers. So, the more institutional discourse of the opening section and the personal discourse of the latter section do not link together and reinforce each other to prove a single point but rather orient to divergent aspects of his self-presentation. His motivation for applying for the job is questioned and he is rejected.

As well as lack of access to job interview discursive skills, there are complex factors concerning the construction of subjectivity that penalise BME groups. Organisational theorists such as Bell (1990) and Blackwell (1981) have applied du Bois' notion of "double consciousness" (du Bois 1989) to help explain why the synthesis of work-centred and personal identities creates an additional penalty for this group. Bell argues that "compartmentalisation appears to be a strategy for maintaining two distinct cultural spheres so the dynamics of one do not spill over into the other … as a strategy, it may reduce the stress deriving from the bicultural experience" (Bell 1990: 474). This compartmentalisation was evident in the ways in which BME candidates from abroad used contrasting styles to talk about personal and work experience. They also, on occasions, made their ethnicity relevant in ways that oriented to their double consciousness of themselves as "other". Again these markers of idiosyncratic personal identity and specific group membership do not sit comfortably with the synthetic personality of current organisational ideology.

We will now turn to Example 5 where Sara is applying for a junior manager position.

Example 5: Sara, Maltese, Unsuccessful

1. I: {[looking down] how- how do you ensure (.) you know wh- when you're a manager that you (.) you learn from} {[I looks at C] experience and you pick up particular lessons from past mistakes} {[I looks down, begins writing] (1)
(twenty five seconds of talk deleted)

2. C: I mean I'm Maltese {[C moves arms] I <u>tend</u> to <u>talk</u> with my <u>hands</u>} and one thing that's really brought up quite often when I'm talking in a meeting you know I'm sitting there with my]} {[C gesticulates with hands, I looks up and nods] hands flailing away like this} {[I looks down] which puts everybody off because they're looking at you know {[I looks up, C moves arms]what on earth is she doing} {[I looks down] doing this [business

3. I: right]

4. C: so I've made a conscious effort to keep my hands in my lap [I mean

5. I: i-]

6. C: that that is one [thing that somebody told me

7. I: how do you er:m]} {[I looks up] (.) how do you ensure though if you (choose) somebody in your team that maybe they they maybe don't want to be too critical you know they're only really sort of being positive or being nice for the sake of it really is that not a danger some times

8. C: that is a danger but-

9. I: they might not want to say that actually you was pretty- you were just mumbling it was pretty awful but I daren't say that because she's the boss}

10.   (fifteen seconds of talk deleted)

11. I: so can you give me some examples of things you've picked up then from using that

12. C: well I just did that that was the one that comes [to mind

13. I: the one about] are there any other sort of things that

14. C: er:m-

15. I: apart from you know your own sort of body language and things which (.) you know I think from presentations we always there's always things to pickup there

16. C: mm

17. I: sort of ex- examples maybe s- substan- in terms of-

In this interview (which is discussed in more detail in Campbell and Roberts 2007), Sara's perceived inappropriate identity is co-constructed by the candidate and the interviewer. From the beginning (not shown in the data example) difficulties emerge with the lack of uptake of a joke made by Sara and then a long first phase in which she uses only institutional discourses. In the video feedback, the interviewer criticised her in this opening phase for "lecturing him" and "saying what she had been told to say" and this dispreferred style then slips unproblematically into personality judgements of arrogance and insincerity. In the latter part of the interview, Sara uses largely personal discourses, speaking about emotional reactions to colleagues and giving narrativised details of colleagues and friends. The interviewer, in the feedback, commented on this as "excessive and garrulous", indicating a lack of professionalism and discretion, framing these statements with: "I know she's Maltese but ..."

The interviewer responds to the lack of blending of both modes of discourse by shifting into an increasingly institutional mode, thus emphasising his membership of the organisation and the "outsider" status of the candidate. With BME candidates this can mean a double outsider status: outside the organisational culture and outside the majority ethnic community. This heightened institutionalisation is played out by the interviewer with more impersonal comments and stricter relevancy requirements. He also increasingly positions himself as merely a representative of the institution, decreasing eye contact, writing more and becoming an "animator" of institutional terms rather than author or principal (Goffman 1981; Roberts and Campbell 2005). A more detailed discussion of the data now follows.

Turn 1 illustrates the heightened institutionalisation that marks an interview already spiralling downwards. The interviewer fixes his gaze on the table for most of this turn and begins to write even before Sara has started to respond. She then chooses an individual and ethnicised foible, talking with her hands (turn 2), rather than describing homogenised synthetic personal characteristics such as "time-management issues". This self-criticism is evidence of the self-as-other characteristic of "double consciousness". While a reflexive awareness of self is a requirement of management interviews, it has to be conveyed in "euphemised", institutional ways (Bourdieu 1991). However, Sara acts out her bodily conduct in a satire of Maltese behaviour and ventriloquises her colleagues in the reaction at the end of turn 2 "what on earth is she doing". So her overly personal style, combined with the ethnic focus, undermines the theme of the reflexive self and instead positions her as doubly separate.

In the feedback, turn 2 was commented on by the interviewer as "highly personal, effusive and indiscreet". Sara was not considered "professional". The interviewer invoked a binary opposition between her body language and style, on the one hand, and substantive points (turns 11–17), on the other. He implicitly linked her body language, speech delivery, "garrulous" long responses and personal discourses to her ethnic identity so that she comes across as unprofessional and her responses as insufficiently substantive. The new forms of discrimination in which certain ethnicities are seen to be marked by non-professional identity have also been noted by Gaudio and Bialystock (1995).

The interviewer's increasing discomfort with Sara is evident in his slackening of conversational involvement throughout this whole section. In the opening stages of this segment, his gaze is elsewhere, and not on her. Then he reacts to her example by interrupting twice at turns 7 and 9 to interject questions and shifts rapidly to new sub-topics at turns 7 and 11. He responds to her perceived inappropriate personalisation by cranking up the institutional themes of "dealing with staff" and hierarchical asymmetries and downplaying "body language" as matters of presentation only. But he also puts her in a double-bind by replaying what her team members might say to her "you was pretty – you were just mumbling it was pretty awful" (turn 9). So he reconstructs her presentation as "awful", implies that even if she was awful that none of her staff would necessarily tell her (so perhaps she is even more awful than she has been told) and then dismisses presentation skills as lacking in substance as an example anyway, before she can respond to the problem of honest reactions from less powerful staff.

A pattern emerges in this interview similar to that experienced by most unsuccessful candidates. There is low interactional involvement, rapid topic shifting, and increasing institutionalisation on the part of the interviewer as Sara's talk becomes more personalised as she seeks to re-engage him. The duality of her self-positioning, the lack of blending of personal and institutional discourses and her reflexive account of her ethnicity reveal tensions, contradictions and multiple positions that chafe against the institutional regimes of the job interview and the new work order discourses that it instantiates.

6.   Practical relevance

Knapp and Antos, in their introduction to the HAL series discuss the practical relevance of research as "science under pressure to succeed" with application at the heart of research in the new century. Simultaneously, there is increasing interest in evidence-based policy and practice. So, as research becomes more action-oriented and users are persuaded to use more research-based evidence, we may have arrived at a time when practically relevant research reaches out to both researchers and users. Indeed, practical relevance is embedded in the notion of applied linguistics. Research that only travels as far as applied linguistic conferences and journals is hardly worthy of its field. And since gatekeeping interviews in general, and employment selection interviews in particular, have such a crucial impact on individuals' life chances and the production of inequality, such research must be judged by its contribution to change in this area.

Bloor's (1997) paradigms of "engineering", "enlightenment" and "critical" social science research can all be drawn on in developing a model of action-oriented research. But such a model should also include the processes of working with people who do not think like applied linguists – in other words working with different epistemologies and discourses – a model not so much of knowledge transfer but knowledge exchange. In the specialised field of recruitment and selection interviewing, these different epistemologies and discourses tend to be those of occupational psychology where notions of personhood as something fixed and measurable are at odds with a socially constructed view of the individual typical of critical social and applied linguistics.

Some of the research on the employment interview takes as its goal a critical understanding of the interview as a site of the production and maintenance of social and institutional order. The ritual of the interview determines people's subjectivity (Habermas 1979) and like any examination tends to reproduce the existing order. Other research, while using critical theory, also builds both joint problematisation and problem solving into the early design of the research (Roberts and Sarangi 1999). "Crosstalk" broadcast on BBC television in 1979 is an early example of turning interactional sociolinguistic research into practical insights for a general public (Gumperz, Jupp and Roberts 1979). Practical relevance, therefore, can be anywhere on a continuum from asking HR and government departments to consider fundamental questions of the function, effectiveness and fairness of selection interviews to using research to produce new training approaches and materials. The latter can be used both for training interviewers and in preparation courses for school leavers and adult job seekers.

An example of both ends of the continuum is the research detailed above (Roberts and Campbell 2006). The analysis of 70 real job interviews, the majority for low paid work, established that there was an unfair linguistic penalty for candidates born abroad and that there was a clear gap between the communicative demands of the job interview and those of the job applied for. Within British law this meant that the job interview for such low paid jobs was indirectly discriminatory. We, therefore, argued that other procedures for recruitment should be used. However, we also recognised that the whole scale demolition of the job interview for entry level jobs was unlikely to happen in the near future. So, we also exploited the unique data base of real interviews to produce two DVDs: "Successful at Selection" for job interviewers (Roberts et al. 2007) and "FAQs: Frequently Asked Questions" for job seekers, particularly those born abroad (Roberts et al. 2007), and both DVDs have been disseminated nationally through the Department of Work and Pensions in the UK.

The employment interview both produces and reproduces institutional and social order and its consequent inequalities. So it is both a site for the development of critical social linguistic theory and a gatekeeping encounter that needs to be exposed as perpetuating some of the small tragedies of everyday life. Social class and ethnicity are salient in explaining how this "quiet sorting" process can systematically disadvantage individuals. Its very quietness masks the corporate ideology that leaks into its design and the inherent contradictions of the game. Candidates have to display an understanding of this game and the fact that it is one. A further irony is that the more recent attempts to design a fairer interview, using competency based frameworks and "equal opportunity" formats, themselves play into the disadvantage experienced by various groups.

The "linguistic penalty" of the selection interview stems from its culturally-specific rituals at four levels: expected interview discourses, hidden assumptions about purposes and roles, interactional constraints and different communicative styles. The methodologies of Interactional Sociolinguistics and ethnography, together with a more general critical discourse analysis, provide the tools for exploring this linguistic penalty. The data examples analysed illustrate how candidates, especially BME candidates, are challenged by the interview regime which requires a synthesis of institutional and personal discourses. It shows how judgements of candidates, both during the encounter and in ethnographic data collected later, produce an increasingly interactionally difficult environment which in turn feeds into further negative evaluations. The interview demands a specific set of discursive skills and a particular kind of subjectivity. These are often unnecessary requirements of the job itself and are more about maintaining the organisation than selecting the right candidate. Whether job interviews for this level of work are a requirement at all is, therefore, questionable. Research of the kind described in this chapter can communicate this message to those who design and use interviews. However, any impact on this user group is likely to be glancing or, at best, effective but slow. So educational interventions, based on the analysis of real encounters, that can make the interview a fairer and more understandable activity are a worthwhile and indeed necessary activity.

Appendix

Transcription conventions

[	beginning of overlap
	eg [anywhere
	[well
]	end of overlap
	eg anywhere he]
	well its]
=	latching
(.)	micro pause
(2)	timed pause in seconds
:	sound stretch
No	emphasis realised in volume and intonation
(unsure)	unclear speech
((low pitch))	description of characteristics of talk
((laughs))	description of non-verbal sounds
[looks down]	description of bodily conduct
{They used to say[looks up] I used my arms too much}	the stretch of speech that occurs at the same time as the bodily conduct

References

Adelswärd, Viveka
  1988   *Styles of Success: On Impression Management as Collaborative Action in Job Interviews*. Linköping Studies in Arts and Science 23. Linköping: University of Linköping.

Agar, Michael
  1985   Institutional Discourse. *Text* 5(3):147–168.

Akinnaso, F. Niyi and Cheryl Ajirotutu
  1982   Performance and ethnic style in job interviews. In: John Gumperz (ed.), 119–144.

Auer, Peter
  1998   Learning how to play the game: An investigation of role-played job interviews in East Germany. *Text* 18(1): 17–38.

Auer, Peter and Friederike Kern
  2000   Three ways of analysing communication between East and West Germans as intercultural communication. In: Aldo Di Luzio and Susannah Günthner (eds.), 89–116.

Bell, Ella L.
  1990   The bicultural life experience of career-oriented black women *Journal of Organizational Behaviour (Special Issue: The Career and Life Experiences of Black Professionals)* 11(6): 459–477.

Birkner, Karin
  2004   Hegemonic struggles or transfer of knowledge? East and West Germans in job interviews. *Journal of Language and Politics* 3(2): 293–322.

Blackwell, Lewis
  1981   *Mainstreaming Outsiders: The Production of Black Professionals*. New York: General Hall.

Bloor, Michael
  1997   Addressing social problems through qualitative research. In: David Silverman (ed.), *Qualitative Research: Theory, Method and Practice*, 221–238. London: Sage.

Bourdieu, Pierre
  1991   *Language & Symbolic Power*. Edited by John Thompson, translated by Gino Raymond and Matthew Adamson. Cambridge, MA: Harvard University Press.

Button, Graham
  1992   Answers as interactional products: Two sequential practices used in job interviews. In: Paul Drew and John Heritage (eds.), 212–231.

Campbell, Sarah and Celia Roberts
  2007   Migration, ethnicity and competing discourses in the job interview: Synthesising the institutional and personal. *Discourse & Society* 18(3): 243–271.

Campion, Michael, Elliott Pursell and Barbara Brown
  1988   Structured interviewing: Raising the psychometric properties of the employment interview. *Personnel Psychology* 41: 25–41.

Campion, Michael, James Campion and Peter Hudson
  1994   Structured interviewing: A note on incremental validity and alternative question types. *Journal of Applied Psychology* 79: 998–1002.

Chafe, Wallace
  1980   *The Pear Stories: Vol III Advances in Discourse Analysis*. New York: Ablex.
Di Luzio, Aldio, Susannah Günthner and Franca Orletti (eds.)
  2000   *Culture in Communication: Analysis of Intercultural Situations*. Amsterdam: John Benjamins.
Drew, Paul and John Heritage
  1992   *Talk at Work: Interaction in Institutional Settings*. Cambridge: Cambridge University Press.
Du Bois, William
  1989   *The Souls of Black Folk*. New York: Bantam.
du Gay, Paul
  1996   *Consumption and Identity at* Work. London: Sage.
du Gay, Paul
  2000   *In: Praise of Bureaucracy: Weber/Organizaton/Ethics*. London: Sage.
Erickson, Frederick
  1986   Listening and Speaking. In: Deborah Tannen and James Alatis (eds.) *Language and Linguistics: The Interdependence of Theory, Data and Application*, 294–319. Washington DC: Georgetown University Press.
Erickson, Frederick and Jeffrey Schultz
  1982   *The Counsellor as Gatekeeper: Social Interaction in Interviews*. New York: Academic Press.
Fairclough, Norman
  1992   *Discourse and Social Change*. Polity Press: Cambridge.
Fitzgerald, Helen
  2003   *How Different are We?* Clevedon: Multilingual Matters.
Foucault, Michel
  1978   *History of Sexuality: Volume One: An Introduction*. Translator Robert Hurley. New York: Vintage Books.
Gaudio, R. and S. Bialystok
  2005   The trouble with culture: Everyday racism in white middle class discourse. *Critical Discourse Studies* 2(1): 51–69
Gee, James, Glenda Hull and Colin Lankshear
  1996   *The New Work Order: Behind the Language of the New Capitalism*. St. Leonards: Allen & Unwin.
Goffman, Erving
  1981   *Forms of Talk*. Oxford: Blackwell.
Goffman, Erving
  1983   The interaction order. *American Sociological Review* 48: 1–17.
Gumperz, John (ed.)
  1982a   *Language and Social Identity*. Cambridge: Cambridge University Press.
Gumperz, John
  1982b   *Discourse Strategies*. Cambridge: Cambridge University Press.
Gumperz, John
  1992   Interviewing in intercultural situations. In: Paul Drew and John Heritage (eds.), 302–327.

Gumperz, John
 1996   The linguistic and cultural relativity of conversational inference. In: John
           Gumperz and Stephen Levinson (eds.) *Rethinking Linguistic Relativity*,
           374–406. Cambridge: Cambridge University Press.
Gumperz, John
 1999   On interactional sociolinguistic method. In: Srikant Sarangi and Celia
           Roberts (eds.), 453–471.
Habermas, Jürgen
 1979   *Communication and the Evolution of Society*. Translator Thomas Mc-
           Carthy. London: Heinemann.
Gumperz, John, Tom Jupp and Celia Roberts
 1979   *Crosstalk*. London: National Centre for Industrial Language Training.
Hawthorne, Lesley
 1992   Migrant engineers' job interview performance: A cross cultural analysis.
           Annual Review of Applied Linguistics 15(2): 90–119.
Heath, Anthony and Dorren McMahon
 1997   Education and occupational attainments: The impact of ethnic origins. In:
           V. Karn (ed.), *Ethnicity in the 1991 Census, vol 4: Education, Employment
           and Housing*. London: HMSO.
Heritage, John
 1985   Recent developments in Conversation Analysis. *Sociolinguistics* 15: 1–19.
House, Juliana, Gabriele Kasper and Steven Ross (eds.)
 2003   *Misunderstanding in Social Life: Discourse Approaches to Problematic
           Talk*. London: Longman.
Hubbuck, Jim and Simon Carter
 1980   *Half a Chance: A Report on Job Discrimination Against Young Blacks in
           Nottingham*. London: Commission for Racial Equality.
Huffcutt, Allen and Phillip Roth
 1998   Racial group differences in employment interview evaluations. *Journal of
           Applied Psychology* 83(1): 179–189.
Iedema, Rick
 2003   *Discourses of Post-Bureaucratic Organisation*. Amsterdam: John Benja-
           mins.
Iedema, Rick and Hermine Scheeres
 2003   From doing to talking work: Renegotiating knowing, doing and talking.
           Applied Linguistics 24: 316–337.
Jenkins, Richard
 1986   *Racism and Recruitment: Managers, Organisations and Equal Opportun-
           ities in the Labour Market*. Cambridge: Cambridge University Press.
Jupp, Tom, Celia Roberts and Jenny Cook-Gumperz
 1982   Language and disadvantage: The hidden process. In: John Gumperz (ed.),
           Language and Social Identity, 232–257. Cambridge: Cambridge University
           Press.
Kerekes, Julia
 2003   Distrust: A determining factor in the outcomes of gatekeeping encounters.
           In: Juliana House, Gabriele Kasper and Steven Ross (eds.)

Kerekes, Julia
  2006   Winning an interviewer's trust in a gatekeeping encounter. *Language in Society* 35: 27–57.
Komter, Martha
  1991   *Conflict and Co-operation in job interviews.* Amsterdam: John Benjamins.
Latham, Gary
  1989   The reliability, validity and practicality of the situational interview. In: Robert Eder and Gerald Ferris (eds.), *The Employment Interview: Theory, Research and Practice*, 169–182. Newbury Park, CA: Sage.
Levinson, Stephen
  1979   Activity types and language. *Linguistics* 17(5): 356–399.
Linde, Charlotte
  1993   *Life Stories: The Creation of Coherence.* Oxford University Press: New York.
Linell, Per and Persson Thunquist
  2003   Moving in and out of framings: Activity contexts in talks with young unemployed people within a training project. *Journal of Pragmatics* 35: 409–434.
Longmire, Jean
  1992   Communicating social identity in a job interview in a Cambodian-American community. *Journal of Asian Pacific Communication* 3(1): 49–58.
Mäkitalo, Äsa and Roger Säljö
  2002   Talk in institutional context and institutional context in talk: Catagories and situational practices. *Text* 22(1): 57–82.
Miller, Peter
  1994   Accounting as social and institutional practice: An introduction. In: Anthony G. Hopwood and Peter Miller (eds.), *Accounting as Social and Institutional Practice*, 1–39. Cambridge: Cambridge University Press.
Morales-López, Esperanza, Gabriella Prego-Vázquez and Luzia Domínguez-Seco
  2005   Interviews between employees and customers during a company restructuring process. *Discourse & Society* 16(2): 225–268.
Murray, Alan and Ranjit Sondhi
  1987   Socio-political contexts of intercultural communication. In: Karlfried Knapp, Werner Enninger and Annelie Knapp-Potthoff (eds.), *Analyzing Intercultural Communication,* 17–33. Berlin / New York: Mouton de Gruyter.
O'Grady, Catherine and M. Millen
  1994   *Finding Common Ground: Cross-cultural Communication. Strategies for Job Seekers.* Sydney: NCELTR, Macquarie University.
Palmer, David and James Campion
  1997   A review of structure in the selection interview. *Personnel Psychology* 50: 655–702.
Posthuma, Richard, Frederick Morgeson and James Campion
  2002   Beyond employment interview validity: A comprehensive narrative review of recent research and trends over time. *Personnel Psychology* 55: 1–81.
Rehbein, Jochen
  2000   Intercultural negotiation. In: Aldo di Luzio and Susanna Günthner and Franca Orletti (eds), 173–207.

Roberts, Celia
   1985   *The Interview Game.* London: BBC.
Roberts, Celia and Sarah Campbell
   2005   Fitting stories into boxes: Rhetorical and textual constraints on candidates'
            performances in British job interviews. *Journal of Applied Linguistics* 2(1):
            45–73.
Roberts, Celia and Sarah Campbell
   2006   *Talk on Trial: Job Interviews, language and ethnicity.* Department of Work
            and Pensions Report 344. http://www.dwp.gov.uk/asd/asd5/rrs2006.asp#t
            alkontrial.
Roberts, Celia, Sarah Campbell and Yvonne Robinson
   2008   *Talking Like a Manager.* Department of Work and Pensions Report 510.
            http://www.dwp.gov.uk/asd/asd5/rrs2008.asp#talkinglikeamanager.
Roberts, Celia, Sarah Campbell, Joanna Channell, John Twitchin and Camilla Lailey
   2007   *Successful at Selection.* Department of Work and Pensions and the Depart-
            ment of Education and Professional Studies, King's College London.
Roberts, Celia, Melanie Cooke, Sarah Campbell and Julian Stenhouse
   2007   *Frequently Asked Questions.* Department of Work and Pensions and the De-
            partment of Education and Professional Studies, King's College London.
Roberts, Celia and Srikant Sarangi
   1999   Hybridity in gatekeeping discourse: Issues of practical relevance for the
            researcher. In: Srikant Sarangi and Celia Roberts (eds.), 473–504.
Roberts, Celia, Srikant Sarangi, Lesley Southgate, Richard Wakeford and Valerie Wass
   2000   Oral examinations – equal opportunities, ethnicity and fairness in the
            MRCGP. *British Medical Journal* 320: 370–374.
Roberts, Celia and Peter Sayers
   1987   Keeping the gate: How judgments are made in interethnic interviews. In:
            Karlfried Knapp, Werner Enninger and Annelie Knapp-Potthoff (eds.),
            Analyzing Intercultural Communication, 111–135. Berlin / New York:
            Mouton de Gruyter.
Sarangi, Srikant
   1994   Intercultural or not? Beyond celebration of cultural differences in miscom-
            munication analysis. *Pragmatics* 4(3): 409–427.
Sarangi, Srikant
   1996   Conflation of institutional and cultural stereotypes in Asian migrants' dis-
            course. *Discourse & Society* 7(3): 359–387.
Sarangi, Srikant and Celia Roberts (eds.)
   1999   *Talk, Work and Institutional Order: Discourse in Medical, Mediation and
            Management Settings.* Berlin / New York: Mouton de Gruyter.
Sarangi, Srikant and Stef Slembrouck
   1997   Confrontational asymmetries in institutional discourse: A socio-pragmatic
            view of information exchange and face management. In: Jan Blommaert
            and Chris Bulcaen (eds.), *Political Linguistics,* 255–275. Amsterdam: John
            Benjamins.
Scheuer, Jann
   2001   Recontextualisation and communicative styles in job interviews. *Discourse
            Studies* 3: 223–24.8

Scollon, Ron and Susan Scollon
    1995   *Intercultural Communication: A Discourse Approach.* Oxford: Blackwell.
Silverman, David and Jill Jones
    1976   *Organizational Work: The Language of Grading, the Grading of Language.* London: Collier Macmillan.
Tetlock, Phillip and Richard Boettger
    1989   Accountability: A social magnifier of the dilution effect. *Journal of Personality and Social Psychology* 57: 388–398.
Thornborrow, Joanna
    2002   *Power Talk: Language and Interaction in Institutional Discourse.* Longman: London.
Weber, Max
    1947   *The Theory of Social and Economic Organisation.* New York: Oxford University Press.
Wodak, Ruth
    1996   *Disorders of Discourse.* Longman: London.
Wong, I. and L. Pooh-Ching
    2000   Chinese cultural values and performance at job interviews: A Singapore perspective. *Business Communication Quarterly* 63(1): 9–22.
Wood, Robert and Tim Payne
    1998   *Competency Based Recruitment and Selection.* Chichester: John Wiley.
Young, Linda
    1994   *Crosstalk and Culture in Sino-American Communication.* Cambridge: Cambridge University Press.
Zimmerman, Don H.
    1998   Identity, context and interaction. In: Charles Antaki and Susan Widdicombe (eds.), *Identities in Talk*, 87–106. Sage: London.

18.   The gatekeeping encounter as a social form and as a site for face work

Frederick Erickson

Abstract

"Gatekeeping" is a metaphor used in social research to refer to situations in which the worthiness of a person to gain access to new resources or to a new social status is assessed, and then granted or withheld, by an institutional officer. Gatekeeping judgments affect the social mobility and life chances of the person who is assessed. Gatekeeping can be done by judging a dossier or it can be done in a face to face encounter. Examples of face to face gatekeeping situations include job interviews, clinic visits with a physician, lawyer-client conferences, and academic advising interviews. Sociolinguistic microanalysis of gatekeeping interaction shows that gatekeeping discourse does not take place in value neutral or emotionally neutral ways. Rather, rhetorics of self-presentation are employed by both the person being assessed and by the gatekeeper – often using indirect verbal tactics of persuasion through indexical expression and allusion. "Face work," in Goffman's sense, is thus ubiquitous in gatekeeping encounters. The presence or absence of "comembership" – features of shared social identity between interlocutors – has a powerful influence on the gatekeeping judgments that are made and on the relative candor of the talk that occurs – the directness or indirectness of the face work that is taking place.

1.   Introduction

Scene – Academic advisor's office in a public junior college – a two year college – in a large city in the United States. The student (S), a working class African-American physical education major who is attending the college on an athletic scholarship, tells the white advisor (A) that his long term goal is to become a school counselor (see Appendix for transcription conventions):

A: Do you plan on continuing along this P.E. major?

S: . . . . Yeah I guess so, I might as well keep it up [. .

A: [mhm/

S: my P.E. and . I wanna go into counseling too see . .
A: Well it's . . this is ah . . . . it'll depend on different . . .

it'll vary from different places to different places . .
but essentially what you'll need . . . .
first of all you're gonna need state certification/state teacher certification
in other words you're gonna have to be certified to teach in some area
History or English or whatever else happens to be your bag . . P.E.
. . . . secondly you're gonna have to have a master's degree
(*single laugh token*)
. . ha/ . . . . which as you know is an advanced degree . .
that's what you have to do to be a counselor

The advisor, acting as an academic gatekeeper, could be encouraging the student in his desire to become a counselor in the future, or the advisor could be discouraging the student from his stated career goal. On the face of it, the gatekeeping message is not clear. The advisor does not say in so many words, "counseling is not for you". But what might he have been implying?

In the excerpt from an academic advising interview that appears above there is ambiguity concerning the advisor's intent as a gatekeeper – was he opening a gate to future social mobility and academic opportunity for the student, or was he closing it? In the advising interview the gatekeeping action of the advisor was metaphoric and indirect. The gatekeeping action, and its "message", is much more clear and direct in a literal situation of gatekeeping, as portrayed by Franz Kafka (1925):

> Before the law sits a gatekeeper. To this gatekeeper comes a man from the country who asks to gain entry into the law. But the gatekeeper says that he cannot grant him entry at the moment … The gatekeeper gives him a stool and allows him to sit down at the side in front of the gate. There he sits for days and years. He makes many attempts to be let in, and he wears the gatekeeper out with his requests. The gatekeeper often interrogates him briefly … and at the end he always tells him once more that he cannot let him inside yet.
> (Kafka 1925)

This passage comes from a short story inserted by Kafka in his novel *The Trial* under the title "Before the Law". It is told as a parable of the mute intransigence of bureaucracy – an aspect of the insanity of modern life. In the gatekeeping scene that Kafka portrayed an actual gate is physically present, tended by a person who is explicitly designated as a gatekeeper. The gatekeeper keeps his gate closed, blocking the appellant from access to legal processes that might provide redress for some injury the appellant has presumably received in the world outside the gate.

In social research, *gatekeeping* as a metaphor has been applied more broadly to situations of face to face interaction in which some issue of institutionally authorized social selection is involved – inclusion or exclusion at an institutional boundary that is based on an institutional officer's judgment of the worthiness of the person who is being considered for inclusion. Many situations of institutional interaction involve aspects of gatekeeping – a partial list of examples includes job interviews, promotion/retention reviews, lawyer-client conferences, home-life inspection visits by a social worker, clinic visits with one's physician, classroom interaction within which teachers form judgments of students concerning grading or streaming within the school system, and selection or promotion for participants in performance groups – teams in sports, an ensemble in music, the cast of a play. Gatekeeping judgments affect the later life course of the person that is being assessed – such assessments may have consequences for the social mobility and life chances of the gatekept. Gatekeepers are also assessed by the gatekept, but given the tilted playing field of the institutional gatekeeping encounter, the assessments of the gatekept by the gatekeeper are visible institutionally – and in terms of future life chances – whereas the assessments of the gatekeeper by the gatekept remain invisible – an aspect of the "hidden transcripts" in relations between the dominant and the dominated (see Scott 1990).

Because the "worth" of the gatekept person is under scrutiny, gatekeeping situations of interaction differ from ordinary social interaction in a number of ways that make it of interest for sociolinguistic study of language use and interaction process. In Kafka's portrayal of gatekeeping there was little interaction between the supplicant and the gatekeeper, and no attempts at persuasion by the supplicant had any effect. Yet in ordinary gatekeeping interaction attempts at persuasion are ubiquitous. There is special pressure on persuasion – rhetorics of self-presentation by the gatekept person and by the gatekeeper as well. This self-presentation is interactionally accomplished because what the gatekeeper does vis-à-vis the gatekept person can make it easier or more difficult for the gatekept person to make a positive self-presentation, and the same applies to the gatekeeper vis-à-vis the gatekept person. The gatekeeping encounter is fraught with potential for face-threat – in gatekeeping interaction both the gatekept person and the gatekeeper are vulnerable to loss of face, and so some of their attempts at persuasion are reciprocal – the supplicant attempts to present a self that has worth and dignity (unlike Kafka's fictional account); the gatekeeper attempts to present a self that is respectful of the self that the applicant is presenting. There are also matters of overall situational framing that lead to more and less charitable "readings" of the case at hand by the gatekeeper and more and less candid and direct presentations by the supplicant of his or her case for entry past the gate.

In the introductory discussion above I have begun to discuss key aspects of the conduct of literal and metaphoric gatekeeping in social interaction. In the section that follows I will extend a bit further the discussion of gatekeeping interaction as a social form. I will then present specific illustrative examples of interaction in gatekeeping – encounters that take place as interviews in particular institutional settings – academic advising, medical interviews, and a job interview. In each specific instance I will consider certain rhetorics of self presentation in talk by the gatekeeping interviewer and the interviewee. I will also consider circumstances of framing that affect the more or less "charitable" readings of the self presentations of the interlocutors.

2.   Gatekeeping as a social form

Let us consider some general conditions of gatekeeping interaction as a set of reciprocal social practices. The force of the gatekeeping metaphor, as applied to situations of face to face social selection in institutional settings, comes from the circumstances of literal gatekeeping, as illustrated by Kafka's parable. In that portrayal there is an actual gate, with a person tending it who has the authority to open or close it. The gate provides access to an interior space, within which access is available to certain goods – to rights/privileges/services/network connections – that are either not available at all outside the gate or are available in only small quantities compared with their availability inside the gate. In consequence, entry through the gate constitutes access to certain advantages and denial of entry prevents access to those advantages.

The simplest kind of literal gatekeeping is one in which the goods behind the gate are in abundant supply – as in a mass transit system or a general admission seat in a sports arena – and the qualification for entry is also in abundant supply. In such a situation the gatekeeping decision process is very simple. Review of credentials of worth is minimal. If the applicant possesses an access ticket (or buys one on the spot) and does not look dangerous he or she is admitted. Without the ticket entry is denied. Indeed, a machine can be programmed to replace the gatekeeper, accomplishing the gatekeeping function automatically, as at a subway entrance. When the applicant inserts the proper ticket or token, the gate opens. (As a service encounter, interaction with a live ticket seller is only slightly more complex – if an applicant presents the right amount of money, usually the access pass can be issued by the sales clerk without any exchange of words with the purchaser.)

Literal gatekeeping interaction becomes more complex when there are limited numbers of "slots" available for accessing the goods on the inside of the gate, or when multidimensional credentials of worth are required of the applicant, involving some ambiguity – multiple tokens of worth, some of which are so indexically signalled as badges of social identity that they are not obvious in their meaning. This increases both the rhetorical complexity of self presentation by the applicant and the inferential complexity of the assessment task for the gatekeeper. Various written pieces of evidence may need to be considered and many verbal exchanges may occur before a gatekeeping judgment can be rendered.

Most metaphoric gatekeeping encounters present some of the complexity of the literal gatekeeping situation in which there is either limited availability of slots, or high cost of admission, in terms of large amounts of evidence of the applicant's worth being required. But further complexity comes in metaphoric gatekeeping situations when the role of the gatekeeper as an institutional officer involves both representing the best interests of the institution *and* the best interests of the applicant (as Roberts points out in her chapter on job interviews in this volume, the doorkeeper God Janus was seen as facing two ways at once). This duality of attention and allegiance is especially apparent in gatekeeping in "caretaking" occupations – e.g. ideally a physician should provide medical services to a patient, not withhold them. Yet in a "triage" medical decision situation, where the need for medical services far exceeds the capacity of the medical system to deliver services to all who need them, some exclusionary gatekeeping decisions must be made by the physician. Analogously a defense attorney should advocate for the client, not side with the prosecution, but sometimes the attorney will counsel the client to plea bargain; and while an academic advisor should provide advice and support to a student, sometimes the advisor's role on behalf of the school may be to say that the student is not qualified for admission through a particular academic gate. Moreover, for "caretaking" gatekeepers, there is face threat potential in not appearing to the applicant as sufficiently "caring" – putting the interests of the institution above those of the appellant. In contrast, in a simpler gatekeeping situation such as a job interview, the gatekeeper's role is relatively unitary – as an institutional officer whose primary obligation is to maintain the best interests of the institution – and, it would seem, the job interviewer could keep the employment gate closed without losing face. (As we will see, however, in actual gatekeeping interaction certain face threat conditions obtain even for a job interviewer.) Finally, in complex situations of gatekeeping in face to face interaction, the tactics of persuasion in positive face maintenance by both the gatekeeper and the gatekept person tend toward indirection and implicit rhetorics rather than toward direct, explicit expression, avoiding a bluntness that might appear to be less than appropriately tactful. The implicit, allusive character of positive self-presentation in gatekeeping interaction thus presents another topic of interest for sociolinguistic description and analysis.

I have mentioned "self-presentation" and "face threat" in the discussion above, and I mean that precisely in terms of Goffman's theoretical account of basic processes in social interaction. In his classic paper "On Face Work" Goffman (1955) claimed that interlocutors shared an interest in protecting one another's positive identities in the interaction at hand. Since both parties were potentially vulnerable to the negative consequences that might follow if their defects became salient in the encounter, Goffman contended, interlocutors would avoid to the greatest extent possible doing or saying things that would threaten the other's "face". (This can be thought of as a microsocial version of the Cold War process of "deterrence" in the use of nuclear weapons – a process based on mutual recognition of "mutually assured destruction".) We can see how attempts at mutual avoidance of face threat happen in actual gatekeeping encounters.

3.   Illustrative examples of gatekeeping interaction

The first example is taken from an academic advising interview in an urban public community college in the United States – a two year school offering an "associate" degree rather than a baccalaureate degree. These advising interviews typically began with the advisor and student reviewing and updating the student's cumulative record (this was before the days of digital record keeping). This was an academic history-taking phase in the interview, which was typically followed by a statement of an intended future goal, which in turn was followed by advice on what steps to take in order to reach that goal. (For further discussion of this example, and of the study in which it was collected, which was done in the early 1970s in a large American city, see Erickson [1975] and Erickson and Shultz [1982: 110–121]). In this example the interviewer was white and the student was African-American. The student had adequate grades and was a basketball star – in the previous year his team had won the national championship for two-year colleges.

The transcript begins as the advisor (A), having summed up the number of credits in courses the student had completed in the previous semester, asked about the student's (S) plans for a course of study in the next academic term:

A: Do you plan on continuing along this P.E. major?

S: . . . .   Yeah I guess so, I might as well keep it up [. .

A: [mhm/

S: my P.E. and   . I wanna go into counseling too see   . .
    . . . . you know . . . to have . .
    two way . . like equal balance]

A: [I see . ah .
    what do you know about counseling?

S: Nothing[

A: [O.K.]

S: [I know you have to take psychology courses
    of some sorts . . . and counseling . .

(shifts in chair)
A: Well it's . . this is ah . . . . it'll depend on different . . .
it'll vary from different places to different places . .
but essentially what you'll need . . . .
first of all you're gonna need state certification/state teacher certification
in other words you're gonna have to be certified to teach in some area
History or English or whatever else happens to be your bag . . P.E.
. . . . secondly you're gonna have to have a master's degree
(single laugh token)
. . ha/ . . . . which as you know is an advanced degree . .
that's what you have to do to be a counselor

As the academic history-taking phase of the interview concluded, the advisor had asked about the student's future goal, "Do you plan on continuing along this P.E. (physical education) major?" The student replied in the affirmative but added rather abruptly that he wanted in addition to become a counselor, "You know, to have . . two way – like equal balance." After a question about what the student knew about study in the field of counseling, to which the student gave a minimally informative reply, the advisor shifted his position in his chair rather awkwardly and, after a series of uncomfortable vocal hesitations and false starts, launched into a long and rather convoluted explanation of how one became a counselor: ". . . it'll vary from different places to different places but essentially what you need . . First of all you're gonna need certification/ state teacher certification . . In other words you're gonna have to be certified in some area . . English, or History, or whatever else happens to be your bag. P.E. . . . . Secondly you're gonna have to have a master's degree – which as you know is an advanced degree."

Ordinarily when a student had identified a future goal that advisor would say something like the following: "O.K. then next term take Courses X and Y and the following term take Z." Here is what he had said in immediate response to a student who said he wanted to transfer to a local university (i.e. one offering a baccalaureate degree): "Check with [University name]." In other words, the time sequence of advice would be "do this now, then do that next" and so on, stepwise out from the present moment into the future.

In contrast, in this example with the student who said he wanted to be a counselor, the advisor reversed his typical time sequence for giving advice (First you need teacher certification. Second you need a master's degree.). Teacher certification and a subsequent master's degree were not "first" at all. What would have been "first" was something the student could do in the immediate next semester. Given that the student was in his second year at the community college and that therefore state teacher certification for him (requiring a baccalaureate degree) could occur no sooner than two years after the completion of the current academic year, with a master's degree possible no sooner than a year or two after that, the advisor had begun his advice by skipping forward to a point in time far in the future.

By producing this temporally reversed sequence of advising talk, the advisor was hedging. There was something he could have said directly right then but he didn't. (N. B. I knew this because I had conducted a "viewing session" with this advisor, during which we reviewed together a videotape of his encounter with the student. The advisor could stop the tape whenever he wished, and make comments on the interaction process, which were audio recorded and transcribed. In an interview with me, we reviewed together the videotape of his advising session with the student.) In a viewing session the advisor stopped the tape at the end of his explanation: "a master's degree. Which as you know is an advanced degree." At that stopping place the interviewer made two comments. First, he said that during the few weeks previous to the videotaped advising session a number of students had come to him telling him that they wanted to be a counselor. "I think I went into an automatic explanation of how to become a counselor", the interviewer said. In other words, the advisor recognized that there was something a bit odd in the way he had explained to the student what would be involved in the student's achieving his career goal. Second, the advisor said "and he's a little ahead of himself in wanting to change to counseling right now". The advisor went on to say very directly to me that this was an example of how his employer, the community college, was taking advantage of African-American students who were skilled athletes. (The counselor used a strong term, "victimized", to characterize this.) Each semester the basketball coach reviewed the proposed courses of study for all members of his team – plans for course registration in the next term that had been constructed with the students' advisors and had been approved by them. The coach then adjusted the programs of study to eliminate courses that he knew had major assignments or tests that conflicted with the team's "big game" schedule. The coach would then over-ride the advisorws – approved plans and re-register the students for courses whose assignment and test schedules did not conflict with his game schedule. (Because the coach had winning teams, with national championships, the central administration of the college allowed him to over-ride the planning work of the advisors.) These actions by the coach resulted in basketball team members having programs of study that "didn't add up" – they were anomalous. And this particular star basketball player had had his schedule altered by his coach. Even though his grades were adequate, it would take him extra time to complete courses he should have already completed in order to follow through on his intention of becoming a counselor.

But in the advising interview, as the topic of the student's future goal came up the counselor didn't say anything about the coach, forthrightly, to the student, nor did he point out the anomalies in the student's record that had resulted from the coach's interference. Instead the advisor was indirect – he produced the temporally back-to-front description of first steps: "First of all you're going to have to get certification/state teacher certification …" The advisor had not met this student before. Apparently he felt that it was inappropriate to deliver such "bad news" immediately and explicitly in response to what the student had said. A minute later in the original interview the advisor told the student that he had a problem with changing his course of study and that the problem was due to the wrong actions of the coach.

The counselor's attempt to cushion the "bad news" for the student (and in the process, to maintain his self presentation as an advisor who was not inconsiderate or unduly harsh) was dramatically unsuccessful. In a separate viewing session, similar to the one conducted with the interviewer, the student reviewed the videotape of the interview, stopped the tape at exactly the same juncture as the interviewer had done. The student said of the interviewer: "He's telling me I'm not qualified. But he doesn't just do it POW! like they would in the old days. He put some sugar on it. He used some psychology." In a second viewing of the tape the student stopped again at the same place and said, "He insulted my manhood."

The viewing session comments of the advisor and the student showed very different inferences concerning the meaning of the advisor's explanation about how to become a counselor. In his viewing session comment the advisor characterized his explanation as a bit stilted, but yet as affectively neutral. The student, in his viewing session comment characterized the advisor's explanation as profoundly face-threatening – an implicit rejection of the student's career intention that was so absolute as to be insulting. (A minute later in the original interview the counselor did speak directly to the student about what the coach had done and the problem that had created for the student. But that was too late – the student said in his viewing session that by then he was so angry that he dismissed everything the advisor was saying, for the rest of the interview.)

Unlike Kafka's fictional gatekeeper whose role was unitary, the role of an academic advisor is dual – acting as an institutional officer of the college, committed to the "gatekeeping" obligation of enforcing college rules and standard operating procedures, and also acting as an advocate for the student, with an obligation to further the student's best interests by giving advice and encouragement. The advisor cannot simply help the student at the expense of the institution's interests and standards nor can the advisor simply defend the institution's interests at the expense of the student. In trying for a "minimax" resolution of this inherent role tension, the advisor is obliged to act enough on behalf of the student, and to be tactful enough in pointing out negative features of the student's academic circumstances so that the student's "face" is protected. In so doing the advisor protects his or her own face. That was what went wrong in the advisor's encounter with the basketball star – the advisor had attempted to be tactful by being indirect in his talk, but that attempt was interpreted by the student as an insult.

In the larger study from which this example comes, 26 of these advising interviews were filmed and studied comparatively (see the reports in Erickson [1975] and Erickson and Shultz [1982]). Four male advisors were filmed in encounters with sets of male students who had been routinely scheduled for appointments with them. Both the advisors and students varied in ethnicity so that in some of each advisor's encounters the ethnicity and/or race of the interlocutors was similar and in other encounters it was different. Moreover, the encounters differed in whether or not the interlocutors revealed that they had things in common besides ethnicity or race, and the researchers came to call this *situational comembership*. The encounters differed in overall tone – in some encounters each advisor gave considerable special help to the student and was candid in talking about any academic problems the student might be having, and in other encounters the advisor gave little special help and was indirect in talking about the student's academic problems. We can call the former kind of encounter Type I and the latter kind Type II. Overwhelmingly in the study the Type I encounters were characterized by high comembership (a sharing of background similarities which might include race or ethnicity but not necessarily so) and the Type II encounters were characterized by low comembership. In other words, the presence of comembership in the encounters seemed to establish a frame of mutual positive regard, within which the student and the advisor were more candid with one another and the advisor was more overtly acting as a sponsor of the student than was the case when the comembership relation between the two interlocutors was low. Comembership appeared to be influencing the footing – the alignment – between the advisor and the student (see Goffman 1981: 124–157).

In the example of advising interaction presented above there was low comembership between the interlocutors – they differed in race and had had no previous acquaintance. In that situation the advisor was indirect in identifying an academic problem the student had, and the student interpreted that indirection as a face attack. In contrast, in an encounter characterized by high comembership the advisor was much more direct in talking about a problem – the student's extremely low grade point average:

S: I ah   .   wanted to/ah get straight about my average
   workin' out this semester as far as goin' to [University name]

(A opens file of papers on his desk)

A: I see . . O.K. Lemme . . . .
   I went into the/ah registrar's office a little earlier today and I
   picked and I picked up your most current   . ah . transcript
   . . . .   and I also talked to the registrar about this . .

and you remember when we wrote that letter to [name]
down at . ah . ah/[University name] you said that you
had a one-five-six/well in the meantime . ah . with the
Afro History that you took last semester you've raised it to
one-five-**eight** [. .

S: [mhm]

A: [so/(*slight swallowed laugh outbreath*) it's
a little bit of an improvement . . . . **Now** . .
I talked to [name] who's the registrar here . . and . the way
this thing looks to me . . you're taking Business one forty one

S: Well I dropped the one]

A: [you dropped the one-forty-one . . O.K.
Business one-eleven.

S: Right.
A: ah . Geography one-oh-one?]
S: [right.
A: Business two **thir**ty one]
S: [right
                    (*S nods*)
A: and soh-sci one-oh-**one**[. . anything else?]

S: [yes]

A: [just twelve hours
                    (*S nods*)
thir/P.E. would be thirteen . . O.K. . ah . I talked to [name]
and [name] indicated to me . . that as long as you were taking
these courses **over** again we would take the higher **grade**.
                    [(*S nods*)
        . . in [computing the **grade point** average

In contrast to the first student, who had acceptable grades but an anomalous
program of study, this student had terrible grades – he had previously failed a
number of courses and it had been necessary for him to be "taking the courses
over again". Apparently he had only received minimally passing grades in the
courses that he repeated, since his overall grade point average was now 1.58 on
a four point scale (i.e. a D+ average, in terms of American letter grades). After
such performance in a two year college, admission to a four year school (in this
case, a state university) would be very unlikely, without special advocacy from
someone at the student's two year college. That person was this advisor – over a
period of years he had been overseeing the student's progress, writing letters on

his behalf to the admissions officer at the university, and making sure that student records and other paperwork reached that admissions officer in good order. Over time the advisor had come to identify very positively with this student, and the student was aware of that. (In his viewing session the advisor said, "I feel like a father to him.") Within the frame of high comembership that had been established between these two interlocutors they could talk very directly about the otherwise very face threatening topic of the student's low grade point average. This high comembership relation obtained in spite of a difference in race – the student was African-American and the advisor was white, as was also true for the first example. But what a difference in frame, and in mutual candor, between the first example of an inter-racial gatekeeping encounter and the second one! The difference, for the conditions of face threat, seems to lie in the level of comembership established between the advisor and the student.

A comparable example comes from an interview with another of the advisors we studied at the same community college. The example comes from an encounter that we characterized as the highest in comembership of all the 26 cases we studied. The advisor and student were still in the academic history-taking phase of the interview when the student revealed a serious academic problem:

A: Data processing 101, what did you get for a grade?
S: B.
A: Data processing 111.
S: F/
A: /data processing, that's your **major**, data processing – right?

S: Yeah well I just talked to him [the instructor] and he said
    it was because of excessive absences

A: Good for you! Good for you.

Both the student and the advisor were being very direct in talking about what would seem to have been a seriously face-threatening piece of new information about the student's academic performance – he had not only failed a course, but the course was one in his major field of study. The student stated without any hedging that he had received "F" for a grade and the advisor responded with marked sarcasm, "data processing, that's your **major**." Then the student upped the ante of candor by explaining that it was not that he didn't understand the material in the course; he had simply gotten the failing grade because he didn't attend enough classes. Again the advisor responded ironically, "Good for you!"

What accounts for this strange way of treating a topic with such high potential for face threat? My interpretation is that this is a matter of high co-membership framing. The advisor and the student shared ethnicity – they were both Italian-American. In his viewing session with me the advisor said that he and the student had known each other for a number of years. The advisor had formerly taught at a Roman Catholic high school in the city, where this student had also been a student. At that school the advisor had been the wrestling coach, and this student's older brother had been one of the wrestlers on the advisor's high school wrestling team. In consequence the advisor had been acquainted not only with this student's brother but with his parents. Moreover, since this student had come to the community college the advisor had been counseling him, and had been colluding with the student in a tactic to keep him registered in school. He was now in his seventh semester, when with ordinary progress he would have graduated in four semesters. The year was 1970 and, had this young man not been registered in college he would have been eligible to be drafted. The advisor was helping the student evade the draft and stay out of the war in Vietnam.

A high comembership relation, indeed. What the student would do each semester was register for required courses, then drop one or two of them and fail another, so that he was continually having to register again in the next semester for courses he had not completed the previous semester. Within the frame of shared background and shared understanding that obtained between this particular advisor and student it was entirely appropriate and comfortable for the student to talk directly – and even for the advisor to speak in friendly mockery – about a failing grade in a course in the student's major field of study. They both knew what that was about – it was a tactic to stay registered in school. In a sense this gatekeeping situation can be considered to be a mirror opposite of the one in Kafka's story, for not only was this advisor letting the student though an institutional gate by allowing him to register for the next semester, but he was helping the student to hide behind a "gate" he had already passed through – the gate of admission to the status of registered college student which allowed him to continue to be exempt from the draft. In sum, this encounter showed an extreme of high comembership and an extreme of special help and candor in the interaction between the academic advisor and the student. (For further discussion of this interview and its implications for social theory as well as for sociolinguistic inquiry, see Erickson [2004: 72–85, 172–174].)

The next example comes from a clinic visit in medicine. The mother of an infant had come with her child to an after-hours pediatrics clinic at a community hospital. The clinic was staffed by interns (clinically inexperienced physicians who practice under clinical supervision by an experienced physician). The mother held the infant in her lap as she spoke to the physician in an examining room:

Dr: Dr [name] is your normal physician?

Mo: (nods)

Dr: OK . . so . . . . what brings you here tonight?

Mo: A:h . . yesterday morning when I got him up he felt kind of **warm]** . .

Dr: [mhm]

Mo: [or I thought he felt a little warm right out of the bed

but when I took him to the babysitter he said/she checked him and she she
said he was O.K. . .   and ah . he seemed fine yesterday afternoon .
this morning I got him up
I took his temperature be**fore** I took him to the sitter to make **sure** he was
O.K. . .   no temperature and now when I picked him up she said he had a
real bad day . .   and/and she had given him Tylenol **twice** . . and I took
him home and took his temperature and it was a hundred and **four** . . . .
so I gave him **Tylenol** . . . .   as soon as I got ahold of her to find out if it
was O.K. to give it to him . .   and so it was six **thirty** before he had Tylenol a**gain** . .   I took his temperature at about . .   quarter to **eight** and it
was a hundred and four point **six** . . . .   and so then we .   called the
doctor and they said that we'd better bring him in and have him **checked**
and I've given him/I've bathed him . .   given him a quick bath too I
thought maybe that would help . bring it down . .
he just is tired . droopy . .   falls asleep in your arms . . . .
(*addresses baby*) you're just not happy are yah? . . . .
and I . I he's got a **white** spot on his **goom** and I thought maybe it was
teeth . but he said that he shouldn't run that high a **tem**perature . .
y'know]

Dr: [mhm]

Mo: [just teething . . said we oughta bring him in
to have him **checked** . .

Dr: O . Ka::y . how did the baby sitter say he **act**ed

Mo: a::h she just/she said he just was **fus**sy he . when he slept he just
you know tossed and turned and .

Dr: [Mhm] . . . .
(*low pitch, low volume*)

Mo: [I wish she had called me at **work** but I guess she didn't think it was
necessary . . . .
(*quietly*) (*normal volume*

Dr. O.K. . .   Have there been any other problems?

The interview began by the intern asking the mother why she had come to the
clinic, "So, what brings you here tonight?" This is a routine opening of physician-patient encounters in the United States – an invitation to the patient to
state a "presenting complaint". Such an invitation is intended as a gesture of
politeness by the physician, but it presents the patient with a potentially face-

threatening task – to tell a narrative of the presenting complaint in a way that is medically coherent – consistent with medical standards for medically relevant information, and avoiding details or excursus that is medically irrelevant. Since the physician knows much more about those standards of medical relevance than does the patient, the request to tell the story of the presenting complaint is a bit of a "set-up" – it puts the patient "on the spot" to produce a medically well-formed narrative of the complaint. (For further discussion on this point, see Erickson and Rittenberg [1987].)

The intern was young – he was in his late twenty's or early thirty's – and the mother was about ten years older than he. She had other children, and so it is reasonable to assume that she was more experienced in speaking to pediatricians than was the intern in speaking to the parents of infants. Still, it is remarkable that she produced a narrative of the presenting complaint that was faultless, in terms of the medical relevance of information points in her story. She provided an exact chronology of the (approximately) forty hour course of her observation of the baby's fever, beginning with the morning of the previous day and continuing with major points in time until she had brought the baby to the clinic some time after eight o'clock that evening. She was precise in identifying the various amounts of fever, as its waxing and waning, with an overall pattern of increase over time, was measured on a Fahrenheit scale by a thermometer. She was also precise in identifying the kind of medication the child was given (Tylenol), and the amounts and timing of administration of the doses the baby had received.

I have shown this as an example video to groups of experienced physicians and nurses over the years, as well as to sociolinguists who study physician patient interaction, and they all notice the remarkably well-formed character of the mother's narrative report on the course of the child's fever. In addition, these viewers of the videotape identify a subtext in the mother's story – a narrative theme that is never stated explicitly. There are three characters in the story of the presenting complaint – the mother, her baby, and the baby's caregiver – a woman who tended the child in her own home while the mother was at work. The mother appears to be saying something like the following: "It wasn't my fault the fever reached this level – I'm a good mother, but the woman who helps me with child care was too casual about this." The mother, by the very details of medical relevance contained in her narrative, portrayed her own actions as more attentive to the child's medical condition than had been those of her child care provider. She also concluded her narrative with an explicit though muted criticism of the child care provider, "I wish she had called me at work but I guess she didn't think it was necessary."

Here is a schematic presentation of portions of the mother's narrative that highlights her rhetorical emphasis:

MOTHER FOCUS	BABYSITTER FOCUS
Yesterday morning when I got him up he felt kind of warm	
	But when I took him to the babysitter [she] checked him and she said he was O.K.
This morning I took his temperature before I took him to the sitter to make sure he was OK – no temperature	
and now when I picked him up	
	she said he had a real bad day and she had given him Tylenol twice
I took him home and took his temperature and it was a hundred and four.	
So I gave him Tylenol as soon as I got ahold of her [babysitter] to find out if it was O.K. to give it to him.	
I took his temperature at about a quarter to eight and it was a hundred and four point six. So then we called the doctor and they said we'd better bring him in to have him checked. I've bathed him, given him a bath too . . . . I thought maybe that would bring it down	
And he's got a white spot on his goom and I thought maybe it [the baby's discomfort] was teeth but he [the physician] said he shouldn't have that high a temperature	
Dr: How did the babysitter say he acted?	
	She said he just was fussy . . when he slept he tossed and turned
	I wish she had called me at work but I guess she didn't think it was necessary.

In the mother's account she portrayed herself as responsible and knowledgeable (even to the point of engaging in a bit of "differential" diagnostic hypothesizing – she had volunteered to her primary care physician that the baby's fussiness might have been due to teething, and that hunch had been "ruled out" by the physician.) The mother was obliged to turn over care of her infant to a babysitter during the day, but that was not her fault, nor was the situation that the babysitter may have been less than fully competent as a caretaker – the mother needed to work. My line of inference here about her implicit argument needs to be understood in the context of the American child care situation. The woman's dress and speech style (e.g. her prosody and the locutions "get ahold of her" and "goom") identified her as working class. She was not in a financial position to be able to arrange an ideal child care situation such as employing a nanny at home or placing the child in a day care center staffed by an adequate number of professionals. Thus she was entitled to a cosmetic touch of "poor me" in her self-presentation as a working mother caring for a sick child. (When I showed this video to an audience of pediatricians, nurses, and midwives at the Karolinska Institute teaching hospital in Stockholm they recognized this "poor me" implication by the mother. In fact they indulged in a Swedish version of *Schadenfreude* [taking pleasure in noticing another's misfortune] as they commented at some length on the superiority of Scandinavian systems of provision of child care for working mothers, in contrast to the haphazard and market driven manner of provision that was available to working class mothers in the United States.)

There is another aspect of the subtext of being a good mother that relates to a United States context. When this clinic visit was videotaped (the mid-1970s) state laws had recently been passed that required such professionals as physicians, social workers, and teachers to report cases of suspected child abuse – in legal language such persons were designated as "mandated reporters." This change in the law made the relations between professional care givers and their parent clients more adversarial then they had been before the new laws had been enacted. This could explain why the mother's account was so well crafted medically, and why it emphasized her concern and agency on behalf of her child. In her self-presentation as competent and caring she was trying indirectly to prevent even the appearance of child neglect on her part. If anyone had been neglectful or unskilled it was the babysitter, not the mother. Face threat, in this situation, was not just a matter of maternal narcissism – the mother could have been slightly on the defensive with her child's physician because of the legal ramifications that could follow upon being judged by a gatekeeping physician as something other than a good parent.

It might seem that in a job interview the issue of face threat would be less complicated than in advisor-student encounters, physician-patient encounters, or preceptor-intern encounters. Ideally, the job interviewer is primarily an officer of the organization that is hiring new employees. Hence the job interviewer should have less "care-giving" obligation in dealing with the job applicant than do advisors or physicians or teachers in dealing with their charges. But in the interactional conduct of job interviews, face maintenance is still necessary, as the following example illustrates:

App: (In viewing session)
Int: (*looks down at the application form on his desk*)
Just got your degree . . one year in Rome, huh?

App: Right . . . .
                        (*Int looks up at the applicant . . nods here*)
[University name] offers a junior year abroad program . .
(*Int looks down at the coffee cup and picks it up*)
and . ah . at the moment of accepting or not I decided to go . .
(*I looks at his coffee cup as A shifts uncomfortably in chair*)
to . ah . Rome . ah . .
(*A brings right hand to his eyebrow and wipes eyebrow*)
It was a great experience.

The young man was applying for an entry level position in an insurance company. At the end of the interview the interviewer offered him the job, and so in gatekeeping terms this was a positive story – the "gate" of opportunity was not closed to this applicant by the gatekeeper. Still the opening of the interview held some "bad breath" for the applicant. He appeared to be nervous, hesitating in speech and shifting in his chair. Here is what the job interviewer said as he reviewed the videotape of the interview in a viewing session. He stopped the tape to comment after the student had shifted in his chair:

> I could see he was nervous but that he was interested in talking about Rome. So I thought if I could keep him talking about Rome he'd relax and then we could go on with the rest of the interview.

The applicant, in a separate viewing session, commented on the way the interviewer had appeared to him:

> OK ah. I think I can see it now – he had very lit/right at the beginning he had very little eye contact with me. He was ah, staring at his coffee and at the application. And ah, this signified to me that, you know, he doesn't care, you know. It doesn't matter one way or the other to him. It's just not his job. And he's not going to, you know, get involved deeply with the applicant.

Notice in the transcript of the interview that the interviewer asked the first question in the interview while still looking down at the job application form on his desk. The applicant began to answer and the interviewer then looked up and across at the applicant as he said "offers a junior year abroad program". Then the interviewer broke eye contact and looked down at his coffee cup. As he did that the applicant began to hesitate in speaking and shifted his weight in his chair. The interviewer asked two more questions about the junior year abroad program and the applicant hesitated and shifted uncomfortably again, each time doing so after the interviewer had broken eye contact. The applicant did not stop acting uncomfortable until the interviewer left off asking questions about Rome and went on to describe the work practices involved in the entry level job.

The interviewer was unaware that it was his own listening behavior that was influencing the applicant to act in ways that appeared to the interviewer to be nervous. The applicant had expected more animated listening responses than those he had gotten from the interviewer. (In a subsequent viewing session comment the applicant said that his year in Rome had been the most exciting experience of his life, and that the interviewer's apparent disinterest was puzzling and off-putting. The applicant said, "If you are interested in what someone says you don't just SIT THERE. You move and talk while the other person is talking.") From the applicant's point of view the interviewer had failed to show appropriate engagement and respect during the recounting of a piece of personal information that the applicant regarded as highly interesting. The "face" of the interviewer as one who cares about applicants was damaged by his own actions as a listener. And the "face" of the applicant, who was reporting a significant and life-changing experience, was damaged as well. (Note that this is the same instance that is discussed and cited as Erickson [1986] in the Roberts chapter in this volume – see Erickson [1986] for further discussion on the importance of listening behavior in general and in gatekeeping encounters in particular.)

4.   Conclusion

It would seem from these examples from the late twentieth century in the United States that people do not live in the same gatekeeping universe as that portrayed by Kafka, who was writing from Prague in the early twentieth century. In contrast to Kafka's intransigent gatekeeper, American gatekeepers seem to be obliged not only to be basically affirming but to be nice – an academic advisor should present himself to the student as supportive, a physician should treat a patient as capable of telling a medically coherent story of the presenting complaint (no matter how medically incoherent such a story might actually be), and a job interviewer should treat a young job applicant's recounting of personal experience as interesting, no matter how commonplace the experience might be or how callow was its recounting. In recent statements within the perspective of critical discourse analysis (e.g. Fairclough 1992) the facade of politeness and friendliness that now characterizes many routine institutional encounters in workplaces is seen as a result of changes in late capitalism by which increases in conditions of inequality and domination are masked from those who are being dominated.

Writing a generation earlier, and describing interaction in the 1950s and early 1960s, before capitalism had become quite so "late", Goffman took up lines of explanation that differ from the critical discourse analysis perspective. On the one hand, Goffman noted a particularly North American tendency – and most particularly a tendency in the United States – toward indirectness in the exercise of institutional authority. He described this as "role distancing" – a superordinate masking the directness of the "directives" that are being uttered (Goffman 1961: 106). He saw this as distinctive of the United States, deriving from a long-standing cultural pattern of ambivalence about the face to face exercise of superordination and subordination that was noticed as early as the 1830s by de Tocqueville and reported in the two volumes of his *Democracy in America* (1835, 1840). On the other hand, Goffman made an even more general claim in the essay on face work. This was the claim that protection of face was in the mutual interest of interlocutors in all sorts of situations of face to face interaction, i.e. that face work was a functionally necessary component of an "interaction order". (Goffman 1955, 1983)

In a recent discussion (Erickson 2004) I have maintained that attempts to identify the influences of macro-social processes upon local social action in everyday discourse are more complicated than they may appear at first glance. But whatever the mix of distal and proximal causes of the local social action that takes place in the micro-social realm of face to face interaction might be, there does appear to be a tendency toward role-distancing in the exercise of authority that currently can be found not only in North America but in Britain and in continental Europe as well. In the gatekeeping encounter this tendency can be seen as manifesting in face work that is done by the gatekeeper and also by the gatekept. The gatekeeper tends to a self presentation that involves tactful concern for maintaining the "face" of the supplicant, and in so doing maintains the gatekeeper's own "face" as cordial and fair in the gatekeeping judgments that the gatekeeper must make. The supplicant also makes as positive a self presentation as is possible, "putting one's best foot forward," and hoping for as charitable as possible a reading by the gatekeeper of such a self-presentation. A recent study by Roberts, Campbell, and Robinson (2008) found evidence that the veneer of cordiality and fairness in job interviews is only a front-stage performance, with "backstage" gatekeeping judgments rendered for reasons that are never revealed in the interview. I think that Goffman would concur in such a pessimistic assessment – he never claimed that everyday social interaction was honest and fair; indeed in the essay on face work he argued that a certain disingenuousness was necessary in the conduct of everyday social interaction. We should not be surprised, therefore, to see manifestations of complicated and astute face work in the gatekeeping encounters that take place routinely in institutional settings currently. Moreover, the rhetorics of persuasion in the face work that takes place discursively in gatekeeping encounters are phenomena with distinct sociolinguistic interest – a fruitful ground for continuing research.

Appendix

Transcription conventions

. .   two dots=clause terminal pause ("comma")
. . . .   four dots=sentence terminal pause – approximately 1 second
[   ]   brackets in various combinations indicate latching (no gap or overlap between utterances)
bold   boldface type indicates pitch and volume emphasis
?   indicates question intonation

References

de Tocqueville, Alexis
    1835   *Democracy in America*. Vol. 1. (trans. Henry Reeve) New York: The Colonial Press.
de Tocqueville, Alexis
    1840   *Democracy in America*. Vol. 2. (trans. Henry Reeve) New York: The Colonial Press.
Erickson, Frederick
    1975   Gatekeeping and the melting pot: Interaction in counseling encounters. *Harvard Educational Review* 45: 44–70.
Erickson, Frederick
    1986   Listening and speaking. In: Deborah Tannen and James E. Alatis (eds.), *Language and Linguistics: The Interdependence of Theory, Data, and Application*, 294–319. Washington, D.C.: Georgetown University Press.
Erickson, Frederick
    1999   Appropriation of voice and presentation of self as a fellow physician: Aspects of a discourse of apprenticeship in medicine. In: Srikant Sarangi and Celia Roberts (eds.), *Talk, Work, and Institutional Order: Discourse in Medical, Mediation and Management Settings*, 109–143. Berlin / New York: Mouton de Gruyter.
Erickson, Frederick
    2004   *Talk and Social Theory: Ecologies of Speaking and Listening*. Cambridge: Polity Press.
Erickson, Frederick and Jeffrey Shultz
    1982   *The Counselor as Gatekeeper: Social Interaction in Interviews*. New York: Academic Press.
Erickson, Frederick and William Rittenberg
    1987   Topic control and person control: A thorny problem for foreign physicians in interaction with American patients. *Discourse Processes* 10: 401–415.

Fairclough, Norman
    1992   *Discourse and Social Change.* Cambridge: Polity Press.
Goffman, Erving
    1961   *Encounters: Two Studies in the Sociology of Interaction.* Indianapolis: Bobbs-Merrill.
Goffman, Erving
    1955   On face work: An analysis of ritual elements in social interaction. *Psychiatry: Journal of the Study of Interpersonal Processes* 18: 213–231. Reprinted in Erving Goffman, *Interaction Ritual: Essays in Face-to-Face Behavior*, 5–46. New York: Random House [1967].
Goffman, Erving
    1981   *Forms of Talk.* Philadelphia: University of Pennsylvania Press.
Goffman, Erving
    1983   The interaction order. *American Sociological Review* 48: 1–17.
Roberts, Celia, Sarah Campbell and Yvonne Robinson
    2008   *Talking Like a Manager.* Department for Work and Pensions Research Report No. 510. Norwich: Her Majesty's Stationery Office.
Scott, J.
    1990   *Domination and the Arts of Resistance: Hidden Transcripts.* New Haven: Yale University Press.

Part IV

19. Appreciating the power of narratives in healthcare: A tool for understanding organizational complexity and values

Amanda Taylor, Orit Karnieli-Miller,
Thomas Inui, Steven Ivy and Richard Frankel

Abstract

Storytelling and narrative analysis have become increasingly popular in organizational research as a means of uncovering the human dimensions of organizational life. We present a case study in which employee narratives were used to uncover the values of 150 high-performing employees in a large healthcare organization. We provide a detailed description of our analytic methods, focusing on value-affirming situations in which actions and values were fully aligned, and value-challenging situations in which one's own or others' actions were not aligned with values. We utilized snowball sampling to select and interview high-performing employees from housekeeping to administration, purposefully excluding physicians, whose stories are the subject of a parallel study not reported here. Our approach was based on Appreciative Inquiry (an organizational change strategy that focuses on what works well and how to get more of it rather than what's wrong with an organization and how to fix it). Our analysis focused on the core values mentioned in each story (the plot), the characters (e.g., self, patient, organization), and how they were positioned (i.e., employee connected to the patient or organization?) Lastly, we discuss the importance of the presentation of findings and describe the implications of this approach for narrative research studies.

1. Introduction

"We had a 2 ½ yr old patient that had been here his whole life … He had to be in isolation, due to an infection. I would go in there every night before I left and rock him to sleep, 'cause his mom was a single mom; she couldn't be here a lot and I couldn't stand the thought of him always going to sleep by himself … And there was this Sunday night before he passed away, … and work called and said, "You know he's not doing real well, we're really, really busy, I think he needs to be rocked to sleep, and we were wondering if you would come in." And I said, "Absolutely." So I got in my car and came … he was just sitting there awake. He grabbed the bars and just kinda looked outside and so I went in there and rocked him to sleep."
(Staff coordinator in Pediatrics Specialty Center)

The narrative above illustrates the extent to which a health care professional who is asked by her colleagues to "go above and beyond" her role responsibilities demonstrates self-sacrifice in order to provide a dying child peaceful sleep during his hospitalization. In addition to her actions, the narrative also expresses the teller's values, in this case, the fact that human need trumps the "official" work schedule. In this chapter we take up several related questions about the use of narratives to understand how values operate in a large healthcare organization. These include: What values are present in positive, appreciative, narratives? What values are present in narratives that describe challenging situations? What is the relationship between personal and organizational values contained in these two types of narratives? Perhaps, most importantly, we ask by what methodological standards do we make assertions about the values contained in these narratives?

Since the 1970s researchers have increasingly taken a "discursive turn", using narrative approaches to describe the context, culture and complexity of organizations (Clark 1972; Mitroff and Kilmann 1975, 1976; Rhodes and Brown 2005). This is especially the situation in fields of organizational research (Boje 2001; Czarniawska 1998; Gabriel 2000), where storytelling and analysis have produced a rich body of knowledge (Stutts and Barker 1999). According to Laslett (1999), organizational narratives can illuminate "individual and collective action and meanings, as well as the process by which social life and human relationships are made and changed" (Laslett 1999: 392).

A "discursive turn" is also apparent in medicine and healthcare (Greenhalgh 1999; Greenhalgh and Hurwitz 1999) where narrative approaches are becoming an increasingly popular means of understanding health and illness in terms of first-person experiences. Within the healthcare context narratives have also been used to understand the joys and challenges of medical professionals' day-to-day work experiences (physicians, residents, medical students and nurses (Brady, Corbie-Smith, and Branch 2002; Hunter 1991; Karnieli-Miller et al. 2008; Wengström and Ekedahl 2006); or learning about physicians' experiences as patients (Tierney and McKinley 2002).

Equally exciting is the potential narratives hold to uncover organizational values within the healthcare setting where values are transmitted through messages organizational members send and receive (Meyer 1995). Research has suggested that values constitute the basic assumptions which drive organizational actions and communication (Schein 1985) and provide a sense of common direction and guidelines for all employees in their day-to-day behavior (Deal and Kennedy 1982). Since healthcare organizations are exceptionally value-laden structures, the study of narratives offers an extraordinary opportunity to examine organizational values and the way in which employees espouse these values in their day-to-day work.

As useful as narrative studies in the healthcare setting might be, these studies tend to focus on a single role type or one group of professionals. Few studies have used narratives to understand the broader landscape of organizational culture as it might be expressed by all employee categories from administrators to housekeepers. Fewer studies still have focused on how personal and organizational values come into play at work. Finally, it is often the case that the results of these studies are reported without adequate attention to the analytic methods that produced them. We attempt to address some of these gaps in knowledge in this chapter by describing both the results and methods used to study employees' values in a large health care organization.

1.1.   First the "punch line": Findings from the work-life narratives study

We present a case study in which solicitation and analysis of employee narratives were used to identify the values of a range of high-performing employees in a large (12,000 person) healthcare organization. We begin toward the end of the story by describing the results of our analysis. Having done so, we present details of the methods that we used to reach our conclusions striving to make the method of our narrative analysis as transparent as possible so that others may easily replicate our analytic procedures. Finally, we describe our strategy for initially disseminating the results, as the dissemination of findings is an important, often overlooked piece of the overall research puzzle.

The authors were invited by a large healthcare organization to discover the relationship between its formally stated organizational values and the lived values of high-performing employees. In discussion with the relevant executives, we decided to ask 150 high-performing employees from various organizational positions to tell us stories about (i) a time/situation/occasion when they and the organization were at their best and (ii) also a time when they felt their values were challenged. Our goal was to help the organization discover the *lived* values of high-performing employees in their day-to-day work. The analysis of these employees' personal narratives describing situations in which their values were aligned with the organization's values (i.e. value-affirming stories) and situations in which their values were challenged at work (i.e. value-challenging stories), revealed that the everyday work setting is filled with complex and often competing demands. Narrative analysis revealed several important features of the organization we studied. These included:

1) Core values in day-to-day work were not always aligned with the organization's formally espoused values.
2) Many of the value-challenging conflicts that arose were not discussed and were often left unresolved.
3) Many of the value-challenging conflicts involved interpersonal respect and its absence.
4) Employees were willing to risk their jobs in order to "do the right thing", that is, to act in accordance with their values when they experienced challenges.

1.1.1.   Employee values were not always aligned with the organization's values

Organizations often create a formal statement of organizational values they disseminate among employees and publish to codify and express their core values, purpose, and practices. Most commonly these values are listed as a part of the organization's mission statement (Bart and Tabone 2000). Little is known, however, about how these values are actually embodied in day-to-day work. Our analysis showed that stated values of the organization were not always aligned with the values employees identified as most important to them. For example, the value of teamwork and collegiality was mentioned repeatedly by the front line employees as a motivator or a challenge, while it is not mentioned in the stated mission. Following is an example of a value-affirming short story about teamwork:

> "We have had so many days in which we have patients who are extremely sick, emergencies going on all over our unit, and when we are at our best, which is much of the time, we're all clicking together as the teamwork aspect, everybody supporting each other, and that's how we get through those days ..."
> (Staff nurse in the pre-operative care department)

We found that some of the values that emerged in employee narratives were not found in the organization's published values, and some of the organization's formally published values were not mentioned by high-performing employees. In fact, only four of the organization's seven published mission elements were actually expressed in the narratives we collected. Interestingly, employees frequently could not articulate the formal values of the organization when asked. Despite these differences, most still expressed a belief that their own values were aligned with those of the organization.

1.1.2.   Many of the value-challenging conflicts that arose were not discussed and were often left unresolved.

A second important finding revealed that most of the value-challenging stories told by employees remained unresolved (i.e. no satisfying conclusion was achieved in the story; see Table 1). In fact, only 17 % of the value-challenges, as reported, were entirely resolved. Often employees felt most challenged when they, their professional role, or patients were not respected or when the rigidity of the hospital rules and regulations prevented them from providing what they considered to be the highest quality of patient care. An example of an unresolved conflict between two colleagues appears below. In this case the values-conflict is based on a hierarchical relationship between the storyteller and a supervisor or physician. In these types of situations employees felt less control and were less likely to take action:

"I had a situation with a physician and we did not agree on the approach with a patient at all. And I felt very confident in mine. During that interaction, though, you know, I think we were discussing my area of practice, so I feel like I'm the expert in my area of practice. I just felt not listened to; and I respect the physician and they are the overseer of the patient, but I wasn't listened to, and I didn't feel respected … instead I was being talked down to … yelled at, but it wasn't pleasant. And then, having that situation happen, then comments were made when I wasn't there, and things were written in the chart that were downplaying my abilities and my role with this patient. And I didn't find it appropriate, and it, gosh, I was really upset."
(Physical therapist)

Despite not feeling respected, this employee did not take action to talk with the physician or advocate on behalf of the patient because s/he viewed the physician as having the ultimate say in the patient's course of treatment. In effect, this employee continued to feel as though the interaction had, and would continue to have, a negative impact on their relationship with the physician. Unresolved values-conflicts and a feeling of unfair treatment of self and others, as revealed in the story above, can obviously result in negative feelings toward the organization, a supervisor and/or the team members. These feelings could, in turn, compromise patient care and lead to feelings of work dissatisfaction and turn-over.

Table 1. Conflicts in value-challenging stories and their degree of resolution

	No Resolution	Partial Resolution	Complete Resolution	Unclear Resolution
Interpersonal Axes of Conflict				
Self-organization	12	6	5	2
Self-team	15	6	2	1
Self-patient's family	7	3	1	
Self-patient	13	1	7	
Self-supervisor	6	1	1	
Self-doctor	2	3		1
Patient-organization	7	3		4
Patient-team	4	3	3	
Patient-doctor	2		1	
Organization-team	3		1	
Totals	71 (56%)	26 (21%)	21 (17%)	8 (6%)

1.1.3. Many of the value-challenging conflicts involved interpersonal respect and its absence.

The largest proportion (45 %) of value-challenging stories were about giving and receiving interpersonal respect. This is in stark contrast with the value-affirming employee stories where respect was only mentioned 1.1 % of the time. In effect, the issue of respect was explicitly mentioned either when employees felt that they were not respected, when others made judgments about co-workers, or when co-workers were not accepting of patients' different beliefs or behaviors, as illustrated in the following narrative:

> "There was a transgender individual on our unit. There were two staff members that weren't tolerant of the situation and in return I was pretty adamant about how I felt that they became very judgmental. I guess I was trying to be supportive of this person … The other staff member made a comment about Jesus and fags, and I was just like, 'Oh, we don't use that word.' And she thought it was very acceptable to say that about a patient … [and] refused to address that patient as whatever gender they had decided that they were."
> (Registered nurse in critical care)

It is clear from this story that the teller experienced a colleague's behavior as disrespectful and that her attempts to resolve the issue were unsuccessful. As a result there is a "residue" of unresolved negative feelings about the event and her colleague which certainly creates a non-optimal situation for delivering patient care as a team.

1.1.4. Employees were willing to risk their jobs in order to act in accordance with their values when they experienced challenges.

One of the more striking findings from our analysis revealed the risks employees were willing to take in order to protect and maintain values that they felt were important to them. When employees' values were challenged, some experienced negative emotions (such as feeling uncomfortable or having thoughts of quitting work); others took action to try and remedy the situation (such as advocating for patients' best interests, crossing personal boundaries to make patients more comfortable). In fact, narratives where a resolution occurred (17 %) included situations where employees bent the rules or regulations to help patients receive what they considered to be the best quality of care. In situations where employees felt that the value conflict could have significant negative implications, they were often willing to risk their jobs by violating organizational written or spoken rules in order to advocate for patients and maintain alignment with their values. For instance, the nurses in the following story risked their jobs to act according to their values:

"A little boy fell off a lawnmower and his arm had been cut off ... and this was a very nasty complete amputation. We had the limb in a cooler and the surgeon took a look at it and said to the father 'I can't put that back on because this kid will be frustrated with it and he will be better off with a prosthesis ...'. As they were leaving the father picked up the cooler and I said: 'you can just leave that here' and he said 'no I'm taking that' and I said 'why don't you let me take care of it and I'll clean up the cooler and bring to you'. He said, 'no I'm taking it' and I said 'could you tell me what you're going to do with it' and he said 'those are the five little fingers that I kissed and wrapped those fingers around my fingers and I'm not going to let you throw them away'. Another nurse and I said simultaneously – 'what cooler?' I said that we have some things to do over here and you just go out in the hall and we'll have someone take you to surgery. I think even if I had known if I would have got fired [for doing that], it wouldn't mean anything to me."
(Manager of clinical operations in an emergency department)

This story illustrates the great lengths employees were willing to go to in order to maintain their value system and fulfill patients' wishes. In actuality, they violated a hospital policy that mandates that any tissue taken from patients has to be retained and given to pathology for examination and proper documentation. It is important to note that this story was told as a value-affirming story, where an employee chose to act in a way that fit her own value system, the value of humanism, in the search of a humane way to help others during a stressful life experience.

2.   How did we arrive at these conclusions? Our analytic method

This work-life narratives study is qualitative and based on organizational and personal story-telling. Data-gathering required one-hundred and fifty, 30–45 minute, face-to-face, semi-structured interviews, with high-performing employees in the organization. The interview questions focused on day-to-day experience, values and organizational climate. Designing the interview was a collaborative process that involved a Senior Vice President of the hospital system (SSI) and the research team (RMF and TSI).

2.1.   Semi-structured interviews

The semi-structured interviews followed a predetermined guide with a specific order of questions and wording, but were viewed as only moderately restrictive, since they also encouraged two-way, responsive communication. The use of a semi-structured interview and interviewer training allowed us to standardize the questions that were asked to each participant (to allow for comparability of interview content) while still providing some flexibility for interviewers to pursue certain topics in more depth by probing with follow-up questions and clarifications.

The interview guide (Appendix A) touched upon several different topics, including personal meaning and commitment, personal strength and gifts, value-challenging situations, personal values and the relationship between personal values and the healthcare system's stated values. All interviews were digitally recorded. The recordings were transcribed verbatim.

2.2.   Interviewers

Twenty volunteers from within the organization conducted the interviews: sixteen chaplains, three program directors and one social worker. All were trained in Appreciative Inquiry (AI), an approach that focuses on organizational change through positive story telling during a single three-hour session. Topics touched upon in this session included an introduction to AI; recommended interviewer conduct to avoid inadvertent biasing of responses; suggested questions to explore a story in more detail; learning how to deal with negatives (e.g. postponing; empathic listening; redirecting); and assuring anonymity.

2.3.   Sampling

Sampling is a critical issue in qualitative research and varies based on the questions asked and the resources available to conduct the study (Patton 1990). "Snowball sampling" was used to select an enriched sample of high-performing front-line staff. A list of "outstanding" employees was made available by the human resources department of the healthcare system to aid in the initial selection. In the interviews themselves, each participant was asked for the names of 2–3 other workers whose work they thought was exemplary and who they believed truly lived the hospital's values (Wengström and Ekedahl 2006). These people were then interviewed and through this process the sample "snowballed".

Our decision to use snowball sampling was based on a desire to identify the "best practices" of a group of high-performing individuals, rather than looking for a representative sample of all employees. We also wanted to sample as many different job categories as we could, excluding physicians, within a limited budget and, therefore, sought nominees from all categories of employment.

2.4.   Participants

The final sample included a diverse group of hospital employees with varying years of service to the organization (see Tables 2 and 3).

Table 2. Interviewees' job titles

Nurses	Managers	Educators/ Human Resources/ Dieticians	Therapists/ Counselors	Office Assistants	Service Personnel	Job Titles not captured
50	15	2 / 5/ 3	15	15	28	17

Table 3. Interviewees' tenure in the organization

<2 years	2–5 years	6–9 years	>10 years	Did not state
22	15	20	66	29

3.   Analysis

The stories were analyzed using an immersion/crystallization method (thematic narrative analysis framework). Employing this method, we immersed ourselves in the data and then reflected with "intuitive crystallizations until reportable interpretations" were reached (Crabtree and Miller 1992). Similar to grounded theory, this qualitative research method begins inductively and allows patterns of meaning to emerge through repeated engagement with the data. The immersion/ crystallization research method requires cognitive and emotional engagement on the part of the researchers to go beyond the usual and obvious interpretations and maintain fluidity at all stages of the research (Borkan 1999). Reflection upon the data also requires a significant amount of time, sometimes days or weeks, before insights occur. As compared with the line-by-line analysis approach of grounded theory immersion/crystallization methods allow the researcher to move back and forth between the entire narrative and its components as a means of identifying categories and themes.

We began our analysis by randomly selecting three employee narratives at a time and immersing ourselves in the data. We used a technique called a "horizontal pass" in which we read the narratives in their entirety searching for themes (Borkan 1999). Three of us each independently highlighted sections of text we believed to represent value statements and gave them provisional names. Next we met face-to-face to discuss what we had done and sought consensus on the segments of text highlighted and the value names they were given. We then repeated this consensus building approach to identify additional values in each block of three narratives. Emergent themes were recorded in a codebook and refined after each batch of coding. The codebook was utilized to help increase the reliability of the coding and was given to each coder after each modification. This process was repeated until consensus was reached on identifying content and themes within the narratives (i.e., trustworthiness).

After we had identified an exhaustive list of 70 value-related themes we stepped back from the data to see if some of them clustered together. One of the coders (OKM) then eliminated repetitive value-themes and divided the remaining themes into eight conceptual groups and recorded them in the codebook. The group then met to refine the coding and added two more conceptual categories. This codebook with the smaller, more fine-grained categories subsumed under the larger conceptual themes, was modified throughout the iterative process (Appendix B).

As a check on the face validity of our larger conceptual categories we conducted a broad literature search focused on professional values and values in action. This search yielded a list of 50 values. This list of values identified in the literature was compared to the values that emerged from our narrative analysis. We then compared and contrasted the narrative-based values and those from the literature. We kept the names of the themes that emerged from the data as we had originally denoted them (see Table 4, left column), and "matched" them with literature-based values to be able to communicate our findings with others in the field (Table 4, right column). The overall result of this process was that each conceptual category was given two names as described in Table 4.

Table 4. 10 Healthcare workers' values and general work values

Values expressed in workers' stories as uncovered by immersion/crystallization method	Related terms from organizational work values literature
Valuing Patients' Well-Being	Altruism
Going Above and Beyond	Being of Service
Treating Others with Dis/Respect	Respect
Helping and Healing	Humanism
Doing the Right Thing	Professionalism
Feeling Part of Organization and Team	Citizenship
Expressing Passion and Emotion	Vitality
Gratitude and Appreciation	Recognition
Growing and Developing	Love of Learning
Believing in a Higher Power	Affirming a Calling

As a final check on the trustworthiness of the coding scheme another member of the research team (TSI) conducted an independent analysis and then compared his findings to those of the other three coders. Consensus on category names and rules for accurate coding of content was achieved between the independent coder and the rest of the team after 10 % of interviews were reviewed (i.e., after 15 interviews). At this time the codebook was felt to be complete and two of the coders (ACT and OKM) coded the remaining narratives.

The following is an example of the analysis procedure carried out on a value-affirming story that contains multiple values. In the first step, all values were highlighted and named:

Table 5.

Narrative	Coding
We had a 2 ½ yr old patient that had been here his whole life … He had to be in isolation, due to an infection. I would go in there every night before I left and rock him to sleep, 'cause his mom was a single mom; she couldn't be here a lot and I couldn't stand the thought of him always going to sleep by himself … And there was this Sunday night before he passed away, … and work called and said, "You know he's not doing real well, we're really, really busy, I think he needs to be rocked to sleep, and we were wondering if you would come in." And I said, "Absolutely." So I got in my car and came … he was just sitting there awake. He grabbed the bars and just kinda looked out-side and so I went in there and rocked him to sleep.	Caring Holistic care Commitment/ Self sacrifice Caring

In this narrative, four values were expressed: caring (twice), holistic care, com-mitment, and self-sacrifice. We asked ourselves, "What was the storyteller try-ing to convey to us? Is this a story about her willingness to serve or about the storyteller caring about the dying child's needs (see also Section 4)?

In trying to answer these questions we re-examined the "plot". Was it the employee's willingness to come to the hospital on her day off, or the caring for the child's needs that is the main thrust of the narrative? Who were the char-acters (e.g. self, mother, patient, organization)? And how are they positioned relative to one another (i.e. has the employee has an ongoing relationship to the mother and the child?)? In this example, willingness to come to the hospital on her day off is less the focal point of the story than caring about comforting a dying child. In our approach each value statement is coded into a category and the corresponding characters from the narrative are also identified for each value statement. We decided to categorize the narrative above under the theme of *Valuing Patients' Well Being / Altruism*, because it emphasized the overriding importance of caring for another and the willingness of the employee to put the child's needs above her own.

After identifying and highlighting sections of text considered to be value statements, the stories were imported into a qualitative software program, Nar-ralizer, for data storage, retrieval, and quantification (Shkedi 2005). Narralizer allowed us to code these more fine-grained categories under the larger, conceptual categories, such as "Feeling Part of Organization and Team/ Citizenship" in the previous example.

Once all of the narratives had been coded using the Narralizer, we again bracketed our assumptions about the data and attempted to examine them through a different lens. When we looked at the value statements and characters in each narrative and how they were connected it quickly became apparent that the values, characters, and their positions were different in the value-affirming stories versus the value-challenging stories. This observation eventually led us to a second analysis of the data.

3.1.   Second analysis

In the second analysis, we divided the stories into value-affirming and value-challenging databases. This allowed us to compare and contrast the two in a "vertical pass" at the data, concentrating on one section at a time (Borkan 1992). As a result of this process different trends then began to emerge. For example, we began to see that the affirming and challenging stories involved different patterns of relationship between the core values mentioned (the plot) and the characters. This analysis revealed that many of the value-challenging stories represented conflicts between the employee and the supervisor/physician/ or organization, as opposed to the majority of value-affirming stories that were focused on experiences between the employee and the patient or family. During this analysis we could ask if the same or different values came into play in the two types of stories and if so, how the values were acted upon.

Using the approach described above, we noticed that value-challenges involved many conflicts that often went unresolved. To better understand this phenomenon we took another "vertical pass" at the data and coded the challenge narratives into conflicts that were resolved, i.e., where there was an explicit statement by the story teller that the issue or concern had been explicitly addressed; conflicts where there was some but not complete resolution; and unresolved conflicts. This strategy led us to observe that the "best" high-performing employees of the organization frequently experienced challenges that went unresolved for a variety of reasons. From a patient safety and quality perspective unresolved conflict is a contributor to errors and adverse events since people in conflict often go out of their way to limit or avoid communication with one another (Andrew 1999). If the "best" employees were experiencing such difficulties in their day-to-day work, it seemed certain that hospital leadership would want to know and perhaps find ways to alleviate these situations.

To summarize, we began this study noting the usefulness of narrative methods in uncovering organizational values as espoused in the day-to-day work of front-line employees. Our method of analyzing the narratives of 150 high-performing employees was designed to tell us what values come into play when things go right and when they are challenging. We approached the data without making *a priori* assumptions about what we might find. Instead we attempted to maintain fidelity to the material as we reduced it to manageable proportions. With a number of quality control measures built in we were able to ask questions of interest to us as analysts and at the same time of interest to the organization. As patterns emerged from coding the data we were able to ask new questions and compare values across types of stories (value-affirming *versus* value-challenging). In the end, we believe that we engaged in a process that would produce much the same result if undertaken by another team of researchers, one of the main goals of any scientific enterprise be it quantitative, qualitative or multi-method (Inui 1996).

4.   Methodological issues

There were several methodological issues we faced and resolved in decisions about data collection and analysis of employee narratives. One of these choices included identification and training of interviewers. We chose to use chaplains and social workers to conduct the interviews. We did so believing that pastoral care professionals and social workers are known in the organization (and more generally) for their ability to listen empathically and without judgment. We assumed that our selection of interviewers would increase the likelihood that study subjects would agree to be interviewed and would feel comfortable in telling their story. Our assumption appears to have been correct as we had very few employees who were asked to share stories and declined the opportunity.

Should an interviewer be an insider (i.e. an employee from within the same organization), or outsider, unknown to the interviewees? We chose to utilize a combination of the two attributes – organizational insiders who were, however, not immediately well-known to the interviewee. The interviewers employed in our study came from inside the organization, but were asked to interview people from departments outside their own in order to decrease the likelihood that a prior relationship would influence the course and/or direction of the interview. Having interviewers interview employees outside their own department, we reasoned, might also help interviewees feel more open to respond honestly and less likely to provide socially desirable answers.

Another important issue that arose in our study was how to handle multiple values expressed in one narrative. Many of our narratives contained more than one value statement. Coding for multiple values, while valuable in terms of breadth, creates more complexity when developing a reliable and reproducible coding structure. In the interest of parsimony, we decided to code each story for the single most salient value. Consequently, each story was coded into only one

core value category. The questions we asked in order to determine the most salient core value in each story was: "What is the story teller trying to tell us?" and
"What was the most important value for him/her?" Using this approach, we
were able to reach a high level of consensus and coding reliability.

5.   Presentation of findings

Presentation of study findings is often an overlooked, but crucial aspect of the
"success" of a study. Did the study findings reach the intended audience? Did
the study findings evoke the anticipated reaction from that audience? Did the
study findings result in any actions taken? We found that the mode of presentation of our findings was just as influential as our actual data collection and
analysis. Our intended audience was the health care organization's Board
members, and we tailored the presentation to this audience. Before we presented our findings, we met to select a sample of the most powerful employee
stories we had encountered. Among these narratives, we chose one story to represent each value that emerged in our data analysis and then printed each story
on a separate sheet of paper. Each story was printed in a different font style and
size and given a unique title. These narratives were stapled together and were
presented as a packet to each board member. The Principal Investigator (RMF)
provided Board members with a PowerPoint presentation summarizing our
study methods, the rationale for our methodology, and our findings. As he discussed employees' values, he invited Board members to read aloud the corresponding employee narrative that we had pre-selected, rather than simply sending the Board members home with the packet of stories and trusting that they
would take the time to read them individually. Including Board members in the
presentation in this manner seemed to have a profound effect on their reception
and moved some to tears. Reading the stories aloud brought the narratives to life
and allowed an emotional connection to be made between the characters and the
Board. Reading aloud also permitted Board members to assume the persona of
the storyteller and permitted them to get "inside the storyteller's head", to gain a
fuller understanding of their actual day-to-day experience in their healthcare organization. In fact, the Board decided that our findings were so remarkable and
important they have asked us to conduct a second study focusing on physicians'
values (the only population not represented in the first phase of the study).

Other presentations were made by SSI to the chaplaincy staff and other interviewers and to the senior executive group. In addition to reporting the results
of the study, the chaplaincy presentation emphasized their role in supporting
such story-telling in team meetings and leadership settings. Their feedback centered on the energy generated by the interviews. Furthermore, one chaplain reported how a nurse with one of the "unresolved stories" had taken initiative to

seek a resolution after telling the story. The senior executive presentation focused on ways to generate such story-telling in support of morale and cohesive teams. Additionally, the unresolved stories led to a renewed focus on establishing a safe culture, including reducing the effects of hierarchy and power differentials. Another, shorter, presentation to all leaders and managers was provided by RMF.

6.   Limitations and areas for improvement

This study had many positive qualities and strengths. However, there are clearly also some limitations in our data collection and analysis. One limitation is that while using a script with specific wording of questions resulted in more control over the comparability of queries and responses, the interviewers, at times, did not further prompt or probe about specific topics the interviewees mentioned, because it did not fit the script. As a result of this limitation we have decided to strengthen this portion of our interviewer training for our upcoming investigation and will create a document with example questions that may be helpful for interviewers to use when they require further clarifications. We believe this will help result in more thorough interviews and thus help ensure that we have accurately captured the deeper meanings our interviewees intend to communicate with their stories.

A second limitation is that the findings described in the first part of this chapter may not be representative of all health care workers, even the workers of the specific organization we studied as we deliberately selected high-performing employees to study, not a random sample of all workers. Our study results do not tell us anything about groups of employees in this organization, other than those who are high-performing.

There are also limitations in the consensus-building approach we utilized to analyze these narratives. As in all qualitative approaches, our categories may represent our own biases and limited understanding of the materials we analyzed. It is possible that the values we clustered under our provisional categories might be arranged differently by different investigators, leading to the identification of different values, even though we were four investigators from different fields (psychology, social work, medicine and behavioral science) triangulating and challenging our assumptions during each step of the analysis. The fact that we were careful in creating our categories and worked to codify them in a detailed codebook makes any differences that might occur if another team were to analyze the data principled and systematic rather than difference due to random variation and lack of specificity in the work we conducted.

7.   Conclusion

Narratives are one way in which employees make sense and meaning out of their everyday life experiences. As such, analysis of work-life narratives opens a powerful window into the ways in which organizations and employees communicate their identities, priorities, values, and directions (Gergen 1994). The stories in this analysis were of human relationships, connections and efforts to create a better day-to-day experience. In telling their stories, our worker interviewees shared their own touching experiences and exposed their vulnerabilities, beliefs and values.

As the narratives illustrate, work in a modern day hospital involves many complex and competing demands. At the center of every healthcare organization is the patient. The employees of such organizations are oriented toward "patient-centeredness" (Sarangi 2007), an ideology that guides their behaviors and attitudes. What became evident in our analysis were the conflicts that arose among employees and between employees and organizational/bureaucratic rules when they struggled to do what they felt was best for the patient. The value placed on patient-centeredness led many employees to feel a sense of professional responsibility to place patients' needs and best interests, as they saw them, ahead of institutional standard operating policies, regardless of the potential personal consequences. This finding resonates with the observations of McDonald et al. (2006), who found that medical personnel take on a cultural identity in which they value being able to "think on their feet", respond flexibly and to use their professional experience over the presence of formal rules and clinical guidelines to respond to patient need. In our case, the healthcare system's staff took actions they believed were "doing the right thing". Understanding the complexity of work inside healthcare organizations, and the values that draw personnel to work in them, is one step toward understanding organizational "culture" — the sum of the conversations that make up the organization, some of which are in plain view and some of which are very private.

Careful analysis of employees' narratives can be a powerful method for "taking the pulse" of an organization, and sharing the results of such an analysis can create conditions for positive change. As Meyer (1991) suggested, values need to be communicated throughout the organization in order to become a reality. These values may be discovered in the messages organizational members send and receive, especially in the stories they tell about work. Once discovered, sharing the value-affirming or appreciative stories should promote a positive atmosphere that encourages others to take their own actions to improve organizational climate (Cooperrider et al. 2001). Our goals in this chapter were three-fold. First, we sought to contribute to the field of organizational development and change by uncovering important values in the day-to-day work of a group of high-performing employees in a large healthcare system. Our second goal was to contribute to the field of applied linguistics and professional/organizational communication research by describing, in some detail, the approach we used to gather narratives and the analytic methods we used to arrive at our conclusions. In this way we hope to draw a more explicit connection between the destination (i.e., our conclusions) and the journey (i.e. the methods we used to get there). Lastly, we desired to be a catalyst for change through the dissemination of our findings. Careful attention to the presentation of our findings ensured our findings did in fact reach, and evoke action from the intended audience.

Appendix A. Interview guide

Personal Meaning and Commitment

People do their best work when they are doing things that they find personally meaningful, and when they feel that their work makes a difference. During your time at [____], there have no doubt been highs points and lows, peaks and valleys. For now, I'd invite you think of a time that stands out for you as being particularly meaningful; a time that brought out the best of who you are, in which you felt connected to your values and your sense of purpose.

Please tell the story of that time.

Without worrying about being modest, please tell me what was it about you – your unique qualities, gifts or capacities; decisions you made; or actions you took – that contributed to this experience?

What did others contribute?

What aspects of the context or situation contributed (setting, time, background circumstances, etc.)?

Using the same framework as above, Tell me a story about a time in your work at when you and/or your values were challenged?

Strengths and gifts

We each have different qualities, gifts and skills we bring to the world and to our work. Consider for a moment the things you value deeply about yourself, the nature of your work, and the hospital.

a) Yourself: Without being humble, what do you most value about yourself, your unique gifts and special capacities as a person, a friend, a son or daughter, a parent, a spouse, a citizen, a professional?

b) Your work: When you are feeling most positive about your work or your learning, what do you value about the task itself?

Personal values

How do your personal values match those of the hospital?

If you had a camera in hand where would you take pictures of places and/or people that best reflect our values?

Please name two or three other people that you believe truly live the hospital's values.

Appendix B. Values codebook

Valuing Patients' Well-Being

An attitude or way of behaving marked by unselfish concern for the welfare of others.

Unselfishness/self-sacrifice/selflessness/giving of ones' self

Humanity / Humanism – a concern with the needs, well-being, and interests of people

Caring / Care for others (compassion, kindness) – compassionate or showing concern for others

Generosity – willingness to give money, help, or time freely (magnanimity)

Diligence – persistent and hard-working effort in doing something

Self-awareness (putting oneself in others' shoes)

Facilitating relationships

Dedication

Going Above and Beyond

Enthusiasm – excited interest – passionate interest in or eagerness to do something

Excellence – the quality or state of being outstanding and superior

Social intelligence – (emotional intelligence, personal intelligence) – being aware of the motives and feelings of others and oneself

Trying to understand patients' and families' perspectives – a particular evaluation of a situation or fact from another person's point of view

Adaptability/ flexibility – to adjust oneself readily to changing conditions and to remain viable during ongoing change

Creativity – originality, ingenuity – thinking of novel and productive ways to conceptualize and do things (e.g., turning bed, buying hats, bringing dog)

Being an advocate

Get it done

Being of service

Treating Others with Dis/Respect

A non-judgmental approach to the inherent worth, dignity, uniqueness and human rights of every individual.

Equality – giving the same rights irrespective of privileges, or status

Acceptance

Fairness – the condition of being just or impartial. Justice – fairness or reasonableness, especially in the way people are treated or decisions are made.

Honesty/integrity

Trustworthy

Responsibility

Reliability/dependability

Feeling Part of an Organization or Team

Commitment to teamwork and collaboration: the concerted effort of individuals and groups to attain a shared goal; to address the health needs of the patient and the public.

Leadership – encouraging a group in which one is a member to get things done and at the same time maintain good relations within the group

Citizenship – (social responsibility, loyalty and teamwork) – working well as a member of a group or team. Being loyal to the group.

Loyalty

Teamwork

Teaching/educating

Compromise

Honor

Helping and Healing

Humanism

Acceptance and acknowledgment of death and dying (a shared human condition)

Hospitality – a friendly welcome and kind or generous treatment offered to guests or strangers.

Helpfulness – providing or willing to provide assistance, information, or other aid

Golden Rule

Connecting with others (e.g., through personal experiences, ability to develop relationships, etc.)

Personal experience

Hospitality

Presence

Creating intimacy

Holistic care – family orientation, continuity of care

Perspective – wisdom – being able to provide wise counsel to others; having ways of looking at the world that make sense to oneself and to other people (e.g. acceptance of death and moving on)

Non-verbal communication (e.g., touch)

Esthetics – qualities of objects, events, and persons that provide satisfaction (e.g. adapts the environment so it is pleasing to the patient; creates a pleasant work environment for self and others; presents self in a manner that promotes a positive image of nursing

Commitment

Using my own talents and knowledge

Expressing Passion and Emotion

Happiness/joy – feeling or showing pleasure, contentment, or joy; causing pleasure, contentment or joy.

Love – valuing close relations with others, in particular those in which sharing and caring are reciprocated.

Sympathy – sharing somebody else's feelings.

Hope – (optimism, future-mindedness, future orientation) expecting the best in the future and working to achieve it.

Emotional investment

Growing and Developing

Mastering new skills, topics, and bodies of knowledge, whether on one's own or formally.

Growth and development

Expertise

Love of Learning

Believing in a Higher Power

Faith – belief in, devotion to, or trust in somebody or something, especially without logical proof.

Spirituality – (purpose) – having coherent beliefs about the higher purpose, the meaning of life and the meaning of the universe

Religiosity

Doing the Right Thing

Doing the right thing – even if it means risking your job.

Gratitude and Appreciation

Gratitude and appreciation – being aware of and thankful of the good things that happen

Acknowledging work well done

Challenges

Dealing with challenges: Conflict of interest for employees – Employees strive to resolve such conflicts in ways that ensure patient safety, guard the patient's best interests and preserve the professional integrity.

Competing loyalties in the workplace, including situations of conflicting expectations from patients, families, physicians, colleagues, and in many cases, health care organizations and health plans.

Conflicts arising between their own personal and professional values, the values and interests of others who are also responsible for patient care and health care decisions, as well as those of patients.

References

Andrew, Louise B.
  1999   Conflict management, prevention, and resolution in medical settings. *Conflict Management* (Physician Executive, June–July): 1–9.
Bart, C. and J. Tabore
  2000   Mission statements in Canadian not-for-profit hospitals: Does process matter? *Health Care Management Review* 25 (2): 45–53.
Boje, David M.
  2001   *Narrative Methods for Organizational and Communication Research.* London: Sage.
Borkan, Jeffrey Michael
  1999   Immersion/crystallization. In: Benjamin R. Crabtree and William L. Miller (eds.), *Doing Qualitative Research.* 2nd edn. 179–194. London: Sage.
Brady, Donald W., Giselle Corbie-Smith and William T. Branch
  2002   "What's important to you?" The use of narratives to promote self-reflection and to understand the experiences of medical residents. *Annals of Internal Medicine* 137: 220–223.
Clark, Burton R.
  1972   The organizational saga in higher education. *Administrative Science Quarterly* 17: 178–184.
Cooperrider, David, Peter F. Sorensen, Therese F. Yaeger, and Diana Whitney
  2001   *Appreciative Inquiry: An Emerging Direction of Organization Development.* Champaign, IL: Stipes Publishing Company.
Crabtree, Benjamin R. and William L. Miller
  1992   *Doing Qualitative Research. Research Methods for Primary Care. Vol. 3.* Thousand Oaks, CA: Sage.

Czarniawska, Barbara
    1998   *A Narrative Approach to Organization Studies.* Thousand Oaks, CA: Sage.
Deal, Terrence E., and Allan. A. Kennedy
    1982   *Corporate Cultures.* Reading, MA: Addison Wesley.
Gabriel, Yiannis
    2000   *Storytelling in Organizations: Facts, Fictions, and Fantasies.* Oxford: Oxford University Press.
Gergen, Kenneth
    1994   *Realities and Relationships: Soundings in Social Construction.* Cambridge, MA: Harvard University Press.
Greenhalgh, Trisha
    1999   Narrative based medicine: Narrative based medicine in an evidence based world. *British Medical Journal* 318: 323–325.
Greenhalgh, Trisha and Brian Hurwitz
    1999   Narrative based medicine: Why study narrative? *British Medical Journal* 318: 48–50.
Hunter, Kathryn Montgomery
    1991   *Doctors' Stories: The Narrative Structure of Medical Knowledge.* Princeton, NJ: Princeton University Press.
Inui, Thomas S.
    1996   The virtue of qualitative and quantitative research, editorial comment. *Annals of Internal Medicine* 125(9): 770–771.
Karnieli-Miller, Orit, Robert Vu, Alexander Djuricich, Lisa Logio, and Thomas Inui
    2008   *NBME narrative analysis: A qualitative analysis of the content of professionalism narratives in the IUSM medicine clerkship.* Indianapolis: Indiana University School of Medicine.
Laslett, Barbara
    1999   Personal narratives as sociology. *Contemporary Sociology* 28(4): 391–401.
Mc Donald, R., J. Waring and S. Harrison
    2006   Rules, safety and the narrativisation of identity: A hospital operating theatre study. *Sociology of Health + Illness* 28 (2): 178–202.
Meyer, John C.
    1995   Tell me a story: Eliciting organizational values from narratives. *Communication Quarterly* 43(2): 210–224.
Mitroff, Iian I. and Ralph Kilmann
    1975   Stories managers tell: A new tool for organizational problem solving. *Management Review* (July): 18–22.
Mitroff, Iian I. and Ralph H. Kilmann
    1976   On organizational stories: An approach to the design and analysis of organizations through myths and stories. In: Ralph H. Kilmann, Louis R. Pondy and Dennis P. Slevin (eds.), *The Management of Organizational Design (Vol. 1.)*, 189–207. New York: North Holland.
Patton, Michael Quinn
    1990   *Qualitative Evaluation and Research Methods* (2nd edn.). Newbury Park, CA: Sage.
Rhodes, Carl and Andrew Brown
    2005   Narrative, organizations and research. *International Journal of Management Reviews* 7(3): 167–188.

Sarangi, Srikant
    2007   Other-orientation in patient-centred healthcare communication: Unveiled ideology or discoursal ecology? In: Giuliana Garzone and Srikant Sarangi (eds.), *Discourse, Ideology and Ethics in Specialised Communication,* 39–71. Berne: Peter Lang.

Schein, Edgar H.
    1985   *Organizational Culture and Leadership.* San Francisco: Jossey Bass Publishers.

Shkedi, Asher
    2005   *Multiple Case Narrative: A Qualitative Approach to Studying Multiple Populations.* Herndon, VA: John Benjamins.

Stutts, Nancy B. and Randolph T. Barker
    1999   The use of narrative paradigm theory in assessing audience value conflict in image advertising. *Management Communication Quarterly* 13(2): 209–214.

Tierney, William M. and Elizabeth D. McKinley
    2002   When the physician researcher gets cancer: Understanding cancer, its treatment, and quality of life from the patient's perspective. *Medical Care* 40(6 Suppl.): 20–27.

Wengström, Yvonne and Marieanne Ekedahl
    2006   The art of professional development and caring in cancer nursing. *Nursing & Health Science* 8(1): 20–26.

20. Family support and home visiting: Understanding communication, "good practice" and interactional skills*

Stef Slembrouck and Christopher Hall

Abstract

The chapter examines professional-client communication in home visits by health and social care professionals. It reviews the professional literature on communication skills and detects a series of assumptions on what constitutes "good practice" but little consideration of the insights of discourse analysis or the study of actual encounters. Next, a pilot study is described in which professionals examine their own communicative practices. It is suggested that discourse analysis has a great deal to offer but that it needs to engage more systematically with professional understandings, concerns and dilemmas.

1. Introduction

A professional describes her communication strategy with a mother:

> See M's a funny one, she wouldn't necessarily bring it up I don't think, I would always ask her. I always try and follow things up with her. So I talked about that last week how it was going or have you had a chance to try it and have you have a chance to do this. And she was usually quite honest you know if she hadn't a chance to try it she would ('ve) just said this week I haven't had a chance or I've been feeling a bit rubbish and then sometimes she would be something about this week and tell me about something new and then we'll talk about that instead. So yeah she was never very forthcoming. With her you know you had to kind of pull things out of her, but that was part of her personality and sort of things that happened to her in the past. She was very sort of reserved and wouldn't just come out and say things.

How professionals communicate with clients is of central importance to the success of interventions in health and social care. As demonstrated above, it is something to which they give considerable attention, but often without the opportunity to examine their actual interaction. The chapter considers the professional literature on communication skills and how discourse analysis can engage with professionals' concerns.

Most of the study of communication between professionals and clients, patients and end users in the human services has focused on medical interaction, therapy, and counselling. Other parts of the human services have been less well documented. A wide variety of professionals – health visitors, family support workers, housing workers and social workers – provide an extensive range of services by visiting individuals and families in their homes. Pithouse (1987) calls social work an "invisible trade" to denote this orientation to the family home, away from the office and managerial scrutiny. Such workers are employed by various agencies – health, education, social care, housing, voluntary organisations, with different professional qualifications and work experience.

Home visiting suggests a wide range of interactional complexities which are different from the straightforward medical setting. Whilst medical communication has much to offer to the study of other human services, there are particular characteristics to the home visit. Gray (2002: 13) sees home visiting as the institution going into the private household. Barlow et al. (2003: 178) consider that it promotes more democratic partnership rather than an "expert model", prototypically associated with doctors. A key concern is the establishment of a "good relationship" between the professional and client. Yet, the home visit is not centrally constituted by a therapeutic relationship, utilising psychological techniques (Mead et al. 1997: 885). Rather, home visitors rely on their interpersonal capacities to engage with clients, establishing trust, empathy, active listening, displaying genuineness and respect (Barlow et al. 2003: 178).

In Section 2, we review work on communication skills and its underlying orientation to "good/bad practice". Section 3 will contrast such an approach with a discourse analytic approach to professional-client communication. In such research, professional formulations of what is happening during encounters are typically replaced by an analysis of interactional sequence. Action is seen as a product of interactional imperatives and logic, rather than the enactment of particular professional ambitions. Section 4 will make the case for drawing on both analytic and professional understandings of communicative practice. It will report on a pilot study in which professionals have examined their own communication with clients by reading and discussing transcriptions of the audio recordings of their home visits. The focus is on examining with the professionals how the interaction works in relation to stated aims, identified instances of good practice and professional strategies in situated encounters. It will be suggested in the Conclusion that professionals and discourse analysts can learn from one another about seeing and understanding talk and communication.

2.   Literature on communication skills

The investigation of and training in communication skills has become central to professional practice. Much has been written by trainers and policy makers in the human services which exhorts professionals to examine and reflect critically on their communication with clients. Communication is seen as central to the delivery of services. For example, the Social Care Institute for Excellence considers communication to be fundamental while also identifying it as a problem:

> Learning to communicate in a professional manner in a variety of contexts with people from a diverse range of backgrounds can be difficult, but it is a fundamental skill without which it is difficult to perform many other social work tasks or, perhaps the social work role at all.
> (Social Care Institute for Excellence 2004: 1)

Forrester et al. (2008) identify a key perceptual gap: while communication skills are often taken for granted, research findings often suggest that professionals are not communicating well with clients. In a similar vein, Koprowska (2005: 5) stresses that communication skills "don't come naturally" and professionals are cautioned not to "rest on their laurels" (Thompson 2003: 102). Bowles et al. (2001: 348) express similar concerns in the context of nursing.

Many of the publications which produce proscriptions of good practice in professional communication contain few if any descriptions of actual communication in the workplace. Books by Koprowska (2005), Thompson (2003) and Williams (1997) include no examples of talk, but many descriptions of hypothetical communication scenarios. Similarly, there is little discussion of research findings from sociolinguistics or sociology, an absence noted by Cameron (2000: 30). Instead, as Lishman (1994: 3) observes, questions about communication skills are mostly discussed within an evaluative framework.

2.1.   Definitions of communication skills in the human services

First, much of the communication skills literature promotes a deficit model. It assumes that there is "good" and "bad" communication, so the aim is to enable professionals to avoid pitfalls and mistakes, while improving their skills. There are strong views about what constitutes good practice, although the basis for such judgements is not often made clear. As Cameron notes:

> Whether some person or group of people, has good, bad or indifferent communication skills is entirely dependent on what "communication" is taken to be, and what is thought to constitute "skill" in it.
> (Cameron 2000: 145)

In her analysis of 15 instructive texts, she notes a series of recurrent assumptions which underline how the phrase "communication skills" names a cultural construct. Examples include: it is good to encourage the expression of emotion and to avoid interruptions. Active listening must be promoted. Open questions are preferred over closed ones.

Second, communication is often situated at a different level than actual instances of communication examined by linguists or discourse analysts. Koprowska (2005: 8) makes a distinction between "first- and second-order skills".

While first-order skills are required in direct communication itself, second-order skills are those employed in the planning of communication strategy. They include thinking about what we are doing, observing interactions, reviewing what has happened and modifying our next and future communications accordingly. The writer is less interested in the actual conversation between the worker and client, concentrating instead on the professional and institutional strategy behind the communication. The book takes the reader through various ways of achieving these objectives, and it does so by referring to evaluative concepts such as "empathy", "clarity", "reliability", with suggestions of what to say in particular circumstances. The actual sequence of words, utterances and turns of speaking are less important than the strategy behind the communication.

Communication skills then are a focus for debates about what constitutes the essence of professional practice at a strategic level. It is in this light that for instance Forrester et al. (2008: 42) are rather dismissive of the discourse analytic approach adopted by van Nijnatten et al. (2001) as "not interested in evaluating the skills the workers used", but nonetheless providing "interesting qualitative data on how social workers managed the tension between care and control."

A third approach is to see the professional as constrained in their communications with clients by structural factors and cultural features. Class, race, gender and power are seen as barriers to communication, creating asymmetric and discriminatory positions. For some, this is seen as a concern about "linguistic sensitivity". Thompson (2003: 139) identifies "problematic forms of language [which] excludes, depersonalizes, stigmatizes, reinforces, stereotypes and legitimizes discrimination". For others, communication reinforces underlying values and belief systems. Robinson (2004: 116–7) notes: "A white practitioner with a monocultural perspective will view any behaviours, values and lifestyles that differed from the Euro-American norm as deficient (cultural racism)." There is also a related view that wider contextual constraints on the encounter determine what can be said. Richards et al. (2005) make a distinction between a social work encounter based on empathy and a helping relationship and one based on bureaucracy and managerialism. The former is seen as preferable but increasingly compromised: "Crucially, from a communication skills perspective the emphasis on understanding individuals and their problems through bureaucratic procedures serves to undermine the process of interpersonal communication itself" (Richards et al. 2005: 414).

2.2.   Research on communication skills

Empirical research on communication skills in home visiting that does exist appears to be based on similar views of good practice, the talk being scrutinized for its alignment with professionally-defined therapeutic processes. For instance, Nerdrum (1997) followed up students on a communication skills course and tested their "empathetic communication" before and after the course and then again after 18 months. Students were asked to submit written answers to videotaped client situations and their answers were rated on a five point scale by two experienced teachers: a social worker and a clinical psychologist. An example of how the rating is administered is provided:

> Student A's answer before training is an attempt to dismiss the expression and experience of the client. It does not confirm any of the feelings of doubt or insecurity in the question and probably serves to protect the student himself ... There is a tinge of aggressiveness in this way of answering the client's questions.
> (Nerdrum 1997: 715)

Such a method of analysis bears little resemblance to engaging with the complexities of actual professional-client communication. It is being evaluated in the experimental situation of video scenarios and written responses rather than the exigencies of a real encounter. Furthermore, the method of assessment echoes notions of deficits in communication. Ways of talking are not analyzed in their own right as part of interaction. Interestingly, the answers which receive higher ratings are those which turn the client's question into a question back to them: "This is a good question but why are you wondering about it?" (Nerdrum 1997: 714).

Forrester et al. (2008) also base their analysis on counting preferred and dispreferred items. They use simulations of social workers' talk with actors, maintaining that sensitive encounters are not amenable to recording (2008: 43). The findings are presented as critical:

> Many social workers were not skilled communicators ... To find that workers use predominantly closed questions, that they use few reflections, that they rarely recognise strengths and that they tend to lack empathy is profoundly concerning. It is good that workers almost universally managed to raise difficult issues and that they were able to be clear about concerns with the parent. However, the way in which this was done often appeared unskilled and, in a few instances, virtually abusive to the parent.
> (Forrester et al. 2008: 48)

In summary, communication skills are seen as important but also problematic. The approach is essentially evaluative, associated with preferred versions of practice – e.g. "client-centred" or "relationship-based". A particular dilemma is whether home visiting practice should be measured against the standards of counselling skills (e.g. Bowles et al. 2001: 341; Ruch 2005: 111). The level of analysis is set above the actual talk between client and professional, concerned more with the professional's strategy in the encounter than the dynamics of the interaction. It is also concerned with structural influences that constrain the communication, again situated above the interaction. When some of the concepts are operationalised in research, they are seen in terms of (dis)preferred actions around evaluative concepts – empathy, reflection, open/closed questions, interruptions. Actions are often treated as countable units, rather than occurrences which are analysable in terms of a layered flow of interaction. Research rarely looks at actual encounters, more often using simulations or vignettes.

3.   Discourse analysis of professional communication

Discourse analytical literature on communication within the professions is extensive, in particular the literature on medical encounters. Other areas involving health and social care include counselling (e.g. Erickson and Schultz 1982), psychotherapy (e.g. Buttny 1996), social work (e.g. Hall, Slembrouck and Sarangi 2006) – often with specific "sub-themes" which cross more than one field of professional practice, for instance, genetic counselling (e.g. Sarangi and Clarke 2002), health visiting (e.g. Heritage and Sefi 1992), judicial cross-examination of child witnesses (e.g. Brennan 1994) and employment counselling (e.g. Olesen 2003).

From a professional perspective, the discourse analytical literature has mostly stayed within an academic tradition (for an overview, see Sarangi [2005]). Disseminated findings are (often implicitly and exclusively) voiced as expert corrections of the non-expert understandings. For instance, a key study in the literature criticises advice giving on a radio broadcast as "unwarranted affiliation compounded by inept servicing" (Jefferson and Lee 1992: 546). Some assume that merely by introducing professionals to discourse analysis, their practice will improve (Heritage and Maynard 2006: 21; Housley and Fitzgerald 2007: 14). Exceptions can be noted: Silverman (1987: 263) criticizes one-directional notions of "enlightenment", while Harper (2003: 84) describes the "curious dualism" of being a practitioner and discourse analyst as "like a tightrope walker … both an asset and impediment".

The concepts deployed by the discourse analyst often do not connect well with the everyday dilemmas of professionals. Bryans (2000: 5) sees conversation analysis as attractive but "not entirely appropriate" for research on community nursing. Nor is discourse research generally oriented towards developing training courses and few publications engage explicitly or dialogically with professionals' understandings of communicative practices (for an example in relation to nursing and applied health, see Candlin [2008]). Not surprisingly, exceptions often start from conversation analysis, a tradition which stresses members' social-interactional competence and views sequences of talk as resulting in interactional accomplishments which talkers orient to without necessarily noticing the complexity and richness of sequential detail. For Silverman (1997a) 249–251, a discourse analysis which lays bare the communicative-interactional patterning routinely attended to by talkers can be understood in terms of an aesthetics of the micro which reveals the massive regularity of ordinary conduct. Such an approach defies the immediate gratification of simple grand (policy) narratives about exciting "incidents". Here, Silverman invokes the later Wittgenstein as consciously rejecting "big" questions and global answers in favour of a meticulous examination of apparently unremarkable examples. "Rather than shock us with tabloid examples, he shocks us by reminding us of the complexities of what we know already" (Silverman 1997: 250).

Professionals are thus likely to gain from a discourse analytic concept of "interactional accomplishment" which holds irrespective of professional assessments of "good" or "bad" practice. One can add to this: discourse analysts are likely to further an awareness that interaction is not atomistically "all over the place", but that instead it is "patterned" and "layered", that it "unfolds sequentially" and it is "attended to constantly, be it often routinely". A third advantage derives undeniably from the constraint that research has to be replicable. Indeed, the invitation for professionals is towards greater detail, precision and depth than the views customarily obtained in much communication research.

Some discourse researchers have addressed the relationship of analysis to professionals' own normative understandings and theories about professional interaction – their "stocks of interactional knowledge" (Peräkylä and Vehviläinen 2003). For instance, Peräkylä (1995: 332–338) notes the overlap between, on the one hand, categories of conversation analysis and, on the other hand, family systems and other theories developed by counselling practitioners. The critical question he thus poses is: can Conversation Analysis say anything about counselling that the professionals have not already addressed? Various kinds of surplus value are noted: (i) laying bare how the counsellors' own practices may be more sophisticated than their own theory; (ii) demonstrating the usefulness of particular interactional techniques beyond the objectives stated in the professional theory; (iii) examine at a level of precision how key professional concepts work out in actual interaction (cf. Hall and Slembrouck [2001] on the statutory concept of "parent participation" in child protection conferences in the UK); and (iv) bring out how the professional and the discourse analyst have similar enterprises. Within sight comes the more hybrid role of a practitioner who is also trained in discourse analysis (Clarke 2003: 375).

4.   Making connections between analysis and professional understandings

In an attempt to make a bridge between professional and discourse analytic concerns with communication, we have started to examine examples of client-professional communication together with home visiting professionals, as one way towards joint agenda-setting which renders discourse analysis relevant and meaningful to a community of practice. The professionals audio recorded a home visit to the family. The researchers used transcriptions of the interaction as a basis for an interview with the individual professional. It is the latter set of data that we draw on here, plus a focus group discussion attended by most of the professionals in the group. The key features of the joint research process was that the discussion was set up as non-evaluative, "good practice" being more a matter of description than evaluation. In their turn, the researchers introduced particular ways of illuminating the data, drawing attention to interactional patterns and the existing professional literature.

All the professionals involved found the process interesting and worthwhile. Most stressed the lack of opportunities to engage explicitly with their communicative practices.

> Professional 2: I wouldn't say it's standard as part of health visitor training yet so much of our work is client face-to-face contact, clinics, home visits, constantly getting information, getting advice, listening to people

> Professional 1: it's almost down to personality rather than sort of what you have learned or what you've been taught.

Moreover, despite reassurances of the non-evaluative orientation, observing one's own practice was approached with some trepidation. The transcripts are the professionals at work and lay bare professional practices:

> Professional 1: I mean I did linguistics at University but it's been a long time since I've looked at transcriptions and things so I was quite nervous looking at myself. I'm quite happy to look at other peoples'

> Professional 3: It's been very interesting and as I said I was a little bit apprehensive and I like a challenge

The first reaction was often surprise at what the transcripts revealed. Professionals were especially self-critical of the relative quantity and salience of their contributions:

> Professional 5: I suppose the things that I didn't realize maybe that I said quite so much and whether I feel like that's positive or negative but I did say "yes" quite a lot and I did wonder whether sometimes when I was reading through it whether I interrupted her sometimes half way through her sentences

> Professional 1: I seem to ramble on

This stance extended into observations about being too close to the talk and being guarded in exploring it in detail.

> Professional 2: I read that as oh she wasn't listening to me there I just carried on and waffled a bit, whereas actually you pointed out that she was listening.

In the various discussions, certain themes were selected and highlighted for detailed attention. In succession, we will now examine what the professionals had to say about communicative behaviour in relation to role, client categorization, displays of affiliation and "good practice".

4.1.   Professional role boundaries and their interactional dynamics

There are instances in the client interviews where particular problems are discussed in terms of who should address them. Talk about professional role boundaries is more complex than saying "if you want to talk about A you have to talk to X" and can on occasion become part of an ongoing assessment of the client's well-being. The nursery nurse had to handle relationship and health problems, clearly issues outside her professional remit. However, she insists on facilitating talk about such issues.

> Professional 4: Because I know I'm aware that okay I can link them to services, but this is not my expertise area but I don't want to abandon this family (Researcher: no no sure) I know they been through a lot (Researcher: sure) I built up this relationship with them and they've told me things they've never told anybody else so we're in it for the long haul together so to speak.

Compare also with the view of another health visitor:

> Professional 5: I think it's quite common I went with my agenda of it was to review in terms of postnatal depression screening and I got sidetracked by a few different issues but that's fine to do that and I did still manage to achieve what I wanted to achieve.

Interestingly, during the client interview the health visitor asks the standard questions, followed by a series of apparently unrelated questions which screen indirectly: Is the client looking forward to a visit from a relative? Answers to these screening questions are not enough in themselves, but have to be taken in the round, adducible in support of a general opinion about the client.

> Professional 5: If she was presenting in a different way then probably I would have probed a bit more but she presented in quite a positive upbeat way and wanted to access other services I see her at clinic quite regularly as well and she always presents very well.

The point of access to services (which is part of negotiating role boundaries) is not only addressed in its own right, but also becomes part of a process of general assessment through which a particular picture of the client is built up.

Another worker also recognizes the need to allow the client to talk about issues which concern them, even if it covers issues where they cannot help:

Professional 3: I feel people need to off-load and they do off-load on me quite a lot, but I have to, I do have to bring it to a close somewhere because it can go on for long and I mean, there is one particular mum I know, I always have to, right that's it, you know, time there. But in a nice, polite, respectful, em, but by changing the subject slightly I have to move her on and that's when I was saying I won't keep you much longer.

Whilst professionals are acutely aware of the specifics of their role and purpose, we can see how they negotiate appropriateness, at the same time allowing talk which ventures beyond their professional brief. Analytical caution thus has to be invited when discourse analysts too easily read client-professional data in terms of a particular intervention with a limited scope which follows straightforwardly from the professional's mission or a case-specific brief. Professional practice in any one encounter can head off in different directions – and with this a case may change character. Professionals appear to be prepared for and prepared to accept such re-framings. This potential open-endedness comes with its own set of interactional dilemmas, not only in terms of the appropriate use of a busy professional's time, but also whether the formality of, for instance a line of questioning is at odds with developing a helping relationship (Cowley et al. 2004). Managing such interactional dilemmas is critical for professional learning.

4.2.   Adjusting the talk to a particular kind of client

Traditionally, discourse research focuses on patterns and regularities beyond individual situated occurrences. What follows from this is often a view that interactional processes will be the same, whatever the characteristics of the participants involved. The professionals resisted this view. In fact, much of the discussion revolved around "what the client is like" and "what I'm like". In one interview, the professional explains her communicative relationship with the client by mentioning that she had been in care, by referring to the client's church membership as a strong influence, and invoking her relationship with her mother. As noted in the interview extract which opened this chapter, professionals describe adjusting their interactional strategies to the client's interactional characteristics:

Professional 2: (when I'm doing) an initial assessment I would definitely be aware of how I could ask those questions to that particular client. I think with the one I did know that she was the sort of person I could ask probably whatever I wanted to ask whereas and also then complete the assessment, whereas there's other people who maybe I would only be able to discuss feeding whereas actually I wanted to try and discuss how they made their environment safe. It does impact on who you are going to see.

Professional 4: I'm not sure if [father's] comprehending what [mother's] saying at all or if he's just shut down, cos a lot of the time he'd just shut down and I've been there when he has fallen asleep when we're talking, so on previous visits … I always want to make sure he understands absolutely everything.

Other comments related to what the workers see as their personal investment in particular styles of reacting to clients.

Professional 3: Yeah. I just feel that, that is something that it's me. I have to allow a little bit of them to give me their troubles, tell me what's going on and then I can bring them back. But a lot of the places that they go to, it's a case of, why are you here, what do you need to be done, this is it, you know, you don't have enough points, can't really help you, goodbye and I've had too many people tell me that.

Forming a positive relationship with the client is critical to successful work for this group of professionals. It is not an adjunct, and often it is an end in itself (see Candlin and Candlin 2002: 118). It is difficult to explore such professional-client talk in the absence of a professional viewpoint which locates personal formulations of people as an interactional prerequisite.

4.3.   Looking for displays of affiliation

In the existing literature, affiliation has been mainly explored through identifying the extent to which the client accepts advice or diagnosis (e.g. Heritage and Sefi 1992). In this example, affiliation with the client is identified at the point where a worker takes the applicants' complaints while persuading them that the process can be slow:

Researcher 2: And then what you say is, I'm glad that em, glad that you've started realising that it can take a long time.

Professional 3: Yeah because some of those people are talking to me and I'm telling them things, but sometimes it's difficult for them to actually hear what I'm saying and absorb it. What she's saying is you know, it's taken a long time for me to get on that system and then I think she realises and I said well that's it, you can see there has been this long gap.

What the professionals noted here was the way in which affiliation involved the development of a helping relationship. The professionals are aware of different forms of talk during the home encounters, friendly or business-oriented. In many cases, it is the client who established the move towards more informal friendly talk. The idea of developing a relationship often appears to be accomplished alongside institutionally-prescribed activities, although professionals and clients believe it is vital and that it should happen:

Researcher 2: the impression that you're giving me is that these sorts of little incidents are quite nice the fact that you've got to fill this long complicated form doesn't really allow that sort of more familiar form of interaction to take place too often

Professional 2: no no probably not and I think that interaction is very dependent on the client I think it's not something we would maybe (.) I think we would probably do it but I think I would maybe do it as a little bit at the beginning to try and sort of allow people to feel they can talk to me and maybe possibly a little bit at the end but it's not something I would do consciously I think

Affiliation is also about client alignment with professional advocacy. Professionals are not necessarily explicitly looking for affiliation where they might. For instance, in one of the client interviews there were various instances where the professional did not check for confirmation across child-initiated interruptions, because the mother's role in the child's development was the focus of intervention. In other cases, although it looked like a piece of advice had been taken on, it took a long time to become manifest in the interaction:

Researcher 2: she accepted the advice it seemed to me
Professional 5: ok yeah but it took quite a while

Looking at the transcript, the professional highlights the number of turns in between. Similarly, a sequence may end without any indication that the advice has been accepted. Sometimes workers resort to very explicit positions of advocacy which establish their professional authority.

Researcher 2: is she prepared for that, does she say yes I'll do that then which you suggest

Professional 2: being forced to do it I think sometimes I say things like that and I take that as your health visitor stance because it's I'm really relinquishing responsibility to the title of my role and profession but I am saying I almost use that as a bit of power

Professionals recognize the need to explore the nature of "advice" further, for instance, in terms of subtle gradations of investment in the problem.

Professional 5: I suppose maybe at this stage then I could have checked with her maybe what she thought the problem was and then had a discussion about that I don't know but she said what the problem is and I suppose it's whether or not she's wanting advice which I think she is saying that that by saying she came to see the health visitors but maybe it's not this isn't advice this is actually reassurance

The question here may be whether the talk is framed in terms of "troubles talk within action" or "imperatives that require action" (cf. Jefferson and Lee 1992). Sequences can be ambiguous between the two but framed subsequently. In one sequence an inquiry about whether or not to have a single MMR injection was responded to with a long turn by the professional which resulted in a clear advocacy. This was an issue that the worker saw as important and could not leave to a mere reassurance that the client is doing fine and that the choice is hers (cf. Silverman [1997] on health promotion talk being occasioned by a strong imperative to put the advice into the interaction). In contrast, Professional 5 questions the researcher's straightforward interpretative identification of a particular sequence as one of advice giving. To this extent, the distinction between interpersonal and professional forms of talk is hard to maintain (cf. Candlin and Candlin 2002: 124).

5.   Conclusion

This project suggests professionals and discourse analysts stand to learn from a dialogic enterprise, some of the contours of which have emerged in the pilot study reported here. While professionals are likely to be primarily interested in recommendations towards "good practice", they are likely to benefit from explicit micro-sequential analysis which is conducted in the less evaluative terms of discourse analysis, analysis which makes explicit and deepens their understanding of what they do routinely. Likewise, discourse analysts stand to gain from avoiding the pitfalls of an engagement with dissemination which is cut off from practitioners' views, interpretations and understandings. In the three topics we have explored through examining home visiting, we can detect a professional concern for formal procedure which is informed by professional mission and/or institutional brief but which is pushed forward by a helping and befriending relationship with the client, as well as being set in a context of professional judgment which is sensitive to the specific characteristics of the client. Professionals listen widely for and engage with all kinds of relevant client experiences.

Moreover, our analysis has revealed some of the tensions that derive from the contradictory pulls of two kinds of "client-orientedness": at one end, there is (i) client-centredness in the sense of a sensitivity to client experiences, their expectations, the way they make sense of themselves and others around them and their agency in decision-making. At the other end, there is (ii) client-centredness as a specific imperative that follows from professional vision as to what is "in the best interest of the client". For the professionals in this study, good practice attends equally well to both dimensions. Interactional skills and strategies are selected and deployed in context: strategies are both client-specific and informed by professional brief, and they come with a readiness to engage with whatever emerges as relevant in the shorter and longer run of the contact with the client. We have reason to believe that this complex dynamics (and the polarities that inform it) is likely to apply (and be debated) across professional domains such as health, welfare, law, the labour market, etc. Obviously, more research into this aspect is needed and not just research which concentrates on home visiting.

One specific challenge thus lies in the pursuit of a professional perspective beyond the a-personal sequential minutiae of exchanges. Such an exercise is premised on a fuller engagement still with professionals' situated understandings of a client case and its specific interactional dynamics. We can state more generally with Cicourel (1992) – cited in Candlin and Candlin (2002: 119) – that professional judgement is "never abstracted from context, both local and more broadly-conceived. In our view, it is always situated against some specific *cost-benefit analysis*, and realized through some event- and person-sensitive *performance*". In other words, while the deployment of discourse analytical methods easily leads us on the path of a-personal generalisations, it can be observed how professionals mostly talk about their own communicative practices through case- and category-specific lenses: what sort of communicative approach does this kind of condition, client or situation invite? Thus, equally needed is a discourse analytical sensitivity to what professionals are really saying about their own communicative practices and the need for such to be ethnographically detailed (Candlin 2003: 389). This includes precision in the description of professional communicative concepts, and with that, a readiness to venture into understandings of communicative practice which are informed both by profession-, client- and case-specific reasoning and concerns.

Note

* This paper was completed in collaboration with Lucy Bowen, Anita Lee, Nicole Wakely-Griffiths, Victoria Warren, Muriel George and Emma Haigh. The fieldwork was completed in the context of a larger study of professional practice, "e-Assessment in Child Welfare", funded by the ESRC e-Society programme (Award No: 341-25-0023).

References

Barlow, Jane, Neil Brocklehurst, Sarah Stewart-Brown, Helen Davis, Claire Burns, Helen Callaghan and Joanna Tucker
    2003   Working in partnership: The development of a home visiting service for vulnerable families. *Child Abuse Review* 12: 172–189.

Bowles, Nick, Caroline Mackintosh and Alison Torn
  2001   Nurses' communication skills: An evaluation of the impact of solution-fo-
             cused communication training. *Journal of Advanced Nursing* 36: 347–354.
Brennan, Mark
  1994   The discourse of denial: Cross-examining child victim witnesses. *Journal
             of Pragmatics* 23: 71–91.
Bryans, Alison
  2000   Providing new insight into community nursing know-how through quali-
             tative analysis of multiple sets of simulation data. *Primary Health Care
             Research and Development* 1: 79–89.
Buttny, Richard
  1996   Client's and therapist's joint construction of the client's problems. *Research
             on Language and Social Interaction* 29: 125–153.
Cameron, Deborah
  2000   *Good to Talk? Living and Working in a Communication Culture*. London:
             Sage.
Candlin, Christopher and Sally Candlin
  2002   Discourse, expertise and the management of risk in health care settings.
             Research on Language and Social Interaction 35: 115–137.
Candlin, Sally
  2003   Issues arising when the professional workplace is the site of applied lin-
             guistic research. *Applied Linguistics* 24: 386–394.
Candlin, Sally
  2008   *Therapeutic Communication: A Lifespan Approach*. Melbourne: Pearson
             Education.
Clarke, Angus
  2003   On being an object of research: Reflections from a professional perspective.
             Applied Linguistics 24: 374–385.
Cowley, Sarah, Jan Mitcheson and Anna Houston
  2004   Structuring health needs assessments: The medicalisation of health visiting.
             Sociology of Health and Illness 25: 503–526.
Erickson, Frederick and Jeffrey Schultz
  1982   *The Counselor as Gatekeeper: Social Interaction in Interviews*. New York:
             Academic Press.
Forrester, Donald, Sophie Kershaw, Helen Moss and Laura Hughes
  2008   Communication skills in child protection: How social workers talk to par-
             ents? *Child and Family Social Work* 13: 41–51.
Gray, Benjamin
  2002   Emotional labour and befriending in family support and child protection in
             Tower Hamlets. *Child and Family Social Work* 7: 13–22.
Hall, Christopher and Stef Slembrouck
  2001   Parent Participation in social work meetings: The case of child protection
             conferences. *European Journal of Social Work* 4: 143–160.
Hall, Christopher, Stef Slembrouck and Srikant Sarangi
  2006   *Language Practices in Social Work: Categorization and Accountability in
             Child Welfare*. London: Routledge.

Harper, David
  2003   Developing a critically reflexive position using discourse analysis. In:
          Linda Finlay and Brendan Gough (eds.), *Reflexivity: A Practical Guide for
          Researchers in Health and Social Sciences*, 78–92. Oxford: Blackwell.
Heritage, John and Douglas Maynard
  2006   Introduction: Analysing interaction between doctors and patients in pri-
          mary care. In: John Heritage and Douglas Maynard (eds.), *Communication
          in Medical Care: Interaction Between Primary Care Physicians and Pa-
          tients*, 2–21. Cambridge: Cambridge University Press.
Heritage, John and Sue Sefi
  1992   Dilemmas of advice: Aspects of the delivery and reception of advice in in-
          teractions between health visitors and first-time mothers. In: Paul Drew and
          John Heritage (eds.), *Talk at Work: Interaction in Institutional Settings*,
          359–419. Cambridge: Cambridge University Press.
Housley, William and Richard Fitzgerald
  2007   *Conversation Analysis, Practitioner Based Reseach, Reflexivity and Reflec-
          tive Practice: Some Exploratory Remarks* (Cardiff Working Paper 89.) Car-
          diff: School of Social Sciences, Cardiff University.
Jefferson, Gail and John Lee
  1992   The rejection of advice: Managing the problematic convergence of a
          "troubles-telling" and a "service encounter". In: Paul Drew and John Heri-
          tage (eds.), *Talk at Work: Interaction in Institutional Settings*, 521–548.
          Cambridge: Cambridge University Press.
Koprowska, Juliet
  2005   *Communication and Interpersonal Skills in Social Work*. Exeter: Learning
          Matters.
Lishman, Joyce
  1994   *Communication in Social Work*. Basingstoke: Palgrave.
Mead, Nicola, Peter Bower and Linda Gask
  1997   Emotional problems in primary care: What is the potential for increasing
          the role of nurses? *Journal of Advanced Nursing* 26: 879–890.
Nerdrum, Per
  1997   Maintenance of the effect of training in communication skills: A controlled
          follow-up study of level of communicated empathy. *British Journal of So-
          cial Work* 27: 705–722.
Olesen, Sören Peter
  2003   Client, user, member as constructed in institutional interaction. In: Chris-
          topher Hall, Kirsi Juhila, Nigel Parton and Tarja Pösö (eds.), *Constructing
          Clienthood in Social Work and Human Services. Interaction, Identities and
          Practices,* 208–222. London: Jessica Kingley.
Peräkylä, Anssi
  1995   *AIDS Counselling. Institutional Interaction and Clinical Practice.* Cam-
          bridge: Cambridge University Press.
Peräkylä Anssi and Sanna Vehviläinen
  2003   Conversation analysis and the professional stocks of interactional knowl-
          edge. *Discourse and Society* 14: 727–750.

Pithouse, Andy
   1987   *Social Work: The Organisation of an Invisible Trade.* Aldershot: Gower.
Richards, Sally, Gillian Ruch and Pamela Trevithick
   2005   Communication skills training for practice: the ethical dilemma for social
             work education. *Social Work Education* 24: 409–422.
Robinson, Lena
   2004   Beliefs, values and intercultural communication. In: Martin Robb, Sheila
             Barrett, Carol Komaromy and Anita Rogers (eds.), *Communication, Rela-
             tionships and Care: A Reader,* 110–120. London: Routledge.
Ruch, Gillian
   2005   Relationship-based practice and reflective practice: Holistic approaches to
             contemporary child care social work. *Child and Family Social Work* 10:
             111–123.
Sarangi, Srikant
   2005   The conditions and consequences of professional discourse studies. *Jour-
             nal of Applied Linguistics* 2: 371–394.
Sarangi, Srikant and Angus Clarke
   2002   Constructing an account by contrast in counseling for childhood genetic
             testing. *Social Science & Medicine* 54: 119–132.
Silverman, David
   1987   *Communication and Medical Practice: Social relations in the clinic.* Lon-
             don: Sage.
Silverman, David
   1997   Towards an aesthetics of research. In: David Silverman (ed.), *Qualitative
             Research: Theory, Mothod and Practice,* 239–253. London: Sage.
Silverman, David
   1997   *Discourses of Counselling: HIV Counselling as Social Interaction.* Lon-
             don: Sage.
Social Care Institute for Excellence
   2004   *Teaching and Learning Communication Skills in Social Work Education
             Knowledge Review.* London: SCIE.
Thompson, Neil
   2003   *Communication and Language: A Handbook of Theory and Practice.* Bas-
             ingstoke: Palgrave Macmillan.
van Nijnatten, Carolus, Mariette Hoogsteder and Jeanie Suurmond
   2001   Communication in care and coercion: institutional interactions between
             family supervisors and parents. *British Journal of Social Work* 31: 705–720.
Williams, Diana
   1997   *Communication Skills in Practice: A Practical Guide for Health Profes-
             sionals.* London: Jessica Kingsley.

21. Crossing the boundary between finance and law: The collaborative problematisation of professional learning in a postgraduate classroom

Alan Jones and Sheelagh McCracken

Abstract

The authors, an applied linguist and an academic lawyer, describe how they collaboratively problematise and co-develop conceptual learning materials for finance professionals enrolled in a postgraduate study-unit called Legal Risk in Finance. Activities are designed to function as "boundary objects" bridging the gap between two professional visions. These "objects" are intended to help the finance professionals engage for the first time with categories of meaning and discursive practices that are often represented in terms superficially similar to those of their own professional domain. The authors also document their own cross-disciplinary collaboration, which takes place in sites of engagement that together constitute a "back region" relative to the classroom's "front region" (Goffman 1959). In this "second site" the applied linguist qua discourse analyst identifies areas of conceptual difficulty and potential misunderstanding. There have been numerous studies of professional acculturation and socialisation, especially in the medical and legal domains; but as yet little in the realms of finance and finance law. Moreover, the classroom is rarely seen as the site of such processes. Yet for many postgraduate students that is precisely where they first confront the categories of a new professional domain. The role of applied linguists in tertiary curriculum development is another neglected research topic involving cross-boundary professional partnerships.

1. Introduction

Consider the following email exchange between the two authors, an applied linguist and an academic lawyer, which originated in a discussion of a legal judgment:

> Applied Linguist: I've been trying to get my head around the [Bank] case before looking at the notes – fascinating story of the inner workings of a bank, and a beautiful example of an "unstructured problem" … Can you check my understanding so far? Firstly are my calculations correct – [Bank] only stood to lose some $7000 over the difference in exchange rates?

Academic Lawyer: Yes, my finance colleagues always get excited about the figures. When teaching this case, I say to the students that from a legal perspective it is simply important to appreciate that they were two different numbers – x dollars and y dollars and that x does not equal y! The legal issue lies in whether there was a contract or not rather than the rate of exchange at which the deal was purported to be done. Note on p. 178 that the bank only alleged the .6626 rate in May 1986. The initial fight was whether there was a contract for purchase at 28 June. In May 1986 the bank amended their claim to argue that there was a contract as at 26 June. The bank was desperate to find a contract – at whatever rate.

As can be seen, the applied linguist has to grapple with the underlying financial and legal parameters of a dispute between a bank and its corporate customer. He needs to familiarise himself with the kinds of issues encountered in a very particular classroom environment: one in which experienced finance practitioners are attempting to cross the professional boundary between finance and law. Here they engage with an academic lawyer in an inter-professional meaning making exercise, in a course on Legal Risk in Finance (taken as part of a postgraduate program in applied finance at an Australian university).

The question posed by the applied linguist in the above email echoes that asked by most finance professionals who, when confronted in the classroom with the facts of that particular dispute, commonly home in on the exchange rates at which the trade is done. They overlook, thereby, the critical legal issue of whether or not a contract exists. This inadvertent replication of the finance professionals' approach highlighted to us the ability of the applied linguist to perform the role of a novice in the targeted field. It prompted us to explore the potential for exploiting the new subject position and the developed process knowledge (as distinct from the perhaps more usual content knowledge) of the applied linguist in designing learning materials for use in this type of classroom.

This chapter describes the resulting collaborative problematisation and design of textualised and scaffolded learning materials in a site of engagement which can be characterised as a "back region" relative to the site of engagement represented by the classroom, which is a "front region" (in terms made familiar by Goffman 1959). Because of the preparatory and occluded nature of the interactions and design processes taking place in the back region, we refer to this space as the second site. While discursive phenomena of the first site have become reasonably familiar to applied linguists through analyses of classroom discourse, including that of the legal classroom (see especially Mertz 2007), discourses of the second site remain relatively unexplored. We describe the interactions characteristic of this second site and how these led us to conceptualise the learning materials produced by us in this site (i.e. the exercises, the tasks, the problems and the "cases") as *constructed boundary objects* (Star and Griesemer 1989; Star 1990; Bowker and Star 1999; Wenger 1998).

Although the communicative and meaning-making activities generated in the second site are directed, at a practical level, towards producing learning materials for use in the first site to mediate and scaffold interactions between the academic lawyer and the finance professionals, their implications at a broader level for an understanding of professional socialisation should not be overlooked. The planning and design processes in this second site highlight ways in which meanings and discursive practices germane to one type of professional practice (in our case, finance) can become laminated with meanings and discursive practices drawn from another (law). Studies of professional socialisation, which until now have concentrated largely on the medical and legal domains rather than that of finance, have not as yet examined how professionals in one domain might, as part of their socialisation into that domain, benefit from exposure to and peripheral socialisation into another relevant domain (cf. Lave 1991).

2.   Background to the intervention

Our approach has entailed a prolonged collaboration between an applied linguist and a subject area specialist. Through a sustained dialogue, we have problematised the teaching practices of the academic lawyer. The approach we have gradually developed has its inspiration in several converging traditions within the field of applied linguistics, but particularly Content Based Instruction (CBI). The goal of integrating the teaching of content with language teaching has been adopted by growing numbers of language teachers practising in the areas known as English for Specific Purposes (ESP), including English for Academic Purposes (EAP), where linguistic proficiency (albeit of specialised kinds) is still the intended outcome. This goal has also been adopted, however, by subject area teachers and language teachers, often working together, in secondary and tertiary level education, where language learning is regarded as ancillary to content learning, rather than as the prime objective (cf. Mohan 1986; Crandall 1987; Snow, Met and Genesee 1988; Brinton, Snow and Wesche 1989; Krueger and Ryan 1993; Stoller 2004; Wilkinson 2004; Wilkinson and Zegers 2007).

The trend towards Content Based Instruction has resonated with the writing-to-learn movement, popular on many US campuses, which is allied with two other widespread movements: Writing in the Disciplines (WiD) and Writing Across the Curriculum (WAC). In most European countries, and in some parts of Australia, the principles of Content and Language Integrated Learning (CLIL) have been adopted either as part of mainstream school education or in the form of pilot projects (see Eurydice 2006: 14). This development has been stimulated in part at least by the mooted success of immersion language teaching in Canada, and is helped along by increasing numbers of international stu-

dents attending universities in countries where instruction takes place in students' second (or third, etc.) language.

As a consequence, language professionals are often working more closely
and for more sustained periods with subject-area specialists in higher education,
forging relationships that increasingly involve collaborative research and joint
publications as well as collaborative curriculum development. The aim of such
collaborations is often twofold. On the one hand, applied linguists can assist
subject-area specialists to scaffold the acquisition of subject-specific conceptual
knowledge through language-based learning activities. On the other, they can
ensure that certain activities scaffold communicative responses to issues and
problems likely to be important in professional practice (e.g. the learning materials in Jones and Sin 2003; cf. also Jones and Sin 2004; Jones and McCracken
2007; Sin, Jones and Petocz 2007).

Interpersonal and interdisciplinary partnerships of the kind in question here
are frequently problematic. A lack of shared premises about how knowledge
is constituted and/or the role of language in knowledge constitution may
compound other, more mundane, forms of incompatibility (see Jacobs 2005).
Hence, in this chapter, we comment on the processes whereby we reached a mutual understanding about interests, aims and methodology. This may prove
instructive for other collaborations where a disciplinary expert embarks on a
problem-focused reflexive enterprise in partnership with an applied linguist.
(For recent discussions of collaborative processes and procedures, in a variety
of contexts, see Gollin [1999] and Crossling and Wilson [2005]; for discussions
of interdisciplinarity see Klein [1996] and [2005], and the edited collection by
Derry, Schunn and Gernsbacher [2005].)

Our own collaboration has been characterised by self-reflective dialogical-
ity. We each have had to take on shifting roles, as we are alternatively expert or
novice, changing our professional and disciplinary footings and perspectives
often from one moment to the next. In this way we attempt to anticipate the
kinds of problems likely to be faced by the finance professionals when engaging
with the meanings and discursive competencies of a lawyer. This process can
best be understood as a "joint problematisation" (Roberts and Sarangi 1999a:
399; 1999b: 473–474) of the linguistic and discursive aspects of a complex professional practice which has both financial and legal ramifications. The concept
and the rationale for joint problematisation as a principle of interprofessional
practice runs throughout Sarangi (2002) and Sarangi and Candlin (2001). We
enlarge this concept by going beyond the problem and jointly scaffolding learning trajectories designed to maximise the ease with which learners acquire a
laminated understanding of financial transactions and the ability to reason about
them persuasively from a legal standpoint. Meanwhile, our dialogue continually
implicates and ventriloquises the viewpoint of an absent third party – the finance
professional.

3.   Where interests and discourses combine: the second site

Interactive spaces frame moments of time in which social and discursive practices intersect, producing mutuality of engagement and the negotiation of meanings. Scollon (1998) described these communicative space-times as "windows", and termed them "sites of engagement". Our first "site" – spatially defined – is a postgraduate classroom frequented by members of the finance industry who need to become familiar with the discourse of the specialised area of finance law. With the continuing sophistication of financial markets, finance professionals are increasingly required to understand the application of the law to their activities and to be able to determine where legal risk may lie. This ability will assist them to manage that critical risk in daily business operations. It will also improve their ability to communicate more clearly with their lawyers and to work together with those lawyers to address that risk. Our second site is sometimes an office and sometimes a quiet restaurant or café, where the academic lawyer sits down with the applied linguist to openly and critically discuss and collaboratively problematise her teaching practices and learning materials, and to design new learning materials to be used either as the focus of classroom interactions or as resources for independent learning.

In contrast to what happens in the first site, where the explicit aim is to align two non-competing disciplinary discourses, in the second site two professional knowledge-based and practice-based discourses are frequently in conflict as the proponents of each attempt to find common interests (Latour 1987: Chapter 3) and understandings and a viable modus operandi (Star and Griesemer 1989: 388). Our common interests are defined in relation to the absent third party. The second site resembles a type of interaction that is referred to as a lesson planning meeting, or a curriculum planning meeting. We would describe what happens here, in more object-oriented terms, as a learning-process design meeting. And we would emphasise the fact that the first site is *functionally dependent on* the second.

Prior to our collaboration and the collaborative problematisation of the academic lawyer's approach to teaching and learning in the second site, she relied on an interactive pedagogy designed to create a space for negotiated meanings in the classroom. By some measures this was very successful. The negotiation of meanings took the form of dynamic interactions between individual finance professionals and herself (of the kind known in legal circles as *Socratic*). On the whiteboard, ad hoc diagrams of the kind lawyers frequently use to map out and disambiguate transactions would form the focus of negotiated understandings. The need for a second site in which additional learning materials could be designed first became apparent when she was faced with developing the course to be taught in China. The initial concern that motivated her to approach the applied linguist was a "linguistic" one: how would this new body of students manage the highly technical, abstract and elevated level of language in which legal concepts tend to be expressed? At that stage, she envisaged the role of the applied linguist as a supportive one, helping her to produce transparent and more readily comprehensible learning materials (see Jones and McCracken 2007).

Preliminary discussions with the applied linguist resulted, however, in a critical change of direction: from a narrow and exclusive focus on central concepts and principles of the legal discipline, to the identification, explication and scaffolding of potentially problematic concepts, and modelling of the types of discursive reasoning through which they can be tested against actual cases. A collaborative rethinking of the curriculum and of the materials used to implement it (carried out in the second site) resulted in exercises and tasks that identified and began with "threshold" concepts (cf. Meyer and Land 2003; Davies 2006) and explicated both the internal structure and external conceptual linkages of these concepts while highlighting their practical implications. It was soon realised that exercises designed to scaffold problematic concepts in the manner just described – along with the discursive practices in which they are characteristically embedded – would benefit not only students from a non English speaking background but also native speakers (Jones and McCracken 2007). The key issues, common to both groups, were conceptual understanding and the ability to recognise the consequences of the concepts and principles for real-life actors and situations. Hence we used the second site to jointly unpack the legal concepts and explore the legal principles that they supported, and then to produce exercises and tasks based on our analyses which would scaffold the concepts and (whenever possible) also model the kinds of legal reasoning used for legal problem-solving in finance contexts. We introduced rich contextualisation through mini-cases. Interactions and activities characterising the first and second sites are represented schematically in Figures 1 and 2, which also show the relationship between the two sites before and during the intervention.

The whiteboard diagrams – and the talk around them – thus became the predecessors of the learning materials that we now design in the second site, negotiating understandings across our own disciplinary boundaries, and on the basis of our different knowledge of financial discourse. The nature of this collaboration in the second site has been somewhat unusual. As "discourse practitioners" (Sarangi 2002), our normal allegiances are to very different "discourse communities" (Nystrand 1982; Swales 1990). For present purposes, the discourse communities can be understood as corresponding to the "social worlds" of Strauss (1978, 1984) and, more pertinently, the "epistemic cultures" of Knorr-Cetina (1999). To add a layer of discursive complexity, we are designing and constructing learning materials for use, not by members of one or other of our own discourse communities, but by members of a third, entirely distinct community, world, or culture, that of the finance professionals.

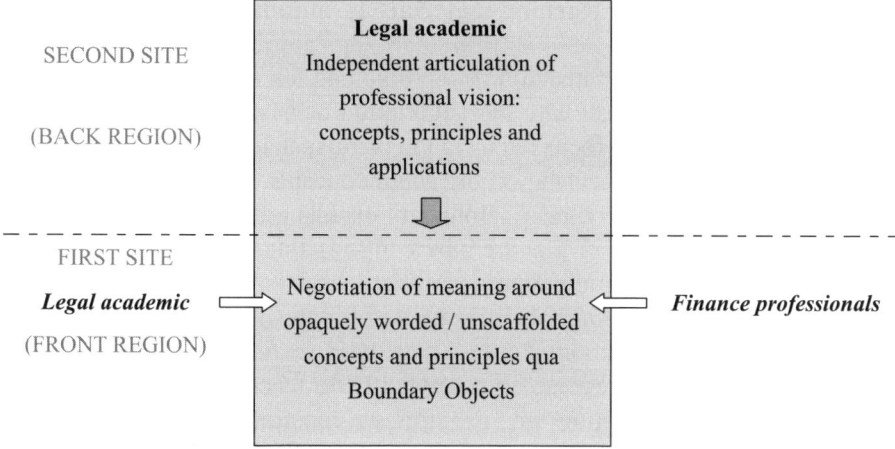

Figure 1.   STANDARD PRACTICE – independently designed, unscaffolded learning
materials

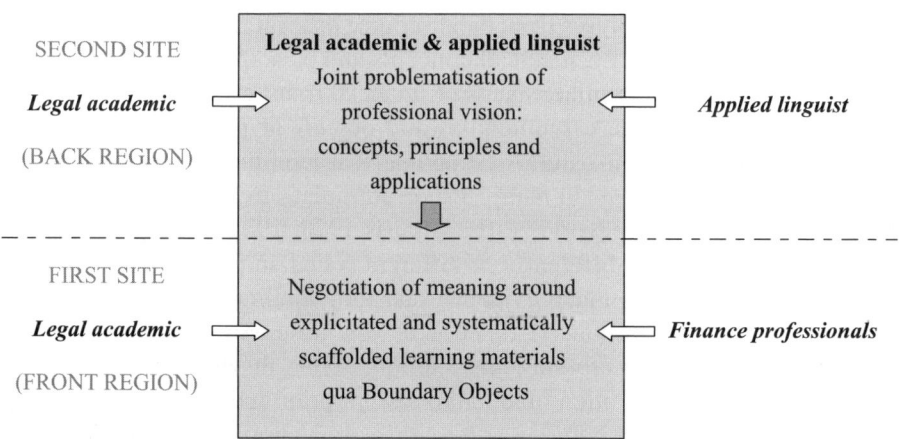

Figure 2.   INNOVATED PRACTICE – collaboratively designed, scaffolded learning
materials

4.   Conceptualising learning materials as boundary objects

The collaborative problematisation of teaching and learning in our second site focused on the need to facilitate the negotiation of new meanings in the first site – the classroom. This focus led us to the premise that the learning materials developed here, ideally focusing on threshold concepts, can profitably be conceptualised as "boundary objects". Boundary objects are usually understood as real-world events or "cases" that are inherently capable of being interpreted in different ways. For pedagogical purposes these are ideally re-presented as objectively as possible; (failing that) constructed events can be closely modelled on real ones. In our classroom, "cases" have been textualised – sometimes by the courts and sometimes by ourselves explicitly for teaching purposes. Around these cases sets of instructions and prompts are constructed, and these are designed to scaffold a series of learning conversations (Pask 1976) which may be either rehearsed in class or carried on internally, as it were, between the inner voice of the learner and the textualised voice of the teacher. In explicitly conceptualising learning materials in this way, we were compelled to recognise the voice of the absent third party; and this recognition constrained us to design dialogical and dynamic learning materials that would support actual or virtual teaching-learning interactions. The textually represented problem situations are taken from, or based on, actual legal cases. In these, to borrow the words of Star and Griesemer (1989), we "translate, negotiate, debate, triangulate, and simplify" constructs and analyses from the discourse of legal risk; and we link them to, and enrich conceptually, financial concepts and principles normally thought to account for all the essential aspects of financial transactions.

Boundary objects are essentially natural objects or phenomena that have been extracted from their natural setting and that lend themselves to multiple analyses or interpretations. In many current formulations they are said to exist in more than one "social world" (after Strauss 1978, 1984), which means that they can be interpreted differently in different social and/or professional contexts. However, there is much evidence that they facilitate the negotiation of shared understanding or concerted action across those worlds. In other words, they facilitate boundary crossing and learning across disciplinary and professional boundaries. They often function to disrupt prior understandings, thereby creating the necessary *conditions of possibility for learning to occur* (cf. Fairclough 2004).

Different types of boundary objects are listed in Star (1990) and Star and Griesemer (1989), though the lists were not intended to be exhaustive. Significantly, Star and Griesemer noted that boundary objects may be "abstract or concrete" (1989: 393). Since the original formulation (in Star 1990; Star and Griesemer 1989), the definition of boundary objects has been expanded in practice to encompass not only technologies and other "objects" but also human beings.

According to Frost, Reich, and Fujisaki (2002: 92), "boundary objects can be things, ideas, processes, and they can also be people" (see also Star 2005). Engineers, architects and draughtsmen have widely applied the concept to representations, drawings, models – both virtual and physical – and prototypes. Thus, according to our premise, the concept covers certain types of "reportative" texts and – more precisely – the problems and cases re-presented in the texts.

Recent work suggests that even artificial objects and created phenomena – i.e. artefacts and simulations – can function as boundary objects for cross-boundary learning and teaching. In a recent application relevant to training and education, Fleischmann (2006: 78) describes the use of cyber-cadavers (human anatomy simulations) in a medical training context, categorizing educational computer simulations as "boundary objects that arise at the intersection of the social worlds of education and information technology." The technology was viewed by the educational administrators as a "comprehensive, self-directed learning resource" (Fleischmann 2006: 81). More recently, Falconer (2007: 155) has worked on the level of knowledge acquisition or learning and has problematised "the practical operation of mediating concepts" (cf. Löwy [1992] on "boundary concepts" and Davies [2006] on "threshold concepts"); she argues that "for effective transfer of concepts between communities, the communities need to overlap to the extent that a single representation is comprehensible to both". Falconer goes on to claim that "[t]his representation may be viewed as a boundary object that is used to negotiate understanding" (2007: 155). Another recent discussion of boundary objects sees them as pushing boundaries and destabilising protocols, rather than sailing across them to facilitate communication and coordination (Lee 2007: 307). This implies category change and conceptual development, or learning.

All of the applications referred to above resonate with the developing nature of our own project in the second site, where we have found that the reconceptualisation of the texts around which teaching-and-learning materials (such as exercises, problems and tasks) cluster as *boundary objects* potentially leads to subtle but far-reaching changes in the management of these boundary objects and of the interactions that are designed to accompany them. These interactions, cognitive and/or verbal, constitute a narrative of the way that each learner traces a unique journey through the set of designed options. That narrative will consist of (for example, and in any order) reading critically and analytically, writing summary answers, reflecting on apparent contradictions or anomalies, applying concepts in simulated contexts of situation, making decisions and/or advising imagined clients. Such activities are illustrated by our own teaching-and-learning materials.

Its many applications also attest to the heuristic power of the boundary object concept for applied linguistics and in particular for a reconceptualisation of pedagogical design and the nature of learning materials. It has already been used in discourse analytical research (see Atkinson, Parsons and Featherstone 2001). It builds usefully on the work of Goodwin (1994: 606) who characterised pre-interpreted objects of potential professional interest as "domains of scrutiny". For Goodwin, a disciplinary "object of knowledge" emerges through the interplay between a "domain of scrutiny" (which may be anything from a patch of ground to an observed and recorded real-time event) and a set of "discursive practices" (which divide up the domain of scrutiny, by applying specific coding schemes, within a *specific activity* (e.g. mapping a terrain, arguing a legal case, etc.). That is, domains of scrutiny are subject to discursive interpretation, within generic sites of engagement, before becoming meaningful "objects" for a particular profession or discipline. Goodwin's domains of scrutiny thus correspond rather closely to the boundary objects of those working in different paradigms (especially symbolic interactionism). Moreover, they have the potential to be recursively and reflexively co-problematised by professional and/or disciplinary specialists working within different professional or disciplinary discourses, leading to boundary crossings and even the partial erasure of those boundaries. Meanwhile, Goodwin's discursive practices clearly resonate with Cicourel's "interpretive procedures" (Cicourel 1974; Sarangi 2007), albeit reconceptualised as germane to a professional discourse grounded in networks and taxonomies of more or less well-defined technical concepts.

5.   Scaffolding boundary objects to mediate teaching-and-learning

One of the most problematic areas for teaching-and-learning across the boundaries of individual disciplines and professions, within which relatively stable terminologies and standard definitions are used to categorise real-world situations and to identify and solve problems, is the existence of terms that have a different sense and *valeur* in the different disciplinary or professional discourses. Relevant examples here are *authority*, *consideration* and *liability*. In selecting or designing learning materials to facilitate professional boundary crossings by finance professionals, and in constructing interactive exercises and tasks around these, it is necessary to lead the finance professionals away from their own uses of such key terms and to introduce them to their crucial legal dimensions and uses. The academic lawyer has, through collaborative problematisation in the second site, become increasingly sensitised to the need to check for possibly disparate understandings of fundamental terms/concepts. Sometimes the distinct conceptual meanings of shared terms are obvious; on other occasions, crucial differences are only teased out in reflective interaction with colleagues or through misconceptions that become evident in classroom discussions (a natural place for this to happen, according to Davies [2006]). In either case, overlapping terms such as these present us with teaching opportunities as well as challenges, representing boundary concepts that "are adaptable to local sites and may facilitate communication and cooperation"; they "simultaneously delimit and link" territories and discourses (Löwy 1992: 374–375).

The term *liability* (and *liabilities*) will provide a useful illustration (see Jones and McCracken [2007] on *authority*). The term has a relatively ill-defined but generally understood meaning (i.e. anything that acts as a hindrance or disadvantage), while also appearing in the two different professional discourses under discussion with very different specialised meanings and with different connotations. The initial issue for the academic lawyer, before she can attempt to teach the content of the substantive legal rules relating to possible liability, is how she can enable the finance professionals to recognise the subtle and shifting legal usage of these terms and to appreciate the need to start looking at their habitual actions in a new way. Finance professionals for the most part understand these terms very concretely, as meaning "amount or amounts owed", picturing *a debt* as a common example. If the term is used in the plural, they may visualise a company balance sheet showing assets and liabilities. They frequently characterise liabilities as the opposite of assets, reasoning that if an asset is "what you own", a liability may be described as "what you owe" (Carew 1985). The notion of "owing" appears in fact to be critical to the finance professionals and is encompassed in other common explanations of the term which they provide, such as "an obligation to make payment to another" (Gastineau and Kritzman 1999). Sometimes a more general reference can be found, as in the description "anything owing to somebody else" (Hindle 1985). The latter description starts to encroach on the legal understanding of *liability*. While legally the term may certainly mean an amount owed, it is most often used in the more abstract sense of a duty or obligation (see e.g. *Oxford Dictionary of Law* 2003) or even the state of being subject to an obligation (Bone and Osborn 2001). The term is frequently described judicially as "chameleon-hued" (a phrase introduced into legal debates about legal and non-legal language by Hohfeld [1913]). Several fairly distinct usages in common legal parlance can easily be identified:

> ... there are at least three main senses in which lawyers speak of a liability or liabilities. The first, a legal obligation or duty; the second the consequence of a breach of such an obligation or duty; the third a situation in which a duty or obligation can arise as the result of the occurrence of some act or event.
> (Windeyer, Ogden Industries Pty Ltd v Lucas, 1967)[1]

However, the terminological ambiguity of *liability* runs deeper than this insofar as the term is always interpreted contingently in specific contexts of use, using more or less explicit discursive practices or interpretive procedures. It can be, moreover, interpreted strategically (both by participants and commentators); though its actual meaning-in-use is typically negotiated in interaction with other stakeholders or interlocutors. The interactional context is acknowledged to be critical by lawyers (McHugh 1999)[2] just as it has been by ethnographers since Malinowski (1923) and discourse analysts with a commitment to ethnography (Duranti and Goodwin 1992). Cicourel (1992: 223) has drawn particular attention to the role played by "systematically codified knowledge" as well as to the training processes and professional experience through which this knowledge is turned into practical reasoning. Cicourel (2007: 746) also refers to the "coding strategies" involved in the actual use of codified knowledge (while emphasising the institutional force exercised thereby).

Exercises must therefore be developed which will probe the meaning of liability in the sense used by lawyers. One typical exercise is set out below by way of example. It may be viewed as the equivalent in a language learning context to a comprehension passage. Under a *linguistically scaffolded curriculum* (a term introduced in Jones and McCracken [2007]), passages that in a language program would be regarded as comprehension exercises can be used to test understanding of a concept. Appropriate passages can be taken from legal texts, such as statutes or court judgments or created to suit a particular topic. Often it is necessary to start with a passage that is specially created for the purpose in order to introduce the concept and to highlight the differences in meaning, depending on the perspective.

Examine the following narrative closely. Try to imagine yourself in the role described. Can you identify elements of the narrative that indicate or suggest a possible liability for any person?

You work for Rainco Ltd, a company specialising in water installation systems. You attended a corporate function last night and overheard Rainco's chairman telling several potential joint venturers that Rainco was going through a period of growth and that its balance sheet was healthy. You mention this to your manager who is Rainco's CFO. You know she has been concerned about the company's cash-flow problems over the last 6 months. These have been caused in part by an unusually high number of customers failing to pay invoices on time. Some $200,000 is currently outstanding. She tells you not to worry about the conversations and to carry on with finalising the arrangements for delivery of some new high-tech machinery which she bought last week at a trade fair. She deposited $100,000 with the supplier, but the balance is due at the end of this week. She suggests you contact Rainco's bank and arrange for a funds transfer from the operating account.

In the passage above, we constructed a boundary object designed to activate and contextualise the legal concept of liability and the knowledge schema that it implicates. This object takes the form of a short narrative text. Written in the second person singular, it inserts the reader into a dynamic situation susceptible of being interpreted in terms of the focal concept, liability. At the same time use of the second person singular allots the reader a central role in deciding how that situation will unfold (the positive effects of assigned roles on legal "problem detection" have been highlighted by Stratman 2002). Two of the prompts are directive and act to guide cognition. The third is in the form of a request and a challenge. To satisfy the challenge, the finance professional (in the simultaneous roles of imagining learner and virtual participant) must activate previously acquired knowledge, including definitions of liability (see above), and find elements of the events described that implicate that concept. This task is designed to assist learners to acknowledge the specialised way in which they themselves ordinarily use the term, *in contrast to legal usage*. Having begun (through this exercise) to recognise that liability in the legal sense can extend beyond amounts due and owing, a finance professional next needs to reflect on *the extent* of liability that arises in a particular situation and to consider how that may be defined and constrained by law.

Another more complex boundary object (containing two authentic texts) is illustrated by the following exercise. It is designed to test learners' familiarity with both statutory and judicial terminology and discourse relevant to a company director's liability and their capacity to interpret specific legal rules in that regard. A fairly long and internally complex text setting out a certain statutory provision is provided for examination by the finance professionals; this is followed by a passage of judicial reasoning taken from a court judgment that can be used to assist in interpreting that provision (although it in fact related to an earlier version of the provision). The prompt that follows these two texts requires the finance professionals to do two things. They must answer a particular question on the provision, so they will need to process that first text very thoroughly. And, secondly, they are required to recapitulate the court's reasoning, so they will need to follow some very abstract legal argumentation and (to some extent) make it their own by enacting it. The two tasks together constrain learners to absorb a very complex stipulation – made complex by the number of contingencies the reader is asked to process and recall – and then to understand how a court would apply it.

What follows is a section of the Australian Corporations Act 2001. Study it carefully.

Section 197(1) of the Corporations Act 2001 (Cth) states:

> *A person who is a director of a corporation when it incurs a liability while acting, or purporting to act, as trustee, is liable to discharge the whole or a part of the liability if the corporation:*
>
> *(a) has not discharged, and cannot discharge, the liability or that part of it; and*
>
> *(b) is not entitled to be fully indemnified against the liability out of trust assets solely because of one or more of the following:*
>
> > *(i)   a breach of trust by the corporation;*
> >
> > *(ii)   the corporation's acting outside the scope of its powers as trustee;*
> >
> > *(iii)   a term of the trust denying, or limiting, the corporation's right to be indemnified against the liability.*
>
> *The person is liable both individually and jointly with the corporation and anyone else who is liable under this subsection.*
>
> *Note: The person will not be liable under this subsection merely because there are insufficient trust assets out of which the corporation can be indemnified.*

The next text is an (abbreviated) judgment in which the judge, considering an earlier version of the provision, explains the purpose of the provision (Phillips J, *Young v Murphy*, 1994).[3]

> *The section operates, in my view, not simply because the trustee "incurs a liability", but because, in the circumstances of the case, the trustee is precluded from having resort to the assets of the trust in respect of that liability. The section creates an alternative source for the satisfaction of the liability, where the liability is not to be met out of the assets because of the circumstances in which the liability was incurred. ... [T]he section had in contemplation, by its very terms, that the assets might have been reached for the purpose of indemnifying the trustee in respect of the liability, had it not been for the circumstances in which the liability was incurred ... [W]here the trustee is sought to be made liable to the beneficiaries for breach of trust, it is not the case that the assets might have been used for the purpose of indemnifying the trustee, were it not for the trustee's breach of trust.. [T]he section is there for the benefit of the creditors, not for the benefit of the beneficiaries ... [T]he section is to meet a liability incurred in breach of trust, but not a liability incurred for breach of trust.*

Your question is: To whom are the liabilities owed – the beneficiaries under the trust or the creditors of the trustee? Study the wording of the provision and the judgment and prepare an answer along with a justification for that answer.

6.   Conclusion

We have focused in this paper on the role of an applied linguist in jointly prob-lematising, in a second site, with an academic lawyer, the task of enabling those from outside a specific professional discourse community – i.e. "non-members" – to cross a professional boundary so as to access and acquire the fundamental concepts and principles of the legal discourse of risk while remaining outside the legal discourse community. We have effectively shown that close collabor-ation between an applied linguist and a subject specialist within a targeted dis-ciplinary or professional discourse can radically modify the latter's pedagogical approach to and design of learning materials. The changes involve the construc-tion or selection of focal texts, and construction of the prompts that accompany them. These prompts embody the instructor's voice, but it is a *voice tempered by interactions with the applied linguist in the second site.* We have argued that the constructed or authentic texts around which carefully scaffolded task environ-ments have been constructed function as *boundary objects,* mediating com-munication and learning between discourse communities, and rendering dis-parate discourse systems visible to one another while subtly *destabilising them* in an effort to create the necessary conditions of learning.

In the collaborative problematisation that takes place in the second site, the applied linguist sometimes adopts a passive and reactive role and sometimes an active one, often finding himself in the role of the novice learner, albeit with the space and confidence to express incomprehension when faced with unwarranted assumptions of successful learning or prior knowledge. The ability to perform this role is an essential feature of effective pedagogy (Marton and Booth 1997: 179): the teacher "takes the part of the learner" and in this way "becomes aware of the experience through the learner's experience". The second site is a space apart where key legal concepts pertaining to finance are explained, decon-structed, queried or challenged. It is a *critical* space in which alternative mean-ings are juxtaposed and represented situations and events are given alternative interpretations. And it is a space where the ground is laid for emergent forms of interprofessional discursivity in the first site. The learning materials developed in this second site are primarily for use in the teaching of conceptual and decla-rative knowledge *through* language, but it would be surprising if the linguistic proficiency and discursive skills of the students did not simultaneously improve.

Although our current project targets finance professionals and their under-standing of legal risk, we would argue that similar collaborations, and linguisti-cally scaffolded learning materials, could be equally useful in other interdisci-plinary or interprofessional learning contexts *where conceptual understanding and declarative knowledge are key learning objectives.* This is a comparatively new frontier for linguists, qua applied linguists, raising questions about the roles that linguists can and perhaps should be playing in the complex, increasingly specialised society of the 21st century. Professional boundaries are as strongly enforced as before, but individual expertise is increasingly interdisciplinary and *layered*. The collaboration described here suggests new ways in which the sharing of linguistic expertise and the building of language awareness can contribute to a wide range of problem-solving and teaching/learning practices, in an array of old and new occupations, professions and fields, and (as here) to the design and use of boundary-spanning learning objects, activities and curriculum.

Notes

1. *Ogden Industries Pty Ltd v Lucas* [1967] HCA 30 paras 14, 20 per Windeyer J.
2. See *Crimmins v Stevedoring Industry Finance Committee* [1999] HCA 59 paras 137–139 per McHugh J.
3. *Young v Murphy* [1994] 13 ACSR 722 at 760 per Phillips J.

References

Atkinson, Paul, Evelyn Parsons and Katie Featherstone
    2001   Professional constructions of family and kinship in medical genetics. *New Genetics and Society* 20(1): 5–24.
Bone, Sheila and Percy G. Osborn
    2001   *Osborn's Concise Law Dictionary,* 9th revised edn. London: Sweet & Maxwell.
Bowker, Geoffrey and Susan Leigh Star
    1999   *Sorting Things Out: Classification and its Consequences*. Cambridge MA: MIT Press.
Brinton, Donna M., Marguerite Anne Snow and Marjorie Wesche
    1989   *Content-Based Second Language Instruction*. New York: Newbury House.
Carew, Edna
    1985   *The Language of Money*. Sydney: Allen and Unwin.
Cicourel, Aaron V.
    1974   *Cognitive Sociology: Language and Meaning in Social Interaction*. New York: Free Press.
Cicourel, Aaron V.
    1992   The interpenetration of communicative contexts: examples from medical encounters. In: Alessandro Duranti and Charles Goodwin (eds.), *Rethinking Context: Language as an Interactive Phenomenon,* 291–310. Cambridge: Cambridge University Press.
Cicourel, Aaron V.
    2007   A personal, retrospective view of ecological validity. *Text & Talk* 27(5/6): 735–752.
Crandall, JoAnn (ed.)
    1987   *ESL through Content-Area Instruction: Mathematics, Science, Social Studies*. Englewood Cliffs, NJ: Prentice-Hall.

Crossling, Glenda and Anne V. Wilson
   2005   Creating a rich environment: Cooperation between academic support and disciplinary teaching staff. Papers from *Language and Academic Skills in Higher Education Conference*, Australian National University, November 24–25, 2005. https://academicskills.anu.edu.au/las2005/las_papers.php (accessed 8–1–08).

Davies, Peter
   2006   Threshold concepts: How can we recognise them? In: J. H. F. Meyer and Ray Land (eds.), *Overcoming Barriers to Student Learning: Threshold Concepts and Troublesome Knowledge*, 70–84. London, Routledge.

Derry, Sharon J., Christian D. Schunn and Morton Ann Gernsbacher
   2005   *Interdisciplinary Collaboration: An Emerging Cognitive Science.* Mahwah, NJ: Lawrence Erlbaum Associates.

Duranti, Alessandro and Charles Goodwin (eds.)
   1992   *Rethinking Context: Language as an Interactive Phenomenon.* Cambridge: Cambridge University Press.

Eurydice
   2006   Content and language integrated learning (CLIL) at school in Europe: Comparative studies. Brussels: Eurydice. http://www.eurydice.org/ressources/eurydice/pdf/0_integral/071EN.pdf (accessed 6 June 2008).

Fairclough, Norman
   2004   Semiotic aspects of social transformation and learning. In: Rebecca Rogers (ed.), *New Directions in Critical Discourse Analysis: Semiotic Aspects of Social Transformation and Learning,* 225–236. Mahwah, NJ: Lawrence Erlbaum Associates.

Falconer, Isobel
   2007   Mediating between practitioner and developer communities – the Learning Activity Design in Education experience (LADiE). *ALT-J [Association for Learning Technology Journal] – Research in Learning Technology* 15(2): 155–170.

Fleischmann, Kenneth R.
   2006   Boundary objects with agency: A method for studying the design-use interface. *The Information Society* 22: 77–87.

Frost, Laura, Michael R. Reich and Tomoko Fujisaki
   2002   A Partnership for Ivermectin: Social worlds and boundary objects. In: Michael R. Reich (ed.), *Public-Private Partnerships for Public Health.* Cambridge, MA: Harvard Centre for Populations and Development Studies.

Gastineau, Gary L. and Mark P. Kritzman
   1999   *Dictionary of Financial Risk Management,* 3rd edn. New York: John Wiley + Sons.

Goffman, Erving
   1959   *The Presentation of Self in Everyday Life.* New York: Doubleday Books.

Gollin, Sandra
   1999   Why? I thought we'd talked about it before: Collaborative writing in a professional workplace setting. In: Christopher N. Candlin and Ken Hyland (eds.), *Writing: Texts, processes, practices*, 267–290. London: Longman.

Goodwin, Charles
   1994   Professional Vision. *American Anthropologist* 96(3): 606–633.
Hindlc, Tim
   1985   *The Economist Pocket Banker*. New York and London: Blackwell and The Economist.
Hohfeld, Wesley N.
   1913   Some fundamental legal conceptions as applied in juridical reasoning. *Yale Law Journal* 23: 16–59.
Jacobs, Cecilia
   2005   On being an insider on the outside: New spaces for integrating academic literacies. *Teaching in Higher Education* 10(4): 475–487.
Jones, Alan and Samantha Sin
   2003   *Generic Skills for Accounting: Competencies for Students and Graduates*. Sydney: Prentice Hall / Pearson Education.
Jones, Alan and Samantha Sin
   2004   The integration of language and content: Action research based on a theory of task design. *Journal of Applied Linguistics* 1(1): 95–100.
Jones, Alan and Sheelagh McCracken
   2007   Teaching the discourse of legal risk to finance professionals: Foundations for a linguistically scaffolded curriculum. In: Robert Wilkinson and Vera Zegers (eds.), *Researching Content and Language Integration in Higher Education*, 122–136. Nijmegen, Maastricht: Valkhof Pers and Maastricht University.
Klein, Julie Thompson
   1996   *Crossing Boundaries: Knowledge, Disciplinarities, and Interdisciplinarities*. Charlottesville, VA: University Press of Virginia.
Klein, Julie Thompson
   2005   *Humanities, Culture, and Interdisciplinarity: The Changing American Academy*. Albany, NY: State University of New York Press.
Knorr Cetina, Karin
   1999   *Epistemic Cultures: How the Sciences Make Knowledge*. Cambridge, MA: Harvard University Press.
Krueger, Merle and Frank Ryan
   1993   *Language and Content: Discipline- and Content-Based Approaches to Language Study*. Lexington, MA: Heath and Company.
Latour, Bruno
   1987   *Science in Action: How to Follow Scientists and Engineers through Society*. Cambridge, MA: Harvard University Press.
Lave, Jean
   1991   *Situated Learning: Legitimate Peripheral Participation*. Cambridge: University of Cambridge Press.
Lee, Charlotte P.
   2007   Boundary Negotiating Artifacts: Unbinding the Routine of Boundary Objects and Embracing Chaos in Collaborative Work. *Computer Supported Cooperative Work* 16: 307–339.
Löwy, Ilana
   1992   The strength of loose concepts: Boundary concepts, federative experimental strategies and disciplinary growth: The case of immunology. *History of Science* 30(4): 371–96.

Malinowski, Bronislav
1923   The problem of meaning in primitive languages. In: Charles K. Ogden and
        Ivor A. Richards (eds.), *The Meaning of Meaning,* 146–152. London: Rout-
        ledge and Kegan Paul.
Marton, Ference and Shirley Booth
1997   *Learning and Awareness.* Mahway, NJ: Lawrence Erlbaum Associates.
Mertz, Elizabeth
2007   *The Language of Law School: Learning to "Think Like a Lawyer".* New
        York: Oxford University Press.
Meyer, Jan and Ray Land
2003   *Threshold concepts and troublesome knowledge: Linkages to ways of think-
        ing and practices within the disciplines. Occasional Report 4.* Edinburgh:
        ETL Project.
Mohan, Bernard A.
1986   *Language and Content.* Reading, MA: Addison-Wesley.
Nystrand, Martin (ed.)
1982   *What Writers Know: The Language, Process, and Structure of Written Dis-
        course.* New York: Academic Press.
Oxford Dictionary Of Law (5th edn.)
2003   Oxford: Oxford University Press.
Pask, Gordon
1976   *Conversation Theory: Applications in Education and Epistemology.* Am-
        sterdam: Elsevier.
Roberts, Celia and Srikant Sarangi
1999a   Introduction: Revisiting different analytic frameworks. In: Srikant Sarangi
        and Celia Roberts (eds.), *Talk, Work and Institutional Order: Discourse
        in Medical, Mediation and Management Settings,* 389–400. Berlin / New
        York: Mouton de Gruyter.
Roberts, Celia and Srikant Sarangi
1999b   Hybridity in gatekeeping discourse: Issues of practical relevance for the
        researcher. In: Srikant Sarangi and Celia Roberts (eds.), *Talk, Work and
        Institutional Order: Discourse in Medical, Mediation and Management
        Settings,* 473–503. Berlin / New York: Mouton de Gruyter.
Sarangi, Srikant
2002   Discourse practitioners as a community of interprofessional practice: Some
        insights from health communication research. In: Christopher N. Candlin
        (ed.), *Research and Practice in Professional Discourse,* 95–135. Hong
        Kong: City University of Hong Kong Press.
Sarangi, Srikant
2007   The anatomy of interpretation: coming to terms with the analyst's paradox
        in professional discourse studies. *Text & Talk* 27(5/6):567–584.
Sarangi, Srikant and Christopher N. Candlin
2001   "Motivational relevancies": Some methodological reflections on social the-
        oretical and sociolinguistic practice. In: Nikolas Coupland, Srikant Sarangi
        and Christopher N. Candlin (eds.), *Sociolinguistics and Social Theory,*
        350–388. London: Pearson.
Scollon, Ron
1998   *Mediated Discourse as Social Interaction.* London: Longman.

Sin, Samantha, Alan Jones and Peter Petocz
    2007   Evaluating a method of integrating generic skills with accounting content based on a functional theory of meaning. *Accounting & Finance* 47(1): 143–163.
Snow, Marguerite Anne, Myriam Met and Fred Genesee
    1987   A conceptual framework for the integration of language and content in second/foreign language instruction. *TESOL Quarterly* 23(2): 201–217.
Star, Susan Leigh
    1990   The structure of ill-structured solutions: Boundary objects and heterogeneous distributed problem solving. In: L. Gasser and M. Huhns (eds.), *Distributed Artificial Intelligence*, Vol. II (Morgan Kaufmann Series in Research Notes in Artificial Intelligence), 37–54. London: Pitman.
Star, Susan Leigh
    2005   Categories and cognition: Material and conceptual aspects of large-scale category systems. In: Sharon J. Derry, Christian D. Schunn and Morton Ann Gernsbacher (eds.), *Interdisciplinary Collaboration: An Emerging Cognitive Science*, 167–186. Mahwah, NJ: Lawrence Erlbaum Associates.
Star, Susan Leigh and James R. Griesemer
    1989   Institutional ecology, "Translations" and boundary objects: Amateurs and professionals in Berkeley's Museum of Vertebrate Zoology, 1907–1939. *Social Studies of Science* 19(3): 387–420.
Stoller, Frederika L.
    2004   Content-based instruction: Perspectives on curriculum planning. *Annual Review of Applied Linguistics* 24: 261–283.
Stratman, James F.
    2002   When law students read cases: Exploring relations between professional and legal reasoning roles and problem detection. *Discourse Processes* 34(1): 57–90.
Strauss, Anselm
    1978   A social world perspective. *Studies in Symbolic Interaction* 1: 119–128.
Strauss, Anselm
    1984   Social worlds and their segmentation processes. *Studies in Symbolic Interaction* 5: 123–139.
Swales, John
    1990   *Genre Analysis*. Cambridge: Cambridge University Press.
Wenger, Etienne
    1998   *Communities of Practice: Learning, Meaning, and Identity.* Cambridge: Cambridge University Press.
Wilkinson, Robert (ed.)
    2004   *Integrating Content and Language: Meeting the Challenge of a Multilingual Higher Education.* Maastricht: Maastricht University Press.
Wilkinson, Robert and Vera Zegers (eds.)
    2007   *Researching Content and Language Integration in Higher Education.* Nijmegen, Maastricht: Valkhof Pers and Maastricht University.

22. Analytic challenges in studying professional learning

David Middleton[1]

Abstract

This chapter discusses how communicative analysis was introduced and used by a research team located across four UK Universities engaged in a longitudinal multi-site intervention study of professional learning. The research project, "Learning in and for interagency working" faced a number of analytical challenges. These included how to move from framing inter-professional communication as descriptions corresponding to states in and of the world to an analytic focus on the sequential organization of communicative action – a shift of focus aimed at revealing the emergence of professional learning in children's services responding in a multi-agency way to the complex phenomena of social exclusion.

We then describe an analytic protocol focused on emergent issues and distinction designed to support a multi-centred cross-site analysis of what it was to learn to work in a multi-agency way as the research sites were moving on from carefully targeted children's services and were instead introducing more fluid ways of working. This work highlights the reflexive relationship between analysis and emergent findings in a longitudinal study of professional learning.

1. Background

This chapter discusses how communicative analysis was introduced and used by a research team located across four UK Universities engaged in a longitudinal multi-site intervention study of professional learning. It draws upon a UK Economic and Social Research Council (ESRC) funded project: "Learning in and for interagency" (LIW). This research project focussed on how professionals were learning to respond in a multi-agency way to the complex phenomena of social exclusion. Such professional learning was in response to the British Government's Children Act of 2004 demanding that practitioners from different professions collaborate to prevent the social exclusion of children and young people. Between 2004 and 2007 we worked with educational psychologists, children and families workers, teachers, education welfare officers, health professionals, speech and language therapists and voluntary sector workers who were working together in new ways. We selected research sites that were moving on from carefully targeted services; and were instead introducing more fluid ways of working which recognised the complexity of children's trajectories of social exclusion. The sites offered different configurations of professionals including new multi-professional teams and more loosely coupled arrangements of team-working for specific groups of children, enabling us to look across the options of service configuration emerging after the Children Act.

2.   Research scenario

As a central element in the study we set up series of structured intervention sessions in the case-study sites. Using the analytic resources of Cultural Historical Activity Theory professionals identified contradictions in their own everyday understandings of practice. Over a period of twelve months professionals at each of the main case sites were provided with the analytic resources to enable them to explore and identify the challenges they faced in learning to work in a multi-agency way.

For the purposes of this chapter it is not necessary to go into the details of Cultural Historical Activity Theory (CHAT) (see for example Engeström 1987, 2001, 2007) rather the aim is to illustrate and reflect on how a form of communicative analysis was introduced to enable us to examine the emergence of professional learning in a longitudinal multi-site study.[2] As a multi-centred project located across four Universities employing both University based research officers and also those who were seconded from the study sites we therefore faced a number of analytical challenges.

The intervention sessions had resulted in an extensive corpus of conversational data reflecting upon and developing the multi-agency practices at each site. As the intervention progressed at each site we had engaged in detailed CHAT based analysis for selecting material for use in subsequent sessions. However, once all the data was in we needed to identify how work based learning emerged at each site. In order to do this we needed a comprehensive analysis of the organisation of communicative action in the intervention sessions. Members of the research team were mostly familiar with, and expert in the use of CHAT based analysis used in the research. However, such analysis tends to take a top down approach to selected data in applying theoretical and conceptual resources. One of the key analytical challenges of the study was to move from a top-down selective analysis based in the CHAT concepts used in the intervention phase of the project, to a "bottom-up" comprehensive analysis of the organisation of communicative action in the intervention sessions.

The majority of the research team were unfamiliar with ways of analysing session talk as a communicative accomplishment. We therefore faced the general analytic challenge of how to introduce the *raison d'etre* for communicative analysis to research team members drawn from four universities working across three research sites – sites which were also represented by a local research associate who facilitated and engaged in the research interventions. Each site had an analytic team of two research officers, a senior research discussant and a local research associate. We also needed to address the particular research challenge of how we might develop an analytic heuristic, or protocol, for within, and cross-site, analysis of communicative action in the CHAT based intervention sessions.[3]

3.   Orienting the research team to communicative analysis

We introduced the research team to the general analytic framing of communicative analysis by describing how it involved a shift from the "given" to the "to-be-established". For example, we discussed how "what-it-is-to-do multi-agency work" or "to learn" need not be assumed as an analytic "a priori" (Middleton 2004). Rather such issues are approached as participants' concerns or "members categories" (Sacks 1992; Edwards and Stokoe 2004; Stokoe 2006). This analytic shift aimed to move from framing communication as descriptions corresponding to states in and of the world, to the performative organization of communicative action. In other words, what professionals did with talk and text can be analysed in terms of what it accomplishes (Potter and Wetherell 1987; Edwards and Potter; Edwards. 1992). For example, how do professionals use, account for, and warrant what it is to do multi-agency work, or what it is to be a team member? We emphasised that addressing such issues required a focus on the sequential and contingent organisation of talk in the intervention sessions.

As part of the move to communicative analysis we also illustrated the sorts of communicative devices people use. For example: how second stories are used to substantiate points (i.e., when one person produces an account others produce similar but different accounts. The differences between the 1st and 2nd stories (Sacks 1992) both legitimate and warrant claims to experience and provide an analytic resource for examining the stake and interest of those involved). In drawing analytical attention to the significance of claims to experience we were also able to highlight the temporal organisation of communicative action. As Mercer (2004) points out in his presentation of what he terms "socio-cultural discourse analysis", the performative aspects of communicative action extend beyond the immediacies of the situation of production.

> Things that are said may invoke knowledge from the joint past experience of those interacting (e.g. their recall of previous activities they have pursued together), or from the rather different kind of "common knowledge" which is available to people who have had similar, though separate, past experiences.
> (Mercer 2004: 140)

Just as Mercer develops an analytic framework for the analysis of the development of common understandings in classroom interactions, we also used forms of communicative analysis to trace the emergence of what can be taken as the collective and distributed knowledge of people who are charged with the task of working together. Our aim was to introduce and use communicative analysis for tracking how relevant distinctions concerning multi-agency working were established and made to stick in the emergent learning of what it takes to practice such forms of working. In other words, we aimed to track the emergence practical epistemologies (cf Wickman and Östman 2002; Wickman 2004) that come and need to be taken-as-given in order to take account of hitherto unaddressed gaps in the realisation of multi-agency practice. Such gaps were identified and worked on through participation in six intervention sessions held over a twelve-month period at each research site.

As we have already indicated the general analytical challenge was how to introduce and engage the whole of the research team in the conduct of analysis focused on the organization of communicative action. In order to do this research team members were given an induction and orientation to communicative analysis. This focused on two lines of analysis. First, what forms of communicative action went into the production of the sessions as a context for intervening and research. Once we had oriented the research team to what might be accomplished with and through the analysis of communicative action we turned to a second phase of piloting, comparing, refining, applying, cross-site collating of the research data. The primary focus of this was on the emergence of what-it-is-to-learn as an analytic object across the sessions.

In summary, the induction and orientation to communicative analysis focused on what the interactive and sequential organisation of professional talk could tell us about the emergent organisation of the intervention sessions. In addition we also examined the emergent engagement of participants as the sessions progressed.

4.   Visibility of learning in communicative action

As we have already discussed, the aim of the intervention sessions was to build upon professionals' "everyday" understandings of multi-agency working, juxtaposing these with reflective analyses based in concepts derived from CHAT. The whole point of the sessions was to provide a forum where participants in multi-agency working could interrogate how their current working practices either enable or constrain the development of innovative multi-agency working. And on the basis of that interrogation we aimed identify how their work could or should be reconfigured in practice. Having equipped the research team with a basic perspective on how to approach the data in terms of the communicative analysis of participation, we turned to how we might look for communicative evidence of "learning". How might we examine the data for how participants formulated and made visible the consequences for them of session participation, as professionals who were mandated to work across professional boundaries and in relation to what they took to be their own professional competence? What forms of communicative action could we identify as demonstrating participants making visible "what-it-is-to-learn"? In the first instance we approach the data with what could be termed a minimal operationalisation of what-it-is-to-learn from a participant's perspective. We examined the data for ways participants signalled some forms of awareness that theirs or others' knowledge state is at issue. Identifying "news receipts", "announcements" and "noticings" provided a way of searching the data for claims concerning knowledge states. Discussing example forms of these brought into focus the notion of participant formulation of knowledge states. For example, claims can be made concerning "what-it-is-to-be-in-the-know".

Site A Session 3	*Lead Education Officer (LEO)*: I did not know that
Site B Session 2	*Education Welfare Officer (EWO)*: Don't ask me what they do I haven't got a clue
Site C Session 5	*Educational Psychologist (EP)*: I'll tell you what I've really noticed recently is …
Site A Session 5	*Social Worker (SW)*: Are we sharing that today – is that new?

Claims concerning knowledge states do of course need to be analysed in the context of their production for the work that they do. To claim not-to-know can be used, for example, in mitigation of individual and or collective failure to act, to account for some form of discursively marked error in terms of previous turns. Likewise to request, or question, the status of news would need to be analysed also in terms of its context of production. For example, formulating the collective significance of whether something is new ("Are we sharing that today – is that new?") provides a basis for making others accountable for the production of that news. The final example quoted above concerned the development of a new procedure involving social workers in facilitating the invitation of foster carers and children to health appointments. One of the social workers is explaining a potential mechanism for doing this.

Social Worker 1: With a copy letter to the social worker. There's no extra task for the social worker.

Social Worker 2: Are we sharing that today – is that new?

Social Worker 1:   Well I understand it's come – I mean it's just being introduced I think this month, or in September so it's not quite
this month, you know, it's just been introduced in September.

The response by the second social worker to the procedure in terms of "is that
new" (as the receipt of "news") positions the first social worker as accountable
for giving news. We see how the first social worker goes on to hedge or attenu-
ate any accountability for someone else not being-in-the-know in terms of how
recently the innovation in practice had been introduced. Claims concerning
states of knowledge are a marker of where participants make relevant some
form of distinction. If such claims to knowledge state changes are to matter in
the context of participation in the intervention sessions then we needed to develop a way of taking the analysis further in the pursuit of the visibilities of
learning in communicative action.

5.   Distinctions as a communicative accomplishment

One way to do this is to examine the ways in which distinctions concerning the
details of practice were worked up to make a difference. In other words, we focussed the research teams' analytic attention on how participants worked up the
significance of details of practice in ways that came to make the difference (cf.
Bateson 1972). The next example illustrates what we mean by a "distinction",
and how such distinctions were used by the participants in the sessions.

The following sequence is part of an extended discussion of what sort of
"rules" govern allocation of professional resources to schools that have on their
rolls numbers of children who are in public care and to what extent such "rules"
could be redefined or be subject to "bending" according to prevailing circumstance of need. The particular focus of attention at this point in the discussion
was on the service provision of educational psychology in those schools. All the
participants were professionals whose remit was to provide services to children
in public care – a group of children with recognised risks of social exclusion.

Site A Session 3
Participants: Teacher (T); Senior Educational Psychologist (SEP); Lead Education Officer (LEO)
T: Can I ask how is the time allocation to schools awarded? Do
you know what I mean, is it on like um previous problems in the
school or is it on exam results, or is it on percentage of free school
dinners?
SEP: yeah it's just on size of school mostly and a social indices. So um
primary schools get slightly more than secondary schools in terms

of size because they're smaller, but there's a baseline of number of sessions per annum that every school gets. And then it's done on free school meals, which are social indicators and, er and um size of school um …

LEO: I didn't know that.

T: So do "looked after" children appear in that equation at all?

SEP: No, no

LEO: Because if that's so they don't come from the area that they're actually being schooled in, do they necessarily.

SEP: No it's free school meals versus the school roll and the …

LEO: They're not necessarily on free school meals. And like you've got a school there that, I mean you are in an area that is classed as being high levels deprivation, but had you not been and you had 13 "looked after" children then that wouldn't necessarily be a good equation of time spent would it? And there's supported transfer system where you've got them going all over the show.

The teacher's question concerning the basis on which educational psychology resources are allocated to schools both identifies (nominates) time as a relevant distinction and sets up two candidate metrics on which allocation might be based ("problems in the school" or "percentage of free school dinners"). The Senior Educational Psychologist provides a detailed account of how both these are relevant in terms of time allocation. The metric is complex. Both "size of school" and "social indices" matter. However, it is more complicated than that. Relative to school size primary schools receive more sessions than secondary schools because all schools – no matter what their size – receive a "baseline number of sessions per annum". Furthermore, "free school dinners" are indeed one of the social indices that count towards the metrical allocation of educational psychology resources. The distinctions identified in the question have opened up a whole discursive space for delineating, defining and qualifying the ordering of educational psychology resources.

SEP's elaboration of this metric is received as news by the Lead Educational Officer ("I didn't know that") and in the second part question the Teacher identifies a further distinction concerning "looked after children" ("So do looked after children appear in that equation at all?"). SEP confirms that this is indeed so and we then see further delineation on the part of LEO expansively qualifying what is missing from the "equation" – "looked" after children do not necessarily live in the area in which they are schooled. SEP's ratification that this is the case provides a basis for further deliberation and consensus on the emergent problematic concerning these children ("No it's free school meals versus the school roll"). A further distinction is then drawn concerning these children's exclusion from the reckoning concerning the allocation of the Educational Psychology service's time. There is no necessity for "looked after" children" to be "on free school meals". Furthermore, you could have a "school that was classed as being high levels of deprivation" but unless you visited then you need not be aware that it had large numbers of "looked after" children. We see a deliberative consensus emerging concerning "equation of time" as not being "necessarily good". This putative conclusion is further evidenced in terms of yet another distinction, revealing a potential contradiction in current practice concerning a "supported transfer where you've got the children going all over the show". The key point is that the discussion is organised in terms of a series of emergent distinctions. Those distinctions are what make the difference. A difference that makes visible contradictions in practice that potentially should be attended to in terms of taking into account in the allocation of Educational Psychology services in relation to the presence of "looked after" children in schools.

Learning is clearly at issue here in the sense that such noticings provide the resource that engages the participants in their definition, delineation, and deliberation of the nature of the practices that make up their multi-disciplinary work. In the data we could identify many such strands of marking such distinctions that make the difference. Indeed this sort of analysis provided us with a basis for defining a protocol for guiding interrogation and analysis of the data in terms of the sequential organisation of such strands. The research team's analysis was therefore initially guided in terms of the following protocol:

Deixis: identify when there is some nomination or "pointing" to a particular issue in terms of drawing attention to a distinction that is then worked up to make a difference in subsequent turns.

Definition and delineation: look for how that issue is elaborated in the uptake of others in terms of how the following are warranted and made relevant through: (i) qualifications identifying further distinctions; (ii) orderabilities in the organisation and delivery of past, present and future practice; (iii) expansive elaborations of the problems of practice.

Deliberation: identify how some working consensus on what is the case emerges in terms of evoking both particularities and generalities of marking distinctive features of past, present or future practice.

The analysis then turned to examining the ways in which such sequences mattered. If we identified strands of deixis, definition/delineation and deliberation, what were their contingent consequences for participants? Did they make visible distinctions that made the difference in ways that participants could be identified as attending to what it was necessary to attend to in order to learn to do multi-agency working? In other words, did they lead to some form of departure or development in claims concerning the practice of the participants? This set of questions enabled us to complete the definition of the protocol with:

Departure: identify shifts towards qualitatively different position in practices in terms of the formulation of emergent distinctions.

Development: identify when participants specify new ways of working that provide the basis for becoming part of, or have become part of, what they take to be and warrant as a significant reformulation of their practices.

Overall the protocol itself emerged as an analytic rubric (what we termed the "D-Analysis" protocol) for identifying strands of learning in terms of the emergence of distinctions that made the difference for participants in their working towards multi-agency working. This is illustrated in the next section.

6.   Making distinctions matter

The following sequence is from the fourth intervention session at Site 3 – an "extended school" developing multi-agency service provision (see for example Wilkin, White and Kinder 2003). The sequence demonstrates a major shift in relation to how participants from different agencies and from within the school positioned themselves in terms of the use of a Common Assessment Framework (CAF). The development of the CAF forms part of the recommendations outlined in the Green Paper *Every Child Matters* (DfES 2003), and the Children Act (2004) guidance on how to move toward multi-agency working. CAF emerges as a tool for sharing information about families who are the clients of multi-agency services. At the time of the sessions the participants had not started to explore the implications of developing and using a CAF as part of their multi-agency work in an "extended school" setting. The sequence starts at the point where a new distinction is made relevant. This concerns the potential confusion of families when numbers of professionals converge on them in relation to the multi-agency services on offer. Applying the D-Analysis protocol provided a means to interrogate the data for sequences where distinctions were identified as mattering in terms of the ways in which multi-agency work could be accomplished. CAF emerges and is warranted as significant tool for both information sharing and the coordination of service provision.

Site 3 Session 4

Participants: Social Care and Health Support Worker (SCHS); Extended Schools Adviser 1 (ESA1); Extended Schools Adviser 2 (ESA2); Facilitator (F); Extended School Vice-principal (ESVP)

SCHS	It's a little bit as well about sharing information that a whole range of professionals may have about one family, um, and sharing that information just to let each other know what they are doing for this family. And to … as an example I think one was put forward where there were four different professionals visiting this one home on the same day all offering a very similar service, and no wonder the family, you know, they could be totally confused. And although all the help was being offered it may in the end not have been very helpful because of the confusion element.	*Deixis*: information sharing nominated as an issue and an example given
ESA1	And they have to repeat their story every time. [talking together].	*Delineation*: *Qualification* of the consequences of multiple visits from professionals resulting families having to repeat themselves
SCHS	Repeating the assessment of the family, so in a way they get sort of done to death, if you like, to find out what they're asking for. So in a way it's preventing that. It's simplifying things, making services available that make sense to families, er, and are easily accessible to them. And it's finding out the right person to do the right task depending on the problem that's being presented. We've all got strengths, we all, you know, have got lots of skills and expertise and we all do different things. So depending on the problem there's bound to be one that knows how to deal with that more than another.	*Delineation: Orderabilities* in the ways in which delivery could be "simplified" in terms of finding the right person for the task in hand vis-a-vis a particular family

F	So is that … I mean I absolutely agree with you, you put it beautifully and succinctly, but is that where this has gone, I mean, can you actually say that now Liberton is moving towards …	
SCHS	I think moving towards is better than gone, yes. So moving towards that. And I think …	
ESA2	It's the Common Assessment Framework really isn't it?	*Departure* in terms of identifying CAF as a tool for information sharing and coordinated consultation
SCHS	Yes.	
ESA2	I mean obviously the rollout of the Common Assessment Framework and lead professional will [unclear – 00:28:26], but will make a difference. And it could be that some of the preventative work that you talk about, um, needing to be done will happen through CAF and through the lead professional. And also it might be done before we even get to there. It might be done through Children's Centres or the primary schools. Um in a sense if we're looking at adolescent issues one would hope that if we can get this sorted, I know I'm talking long term, but they might have been identified and nipped in the bud pre adolescence.	*Development:* In terms of warranting the significance of developing the use of CAF
ESVP	That's what we hope isn't it?	

Having identified such a sequence where emergent distinctions are warranted as mattering in relation the development of multi-agency working, it was then possible to track through the subsequent discussion for how participants picked up and extended their discussion of CAF. In subsequent material from this session and the two further sessions held at the extended school site CAF was identified by participants not just as a means for sharing and coordinating visits but an object of work in and of itself. For example, how through their further refinement of CAF procedures they could involve parents directly in the ways that would enhance their access to the multi-agency service provision.

7.   Conclusion

This chapter has described the introduction and use of communicative analysis by a research team studying professional learning in multi-agency. We also described how we developed and applied an analytic protocol for the cross-site analysis of communicative action (what we termed "D-Analysis"). This was designed to focus the analytic attention of the research team on emergent distinctions that were argued by participants to matter as they engaged in the research interventions devised for use across each of the final three research sites. This protocol was used as a unit of analysis for examining the sequential organisation of session talk in terms of identifying distinctions that make the difference for participants in learning to do multi-agency work. It provided a basis for tracking the emergence of what-it-is-to-learn as an analytic focus of concern across sessions at each site. Its cyclical use enabled reading, reviewing, interrogating, collating and comparing all the audio-visual evidence from the intervention sessions in order to identify the emergent strands of learning.

The use of communicative analysis re-focussed research teams analytic attention in two main ways. First, it provided a means for making visible emergent forms of professional learning in longitudinal research intervention. Secondly, it also made visible the reflexive relationship between such analysis and the research team's emergent conceptual framing of the research findings. This allowed the analysis to be taken to the next stage (Daniels et al. 2005) where we addressed the question of how complex and highly contested social dilemmas (Billig 1996) were locally constituted as objects for institutional activity. In other words, how they became part of an institutional order (Smith 2005), which had no ready-made strategy for dealing with such dilemmas. The overall challenge of the project was to show how institutionally established categories and ways of arguing could be reformulated and transformed into new strategies and activities as part of learning what it is to become engaged with and in multi-agency work. However, without the comprehensive analysis of the communicative action within the sessions across all the research sites we would not have been able to progress to the final analysis of those transformations (see Daniels 2006).

Notes

1. In association with Steven Brown (Leicester University), Harry Daniels (Bath University), Anne Edwards (Oxford University), Jane Leadbetter (Birmingham University), Paul Warmington (Birmingham University).
2. Please see Edwards et al. (2008) for a full presentation of how CHAT was used in the project directed by Harry Daniels (Bath University) and Anne Edwards (Oxford University). The project was one of a twelve that comprised Phase III of ESRC's Teaching

and Learning Research Programme (TLRP) and ran from January 2004 to March 2008. Two years into the study, a research team led by Tony Gallagher (Queen's University, Belfast), received TLRP funding to extend the LIW work in Northern Ireland.
3. It should also be noted that in order to handle the diversity of material gathered at the empirical sites, and to coordinate analysis across four universities, it was necessary to develop accessible archiving of the primary data and clear protocols for maintaining the coherency of the analysis across the centres. Systematic archiving protocols were developed to support in-depth communicative analysis of the audio and video taped recorded material. All recordings were made on the basis of maintaining the confidentiality of the participants. Permissions allowed use of anonymised transcripts. To facilitate secure access to primary data sources (video and audio recordings and transcriptions) we used web based virtual learning environments (VLE's) for archiving resources that were available at two of the University sites ("WebCT" at one and "Moodle" at the other). These VLE's provided us with generic tools for archiving and granted secure on-line access to the research team members at distributed sites.

References

Bateson, Gregory
    1972   *Steps to an Ecology of Mind.* Chicago: University of Chicago Press.
Billig, Michael
    1996   *Arguing and Thinking: A Rhetorical View of Social Psychology.* Cambridge, England: Cambridge University Press.
Daniels, Harry, Steven D. Brown, Anne Edwards, Jane Leadbetter, Deirdre Martin, David Middleton, Sarah Parsons, Ana Popova and Paul Warmington
    2005   Studying professional learning for inclusion. In: Katsuhiro Yamazumi, Yrjo. Engeström and Harry Daniels (eds.), *New Learning Challenges: Going Beyond the Industrial Age System of School and Work*, xx–xx. Kansai: Kansai University Press.
Daniels, Harry
    2006   Analysing institutional effects in Activity Theory: First steps in the development of a language of description. *Outlines: Critical Social Studies* 2: 43–58.
Edwards, Anne, Harry Daniels, Tony Gallagher, Paul Warmington and Jane Leadbetter
    2008   *Improving Inter-professional Collaboration: Learning to do Multi-agency Work.* London: Routledge.
Edwards, Derek and Neil Mercer
    1987   *Common Knowledge.* London: Routledge.
Edwards, Derek and Jonathan Potter
    1992   *Discursive Psychology.* London: Sage.
Edwards, Derek and Elizabeth Stokoe
    2004   Discursive psychology, focus group interviews, and participants' categories. *British Journal of Developmental Psychology* 22: 499–507.
Engeström, Yrjo
    1987   *Learning by Expanding: An Activity-theoretical Approach to Developmental Research.* Helsinki: Orienta-Konsultit.

Engeström, Yrjo
    2001   Expansive learning at work: Toward an activity theoretical reconceptualiz-
            ation. *Journal of Education and Work* 14(1): 133–156.
Engeström, Yrjo
    2007   From stabilization knowledge to possibility knowledge in organizational
            learning. *Management Learning* 38(3): 1–5.
Hall, Christopher, Stefaan Slembrouck and Srikant Sarangi
    2006   *Language Practices in Social Work: Categorisation and Accountability in
            Child Welfare.* London: Routledge.
Leadbetter, Jane, Harry Daniels, Steven D. Brown, Anne Edwards, David Middleton,
            Ana Popova, Apostol Apostolov and Paul Warmington
    2007   Professional learning within multi-agency children's services: Researching
            into practice. *Educational Research* 49(1): 83–98.
Mercer, Neil
    2004   Sociocultural discourse analysis: Analysing classroom talk as a social
            mode of thinking. *Journal of Applied Linguistics* 1(2): 137–168.
Middleton, David
    2004   Concepts, learning and the constitution of objects and events in discursive
            practice. In: Anne-Nelly Perret-Clermont, Clothilde Pontecorvo, Lauren B.
            Resnick, Tania Zittoun and Barbara Burge (eds.), *Joining Society: Social
            Interaction in Adolescence and Youth*, 204–215. Cambridge: Cambridge
            University Press.
Potter, Jonathan and Margaret Wetherell
    1987   *Discourse and Social Psychology: Beyond Attitudes and Behaviour.* Lon-
            don: Sage Publications.
Sacks, Harvey
    1992   *Lectures on Conversation, Vols. I and II.* Oxford: Blackwell.
Smith, Dorothy
    2005   *Institutional Ethnography: A Sociology for People.* Oxford: AltaMira Press.
Stokoe, Elizabeth
    2006   On ethnomethodology, feminism, and the analysis of categorial reference to
            gender in talk-in-interaction. *Sociological Review* 54(3): 467–494.
Warmington, Paul, Harry Daniels, Anne Edwards, Steven D. Brown, Jane Leadbetter,
            Deirdre Martin and David Middleton
    2005   Interagency Collaboration: A Review of the Literature. http://www.
            education.bham.ac.uk/research/projects1/liw/publications.shtml (accessed
            01–12.10).
Wickman, Per-Olof and Leif Östman
    2002   Learning as discourse change: A sociocultural mechanism. *Science Edu-
            cation* 86: 601–623.
Wickman, Per-Olof
    2004   The practical epistemologies of the classroom: A study of laboratory work.
            Science Education 88: 325–344.
Wilkin, Anne, Richard White and Kay Kinder
    2003   *Towards Extended Schools: A Literature Review.* Report RR408. Notting-
            ham, England: DfES Publication.

23. Applying linguistic research to real world problems: The social meaning of talk in workplace interaction

Janet Holmes, Angela Joe, Meredith Marra,
Jonathan Newton, Nicky Riddiford and Bernadette Vine

Abstract

Focusing on the communication challenges facing migrants with professional qualifications, this chapter describes how linguists can work with lay-people to identify and research areas of mutual concern, presenting research which is paradigmatically "applied linguistics applied" (Roberts 2003). The research was designed around a course aimed at providing well-educated migrants with the socio-pragmatic skills they need to analyse workplace interactions for themselves. Incorporating a critical dimension helps prepare learners for encounters beyond those presented in class, and encourages them to engage with native speakers from a position of strength. The course includes both classroom instruction and workplace experience, and draws on previous analyses of effective workplace communication by the research team, as well as current workplace interactions in which the learners are involved. The course and the related research involves people who are fundamentally disadvantaged in a wide variety of ways when they join a new society, because of their lack of social power, as well as their unfamiliarity with societal norms. The research adopts an approach which aims to empower, rather than simply attempting to make skilled migrants fit into the host culture.

1.   Introduction

Consider this exchange between a skilled migrant and a colleague in a New Zealand workplace.

A workplace scenario[1]
Context: The first day of Helena's (Hel) internship. Edward (Edw) is explaining the job to her.

1.   Edw: how about p cs two p cs mm three two eight five (4)
2.   mm where do you go where do you come from
3.   where do you er you where in wellington are you

4. Hel: lower hutt //+ yeah so\
5. Edw: /oh okay\\
6. Hel: I catch a train and then I went on to the campus
7.   to do some um school work [laughs] …
8. Edw: wow [laughs]
9. Hel: what about you where do you //+ live\
10. Edw: /oh\\ in churton park
11. Hel: churton park so you //+ own your own transport\
12. Edw: /yeah (   )\\ no I ride a bus
13. Hel: oh yeah
14. Edw: um we can't (afford to use the car) +++ [laughs]
15. Hel: so when you do the offshore one +
16.   I think they'll be much more difficult
17.   than this one + yeah

This short excerpt of typical everyday workplace talk illustrates some fundamental issues for exploring ways in which learner-centred research can inform pedagogy. As we will demonstrate in this chapter, the data collection method, which involves both the migrant worker and her colleague, not only provides authentic material for teaching resources, but also provides a basis for generating valuable insights involving both participants and the researchers.

In this short excerpt, Helena, the skilled migrant, not only makes an appropriate contribution to the small talk (lines 6–7), she also adeptly and considerately returns the interactional baton to Edward after she has made her contribution (line 9). Moreover, she also has the confidence to shift the talk back to transactional matters (their offshore accounts) after a pause which serves as a possible transition point (lines 15–17). While this interaction may seem unremarkable and mundane, it indicates considerable learning and reflection on Helena's part, based on familiarity with similar conversations she has studied in preparation for working in a New Zealand workplace.

Clyne (1994) has discussed the puzzlement of migrants in Australian factories when faced with the expectation that they would engage in small talk while at work. Migrants from Vietnam, for example, interpreted friendly social talk as intrusive cross-questioning about personal matters (Clyne 1994: 180). Given our awareness of the importance of social talk in New Zealand workplaces, as indicated by our extensive participatory research (Holmes and Stubbe 2003), Helena had been well-prepared to engage appropriately in small talk at work. Her ability to contribute appropriately, as illustrated in this scenario, is good evidence of the value of using authentic pedagogical materials, and for engaging learners in the research process in order to encourage reflection on the differences between the norms of workplace interaction in their own cultures and those of their new country. This short and seemingly inconsequential extract thus contains many features of relevance to understanding the social meaning of talk in workplace interaction.

Scenarios such as this, but based on talk between native speakers, are presented to students attending Victoria University of Wellington's course for professional migrants with English as an Additional Language. Students are asked to reflect on aspects of different scenarios in order to develop their socio-pragmatic awareness. Learners' attention is directed to a number of aspects of the discourse, including the way that small talk in seamlessly integrated with work talk, with few and often very subtle signals at transition points. Course members are also asked to compare the authentic materials from New Zealand workplaces with their experience in their own cultures, and to discuss possible reasons for the differences they identify.

Scenarios used in the course, are taken from the corpus of authentic workplace recordings of the Wellington Language in the Workplace Project (LWP).[2] The LWP database has been collected over the last fifteen years from a range of different types of workplaces, including government departments, commercial organisations and factories. The data for the professional migrants' communication course is drawn from white-collar workplaces. In this chapter we examine the value of using authentic data to develop teaching materials, and outline how scenarios like this are used in the course. As advocated by Byram (1997: 20–21), we incorporate an empowering critical dimension which helps prepare learners for encounters beyond those presented in class, and encourages them to see their role not as imitators of native speakers, but as "social actors" interacting with others in a specific style and context which can be distinguished from the way in which native speakers interact.

A number of scholars have addressed the issue of how research using Discourse Analysis can be applied in the production of suitable pedagogical training materials for those entering workplaces in a new culture, using a second language. However, few have examined what sociolinguistic research can offer in developing applied linguistics education and training. In what follows we demonstrate how linguists can work with lay-people to identify, research and illuminate areas of mutual concern and interest, with the goal of providing learners "with the means to analyse and thereby understand and relate to, whatever social world their interlocutors might inhabit" (Byram 1997: 20).

2.   Socio-pragmatic skills in workplace interaction

A growing body of research has focused on the development of pragmatic awareness and ability in second language learners. More than twenty years ago, Leech (1983) and Thomas (1983, 1995) identified the importance of socio-pragmatic features of interaction, demonstrating their significance in interpreting social meaning, and the potential problems they posed in intercultural interaction. Leech's analytical dimensions of power, social distance and cost-benefit (cf. Brown and Levinson's 1987 Politeness model), together with his Politeness Maxims, provided a rich basis for analysing social interaction. Thomas's (1983) distinction between pragmalinguistic failure (failure to select the appropriate linguistic strategies to express particular social meanings) and socio-pragmatic failure (failure to accurately interpret the socio-cultural values expressed in an interaction) has proved invaluable in developing useful pedagogic materials for ESL classrooms. Similarly the pioneering work of Willing (1992) on sociolinguistic dimensions of workplace interaction, and the extensive work of Clyne (1994, 2006) on pragmatic issues facing migrants in Australian workplaces, has informed the ways in which migrants for whom English is an Additional Language have been prepared for the sociolinguistic demands of the workplace. (See Hogarth and Burnett 1995 for teaching/learning materials based on Willing's research). Overall, this research has led to much greater attention to socio-pragmatic aspects of interaction, and to the pragmatic strategies and linguistic forms used to express particular social meanings.

In Britain, Gumperz, Roberts and colleagues have been investigating intercultural communication for many decades, using an interactional sociolinguistics approach (Gumperz and Roberts 1991; Roberts, Davies and Jupp 1992). Their self-reflexive techniques, involving direct engagement with issues of relevance to the wider community, have focused in recent times on job and promotion interviews for immigrants working in professional contexts (Roberts, Campbell and Robinson 2008). They identify discursive and cultural issues as key to discrimination, and draw attention to the fact that interviews are "highly culturally specific events, reflecting the normative values and styles of the majority ethnic organisational culture" which transform "ordinary workplace talk into an intense regime of display and judgement where acceptability is narrowly and implicitly defined" (Roberts, Campbell and Robinson 2008: 3). Socio-cultural differences in the ways pragmatic meanings are appropriately expressed lie at the heart of the issues they identify as problematic.

In the area of instruction in second language pragmatics, recent research indicates positive effects of classroom input and intervention (Bardovi-Harlig 2001; Kasper and Rose 2002; Koike and Pearson 2005). It is clear that providing learners with explicit instruction at a metapragmatic level is more effective in assisting them to acquire target language norms than simply exposing them to target language features (Kasper 2001; Rose 2005; Takahashi 2001). These findings reinforce Schmidt's (1993: 36) view that exposure to the target language is usually not enough, since pragmatic features are not sufficiently noticeable to second language learners, and are therefore not likely to be integrated even after considerable exposure. Our own recent research with skilled migrants also supports this position, as the initial scenario indicated. Course participants need to have their attention drawn, for example, to the many subtle ways in which native speakers construct collegial relationships at work, as well as the indirect ways in which they construct their professional identity (Holmes 2008). Before describing this research, however, we provide some information on the broader context within which the research was undertaken.

3. Language in the Workplace (LWP) research: Identifying "real world" issues in collaboration with "real world" partners

From its beginnings, the LWP research has been applied in conception, not only in developing applications of the analyses for addressing real world problems, but also in working in partnership with workplace practitioners in exploring real world issues (Bygate 2004: 18). We identify issues of mutual interest, drawing on our knowledge of the way language works, and especially our awareness of the immensely important influence of contextual factors on communication in researching those issues. Basing our design as far as possible on the action research principle of research "for and with" our participants (Cameron et al. 1992: 22), we adopt a research process which is as open and empowering as possible, and which avoids exploitation of those we work with.

Our first step involves identifying organizations with an interest in workplace communication, who perceive the possibility of learning more through a partnership with us. Considerable discussion often takes place to identify issues of mutual concern and interest. Moreover, as noted in Holmes and Stubbe (2003: 20), "[e]ven though the participating organisations were convinced that the research had the potential to be useful in the longer term, most still expected a more immediate, concrete benefit in return for their investment of staff time and goodwill". This demand for what Sarangi and Candlin (2003: 277) aptly characterise as "hot" feedback, so that people "do not wait for too long to know what relevant findings can be put into practice" is quite typical of all our workplace research, encouraging reflexivity at every point in the research process.

Our data collection method has been thoroughly described elsewhere (Holmes and Stubbe 2003; Marra 2008). Its most distinctive feature is that the participants themselves audio-record their everyday workplace talk with as little interference from us as possible (see also Willing 1992; Clyne 1994). We also video-record meetings, using cameras which are fixed in place, switched on in advance, and left running for the whole meeting. As far as possible, our policy is to minimise our intrusion as researchers into the work environment. This is the broader context in which we began to research with migrant workers, adopting a process which is described in the following sections.

4.   Using the Language in the Workplace (LWP) corpus for teaching migrant workers

In 2005, the New Zealand government set aside $60 million for a four year migrant and refugee settlement strategy (Department of Labour 2005: 6). This was partly a response to difficulties encountered by recently arrived migrants with professional qualifications and skills who had been attracted to New Zealand because of the country's shortage in certain professions, specifically those identified as important by the New Zealand Immigration Service. On arrival in New Zealand these migrants report a range of difficulties, some of which are clearly intercultural communication problems. These include: (i) unfamiliarity with aspects of local New Zealand culture which makes social exchanges difficult (e.g. ignorance of suitable topics of small talk such as weekend sporting events which are crucial in order to participate in morning tea conversations in some workplaces); and (ii) unfamiliarity with the communicative norms of the workplace culture in which they are expected to operate which generates problems with workplace interaction (e.g. the degree of informality which characterises much New Zealand interaction, see also Riddiford and Joe 2005).

Our LWP corpus of interactions collected in professional workplaces provides an ideal resource for developing teaching and learning materials to assist such migrant workers. We secured a contract with the Tertiary Education Commission to provide language-focused training courses for skilled migrants who had been unable to find work in their chosen professions in New Zealand for at least two years. Applicants for the course are required to be proficient in English at a level comparable to at least an IELTS score of 6.0 (roughly equating to intermediate proficiency), and to be trained and experienced in a profession. Professions represented by migrants in the program include law, stockbroking, finance and economics, teaching, academia, design, accountancy, IT and telecommunications, banking, engineering and policy analysis.

4.1.   Structure of the course

The twelve-week course is divided into a five-week in-class block followed by a six-week workplace placement (with half a day per week spent back in class), and concludes with a final week in class (see Prebble 2007 for more detail). The initial five week block includes a component which focuses on developing awareness of socio-pragmatic aspects of communication in the New Zealand workplace in preparation for the work placement. The course aims to provide the well-educated migrants with the socio-pragmatic skills they need to analyse workplace interactions for themselves. As mentioned above, the course incorporates an empowering critical dimension which helps prepare learners not just to "fit in", but also to actively construct themselves as skilled professionals in

New Zealand workplaces, and as outlined above "as social actors engaging with other social actors in a particular kind of communication and interaction which is different from that between native speakers" (Byram 1997: 20–21).

The course materials are also designed to develop awareness of how New Zealand English is used for particular purposes, such as to establish or maintain social relationships, to access information, to direct others, and to disagree or refuse without causing *unintended* offence. In other words, they are designed to provide the means for people to negotiate, disagree, and, if they choose to do so, to question, flout, contest and resist. Again the critical dimension is fundamental, involving recognition of the dynamic aspects of interaction and the capacity for negotiation.

To meet these goals, teaching and learning materials have been developed based on authentic interactions from the LWP corpus between native speakers engaged in workplaces which resemble those in which the skilled migrants will be placed as interns. These materials provide a basis for developing awareness of relevant socio-pragmatic dimensions of analysis, acquiring skills in analysing what is going on in the interaction from a socio-pragmatic perspective, and for considering alternative ways of enacting a comfortable professional identity in such contexts. As Bardovi-Harlig (2001) observes, one cause of non-target-like pragmatics is misleading input in teaching materials. Kasper (1997: 11) also notes that input from authentic interactions is important for pragmatic learning: "Because native speaker intuition is a notoriously unreliable source of information about the communicative practices of their own community, it is vital that teaching materials on L2 pragmatics are research-based". Hence the course draws on the authentic data and the socio-pragmatic analyses of a range of speech acts undertaken by the research team (e.g. Holmes and Stubbe 2003; Holmes 2005a, Holmes 2005b; Vine 2004).

4.2. Designing the course

Newton (2007) describes the steps adopted in designing the course. These include: (i) identifying socio-pragmatic targets for instruction; (ii) selecting samples of workplace talk; and (iii) choosing instructional methods to make best use of authentic workplace talk.

4.2.1. Identifying socio-pragmatic targets for instruction

The course concentrates on assisting course members to acquire competence in analyzing, interpreting and expressing potentially confrontational speech acts, such as requests, disagreements, refusals and complaints, in ways that will not cause unintended offence. Because culture plays a role in shaping the strategic and linguistic realizations of politeness and face-work (Gass and Neu 1996;

Spencer-Oatey 2008), these areas typically prove particularly challenging for second language learners. For our professional migrant employees, knowledge of the tasks involved in their jobs was generally not an issue, whereas learning how to relate to colleagues and superiors at work in ways that were considered socio-pragmatically appropriate was typically much more taxing. Moreover, a focus on these areas is compatible with the goal of empowering people to question and critique what is going on in the workplace, rather than providing them with formulas to better fit them into a social category. So, for example, learning how to challenge and disagree effectively in a new community of practice draws attention to, and makes it possible to, question underlying taken-for-granted assumptions and values. Once these underlying values are identified, migrant workers have an opportunity to choose to articulate different values and enact different identities. In this kind of empowering and enabling learning context, we as researchers also become much more aware of the usually unexamined assumptions which underlie much of our automatic behaviours and interpretations. Reflecting on the reasons for the behaviours captured in the recorded interactions of the migrant workers during their internships further promotes learning on both sides (Holmes 2008).

4.2.2. Selecting samples of workplace talk

Selecting suitable materials involves a careful search of our rich LWP database. Our two primary criteria for selecting useable interactions are first, that an interaction contains salient examples of relevant socio-pragmatic features, and second, that the speech act occurs within a coherent bounded speech event that can be comprehended as a stand-alone episode. Scenario One illustrates the use of small talk embedded within transactional talk at work. But relatively clearcut examples such as this are the exception rather than the rule. The highly situated and contextualized nature of spoken discourse produces meanings that emerge from shared physical context, shared histories, and previous conversations, all of which are difficult for a third party, and especially a non-native speaker, to access. Despite these challenges, we make every effort to select material which resembles as closely as possible the workplace contexts of the migrants on our language-focused training courses. Ultimately, this has proved one of the greatest strengths of the process adopted in applying linguistic research to "real world" problems.

4.2.3. Choosing instructional methods

Choosing appropriate instructional methods involves consideration of pedagogical principles. Our approach involves an exploratory and cyclical model (Liddicoat et al. 2003: 24–25), involving *awareness raising* (cf. Schmidt 1990;

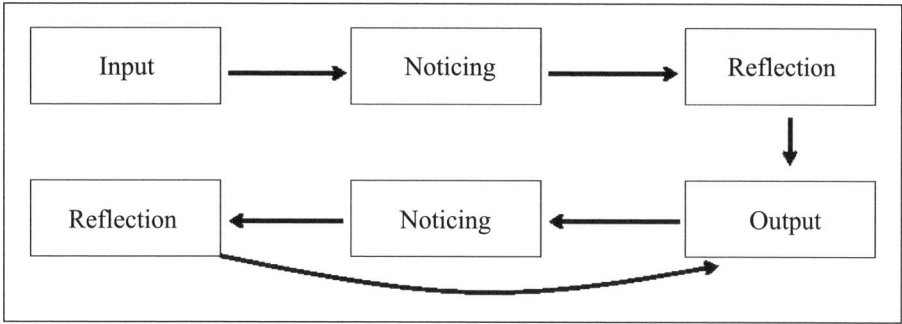

Figure 1. A pathway for developing intercultural competence (Liddicoat et al. 2003: 20)

Gass 1997; Ellis 1997), *experimentation, production,* and *feedback.* The model presupposes a starting point of exposure to the kind of authentic discourse provided by the LWP data.

As represented in figure 1, using transcripts of interactions course members are first encouraged to notice features of language that are not in their usual repertoire (Awareness raising/Noticing). They then discuss possible reasons for these features as well as their personal response to them (Reflection). Opportunities for communication follow (e.g. role play), allowing them to experiment with new forms, expressions or strategies derived from the earlier input (Experimentation). Next they attend to how "comfortable" these feel, and assess how successful the communication was interpersonally (Noticing again).

Course members then integrate the information they have acquired by engaging in interaction with native speakers in real workplaces (Production). Teacher feedback and discussion among course members encourages the exploration of how they felt about speaking and acting in a particular way (Feedback). A final reflection involves deciding on whether material from the input is worth adopting. Through this exploratory and collaborative process, course members are guided to interpret and construct their own models of culture.

In sum, the materials developed for the professional migrants' communication course are designed to encourage course members to notice and explicitly comment on socio-pragmatic aspects of workplace interaction which differ between their first language and the New Zealand English contexts they are exposed to through the authentic LWP excerpts. They are encouraged to reflect on the multiple interpretations which are often possible, as well as the implications of differences noted, and to develop their critical awareness of the assumptions and values that lie beneath utterances and behavior in each culture. The goal is to help develop the analytical, reflective and critical skills which will enable course members to make informed choices about how to construct their social and professional identities in the new culture, and which will assist them in deciding to what extent to accept or challenge the socio-pragmatic norms of their new communities of practice.

5.   Experience in New Zealand workplaces

The second part of the course involves direct workplace experience for course members through placements or internships organised with participating workplaces. Insights gained through the analysis of the LWP data and the findings of the LWP research can thus be tested against the personal observations and experiences of the course members in their workplaces. The course members continue with one weekly classroom session during this phase of the course, where they discuss their experiences, as well as any critical incidents involving communication difficulties that they have encountered.

Course members report, for instance, being initially sceptical of advice about the value of conforming to the politeness norms of New Zealand white collar workplaces. However, their direct experience of the uncooperative or even antagonistic responses elicited by unmitigated directives typically lead to discussion and experimentation with alternatives. A Chinese professional accountant, for example, reported a negative response when she said to her mentor and colleague, "You must meet me tomorrow to discuss this". The direct form seemed perfectly clear and appropriate to her. Her colleague responded, however, by resisting her "request"; he presumably interpreted it as an unwarranted directive given her position as an intern. Another intern reported that he was treated very coldly when he refused to help with moving heavy boxes from one office to another (McCallum 2008). In discussing this interaction with our researchers, he explained that he had a bad back and so he tried to avoid lifting heavy items. However, he had not mentioned this fact in the workplace context since he considered it a private matter which was not relevant to his refusal. Unpacking the assumptions and alternative socio-pragmatic norms underlying such "critical incidents" is useful both to the interns and to the researchers, nicely instantiating the kind of productive, collaborative partnership between researchers and researched that Sarangi (2006: 215) advocates.

Often these discussions lead to action plans for future handling of such situations, including guidance on how to challenge and contest what is being required or expected if the learner requests this. In the first example above, the intern agreed to try out some alternative phrasings of requests, and to note the different reactions they elicited. She was astonished to discover that the introductory phrase "I was wondering if …" made a great difference to the response she elicited. Thus the value of hedging and mitigation was learned through experience. But it was not just the formula which was acquired; she also internalised the importance of assessing the relevant social dimensions in the context of in-

teractions. In other contexts, such as when addressing her administrative assistant, her more direct approach worked perfectly well and, from her perspective,
this satisfactorily validated her professional identity in the new work context.

The weekly opportunity to question and discuss the socio-pragmatic norms
of the work groups in which they are interacting proves very valuable for the
migrant workers. Moreover, challenging norms which New Zealanders take for
granted in a supportive and scholarly environment is useful not just for the interns but also for the researchers. This comment from a Vietnamese skilled migrant illustrates the kind of learning that is facilitated by our approach.

> The way New Zealanders deal with [a] complaint is really surprising me. In my
> mind, if a waitress did not have good customer service skills, then she should be
> complained [to] directly. This will make her improve.

Through such reflections, we learn a good deal about what we assume to be
"normal" compared to those working in different cultural contexts.

6.   Sociolinguistics applied in the "real world"

With typical lucidity, Chris Brumfit (1995: 27) defined applied linguistics as
"the theoretical and empirical study of real world problems in which language
plays a central role" (see also Brumfit 2001: 186). The previous sections have
provided a specific illustration of how sociolinguistic research can be applied to
"real world" problems. Working with people who are fundamentally disadvantaged in a wide variety of ways when they join a new society, because of their
lack of social power, as well as their unfamiliarity with societal norms, inevitably increased our sensitivity to the problems that new migrants face. Consequently, as indicated above, we were predisposed to explore approaches which
could empower such people, rather than approaches which attempted to make
them "fit" (see Pennycook 2001).

The same approach characterises other areas where we have developed applications for our research. Data collected in factory environments has resulted
in materials to improve the communication skills of new factory workers
(Stubbe and Brown 2002), as well as more specific materials for use with migrant workers from non-English speaking backgrounds (Newton 2004; Brown
2005). Analyses of recorded interactions between nurses, doctors and patients
in a hospital ward have led to the development of course materials for nurses for
whom English is an additional language (Malthus, Holmes and Major 2005).[3]

In another application of the LWP research, collaborating with colleagues
teaching young workers with an intellectual handicap (Holmes and Fillary
2000), we have produced resources for assisting them to develop workplace
communication skills. Interactions recorded in their workplaces identified so-

cial skills as a crucial area for establishing good work relationships. Our research provided detailed information for these young people about the specific
workplace norms in their places of employment, such as accepted ways of addressing and greeting others, and appropriate topics of small talk. This data provided the basis for exercises and role plays designed to provide the young
workers with the socio-pragmatic knowledge and sociolinguistic skills which
would enable them to better integrate with their colleagues if they wished to do
so. All these applications are designed to address real world problems and to
provide constructive and empowering solutions.

7.   Conclusion

Compared to SLA research, language in the workplace is a "relatively under-ad-
dressed field of research interest in applied linguistics", as Sarangi and Candlin
(2003: 271) note. Yet communication problems at work are self-evidently important and relevant potential research areas for applied linguists. Our research
on workplace discourse provides one possible approach for applied linguists
concerned to use their skills in linguistic analysis to address real world issues.
We address issues that are of direct interest to people other than fellow academics
and engage with those people in discussing the data and analyses. We collaborate
with workplaces in identifying and addressing issues of mutual interest and
concern, and providing feedback to these workplaces; and we use the results of
our analyses to develop teaching and learning materials for new employees, and
especially those from non-English-speaking backgrounds. In other words, our
research not only addresses real world problems, it also has what Bygate calls "a
real world role" (2004: 18).

Our research methodology is as genuinely collaborative as we can make it.
Appraising applied linguistics and professional discourse studies, Sarangi
(2006: 201) usefully distinguishes between the "consultancy and consultative
models of research" on the basis of the relationship between the researcher and
the researched, as well as "the ways in which the research findings may be presented and disseminated for potential uptake". In this context, we have adopted a
consultative model as most useful in empowering our participants as co-re-
searchers.

Finally, the applied linguistics research outlined in this chapter aims to "inform social action" (Byrne 1998: 167). It is "doubly applied" in Bygate's terms
(2004: 18), or "applied linguistics applied" in Roberts' (2003) terminology:
applied linguistics has influenced both the nature of the problems selected
for study, and the ways in which the results have been used to address the issues
identified. Moreover those uses have been tested out with real world participants, and evaluated by them.

Engaging with the real world is a demanding goal. We have outlined in this chapter a range of valuable ways in which applied linguists can do this, and as a result can make a difference to the quality of people's working lives, and especially to the prospects of job satisfaction for the potentially disempowered.

Notes

1. The following transcription conventions have been used:

[laughs]	Paralinguistic features and other information in square brackets
+	Pause of up to one second
(2)	Longer pause, measured in seconds
... //......\...	Simultaneous speech, superscript numbers used
... /.......\\...	for multiple overlaps
(hello)	Transcriber's best guess at an unclear utterance
...	Section of transcript omitted

   All names used in examples are pseudonyms.
2. The research reported here was largely funded from grants received from the New Zealand Foundation for Research, Science and Technology and Victoria University of Wellington. We express our appreciation to all those who allowed their workplace interactions to be recorded. We acknowledge Work and Income (Wellington), Ministry of Social Development, for funding the six-week work placements for four of the five intakes. We also thank other members of the Language in the Workplace team who participated in the data collection and transcription.
3. See Holmes and Stubbe (2003: Chapter 8) for a description of the Communication Evaluation Development (CED) model, another application of the LWP research.

References

Bardovi-Harlig, Kathleen
    2001   Empirical evidence of the need for instruction in pragmatics. In: Kenneth
              R. Rose and Gabriele Kasper (eds.), *Pragmatics in Language Teaching*,
              13–32. New York: Cambridge University Press.
Brown, Penelope and Stephen C. Levinson
    1987   *Politeness: Some Universals in Language Usage*. Cambridge: Cambridge
              University Press.
Brown, T. Pascal
    2005   *Authentic Spoken Workplace Texts in the Classroom*. (Professional Devel-
              opment Collection.) Sydney: The National Centre for English Language
              Teaching and Research (NCELTR), Macquarie University.
Brumfit, Christopher J.
    1995   Teacher professionalism and research. In: Guy Cook and Barbara Seidl-
              hofer (eds.), *Principle and Practice in Applied Linguistics*, 27–41. Oxford:
              Oxford University Press.

Brumfit, Christopher J.
    2001   *Individual Freedom in Language Teaching: Helping Learners to Develop a Dialect of their Own.* Oxford: Oxford University Press.
Bygate, Martin
    2004   Some current trends in applied linguistics: Towards a generic view. In: Susan M. Gass and Sinfree Makoni (eds.), *World Applied Linguistics (AILA Review 17)*, 6–22. Amsterdam: John Benjamins.
Byram, Michael
    1997   *Teaching and Assessing Intercultural Communicative Competence.* Clevedon: Multilingual Matters.
Byrne, David
    1998   *Complexity Theory and the Social Sciences.* London: Routledge.
Cameron, Deborah, Elizabeth Frazer, Penelope Harvey, M. B. H. Rampton and Kay Richardson
    1992   *Researching Language: Issues of Power and Method.* London: Routledge.
Clyne, Michael G.
    1994   *Inter-Cultural Communication at Work: Cultural Values in Discourse.* Cambridge: Cambridge University Press.
Clyne, Michael G.
    2006   Some thoughts on pragmatics, sociolinguistic variation, and intercultural communication. *Intercultural Pragmatics* 3(1): 95–105.
Department of Labour
    2005   News in brief. *LINKZ* 29: 6.
Ellis, Rod
    1997   *SLA Research and Language Teaching.* Oxford: Oxford University Press.
Gass, Susan M.
    1997   *Input, Interaction, and the Second Language Learner.* Mahwah, N.J: Lawrence Erlbaum.
Gass, Susan M. and Joyce Neu (eds.)
    1996   *Speech Acts Across Cultures: Challenges to Communication in a Second Language.* Berlin / New York: Mouton de Gruyter.
Gumperz, John J. and Celia Roberts
    1991   Understanding in intercultural encounters. In: Jan Blommaert and Jef Verschueren (eds.), *The Pragmatics of Intercultural and International Communication*, 51–90. Amsterdam: John Benjamins.
Hogarth, W. and L. Burnett
    1995   *Talking it through. Teachers' Guide and Classroom Materials.* Sydney: NCELTR, Macquarie University.
Holmes, Janet
    2005a   Socio-pragmatic aspects of workplace talk. In: Yuji Kawaguchi, Susumu Zaima, Toshihiro Takagaki, Kohji Shibano and Mayumi Usami (eds.), *Linguistic Informatics – State of the Art and the Future: The First International Conference on Linguistic Informatics*, 196–220. Amsterdam: John Benjamins.
Holmes, Janet
    2005b   When small talk is a big deal: Sociolinguistic challenges in the workplace. In: Michael H. Long (ed.), *Second Language Needs Analysis*, 344–371. Cambridge: Cambridge University Press.

Holmes, Janet
   2008   Relational talk at work: From the workplace to the classroom and back
           again. Plenary paper presented at Partnerships in Action: Research, Prac-
           tice & Training Inaugural Conference of the Asia-Pacific Rim LSP and Pro-
           fessional Communication Association, Hong Kong 9–10 December 2008.
Holmes, Janet and Rose Fillary
   2000   Handling small talk at work: Challenges for workers with intellectual dis-
           abilities. *International Journal of Disability, Development and Education*
           47(3): 273–291.
Holmes, Janet and Maria Stubbe
   2003   *Power and Politeness in the Workplace*. Harlow: Pearson.
Kasper, Gabriele
   1997   *Can Pragmatic Competence be Taught?* (NFLRC NetWork 6.) Second Lan-
           guage Teaching and Curriculum Center. http://nflrc.hawaii.edu/NetWorks/
           NW06/ (accessed 28 July 2006).
Kasper, Gabriele
   2001   Four perspectives on L2 pragmatic development. *Applied Linguistics*
           22(4): 502–530.
Kasper, Gabriele and Kenneth R. Rose
   2002   Pragmatic development in a second language. *The Language Learning
           Monograph Series* 52(s1): 1–339.
Koike, Dale and Lyn Pearson
   2005   The effect of instruction and feedback in the development of pragmatic
           competence. *System* 33(3): 481–501.
Leech, Geoffrey
   1983   *Principles of Pragmatics*. London: Longman.
Liddicoat, Anthony J., Leo Papademetre, Angela Scarino and Michelle Kohler
   2003   *Report on Intercultural Language Learning*. Canberra: Department of Edu-
           cation, Science and Training. http://www1.curriculum.edu.au/nalsas/pdf/
           intercultural.pdf (accessed 16 August 2006).
McCallum, Judi
   2008   Critical Incidents from internships for skilled migrants in NZ workplaces.
           Paper presented at Community Languages and English for Speakers of
           Other Languages (CLESOL) Conference, Auckland, 2–5 October.
Malthus, Caroline, Janet Holmes and George Major
   2005   Completing the circle: Research-based classroom practice with EAL nurs-
           ing students. *New Zealand Studies in Applied Linguistics* 11(1): 65–89.
Marra, Meredith
   2008   Recording and analysing talk across cultures. In: Helen Spencer-Oatey
           (ed.), *Culturally Speaking: Managing Rapport through Talk Across Cul-
           tures 2nd edition*, 304–321. London: Continuum.
Newton, Jonathan
   2004   Face-threatening talk on the factory floor: Using authentic workplace inter-
           actions in language teaching. *Prospect* 19(1): 47–64.
Newton, Jonathan
   2007   Adapting authentic workplace talk for workplace communication training.
           In: Helga Kotthoff and Helen Spencer-Oatey (eds.), *Handbook of Intercul-*

tural Communication (Vol. 7: Handbooks of Applied Linguistics), 519–537. Berlin / New York: Mouton de Gruyter.

Pennycook, Alastair
2001   *Critical Applied Linguistics: A Critical Introduction.* Mahwah, NJ: Lawrence Erlbaum.

Prebble, John
2007   *Workplace Communication for Skilled Migrants: English for Professional Purposes* VUW ELIN 941. www.victoria.ac.nz/lals/programmes/english-prof/workplace-communication.aspx (accessed 31 October 2007).

Riddiford, Nicky and Angela Joe
2005   Using authentic data in a workplace communication programme. *New Zealand Studies in Applied Linguistics* 11(2): 103–110.

Roberts, Celia
2003   Applied linguistics applied. In: Srikant Sarangi and Theo van Leeuwen (eds.), *Applied Linguistics and Communities of Practice*, 132–149. London: Continuum.

Roberts, Celia, Sarah Campbell and Yvonne Robinson
2008   *Talking like a Manager: Promotion Interviews, Language and Ethnicity.* Department for Work and Pensions Research Report No 510. http://www.dwp.gov.uk/asd/asd5/rrs-index.asp (accessed 30 September 2008).

Roberts, Celia, Evelyn Davies and Tom Jupp
1992   *Language and Discrimination: A Study of Communication in Multi-ethnic Workplaces.* London: Longman.

Rose, Kenneth R.
2005   On the effects of instruction in second language pragmatics. *System* 33(3): 385–399.

Sarangi, Srikant
2006   The conditions and consequences of professional discourse studies. In: Richard Kiely, Pauline Rea-Dickens, Helen Woodfield and Gerald Clibbon (eds.), *Language, Culture and Identity in Applied Linguistics* (*British Studies in Applied Linguistics 21*), 199–220. London: Equinox.

Sarangi, Srikant and Christopher N. Candlin
2003   Trading between reflexivity and relevance: New challenges for applied linguistics. *Applied Linguistics* 24(3): 271–285.

Schmidt, Richard
1990   The role of consciousness in second language learning. *Applied Linguistics* 11: 129–158.

Schmidt, Richard
1993   Consciousness, learning and interlanguage pragmatics. In: Gabriele Kasper and Shoshana Blum-Kulka (eds.), *Interlanguage Pragmatics*, 21–42. Oxford: Oxford University Press.

Spencer-Oatey, Helen
2008   *Culturally Speaking Culture: Communication and Politeness Theory*, 2nd edn. London: Continuum.

Stubbe, Maria and Pascal Brown
2002   *Talk that Works: Communication in Successful Factory Teams: A Resource Kit.* Wellington: School of Linguistics and Applied Language Studies, Victoria University of Wellington.

Takahashi, Satomi
  2001   The role of input enhancement in developing pragmatic competence. In:
             Kenneth R. Rose and Gabriele Kasper (eds.), *Pragmatics in Language
             Teaching,* 171–199. Cambridge: Cambridge University Press.
Thomas, Jenny
  1983   Cross-cultural pragmatic failure. *Applied Linguistics* 4(2): 91–112.
Thomas, Jenny
  1995   *Meaning in Interaction: An Introduction to Pragmatics.* London: Longman.
Vine, Bernadette
  2004   *Getting Things Done at Work: The Discourse of Power in Workplace Inter-
             action.* Amsterdam: John Benjamins.
Willing, Ken
  1992   *Talking it Through: Clarification and Problem-solving in Professional
             Work.* Sydney: NCELTR, Macquarie University.

24. Changes in professional identity: Nursing roles and practices

Sally Candlin

Abstract

Nurses' identities are constructed through their institutional belonging and the exercise of particular roles in the context of professional practices. Such roles and practices are themselves in part constituted through the performance of particular discourses. Research into such practices requires discourse analysts to become aware of and to understand the institutional and professional histories of those participants with whom they work, against which their professional practices are set. A collaborative exploration of how such professional participants, in this case, nurses, categorise their communities of practice is one way in which this understanding can be attempted. Such a process poses challenges both to discourse analysts and to nurse professionals which may be met by close and collaborative inquiry.

1. Introduction

> … in Australia nurse education is now in the tertiary sector of education and takes its place alongside other professions such as medicine, physiotherapy, occupational therapy, and so on. It means that nursing practice is not just a matter of "doing" and "doing as we are told", but doing with understanding and thoughtfulness. It means being critical and reflective about what we do, analysing what we have done, and working out how we can improve practice, pushing back the frontiers of knowledge and thus improving patient care …
>
> (Nurse academic, cited in Candlin and Candlin [2007: 203])

There are a number of ways in which the identities of professional practitioners can be explored. One such, as evidenced in the quotation above, is to draw upon their narratives of experience, especially, as here, where they reflect on the impact on their practice of institutional changes in their professional lives. Such narratives formed the basis of a previous study exploring the community of practice of nursing over time and space (Candlin and Candlin 2007). Such changes are also reflected however in the discourses of practitioners in their professional lives, especially as a means of exploring their heightened awareness of their professional identities in the performance of their varied professional roles. This is the focus of this chapter. Against a context which is at once institutional, professional and personal (Sarangi and Roberts 1999), I explore how nurses are not only identified institutionally and professionally by their area of specialty practice but also by the specific roles they undertake at any given time within that practice. A nurse may, for example, be identified institutionally and professionally as an aged care nurse, but also, for example, as a counsellor, a patient educator, a healer, among a number of other roles (Candlin 1997). The adoption of one or another of these roles often depends upon the healthcare context. A nursing administrator, for example, would not need to adopt the identity of healer or carer in a management meeting; neither might the nurse academic need to adopt the identity of a carer when in the academy, but would readily do so if in the clinical practice area.

For discourse analysts to understand these different and evolving identities of nurses as their roles are affected by those social and institutional changes which impact on the practices of nursing care, requires a familiarity with the institutional and professional context in which such roles are set. The following matters are especially relevant to such an inter-professional inquiry. They are well outlined in the work prepared by Saltmarsh, North and Koop (2002) in their account of student expectations of nursing education, to which I refer further below. As in the discussion of professional identity and membership more generally, the rights and responsibilities of nurses, the holding of particular beliefs and the adoption of appropriate behaviours, all derive as a condition of that membership. Indeed, such identity derives its meaning in large part in apposition to that of other professionals, as, for example, where nurses are expected to demonstrate different professional behaviours from teachers, lawyers and allied health professionals, and enjoy different rights and privileges.

What is relevant for the study of nursing identity seen through discursive eyes is that these identities are realised and become relevant in the adoption of a complex of interconnected roles in particular situated institutional contexts. Further, these identities are *professionally* constructed not only by nurses themselves but also by patients – who are recipients of nursing care – and by other health professionals. At the same time, in that nursing is a public institution whose members in the course of their professional practices and behaviours display a public face, such nursing identities are socially constructed and subject to the beliefs and expectations held by societal members about what a nurse is and what a nurse does. These beliefs and expectations are not fixed: nursing, and the identities of its practitioners, as with all professions, is subject to evolutionary change as a consequence of responses to changing demographics, increasing cultural diversity, socio-political developments, and advances in medical science. As the institution and profession evolve over time so the identities of its members change. At the same time, the identities of nurses as persons change as they themselves engage with their professional and institutional identities in particular moments in time and space.

Role relationships are thus determined in part not only by the responsibilities which a person carries as a member of an institution, but also as a member of the specific community of practice in which s/he is professionally engaged. At the same time, and in different locations and sites such as home or community, relationships with members of the family group or a community group must be negotiated. As the person's role relationships and responsibilities change with age and family/social structure and circumstances, so too they change within the institution. For the nurse, for example, they change as a result of professional education and experiences – both within and across specialty areas of practice. The nurse is, in effect, experiencing a variety of professional practices and engaging in a community of practice (COP), where COP can be defined as

> ... an aggregate of people who come together around mutual engagement in an endeavour. Ways of doing things, ways of talking, beliefs, values, power relations – in short practices – emerge in the course of this mutual endeavour. As a social construct, a community of practice is different from the traditional community, primarily because it is defined simultaneously by its membership and by the practice in which that membership engages ...
> (Eckert and McConnell-Ginet 1992: 464)

As a result of the nurse's membership in a COP, we can then expect changes in her identity as she "moves" from being, say, a "general medical surgical" nurse to, for example, a palliative care nurse, community nurse, midwife, and so forth. In each of these communities the nurse will draw upon resources gained from an accumulation of life experiences which include professional education and training programs, clinical experiences, and social relationships with nurses and other health professionals. We can usefully identify these resources in Fairclough's terms, as "members resources" (MRs):

> ... what people have in their heads and draw upon when they produce or interpret texts – including their knowledge of language, representations of the natural and social worlds they inhabit, values, beliefs, assumptions and so on ...
> (Fairclough 1992: 244)

Such resources are not, of course, the property of the nurse only. Assumptions and beliefs about nursing on the part of all involved in the healthcare process base themselves upon experiences of self or others to the world of health and illness, but they can also be impacted by exposure to the media. Public perceptions of health, disease, bureaucratic and nursing institutions have all contributed to a folk history of myths, beliefs and expectations surrounding nursing identity, and are confirmed or changed by what Thompson (1984) refers to as the "mediazation" of the health care system. It is to be expected therefore that the MRs of lay people, patients, novice nurses and experienced nurses will be quite disparate, affecting individual understanding, including that of discourse

analysts, of nursing situations, and by implication, of their characteristic interactions, whether between novice nurses and patients or between experienced
nurses and patients (see Candlin 2000). Accordingly, as the narrative excerpt at
the outset of this chapter indicates, identities reflect change both in the institutional order, that of nursing as a profession and institution, but also in the interaction order in particular sites and moments of practice.

How such identities shift and change in the contexts of an evolving profession presents an opportunity for, and a challenge to, the descriptive, interpretive
and explanatory analysis of the discourses of nurses and patients in occasions of
health care practice. Such data offer possibilities of exploring how, in the context of action, professional, institutional and personal identities are drawn upon
by nurses in the delivery of care. What is clear is that even a surface analysis of
such discourses reveals not only the considerable complexity of role and practice inherent in such interactions, but just how challenging to discourse analysts
such data is, given their "outsider" status (see Sarangi 2007) in relation to the
professional knowledge and experience and expertise inherent in, and therefore
likely to be explanatory of, the nurse's roles. Note, as one small example, how in
Extract 1 below, Cheryth, the attending nurse, shifts roles (and professional
identity) with ease as she moves from that of a healer to a carer, educator and advisor. At the same time, the challenges posed by the interpretation of such data
need always to be borne in mind. Here, Sarangi's identification of what he calls
the *analyst's paradox* (Sarangi 2007) becomes relevant as it relates to the activity of obtaining members' insights to inform analytic practice. This paradox relates to interpretation by all participants of the data. What this means in practice
is that what one hears or reads explicitly as an analyst, or sees "going on", may
not be what the participants implicitly understand by "professional practice". So
we may have a distorted vision of the encounter. This is generally true, Sarangi
argues, but particularly so in professional encounters where we may not appreciate fully what the core practices are, what is considered "frontstage" or
"backstage" (Goffman 1969). In professional-client encounters we may be
better positioned because we have experience of being "clients", but even there
we cannot avoid the paradox. As the knowledge gap increases between analysts
and participants as a consequence of new domains of inquiry, and new contexts,
analysts are increasingly unable to categorise events *without* participant involvement, here from those intimately familiar with the practices of nursing
over time and space.

2.   Categorising nursing identities over time and space

Returning to the matter of the need of the discourse analyst to augment his or her awareness of professional background as a basis for any analysis, we can turn, for example, to accounts of such practice by nurses and nurse educators and nursing researchers. One such account is provided by Burkitt et al. (2001: 3) of nursing education in the context of nursing seen as a community of practice. Their key argument is that developing into a nurse involves more than the learning of a body of knowledge and a range of skills; it involves what they refer to as "becoming" a nurse, a certain type of person whose very identity is constructed and maintained through nursing practice. The process of "becoming" a nurse for them is demonstrated in ways of doing things, talking, negotiating power relations, and selecting and developing a set of values and beliefs which are drawn from a variety of experiences both from the academy and from a vast array of clinical experiences. These are the environments within which the nurse develops and then fuses her own personal and multiple identities so that the overarching identity becomes, in their words, that of the nurse, an identity shared with others in the community of practice of nursing.

In their evaluation of the cognitive and affective processes developed in the educational preparation of nurses, Burkitt et al. argue that:

> ... at the core of nursing commitment and professional self-regard there is a strong shared identity. This inclusive identity of "nurse" has at its heart a commitment to caring and to delivering holistic individualised care ... caring, compassion and empathy were regarded as essential characteristics of this generic nurse identity.
> (Burkitt et al. 2001: 4)

Such a "generic nurse identity" has of course to be seen against the institutional specialisation I refer to earlier, with the emergence of a range of new categorisations such as Specialist Nurses, Consultant Nurses, Nurse Practitioners. Nonetheless, despite this diversity, at the heart of this "generic identity" sits the functions that nurses undertake in their various roles within the course of their practice. Roles in which they are identified professionally, variously and simultaneously, as a healer, educator, advisor, advocate, counsellor, or as a leader etc. (see Candlin 1997). These identities and their performing roles are negotiated interactionally within the frame which is set by the participants. Within nursing practice, identities evolve as participants identify and pursue their goals. Seen in this light, exploring the identity of nurses through an observation of their practice becomes a natural theme for discourse analysis, allowing researchers to draw on Goffman's (1974) theories of frame and footing to explain how shifts in those constructs in the discourses of professional practice may be closely relatable to shifts in identity. In such a way these identities underpin what Roberts and Sarangi (2005) refer to as the *focal* themes of a given profession and as such offer a resource for what they call the *analytic* themes of inter-professional and collaborative analysis of discourse.

Nevertheless, understanding the significance of these focal themes does not emerge from any observation of the data alone. Appraising such significance can only arise from a rich understanding of the principles, values and practices of the profession. In short, achieving such understanding is a necessary pre-requisite for the explanatory analysis of discourse data and is unlikely to be achieved without undertaking what Sarangi (2005), as a counterpoint to Geertz's "thick description" (Geertz 1973), refers to as "thick participation". As a brief and skeletal example of what achieving such understanding might entail, Table 1 draws on Candlin (1997) to offer a characterisation of a set of just seven nursing identities with brief descriptors of each.

Table 1. Some suggested nursing identities

Identity	Function	efined as and exemplified by:
Healer	Healing	Empathetic acknowledgement of the multidimensional effects of a painful event
Carer	Caring	Action to (or facilitate the termination of) terminate a painful event (physical, social, psychological, emotional, spiritual)
Educator	Educating	Giving information and facilitating behaviour change
Advisor	Advising	Offering advice to improve a situation
Counsellor	Counselling	Listening to painful self-disclosures demonstrating empathic understanding, facilitating person's understanding of situation
Manager	Managing/ Administration	Time management, management of resources or people, aimed at improving a situation (whether related to a person, group or institution)
Advocate	Advocacy	Presenting a person's situation to significant others

Now, as a counterpoint, as I argue earlier, such identities need grounding in particular examples of discourse data if they are to make sense to discourse analysts, (and indeed if they are to constitute evidence and warrants for claims concerning nursing practice and, as I indicate at the close of this chapter, if they are to serve as exemplification in nursing education). Accordingly, I offer a number of such examples (below) drawn from the discourse of nurses and patients in the context and setting of health assessment in which I seek to bring together institutional roles and professional practice. In each example, the nurse in question is identified, institutionally, as a Community Nurse, i.e. her speciality and particular community of practice is that of Community Nursing. However as each interaction proceeds, what we may notice is that a range of her professional identities emerges and are drawn upon, as she takes on the various roles of healer, carer, educator, advisor, and within these roles shifts her frame of reference and footing. (For convenience, I have highlighted these in the margin in plain font together with the discourse type drawn on in the realisation of these professional identities, in italics.)[1]

Example 1[2]

Cheryth is a registered nurse visiting Mrs S in her home following an accident in her garden. Cheryth has been eliciting information about the circumstances of the situation. The conversation continues:

Cheryth:	45 Right and the pain is starting to ease off now?	**Healer** *questioning*
Mrs S:	46 It's eased off considerably yes thanks	Sick role identity *signals agreement*
Cheryth:	47 And how often did your doctor say to take them *(tablets)*?	**Carer** *questioning*
Mrs S:	48 Four hourly	
Cheryth:	49 Four hourly. Did the doctor tell you that they'll probably	*Change of footing*
	50 make you constipated?	and identity to **Educator** *i) giving information*
Mrs S:	51 //No//	
Cheryth:	52 //sympathetic laugh// They will so// keep //a good eye	*ii) re-enforcing and*
	53 on that.	*iii) advising*
Mrs S:	54 //oh//I get very I've	Confirming **sick role** identity
	55 got a lot of trouble like that because I'm on	*offering more information*
	56 on X tablets as I'm on X tablets as well	
Cheryth:	57 You don't. You might need to take something so keep a good	**Advisor**
	58 eye on it and em (…) you probably need some (?) …	*giving information*

Example 2
Jane is a registered nurse assessing Mrs C in her home

Jane:	1 Thank you for taking part in this re-search today. We're just	***Creating frame***
	2 going to be talking about you (…) and how you are. How	1) **"informal talk"** frame
	3 you manage at home that sort of thing. We've been coming	2) **research** frame
	4 to you for some months now haven't we?	*Explaining and questioning*
Mrs C:	5 Yes	*Response token*
Jane:	6 Helping you with your showering. You're starting to feel	**Change of footing** to
	7 better about that now aren't you?	**"patient"/sick role identity**
Mrs C:	8 Oh yes feeling more confident too	*Response – agreement*
Jane:	9 Mm that's good	*acknowledgement token*
Mrs C:	10 But as I say you know if I didn't feel well and I was (?)	*Response –* **expansion of**
=	11 wouldn't have	**sick role**
Jane:	12 =that's right. You're better off not to on those odd days	*acknowledgement token*
	13 you're sure that there's a nice support in the shower	**Manager** *confirming*
	14 with the rail and all that in it?	*resources –*
Mrs C:	15 Yes	
Jane:	16 And the rubber mat now that you've //got	*confirming resources*
Mrs C:	17 //my stick has been in 18 the kitchen for two days not used=	*Response – expansion*
Jane:	19 =right so you're becoming stronger// that's//good isn't it	**Carer –** *encouragement token*
Mrs C:	19 //yes //	

Example 3
Mary, a registered Nurse is talking with Mr and Mrs R in their home where Mrs R is recovering from a stroke.

Mary:	9 So do you both feel that given your current position and time frame 10 that has gone on since your stroke that you are both coping. On a 11 scale of 1–10 where would you see yourselves	**Counsellor** *i) Probing*
Mr R:	12 Well considering all the difficulties I would think that we'd 13 be up around the 8 mark wouldn't we Jean?	Confirming identity **patient/sick role** *Statement (opinion)*

Following another 18 exchanges, 3 of which were only brief interjections by the nurse, the interaction continues

Mary:	14 well on a score of 1–10 as far as coping you you've (?) what do you think	**Counsellor** *ii) Probing*
Mr R:	15 What do you think?	
Mary:	16 I would give you a 10	**Counsellor** *iii) Encouraging*
Mr R:	17 Would you? Well you're marvellous aren't you *(to Mrs R)*	*response/opinion*
Mrs R:	18 Well Mary looks for other values too Jim. She looks for 19 different things you know	*Response/ explanation*
Mary:	20 I think you've both coped extremely well. I think you are very 21 much in tune with yourselves and your own needs and have a 22 realistic outlook for the future	**Counsellor** *iv) Justifying and* *encouraging)*

After further exchanges the interaction closed with:

Mrs R:	23 I never thanked you for coming to see me so much in the past	**Sick role/patient**
Mr R:	24 Yes that was marvellous thankyou	*Gratitude token*
Mrs R:	25 I really needed to see you there. That was when 26…	*acknowledgement*

Mary:	27 And that was when I introduced you to S.B.	**Advocate** *presenting patient to another health worker*
Mrs R:	28 You took me across in the wheelchair	*Response/expansion*
Mary:	29 Well I'd like to thank you both very much indeed for your	
	30 generous contribution and for the sake of posterity	**Researcher** *(referring to the study)*
Mrs R:	31 And we want to thank you for every-thing. Just knowing	*Evidence of*
	32 you is enough	*effective caring*
Mary:	33 Oh thank you	

In exploring our theme of participant identities, specifically those of the nurses, evidenced through these three extracts of data, and in the context of the effect on identity perception of professional and institutional change over time, the following historical comment from the American Medical Association in 1906, reproduced in Aaronson is relevant.

> … every attempt at initiative on the part of the nurse … should be reproved by the physician, and hospital administration. The programs of nursing schools … should be (limited) strictly to the indispensable matters of instruction … without going extensively into purely medical matters …
> (Aaronson 1989: 275)

It appears here that one profession (medicine) was constructing not only the training and direction of another profession (nursing), but defining its identity. Medicine was identifying the nurse, usually female, as a "handmaiden", and subservient to the doctor, usually male. That this stance is, however, not entirely historical is evidenced in the recent brief interview excerpt below with a nurse academic:

> What we learned really was how the hospital ran its wards. The language was very medical. We followed the orders given by the sister and she got her orders from the doctor … The language was medical language … We didn't talk to doctors. Only the Sister talked to the doctor. We were taught that doctors were addressed as "sir" and we stood with out hands behind our backs when we talked to them … we couldn't have relationships with doctors or porters. There was a hierarchy of behaviours. We could joke with a porter, and an Honorary could joke with a nurse but not vice versa … We had to keep our distance from patients. We had to be objective and impersonal. We were there for a reason. We could be kindly but not involved. We couldn't show emotion. We had to leave our personal life at the front door. We couldn't call patients by their given names.
> (Nurse academic cited in Candlin and Candlin [2007: 208])

Whatever our stance is to these two statements of position, what is important for the analysis of discourse is to take such historical accounts (among many others) as a basis from which we can come, as analysts of discourse, to our understanding of professional discourse through our appraisal of participant roles and responsibilities. One important way of approaching such appraisal is to grasp that in identifying participants according to their roles, we are effectively *categorizing* them. Here a recent Editorial in the journal *Health, Risk and Society* by Sarangi and Candlin (2003: 117) has some relevance. Following Lakoff (1987), they suggest that "categories are spectacles through which we routinely, albeit largely unconsciously, observe and classify events and experiences". According to Sarangi and Candlin, categorization is

> ... generally understood as definition of situations (including events, actions, roles/identities, knowledge claims etc) in everyday and professional/institutional settings ... [it is] a meaning making activity, deeply embodied in human experience and understanding. Language and discourse play a significant part in how we categorize events and things in discipline-specific ways.
> (Sarangi and Candlin 2003: 115)

The significance of this statement for this chapter lies not only in its emphasis on the part that discourse plays in the categorization process but, importantly, on the knowledge by the analyst it requires of the discipline within which the professional activity is being played out. Herein lies the problem for the discourse analyst, since, as I have alluded to earlier, we cannot assume that these analysts are conversant with the knowledge base of another discipline, or indeed fully understand the professional practices which are indicative of the specific discipline. Schegloff in a recent paper (2007), when referring to the work of Harvey Sacks, specifically his essay titled, "The search for help" (based on the utterance of a caller to the Suicide Prevention Centre, "I have no one to turn to"), discusses the problem which Sacks himself identified much earlier, namely

> ... how to understand "no one to turn to" as a seriously methodically arrived at report of the result of a process or a set of practices. The solution was this: when you are in trouble, there are people who have rights (and *obligations*) to turn to, and people you *do not*.
> (Schegloff 2007: 482)

Sacks called these two classes of people Rp and Ri – short for *Relationship proper* and *improper* respectively. After discussing which categories, *improper* or *proper*, that persons fell into, Sacks proposed another collection of categories, grounded not in relationships but in knowledge, specifically *professional* knowledge. Thus the categories Kp and Ki emerged. These collections of categories are what Sacks (1972: 31) refers to as *categories of member*, when he writes "among the basic resources we need in order to describe the materials we have collected are some collections of membership categories".

The issue for Sacks was that having proposed membership categories, how might they be applied as categories of analysis. Here Sacks proposed an apparatus, a set of resources and practices, which he termed *membership categorisation devices* (MCD). Such categories, e.g. men, women, vegetarians, Protestants, dog-lovers, Germans etc. could be organised into collections of categories, as it were in a set, "for example, [male/female], [Buddhist/Catholic/Jew/Muslim/Protestant]". My presentation of health professionals (nurse, physiotherapist, occupational therapist, doctor etc) in this chapter would be a precise correlate to Sacks' list. Indeed, such a list can be usefully further extended; in the light of earlier discussion, we might consider generalist nurse, paediatric nurse, midwife, consultant nurse etc as yet another collection of categories. However, while identifying such professional categories is of interest, the question remains as to its explanatory value. In short, its relevance. Schegloff's (2007) view in his "tutorial on membership categorization" continues to be significant here since he, along with Sacks, believes that such categories are more than mere labels – they allow one to categorize people (members) by their features, and it is by knowing and understanding these features that a person can identify fellow (and other) members of a community of practice. It would enable one to distinguish, for example, nurses from physiotherapists, but also among different categories of nurse. But how does going beyond the labelling offer explanatory potential to the discourse analyst? Recall that in the data extracts above we have categorized nurses as: counsellor, manager, healer, carer, educator. Schegloff suggests three facets of his categories which offer more explanatory ways of understanding how these roles are constructed in part through interaction: firstly, through what he calls *Inference-richness*; secondly, through what he refers to as *Protected against induction;* and thirdly, through what he identifies as *Category-bound activities.* I examine each in turn below from the perspective of understanding nursing identity in context and in action.

Membership categories for Schegloff are *inference-rich*:

> They are the store house and the filing system for the common-sense knowledge of ordinary people – that means ALL people in their capacity as ordinary people – have about what people are like, how they behave etc. …
> (Schegloff 2007: 469)

For a lay person (and by this I include discourse analysts) to understand a broad and superordinate professional category such as nursing (or its various sub-categorisations) requires, as I have argued earlier, a certain knowledge of not only professional structures but also of changes over time and place in the health care system, disease patterns, advances in medical science and nursing practices. As we saw from the data extracts earlier, nurses perform certain functions at any one time as and when appropriate (see Table 1 and Examples 1–3). For the lay person who will understand the nursing world only from limited personal experience, and often perhaps only from the perspective of a hospital environment, the depth and breadth of professional practice might be surprising. Such understanding is fundamental to an inference-rich evaluation of the discourses of nursing practice and the identification of nursing identities.

Schegloff continues in relation to the facet *Protected against induction*:

> The common sense knowledge organised by reference to membership categories is *protected against induction*. If an ostensible member of a category appears to contravene what is "known" about members of the category, then people do not revise that knowledge, but see the person as "an exception", "different", or even a defective member of the category.
> (Schegloff 2007: 469)

However, that this facet of *protection against induction*, although illuminating, may not necessarily apply in a particular moment in a professional context such as nursing, is evidenced in Example 3 above when Mrs R gently corrects her husband (lines 18–19: "Well Mary looks for other values too Jim, she looks for different things you know"). This seems to suggest that Mrs R has been made aware of, and acknowledges nursing practices, which her husband is not understanding. Note that the extract does not, overall, suggest that the patient and her husband believe this particular nurse to be an exception or different. Rather, they have accepted the expertise and knowledge on the part of the nurse which are necessary for Mrs R's care. Mr and Mrs R are aware that nurses' identify need and make use of resources which are available as a result of their membership of a specific COP (see lines 9–10 in Example 3). I argue that once a person becomes a patient, then an opportunity is presented for them to view nurses (or the category in question) with increased understanding as a result of their exposure to this COP. In such situations people can, and *do*, revise their knowledge.

Schegloff's third facet is that of *category-bound activities*. He writes:

> Among the items that compose category-based common sense knowledge are kinds of activities or actions or forms of conduct taken by the common-sense or vernacular culture to be specially characteristic of a category's members ... what Sacks termed category-bound activities ...
> (Schegloff 2007: 470)

This facet is of particular explanatory relevance when discourse analysts (or patients for that matter) discuss nursing activities, if only because such people often express surprise at the extent of nursing knowledge and nursing practices required for their understanding, suggesting that common-sense or popular beliefs inadequately reflect professional reality. As Mr R (from the source of Example 3 but not reported in this data) stated when reflecting on recent health experiences, "I knew I didn't know much, but I didn't know I knew *less* than nothing".

At the very least, then, Sacks' and Schegloff's work on membership categorisation and the facets above raises issues concerning the explanatory adequacy of analyses based only on common-sense knowledge. Almost axiomatically, as Hak (1999) points out, the knowledge level of the analyst has the potential to affect the richness, if not the adequacy of the analysis. What is clear, following on Sacks' proposition, is that Cheryth, Jane and Mary are in professional relationships with Mrs S, Mrs C, and Mr and Mrs R respectively, and are identified by the patients as the persons to whom they each had a right and obligation to turn to with their health needs. The nurses therefore fit into the Rp (Relationship proper) category. They also fit into another category, Kp, i.e. the proper person based on professional knowledge.

3.   Towards collaborative understanding

The discussion so far has focused on what is required of discourse analysts in terms of understanding nursing identities and roles across time and space. Although mentioned earlier in this chapter but not yet explicitly canvassed, the logic of the position of "sharing knowing" is for discourse analysts and nursing professionals to engage in a practice of *collaborative* understanding. Such understanding of identity in practice is not, however, the responsibility of discourse analysts alone. Identifying identity on the part of nurses needs equally to be self-initiated and self-focused. After all, it is only reasonable to propose that the education, and experiences in practice of nurses impacts on the care of patients and is reflected in their discourse and the manner in which they are identified, and that drawing on that education and experience will offer a basis for explanatory accounts.

How can nurses be prepared for changes in their perceptions of their nursing identities and in the perceptions of others? Saltmarsh, North and Koop (2002) are quite clear that nursing education requires nursing to be seen as a process – a "work in process" – where nurses need to conceptualise themselves through "first-hand experience … within a diverse array of contexts":

> Educational institutions such as universities, and social institutions such as hospitals, may be seen as discursive participants in nursing education, which construct identities for themselves, as institutions, and in that process, play an important role in informing the constructed identities of nursing students.
> (Saltmarsh, North and Koop 2002: 5)

In the light of the discussion earlier on the requirements on understanding for analysts of professional discourse, one can pose a similar and parallel challenge to nurses. How familiar can they become with these *analytic themes* (see Roberts and Sarangi 2005) of discourse analysis as a means of explaining how their professional and focal themes are constructed and played out through discourse? Such an objective has long been targeted by raising nurses' awareness of the nature of the patient-nurse relationship through monitored audio-visual displays of professional practice in action (see Faulkner [1992] as one example). What more recent discussion suggests is that such awareness can be usefully extended and channelled into a richer professional development program, one which acknowledges that participants are continually constructing their identities as their nursing and their associated discourse goals are identified. Such a process would be indicative of the nurse applying her knowledge of the principles of what we might term *therapeutic communication,* so that the discourse, the vehicle for nursing care in this instance, is not only revealed as context and participant-sensitive, but also as eliciting that rich and appropriate information for relevant professional goals to be identified and related interventions planned/implemented. We see this in the Examples excerpted above in the case of the Community Nurse. In each instance she is demonstrating the skills of an expert nurse as identified by Benner (1984). In particular, how as an expert nurse, she demonstrates her therapeutic communication skills to a level where her identity/identities are unambiguous, so that care is sensitive, safe and effective.

How can such therapeutic communication be addressed as part of professional development programs, whether for nurses or for discourse analysts? In essence, by means of a *parallel* pattern and system, focused on the awareness, analysis and evaluative explanation of a range of therapeutically directed communicative strategies and skills, within a problem-based curriculum. Such a curriculum would take an experientially based learning approach drawing on a total-situation focused learning methodology (based on the principles of problem based learning). Such a methodology involves making discourse meaningful by engaging in a data-driven analysis of interactions between nurse and patient, nurse and nurse, nurse and other health care professionals. Its aim is to develop a sensitivity to, and understanding of, the process of "therapeutic communication" in the health care workplace. By analysing discourse in the context of the total situation – the patient's socio-cultural-economic background, education, ethnicity, language background, health situation etc drawing on authentic and/or simulated interactions between nurses and patients or nurses and other nurses/other professionals, both parties – nurses and discourse analysts – can come to collaborative understandings of how such interactions are discursively constructed, but always against a background of institutional and professional knowledge over time and place. In doing so, such a curriculum would go some considerable way to setting the conditions for the exploration of what Cicourel, in a number of places (Cicourel 2003, 2007), refers to as *"ecological validity"* in research (and, we may say, in education and professional development).

4.   A way forward in collaborative practice

Health care has long been the site of much useful research, traditionally with its focus centered on the doctor-patient relationship (Candlin and Candlin 2003). More recently, nurse-patient relationships and interactions have been the site of investigation, much of this being conducted by nurses, with a few taking a discourse analytical perspective. At the same time, as Candlin and Candlin (2003) also indicate, there has been little research undertaken by discourse analysts in the fields and themes of nursing. As this chapter has argued, such a lack poses challenges to both professions: for the discourse analyst to engage meaningfully in the analysis of the professional discourse of nursing calls for more than that "common-sense understanding" of the profession which Sacks (1972) refers to. Equally, for the nurse to collaborate effectively in such an inter-professional endeavour effectively requires her to be engaged in what Gumperz refers to as:

> … an ongoing process of negotiation, both to infer what others intend to convey and to monitor how one's contributions are received … at issue are shared interpretations rather than just denotational meaning … And background knowledge that goes beyond overt lexical information always plays a key role in the interpretative process. (Gumperz 1999: 454)

To enhance her own professional practice, the nurse must be prepared to view the world through another lens, and for researchers, such as discourse analysts, in *their* professional practice there must be an awareness that such mutual understanding is fundamental to their inquiry. Not only do nurses need to reflect on their practice by appraising their professional identities, but so too do discourse analysts if they are to derive relevant and explanatory meanings from professional discourse. In this way inter-professional practice mirrors professional practice. The interpretation of discourse in interaction becomes thus not just a matter shared between patient and nurse, but also between nurse and analyst as a collaborative endeavour where nursing practitioners and discourse practitioners work at entering the world and culture of the other, mutually engaging "in a journey of discovery" (see Candlin 2003: 392). Such a partnership of professional interests can then be effectively translated into professional development support materials in nursing education, as is evidenced, for example, in Candlin (2008).

Such a journey presents challenges to both parties. Not only in terms of the pragmatic and ethical issues (e.g. issues of confidentiality, beneficence, non-maleficence, self-determination and informed consent of all parties) to be addressed, but also in terms of that willingness which is required to develop insights into another discipline, and an acceptance by each of the others' expertise. That such collaboration, both institutionally and professionally, can be successfully achieved is evidenced by a number of discourse analysts working with health care professionals (as one example, see Peräkylä 1995). Further investigation by multi-disciplinary teams, consisting of nurses (either investigating their own communicative practices, or observing others) and discourse analysts, can add depth and knowledge to practice areas and can illuminate and offer explanations for professional practitioners of what might be regarded as common sense knowledge. Such a process is not only likely to increase a mutual awareness of the complexity of the interactive dimension of nursing practice, but by means of its deriving from, and its application to, context can enhance professional practice in patient care.

Notes

1. Transcription conventions:
   // overlapping speech
   = = latching
2. All names in data extracts are fictitious to maintain confidentiality of participants.

References

Aaronson, Lauren. S.
    1989   A challenge for nursing: Reviewing an historic competition. *Nursing Outlook 37*(6): 264–279.
Benner, Patricia
    1984   *From Novice to Expert. Excellence and Power in Clinical Nursing Practice*. Menlo Park: Addison-Wesley.
Burkitt, Ian, Charles Husband, Jennifer Mackenzie and Alison Torn
    2001   *Nurse Education and Communities of Practice*. Research Report Series. London: English National Board for Nursing, Midwifery and Health Visiting.
Candlin, Sally
    1997   *Towards Excellence in Nursing: An Analysis of the Discourse of Nurses and Patients in the Context of Health Assessments*. Unpublished PhD dissertation, Department of Linguistics, University of Lancaster.
Candlin, Sally
    2000   New dynamics in the nurse-patient relationship. In: Srikant Sarangi and Malcolm Coulthard (eds.), *Discourse and Social Life*, 230–245. London: Longman.
Candlin, Sally
    2003   Issues arising when the professional workplace is the site of applied linguistic research. *Applied Linguistics* 24(3): 386–394.
Candlin, Sally
    2008   *Therapeutic Communication: A Lifespan Approach*. Sydney: Pearson Education.

Candlin, Christopher N. and Sally Candlin
    2003   Health care communication as a problematic site for applied linguistic re-
            search. *Annual Review of Applied Linguistics* 23: 134–154.
Candlin, Sally and Christopher N. Candlin
    2007   Nursing through time and space some challenges to the construct of com-
            munity of practice. In: Rick Iedema (ed.), *The Discourse of Hospital Com-
            munication: Tracing Complexities in Contemporary Health Care Organiz-
            ations,* 244–267 Basingstoke: Palgrave Macmillan.
Cicourel, Aaron V.
    2003   On contextualizing applied linguistic research in the workplace. *Applied
            Linguistics* 24(3): 360–373.
Cicourel, Aaron. V.
    2007   A personal, retrospective view of ecological validity. *Text and Talk* 27(5):
            735–752.
Eckert, Penelope and Sally McConnell-Ginet
    1992   Think practically and look locally: Language and gender as community-
            based practice. *Annual Review of Anthropology* 21: 461–90.
Fairclough, Norman
    1992   *Discourse and Social Change.* Cambridge: Polity Press.
Faulkner, Anne
    1992   *Effective Interaction with Patients.* Edinburgh: Churchill Livingstone.
Geertz, Clifford
    1973   *The Interpretation of Cultures.* New York: Basic Books.
Goffman, Erving
    1969   *Strategic Interaction.* Philadelphia: University of Pennsylvania Press.
Goffman, Erving
    1974   *Frame Analysis: An Essay on the Organization of Experience.* New York.
            Harper Row
Gumperz, John J.
    1999   On interactional sociolinguistic method. In: Srikant Sarangi and Celia Ro-
            berts (eds.), *Talk, Work and Institutional Order: Discourse in Medical,
            Mediation and Management Settings,* 453–471. Berlin / New York: Mouton
            de Gruyter.
Hak, Tony
    1999   "Text" and "con-text". Talk bias in studies of health care work. In: S. Sar-
            angi and C. Roberts (eds.), *Talk Work and Institutional Order: Discourse in
            Medical Mediation and Management Settings,* 427–451. Berlin / New
            York: Mouton de Gruyter.
Lakoff, George
    1987   *Women, Fire and Other Dangerous Things: What Categories Reveal about
            the Mind.* Chicago: University of Chicago Press.
Peräkylä, Anssi
    1995   *Aids Counselling: Institutional Interaction and Clinical Practice.* Cam-
            bridge: Cambridge University Press.
Roberts, Celia and Srikant Sarangi
    2003   Uptake of discourse research in interprofessional settings: reporting from
            medical consultancy. *Applied Linguistics* 24(3): 338–359.

Roberts, Celia and Srikant Sarangi
  2005   Theme-oriented discourse analysis of medical encounters. *Medical Edu-
            cation* 39: 632–640.
Sacks, Harvey
  1972   An initial investigation of the usability of conversational data for doing
            Sociology. In: David Sudnow (ed.), *Studies in Social Interaction*, 31–74.
            New York: Free Press.
Sarangi, Srikant and Celia Roberts (eds.)
  1999   *Talk, Work and Institutional Order: Discourse in Medical, Mediation and
            Mangement Settings*. Berlin: Mouton de Gruyter.
Sarangi, Srikant
  2005   The conditions and consequences of professional discourse studies. *Jour-
            nal of Applied Linguistics* 2(3): 371–394.
Sarangi, Srikant
  2007   The anatomy of interpretation: Coming to terms with the analyst's paradox
            in professional discourse studies. *Text and Talk* 27(5): 567–584.
Sarangi, Srikant and Christopher N. Candlin
  2003   Categorization and explanation of risk: A discourse analytical perspective.
            Health Risk and Society 5(2): 115–124.
Saltmarsh, David, Sue North and Tony Koop
  2002   Student expectations of nursing education. *National Review of Nursing
            Education. Nurse Education and Training Vol.1: 5–31*. Canberra: Com-
            monwealth Department of Education, Science and Training.
Schegloff, Emanuel A.
  2007   A tutorial on membership categorization. *Journal of Pragmatics* 39:
            462–482.
Thompson, John B.
  1984   *Studies in the Theory of Ideology*. Cambridge: Polity Press.

25. Crossing the practitioner-researcher boundary: Working with another discipline to examine one's practice

Angus Clarke

Abstract

Long-term collaboration between a practitioner and a discourse analyst researcher is unusual and brings real benefits but requires a substantial investment of effort by both parties. Opening a specialist area of clinical practice to scrutiny by researchers has the potential to provide helpful feedback to practitioners and may thereby improve practice. One further development of joint working can be that the practitioner conducts "social research" interviews with individuals and families already known to him/her through more medical encounters based in practice or research; these interviews inevitably become hybrid activities as the professional's orientation as a practitioner cannot be discarded. Even so, and despite the possible complexities, such hybridity has many more advantages than disadvantages.

1. Introduction

This paper is written from the perspective of a clinical geneticist who has developed collaborations with social science researchers so that his clinical practice can be examined and the impact of genetic disease and genetic information on families can be explored.

We start with a brief extract from a research interview conducted by the author with several members of a family affected by X-linked hypohidrotic ectodermal dysplasia (XHED). This is a sex-linked condition, predominantly affecting males but transmitted through females, that results in the impaired development of sweat glands, teeth and hair. This can result in both medical hazards in early childhood and social, cosmetic challenges in the teens and twenties. The interview from which this extract is taken happens to be the most recent of a series of some twenty interviews with members of XHED families. It is important to note that the researcher was interviewing individuals whom he had met in the past on several occasions over more than 20 years; he spent 18 months during the 1980s conducting a clinical and molecular genetic research project into XHED. For this, the researcher visited families around the UK so as to examine affected and carrier individuals and take blood samples for genetic research. This entailed many visits to the homes of family members, in which the researcher was the guest of each family and during which he heard many family stories about the condition and about coping with the condition. So the participants of this interview have a longstanding relationship; this occasion is just the latest in a long series of encounters.

(Interview One): Finding out about being a carrier
(M, K and T are the adult carrier daughters of N, whose son S – the brother of the three sisters – is affected by XHED. R [not present] is K's husband; R and K have an affected son, C.)

1   Int: Were you sort of like, you sat down and told one day, you know, or was it something that you just sort of picked up slowly …?
2   M: I just picked it up slowly I think. Cos Mum [i.e. N] used to always say didn't she like, … er …
3   K: She used to always go on, going, "You lot, you lot are all carriers so you might have a baby like S" [N's Son]. And she always said that.
4   M: It were quite young weren't it?
5   K: It's probably from when *you* [i.e. the researcher-interviewer] came to see us, 'cos we probably asked her, why is that man coming? And she's just said, "oh, he's coming to see if you can, if you've all got the gene", or whatever, or however she explained it when we were, "to see if you'll have a baby like S [N's Son] when you're bigger". And we probably knew it from then really didn't we.
6   Int: But that wasn't something that sort of, you know, weighed you down?
7   K: No
8   M: No
9   Int: You just accepted it, and that's the way it is?
10   K: I think if you tell them maybe when they're younger they sort of go, "Oh alright then, fair enough".
11   Int: Yeah
12   K: And then you don't bother about it, but I think if when you're told, like R [K's Husband], 'cos it were like R [K's Husband] knew it was always a possibility we'd have a little boy, and he would have the same as S [N's Son], but in the background of his mind he's still thinking, "Oh no we won't, it'll be alright." So when we did, I think it was more of a shock for him, don't you? [asking her sisters]. And he was more like more taken aback by it, and it took R [K's Husband] a lot longer to get used to, not that he didn't want C [affected son of R and K], but just getting his head round the fact that his child had something wrong with him.

This extract is of interest for several reasons. First, three sisters and their mother and aunt give a collaborative account of how they (the sisters) found out that they were carriers of ectodermal dysplasia (XHED) and they contrast their ready understanding of the situation with the husband's difficulty in accepting that his son was affected. The sisters explain that they knew that they might well have a son affected by the condition because they had been told this many times from an early age. On the other hand, R (K's husband) also knew about this possibility but (as recounted in his absence) his "knowledge" was only superficial, so that he could accept this possibility at one level but did not *believe* it in a deeper sense. (Here, the dialogue enters the domain of epistemology, elaborating the claim that there are several different types of "knowledge", or that declaring that one knows something may serve several different functions.)

In the process of this dialogue as set out above, the sisters advocate informing children at an early age about their genetic carrier status, at least if this is known. (This would be to give them information about the possibility of their having a son affected by the condition.) It becomes clear that the interviewer is referred to in the dialogue as a character in the family script from an episode more than twenty years earlier. This would be a very unlikely occurrence in most research interviews. It occurred here, and in other interview extracts to be discussed below, because my work as a practitioner has led me to collaborate with social researchers. This, in turn, has led me at times to straddle the territory between medicine and the social sciences. As part of these collaborations, I have carried out social research interviews, in which my knowledge both of the condition and of the individual family over the years seems to me often to have enriched the interview.

A number of potential issues or concerns might arise at this point, especially the question of consent to participation (would there be an unfair pressure to participate?) and the reliability and validity of the research (would the findings be distorted by the previous acquaintance?) Of course, there is also the (hoped for) possibility that families would be more willing to participate precisely because of their long-standing relationship with the researcher and that the previous acquaintance of interviewer and interviewees would enrich the interview rather than detract from it. Will families find it easier or more difficult to talk about delicate or sensitive topics with someone whom they already know? (They will surely talk about such topics differently in different settings – within the family, with their family doctor, with an unknown researcher or with a familiar researcher-practitioner.) How can an interview be conducted so as to make accessible the most "natural", "genuine" or "insightful" dialogue?

This raises some additional questions about the conduct and the outputs of research conducted by such hybrid researcher-practitioners. First, how have these collaborations with social researchers worked out? As a practitioner working in the fields of clinical genetics and genetic counselling, how have I found the process of collaborative research with scholars from the fields of communication, discourse and the social sciences? And, second, how have these collaborations worked *as research*? We will first explore my responses to the early phase of collaboration, when I invited social researchers into my clinic. We will then return to look at other aspects of the joint work, examining further extracts from my social research interviews: how have my forays across the border into social research worked *as research?* Are there any more general implications for hybrid (practitioner-researcher) research?

2.   Being observed

One immediate consequence of being observed is the presence in the clinic of researchers, with or without recording equipment. As with many clinicians, we in clinical genetics are accustomed to the presence of "others" in the clinic – colleagues, students and family members other than those centrally involved in the consultation. It is not difficult for a researcher to blend into the setting with minimal impact on the proceedings, as long as they adopt an appropriately tidy but inconspicuous appearance and pattern of behaviour, as if they were from one of the healthcare professions. This is not a question of disguise – the patient or client has given consent to a researcher being present and the researcher is introduced as such – but it is important for the observer not to intrude further into the occasion once their presence has been noted and accepted. The observer should avoid "trying too hard" to detach themselves from the encounter; too active an effort to mark their non-participation in the clinic results in a paradoxical intrusiveness as their presence then becomes unfamiliar, awkward and unnatural (Clarke 2003; see also Sarangi [2007] on "participant paradox").

Simply having an additional trained observer in the room is conducive to constructive reflection and discussion in the gaps between consultations and at the end of a clinic; this may be termed "reflections on practice" (Schön 1983) or "hot feedback". The opportunity to elicit comments from the observer, which may then lead into a detailed discussion of practice, is itself a good reason for opening one's practice to observation. The subsequent access to transcripts of consultations may be another practical benefit, which can be of great value during clinical supervision as well as for simple reflection on one's practice. One can identify key moments in a consultation and consider, "How could I have done that differently?" And of course it is always flattering to have someone take an active interest in what one does and thinks.

3.   Feedback on practice from different perspectives

Beyond this, engagement with colleagues from a different tradition of research is stimulating and has the potential to give additional insights. There is good research to be done into the nature of "feedback and discussion" from different perspectives – from psychotherapy, from "counselling", from ethics, or from discourse analysis. How does feedback and discussion about a clinic consultation differ if it is provided and led from a social research (perhaps discourse) perspective, as opposed to when it is led by a psychotherapist, a counsellor, an ethicist or an experienced colleague? Are the differences the result of the different disciplinary patterns of thought or of the inevitably different personalities of the individuals?

An ethicist will attempt to dissect out, and adjudicate upon, the ethical issues of a case – the principles or virtues at stake balanced against his/her evaluation of the likely consequences of the possible courses of action. The psychotherapist will examine the relationships between those involved in the consultation – and perhaps others absent from the occasion. The counsellor will focus on and assess the interventions of the counsellor, i.e., what could have been done differently. How can the various perspectives each contribute to the support and development of practitioners?

The issues that a practitioner takes to an ethicist will perhaps be different from those s/he takes to a psychologist or counsellor for supervision. S/he will perhaps take to the ethicist a different type of discomfort from that s/he would take to a psychotherapist or a counsellor. In what way are these differences important? How do we distinguish an ethical discomfort about the abstract principles of a case from a personal-emotional feeling that our client is doing something that we regard with distaste or horror? Or, that our client is perhaps being dishonest or manipulative towards his/her partner or towards us, the professionals? Are these differences as real as may at first sight appear – or are our ethical concerns "really" emotional responses that we wish to regard as objective and externally valid? It is of interest that a practitioner will regularly take a problem to a counsellor, a psychotherapist or an ethicist for discussion but it would be unusual for them to take a specific problem to a discourse analyst. Indeed, what type of "problem" would be appropriate for a practitioner to take to a discourse analyst? These reflections serve to indicate an area for more detailed attention in the future.

4.   Cross-disciplinary collaboration and its difficulties

The early stages of collaboration involve the researcher in attending the clinic for an initially intensive familiarisation, with the clinician explaining to the researcher the terminology and giving background information about a range of diseases and the events within the clinic. Equally, the clinician has much to learn about the researcher's perspective – how communication in the clinic has parallels with communication in other settings and what questions may be of interest within the researcher's discipline. There has to be a substantial investment of time and effort by both parties, which needs to be sustained over a number of years if it is to bear fruit. Through spending time together, clinician and researcher can discuss what has been taking place in clinic and work towards a common understanding of the events observed and a joint problematisation (Roberts and Sarangi 1999) of what needs to be explained and accounted for. Both parties need to learn to make sense of the professional language of the other – not only the vocabulary and the formal grammar but the patterns of discourse and interactions as well, i.e. the interaction order; this can happen very effectively in post-consultation discussion of what has just happened in the clinic (for an example, see Sarangi 2002). In addition, attendance at the meetings of each others' professional bodies takes a commitment of both time and effort but may be an excellent way of promoting mutual intelligibility. Where this leads to the emergence of a new hybrid, interdisciplinary discourse, let us hope that it would be readily comprehensible by both groups.

Some researchers or commentators might not see the need for this familiarisation process; they wish to make their contribution towards improving clinical practice without much knowledge or experience of the clinical context. These researchers will be unable to comment upon the details of practice, of setting, of context, of gesture or of nuance. They will not be able to contribute to thinking about the interactions in clinic or the professional-client (doctor-patient) relationships; their contributions will not be readily applicable to an individual case.

There are great benefits if the social science researcher is able to learn some of the science employed in the clinic – by a mixture of reading, watching TV documentaries, explanation or even instruction by the collaborating clinician and colleagues, and (the most difficult to characterise) the slow absorption of facts through "osmosis" (see also the value of long term, informal ethnography in the form of "thick participation", Sarangi [2007]). Similar considerations can apply to social science research on the conduct of other types of natural scientific research or clinical practice. Without good background knowledge of the science or the clinical context, the ability of a social science researcher to engage a participating scientist or practitioner in an interview about their work may be very limited (Collins and Evans 2003). The scarcity of such individuals trained (or at least conversant) in both disciplines has arguably been holding back further progress across a wide range of cross-disciplinary research.

The relationship between clinical practitioner and social researcher will not always work well. Some researchers will gain access to a privileged clinical site, collect data and then retreat into the distance to report their observations without involving the practitioners. They often make crass and easily avoidable errors of interpretation of the events they have witnessed, which will not be corrected in the peer review process if the reviewers are equally ill-informed. Clinicians who have experienced such discourtesy and arrogance in the past can feel reluctant to expose themselves and their patients to another such "smash-and-grab" raid.

Clinicians can also feel that some traditions of "critical" social science research focus excessively on the mere demonstration of inequalities of power in the clinic without recognising that differences in knowledge, experience and judgement are inevitable (and indeed necessary) and underlie much of the difference in authority or power. Indeed, without such inequalities, there would be little point in a patient seeking medical attention or advice. The point, surely, is to examine these inequalities carefully and look at how they play out in the interactions between the various parties. Does the professional use expertise and professional authority constructively, courteously and for the benefit of the patient or client – or not? How is the appropriate use of "power" accomplished, when it happens, and how can we recognise when it is (or is not) occurring and when and how it contributes to the "successful" outcome of the consultation?

5.   Taking account of practitioners' perspectives

Health professionals in many countries, including the UK, are now subject to surveillance in their professional work by an array of mechanisms imposed by our "audit society". Those who open their practice to inspection by researchers – yet another type of surveillance – will often need to be persuaded that there is some potential for benefit from such participation. This benefit could take the form of a realistic prospect of improved patient care and the management of "difficult cases", of improved approaches to the training of healthcare students, of research output, of professional development or of pure interest. Professionals willing to expose themselves in this way should be listened to by the social science researchers so that due account is taken of their perspective. This need not entail the social scientist "caving in" to the demands of an arrogant professional, insisting upon complete control over the research. One aspect of this is the willingness of the researcher to utilise the local knowledge of the practitioner, with due acknowledgement of the "analyst's paradox" (Sarangi 2007); this can be especially important if the findings of the social research are to appeal as interesting and relevant to an audience of practitioners. For example, in working with Sarangi and others on genetic counselling, we used the term "reflective frame" rather than "therapeutic frame" although the latter term was already long established in discourse studies; this is because it would most probably have resulted in professionals misinterpreting both the title and the findings of our publications (Sarangi et al. 2003; Sarangi et al. 2004).

Listening to the practitioners' understandings of an interaction in clinic can also add very substantially to the researcher's understanding of the events observed (Cicourel 2007). How else could the institutional and professional press-

ures operating on a clinician – and influencing their choice of words in a consultation – be given voice and become apparent? One may liken these pressures
to a parrot sitting on the practitioner's shoulder and whispering: "How are you
going to justify this decision to your colleagues when you discuss the case in a
clinical meeting?"; "How will this influence your waiting list for new refer-
rals?"; "Might this make you vulnerable to litigation?" Unless the researcher
discusses the consultations with the practitioner, how would s/he become aware
of this "unspoken voice" simply through analysing the practitioner's speech in
the consultation? The researcher could very easily be entirely oblivious of a
major player in the interaction.

6.   Physical realism or social constructionism?

If researchers are going to benefit from such practitioner insights, they will need
to see the research as a joint construction and therefore respect the clinician's
sensibilities over terminology and even epistemology. Clinicians will generally
adopt a positivist, realist approach to the understanding and management of disease and genes. They (we!) will insist upon the material reality of the human
body, DNA and disease processes. Social factors clearly influence people's
understandings of these phenomena, however, and how these understandings are
constructed through prolonged and complex negotiations, and are then acted
upon within society.

This view could be summarised as being positivist about the physical world
but social constructionist about our knowledge and understanding of it and our
individual and collective responses to the challenges that this presents (Bhaskar
1975). In order to work well together, do clinicians and social scientists need to
share some such explicit theoretical framework? Probably not, but working out
common approaches on these theoretical concerns may enhance cross-disciplinary working.

7.   Joint problematisation

We will now continue this brief digression into the scope for joint working between practitioners and researchers. One benefit of research collaborators discussing specific instances of interaction in a clinical setting is that this can lead
to a shared perspective not only on the theoretical issues but also on "what is at
stake" in the individual case. This amounts to working out a balanced and inclusive approach towards the matter in hand, which can become a joint problematisation (Roberts and Sarangi 1999). Areas, where collaboration between
social/communication researchers and clinician-practitioners is likely to be es-

pecially productive, include the understanding of multi-professional discussions, where multiple voices refer to the same topic but from different practitioner perspectives. Research methods from the "language and communication" stable will be especially helpful at identifying and evaluating the different voices in these multiparty discussions.

8.   Research to inform practice

"Applied" social research is driven by a wish to inform – and improve – practice. So we must consider what types of social research are most likely to contribute to practitioner self-awareness and professional development. In the process, we may hope that clinical practice will be improved. What are the different approaches able to illuminate?

The microanalysis of very brief, recurrent exchanges in a conversation is unlikely to interest the clinician because so much of the context is ignored (Clarke 2005). Observation of clinical areas and consultations can clarify social processes but, if it does not focus on the content of what is being said, it will miss the significance of much that is happening in the healthcare setting. What is likely to be more influential with practitioners is a focus on what the physician or other practitioner is able to achieve with their talk within a setting that has been studied in an attempt to grasp the "talk-in-context" as a whole. A combination of (i) close observation of the scene and the nonverbal interactions, (ii) discourse analysis of spoken practitioner interactions with clients and (iii) interviews to gain the understandings of the various actor-participants will often be required to achieve this. This amounts to something like the "ecological validity" of Cicourel (2007), permitting the investigator to make a broad assessment of what is happening in real life in order to understand the patterns of conversation and interaction either in clinic or in the research interview – listening to what is said while taking account of what is not said but performed (e.g. maintaining face, displaying professional competence, etc). This approach to discourse is the natural methodological ally of the clinician, who will also be attempting to gain as rounded and complete an appreciation of the setting as can be achieved.

9.   The hybrid researcher "in the family script"

We return now to consider what may be gained when a clinical practitioner enters the world of social research and draws upon their professional insights while doing social science. To illuminate the issues raised earlier, we will look at data extracts from research interviews conducted by the author, who was hoping by these means to enhance his understanding of his patients and their families.

The goal here is not for the practitioner to become a convert – to conduct research as if his or her primary discipline and commitment were in the social sciences – because such research could be conducted as well or better by a scholar from the social sciences. Indeed, for a practitioner to become as conversant with the literature and theoretical frameworks across a range of the social sciences as would be expected of a social scientist, while simultaneously maintaining their professional competence, would be a major challenge. Rather, the point is to see whether a hybrid researcher can add anything to social science research beyond acting as a local informant for the social scientist.

The discussion that led to my conducting these interviews was lengthy because the issues raised had necessarily been discussed in relation to funding (through the Wellcome Trust) and the process of research ethics committee approval. It was necessary to consider whether families might feel coerced into participation through prior acquaintance with the researcher-physician and an undue sense of obligation.

The clinical background to the research was my long-standing interest in the uncommon sex-linked disorder, XHED. As referred to earlier, this condition is characterised by the (complete or partial) absence of sweat glands and teeth and by sparse, fine hair on the scalp and the body. It is important to understand that there are at least two distinct ways of viewing this condition because of the different ways in which it may be experienced at different ages. In infancy, XHED can be fatal from overheating in the absence of adequate mechanisms to cool the body and there is often also a long period, sometimes as long as two years, of repeated infections and feeding problems during which the young child can be highly vulnerable. In contrast, while older boys and men do often continue to suffer some symptoms of overheating, they generally learn to cope tolerably well. Instead, it is the stigmatising quality of their physical appearance that most often troubles the adolescents and young adults, especially the sparse hair, the lack of teeth (average of four teeth in total in an affected male) the general dryness of the skin and the wrinkling and pigmentation of the skin around the eyes. While the risk of death falls away after early childhood, especially once an individual is able to recognise their own need to cool down when overheating, the difficulties of coping with stigma remain.

My initial listening to the stories of the families I was visiting as a biomedical researcher, told in their homes in the 1980s to me as their guest, laid the ground for the later phase of socially-oriented research. More recently, I have revisited a number of these families – after twenty years or more – and have been impressed by the families' continued willingness to address difficult and sensitive topics. It was uncertain just how the families would respond to my role as a social researcher, when many of them already knew me from two decades earlier as a clinical genetics researcher. While my knowing some families might have helped to gain access for these interviews, how would it impact on other aspects of the research, such as the ways in which family members would report their feelings and account for their behaviours?

We look at further extracts selected from twenty interviews in which the role of the interviewer was evident as straddling the roles of practitioner and social researcher. While Data Extract 1 was chosen because the interview had been the most recent at the time, Data Extract 2 was chosen because it addressed the question of the affected male's sense of identity.

Data Extract 2 (Interview Two): "Taken to a meeting of the ectodermal dysplasia society"
(Interviewer [Int]; Affected Male [AM])

1 Int: And (.) has that (.) sort of made you (.) um (.) feel like a, you know, an object of curiosity? has it sort of made you feel a bit sort of, "Hey what's going on?"
2 AM: No I mean (.) like anything you study (.) you study I mean people study people for human behaviour and interaction
3 Int: Yeah
4 AM: Like people that have lost their parents young people study them, people will study how they react and interact later on as adults
5 Int: Mm
6 AM: For psychologically purposes or psychology or sociology or whatever (..) same sort of thing really isn't it (.) I mean same as you talk to my Mum or my Nan because they were carriers
7 Int: Mm
8 AM: The the one thing I do find when we had that first meeting as a child
9 Int: Yeah
10 AM: I didn't want to go, I didn't want to go
11 Int: No
12 AM: I just thought said to my Mum
13 Int: You were dragged along
14 AM: I said, "What have I got in common with these people?"
15 Int: Mm
16 AM: And my Mum said, "Well it's not for them it's for the Doctor." And I was like (..) okay I only agreed because it was for you (.) said it was to try and help and that that was it (.) but I didn't
17 Int: I mean I didn't see (.) as far as I was concerned that meeting (.) was you know for the Society and the people to meet up not and I was there [(but to talk)]
18 AM: [right]

19 Int: It wasn't for me
20 AM: You see I didn't want that (.) yeah
21 Int: At least that's how I saw it
22 AM: Yeah (.) you see that that's the the the part I I thought I don't want to be in a group like this (.) group of misfits ((laughs))
23 Int: You don't want to (.) how you ?? identified
24 AM: Yeah I just thought, "Well (..) I don't know these people I'm never going to see them again after that time." I I like I say (.) I stayed in touch with one kid um saw him once or twice and that was it (..) and it's not a reason to stay together

My personal knowledge of individuals and events in the family – my history of contact with the family over decades – appears prominently in this extract. My current contact with others in the family is mentioned in Turn 6, but my previous contact with the family is presented in Turn 16: it appears that I was invoked by this young man's mother, decades ago, as a reason for his having to attend a meeting of the Ectodermal Dysplasia Society (EDS). There is no pretence here of escaping the observer's paradox (known in the social sciences as the Hawthorne effect, in particle physics as Heisenberg's Uncertainty Principle). But the fact that this informant is talking with me, whom he has met on a number of occasions over two decades and whom he knows to be well-informed about XHED, means that he can confidently make reference to events and people because he could trust me to understand without the need for lengthy explanations. This is participation by the researcher that is thicker than thick – beyond merely "thick" participation (Sarangi 2007)!

How has my role impacted on the conduct of these interviews and on what has emerged from them? It is likely that at least some participants agreed to a research interview because they already knew me. Their discussion of events may have been helped by the assumption of shared background knowledge of people and places and of the condition; it is also possible that some interviewees felt able to express feelings that might not have been revealed at all if they had not known the interviewer. In this extract we can see the young man's willingness to discuss his ambivalent feelings about participation in the ED support group.

We next return to the first interview some fifty turns earlier than in Data Extract 1. We find an exchange in which I was asked some clearly medical questions relating to one of my earlier encounters with the family as a clinical researcher. This extract consists, in effect, of my explanation to three sisters, their mother and their aunt about the sweat tests I had performed decades earlier to see how good a test the sweat test was at identifying carriers. As such, the focus here is on my past interactions with the family. So the interviewer has himself become the principal topic within this section of the interview.

Data Extract 3 (Interview One): Explanations about who is a carrier
(Present are three carrier sisters [M, K, T] and their carrier mother, N, as well as N's sister – here silent – and the interviewer [Int])

1   M: Would the girl definitely be a carrier?
2   Int: Yeah, yeah.
3   N: Yeah, yeah. And it obviously, he would probably look into that more ( ) if he ever comes to father a child. You know. Probably think then you know, and start looking into it more but.
4   K: You know when we was younger and we had the tests done, are we all carriers?
5   Int: I think, as I remember it, I think, you all had teeth, some teeth missing at …
6   N: Yeah
7   Int: And, so, so that sort of means that you pretty well have to be carriers I think. So I don't, I don't. I, from ( ) some of you I took blood samples didn't I, and used that so, knowing that you were carriers I used that to help work out where the gene was. So rather than the other way round. So I don't think you've actually had a test. We'd have to go back to the old samples, or get new ones, whatever, and prove that you had it, if you wanted it done. It would be easy enough to do, but I think with the teeth being so definitely affected it didn't seem much point.
8   N: Yeah, cos it was all under Mr J. The three girls and he built the teeth up didn't you? On all of them. And G [Name of Cousin], G was the same. Not under the dental hospital, she had missing teeth.
8   Int: So I think it looks so clear, that I was using that. I was taking that for definite, and using that to help work out. Help learn about the genes. Not the other way round, so, but (if) someone wanted to get it tested then () then someone would easy ?? fix that, but there's probably not much point.
9   K: No
10 N: Can you remember did he do his sweat test as well?
11 Int: And that was also, that was really for me. That was to, 'cause what I wanted to do was look at how good the sweat test was at showing carriers. So I was sort of assuming that you carried it and wanted to see how good is this test you know. How many () someone who might be a carrier and I do the test, and if it shows they're a carrier, that's fine, but, if it doesn't, how reliable is it that they're not?
12 K: Yeah, yeah.

Is it a problem that the interviewer (in his role as a medical practitioner) has become the topic of discussion? I would suggest that it is not. While it is a hybrid activity, certainly, the discussion demonstrates a family making sense of the genetic condition that confronts them and the medical and genetic information they have been given. As such it is of interest from a social and discourse perspective. There are very different opinions expressed by the grandmother N and her daughter, K, about the influence of the condition on plans for having further children. In other sections of the same discussion, the sisters raise further medical questions and, when I noted a possible misunderstanding, I corrected it, despite that intervention crossing the boundaries of a social research interview. One of the ethical challenges of qualitative interviewing for social scientists in a medical context is the problem experienced by the researcher of how to respond when they have noticed a misunderstanding on the part of the interviewee. When the interview is conducted by a practitioner, this challenge may be resolved more simply.

In the following two extracts, however, the situation is different. These two extracts were chosen because they include explicitly medical questions, put to me by a family member:

Data Extract 4 (Interview Three): Asking a medical question
(AM is the affected male; MO is his mother, whose nephew Peter also has XHED; interviewer [Int.])

1   MO: Our Peter (.) our nephew gets asthma (.)
2   Int: Yes
3   MO: Really quite severely. Is that connected?
4   Int: I think there's a lot of asthma about anyway.
5   MO: Yes
6   Int: A lot of children have that now. But I think it is more common in people with this.
7   MO: Right
8   Int: I think it's probably because, (.) in the same way that the skin doesn't make as much sweat, the airways don't make as much mucus. So that little bits, particles – pollen and stuff – that goes down on the chest and instead of getting trapped in the mucus and just come (.) being brought up, you know, when you cough and clear your throat it, sort of, stays in the lungs more and that can trigger an allergy more. So I think it is more common in people with ED but, I mean, it still, sort of, there are plenty of people with ED who don't have it.
9   AM: ((hh-hmm))
10 Int: Who don't have asthma.
11 MO: And are they more prone to be sensitive? Because [name of AM] has a nut allergy as well.
12 Int: I think the same is true in the gut. Yeah.

Here we have the researcher giving a medical opinion, with the social research agenda very much laid to one side for that moment. The family is using this occasion as a home visit (a "domiciliary consultation") by an interested clinician. In other words, the "research interview" becomes blurred with a "consultation" as far as the participants are concerned. Is this, then, purposeless as far as the social research agenda is concerned? Consider the next data extract too.

Data Extract 5 (Interview Four): Providing Information about the origin of ED in females
(Discussion between the mother [MO] of a boy affected with XHED and the researcher [Int], about a meeting of a family support group at which several affected girls were present. The mother [MO] has explained that they appeared more severely affected than most female carriers of XHED.)

1 Int: So, I think, the girls that you might have seen who had really quite marked problems probably had a totally different condition.
2 MO: A totally (.) yeah.
3 Int: Another type of ED
4 MO: Oh, right.
5 Int: But a totally different type of ED that <u>will</u> affect girls as much as boys.
6 MO: 'Cause can it be – I don't know if this is the right terminology – like a mute gene that it will suddenly start in a family?
7 Int: It can (.) yeah (.) it can sometimes just crop up out of the blue as a new change in the genetic material
8 MO: Right.

This extract shows a discussion about ectodermal dysplasia in general – that it is not one condition and that some types affect boys and girls to much the same extent. Here again the researcher is giving medical information and straying away from the "pure" social research agenda and his role as a researcher.

Data Extract 6 (Interview One)
(K is a carrier mother of one affected male, brother of another)

1 K: I've already thought to myself now, now I've had [Name of Daughter], I've already thought, well she must be a carrier if I've got C [Name of Affected Son].
2 Int: Well she may be, but she may not be ..

Do these interludes have value in relation to the social research agenda? They do give an indication as to the level of understanding of the science that has been achieved by family members in these interviews – and that is of interest. The questions posed by the family in Data Extract 5 can be answered by the interviewer most convincingly because he was present at the family support group meeting discussed in the extract. But that need not be of great value for the social research, if conceived of narrowly.

Also in Interview One, however, we can point to occasions where the researcher's previous knowledge of the family was most likely of great value in allowing important material to emerge in the flow of conversation. One can never know what would have emerged in different circumstances but these sections are of real interest.

Data Extract 7 (Interview One)
(N is carrier mother of one affected male, grandmother of another)

1   Int: And is it the worry about how the boys will do physically or …
2   N: No, I think they'll do very well, you know, physically or mentally, …
3   Int: Or the name calling and this sort of …
4   N: It's, I don't really want them to have children with it
5   Int: Just because it's, because it's a problem and you'd rather see it go no further …
6   N: Yeah, yeah.
7   Int: Whatever it was really
8   N: Yeah, I just really rather not have them [Affected Boys], which they [Carrier Daughters] would as well, but, if they had them they had them but you know, I don't know what it is, it's just really affected me the last few years obviously …

This poignant disclosure is a moment of sadness for N, but is later contradicted or overruled by one of her daughters, K, after some forty turns:

Data Extract 8 (Interview One)

1   K: If I were, we said this, if I was at home and we could afford for me to stay at home then maybe we would have had more, but I think with the sleepless night, actually our [Patient name] was quite a good sleeper apart from when he was ill, and, [K's daughter]'s terrible so it's put us off. ((laughter)) And I just like, I quite look forward to not having that baby issue again. ((laughter)) So now we've said, the four of us is just nice, so yeah, but it's nothing to do with
2   Int: But it's not particularly to do with this.
3   K: Oh, no, nothing at all. That wouldn't bother me at all.

Here we see mother and daughter openly (but gently and respectfully) displaying very different perspectives on the same topic – and in front of other family members and even a researcher. I think that such delicate moments are more likely to be shared with a researcher already well known to the family, although one cannot be certain of this. Indeed, there may be circumstances where "anonymity" – not knowing the researcher – may promote openness more effectively.

10.   Conclusion

This paper has reported some of the experiences of a clinician who has engaged with research in the social sciences, making explicit some of the practical consequences of doing so. While not always comfortable, the exercise is worthwhile and helpful.

In addition, we have discussed the further engagement of a clinician in social research through an examination of interviews conducted by the author. The boundaries between clinical consultation and social research interview are not rigid but they do seem to be transgressed in these interviews. Taking the interviews in the round, however, it can be argued that attending to the interviewees' topics – the clinical disorder and the family's understandings of its inheritance and its scientific basis – is not so much a distraction as an opportunity for the social research agenda to be explored while the hybrid researcher keeps faith (as a health professional) with the families. The "interviews" contain elements of several distinct activity types – consultation in the form of home visit, social reunion and social research interview. We can see that it was possible for the interviews to cover very delicate ground and make explicit some disagreements – at least, some differences of perspective – within otherwise very cohesive families.

In these interviews, it would be unnatural and perhaps even unprofessional for the practitioner-interviewer not to digress from the social research agenda to respond helpfully to requests for clinical information and clarification. This must of course be within his competence and he should also take care not to give opinions or advice that conflict unhelpfully with those of the medical professionals responsible for the care of family members. These "digressions" can be really helpful for the family; they may be regarded by the researcher as a distraction from the social research but as being worthwhile nevertheless. If the goal of the interview is discussion along the social agenda, then these interruptions can be seen as necessary to maintain the flow of that social agenda as it would appear quite unnatural to both parties if the interviewer refused to address any of the medical or genetic questions of the interviewee. These digressions must then, I would argue, be accepted as inevitable if one is to gain the research benefits of using practitioner professionals to conduct social research interviews with patients or families whom they already know or with patients affected by a disease with which they have some considerable experience.

While some health professionals – and doubtless some social researchers – will regard this hybrid interviewing as deeply unsatisfactory, I would counter by arguing that it can operate to the benefit of both parties. The questioning of the family can be informed by insights that most other researchers would most likely not share, and the experience of such socially-oriented interviewing may be of real benefit to the development of the practitioner – it can inform his/her future clinical work as well as contributing to (social science) research.

Appendix

Transcription conventions
Italics and/or **Bold** indicate emphasis
Quotation marks "....." indicate constructed speech presented as direct reported speech.
Dots ..... indicate a slight pause with voice trailing, often taken to indicate the end of a turn
Brackets with dot (.) or dots (...) shorter or less short pauses that interrupt the flow of a turn
Empty brackets (   ) not transcribed because unclear
Double brackets ((   )) other sounds, i.e. "noises off"
Square brackets [person or relationship] substitute for names in the interests of anonymisation

References

Bhaskar Roy
    1975   *A Realist Theory of Science*. London: Verso.
Cicourel, Aaron. V.
    2007   A personal, retrospective view of ecological validity. *Text & Talk* 27(5): 735–752.
Clarke Angus
    2003   On being an object of research: Reflections from a professional perspective. *Applied Linguistics* 24(3): 374–385.
Clarke Angus
    2005   Commentary: Professionals' theories and institutional interaction. *Communication & Medicine* 2(2): 189–191.
Collins Harry M and Robert Evans
    2003   The third wave of science studies: Studies of expertise and experience. *Social Studies of Science* 32: 235–296.
Roberts, Celia and Srikant Sarangi
    1999   Hybridity in gatekeeping discourse: issues oof practical relevance for the researcher. In: Sarangi, S. and roberts, C. (eds.) *Talk, Work and Institutional Order: Discourse in Medical, Mediation and Mangement Settings* 473–503. Berlin: Mouton de Gruyter.

Sarangi, Srikant
    2002   Discourse practitioners as a community of interprofessional practice: Some
            insights from health communication research. In: Christopher N. Candlin
            (ed.), *Research and Practice in Professional Discourse*, 95–135. Hong
            Kong: City University of Hong Kong Press.
Sarangi, Srikant
    2007   The anatomy of interpretation: Coming to terms with the analyst's paradox
            in professional discourse studies. *Text & Talk* 27(5/6): 567–584.
Sarangi, Srikant, Angus Clarke, Kristina Bennert and Lucy Howell
    2003   Categorisation practices across professional boundaries: Some analytic in-
            sights from genetic counselling. In: Sarangi, Srikant and Theo van Leeuwen
            (eds.), *Applied Linguistics and Communities of Practice*, 150–168. London:
            Continuum.
Sarangi, Srikant, Kristina Bennert, Lucy Howell, Angus Clarke, Peter Harper and
            Joanthon Gray
    2004   Initiation of reflective frames in counselling for Huntington's disease pre-
            dictive testing. *Journal of Genetic Counseling* 13: 135–155
Schön, Donald
    1983   *The Reflective Practitioner: How Professionals Think in Action*. New York:
            Basic Books.

26.   The linguist in the witness box

Malcolm Coulthard

Abstract

This chapter looks at some of the problems faced by linguists who choose to act as expert witnesses and some of the solutions they have produced. The chapter begins with an illustration of linguistic evidence presented in a famous American trademark case. It then moves on to discuss the laws on expert evidence in different English speaking adversarial jurisdictions, concentrating in some detail on the American Daubert criteria and their significance for linguistic evidence. The chapter then examines and evaluates differing ways of expressing opinions, the semantic and the statistical, and ends with examples of the presentation of evidence in two English Appeal Court cases.

1.   Scenario

In 1997 McDonald's Corporation took Quality Inns International, Inc, to court claiming they had ownership not simply of the name McDonald's but also of the initial morpheme "Mc" and therefore could prevent its use in other trademarks. Quality Inns had announced they were going to create a chain of basic hotels and call them McSleep, claiming, when challenged, that they hoped the "Mc" prefix would evoke a Scottish link and with it the Scots' well-known reputation for frugality. McDonald's, who had previously successfully prevented the use of the name McBagel's, when a judge had decided that the prefix could not be used in conjunction with a generic food product, decided to challenge the McSleep mark, claiming it was a deliberate attempt to draw on the goodwill and reputation of the McDonald's brand.

   In supporting their case McDonald's pointed out that they had deliberately set out, in one advertising campaign, to create a "McLanguage" with Ronald McDonald teaching children how to "Mc-ise" the standard vocabulary of generic words to create "McFries", "McFish", "McShakes" and even "McBest".

   Fanciful as this linguistic imperialism might seem to be to ordinary users of the language, particularly to those of Scottish or Irish descent, who would seem to be in danger of losing their right to use their own names as trademarks? The lawyers took the claim very seriously. Quality Inns' lawyers asked linguist Roger Shuy to help with two linguistic arguments, firstly, that the morpheme "Mc" was in common use productively, in contexts where it was not seen to be linked in any way to McDonald's; and secondly, that such examples showed that the prefix, originally a patronymic and equivalent in meaning to the morpheme *son* in John*son*, had become generic and thus now had a meaning of its own, which was recognisably distinct from both of the other major meanings, "son of" and "associated with the McDonald's company".

Shuy chose a corpus linguistics approach and searched to find real text instances of what one might call "Mcmorphemes". Among the 56 examples he found were general terms like McArt, McCinema, McSurgery and McPrisons, as well as items already being used commercially such as the McThrift Motor Inn, a budget motel with a Scottish motif and McTek a computer discount store which specialised in Apple Mac computer products. On the basis of such examples, Shuy (2002: 99) argued that the prefix had become, in the language at large, an independent lexical item with its own meaning of "basic, convenient, inexpensive and standardized". Rather than resort to corpus evidence themselves, McDonald's hired market researchers to access the public's perception of the prefix directly and to do so through interview and questionnaire. The experts reported that their tests confirmed that consumers did indeed associate the prefix with McDonald's, as well as with reliability, speed, convenience and cheapness. Faced with this conflicting evidence, the judge ruled in favour of McDonald's, thereby giving them massive control over the use of the "Mc" morpheme.

Of course, the successful defence of a trademark may occasionally have unwanted consequences. In March 2007 McDonald's went to war against the Oxford English Dictionary, after it described a McJob as "an unstimulating, low-paid job with few prospects, [especially] one created by the expansion of the service sector". The company's Chief People Officer (sic) for Northern Europe suggested the OED should change the definition to make it "reflect a job that is stimulating, rewarding and offers genuine opportunities for career progression and skills that last a lifetime". In fact this is one further skirmish in the constant battle to maintain the mark, because it is insisting that the word "mcjob" can only have one meaning "a job at McDonald's", which is patently not what it is taken to mean by the general population.

2.   Introduction

In the past twenty years, there has been a rapid growth in the frequency with which Courts in a number of countries have called upon the expertise of linguists in cases where there is a dispute about aspects of a written text – I will not treat here the related, but methodologically very different, discipline of forensic phonetics to which a brief introduction can be found in Coulthard and Johnson (2007: Chapter 7) and a much more detailed one in Rose (2002). The cases in which linguistic evidence has been used range from disputes about the degree of similarity in pronunciation and therefore confusability of trademarks (Gibbons 2003: 285–7) and the meaning of individual words in jury instructions (Levy 1993), through the "ownership" of particular words and phrases in a plagiarism case (Turell 2004), to accusations of fabrication of whole texts in certain murder cases (Coulthard 2002). Usually the linguist uses standard analytic tools to reach an opinion, although few cases require exactly the same selection from the linguist's toolkit. Occasionally, though, cases raise new and exciting questions for descriptive linguistics, which require basic research, such as how can one measure the "rarity" and therefore the evidential value of individual expressions (Coulthard 2004) or the reliability of verbal memory (Coulthard and Johnson 2007: 132–5).

3.   On becoming a linguistic expert

For linguists wanting to move into expert witness work the criteria vary from country to country. Australia and Britain share essentially the same position, which is that it is the expert rather than the method that is recognised and so courts can allow expert opinions from anyone considered to have:

> … specialised knowledge based on … training, study or experience [provided that the opinion is] wholly or substantially based on that knowledge.
> (Australian Evidence Act 1995, Sec. 79)

Usually, once an expert has been accepted by one court, s/he will be accepted unchallenged by other courts at the same level. The expert is retained and paid by one side, but even so, legally s/he is "appointed by the court" (Bromby 2002: 21) and since 2007 experts in Britain have had to include in their reports a statement to confirm that they have provided an objective, unbiased opinion.

There are, however, no explicit rules, as there are in the USA following the Daubert ruling (see below), on the nature of the theoretical position or the methodology or the evidence on which the expert bases his/her opinion and so, once an expert has been retained, the court will determine, "*ad hoc,* the sufficiency of expertise and the relevance of that expertise to each case in question" (Bromby 2002: 9). As part of this process both the competence of the expert and the reliability of the method(s) s/he has used can be subjected to detailed examination, which can last for many hours. Even after deciding to allow an expert to give evidence, the judge(s) and/or jury may decide it is not helpful, persuasive or relevant and ignore it and occasionally, at the end of a trial, experts are severely censured by the court and/or particular methodologies deemed to be unacceptable (Hardcastle 1997).

However, the situation in Britain is changing: from 2008 the Council for the Registration of Forensic Practitioners, "set up in 1999 in response to concerns about miscarriages of justice in which deficient scientific evidence was implicated", will begin to register Forensic Linguists following a rigorous peer review of sample case reports (for further information see http://www.crfp.org.uk).

4.   The United States

Unlike the Anglo-Australian system, the American legal system approves the technique(s) that a witness uses rather than the witness him/herself. Rule 702 of the Federal Rules of Evidence allows an expert to testify as a witness if:

> the testimony is based upon sufficient facts or data, [and] the testimony is the product of reliable principles and methods, and the witness has applied the principles and methods reliably to the facts of the case

Rule 702 is designed to take account of the 1993 Daubert Ruling (explained below) which dramatically changed the nature of allowable evidence and distanced the American system even further from the Anglo-Australian one. In what follows, I draw substantially on Tiersma and Solan (2002) and Solan and Tiersma (2004), which readers are advised to study in their entirety.

There have been three stages in defining the admissibility of expert evidence in the United States. Until 1975, the main standard for evaluating expert testimony was the Frye test, named after a ruling in a 1923 case involving the admissibility of lie detector evidence, which required there to be general acceptability of the principles and/or methodology which the expert had used:

> … while courts will go a long way in admitting expert testimony deduced from a well-recognized scientific principle or discovery, the thing from which the deduction is made must be sufficiently established to have gained general acceptance in the particular field in which it belongs …
> (293 F. at 1014, as quoted in Tiersma and Solan [2002: 223])

As time went by, Frye came to be seen as too rigorous. It was argued that scientific knowledge advances by argument and dissent, so there was pressure to allow the judge and/or jury to hear opinions from both sides when there was serious academic disagreement, and in 1975 the Federal Rules of Evidence were introduced with the following observation on the admissibility of expert evidence:

> … if scientific, technical, or other specified knowledge will assist a trier of fact to understand the evidence or to determine a fact in issue, a witness qualified as an expert by knowledge, skill, experience, training, or education, may testify thereto in the form of an opinion or otherwise.
> (Rule 702 as quoted in Tiersma and Solan [2002: 223])

Even so, and confusingly, some federal courts continued to apply Frye until 1993, when the Supreme Court ruled in the case of *Daubert v. Merrell Dow Pharmaceuticals*. The main argument in that appeal was over whether expert evidence could be rejected on the grounds that the experts involved had not published their work and had thereby failed to meet the Frye test. In their ruling the Supreme Court observed that "the adjective 'scientific' implies a grounding in the methods and procedures of science" and then went on to propose four criteria with which to evaluate "scientific-ness":

1. whether the theory ... has been tested;
2. whether it has been subjected to peer review and publication;
3. the known rate of error; and
4. whether the theory is generally accepted in the scientific community.
(509 U.S. at 593 as quoted in Tiersma and Solan [2002: 224])

This ruling left open the question of whether it covered evidence which was descriptive rather than theoretical, but a ruling in 1999, in the case of Kumho Tire Co. v. Carmichael, confirmed that it did:

... the general principles of Daubert apply not only to experts offering scientific evidence, but also to experts basing their testimony on experience.
(119 S.Ct. 1173 as quoted in Tiersma and Solan [2002: 224])

So, where does that leave the American forensic linguist? On the positive side Tiersma and Solan note that:

... courts have allowed linguists to testify on issues such as the probable origin of a speaker, the comprehensibility of a text, whether a particular defendant understood the Miranda warning, and the phonetic similarity of two competing trademarks.
(Tiersma and Solan 2002: 221)

However, in other areas the situation is more problematic, partly, perhaps, because some non-linguists have used some of the linguistic labels for methodologies which are not linguistically sound. For example, the Van Wyk case in 2000 seemed to set a precedent for excluding *stylistic analysis*, as the court refused to allow an expert to give evidence about the authorship of disputed documents, but, as McMenamin (2002) points out, the expert in the case had no qualifications in linguistics. McMenamin (2004) argues a strong case for the scientific nature of his own brand of forensic stylistics and therefore for its acceptability under Daubert. Indeed, he shows, in a case study of the significant documents in the Jon Benet Ramsey case, how to express opinions in terms of statistically calculated probabilities (McMenamin 2004: 193–205). It appears that the linguistic area of *discourse analysis* may have suffered similar loss of credibility through a non-linguist claiming expertise. Tiersma and Solan quote a judge's observation in a 1984 case, *State v. Conway,* following evidence from a psychologist, that discourse analysis is a "discipline allowing [the expert] to determine the intent of the speaker in covertly recorded conversations", which shows just how much re-education needs to be done.

Nevertheless, it must be conceded that, in cases where conclusions depend on observations about the frequency or rarity of particular linguistic features in the texts under examination, many linguists would have considerable difficulty in stating a "known rate of error" for their results, even if this phrase is interpreted as a likelihood ratio. It is for this reason that some linguists will be forced to change their way of reaching and presenting their opinions, while others may choose to see their role more as that of educator/teacher/"tour guide" than of opinion giver (Solan 1998).

5.   Giving opinions

The professional life of the expert linguist, as opposed to that of the academic linguist, can be very lonely, as the majority of experts work alone, on occasional cases and rarely go to court to give evidence: most of them average fewer than ten cases a year and one court appearance every two years. For this reason, giving evidence in person in court is, for the majority of forensic linguists, an uncommon and stressful event. As Shuy observes:

> For those who have never experienced cross-examination, there is no way to emphasise how emotionally draining it can be … Testifying is not for the weak at heart. (Shuy 2002: 3–4)

Nor indeed for the weak at stomach – one colleague eventually gave up, after some 25 years as an expert witness, saying he could no longer cope with the vomiting before every appearance in the witness box.

Once the data analysis has been done and an opinion reached, the linguist is faced with two interactional problems: firstly, how can s/he best transmit the linguistic insights and findings in a written report to an audience of legal professionals, who also consider themselves language experts, and who, despite what was said above about the impartiality of the expert, want to (mis-)use the findings to construct a complicated legal case for innocence or guilt; and secondly, if s/he is called to give oral evidence, the linguist has to cope with the unusual interactional rules of the courtroom which involve lawyers asking questions, notionally on behalf of the court, and the witness being expected to address answers not to the questioning lawyer but directly to the judge and/or jury. Even more difficult can be cross-examination which pits an expert, who has sworn to obey the Gricean maxims of quality and quantity, against a lawyer who is under no such constraints and can apparently at will imply what he may "believe to be false" and say things for which he "lacks proper evidence", as well as cut off the expert in midflow to allow a partially completed truthful answer to imply an untruth.

Maley observes, in an excellent paper examining linguistic aspects of expert testimony, that:

... expert witnesses, particularly if they are new and inexperienced, tend to be quite unaware of the extent to which shaping and construction of evidence goes on ... All too often they emerge frustrated from the courtroom, believing that they have not been able to give their evidence in the way they would like and that their evidence has been twisted and/or disbelieved.
(Maley 2000: 250)

And this despite the fact that experts are generally allowed speaking turns that are on average two to three times longer than those of other witnesses (Heffer 2002).

All experts face these communication problems, but the linguist has the additional and unique problem that everyone is in some senses an expert on language. Indeed it is very difficult to call a linguist to give evidence on word meaning, because courts are mainly interested in two kinds of meaning: *technical*, legally defined meaning, as for instance the meaning of "dusk" in a statute which says "The park gates will be closed at dusk", and where "dusk" will have been given a specific meaning elsewhere in the statute as something like "30 minutes after sunset"; and *commonsense* meaning, which is what a jury, being a collective representative of the common man, thinks a word means – so much so that juries are normally denied dictionaries within the jury room.

When acting as an expert the linguist will typically be asked first to write a report expressing an opinion – (McMenamin [2002: 176–8] has a useful section on report writing) – and then later s/he may be asked to go to court to present and defend that opinion.

In 2002 Stuart Campbell was tried and convicted for the murder of his niece, Danielle. Part of the evidence against him was a couple of text messages sent to his phone from Danielle's phone shortly after she disappeared. The prosecution suspected that he had actually sent them to himself using her phone and I was asked to compare the style of the two suspect messages with a set of 70 which Danielle had sent over the previous three days. Unfortunately there was no similar corpus of texts composed by Campbell to use for comparison purposes.

Below is the first of the suspect text messages:

HIYA STU WOT U UP 2.IM IN SO MUCH TRUBLE AT HOME AT MOMENT EVONE HATES ME EVEN U! WOT THE HELL AV I DONE NOW? Y WONT U JUST TELL ME TEXT BCK PLEASE LUV DAN XXX

It displays a series of linguistic choices which were either absent from, or rare in, the Danielle corpus; for example, the use of capitals rather than sentence case, the spelling of "what" as "wot", the spelling in full of the morpheme "one" in "EVONE", rather than its substitution by the numeral "1", the omission of the definite article in the abbreviation of the prepositional phrase "AT MOMENT" and the use of the full form of the word "text" rather than an abbreviation "TXT" in the phrase "TEXT BCK". The problem was how to reach and then express an opinion on the likelihood that Danielle did or did not produce the message.

6.   Expressing opinions semantically

The majority of forensic linguists (and phoneticians) have traditionally felt that they were unable to express their findings statistically in terms of mathematical probability and so expressed them as a semantically encoded opinion. Indeed, some experts simply express their opinion without giving any indication to the court of how to evaluate its strength, or of how that opinion fits with the two legally significant categories of "on the balance of probabilities" and "beyond reasonable doubt". However, a growing number of experts now use a fixed semantic scale and attach that scale as an Appendix to their report to enable the reader to assess the expert's confidence in the opinion s/he has reached.

At the time of the Danielle case I was using the scale of opinions below, which I had adapted from the 11-point scale devised by members of the International Association of Forensic Phoneticians:

Most Positive
5   "I personally feel *quite satisfied* that X is the author"
4   "It is in my view *very likely* that X is the author"
3   "It is in my view *likely* that X is the author"
2   "It is in my view *fairly likely* that X is the author"
1   "It is in my view *rather more likely than not* that X is the author"
0   "It is in my view *possible* that X is the author"
−1   "It is in my view *rather more likely than not* that X is *not* the author"
−2   "It is in my view *fairly likely* that X is *not* the author"
−3   "It is in my view *likely* that X is *not* the author"
−4   "It is in my view *very likely* that X is *not* the author"
−5   "I personally feel *quite satisfied* that X is *not* the author"
Most Negative

The opinion I gave was −2 on the above scale, i.e. that it was *fairly likely* that Danielle had *not* written the text message, but I agonised long and hard over which semantic label would best convey my assessment of the strength of the evidence as indeed I had with previous cases. Broeders suggested that what was happening in such cases was that:

> … experts, in using degrees of probability, are actually making categorical judgements, i.e. are really saying yes or no. Even if they use a term like *probably (not)*, I think they are subjectively convinced that the suspect did or did not produce the sample material.
> (Broeders 1999: 237)

That was certainly true for me. Broeders went on to observe that the choice of a given degree of likelihood on a scale like this is irremediably subjective, which is why two experts might reach opinions of differing strengths based on exactly the same data. Even so, he stressed that a subjective judgement should not be condemned simply because it is subjective:

> The crucial question is not whether [it] is subjective or objective, but whether it can be relied on to be correct.
> (Broeders 1999: 238).

Nevertheless, a growing body of opinion is opposed to the use of such semantic scales, especially because, even when they *are* accepted by a court, an unsolvable problem remains – how can one be sure that judges and juries will attach the same meanings to the labels as did the experts who chose and applied them? This point was brought home to me in a court martial where I expressed my opinion as "very likely" on the above 11-point scale and another expert expressed her opinion as "very strong support" on a 9 point scale. Neither of us was allowed to tell the jury how many points there were on our respective scales, let alone show the full scale or even gloss the particular category chosen, even though the defence lawyer did his best to persuade the other expert to lower her opinion from "very strong" on the grounds that another expert had evaluated exactly the same evidence as only "strong".

An added complication is that, at the end of the trial, the triers of fact themselves, the jury, are not allowed the luxury of degrees of confidence; they have to work with a binary choice of Guilty or Not Guilty. So, however hedged the individual expert's opinion is when s/he presents it, the judge and jury have ultimately to make a categorical judgement as to whether to interpret the evidence as supportive of the prosecution or the defence case or as simply inconclusive.

7.   Expressing opinions statistically

Broeders (1999) argued that one should be worried about opinions expressed semantically, not because they are subjective, but rather because far too often the experts who use them are expressing their opinions in the wrong way. He, and later Rose (2002), noted that an expert can offer an opinion on two things:

> ... firstly, on the probability of a hypothesis – so in linguistic cases, for example, on the hypothesis that the accused is the speaker/author – given the strength of the evidence which the expert has analysed; and secondly, on the probability that the evidence would occur in the form and quantity in which it does occur, given the *two* hypotheses that the accused is and, crucially, also is *not* the speaker/author.

Both authors recommend the second approach. Indeed Rose quotes Aitken (1995: 4) in arguing that the former type of opinion, which, he says, is tantamount to deciding on the likelihood of the accused being guilty, is the exclusive role of the judges of fact and for this reason responsible scientists must confine themselves to talking about the likelihood of the evidence. Rose supports his argument by pointing out that no expert can make an estimate of the likelihood of guilt or innocence on the basis of the linguistic evidence alone; only those with access to all the available evidence can assess the value of each piece. So, for example, a forensic handwriting colleague of mine concluded, after exhaustive comparisons, that it was very likely on the basis of the evidence he had analysed, that a disputed signature on an Irish will, which had been written with a ballpoint pen, was genuine. But then, fortunately before committing his opinion to paper, he realised that the will was dated before the invention of ballpoint technology!

Broeders and Rose both argue that not only does their approach have logic on its side, but it also has the added advantage that it enables probability to be expressed statistically rather than semantically. Essentially the method involves first looking at the *likelihood* of the prosecution hypothesis given the raw data on each of the particular features being examined. For example, imagine an anonymous letter which includes the non-standard spelling "ofcourse". In attempting to support the prosecution hypothesis that the accused wrote the letter we discover that 80% of a sample of attested letters written by the suspect also display this feature. However, in support of the defence hypothesis that the accused was not the author, we discover that in the general population writers also use the feature 10% of the time. How do we now assess the evidential strength of this finding, i.e. that we would expect the suspect to use it 10% of the time anyway, but that in fact s/he is using it so much more?

To start with, we produce a *likelihood ratio* by dividing one percentage by the other, i.e. 80/10, and so get a likelihood ratio of 8. Interpretation of this ratio, however, is not quite so simple. It is certainly true that, as Broeders (1999: 230) expresses it, "to the extent that the likelihood ratio exceeds 1 the evidence lends greater support to the [prosecution] hypothesis, [while] if it is smaller than 1 it supports the alternative hypothesis". Unfortunately, that does not tell us exactly how much greater support a likelihood ratio of 8 gives – we will return to this question of interpretation below.

A major advantage of this method of expressing the weight of evidence statistically is that it allows the user to combine several pieces of evidence or several likelihood ratios together, by multiplication, in order to produce a composite likelihood ratio: when combined together, all ratios that are greater than 1 will increase the overall likelihood, while any ratio of less than 1 will reduce it. So, to continue our imaginary example, there might be a series of other distinctive features co-occurring in the anonymous and attested letters like *their* spelled as *there*, *you're* spelled as *your* and possessive *its* spelled as *it's*. These features may be found by themselves to have low likelihood ratios of, respectively, 1.4, 1.5, 1.7, but when they are combined with the likelihood ratio of 8 already calculated for *ofcourse*, they produce, by multiplication, the much higher ratio of 28.56. In other words, after examining the four features, we can now say on a principled basis that it is 28 times more likely that the suspect wrote the letter than that a member of the sample general population did.

One strong argument in favour of this statistical approach is that it allows the easy incorporation of counter indications as well. Whereas experts using the "evidence to evaluate the hypothesis approach", as I was in the Campbell case, have to decide what weight to give to any evidence which does not support the indication of the majority of the features analysed – should they, for example, allow such evidence to reduce their opinion by one or two degrees of certainty or by none at all – by contrast, with a likelihood ratio approach, any measurement which supports the defence hypothesis, and so by definition has a likelihood ratio of less than 1, will simply reduce the cumulative ratio. So let us now imagine we add in the feature *whose* spelled as *who's,* which has a ratio for the letters under consideration of 0.85, the cumulative ratio will now fall to 24.28.

While such a statistical approach has obvious attractions, it does present very real problems to both phoneticians and linguists when they try to calculate the defence likelihood ratio. Firstly, how does one establish what is a relevant comparison population of speakers or texts, and how does one get access to, and then analyse, the data from that population, particularly in a world where lawyers and courts are not willing to pay for what might be thought to be basic research. At least in the area of forensic phonetics there are already agreed reference tables for such things as pitch of voice and solid evidence about the effects of telephone transmission on the pitch of the first formants of vowels. In the area of linguistics there is even less reference data, although specialist corpora are being created: McMenamin, for instance, (2002: 154), reports using a corpus of 742 letters for comparison purposes and Grant has created a corpus of text messages. Of course for some purposes, (see Coulthard 1993, 1994) evidence can be drawn from already available general corpora like the Australian National Corpus, the British National Corpus, the Collins Bank of English and the American National Corpus, though the latter at the time of writing, is still being constructed.

But then, even if we are able to calculate the defence ratios, we are still not out of the trees, because we need to know how to evaluate the significance of the resulting composite likelihood ratios. And there is the added problem of whether a lay jury can cope with likelihood ratios, or whether they will simply introduce even more confusion.

Rose (2002: 62) proposes solving this problem by grouping all numerical likelihood ratios, once they have been calculated, into five semantically labelled categories, which, he suggests should be transparent to the jury:

Likelihood ratio	Semantic Gloss
10,000+	Very strong
1,000–10,000	Strong
100–1,000	Moderately strong
10–100	Moderate
1–10	Limited

However, such a translation is by no means universally accepted, and Professor Meadow had a much more persuasive translation – he created what came to be known as "Meadow's Law": "one sudden infant death is a *tragedy*, two is *suspicious* and three is *murder*, unless proven otherwise".

Even if one accepts Rose's argument for the theoretical advantages of his likelihood ratio, there remain two major doubts. Firstly, after rejecting a scale of *opinions* expressed semantically, we have ended up with a scale of *likelihoods* expressed semantically, although admittedly this time, if two experts agree on the facts to be considered, they will necessarily agree on the likelihood ratio, too. Even so, the problem remains of whether juries can and will interpret the semantic expression of the ratios as the expert intended. Secondly, we do not yet know how appropriate the labels are as glosses for the ratios, even though the category cut-off points are numerically neat. On the one hand, courts work with the concept of "beyond reasonable doubt" which does not have a defined likelihood ratio, although a lay juror, along with statistician A. P. Dawid (2001: 4), might be happy to equate the phrase with one chance in a hundred. On the other hand, one area of forensic investigation, DNA analysis, seems to be working with very much higher likelihood ratios:

> His counsel, Rebecca Poulet QC, reminded him of DNA evidence which showed his profile matched that of the attacker, with the chances of it being anyone else being one in a billion.
> (http://news.bbc.co.uk/1/hi/england/3496207.stm)

In principle though, the judicial system should be attracted by the fact that likelihood ratios derived from a variety of types of evidence can be combined to produce a composite likelihood ratio. In an ideal Rosean world, juries would have a statistician to help them weigh all the evidence, and, unlike the individual expert, the jury would be able to take account as well of such *prior odds* as how many possible suspects there are. For example, if there are five suspects, then before any evidence has been considered the odds that one of them is guilty are 1/4 = 0.25, if there are only two suspects the odds are 1/1 = 1.

Despite obvious academic support for the use of likelihood ratios, it may be a long time before they get general acceptance in courts. *The Times* (9 May 1996, p. 36) reported the opinion in an Appeal Court judgement (*R v. Adams*) where, in the original trial, a statistician had been allowed to instruct the jury about both Bayes theorem and underlying likelihood ratios and then how to create and sum the ratios in order to produce a composite ratio. The Appeal Court judges ordered a retrial and observed that, although the likelihood ratio "might be an appropriate and useful tool for statisticians … it was not appropriate for use in jury trials, nor as a means to assist the jury in their task". After a second trial in which the same expert was allowed to instruct a different jury, there was a second appeal, at the end of which the judges opined:

> Introducing Bayes' Theorem, or any similar method, into a criminal trial plunges the jury into inappropriate and unnecessary realms of complexity, deflecting them from their proper tasks. Reliance on evidence of this kind is a recipe for confusion, misunderstanding, and misjudgement.
> (http://www.herkimershideaway.org/writings/bayes.htm)

And that, for the moment, is the situation in the British courts: experts are still able to express opinions without relating them to probabilities or likelihood ratios.

8.   Consulting and testifying as tour guides

So what remains for the linguist whose findings cannot be appropriately presented in a statistical way? Solan (1998) addresses a problem which is unique to experts in linguistics, the fact that the judges of fact, whether they be actual judges or jury members, are seen for most purposes to be their own experts in the area of language use and interpretation – the law is, much of the time, concerned with the meaning(s) that ordinary speakers attach to words and expressions. Even so, there is a role for the linguist, which is to explain and elucidate facts about language and usage as a result of which judge and jury will then be in the same position as the linguist and so can make linguistically informed decisions. In Solan's words:

> … my linguistic training has made me more sensitive to possible interpretations that others might not notice and I can bring these to the attention of a judge or jury. But once I point these out and illustrate them clearly, we should start on an equal footing.
> (Solan 1998: 92)

To expand Solan's observation, linguists are not only "experts in the nature of meaning" but also experts in the nature of linguistic encoding at both lexicogrammatical and textual levels and so there is a guiding role for the linguist in these areas as well, both before and during a trial.

One British example of the expert sensitising the lay audience comes from my evidence in the Appeal of *R v. Robert Brown*. In Brown's disputed statement there occurs the phrase *my jeans and a blue Parka coat and a shirt*. The accused claimed that a monologue confession attributed to him had in fact been elicited

by question and answer and transformed by the interviewing officers into monologue form. As part of my evidence in support of Brown's claim, I focussed on
the two clauses

> I was covered in blood, my jeans and a blue Parka coat and a shirt were full of blood.

To a linguist it is clear that the phrasing of the subject of the second clause is
most unnatural; no one would refer to their own clothes with the indefinite article once they had begun a list with the possessive determiner. The most
likely use of "a" in this context would be to distinguish between "mine" and
"not-mine". For example, "I looked round the room and I saw my jeans and
a blue Parka coat and a shirt, they were full of blood" would be perfectly natural, but that meaning, of course, did not make any sense in a narrative where
all the clothes referred to belonged to the narrator. The phrase "a blue Parka
coat and a shirt" could occur quite naturally, of course, as a result of a careless
conversion of a sequence of short questions and answers into monologue form
and one could see how it might have happened by looking at the following
sequence taken from the record of an immediately preceding interview with
Brown:

> What were you wearing?
> I had a blue shirt and a blue parka

In this context the use of the indefinite article is normal; as just noted above,
when items are introduced for the first time, the indefinite article is the natural
choice. Once the oddity of the phrase and the occurrence of a similar phrase in
the interview had been pointed out the appeal court judges were as competent as
any linguist to draw inferences from this oddity.

9.   A substitute prosecution witness

One of the important points that Solan (1998) makes is that, although juries and
judges may well be able to process words, phrases and even sentences as well as
any professional linguist, they may have problems with long documents or a
series of related documents, because they may not be able to make the necessary
links:

> Of course a jury can read the document[s]. … But not all jurors, without help, can
> focus on a phrase in paragraph 24 of a contract that may have an impact on how an-
> other word should be interpreted in paragraph 55.
> (Solan 1998: 94)

In the Paul Blackburn Appeal it was also important to draw the attention of the
judges to two phrases occurring in two different documents, one a record of a
dictated statement, the other a record of an interview:

i) Statement   I asked her if I could carry her bags she said "Yes"
    Interview   I asked her if I could carry her bags and she said "yes"

ii) Statement   I picked something up like an ornament
    Interview   I picked something up like an ornament

Linguists of most persuasions are in agreement that the likelihood of two speakers independently producing exactly the same phrasing reduces dramatically with the length of the expression and the likelihood of them choosing two or more identical phrasings is even more unlikely. However, the linguist's "knowledge" is the total opposite of lay belief. When faced with the problem of convincing the Appeal Court judges of the significance of the identical expressions, I chose the following procedure.

Firstly, I demonstrated that even short sequences of words can be unique encodings, by looking at the occurrences of the words "I asked her if I could carry her bags" in a series of Google searches. The results at the time were as follows:

Sequence	No. of occurrences
I asked	2,170,000
I asked her	284,000
I asked her if	86,000
I asked her if I	10,400
I asked her if I could	7,770
I asked her if I could carry	7
I asked her if I could carry her	4
I asked her if I could carry her bags	0

Using these examples, I argued that, if there was not a single example of anyone having ever produced this sequence, the chances of even longer sequences occurring twice in different documents was infinitesimal, unless, of course, one was derived from the other. When, writing this chapter, I re-checked the Google figures for "I asked her if I could carry her bags" and found, to my horror, not none but five instances of the phrase. However, as the adage goes, it is the exception that proves the rule. There is now a website devoted to Paul Blackburn's case which carries the disputed statement, so one of the instances is the original saying, three of the others are web-versions of Coulthard (2004) which reports the case and the final instance is a Dutch university PowerPoint quoting the example from Coulthard (2004). In other words the five instances are all quotings of the same single saying.

To strengthen the argument used to the court, I accessed Google to find another case, this time one involving Lord Justice Rose, who was to preside at the trial. On typing in the words "Lord", "Justice", "Rose" and "Appeal" the first three citations I found were concerned with an appeal by a famous British politician – Lord Archer – against his conviction for perjury. The first hit of all was:

Guardian Unlimited | Special reports | Archer loses *appeal* bid
… was not present at today's hearing, had his application for permission to *appeal*
against the conviction rejected within hours. *Lord Justice Rose*, sitting with …
(www.guardian.co.uk/archer/article/0,2763,759829,00.html)

I accessed the full citation, which is reproduced in part below as Text 1, and
from it selected the first phrase quoted from Lord Rose "For reasons we will
give later in the day", which is highlighted in *italics*.

Text 1
Archer loses appeal bid
Lord Justice Rose, sitting with Mr Justice Colman and Mr Justice Stanley Burnton in
London, told Archer's QC Nicholas Purnell: "*For reasons we will give later in the
day* we are against you in relation to conviction".
At the start of the hearing Nicholas Purnell QC, outlining the grounds of appeal,
said: "The submission that we make on behalf of Lord Archer is that *the first and fun-
damental ground* which interconnects with all the other grounds of appeal was that
the learned trial judge wrongly exercised his discretion not to sever the trial of Edward Francis."
Mr Purnell said the decision of the judge, Mr Justice Potts, not to sever the trial of
Francis had an "*unbalancing effect on the equilibrium*" of the trial.
Counsel argued that Mr Francis was "in a position effectively as *a substitute prosecution witness* and a substitute prosecutor".

Given the nature of Appeal Court judgements *for reasons we will give later in
the day* seems to be an unremarkable phrase for an appeal court judge to use,
particularly as a lot of judgements are produced some time after the verdict is
announced. Yet a search returned only seven occurrences. Every single one of
them was about Lord Rose; indeed they were all reports of this same single utterance at the end of the Archer appeal.

I then took three other short phrases which I highlighted in italics in the
extract above, this time from Nicholas Purnell, Lord Archer's lawyer, each of
them apparently not unusual phrases for a lawyer to utter, "the first and fundamental ground", an "unbalancing effect on the equilibrium" of the trial and a
"substitute prosecution witness". For these phrases Google found 7, 10 and 4 instances respectively, but again all the instances were versions of the same single
utterings.

This seemed to be a simple and efficient way of illustrating uniqueness of
expression in court, but when I presented this illustration to the lawyers, they
declined to submit it to the judges and one of them describing it as "whimsical".

10.   Conclusion

However strong the expert feels the evidence to be, its successful presentation in court, indeed whether it is even presented, depends crucially on the lawyers. Sometimes (the expert feels that) the lawyer omits essential facts during the Evidence in Chief questioning, sometimes successful cross-examination neutralises some of the points and sometimes the evidence is used for other purposes in cross-examination. And then there is the use to which no one has access, the jury deliberations. All experts would like to know how best to present their evidence for the benefit of the jury – most would love to receive from the jury some equivalent of those end of module evaluation forms beloved of university administrators.

References

Aitken, Colin
  1995   *Statistics and the Evaluation of Evidence for Forensic Scientists*. Chichester: John Wiley.
Australian Evidence Act
  1995   http://www.comlaw.gov.au/ComLaw/Legislation/ActCompilation1.nsf/ 0/0A3CF7EBACDD51B0CA25719A00060BE6/$file/EvidenceAct1995_ WD02.pdf (accessed 10 January 2008)
Broeders, Ton
  1999   Some observations on the use of probability scales in forensic identification. *Forensic Linguistics* 6(2): 228–241.
Bromby, Michael
  2002   *The Role and Responsibilities of the Expert Witness within the UK Judicial System*. Dissertation presented for the Diploma in Forensic Medical Science, awarded by The Worshipful Company of Apothecaries, London. http://www.caledonian.ac.uk/lss/global/contactmaps/staff/bromby/ DipFMSDissertation.pdf. (accessed 9 January 2008).
Coulthard, Malcolm
  2002   Whose voice is it? Invented and concealed dialogue in written records of verbal evidence produced by the police. In: Janet Cotterill (ed.), *Language in the Legal Process*, 19–34. Basingstoke: Palgrave Macmillan.
Coulthard, Malcolm
  2004   Author identification, idiolect and linguistic uniqueness. *Applied Linguistics* 25(4): 431–447.
Coulthard, Malcolm and Alison Johnson
  2007   *An Introduction to Forensic Linguistics: Language in Evidence*. London: Routledge.
Hardcastle, Robert
  1997   Cusum: A credible method for the determination of authorship? Science and Justice 37(2): 129–138.

Heffer, Chris
    2005   *The Language of Jury Trial: A Corpus-aided Analysis of Legal-Lay Dis-
              course*. Basingstoke: Palgrave Macmillan.
Levi, Judy
    1993   Evaluating jury comprehension of the Illinois capital sentencing instruc-
              tions. *American Speech* 68(1): 20–49.
Maley, Yon
    2000   The case of the long-nosed potoroo: The framing and construction of expert
              witness testimony. In: Srikant Sarangi and Malcolm Coulthard (eds), *Dis-
              couse and Social Life*, 246–69. Harlow. Pearson Education.
McMenamin, Gerald
    2002   *Forensic Linguistics: Advances in Forensic Stylistics*. London: CRC Press.
McMenamin, Gerald
    2004   Disputed authorship in US law. *International Journal of Speech, Language
              and the Law* 11(1): 73–82.
Rose, Phil
    2002   *Forensic Speaker Identification*. London: Taylor and Francis.
Sarangi, Srikant and Malcolm Coulthard (eds.)
    2000   *Discourse and Social Life*. London: Longman.
Shuy, Roger
    2002   *Linguistic Battles in Trademark Disputes*. New York: Palgrave.
Solan, Larry
    1998   Linguistic experts as semantic tour guides. *Forensic Linguistics* 5(2): 87–
              106.
Solan, Larry and Peter Tiersma
    2004   Author identification in American courts. *Applied Linguistics* 25(4): 448–
              65.
Tiersma, Peter and Larry Solan
    2002   The linguist on the witness stand: Forensic linguistics in American courts.
              Language 78: 221–39.
Turell, Teresa
    2004   Textual kidnapping revisited: The case of plagiarism in literary translation.
              International Journal of Speech, Language and the Law 11(1): 1–26.

Biographical notes

Karin Aronsson, Professor at the Department of Child and Youth Studies at Stockholm University (formerly at Linköping University), is engaged in research on identity-in-interaction in various institutional contexts, such as paediatric interviews, family therapy talk, and courtroom disputes about custody and visitation rights. Some of her work concerns bilingual practices in second language classrooms. In a recent set of studies, she has explored inter-generational negotiations in family life encounters.

Ashley Bartell earned a BS in Linguistics and Biochemistry at Georgetown University shortly after the completion of this study. She is currently a dual degree doctoral candidate at Michigan State University, pursuing an MD and a PhD in Linguistics. She is interested in applying sociolinguistic methodology to the study of physician-patient interaction. Her research seeks to quantify discourse-level variation in the context of physician-patient talk, work that she hopes to continue while practicing medicine.

Ellen Barton is a Professor in the Linguistics Program and Department of English at Wayne State University (Detroit, MI, USA). Her research interests are in the discourse analysis of ethics-in-interaction in medical communication and medical rhetoric. She is currently working on a project analyzing the discourse of ethical deliberation in Institutional Review Board meetings. Her work has appeared in *Communication & Medicine, Written Communication,* and *Qualitative Health Research.* She has been a Visiting Fellow in the Centre for Health Communication Research at Cardiff University, Wales (UK).

Kristina Bennert is Research Associate at the School for Social and Community Medicine, University of Bristol, UK. Her background is in qualitative research with an emphasis on discourse analysis. Her work has focused on examining clients' and professionals' experiences of service delivery in a range of healthcare contexts, including genetic counselling, learning disabilities, paediatric diabetes, obstetrics and depression in primary and antenatal care. She has a special interest in the interactional dynamics of healthcare encounters and the application of online interventions to facilitate provider-patient communication.

Lucy Brookes-Howell is Senior Research Fellow at the South East Wales Trials Unit, Department of Primary Care and Public Health, Cardiff University. Her most recent work involved two large qualitative studies (GRACE and CHAMP) funded by 6th Framework Programme of the European Commission, exploring clinician, adult patient and parent beliefs towards antibiotics and antibiotic resistance across Europe. Her research interests include: genetic counselling, the management of common infections, particularly in light of diagnostic uncertainty, qualitative research methods, multi-site/cross-country qualitative research, antibiotic prescribing, and health communication.

Christopher N. Candlin is Senior Research Professor Emeritus in the Department of Linguistics at Macquarie University, Sydney. He has held Professorships at Lancaster, The City University of Hong Kong, The Open University (UK), and Honorary Professorships at the Universities of Lancaster, Nottingham, and Cardiff, and at Beijing Foreign Studies University. His current research is in the field of professional and organisational communication, particularly in healthcare and law. He initiated the postgraduate programme in Communication in Professions and Organisations at Macquarie, and is a member of the Editorial Boards of several international journals and co-edits (with Srikant Sarangi) the *Journal of Applied Linguistics and Professional Practice* (Equinox). He has published widely and has edited or co-edited several collections of original contributions in the fields of professional and institutional discourse, including *Discourses of Deficit* (with Jonathan Crichton, Palgrave 2011).

Sally Candlin is Honorary Senior Research Fellow in the Department of Linguistics Macquarie University, Sydney. She has worked in the UK as a nurse, midwife and health visitor, and in Australia has taught nursing and health sciences particularly in the field of professional communication. She has a PhD in Linguistics from Lancaster University and an MA in Public Health from the University of Hawaii. Her recent book, *Therapeutic Communication: A Lifespan Approach*, has been published by Pearson. She has authored numerous book chapters and journal papers and is currently co-authoring a book titled *Communication for Health Care Professionals*.

Aaron V. Cicourel is Research Professor Emeritus of cognitive science, pediatrics, and sociology at the University of California, San Diego; Professor Emeritus at the University of California, San Francisco, and Visiting Scholar at the University of California, Berkeley (Institute for the Study of Societal Issues). His current research activities include the study of familial and institutional socio-cultural caregiver practices (»scaffolding«) by individuals and groups when caring for patients diagnosed with Alzheimer's Disease and Frontotemporal dementia. An ongoing project follows the diagnostic processes of a neurological clinic with new patients suspected of being afflicted with dementia.

Angus Clarke is Professor in Clinical Genetics, Institute of Medical Genetics, School of Medicine, Cardiff University. Coming from a background in paediatrics, he has worked in clinical genetics at Cardiff since 1989. He has interests in the genetic counselling process and the social and ethical issues around human genetics. He has authored or edited seven books, often with colleagues, including most recently *Genetic Testing: Accounts of Autonomy, Responsibility and Blame* (with Arribas-Ayllon and Sarangi, Routledge, 2011) and numerous research papers and book chapters. He represents Wales on the Human Genetics Commission and directs the Cardiff MSc course in Genetic Counselling.

Malcolm Coulthard was founding Director of the Aston Centre for Forensic Linguistics. He is probably still best known for his work on the analysis of spoken and written discourse, but since the late 1980s he has become increasingly involved with forensic applications of linguistics. He has written expert reports in over 200 cases. Recent publications include *An Introduction to Forensic Linguistics* (2007) and *A Handbook of Forensic Linguistics* (2010) (both with Alison Johnson).

Maria do Carmo Leite de Oliveira is Full Professor of Linguistics in the Pontifical Catholic University of Rio de Janeiro (PUC-Rio) and is senior researcher of the Brazilian National Scientific and Technological Research Council (CNPq). She provides consulting services in organizational communication as part of the interdisciplinary team of the Administration and Management Institute of PUC-Rio. Her main research interest is language and social interaction at work. She is currently working on a project entitled *The Meaning of Work and of Interpersonal Competence*, funded by CNPq.

Frederick Erickson is George F. Kneller Professor of Anthropology of Education Emeritus at the University of California, Los Angeles. A specialist in the use of video analysis in interactional sociolinguistics and microethnography, his work has focused especially on timing and rhythm in the social coordination of interaction, relationships of mutual influence between listening and speaking in interaction, and the signalling of multiple social identities in talk. His publications include (with Jeffrey J. Shultz) *The Counselor as Gatekeeper: Social Interaction in Interviews* (1982) and *Talk and Social Theory: Ecologies of Speaking and Listening in Everyday Life* (2004).

Richard M. Frankel is Professor of Medicine and Geriatrics and a Senior Research Scientist at the Regenstrief Institute, Indiana University School of Medicine. He is also the Acting Associate Director of the Center for Implementing Evidence-Based Practice at the Richard L. Roudebush Veteran's Administration Medical Center in Indianapolis Indiana, USA. He is a qualitative health services researcher and has published more than 175 scientific papers on physician patient communication and related topics.

Giuliana Garzone is Full Professor of English, Linguistics and Translation at Università degli Studi di Milano, and previously at the Faculty of Interpreting and Translation of Bologna University. Her main research interests are in translation and interpreting studies, and in specialized discourse in its different domains (legal, scientific, business). She has co-ordinated several research projects, published in edited collections and journals as well as book-length studies, and has co-edited several volumes. She is General Co-Editor of the book series *Lingua, traduzione, didattica*.

Christopher Hall is Social Care Researcher in the School of Medicine and Health at Durham University. Previously a social worker and team manager in local authority social services, he currently works in a team that provides advice on research design to academics, clinicians and other health professionals. His research interests include child welfare policy and practice, professional communication and narrative and discourse methods. His most recent projects have been two ESRC funded studies of information sharing, assessment and the use of information and communication technologies in child welfare.

Heidi E. Hamilton is Professor and Chair, Department of Linguistics, Georgetown University. She teaches courses in discourse analysis and applications of interactional sociolinguistics. Her research interests focus on issues of language and Alzheimer's disease, language and aging, medical communication, and language learning. Books and co-edited volumes include: *Conversations with an Alzheimer's Patient*; *Language and Communication in Old Age; Blackwell Handbook of Discourse Analysis*; *Linguistics, Language, and the Professions; Doing Foreign Language*; and *Routledge Handbook of Language and Health Communication*.

Sandra Harris is Professor Emeritus at Nottingham Trent University, UK. She has a long-standing interest in institutional discourse, particularly the courtroom, and is the author of two books on business discourse, both with Francesca Bargiela-Chiappini. She has contributed a large number of articles and chapters to a wide range of international journals and edited collections. Her current research interest is in linguistic (im)politeness, especially in institutional, political and legal contexts, and she is one of the original editors of the *Journal of Politeness Research*.

Christian Heath is Professor at King's College London and with Paul Luff leads the Work, Interaction and Technology research group. With colleagues he is currently undertaking projects concerned with social interaction in areas including health care, command and control and museums and galleries. A book entitled the *Dynamics of Auction: Social Interaction and Sales of Fine Art and*

Antiques is forthcoming with Cambridge University Press, and Sage recently published *Video in Qualitative Research: Analysing Social Interaction in Everyday Life* (Heath, Hindmarsh & Luff).

Pamela Hobbs is a Lecturer in Communication Studies at the University of California, Los Angeles, where she received a Ph.D. in Applied Linguistics, and is also an attorney licensed to practice in Michigan, U.S.A. Her research interests include legal discourse, medical discourse, political discourse, language and gender, and the evolution of communication.

Janet Holmes holds a Personal Chair in Linguistics and is Director of the Wellington Language in the Workplace project at Victoria University of Wellington. She teaches and researches in the area of sociolinguistics, specialising in workplace discourse and language and gender. Most recently, with her co-authors, she has been investigating the discourse of skilled migrants as they enter New Zealand workplaces.

Thomas S. Inui is Director of Research, Indiana University Center for Global Health, Professor of Medicine in the Department of Medicine, IU School of Medicine, and Senior Research Scientist at the Regenstrief Institute. He is a multi-method health services researcher with emphases on primary care, chronic disease management, prevention, health behavior and clinical communication.

Steven Ivy is Senior Vice President for Values, Ethics, Social Responsibility, and Pastoral Services with Indiana University Health, an eighteen hospital comprehensive healthcare system based in Indianapolis, Indiana. He also teaches at Christian Theological Seminary and Indiana University School of Medicine. He is clergy and an ACPE supervisor. His research interests include meaning-focused leadership, professional ethics, and professional formation of clergy and others.

Angela Joe is the Director of the English Language Institute in the School of Linguistics and Applied Language Studies at Victoria University of Wellington, a role which incorporates responsibility for courses in workplace communication for EAL skilled migrants and government officials.

Alan Jones is a Senior Research Fellow in the Department of Linguistics, Macquarie University, Sydney. His research interests include discourse analysis, disciplinary knowledge structures, professional and everyday reasoning and account-giving in professional communication. He has collaborated and co-published with specialists in physics, accounting, finance and law, while developing a theoretical framework for linguistically informed curricula. He is currently a Visiting Fellow in the Department of Anthropology, Australian National University.

Orit Karnieli-Miller is Assistant Professor, Department of Community Mental Health; Center for Excellence in Patient-Professional Relationships in Health Care, University of Haifa, Haifa, Israel; and Adjunct Assistant Research Professor of Medicine in Indiana University-Purdue University, Indianapolis. Her expertise is in qualitative methods in the field of medical education, specifically focusing on professionalism, shared decision making and breaking bad news in physical and mental health settings.

Dana Kovarsky is currently Professor and Chair of the Department of Communicative Disorders at the University of Rhode Island. He teaches in the area of language, culture and communication disorders, and child language development. As an ethnographer of communication disorders, his research has focused on the analysis of clinical discourse in a variety of contexts. He has published and presented his work in national and international venues.

Paul Luff is Professor of Organizations and Technology at the Department of Management, King's College London. His research draws upon video recordings of everyday human conduct. With his colleagues, he has undertaken studies in a diverse variety of settings including control rooms, news and broadcasting, healthcare, museums, galleries and science centres and within design, architecture and construction. His research has been reported in numerous articles in the fields of CSCW, HCI, Requirements Engineering, Studies of work practices and ubiquitous and mobile systems. Paul Luff is co-author with Christian Heath of *Technology in Action* (Cambridge University Press).

Sheelagh McCracken is Professor of Finance Law at the University of Sydney. She has lectured extensively on finance law in Australia and the Asia-Pacific region and has a strong research interest in commercial law generally as well as in disciplinary learning and curriculum. Her publications *Banking and Financial Institutions Law* (with Everett, 7th edition, 2009, Law Book Co, Sydney) and *The Banker's Remedy of Set-Off* (3rd edition, 2010, Bloomsbury Professional, London).

Meredith Marra is Research Officer for Victoria University of Wellington's Language in the Workplace (LWP) Project and a Senior Lecturer in Sociolinguistics at the School of Linguistics and Applied Language Studies. Her primary research interest is the language of business meetings, but she has also published in the areas of humour, gender and ethnicity in workplace interactions. Her most recent book (co-authored with the LWP team) is *Leadership, Discourse and Ethnicity* (Oxford University Press, 2011).

Per Måseide is Professor of Sociology at Bodø University College, Faculty of Social Sciences, Norway. He teaches sociology of health and illness, social interaction, social theory and qualitative methodology. He has extensive experience from fieldwork in diverse health care institutions. His research interests lie in doctor-patient interaction, multiprofessional collaboration in medical problem solving, the social organization of medical work, socially distributed cognition and pragmatics.

David Middleton is a Research Consultant and has research affiliations with the Loughborough University Discourse and Rhetoric Group (DARG). His published work includes: *The Social Psychology of Experience: Studies in Remembering and Rorgetting* (with Steven D. Brown, Sage Publications, 2005); *Cognition and Communication at Work* (with Yrjo Engeström, Cambridge University Press, 1996); and, *Collective Remembering* (with Derek Edwards, Sage Publications 1990).

Jonathan Newton is a Senior Lecturer at the School of Linguistics and Applied Language Studies, Victoria University of Wellington where he teaches courses on language teaching methodology and second language acquisition. He has published on a range of topics including second language vocabulary learning, classroom interaction, task-based language teaching, and intercultural and workplace-related language teaching.

Nicky Riddiford is a Senior Language Teacher at the English Language Institute, Victoria University of Wellington. She has taught EAL and EAP in many contexts including at university level, at language schools and at community institutes. She is currently coordinating and teaching a workplace communication course for skilled migrants. She is co-author (with Jonathan Newton) of *Workplace Talk in Action: an ESOL resource*.

Camilla Rindstedt is an anthropologist, employed as Associate Professor at the Department of Child and Youth Studies at Stockholm University. She did her first major fieldwork in Ecuador on peer interaction and language shift. Presently, she is working on a monograph, as well as a series of papers, documenting a fieldwork on doctor-child, nurse-child, and doctor/nurse-parent-child encounters in a paediatric (oncology) setting.

Celia Roberts is Professor of Applied Linguistics at King's College London. Her interests are in language, migration and institutional disadvantage. She also has a particular interest in the practical relevance of research. Her publications include: *Talk, Work and Institutional Order* (with Sarangi, 1999) and *Language Learners as Ethnographers* (with Byram et al, 2001).

Srikant Sarangi is Professor of Language and Communication and Director of the Health Communication Research Centre at Cardiff University. He is also Professor in Language and Communication at the Norwegian University of Science and Technology (NTNU), Trondheim (Norway), Honorary Professor, Faculty of Humanities, Aalborg University (Denmark) and Honorary Professor, Centre for the Humanities and Medicine, The University of Hong Kong. His research interests are in applied linguistics and institutional/professional discourse studies (e.g., healthcare, social work, bureaucracy, education). He is author and editor of twelve books, guest-editor of five journal special issues and has published nearly two hundred journal articles and book chapters. He is the editor of *Text & Talk* as well as the founding editor of *Communication & Medicine* and with (C. N. Candlin) of *Journal of Applied Linguistics and Professional Practice* and three book series[es].

Roger W. Shuy is Distinguished Research Professor of Linguistics, Emeritus at Georgetown University. His research interests include sociolinguistics, medical communication, and the relationship of language to law. He has written ten books on various aspects of language to the law, the most recent being *Creating Language Crimes, Fighting over Words, The Language of Defamation Cases* and *The Language of Perjury Cases,* all published by Oxford University Press, where he is also editor of the scholarly books series, *Language and Law.*

Stef Slembrouck is Professor of English Linguistics and Discourse Analysis at Ghent University, Belgium. He has published widely on the role of discourse practices in the construction of client and professional identities in institutional contexts, also with particular reference to globalization-affected multilingualism. Publications include: *Language Practice in Social Work: Categorisation and Accountability in Child Welfare* (with C. Hall and S. Sarangi, Routledge, 2006) and *Globalization and Languages in Contact: Scale, Migration and Communicative Practices* (with J. Collins and M. Baynham, Continuuum, 2009).

Graham Smart is an Associate Professor in Linguistics and Language Studies at Carleton University, Ottawa, Canada. He has published research on writing in both professional and academic settings, including *Writing the Economy: Activity, Genre and Technology in the World of Banking*, an ethnographic study of the discourse practices of economists at Canada's central bank. His current research focuses on the broad and complex body of discourse jointly created by government, business, and civil-society organizations they advance arguments regarding global climate change.

Amanda C. Taylor is a psychologist at the Edward Hines, Jr. VA Hospital where she works in the Psychosocial Rehabilitation and Recovery Center with veterans with serious mental illness. She received her doctoral degree in Clinical Rehabilitation Psychology at Indiana University-Purdue University, Indianapolis (IUPUI) where she specialized in serious mental illness. Her research interests have included both qualitative and quantitative methods in the areas of physician patient communication, narrative therapy, and medication management.

James R. Taylor is Emeritus Professor of Communication at the University of Montreal. Author or co-author of eight books and more than a hundred refereed articles, his special area of interest is the communicative constitution of organization (CCO). His most recent book is *The Situated Organization* (with E. J. Van Every, Routledge). He is currently working on a new book on the theme of construction of authority in communicative practice.

Bernadette Vine is Corpus Manager of the Archive of New Zealand English, which includes management of the processing, transcription, archiving of databases for the Language in the Workplace Project. Within the area of workplace research, her publications have focussed on a range of factors, including the use of directives at work.

Irene P. Walsh is a Lecturer in Speech and Language Pathology at Trinity College Dublin, Ireland. She teaches in a wide range of areas, including developmental language disorders, communication skills and psychiatric disorders and discourse analysis. Her research interests include the discourse analysis of clinical interactions, especially those involving speech-language pathologists and people with mental health disorders. She has published on this topic in international journals.

David Wastell is Professor of Information Systems at Nottingham University Business School. His research interests are in public sector reform, innovation and design, and cognitive ergonomics. He has extensive public sector consultancy experience and was co-author of the SPRINT methodology for service design and innovation, widely used in local government. His ideas about design and the managerial role are the subject of a recent book titled *Managing as Designing in the Public Services: Beyond Technomagic*.

Sue White is Professor of Social Work (Children and Families) at the University of Birmingham. Her research has focused on the analysis of professional decision-making in everyday practice in child welfare. She has completed two influential Research Council funded studies. Her latest major study has focused on the relationship between the performance management of public services responsible for safeguarding children, and the impact of anticipated blame on those providing these services. She has been centrally involved in the current reform of social work in England.

Subject index